# The Life of the LAW

# The Life of the LAW

Readings on the Growth of Legal Institutions

EDITED BY John Honnold
PROFESSOR OF LAW,
UNIVERSITY OF PENNSYLVANIA

Fp | The Free Press of Glencoe
Collier-Macmillan Limited, London

Copyright © 1964 by The Free Press of Glencoe
A Division of The Macmillan Company

Printed in the United States of America

All rights in this book are reserved. No part of this book
may be used or reproduced in any manner whatsoever
without written permission except in the case
of brief quotations embodied in critical articles and reviews.

FOR INFORMATION, ADDRESS:
The Free Press of Glencoe
A DIVISION OF THE MACMILLAN COMPANY
THE CROWELL-COLLIER PUBLISHING COMPANY
60 Fifth Avenue, New York, N.Y. 10011
COLLIER-MACMILLAN CANADA, LTD., TORONTO, ONTARIO

Designed by Sidney Solomon

Library of Congress Catalog Card Number: 64-16958

# Preface

THIS BOOK grew from the concern that modern lawyers, in their devotion to intensive examination of specific problems, may have dug deep, isolated holes for themselves from which it is hard to see the landscape or the horizon.

One of the casualties in modern law study is a sense for history, a feeling of motion and direction. Not so many years ago we would at least start with the English and early American ancestry of the problem at hand; nowadays the pressure from current problems often crowds out a genetic examination of the rules. The problem is broader than this, for even if the roots of each individual legal problem were uncovered there still would be the need to examine lawmaking institutions—like the judiciary and the legislature—which control the quality of our law.

The first part of the book is designed to sketch in some of the landmarks in the development of legal ideas and institutions which are of current significance. Chapter 1 deals with events in English legal history which have left their mark on our law, like the emergence of the lawmaking role of the judge and the curious division between law and equity. Fortunately we could here meet the standard, which we have tried to maintain throughout the book, of presenting important material with high literary quality, for we could draw heavily on the exquisite writing of Frederic Maitland.

Chapter 2 is devoted to an overview of developments in America during the early "formative" period: the making of homespun law under frontier conditions and the later impact of increasingly complex economic and political forces.

Chapter 3 continues this historical narrative, but in a specific setting: the sharp controversy in the last century over proposals to codify American law. This chapter, while exposing persistent problems concerning the contrasting values of case law and statutes, also helps prepare for the later consideration of some of the salient features of Continental law.

This chapter on codification leads into Chapter 4, which tells the story of the attempt to bring order to the teeming jungle of case law by means of the black-letter propositions of the Restatements. Lawyers and students, I fear, often work with these black-letter rules without a clear view of whether they were brought down from Mount Sinai or had a less mysterious origin. Scholars there are who have been only too pleased to offer a skeptical view of the Restatements' ancestry; the Restaters have stoutly risen to the defense. In this exchange, useful perceptions emerge concerning this significant American phenomenon; the debate also illumines the eternal dilemma between stability and growth.

Then comes a group of four chapters on various human and institutional structures which play a part in modern American lawmaking. Chapter 5 looks at the judge. In the last century a movement swept through the states to "democratize" the selection of the judiciary. To what extent has this supplanted an aristocracy of the bench with political controls which degrade quality and undermine independence? What are the implications of current proposals to divorce the selection of judges from politics?

Chapter 6 turns to the legislature, which at an accelerating tempo is reshaping the legal structure. Is it equipped to attend to deficiencies in the law and to perform a workmanlike job? To what extent have law-revision commissions and similar organs for legislative reform responded to Cardozo's call for a ministry of justice?

The dynamic growth and some of the problems of lawmaking by administrators are examined in Chapter 7. A view of the organized bar's contribution to the law-shaping process closes this group of chapters.

The concluding part of the book is designed to open up perspectives. Both intellectual and legal boundaries are under attack in Chapter 9, with an introduction to legal systems that lie beyond the Anglo-American realm. Law practice increasingly brings American lawyers into contact with problems of foreign law; these readings are designed to provide a basis for further specialized work with specific transnational legal problems. In the final chapter we look briefly at changes in law study which have resulted from the changes in the character of legal institutions.

In bold strokes, such is the plan of the book. The landscape is vast, but the editor submits that each of the vistas is worthy of serious attention.

The book tries to maintain an empirical outlook. For example, we do not try to portray the ideal judge: we want to see what kind of men our judges really are. We are not now dreaming about the ideal for perfect legislative drafting but are examining the tools available at present for lawmaking by legislatures. We are not here indulging in after-dinner ideals for the responsibility of the bar: we want to look at what the bar is doing.

I have tried for something more than a collection of readings; this purports to be a book. Insistence on the development of an integrated subject through writing of literary as well as intrinsic merit has imposed exacting, even exasperating, standards for selection; I can only hope that the reader will share some of the editor's excitement over the literature of the law with which it has been possible to build. To further integrate the book, I have tried to cement the selections together with introductory and connecting passages and with notes which call attention to the relationship between the various chapters and parts. It is against an ambitious objective that the book's deficiencies must be measured.

Do these materials fit into a curriculum? At The University of Pennsylvania Law School, we felt that they were worthy of credit-time as a required course. However, rather than add to the present pressure during the school year, we decided that the book could be read—by the sea or in the mountains—during the summer following the first year; an examination is provided when the students return in the fall. The project thus is based on the radical idea that it is possible to gain education by thoughtful reading. The editor's defense for this intrusion upon summer pleasure must be based on the significance of the institutions which are examined and the quality of the writing.

*Editorial Explanation.* In their original sources, many of the writings are richly documented. In reprinting, footnote references have usually been omitted; those retained have been renumbered. Footnotes indicated by letters have been added by the editor.

*Acknowledgments.* My view of the possibilities of such a book was influenced at an early stage by Professor Spencer Kimball's *Historical Introduction to the Legal System*. In Chapters 2 and 3 I have used some of his "finds" and have borrowed ideas from other collections like Mark DeWolfe Howe's *Readings in American Legal History*. My indebtedness to the authors and publishers whose works are included is all too obvious and is given specific recognition in footnotes to the excerpts.

Several student assistants have given indispensable aid, supported by generous help from the Law School's research funds. This work was too widely shared to permit specific acknowledgment of all of these helpers, but special mention must be made of the contribution, throughout the "formative period" of a temporary edition, of Leonard Orland, Esq., and of the firm hand of Mr. Harold Fitzkee in seeing the manuscript through the final stages of preparation and printing. Mr. Earl T. Britt gave editorial assistance and prepared the index. Colleagues here and elsewhere, with a heart-warming interest in this venture, have furnished valuable suggestions. The secretarial work has been resourcefully discharged by Miss Gloria Watts. To all these helpful people, I take this opportunity to express my gratitude.

JOHN HONNOLD

*Philadelphia*
*June 1963*

# Contents

PREFACE     *v*

## PART ONE: TRENDS

The Place of History in Understanding the Law     3
    OLIVER WENDELL HOLMES, JR.

### Chapter 1. The English Heritage: Tradition and Change

Origins of Legal Institutions     6
    FREDERIC W. MAITLAND

Later Development: Coke and Beyond     27
    FREDERIC W. MAITLAND

The Development of Equity     30
    FREDERIC W. MAITLAND

A View of Equity from *The Commentaries*     37
    WILLIAM BLACKSTONE

The Case-Law System: Historical Factors Which Controlled Its Development     44
    WILLIAM SEARLE HOLDSWORTH

### Chapter 2. Law in the New World

Law and Authority in Early Massachusetts     48
    GEORGE L. HASKINS

| | |
|---|---|
| The Formative Era of American Law<br>ROSCOE POUND | 52 |
| The Administration of Equity through Common-Law Forms<br>SYDNEY G. FISHER | 79 |
| Law and Social Change in the United States<br>CARL A. AUERBACH | 87 |

## Chapter 3. The Codification Movement

| | |
|---|---|
| An Offer to Codify the Law of the United States<br>JEREMY BENTHAM | 100 |
| Report on Codification to the House of Representatives of Massachusetts | 102 |
| The Movement Leading to Codes in the West<br>MAURICE HARRISON | 104 |
| First Report of the Commissioners of the Code (1858)<br>DAVID DUDLEY FIELD, WILLIAM CURTIS NOYES, and ALEXANDER W. BRADFORD | 106 |
| Introduction to the Completed Civil Code (1865)<br>DAVID DUDLEY FIELD and ALEXANDER W. BRADFORD | 109 |
| Reasons for Codification<br>DAVID DUDLEY FIELD | 113 |
| The Proposed Codification of our Common Law<br>JAMES CARTER | 115 |
| The First Half-Century of the California Civil Code<br>MAURICE HARRISON | 122 |
| A Strange Story | 133 |
| The Advisability of Codifying Anglo-American Law<br>ROSCOE POUND | 140 |

## Chapter 4. Codes Without Legislation: The Restatements

Report of the Committee on the Establishment of a Permanent Organization for the Improvement of the Law — 145

How We Did It — 150
WILLIAM DRAPER LEWIS

What Should the American Law Institute Do? — 154
HESSEL E. YNTEMA

The Restatement of the Law of Contracts — 157
CHARLES E. CLARK

A Review of the Property Restatement — 161
MYRES S. MCDOUGAL

The Restatements as They Were in the Beginning, Are Now, and Perhaps Henceforth Shall Be — 162
W. BARTON LEACH

New Law in the Restatements — 169
HARRISON TWEED

Restatement and Codification — 170
HERBERT F. GOODRICH

# PART TWO: LAWMAKING INSTITUTIONS

## Chapter 5. The Judge

The Democratic Revolution in America, 1830–1850 — 184
EVAN HAYNES

Courts and Politics in New York City — 195
WALLACE S. SAYRE and HERBERT KAUFMAN

Magistrates' Courts in Operation: The Philadelphia Story — 220

Judicial Selection 235
SIDNEY SCHULMAN

Federal Judicial Selection—The Role of the American Bar Association 255
BERNARD G. SEGAL

The Bar Reviews the Judicial Appointments of President Kennedy 262
BERNARD G. SEGAL

The Selection of Judges in England: A Standard for Comparison 268
MORSE ERSKINE

Politics, The Bar, and the Selection of Judges 276
FRANCIS D. WORMUTH and S. GROVER RICH, JR.

## Chapter 6. The Legislature

A Ministry of Justice 283
BENJAMIN N. CARDOZO

Legal Research Translated Into Legislative Action: The New York Law Revision Commission 1934–1963 291
JOHN W. MACDONALD

The Makers of our Laws: The State Legislature 315
S. GALE LOWRIE

Twentieth-Century Legislatures for Twentieth-Century Problems 322
RICHARD L. NEUBERGER

The National Conference of Commissioners on Uniform State Laws 324
JAMES W. DAY

The British System 331
HERMAN FINER

The Gap in Lawmaking—Judges Who Can't and Legislators Who Won't 337
HENRY J. FRIENDLY

## Chapter 7. The Administrator

The Development and Role of the Administrative Process     351
KENNETH CULP DAVIS

Changing Attitudes Toward the Administrative Process     381
WALTER GELLHORN

## Chapter 8. The Bar

The Modern Legal Profession     398
A. A. BERLE

The Bar as Lawmaker     403
WHITNEY NORTH SEYMOUR

Comments     424
HARRY W. JONES

Too Little Progress     418
MORRIS L. ERNST

Comments     424
ARTHUR T. VANDERBILT and CHARLES E. CLARK

Equal Access to Justice: The Challenge and the Opportunity     427
ORISON S. MARDEN

The People Behind Legal Aid Statistics     433

The Profession and Practice of the Law in England and America     437
L. C. B. GOWER and LEOLIN PRICE

The Wall Street Lawyers     455
SPENCER KLAW

Review of Levy, *Corporation Lawyer . . . Saint or Sinner?*     468
A. A. BERLE

The Emerging Role of the Corporate Counsel     473
LEON E. HICKMAN

## PART THREE: PERSPECTIVES

### Chapter 9. Beyond the Frontier

| | |
|---|---|
| The Civil Law System: An Historical Introduction<br>ARTHUR T. VON MEHREN | 486 |
| The Code Systems<br>RUDOLF B. SCHLESINGER | 494 |
| French Legal Tradition<br>RENÉ DAVID and HENRY D. DEVRIES | 509 |
| The Approach to German Law<br>MAX RHEINSTEIN | 525 |
| The Comparison of Soviet and American Law<br>HAROLD J. BERMAN | 536 |
| The Dilemma of Soviet Law Reform<br>HAROLD J. BERMAN | 544 |

### Chapter 10. The Goals of Law Study

| | |
|---|---|
| Taught Law Is Tough Law<br>ROBERT A. LEFLAR | 564 |
| The Tapestry Unfolds<br>OLIVER WENDELL HOLMES, JR. | 574 |
| INDEX | 575 |

*The life of the law has not been logic:
it has been experience.*
   —OLIVER WENDELL HOLMES, JR.

*Part One*

# TRENDS

# THE PLACE OF HISTORY
# IN UNDERSTANDING LAW  By Oliver Wendell Holmes, Jr.

THE LIFE of the law has not been logic: it has been experience. The felt necessities of the time, the prevalent moral and political theories, intuitions of public policy, avowed or unconscious, even the prejudices which judges share with their fellow-men, have had a good deal more to do than the syllogism in determining the rules by which men should be governed. The law embodies the story of a nation's development through many centuries, and it cannot be dealt with as if it contained only the axioms and corollaries of a book of mathematics. In order to know what it is, we must know what it has been, and what it tends to become. We must alternately consult history and existing theories of legislation. But the most difficult labor will be to understand the combination of the two into new products at every stage. The substance of the law at any given time pretty nearly corresponds, so far as it goes, with what is then understood to be convenient; but its form and machinery, and the degree to which it is able to work out desired results, depend very much upon its past. . . .

The rational study of law is still to a large extent the study of history. History must be a part of the study, because without it we cannot know the precise scope of rules which it is our business to know. It is a part of the rational study, because it is the first step toward an enlightened scepticism, that is, toward a deliberate reconsideration of the worth of those rules. When you get the dragon out of his cave on to the plain and in the daylight, you can count his teeth and claws, and see just what is his strength. . . .

When a man has working knowledge of his business, he can spend his leisure better than in reading all the reported cases he has time for. They are apt to be only the small change of legal thought. They represent the

---

Reprinted from Holmes, *The Common Law*, pp. 1–2 (Boston: Little, Brown, 1881) and from an address and writings dating from 1897 and 1912 which appear in Holmes, *Collected Legal Papers*, pp. 186–187, 300–301 (New York: Harcourt, 1921).

Oliver Wendell Holmes, Jr. (1841–1935) was Professor of Law at Harvard University; Associate Justice, then Chief Justice, Supreme Judicial Court of Massachusetts; and from 1902 to 1932, Associate Justice, Supreme Court of the United States.

The earlier periods of Holmes' life are brilliantly portrayed in detail by Professor Mark de Wolf Howe in *Justice Oliver Wendell Holmes: The Proving Years, 1870–1882* (Cambridge: Harvard U.P., 1963). For a brief and popular account see Katherine Drinker Bowen, *Yankee from Olympus* (Boston: Little, Brown, 1944).

compromise of the moment between tradition and precedent on the one side and the free conception of the desirable on the other. It is worth while, even with the most mundane ideals, to get as big a grasp of one's subject as one can. And therefore it is worth while to do what we can to enlighten our notions of the desirable and to understand the precedents by which we are constrained. The history of the law stands alongside of sociology and economics as a necessary tool if one is to practise law in a large way. . . .

CHAPTER 1

# The English Heritage: Tradition and Change

WE BEGIN WITH A BACKWARD GLANCE at origins so ancient that they may seem antique. But the developments which emerge in subsequent chapters will show the current significance of early events in English legal history. In Maitland's famous words, "Such is the unity of all history that any one who endeavours to tell a piece of it must feel that his first sentence tears a seamless web. . . . If we would search out the origins of Roman law, we must study Babylon. . . . A statute of limitations must be set; but it must be arbitrary. The web must be rent; but, as we rend it, we may watch the whence and whither of a few of the severed and ravelling threads which have been making a pattern too large for any man's eye."

This chapter is designed to expose some of the threads that have become woven into the patterns of our familiar legal institutions. For example, it will be worthwhile to keep a sharp eye for the forces which produced a legal system in which judges play a central and creative role —a development which, as we shall see later, in the chapter on civil law systems, is less than inevitable. It will also be useful to observe the odd circumstances which led to the enduring distinction between "law" and "equity," and the ways in which fragments of Continental and international mercantile law were woven, without credit for their origins, into the legal fabric.

Fortunately, in the pages to follow we can draw on the writing of the late Professor Maitland, who expressed creative scholarship in writing of clarity and grace.

# ORIGINS
# OF LEGAL INSTITUTIONS     By Frederic W. Maitland

WHEN WE speak of a body of law, we use a metaphor so apt that it is hardly a metaphor. We picture to ourselves a being that lives and grows, that preserves its identity while every atom of which it is composed is subject to a ceaseless process of change, decay, and renewal. At any given moment of time—for example, in the present year—it may, indeed, seem to us that our legislators have, and freely exercise, an almost boundless power of doing what they will with the laws under which we live; and yet we know that, do what they may, their work will become an organic part of an already existing system.

*Continuity of English Law.* Already, if we look back at the ages which are the most famous in the history of English legislation—the age of Bentham and the radical reform, the age which appropriated the gains that had been won but not secured under the rule of Cromwell, the age of Henry VIII, the age of Edward I ("our English Justinian")—it must seem to us that, for all their activity, they changed, and could change, but little in the great body of law which they had inherited from their predecessors. Hardly a rule remains unaltered, and yet the body of law that now lives among us is the same body that Blackstone described in the eighteenth century, Coke in the seventeenth, Littleton in the fifteenth, Bracton in the thirteenth, Glanvill in the twelfth. This continuity, this identity, is very real to us if we know that for the last seven hundred years all the judgments of the courts at Westminster have been recorded, and that for the most part they can still be read. Were the world large enough to contain such a book, we might publish not merely a biography, but a journal or diary, of English law, telling what it has done, if not day

---

The following excerpts were first published as separate articles contributed by Maitland to *Social England*, Vol. 1, pp. 164–172, 274–285, 408–410; and Vol. 2, pp. 32–38, 476–489 (New York: Putnam, 1894). All of Professor Maitland's contributions to that work were later reprinted in *Maitland and Montague, A Sketch of English Legal History*, James F. Colby, ed. (New York: Putnam, 1915).

Frederic W. Maitland (1850–1906) was a professor and lecturer at Cambridge University, and lecturer at Oxford University. Some of his works, in addition to those excerpted in this book, include *Bracton's Notebook* (1887), *History of English Law Before the Time of Edward I* (with Sir Frederick Pollock) (1895), *Domesday Book and Beyond* (1897), *Roman Canon Law in the Church of England* (1898), *The Constitutional History of England* (1908), and *Collected Papers* (1911). In the words of Sir Frederick Pollock, "The bones of the law were dry without history, and the tissue of history was invertebrate without law: the touch of prophetic fire was still wanting. Maitland commanded the dry bones to live, and henceforth they are alive."

by day, at least term by term, ever since the reign of Richard I; and eventful though its life may have been, it has had but a single life.

Beyond these seven centuries there lie six other centuries that are but partially and fitfully lit, and in one of them a great catastrophe, the Norman Conquest, befell England and the law of England. However, we never quite lose the thread of the story. Along one path or another we can trace back the footprints, which have their starting-place in some settlement of wild Germans who are invading the soil of Roman provinces, and coming in contact with the civilization of the old world. Here the trail stops, the dim twilight becomes darkness; we pass from an age in which men seldom write their laws, to one in which they cannot write at all. Beyond lies the realm of guesswork.

## The Early Period

*The First English Code.* About the year 600, Æthelbert, King of the Kentings, by the counsel of his wise men, caused the laws of his people to be set down in writing. He had just received the Christian faith at the hands of Roman missionaries, and it was in imitation of the Romans that he and his folk desired to have written laws. His reign overlaps the reign of Justinian, and perhaps he had heard how in the far east the Roman Emperor had been legislating on a magnificent scale. English law begins to speak just when Roman law has spoken what will, in a certain sense, be its final words.[1] On the Continent of Europe the same thing had been happening. No sooner did the barbarian tribe feel the influence of Rome than it wished for a written code of laws. Æthelbert and his Jutes in Kent are doing what the Salian Franks did a century ago when they wrote down their famous Lex Salica; but while on the Continent the laws of the conquering Germans are written in the Latin language of the conquered, in England the barbarians from the first write down their law in the language that they speak, the language which is to become English.

*Christian Influences.* Æthelbert's laws have come down to us, though only in a copy made after the Norman Conquest. They may seem to us primitive enough. The emperor at Byzantium, could he have seen them, would assuredly have denied that they had any points in common with the Roman law books, save that they were laws, and were in writing.

---

[1] The *Corpus Juris Civilis* which embodied the Roman law in the form which it assumed a thousand years after the decemviral legislation of the Twelve Tables, 450 B.C., and through which mainly it has influenced modern times, was compiled under Justinian and published in 529–34 A.D. [The development of Roman law is explored further in Chapter 9, *infra*.]

Nevertheless, we cannot call them primitive in any absolute sense of that term. They are Christian. . . .

[A] new force is already beginning to transfigure the whole sum and substance of barbaric law, before that law speaks the first words that we can hear. It is a wild plant that has already been torn from its native soil and set to grow in a garden. The change of faith, and the substitution of one order of religious rites for another, would in any case mean much, for we have reason to believe that the old law had in it a strong sacral element; but as it is, they mean the influence of the old civilized world upon the new barbarian world.

Æthelbert's laws consist of ninety brief sentences. Two will serve as samples: "If one man strike another with the fist on the nose—three shillings." "If the eye be struck out let boot [*i.e.*, amends] be made with fifty shillings." To call this brief tariff a code may seem strange, but there are not wanting signs that the wise men of Kent are committing to writing as much of their traditional law as they can remember in the form of abstract propositions. No doubt much more law—in particular, a law of procedure—is known to them implicitly. If a concrete case were to occur, they would be ready with a doom [judgment]; but when asked for general rules, these ninety are all that they can call to mind. Thus we may say that our legal history starts with an act of codification. . . .

*Canute.* It was left for the mighty Canute (1017–35) to bring to a noble close the first great period in the history of English law, the period during which laws were written in the English language, the period which it is convenient to call Anglo-Saxon. Canute's code we must, if we have regard to the age in which it was issued, call a long and a comprehensive code. It repeats, with improvements, things that have been said before; the great Dane was able to enforce as laws rules which in the mouth of his predecessor had been little better than pious wishes; but it also contained many things that had not been said before. The whole economic and political structure of society was undergoing a great change. If by any two words we could indicate the nature of this elaborate process, we might say that tribalism was giving place to feudalism. Had Canute's successors been his equals in vigour and wisdom, perhaps the change might have been consummated peacefully, and by means of written laws which we might now be reading. As it was, there came to the throne the holy but imbecile Edward. . . .

If we say that law serves three great purposes, that it punishes crime, redresses wrong, and decides disputes—and perhaps we need not go into the matter more deeply than this—we may go on to say that in ancient days the first two of these three purposes are indistinguishably blended, while with the third the legislator seldom troubles himself. If he can maintain the peace, suppress violence and theft, keep vengeance within moderate bounds, he is well satisfied; he will not be at pains to enact a law of contract or of inheritance, a law of husband and wife, a law of landlord and tenant. All this can safely be left to unwritten tradition. He has no care to satisfy the curiosity of a remote posterity which will come prying into these affairs and wish to write books about them. Thus, to take one example, the courts must have been ready to decide disputes about the property of dead men; there must have been a general law, or various tribal or local laws, of inheritance. But the lawgivers tell us nothing about this. If we would recover the old rules, we must make the best that we may of stray hints and chance stories, and of those archaisms which we find embedded in the law of later days.

*Folk-right.* The laws of the folk, the "folk-right"—"law" is one of those words which the Danes bring with them—is known to the men of the folk, but more especially to the old and wise. The free-men, or the free land-owners, of the hundred are in duty bound to frequent the "moot," or court of the hundred, to declare the law and to make the dooms. The presiding ealdorman or sheriff turns to them when a statement of the law is wanted. As yet there is no class of professional lawyers, but the work of attending the courts is discharged chiefly by men of substance, men of thegnly rank; the small folk are glad to stay home.

*Characteristics of Early Law.* Also some men acquire a great reputation for legal learning, and there was much to be learnt, though no one thought of setting it in writing. We should assuredly make a great mistake were we to picture to ourselves these old moots as courts of equity, where "the natural man" administered an informal "law of Nature." For one thing, as will be said elsewhere, the law of the natural man is supernatural law, a law which deals in miracles and portents. But then, again, it is exceedingly formal. It is a law of procedure. The right words must be said without slip or trip, the due ceremonial acts must be punctiliously performed, or the whole transaction will go for naught. This is the main theme of the wise man's jurisprudence. One suspects that sometimes the man, who in the estimate of his neighbors has become very wise indeed, has it in his power to amplify tradition by devices of his own. We hear from Iceland a wonderful tale of a man so uniquely wise that though he had made himself liable to an action of a particular kind, no one could bring that action against him, for he and only he knew the appropriate words of summons: to trick him into a disclosure of this precious formula is a feat worthy of a hero. But formalism has its admirable as well as its ludicrous side. So long as law is unwritten, it must be dramatized and acted. Justice must assume a picturesque garb, or she will not be seen. And even of chicane we may say a good word, for it is the homage which lawlessness pays to law. . . .

*The Influence of Rome.* As yet our Germanic law had not been exposed to the assaults of Roman jurisprudence, but still it had been slowly assuming and assimilating the civilization of the old world. This distinction we must draw. On the one hand, there has been no borrowing from the Roman legal texts. We have no proof whatever that during the five centuries which preceded the Norman Conquest any one copy of a Roman law book existed in England. We hear faint and vague tidings of law being taught in some of the schools, but may safely believe that very little is meant thereby. The written dooms of our kings have been searched over and over again by men skilled in detecting the least shred of Roman law under the most barbaric disguise, and they have found nothing worthy of mention. That these dooms are the purest specimens of pure Germanic law has been the verdict of one scholar after another. Even the English Church, though its independence may often have been exaggerated, became very English.

On the other hand, as already said, to become Christian was in a certain sense to become Roman. Whether, had an impassable wall been raised round England in the last quarter of the sixth century, England would not be a barbarous country at this day—that is a question which cannot be answered. As a matter of fact, we had not to work out our own civilization; we could adopt results already attained in the ancient world. For example, we did not invent the art of writing, we adopted it; we did not invent our alphabet, we took the Roman. And so again—to come nearer to our law—we borrowed or inherited from the old world the written legal document, the written conveyance, the will. The written conveyance was introduced along with Christianity; to all seeming Æthelbert himself began the practice of "booking" lands to the churches. We have a few genuine "land-books" from the seventh and eighth, many from the later centuries. For the more part they are written in Latin, and they were fashioned after Italian models; but at the same time we can see that those models have been barbarized and misunderstood; the English scribes pervert the neat devices of Roman lawyers.

Any phrase which draws a contrast between a nation's law and its civilization is of course open to objection. But let us suppose that at the present day a party of English missionaries is setting forth to convert a savage tribe: perhaps no one of them would know enough of English law to carry him through the easiest examination, and yet they would take with them many ideas that are in a certain sort the ideas of English law. Without being able to define murder, they would know that in this country murderers are condemned to death; they would think that a written expression of a man's last will should be respected, though they might well doubt whether a will is revoked by the testator's marriage. So it was in the seventh century. From the days of Æthelbert onwards English law was under the influence of so much of Roman law as had worked itself into the tradition of the Catholic Church.

## English Law under Norman Rule

*English Law under Norman Rule.* The Normans when they invaded England were in one important particular a less civilized race than were those English whom they came to subjugate. We may say with some certainty that they had no written laws. A century and a half ago a king of the Franks had been compelled to cede a large province to a horde of Scandinavian pirates. The pirates had settled down as lords of a conquered people; they had gradually adopted the religion, the language, and the civilization (such as it was) of the vanquished; they had become Frenchmen. . . .

To all seeming, the Conqueror meant that his English subjects should keep their own old laws. Merely Duke of the Normans, he was going to be King in England, and he was not dissatisfied with those royal rights which, according to his version of the story, had descended to him from King Edward.

*The Law Becomes "Common."* As yet the great bulk of all the justice that was done, was done by local courts, by those shire-moots and hundred-moots which the Conqueror and Henry I had maintained as part of the ancient order, and by the newer seignorial courts which were springing up in every village. The king's own court was but a court for the protection of royal rights, a court for the causes of the king's barons, and an ultimate tribunal at which a persistent litigant might perhaps arrive when justice had failed him everywhere else. Had it continued to be no more than this, the Old English law, slowly adapting itself to changed circumstances, might have cast off its archaisms and become the law for after-times, law to be written and spoken in English words. Far more probably [it] would have split into a myriad local customs, and then at some future time Englishmen must have found relief from intolerable confusion in the eternal law of Rome. Neither of these two things happened, because under Henry II (1154–89) the king's own court flung open its doors to all manner of people, ceased to be for judicial purposes an occasional assembly of warlike barons, became a bench of professional justices, appeared periodically in all the counties of England under the guise of the Justices in Eyre.

Then begins the process which makes the custom of the king's court the common law of England. Ever since the Conquest the king's court had been in a very true sense a French court. It had been a French-speaking court, a court whose members had been of French race, and had but slowly been learning to think of themselves as Englishmen. Its hands had been very free. It could not, if it would, have administered the old English written laws in their native purity: for one thing they were unintelligible; for another thing in the twelfth century they had become barbarous—they dealt with crime in a hopelessly old-fashioned way. On the other part, there was, happily, no written Norman code, and the king did not mean to be in England the mere duke he had been in Normandy. And so the hands of his court were very free; it could be a law unto itself. Many old English institutions it preserved, in particular those institutions of public law which were advantageous to the king—the king, for instance, could insist that the sheriffs were sheriffs, and not hereditary *vicomtes*—but the private law, law of land tenure, law of possession, of contract, of procedure, which the court develops in the course of the twelfth century, is exceedingly like a *coutume* from Northern France. Hundreds of years will elapse before any one tries to write about it in English; and when at length this is done, the English will be an English in which every important noun, every accurate term, is of French origin.

*Legal Language.* We may say a little more about the language of our law, for it is not an uninteresting topic. From the Conquest onwards until the year 1731 the solemnest language of our law was neither French nor English, but Latin. Even in the Anglo-Saxon time, though English was the language in which laws were published, and causes were pleaded, Latin was the language in which the Kings, with Italian models before them, made grants of land to the churches and the thegns. In 1066 the learned men of both races could write and speak to each other in Latin. We shall be pretty safe in saying that any one who could read and write at all could read and write Latin. As to French, it was as yet little better than a vulgar dialect of Latin, a language in which men might speak, but not a language in which they would write anything, except perhaps a few songs. The two tongues which the Conqueror used for laws, charters, and writs, were Latin and English. But Latin soon gets the upper hand, and becomes for a while the one written language of the law. In the king's Chancery they write nothing but Latin, and it is in Latin that the judgments of the king's courts are recorded. This as already said, is so until the year 1731; to substitute English for Latin as the language in which the king's writs and patents and charters shall be expressed, and the doings of the law courts shall be preserved, requires a statute of George II's day.

Meanwhile there had been many and great changes. Late in the twelfth or early in the thirteenth century French was beginning to make itself a language in which not only songs and stories but legal documents could be written. About the middle of the thirteenth century ordinances and statutes that are written in French begin to appear. . . . Under Edward I French, though it cannot expel Latin from the records of litigation, becomes the language in which laws are published and law books are written. It continues to be the language of the statute book until the end of the Middle Ages. Under Henry VII [1485–1509] English at length becomes the speech in which English lawgivers address their subjects, though some two hundred and fifty years must yet pass away before it will win that field in which Latin is securely entrenched.

As the oral speech of litigants and their advisers, French has won a splendid victory. In the king's own court it must prevail from the Conquest onwards, but in the local courts a great deal of English must long have been spoken. Then, however, under Henry II began that centralizing movement which we have already noticed. The jurisprudence of a French-speaking court became the common law, the measure of all rights and duties, and it was carried throughout the land by the journeying justices.

In the thirteenth century men, when they plead or when they talk about law, speak French; the professional lawyer writes in French and thinks in French. Some power of speaking a decent French seems to have been common among all classes of men, save the very poorest; men spoke it who had few, if any, drops of foreign blood in their veins. Then in 1362, when the prolonged wars between England and France had begun, a patriotic statute endeavoured to make English instead of French the spoken tongue of the law-courts. But this came too late; we have good reason for thinking that it was but tardily obeyed, and, at any rate, lawyers went on writing about law in French. Gradually in the sixteenth century their French went to the bad, and they began to write in English; for a long time past they had been thinking and speaking in English. But it was an English in which almost all the technical terms were of French origin. And so it is at the present day. How shall one write a single sentence about law without using some such word as "debt," "contract," "heir," "trespass," "pay," "money," "court," "judge," "jury"? But all these words have come to us from the French. In all the worldwide lands where English law prevails, homage is done daily to William of Normandy and Henry of Anjou.

*Henry II's Legal Reforms.* What Henry [1154–89] did in the middle of the twelfth century was of the utmost importance, though we might find ourselves in the midst of obsolete technicalities were we to endeavour to describe it at length. Speaking briefly, we may say that he concentrated the whole system of English Justice round a court of judges professionally expert in the law. He could thus win money—in the Middle Ages no one did justice for nothing—and he could thus win power;

he could control and he could starve the courts of the feudatories. In offering the nation his royal justice, he offered a strong and sound commodity. Very soon we find very small people—yeomen, peasants—giving the go-by to the old local courts and making their way to Westminster Hall, to plead there about their petty affairs. We may allow that in course of time this concentrating process went much too far. In Edward I's day the competence of the local courts in civil causes was hemmed within a limit of forty shillings, a limit which at first was fairly wide, but became ever narrower as the value of money fell, until in the eighteenth century no one could exact any debt that was not of trifling amount without bringing a costly action in one of the courts at Westminster. But the first stages of the process did unmixed good—they gave us a common law.

King Henry and his able ministers came just in time—a little later would have been too late: English law would have been unified, but it would have been Romanized. We have been wont to boast, perhaps too loudly, of the pure "Englishry" of our common law. This has not been all pure gain. Had we "received" the Roman jurisprudence as our neighbors received it, we should have kept out of many a bad mess through which we have plunged. But to say nothing of the political side of the matter, of the absolute monarchy which Roman law has been apt to bring in its train, it is probably well for us and for the world at large that we have stumbled forwards in our empirical fashion, blundering into wisdom. The moral glow known to the virtuous schoolboy who has not used the "crib" that was ready to his hand, we may allow ourselves to feel; and we may hope for the blessing which awaits all those who have honestly taught themselves anything.

*Roman Law in Mediaeval Europe.* In a few words we must try to tell a long story. On the Continent of Europe Roman law had never perished. After the barbarian invasions it was still the "personal law" of the conquered provincials. The Franks, Lombards, and other victorious tribes lived under their old Germanic customs, while the vanquished lived under the Roman law. In course of time the personal law of the bulk of the inhabitants became the territorial law of the country where they lived. The Roman law became once more the general law of Italy and of Southern France; but in so doing it lost its purity, it became a debased and vulgarized Roman law, to be found rather in traditional custom than in the classical texts, of which very little was known. Then, at the beginning of the twelfth century, came a great change. A law school at Bologna began to study and to teach that Digest in which Justinian had preserved the wisdom of the great jurists of the golden age. A new science spread outwards from Bologna. At least wherever the power of the emperor extended, Roman law had—so men thought—a claim to rule. The emperors, though now of German race, were still the Roman emperors, and the laws of their ancestors were to be found in Justinian's books. But further, the newly discovered system—for we may without much untruth say that it was newly discovered—seemed so reasonable that it could not but affect the development of law in countries, such as France and England, which paid no obedience to the emperors.

*Canon Law.* And just at this time a second great system of cosmopolitan jurisprudence was taking shape. For centuries past the Catholic Church had been slowly acquiring a field of jurisdiction that was to be all her own, and for the use of the ecclesiastical tribunals a large body of law had come into being, consisting of the canons published by Church councils and the decretal epistles—genuine and forged—of the popes. Various collections of these were current, but in the middle of the twelfth century they were superseded by the work of Gratian, a monk of Bologna. He called it "The Concordance of Discordant Canons," but it soon became known everywhere as the "Decretum." And by this time the popes were ever busy in pouring out decretal letters, sending them into all corners of the western world. Authoritative collections of these "decretals" were published, and the ecclesiastical lawyer (the "canonist" or "decretist") soon had at his command a large mass of written law comparable to that which the Roman lawyer (the "civilian" or "legist") was studying. A Corpus Juris Canonici begins to take its place beside the Corpus Juris Civilis. Very often the same man had studied both; he was a "doctor of both laws"; and, indeed, the newer system had borrowed largely from the older; it had borrowed its form, its spirit, and a good deal of its matter also.

The canonical jurisprudence of the Italian doctors became the ecclesiastical law of the western world. From all local courts, wherever they might be, there was an appeal to the ultimate tribunal at Rome. But the temporal law of every country felt the influence of the new learning. Apparently we might lay down some such rule as this—that where the attack is longest postponed, it is most severe. In the thirteenth century the Parliament of Paris began the work of harmonizing and rationalizing the provincial customs of Northern France, and this it did by Romanizing them. In the sixteenth century, after the "revival of letters," the Italian jurisprudence took hold of Germany, and swept large portions of the old national law before it. Wherever it finds a weak, because an uncentralized, system of justice, it wins an easy triumph. To Scotland, it came late; but it came to stay.

*Roman Law in England.* To England it came early. Very few are the universities which can boast of a school of Roman law so old as that of Oxford. In the troubled days of our King Stephen [1135–54], when the Church was urging new claims against the feeble State, Archbishop

Theobald imported from Italy one Vacarius, a Lombard lawyer, who lectured here on Roman law, and wrote a big book that may still be read. Very soon after this Oxford had a flourishing school of civil and canon law. Ever since William the Conqueror had solemnly sanctioned the institution of special ecclesiastical courts, it had been plain that in those courts the law of a Catholic Church, not of a merely English Church, must prevail; also that this law would be in the main Italian law.

In the next century, as all know, Henry and Becket fell out as to the definition of the province that was to be left to the ecclesiastical courts. The battle was drawn; neither combatant had gained all that he wanted. Thenceforward until the Protestant Reformation, and indeed until later than that, a border warfare between the two sets of courts was always simmering. Victory naturally inclined to those tribunals which had an immediate control of physical force, but still the sphere that was left to the canonist will seem to our eyes very ample. It comprehended not only the enforcement of ecclesiastical discipline, and the punishment—by spiritual censure, and, in the last resort, by excommunication—of sins left unpunished by temporal law, but also the whole topic of marriage and divorce, those last dying wills and testaments which were closely connected with dying confessions, and the administration of the goods of intestates. Why to this day do we couple "Probate" with "Divorce"? Because in the Middle Ages both of these matters belonged to the "courts Christian." Why to "Probate" and "Divorce" do we add "Admiralty"? Because the civilians—and in England the same man was usually both canonist and civilian—succeeded, though at a comparatively late time, in taking to themselves the litigation that concerned things done on the high seas, those high seas whence no jury could be summoned. So for the canonist there was plenty of room in England; and there was some room for the civilian: he was very useful as a diplomatist.

But we are speaking of our English common law, the law of our ordinary temporal courts, and of the influence upon it of the new Italian cosmopolitan jurisprudence; and we must confess that for a short while, from the middle of the twelfth to the middle of the thirteenth century, this influence was powerful. The amount of foreign law that was actually borrowed has been underrated and overrated; we could not estimate it without descending to details. Some great maxims and a few more concrete rules were appropriated, but on the whole what was taken was logic, method, spirit, rather than matter.

*Glanvill.* We may see the effect of this influence very plainly in a Treatise on the Laws of England which comes to us from the last years of Henry II. It has been ascribed to Henry's Chief Justiciar—Viceroy, we may say—Ranulf Glanvill, and whether or not it comes from his pen (he was a layman and a warrior), it describes the practice of the court over which he presided. There are very few sentences in it which we can trace to any Roman book, and yet in a sense the whole book is Roman. We look back from it to a law book written in Henry I's time, and we can hardly believe that only some seventy years divide the two. The one can at this moment be read and understood by any one who knows a little of mediaeval Latin and a little of English law; the other will always be dark to the most learned scholars. The gulf between them looks like that between logic and caprice, between reason and unreason.

*Bracton.* And then from the middle of the thirteenth century we have a much greater and better book than Glanvill's. Its author we know as Bracton, though his name really was Henry of Bratton.[2] He was an ecclesiastic, an archdeacon, but for many years he was one of the king's justices. He had read a great deal of the Italian jurisprudence, chiefly in the works of that famous doctor, Azo of Bologna. Thence he had obtained his idea of what a law book should be, of how law should be arranged and stated; thence also he borrowed maxims and some concrete rules; with these he can fill up the gaps in our English system. But he lets us see that not much more can now be done in the way of romanization. Ever since Henry II's time the king's court has been hard at work amassing precedents, devising writs, and commenting upon them. Bracton himself has laboriously collected five hundred decisions from the mile-long rolls of the court and uses them as his authorities. For him English law is already "case law"; a judgment is a precedent. While as yet the science of the civilians was a somewhat unpractical science, while as yet they had not succeeded in bringing the old classical texts into close contact with the facts of mediaeval life, the king's court of professional justices—the like of which was hardly to be found in any foreign land, in any unconquered land—had been rapidly evolving a common law for England, establishing a strict and formal routine of procedure, and tying the hands of all subsequent judges. From Bracton's day onwards Roman law exercises but the slightest influence on the English common law, and such influence as it exercises is rather by way of repulsion than by way of attraction. English law at this early period had absorbed so much Romanism that it could withstand all future attacks, and pass scathless even through the critical sixteenth century.

It may be convenient, however, to pause at this point in the development of our judicial institutions, in order to trace the history of our legal procedure.

*History of Trial by Jury.* For a long time past Englishmen have been proud of their trial by jury, proud to see the nations of Europe imitating

---

[2] Bracton, *De Legibus et Consuetudinibus Angliae.*

as best they might this "palladium of English liberties," this "bulwark of the British Constitution." Their pride, if in other respects it be reasonable, need not be diminished by any modern discoveries of ancient facts, even though they may have to learn that in its origin trial by jury was rather French than English, rather royal than popular, rather the livery of conquest than a badge of freedom. They have made it what it is; and what it is is very different from what it was. . . .

*The Earliest Jury Trial.* We have spoken of "trial by jury." That term naturally calls up before our minds a set of twelve men called into court in order that they may listen to the testimony of witnesses, give a true verdict "according to the evidence," and, in short, act as judges of those questions of fact that are in dispute. But it is very long after Henry II's day before trial by jury takes this form. Originally the jurors are called in, not in order that they may hear, but in order that they may give, evidence. They are witnesses. They are the neighbors of the parties; they are presumed to know before they come into court the facts about which they are to testify. They are chosen by the sheriff to represent the neighborhood—indeed, they are spoken of as being "the neighborhood," "the country"—and the neighborhood, the country will know the facts. In the twelfth century population was sparse, and men really knew far more of the doings of their neighbors than we know nowadays. It was expected that all legal transactions would take place in public; the conveyance of land was made in open court, the wife was endowed at the church-door, the man who bought cattle in secret ran a great but just risk of being treated as a thief; every three weeks a court was held in the village, and all the affairs of every villager were discussed. The verdict, then, was the sworn testimony of the countryside; and if the twelve jurors perjured themselves, the verdict of another jury of twenty-four might send them to prison and render them infamous for ever. In course of time, and by slow degrees—degrees so slow that we can hardly detect them—the jury put off its old and acquired a new character. Sometimes, when the jurors knew nothing of the facts, witnesses who did know the facts would be called in to supply the requisite information. As human affairs grew more complex, the neighbors whom the sheriff summoned became less and less able to perform their original duty, more and more dependent upon the evidence given in their presence by those witnesses who were summoned by the parties. In the fifteenth century the change had taken place, though in yet later days a man who had been summoned as a juror, and who sought to escape on the ground that he already knew something of the facts in question, would be told that he had given a very good reason for his being placed in the jury-box. We may well say, therefore, that trial by jury, though it has its roots in the Frankish inquest, grew up on English soil; and until recent times it was distinctive of England and Scotland, for on the Continent of Europe all other forms of legal procedure had been gradually supplanted by that which canonists and civilians had constructed out of ancient Roman elements.

*The Working of Trial by Jury.* If we regard it as an engine for the rediscovery of truth and for the punishment of malefactors, the mediæval jury was a clumsy thing. Too often its verdicts must have represented guesswork and the tittle-tattle of the countryside. Sometimes a man must have gone to the gallows, not because anyone had seen him commit a crime, not because guilt had been brought home to him by a carefully tested chain of proven facts, but because it was notorious that he was just the man from whom a murder or a robbery might be expected. Only by slow degrees did the judges insist that the jurors ought to listen to evidence given by witnesses in open court, and rely only upon the evidence that was there given. Even when this step had been taken, it was long before our modern law of evidence took shape, long before the judges laid down such rules as that "hearsay is not evidence," and that testimony which might show that the prisoner had committed other crimes was not relevant to the question whether he had perpetrated the particular offence of which he stood indicted.

But whatever may have been the case in the days of the ordeal—and about this we know very little—we may be fairly certain that in the later Middle Ages the escape of the guilty was far commoner than the punishment of the guiltless. After some hesitation our law had adopted its well-known rule that a jury can give no verdict unless the twelve men are all of one mind. To obtain a condemnatory unanimity was not easy if the accused was a man of good family; one out of every twelve of his neighbors that might be taken at random would stand out loyally for his innocence. Bribery could do much; seignorial influence could do more; the sheriff, who was not incorruptible, and had his own likes and dislikes, could do all, since it was for him to find the jury. It was easy for us to denounce as unconstitutional the practice which prevailed under Tudors and Stuarts of making jurors answer for their verdicts before the King's Council; it is not so easy for us to make certain that the jury system would have lived through the sixteenth century had it not been for the action of this somewhat irregular check. For the rest, we may notice that the jury of the Middle Ages, if it is to be called a democratic institution, can be called so only in a mediaeval sense. The jurors were freeholders; the great mass of Englishmen were not freeholders. The peasant who was charged with a crime was acquitted or convicted by the word of his neighbors, but by the word of neighbors who considered themselves very much his superiors. . . .

## The Development of Law and Legal Reform under Edward I

*Legislation.* During the period which divides the coronation of Henry II (1154) from the coronation of Edward I (1272) definite legislation was still an uncommon thing. Great as were the changes due to Henry's watchful and restless activity, they were changes that were effected without the pomp of solemn lawmaking. A few written or even spoken words communicated to his justices, those justices whom he was contantly sending to perambulate the country, might do great things, might institute new methods of procedure, might bring new classes of men and of things within the cognizance of the royal court. Some of his ordinances—or "assizes," as they were called—have come down to us; others we have lost. No one was at any great pains to preserve their text, because they were regarded, not as new laws, but as mere temporary instructions which might be easily altered. They soon sink into the mass of unenacted "common law." Even in the next, the thirteenth, century some of Henry's rules were regarded as traditional rules which had come down from a remote time, and which might be ascribed to the Conqueror, the Confessor, or any other king around whom a mist of fable had gathered.

*Magna Carta and Other Statutes.* Thus it came about that the lawyers of Edward I's day—and that was the day in which a professional class of temporal lawyers first became prominent in England—thought of Magna Carta [1215] as the oldest statute of the realm, the first chapter in the written law of the land, the earliest of those texts the very words of which are law. And what they did their successors do at the present day.

The Great Charter stands in the forefront of our statute-book, though of late years a great deal of it has been repealed. And certainly it is worthy of its place. It is worthy of its place just because it is no philosophical or oratorical declaration of the rights of man, nor even of the rights of Englishmen, but an intensely practical document, the fit prologue for those intensely practical statutes which English Parliaments will publish in age after age.

What is more, it is a grand compromise, and a fit prologue for all those thousands of compromises in which the practical wisdom of the English race will always be expressing itself. Its very form is a compromise—in part that of a free grant of liberties made by the king, in part that of a treaty between him and his subjects, which is to be enforced against him if he breaks it. And then in its detailed clauses it must do something for all those sorts and conditions of men who have united to resist John's tyranny—for the bishop, the clerk, the baron, the knight, the burgess, the merchant—and there must be some give and take between these classes, for not all their interests are harmonious. But even in the Great Charter there is not much new law; indeed, its own theory of itself (if we may use such a phrase) is that the old law, which a lawless king has set at naught, is to be restored, defined, covenanted, and written.

The Magna Carta of our statute book is not exactly the charter that John sealed at Runnymede; it is a charter granted by his son and successor, Henry III, the text of the original document having been modified on more than one occasion. Only two other acts of Henry's long reign attained the rank of statute law. The Provisions of Merton (1236), enacted by a great assembly of prelates and nobles, introduced several novelties, and contain those famous words, "We will not have the laws of England changed," which were the reply of the barons to a request made by the bishops, who were desirous that our insular rule, "Once a bastard always a bastard," might yield to the law of the universal Church, and that marriage might have a retroactive effect. Among Englishmen there was no wish to change the laws of England. If only the king and his foreign favourites would observe those laws, then—such was the common opinion —all would be well.

A change came; vague discontent crystallized in the form of definite grievances. After the Barons' War the king, though he had triumphed over his foes, and was enjoying his own again, was compelled to redress many of those grievances by the Provisions of Marlborough (1267) or, as they have been commonly called, the Statute of Marlbridge.

When, a few years afterwards, Henry died (1272), the written, the enacted law of England consisted in the main of but four documents, which we can easily read through in half an hour—there was the Great Charter, there was the sister-charter which defined the forest law, there were the Statutes of Merton and of "Marlbridge." To these we might add a few minor ordinances; but the old Anglo-Saxon dooms were by this time utterly forgotten, the law-books of the Norman age were already unintelligible, and even the assizes of Henry II, though but a century old, had become part and parcel of the "common law," not to be distinguished from the unenacted rules which had gathered round them. Englishmen might protest that they would not change the law of England, but as a matter of fact the law of England was being changed very rapidly by the incessant decisions of the powerful central court.

*The King's Courts.* Slowly the "curia" of the Norman reigns had been giving birth to various distinct offices and tribunals. In Edward's day there was a "King's Bench" (a court for criminal causes and other "pleas of the Crown"); a "Common Bench" (a court for actions brought by one subject against another); an Exchequer, which both in a judicial and an administrative way collected the king's revenue and enforced his fiscal rights; a Chancery, which was a universal secretarial bureau, doing all the writing that was done in the king's name. These various departments had many adventures to live through before the day would come when they would once more be absorbed into a High Court of Justice. Of some few of those adventures we shall speak in another place, but must here say two or three words about a matter which gave a distinctive shape to the whole body of our law—a shape that it is even now but slowly losing.

*Writs.* Our common law during the later Middle Ages and far on into modern times is in the main a commentary on writs issued out of the King's Chancery. To understand this, we must go back to the twelfth century, to a time when it would have seemed by no means natural that ordinary litigation between ordinary men should come into the king's court. It does not come there without an order from the king. Your adversary could not summon you to meet him in that court; the summons must come from the king.

Thus much of the old procedure we still retain in our own time; it will be the reigning King, not your creditor, who will bid you appear in his High Court. But whereas at the present day the formal part of the writ will merely bid you appear in court, and all the information that you will get about the nature of the claim against you will be conveyed to you in the plaintiff's own words or those of his legal advisers, this was not so until very lately. In old times the writ that was drawn up in the King's Chancery and sealed with his great seal told the defendant a good many particulars about the plaintiff's demand. Gradually, as the king began to open the doors of his court to litigants of all kinds, blank forms of the various writs that could be issued were accumulated in the Chancery. We may think of the king as keeping a shop in which writs were sold. Some of them were to be had at fixed prices, or, as we should say nowadays, they could be had as matters of course on the payment of fixed court fees; for others special bargains had to be made. Then, in course of time, as our Parliamentary constitution took shape, the invention of new writs became rarer and rarer. Men began to see that if the king in his Chancery could devise new remedies by granting new writs, he had in effect a power of creating new rights and making new laws without the concurrence of the estates of the realm. And so it came to be a settled doctrine that though the old formulas might be modified in immaterial particulars to suit new cases as they arose, no new formula could be introduced except by statute.

This change had already taken place in Edward I's day. Thenceforward the cycle of writs must be regarded as a closed cycle; no one can bring his cause before the king's courts unless he can bring it within the scope of one of those formulas which the Chancery has in stock and ready for sale. We may argue that if there is no writ there is no remedy, and if there is no remedy there is no wrong; and thus the register of writs in the Chancery becomes the test of rights and the measure of law. Then round each writ a great mass of learning collects itself. He who knows what cases can be brought within each formula knows the law of England. The body of law has a skeleton and that skeleton is the system of writs. Thus our jurisprudence took an exceedingly rigid and permanent shape; it became a commentary on formulas. It could still grow and assimilate new matter, but it could only do this by a process of interpretation which gradually found new, and not very natural, meanings for old phrases. As we shall see hereafter, this process of interpretation was too slow to keep up with the course of social and economic change, and the Chancery had to come to the relief of the courts of law by making itself a court of equity.

## Legal Concepts in the Middle Ages

*Legislation.* The desire for continuous legislation is modern. We have come to think that, year by year, Parliament must meet and pour out statutes; that every statesman must have in his mind some program of new laws; that if his program once became exhausted he would cease to be a statesman. It was otherwise in the Middle Ages. As a matter of fact a parliament might always find that some new statute was necessary. The need for legislation, however, was occasioned (so men thought) not by any fated progress of the human race, but by the perversity of mankind. Ideally there exists a perfect body of law, immutable, eternal, the work of God, not of man. Just a few more improvements in our legal procedure will have made it for ever harmonious with this ideal; and, indeed, if men would but obey the law of the land as it stands, there would be little for a legislator to do. . . .

*Scope of Legislation.* Parliament by its statutes was beginning to interfere with many affairs, small as well as great. Indeed, what we may consider small affairs seem to have troubled and interested it more even than those large constitutional questions which it was always hoping to settle but never settling. If we see a long statute, one guarded with careful provisos, one that tells us of debate and compromise, this will probably be a statute which deals with one particular trade; for example, a statute concerning the sale of herring at Yarmouth fair. The thorniest of themes for discussion is the treatment of foreign merchants. Naturally enough of our lords, knights, and burgesses cannot easily agree about it. One opinion prevails in the seaports, another in the upland towns, and the tortuous course of legislation, swaying now towards Free Trade and now towards Protection, is the resultant of many forces. . . .

On the other hand, the great outlines of criminal law and private law seem to have been regarded as fixed for all time. In the present century students of law will still for practical purposes be compelled to know a good deal about some of the statutes of Edward I [1272–1307]. They will seldom have occasion to know anything of any laws that were enacted during the fourteenth or the first three-quarters of the fifteenth century. Parliament seems to have abandoned the idea of controlling the development of the common law. Occasionally and spasmodically it would interfere, devise some new remedy, fill a gap in the register of writs, or circumvent the circumventors of a statute. But in general it left the ordinary law of the land to the judges and the lawyers. In its eyes the common law was complete, or very nearly complete.

And then as we read the statute roll of the fifteenth century we seem for a while to be watching the decline and fall of a mighty institution. Parliament seems to have nothing better to do than to regulate the manufacture of cloth. Now and then it strives to cope with the growing evils of the time, the renascent feudalism, the private wars of great and small; but without looking outside our roll we can see that these efforts are half-hearted and ineffectual. We are expected to show a profound interest in "the making of worsteds," while we gather from a few casual hints that the Wars of the Roses are flagrant. If for a moment the Parliament of Edward IV can raise its soul above defective barrels of fish and fraudulent gutter tiles this will be in order to prohibit "cloish, kayles, half-bowl, hand-in-hand and hand-out, quekeboard," and such other games as interfere with the practice of archery.

*"The Omnipotence of Parliament."* In the end it was better that Parliament should for a while register the acts of a despot than that it should sink into the contempt that seemed to be prepared for it. The part which the assembled estates of the realm have to play in the great acts of Henry VIII (1509–47) may in truth be a subservient and ignoble part; but the acts are great and they are all done "by the authority of Parliament." By the authority of Parliament the Bishop of Rome could be deprived of all jurisdiction, the monasteries could be dissolved, the king could be made (so far as the law of God would permit) supreme head of the English Church, the succession to the Crown could be settled first in this way, then in that, the force of statute might be given to the king's proclamations. There was nothing that could not be done by the authority of Parliament. And part from the constitutional and ecclesiastical changes which everyone has heard about, very many things of importance were done by statute.

We owe to Henry VIII—much rather to him than to his Parliament—not a few innovations in the law of property and the law of crime, and the parliaments of Elizabeth performed some considerable legal exploits. The statutes of the Tudor period are lengthy documents. In many a grandiose preamble we seem to hear the voice of Henry himself; but their length is not solely due to the pomp of imperial phrases. They condescend to details; they teem with exceptions and saving clauses. One cannot establish a new ecclesiastical polity by half-a-dozen lines. We see that the judges are by this time expected to attend very closely to the words that Parliament utters, to weigh and obey every letter of the written law.

*Statute and Common Law.* Just now and then in the last of the Middle Ages and thence onwards into the eighteenth century, we hear the judges claiming some vague right of disregarding statutes which are directly at variance with the common law, or the law of God, or the royal prerogative. Had much come of this claim, our constitution must have taken a very different shape from that which we see at the present day. Little came of it. In the troublous days of Richard II [1377–99], a chief justice got himself hanged as a traitor for advising the king that a statute curtailing the royal power was void. For the rest, the theory is but a speculative dogma. We can (its upholders seem to say) conceive that a statute might be so irrational, so wicked, that we would not enforce it; but, as a matter of fact, we have never known such a statute made. From the Norman Conquest onward, England seems marked out as the country in which men, so soon as they begin to philosophize, will endeavor to prove that all law is the command of a "sovereign one," or a "sovereign many." They may be somewhat shocked when in the seventeenth century Hobbes states this theory in trenchant terms and combines it with many unpopular doctrines. But the way for Hobbes had been prepared of old. In the days of Edward I the text-writer, whom we call Britton, had put the common law into the king's mouth: all legal rules might be stated as royal commands.

Still, even in the age of the Tudors, only a small part of the law was in the statute book. Detached pieces of superstructure were there; for the foundation men had to look elsewhere. After the brilliant thirteenth century a long, dull period had set in. The custody of the common law was now committed to a small group of judges and lawyers. They knew their own business very thoroughly, and they knew nothing else. Law was now divorced from literature; no one attempted to write a book about it. The decisions of the courts at Westminster were diligently reported and diligently studied, but no one thought of comparing English law with anything else. Roman law was by this time an unintelligible, outlandish thing, perhaps a good enough law for half-starved Frenchmen.

*The Legal Profession: The Inns of Court.* Legal education was no longer academic—the universities had nothing to do with it, they could only make canonists and civilians—it was scholastic. By stages that are exceedingly obscure, the inns of court and inns of chancery were growing. They were associations of lawyers which had about them a good deal of the club, something of the college, something of the trade-union. They acquired the "inns" or "hospices"—that is, the town houses—which had belonged to great noblemen: for example, the Earl of Lincoln's inn. The house and church of the Knights of the Temple came into their hands. The smaller societies, "inns of chancery," became dependent on the larger societies, "inns of court." The serjeants and apprentices who composed them enjoyed an exclusive right of pleading in court; some things might be done by an apprentice or barrister, others required a serjeant; in the Court of Common Pleas only a serjeant could be heard. . . . [T]he inns developed a laborious system of legal education. Many years a student had to spend in hearing and giving lectures and in pleading fictitious causes before he could be admitted to practice.

It is no wonder that under the fostering care of these societies English jurisprudence became an occult science and its professors "the most unlearned kind of most learned men." They were rigorous logicians, afraid of no conclusion that was implicit in their premises. The sky might fall, the Wars of the Roses might rage, but they would pursue the even course of their argumentation. They were not altogether unmindful of the social changes that were going on around them. In the fifteenth century there were great judges who performed what may seem to us some daring feats in the accommodation of old law to new times. Out of unpromising elements they developed a comprehensive law of contract; they loosened the bonds of those family settlements by which land had been tied up. . . . But all this had to be done evasively and by means of circumventive fictions. Novel principles could not be admitted until they were disguised in some antique garb.

---

COMMENT. (1) *Parliament and English Constitutional Law.* In the preceding section only a few words were given to the rise of Parliament; the rest of these materials will be similarly deficient in dealing with English constitutional history in spite of its lasting significance to the contest between the "rule of law" and individualized power. Readers who are not familiar with this story may wish to consult: T. P. Taswell-Langmead, *English Constitutional History* (London: Sweet, 1960); Carl Stephenson and Frederick Marcham, *Sources of English Constitutional History* (New York: Harper, 1937); and M. M. Knappen, *Constitutional and Legal History of England* (New York: Harcourt, 1942).

(2) *Further information* on the development of professional training

at the Inns can be found in Zane's "The Five Ages of the Bench and Bar of England," *Select Essays in Anglo-American Legal History,* Vol. 1, 1907, pp. 625 *et seq.* See also the discussion on the English Bar in Chapter 8, pp. 437–454.

---

## LATER DEVELOPMENT: COKE AND BEYOND

By Frederic W. Maitland

*Coke.* [T]he common law took flesh in the person of Edward Coke (1552–1634). With an enthusiastic love of English tradition, for the sake of which many offences may be forgiven him, he ranged over nearly the whole field of law, commenting, reporting, arguing, deciding—disorderly, pedantic, masterful, an incarnate national dogmatism tenacious of continuous life. Imbued with this new spirit, the lawyers fought the battle of the constitution against James and Charles, and historical research appeared as the guardian of national liberties. That the Stuarts united against themselves three such men as Edward Coke, John Selden and William Prynne, is the measure of their folly and their failure.... Even pliant judges whose tenure of office depended on the king's will, were compelled to cite and discuss old precedents before they could give judgment for their master; and even at their worse moments they would not openly break with medieval tradition, or declare in favor of that "modern police state" which has too often become the ideal of foreign publicists trained in Byzantine law.

*Hale.* The current of legal doctrine was by this time so strong and voluminous that such events as the Civil War, the Restoration and the Revolution hardly deflected the course of the stream. In retrospect, Charles II reigns so soon as life has left his father's body, and James II ends a lawless career by a considerate and convenient abdication. The statute book of the restored king was enriched by leaves excerpted from the acts of a lord protector; and Matthew Hale (d. 1676), who was, perhaps, the last of the great record-searching judges, sketched a map of English law which Blackstone was to color. Then a time of self-complacency came for the law, which knew itself to be the perfection of wis-

---

This excerpt first appeared in the *Encyclopaedia Britannica,* Vol. 28 (10th ed., supp. 1902), and has been reprinted in Helen M. Cam, ed., *Selected Historical Essays of F. W. Maitland* (London: Cambridge U.P., 1957), pp. 112–119.

dom, and any proposal for drastic legislation would have worn the garb discredited by the tyranny of the Puritan Caesar. . . .

*Equity.* But during this age the chief addition to English jurisprudence was made by the crystallization of the chancellor's equity. In the seventeenth century the Chancery had a narrow escape of sharing the fate that befell its twin sister the Star Chamber. Its younger sister, the Court of Requests, perished under the persistent attacks of the common lawyers. Having outlived troubles, the Chancery took to orderly habits, and administered under the name of "equity" a growing group of rules, which in fact were supplemental law. . . . Slowly a continuous series of Equity Reports began to flow, and still more slowly an "equity bar" began to form itself. The principal outlines of equity were drawn by men who were steeped in the common law. By way of ornament a Roman maxim might be borrowed from a French or Dutch expositor, or a phrase which smacked of that "nature-rightly" school which was dominating continental Europe; but the influence exercised by Roman law upon English equity has been the subject of gross exaggeration. Parliament and the old courts being what they were, perhaps it was only in a new court that the requisite new law could be evolved. The result was not altogether satisfactory. Freed from contact with the plain man in the jury box, the Chancellors were tempted to forget how plain and rough good law should be, and to screw up the legal standard of reasonable conduct to a height hardly attainable except by those whose purses could command the constant advice of a family solicitor. A court which started with the idea of doing summary justice for the poor became a court which did a highly refined, but tardy justice, suitable only to the rich.

*Blackstone.* About the middle of the century William Blackstone, then a disappointed barrister, began to give lectures on English law at Oxford (1758), and soon afterwards he began to publish (1765) his *Commentaries.* Accurate enough in its history and doctrine to be an invaluable guide to professional students and a useful aid to practitioners, his book set before the unprofessional public an artistic picture of the laws of England such as had never been drawn of any similar system. No nation but the English had so eminently readable a law book, and it must be doubtful whether any other lawyer ever did more important work than was done by the first professor of English law.[a] Over and over again the *Commentaries* were edited, sometimes by distinguished men, and it is hardly too much to say that for nearly a century the English lawyer's main ideas of the organization and articulation of the body of English law were controlled by Blackstone.

This was far from all. The Tory lawyer little thought that he was

---

[a] A sample of Blackstone's writing appears at p. 37.

giving law to colonies that were on the eve of a great and successful rebellion. Yet so it was. Out in America, where books were few and lawyers had a mighty task to perform, Blackstone's facile presentment of the law of the mother country was of inestimable value. It has been said that among American lawyers the *Commentaries* "stood for the law of England," and this at a time when the American daughter of English law was rapidly growing in stature, and was preparing herself for her destined march from the Atlantic to the Pacific Ocean. Excising only what seemed to savour of oligarchy, those who had defied King George retained with marvelous tenacity the law of their forefathers. Profound discussions of English medieval law have been heard in American courts; admirable researches into the recesses of the Year Books have been made in American law schools; the names of the great American judges are familiar in an England which knows little indeed of foreign jurists; and the debt due for the loan of Blackstone's *Commentaries* is being fast repaid. Lectures on the common law delivered by Mr. Justice Holmes of the Supreme Court of the United States may even have begun to turn the scale against the old country. No chapter in Blackstone's book nowadays seems more antiquated than that which describes the modest territorial limits of that English law which was soon to spread throughout Australia and New Zealand and to follow the dominant race in India.

*Bentham.* Long wars, vast economic changes and the conservatism generated by the French Revolution piled up a monstrous arrear of work for the English legislature. Meanwhile, Jeremy Bentham (d. 1832) had labored for the overthrow of much that Blackstone had lauded. Bentham's largest projects of destruction and reconstruction took but little effect. Profoundly convinced of the fungibility and pliability of mankind, he was but too ready to draw a code for England or Spain or Russia at the shortest notice; and, scornful as he was of the past and its historic deposit, a code drawn by Bentham would have been a sorry failure. On the other hand, as a critic and derider of the system which Blackstone had complacently expounded he did excellent service. Reform, and radical reform, was indeed sadly needed throughout a system which was encumbered by noxious rubbish, the useless leavings of the Middle Ages: trial by battle and compurgation, deodands and benefit of clergy, John Doe and Richard Roe. It is perhaps the main fault of "judge-made law" (to use Bentham's phrase) that its destructive work can never be cleanly done. Of all vitality, and therefore of all patent harmfulness, the old rule can be deprived, but the moribund husk must remain in the system doing latent mischief. English law was full of decayed husks when Bentham attacked it, and his persistent demand for reasons could not be answered. At length a general interest in "law reform" was excited . . . and the great changes in constitutional law which cluster round the Reform Act of 1832 were accompanied by many measures which purged the private, procedural and criminal law of much, though hardly enough, of the mediæval dross. . . .

PROFESSOR MAITLAND HAS ALREADY briefly sketched for us the outlines of the development of equity. But the force of this legal institution is so pervasive that it deserves fuller treatment here. We return to Maitland.

# THE DEVELOPMENT OF EQUITY By Frederic W. Maitland

*What is "Equity"?* I intend to speak of Equity as of an existing body of rules administered by our courts of justice. But for reasons which you will easily understand a brief historical prelude seems necessary. For suppose that we ask the question—What is Equity? We can only answer it by giving some short account of certain courts of justice which were abolished over thirty years ago. In the year 1875 we might have said "Equity is that body of rules which is administered only by those Courts which are known as Courts of Equity." The definition of course would not have been very satisfactory, but nowadays we are cut off even from this unsatisfactory definition. We have no longer any courts which are merely courts of equity. Thus we are driven to say that Equity now is that body of rules administered by our English courts of justice which, were it not for the operation of the Judicature Acts, would be administered only by those courts which would be known as Courts of Equity.

This, you may well say, is but a poor thing to call a definition. Equity is a certain portion of our existing substantive law, and yet in order that we may describe this portion and mark it off from other portions we have to make reference to courts that are no longer in existence. Still I fear that nothing better than this is possible. The only alternative would be to make a list of the equitable rules and say that equity consists of those rules. This, I say, would be the only alternative, for if we were to inquire what it is that all these rules have in common and what it is that marks them off from all other rules administered by our courts, we should by

---

Reprinted from *Equity, Also the Forms of Action at Common Law* (Cambridge U.P., 1909), pp. 1–10, with the permission of the publisher.

way of answer find nothing but this, that these rules were until lately administered, and administered only by our courts of equity.

*Origins.* Therefore for the mere purpose of understanding the present state of our law, some history becomes necessary. . . .

In Edward I's day, at the end of the thirteenth century, three great courts have come into existence, the King's Bench, the Common Bench or Court of Common Pleas and the Exchequer. Each of these has its own proper sphere, but as time goes on each of them attempts to extend its sphere and before the Middle Ages are over a plaintiff has often a choice between these three courts and each of them will deal with his case in the same way and by the same rules. The law which these courts administer is in part traditional law, in part statute law. Already in Edward I's day the phrase "common law" is current. It is a phrase that has been borrowed from the canonist—who used *jus commune* to denote the general law of the Catholic Church; it describes that part of the law that is unenacted, non-statutory, that is common to the whole land and to all Englishmen. It is contrasted with statute, with local custom, with royal prerogative. It is not as yet contrasted with equity, for as yet there is no body of rules which bears this name.

*The Chancellor and the Issuance of Writs.* One of the three courts, namely, the Exchequer, is more than a court of law. From our modern point of view it is not only a court of law but a "government office," an administrative or executive bureau; our modern Treasury is an offshoot from the old Exchequer. What we should call the "civil service" of the country is transacted by two great offices or "departments"; there is the Exchequer which is the fiscal department, there is the Chancery which is the secretarial department, while above these there rises the king's permanent Council. At the head of the Chancery stands the Chancellor, usually a bishop; he is we may say the king's secretary of state for all departments, he keeps the king's great seal and all the already great mass of writing that has to be done in the king's name has to be done under his supervision.

He is not as yet a judge, but already he by himself or his subordinates has a great deal of work to do which brings him into a close connexion with the administration of justice. One of the duties of that great staff of clerks over which he presides is to draw up and issue those writs whereby actions are begun in the courts of law—such writs are sealed with the king's seal. A man who wishes to begin an action must go to the Chancery and obtain a writ. Many writs there are which have been formulated long ago; such writs are writs of course (*brevia de cursu*), one obtains them by asking for them of the clerks—called Cursitors—and paying the proper fees. But the Chancery has a certain limited power of inventing new writs to meet new cases as they arise. That power is consecrated by a famous clause of the Second Statute of Westminster authorizing writs *in consimili casu*. Thus the Chancellor may often have to consider whether the case is one in which some new and some specially worded writ should be framed. This however is not judicial business. The chancellor does not hear both sides of the story, he only hears the plaintiff's application, and if he grants a writ the courts of law may afterwards quash that writ as being contrary to the law of the land.

*Reservoir of Royal Justice.* But by another route the Chancellor is brought into still closer contact with the administration of justice. Though these great courts of law have been established there is still a reserve of justice in the king. Those who can not get relief elsewhere present their petitions to the king and his council praying for some remedy. Already by the end of the thirteenth century the number of such petitions presented in every year is very large, and the work of reading them and considering them is very laborious. In practice a great share of this labour falls on the Chancellor. He is the king's prime minister, he is a member of the council, and the specially learned member of the council. It is in dealing with these petitions that the Chancellor begins to develop his judicial powers.

In course of time his judicial powers are classified as being of two kinds. It begins to be said that the Court of Chancery, "Curia Chancellariae"—for the phrase is used in the fourteenth century—has two sides, a common law side and an equity side, or a Latin side and an English side. Let us look for a moment at the origin of these two kinds of powers, and first at that which concerns us least.

(1) Many of these petitions of which I have spoken seek for justice not merely from the king but against the king. If anybody is to be called the wrongdoer, it is the king himself. For example, he is in possession of land which has been seized by his officers as an escheat while really the late tenant has left an heir. Now the king cannot be sued by action—no writ will go against him; the heir if he wants justice must petition for it humbly. Such matters as these are referred to the Chancellor. Proceedings are taken before him; the heir, it may be, proves his case and gets his land. The number of such cases, cases in which the king is concerned, is very large—kings are always seizing land on very slight pretexts—and forcing other people to prove their titles. Gradually a quite regular and ordinary procedure is established for such cases—a procedure very like that of the three courts of law. . . .

(2) Very often the petitioner requires some relief at the expense of some other person. He complains that for some reason or another he can not get a remedy in the ordinary course of justice and yet he is entitled to a remedy. He is poor, he is old, he is sick, his adversary is rich and powerful, will bribe or will intimidate jurors, or has by some trick or

some accident acquired an advantage of which the ordinary courts with their formal procedure will not deprive him. The petition is often couched in piteous terms, the king is asked to find a remedy for the love of God and in the way of charity. Such petitions are referred by the king to the Chancellor.

Gradually in the course of the fourteenth century petitioners, instead of going to the king, will go straight to the Chancellor, will address their complaints to him and adjure him to do what is right for the love of God and in the way of charity. Now one thing that the Chancellor may do in such a case is to invent a new writ and so provide the complainant with a means of bringing an action in a court of law. But in the fourteenth century the courts of law have become very conservative and are given to quashing writs which differ in material points from those already in use. But another thing that the Chancellor can do is to send for the complainant's adversary and examine him concerning the charge that has been made against him. Gradually a procedure is established. The Chancellor having considered the petition, or "bill" as it is called, orders the adversary to come before him and answer the complaint. The writ whereby he does this is called a subpoena—because it orders the man to appear upon pain of forfeiting a sum of money, e.g., *subpoena centum librarum*. It is very different from the old writs whereby actions are begun in the courts of law. They tell the defendant what is the cause of action against him—he is to answer why he assaulted and beat the plaintiff, why he trespassed on the plaintiff's land, why he detained a chattel which belongs to the plaintiff. The subpoena, on the other hand, will tell him merely that he has got to come before the Chancellor and answer complaints made against him by A.B. Then when he comes before the Chancellor he will have to answer on oath, and sentence by sentence, the bill of the plaintiff. This procedure is rather like that of the ecclesiastical courts and the canon law than like that of our old English courts of law. It was in fact borrowed from the ecclesiastical courts, not from their ordinary procedure but from the summary procedure of those courts introduced for suppression of heresy. The defendant will be examined upon oath and the Chancellor will decide questions of fact as well as questions of law.

I do not think that in the fourteenth century the Chancellors considered that they had to administer any body of substantive rules that differed from the ordinary law of the land. They were administering the law but they were administering it in cases which escaped the meshes of the ordinary courts. The complaints that come before them are in general complaints of indubitable legal wrongs, assaults, batteries, imprisonments, disseisins and so forth—wrongs of which the ordinary courts take cognizance, wrongs which they ought to redress. But then owing to one thing and another such wrongs are not always redressed by courts of law. In this period one of the commonest of all the reasons that complainants will give for coming to the Chancery is that they are poor while their adversaries are rich and influential—too rich, too influential to be left to the clumsy processes of the old courts and the verdicts of juries. However this sort of thing cannot well be permitted. The law courts will not have it and parliament will not have it. Complaints against this extraordinary justice grow loud in the fourteenth century. In history and in principle it is closely connected with another kind of extraordinary justice which is yet more objectionable, the extraordinary justice that is done in criminal cases by the king's Council. Parliament at one time would gladly be rid of both—of both the Council's interference in criminal matters, and the Chancellor's interference with civil matters. And so the Chancellor is warned off the field of common law—he is not to hear cases which might go to the ordinary courts, he is not to make himself a judge of torts and contracts, of property in lands and goods.

*Trusts.* But then just at this time it is becoming plain that the Chancellor is doing some convenient and useful works that could not be done, or could not easily be done by the courts of common law. He has taken to enforcing uses or trusts. . . . No doubt they were troublesome things, things that might be used for fraudulent purposes, and statutes were passed against those who employed them for the purpose of cheating their creditors or evading the law of mortmain. But I have not a doubt that they were very popular, and I think we may say that had there been no Chancery, the old courts would have discovered some method of enforcing these fiduciary obligations. That method however must have been a clumsy one. A system of law which will never compel, which will never even allow, the defendant to give evidence, a system which sends every question of fact to a jury, is not competent to deal adequately with fiduciary relationships. On the other hand the Chancellor had a procedure which was very well adapted to this end. To this we may add that very possibly the ecclesiastical courts (and the Chancellor you will remember was almost always an ecclesiastic) had for a long time past been punishing breaches of trust by spiritual censures, by penance and excommunication. And so by general consent, we may say, the Chancellor was allowed to enforce uses, trusts or confidences.

Thus one great field of substantive law fell into his hand—a fruitful field, for in the course of the fifteenth century uses became extremely popular. Then, as we all know, Henry VIII—for it was rather the king than his subservient parliament—struck a heavy blow at uses. The king was the one man in the kingdom who had everything to gain and nothing to lose by abolishing uses, and as we all know he merely succeeded in complicating the law, for under the name of "trusts" the Chancellors still reigned over their old province. And then there were some other matters that were considered to be fairly within his jurisdiction. An old rhyme[1] allows him "fraud, accident, and breach of confidence"—there were many frauds which the stiff old procedure of the courts of law could not adequately meet, and "accident," in particular the accidental loss of a document, was a proper occasion for the Chancellor's interference. No one could set any very strict limits to his power, but the best hint as to its extent that could be given in the sixteenth century was given by the words "fraud, accident, and breach of confidence." On the other hand he was not to interfere where a court of common law offered an adequate remedy. A bill was "demurrable for want of equity" on that ground.

In the course of the sixteenth century we begin to learn a little about the rules that the Chancellors are administering in the field that is thus assigned to them. They are known as "the rules of equity and good conscience." As to what they have done in remoter times we have to draw inferences from very sparse evidence. One thing seems pretty plain. They had not considered themselves strictly bound by precedent. Remember this, our reports of cases in courts of law go back to Edward I's day—the Middle Ages are represented to us by the long series of Year Books. On the other hand our reports of cases in the Court of Chancery go back no further than 1557; and the mass of reports which come to us from between that date and the Restoration in 1660 is a light matter. This by itself is enough to show us that the Chancellors have not held themselves very strictly bound by case law, for men have not cared to collect cases. Nor do I believe that to any very large extent the Chancellors had borrowed from the Roman Law—this is a disputed matter, Mr. Spence has argued for their Romanism, Mr. Justice Holmes against it. No doubt through the medium of the canon law these great ecclesiastics were familiar with some of the great maxims which occur in the *Institutes* or the *Digest*. One of the parts of the *Corpus Juris Canonici*, the Liber Sextus, ends with a bouquet of these high-sounding maxims—*Qui prior est tempore potior est jure*, and so forth, maxims familiar to all readers of equity reports. No doubt the early Chancellors knew these and valued them—but I do not believe that we ought to attribute to them much knowledge of Roman law or any intention to Romanise the law of England. For example, to my mind the comparison sometimes drawn between the so-called double ownership of England, and the so-called double ownership of Roman law can not be carried below the surface. In their treatment of uses or trusts the Chancellors stick close, marvelously close, to the rules of the common law—they often consulted the judges, and the lawyers who pleaded before them were common lawyers, for

[1] "These three give place in court of conscience, Fraud, accident, and breach of confidence."

there was as yet no "Chancery Bar." On the whole my notion is that with the idea of a law of nature in their minds they decided cases without much reference to any written authority, now making use of some analogy drawn from the common law, and now of some great maxim of jurisprudence which they have borrowed from the canonists or the civilians.

In the second half of the sixteenth century the jurisprudence of the court is becoming settled. The day for ecclesiastical Chancellors is passing away. . . . Ellesmere, Bacon, Coventry, begin to administer an established set of rules which is becoming known to the public in the shape of reports and they begin to publish rules of procedure.

*Conflict with the Common Law.* In James I's day occurred the great quarrel between Lord Chancellor Ellesmere and Chief Justice Coke which finally decided that the Court of Chancery was to have the upper hand over the courts of law. If the Chancery was to carry out its maxims about trust and fraud it was essential that it should have a power to prevent men from going into the courts of law and to prevent men from putting in execution the judgments that they had obtained in courts of law. In fraud or in breach of trust you obtain a judgment against me in a court of law; I complain to the Chancellor, and he after hearing what you have to say enjoins you not to put in force your judgment, says in effect that if you do put your judgment in force you will be sent to prison. Understand well that the Court of Chancery never asserted that it was superior to the courts of law; it never presumed to send to them such mandates as the Court of King's Bench habitually sent to the inferior courts, telling them that they must do this or must not do that or quashing their proceedings—the Chancellor's injunction was in theory a very different thing from a mandamus, a prohibition, a certiorari, or the like. It was addressed not to the judges, but to the party. You in breach of trust have obtained a judgment—the Chancellor does not say that this judgment was wrongly granted, he does not annul it, he tells you that for reasons personal to yourself it will be inequitable for you to enforce that judgment, and that you are not to enforce it. For all this, however, it was natural that the judges should take umbrage at this treatment of their judgments. Coke declared that the man who obtained such an injunction was guilty of the offence denounced by the Statutes of Praemunire, that of calling in question the judgments of the king's courts in other courts (these statutes had been aimed at the Papal curia). King James had now a wished-for opportunity of appearing as supreme over all his judges, and all his courts, and acting on the advice of Bacon and other great lawyers he issued a decree in favour of the Chancery. From this time forward the Chancery had the upper hand. It did not claim to be superior to the courts of law, but it could prevent men from going to those courts, whereas those courts could not prevent men from going to it.

Its independence being thus secured, the court became an extremely busy court. Bacon said that he had made 2,000 orders in a year, and we are told that as many as 16,000 causes were pending before it at one time: indeed it was hopelessly in arrear of its work. Under the Commonwealth some vigorous attempts were made to reform its procedure. Some were for abolishing it altogether. It was not easily forgotten that the Court of Chancery was the twin sister of the Court of Star Chamber. The projects for reform came to an end with the Restoration. Still it is from the Restoration or thereabouts—of course a precise date cannot be fixed—that we may regard the equity administered in the Chancery as a recognized part of the law of the land.

## A VIEW OF EQUITY FROM *THE COMMENTARIES*   By William Blackstone

LET US . . . take a brief, but comprehensive, view of the general nature of *equity*, as now understood and practised in our several courts of judicature. . . .

Equity . . . , in its true and genuine meaning, is the soul and spirit of all law: *positive* law is construed, and *rational* law is made, by it. In this, equity is synonymous to justice; in that, to the true sense and sound interpretation of the rule. But the very terms of a court of *equity*, and a court of *laws*, as contrasted to each other, are apt to confound and mislead us: as if the one judged without equity, and the other was not bound by any law. Whereas every definition or illustration to be met with, which now draws a line between the two jurisdictions, by setting law and equity in opposition to each other, will be found either totally erroneous, or erroneous to a certain degree.

1. Thus in the first place it is said, that it is the business of a court of equity in England to abate the rigor of the common law. But no such power is contended for. Hard was the case of bond-creditors, whose

---

Reprinted from Blackstone, *Commentaries on the Laws of England* (1765–1769), Book 3, Ch. 27, pp. 429–442, in the London edition of 1803.

William Blackstone (1723–1780), on his appointment as Vinerian Professor at Oxford in 1758, instituted the first university lectures on English law; prior to that time only Roman law had been taught at the universities. See Maitland's estimate of Blackstone p. 28; Professor Pound discusses the pervasive influence of *The Commentaries* on United States law at pages 54–55.

debtor devised away his real estate; rigorous and unjust the rule, which put the devisee in a better condition than the heir: yet a court of equity had no power to interpose. Hard is the common law still subsisting, that land devised, or descending to the heir, shall not be liable to simple contract debts of the ancestor or devisor, although the money was laid out in purchasing the very land; and that the father shall never immediately succeed as heir to the real estate of the son: but a court of equity can give no relief; though in both these instances the artificial reason of the law, arising from feodal principles, has long ago entirely ceased. . . . In all such cases of positive law, the courts of equity, as well as the courts of law, must say with Ulpian, *"hoc quidem per quam durum est, sed ita lex scripta est"* [this indeed is exceedingly hard, but so the law is written].

2. It is said, that a court of equity determines according to the spirit of the rule, and not according to the strictness of the letter. But so also does a court of law. Both, for instance, are equally bound, and equally profess, to interpret statutes according to the true intent of the legislature. In general laws all cases cannot be foreseen; or, if foreseen, cannot be expressed: some will arise that will fall within the meaning, though not within the words, of the legislator; and others which may fall within the letter, may be contrary to his meaning, though not expressly excepted. These cases, thus out of the letter, are often said to be within the equity, of an act of parliament; and so cases within the letter are frequently out of the equity. Here by *equity* we mean nothing but the sound interpretation of the law; though the words of the law itself may be too general, too special, or otherwise inaccurate or defective. These then are the cases which, as Grotius says, *"lex non exacte definit, sed arbitrio boni viri permittit"* [the law does not define exactly, but trusts in the judgment of a good man]; in order to find out the true sense and meaning of the lawgiver, from every other topic of construction. But there is not a single role of interpreting laws, whether equitably or strictly, that is not equally used by the judges in the courts both of law and equity: the construction must in both be the same: or, if they differ, it is only as one court of law may also happen to differ from another. Each endeavours to fix and adopt the true sense of the law in question; neither can enlarge, diminish, or alter, that sense in a single tittle.

3. Again, it hath been said, that *fraud, accident,* and *trust* are the proper and peculiar objects of a court of equity. But every kind of *fraud* is equally cognizable, and equally adverted to, in a court of law; and some frauds are cognizable only there; as fraud in obtaining a devise of lands, which is always sent out of the equity courts to be there determined. Many *accidents* are also supplied in a court of law; as, loss of deeds, mistakes in receipts or accounts, wrong payments, deaths which

make it impossible to perform a condition literally, and a multitude of other contingences: and many cannot be relieved even in a court of equity; as, if by accident a recovery is ill suffered, a devise ill executed, a contingent remainder destroyed, or a power of leasing omitted in a family settlement. A technical *trust*, indeed, created by the limitation of a second use, was forced into the courts of equity, . . . and this species of trusts, extended by inference and construction, have ever since remained as a kind of *peculium* in those courts. But there are other trusts, which are cognizable in a court of law: as deposits, and all matter of bailments; and especially that implied contract, so highly beneficial and useful, of having undertaken to account for money received to another's use, which is the ground of an action on the case almost as universally remedial as a bill in equity.

4. Once more; it has been said that a court of equity is not bound by rules or precedents, but acts from the opinion of the judge, founded on the circumstances of every particular case. Whereas the system of our courts of equity is a labored connected system, governed by established rules, and bound down by precedents, from which they do not depart, although the reason of some of them may perhaps be liable to objection. Thus the refusing a wife her dower in a trust-estate, yet allowing the husband his curtesy, . . . and other cases that might be instanced are plainly rules of positive law; supported only by the reverence that is shewn, and generally very properly shewn, to a series of former determinations; that the rule of property may be uniform and steady. Nay, sometimes a precedent is so strictly followed, that a particular judgment founded upon special circumstances, gives rise to a general rule.

In short, if a court of equity in England did really act, as many ingenius writers have supposed it (from theory) to do, it would rise above all law, either common or statute, and be a most arbitrary legislator in every particular case. No wonder they are so often mistaken. . . . But this was in the infancy of our courts of equity, before their jurisdiction was settled, and when the chancellors themselves, partly from their ignorance of law (being frequently bishops or statesmen), partly from ambition and lust of power (encouraged by the arbitrary principles of the age they lived in), but principally from the narrow and unjust decisions of the courts of law, had arrogated to themselves such unlimited authority, as hath totally been disclaimed by their successors for now above a century past. The decrees of a court of equity were then rather in the nature of awards, formed . . . [for the affair immediately at hand], with more probity of intention than knowledge of the subject; founded on no settled principles, as being never designed, and therefore never used, for precedents. But the systems of jurisprudence, in our courts both of law and equity, are now equally artificial systems, founded in the same principles of justice and positive law; but varied by different usages in the forms and mode of their proceedings: the one being originally derived (though much reformed and improved) from the feodal customs, as they prevailed in different ages in the Saxon and Norman judicatures; the other (but with equal improvements) from the imperial and pontifical formularies, introduced by their clerical chancellors.

The suggestion indeed of every bill, to give jurisdiction to the courts of equity (copied from those early times) is that the complainant hath no remedy at the common law. But he who should from thence conclude, that no case is judged of in equity where there might have been relief at law, and at the same time casts his eye on the extent and variety of the cases in our equity-reports, must think the law a dead letter indeed. The rules of property, rules of evidence, and rules of interpretation in both courts are, or should be, exactly the same: both ought to adopt the best, or must cease to be courts of justice. Formerly some causes, which now no longer exist, might occasion a different rule to be followed in one court, from what was afterwards adopted in the other, as founded in the nature and reason of the thing: but, the instant those causes ceased, the measure of substantial justice ought to have been the same in both. Thus the penalty of a bond, originally contrived to evade the absurdity of those monkish constitutions which prohibited taking interest for money, was therefore very pardonably considered as the real debt in the courts of law, when the debtor neglected to perform his agreement for the return of the loan with interest: for the judges could not, as the law then stood, give judgment that the interest should be specifically paid. But when afterwards the taking of interest became legal, as the necessary companion of commerce, nay after the statute of 37 Hen. VIII. c. 9. had declared the debt or loan itself to be "the just and true intent" for which the obligation was given, their narrow-minded successors still adhered wilfully and technically to the letter of the ancient precedents, and refused to consider the payment of principal, interest, and costs, as a full satisfaction of the bond. At the same time more liberal men, who sat in the courts of equity, construed the instrument, according to its "just and true intent," as merely a security for the loan: in which light it was certainly understood by the parties, at least after these determinations; and therefore this construction should have been universally received. So in mortgages, being only a landed as the other is a personal security for the money lent, the payment of principal, interest, and costs ought at any time, before judgment executed, to have saved the forfeiture in a court of law, as well as in a court of equity. And the inconvenience as well as injustice, of putting different constructions in different courts upon one and the same transaction, obliged the parliament at length to interfere, and to direct by the statutes 4 & 5 Ann. c. 16. and 7 Geo. II. c. 20. that,
in

the cases of bonds and mortgages, what had long been the practice of the courts of equity should also for the future be universally followed in the courts of law; wherein it had before these statutes in some degree obtained a footing.

Again, neither a court of equity nor of law can vary men's wills or agreements, or (in other words) make wills or agreements for them. Both are to understand them truly, and therefore both of them uniformly. One court ought not to extend, nor the other abridge, a lawful provision deliberately settled by the parties, contrary to its just intent. A court of equity, no more than a court of law, can relieve against a penalty in the nature of stated damages; as a rent of 5£ an acre for ploughing up ancient meadow: nor against a lapse of time, where the time is material to the contract; as in covenants for renewal of leases. Both courts will equitably construe, but neither pretends to control or change, a lawful stipulation or engagement.

The rules of decision are in both courts equally opposite to the subjects of which they take cognisance. Where the subject matter is such as requires to be determined [according to right and justice], as generally upon actions on the case, the judgments of the courts of law are guided by the most liberal equity. In matters of positive right, both courts must submit to and follow those ancient and invariable maxims [which are traditional]. Both follow the law of nations, and collect it from history and the most approved authors of all countries, where the question is the object of that law. . . . In mercantile transactions they follow the marine law, and argue from the usages and authorities received in all maritime countries. . . .

Such then being the parity of law and reason which governs both species of courts, wherein (it may be asked) does their essential difference consist? It principally consists in the different modes of administering justice in each; in the mode of proof, the mode of trial, and the mode of relief. Upon these, and upon two other accidental grounds of jurisdiction, which were formerly driven into those courts by narrow decisions of the courts of law, *viz.* the true construction of securities for money lent, and the form and effect of a trust or second use; upon these main pillars hath been gradually erected that structure of jurisprudence, which prevails in our courts of equity, and is inwardly bottomed upon the same substantial foundations as the legal system which hath hitherto been delineated in these commentaries; however different they may appear in their outward form, from the different taste of their architects. . . .

With respect to the mode of *relief.* The want of a more specific remedy, than can be obtained in the courts of law, gives a concurrent jurisdiction to a court of equity in a great variety of cases. To instance in executory agreements. A court of equity will compel them to be carried into strict execution, unless where it is improper or impossible; instead of giving damages for their non-performance. And, hence a fiction is established, that what ought to be done shall be considered as being actually done, and shall relate back to the time when it ought to have been done originally: and this fiction is so closely pursued through all its consequences, that it necessarily branches out into many rules of jurisprudence, which form a certain regular system. . . .

The form of a *trust*, or second use, gives the courts of equity an exclusive jurisdiction as to the subject-matter of all settlements and devises in that form, and of all the long terms created in the present complicated mode of conveyancing. This is a very ample source of jurisdiction: but the trust is governed by very nearly the same rules, as would govern the estate in a court of law, if no trustee was interposed; and, by a regular positive system established in the courts of equity, the doctrine of trusts is now reduced to as great a certainty as that of legal estates in the courts of the common law.

These are the principal (for I omit the minuter) grounds of the jurisdiction at present exercised in our courts of equity: which differ, we see, very considerably from the notions entertained by strangers, and even by those courts themselves before they arrived to maturity; as appears from the principles laid down, and the jealousies entertained of their abuse, by our early juridical writers cited in a former page: and which have been implicitly received and handed down by subsequent compilers, without attending to those gradual accessions and derelictions, by which in the course of a century this mighty river hath imperceptibly shifted its channel. Lambard in particular, in the reign of queen Elizabeth, lays it down, that "equity should not be appealed unto, but only in rare and extraordinary matters: and that a good chancellor will not arrogate authority in every complaint that shall be brought before him, upon whatsoever suggestion: and thereby both overthrow the authority of the courts of common law, and bring upon men such a confusion and uncertainty, as hardly any man should know how or how long to hold his own assured to him." And certainly, if a court of equity were still at sea, and floated upon the occasional opinion which the judge who happened to preside might entertain of conscience in every particular case, the inconvenience, that would arise from this uncertainty, would be a worse evil than any hardship that could follow from rules too strict and inflexible. Its powers would have become too arbitrary to have been endured in a country like this, which boasts of being governed in all respects by law and not by will. But since the time when Lambard wrote, a set of great and eminent lawyers, who have successively held the great seal, have by degrees erected the system of relief administered by a court of equity into a regular science, which cannot be attained without study and experience, any more than the science of law: but from which, when understood, it may be known what remedy a suitor is entitled to expect, and by what mode or suit, as readily and with as much precision, in a court of equity as in a court of law.

It were much to be wished, for the sake of certainty, peace, and justice, that each court would as far as possible follow the other, in the best and most effectual rules for attaining those desirable ends. It is a maxim that equity follows the law; and in former days the law has not scrupled to follow even that equity, which was laid down by the clerical chancellors....

It would carry me beyond the bounds of my present purpose, to go farther into this matter. I have been tempted to go so far, because strangers are apt to be confounded by nominal distinctions, and the loose unguarded expressions to be met with in the best of our writers; and thence to form erroneous ideas of the separate jurisdictions now existing in England, but which never were separated in any other country in the universe. It hath also afforded me an opportunity to vindicate, on the one hand, the justice of our courts of law from being that harsh and illiberal rule, which many are too ready to suppose it; and, on the other, the justice of our courts of equity from being the result of mere arbitrary opinion, or an exercise of dictatorial power, which rides over the law of the land, and corrects, amends, and controls it by the loose and fluctuating dictates of the conscience of a single judge.

---

*COMMENT.* Blackstone probably overstated the unity of common law and equity; his views reflected the reforming and unifying approach of Lord Mansfield, from which English law quickly retreated. (See Holdsworth, "Blackstone's Treatment of Equity," *Harvard Law Review*, vol. 43, 1929, p.1, at 22.) But in the longer span, Mansfield's voice was prophetic. The further development of equity in the United States will be considered in Chapter 2. More complete accounts of the development of the English Court of Chancery may be found in Holdsworth, *History of English Law*, 7th ed., Vol. 1, chap. 5 (London: Methuen, 1956); and Spence, "The History of the Court of Chancery," *Select Essays in Anglo-American Legal History*, Vol. 2, 1907, pp. 219 *et seq.*

# THE CASE-LAW SYSTEM: HISTORICAL FACTORS WHICH CONTROLLED ITS DEVELOPMENT  *By William Searle Holdsworth*

THE EVOLUTION of case law gradually gave rise to our modern theory as to the binding effect of decided cases. That decided cases had always possessed authority from the earliest times, is clear from Bracton's *Treatise* and the earliest *Yearbooks*. But, in the Middle Ages and later, the modern theory as to their authority had not emerged. It was not till the style of the law report changed, to meet the changes introduced by the new system of written pleadings, that it could begin to emerge.

The manner in which Coke cites and distinguishes cases in his *Reports* shows that it was beginning to emerge at the end of the sixteenth century; and Bacon, in the *De Augmentis,* could say "judicial decisions are the anchors of the laws as the laws are anchors of the state." By the beginning of the eighteenth century the modern theory had been in substance reached. . . .

It is on the system of case law . . . that the common law of England was very largely based in Blackstone's day. Let us recall Burke's emphatic words: "The English Jurisprudence hath not any other sure foundation, nor consequently the lives and property of the subject any sure hold, but in the maxims, rules, and principles, and judicial traditionary line of decisions contained in the notes taken, and from time to time published (mostly under the sanction of the judges), called Reports . . . To put any end to Reports is to put an end to the law of England." It is true that the English law of today is based less on case law, and very much more on statute law, than it was when Blackstone wrote. But it should be noted that many of these statutes simply codify the results arrived at by case law. What then are the reasons why this unique system of case law was able to develop a legal system, which is fit to be compared, and to be compared in many respects favorably, with the system of Roman Law?

---

Reprinted by permission from William Searle Holdsworth, *Some Lessons from Our Legal History* (New York: Macmillan, 1928), copyright 1928, by Northwestern University. The reprinted material is from a lecture delivered by Holdsworth in 1927 at Northwestern University as one of the Julius H. Rosenthal Foundation lectures.

William Searle Holdsworth, one of the most eminent English legal historians of the past half-century, was Vinerian Professor of Law at Oxford University from 1922 until his death in 1944. For completeness and authority there is no rival to his *History of English Law* (13 volumes, 1903).

## The English Heritage

The a priori reasons are fairly obvious. Case law, developing as it does from precedent to precedent, preserves a continuity in legal development, which is essential to the construction of a system of law. Being based on actual happenings, it keeps the law in touch with reality. There is no room for abstract reasoning on possible events suggested by the ingenuity of academic inquirers. It produces a law which is eminently adaptable to the needs of a changing society. Coke's Reports restated, and adapted to the needs of the seventeenth century, the medieval common law; and, in the nineteenth century, a succession of eminent judges adapted to the needs of that century of change, the common law of the seventeenth and eighteenth centuries. It has some claims to be an eminently scientific way of constructing a legal system; and, on that ground, it may, as Sir Frederick Pollock has said, "fairly claim kindred with the inductive sciences." But these a priori reasons do not tell us why this system of case law has not been adopted in continental countries. Nor do they tell us why, in countries where it has been adopted, it does not always work so well as in England. It is to the reasons for these phenomena that we must look for the essential causes of the success of the English system of case law. These reasons cannot be supplied by any a priori considerations. They can be supplied only by legal history; and, as we shall now see, a system of case law will never be so successful as it has been in England, in the absence of the peculiar conditions in which it originated and was developed. These conditions can, I think, be summarized as follows:

In the first place, a system of case law demands, for its satisfactory working, the presence of a centralized judicial system. This has been a marked feature of English law from the thirteenth century onwards . . . and, at the beginning of the nineteenth century, the English judicial system was more completely centralized than any in Europe. This was inconvenient to the suitor. But it made for the success of the system of case law; for it meant that the number of reports was limited, and that only the considered decisions of competent lawyers were reported. . . . [I]t is clear, as Bacon pointed out, that a system of case law will not work so satisfactorily if the number of courts, whose decisions are reported, is multiplied. The law is likely to be burdened with so great a mass of decisions of different degrees of excellence, that its principles, so far from being made more certain by the decisions of new cases, will become sufficiently uncertain to afford abundant material for the infinite disputations of professors of general jurisprudence.[a] A limitation is needed in the number of reported cases. Since England secured that limitation as the result of the same set of causes which gave us our

[a] See Chapter 4 for a discussion of the Restatements.

common law, English lawyers have hardly realized that it was a condition precedent for the satisfactory working of our system of case law.

In the second place, a system of case law demands a group of learned lawyers, both at the Bar and on the Bench, who are bound together by a common professional tradition. Maitland has said that, in the earliest of our *Yearbooks*, "we see that already the great litigation of the realm . . . is conducted by a small group of men. Lowther, Spigurnel, Howard, Hertpol, King, Huntington, Heyham—one of them will be engaged in almost every case." Their opinions were mentioned with almost as much respect as the opinions of the judges; and Parliament referred difficult points of law to them as well as to the judges. The solidarity of the legal profession was increased by the growth of its organization—the formation of the rank of the serjeants, the rise of the serjeants' Inns, the development of the collegiate life of the Inns of Court. It was these leaders of the profession who made, or who employed the men who made, the anonymous *Yearbooks*. It was they who, in a later age, made the *Reports* which were published under their names. It was they who applied to these reports an intelligent criticism, which has established a professional tradition as to which of these reports are good, which bad, which indifferent. It was they who worked out in theory and applied in practice the subtle rule, to which I have already alluded, that the authority of a decision is attached, not to the words used, nor to all the reasons given, but to the principle or principles necessary for the decision of the case.

In the third place, a system of case law demands an independent well paid bench, which is, on the whole, more able than the bar. "There is no guaranty of justice," says Professor Ehrlich, "except the personality of the judge. . . . The greatest task that can be given a man to discharge, Justice, requires a standard of mental and moral greatness far above the common average." The continental system, under which the judicial profession is a branch of the civil service, and distinct from that of the advocate, is not so successful as the English in securing that standard. Professor Ehrlich has drawn attention to the contrast between the mental outlook of judges appointed under these two different systems, and the effect of that outlook on the development of legal systems. He has no doubt that the best results are attained by our English system. It is true that barristers have sometimes exercised some kind of censorship over the cases which they have reported. It is said that Lord Campbell, when he was a reporter of nisi prius decisions during Lord Ellenborough's tenure of the office of Chief Justice, kept a drawer labeled "bad Ellenborough law," in which he deposited notes of cases which seemed to him to have been wrongly decided. But it is the criticism of the bench, and the use made by the bench of prior decisions, upon which the success of a system of case law in the long run depends. The decisions of the weak judges of Charles II and James II are of less value than the decisions of the judges of any other period of our legal history, because politics then exercised a greater influence upon judicial appointments than at any other period in our history. The change in the quality of the bench after the Revolution, when the influence of politics upon judicial appointments was diminished, and their influence upon the judges' tenure of office came to an end, was the condition precedent for the great work of settling the principles of the modern common law, which was achieved by the judges of the eighteenth century.

---

COMMENT. *A Prognosis for American Case-Law.* Does not Holdsworth's analysis of the conditions necessary for successful case-law development offer a dismal prospect for case law in the United States, in view of the multitude of our courts, a diffuse bar, and the uneven quality of our judicial work? Does Holdsworth's analysis suggest, at least, that the United States will produce case law with different qualities and characteristics than in England? The reliability of this analysis may be tested against the description of the characteristics of American law in the chapter which follows.

*The Biographical Route to Legal History.* The work of Sir Edward Coke has been briefly mentioned. A full and delightful account of his life and times appears in Catherine Drinker Bowen's *The Lion and the Throne* (Boston: Little, Brown, 1957). For the life and work of Lord Mansfield, whose stature grows with time, see C. H. S. Fifoot, *Lord Mansfield* (London: Clarendon, 1936).

An engaging account of the main developments of English legal history in the light of the personalities and the lives of the leading lawyers and judges is Zane's "The Five Ages of the Bench and Bar of England," *Select Essays in Anglo-American Legal History*, Vol. 1, 1907, p. 625. (The origins of legal training at the Inns, 681–684, 701–702; sidelights on Coke and Bacon, 696–699; Mansfield and Bentham, 716–722.) See also Holdsworth, William, *Some Makers of English Law* (London: Cambridge U.P. 1938); Dillon, "Bentham's Influence in the Reforms of the Nineteenth Century," *Select Essays in Anglo-American Legal History*, Vol. 1, 1907, p. 492.

CHAPTER 2

# Law in the New World

IN THE FIRST CHAPTER WE EXAMined some of the forces which shaped English legal institutions. Were these institutions transplanted in the New World? Or did the settlers develop a home-spun, indigenous legal order? The shape of American law which emerged in the Colonies and in the new States during the first three-quarters of a century of Independence is reflected in the legal scene of today. We turn now to this "formative era."

LAW AND AUTHORITY IN
EARLY MASSACHUSETTS             *By George L. Haskins*

THE HISTORY of American law begins, at least in a geographic sense, with the establishment of the first permanent settlements and colonies along the Atlantic seaboard in the seventeenth century. Each of them, whatever the nationality of its inhabitants, of necessity established, or had established for it, some system of laws immediately upon settlement. This was inevitable, since the first colonies were settled not by individual frontiersmen but by groups of men and by families. No social group, not even the family unit, can long subsist without rules of some sort to order and regulate its conduct. In politically organized society those rules, which we call law, are the product of, or a response

---

Reprinted from *Law and Authority in Early Massachusetts* (New York: Macmillan, 1960) pp. 4–8 with the permission of the author and the publisher.

George L. Haskins is a Professor of Law at the University of Pennsylvania and a Fellow of the Royal Historical Society, London. He has written numerous articles on legal and historical subjects and is the author of *The Statute of York and the Interest of the Commons* (1935), *The Growth of English Representative Government* (1948), and *Tradition and Design in the Law of Early Massachusetts* (1960). He is co-author of *American Law of Property* (1952) and *Fiduciary Guide* (1957).

to, complex social and psychological pressures. Their purpose is to secure, limit, and adjust the demands and desires of men with respect to things, to one another, and to the community. Law, in this sense, consists partly of received precepts and ideals and partly of legislative enactments, judicial decisions, and the orders of public officials. So viewed, the law of a particular civilization is a compound of past as well as of present forces; it is both an anchor to tradition and a vehicle for change. Hence, the wisdom of the ancient maxim which spoke of the law as the highest inheritance by which the people are preserved.

Two distinct but related assumptions about early American law have interposed serious obstacles to a comprehensive study of its development. The first is the view, which has become encysted in the tissue of judicial precedents, that the law of the colonies was essentially the common law of England, brought over to the extent applicable to colonial conditions. As early as 1798, a United States Circuit Court announced that the colonists "brought hither, as a birthright and inheritance, so much of the common law, as was applicable to their local situation, and change of circumstances;" and a generation later the Supreme Court stated that they brought with them the general principles of the common law but "adopted only that portion which was applicable to their situation." More recently, it has been asserted that "As soon as the Colonies reached a stage where there was need of any developed system of law, the whole of the English law was introduced in its system of common law and equity, with exceptions that are not important."

Nothing could be more misleading than sweeping statements of this kind, which in effect deny any native legal achievements in the colonial period. It is true, of course, that the colonial charters customarily provided that the laws established should not be contrary to the laws of England. Those provisions undoubtedly established a standard to be observed, but what were the "laws of England" in the seventeenth century? Certainly they included more than the statutes of parliament, more than the law of the king's courts which we call the common law. In the days before the common law had achieved its later ascendancy, the laws of England included the custom of the merchants, the local and divergent customs of towns and manors, as well as the laws enforced by the ecclesiastical tribunals and by numerous other courts and commissions of specialized jurisdiction. Hence, the charters did not prescribe the wholesale introduction of any one form of English law. Indeed, they usually authorized the colony governments specifically to establish their own laws and ordinances, provided they did not violate the announced standard. What constituted a departure from that standard, and what consequences resulted therefrom, depended on the administrative policies of the English government and its relationship at particular times with particular colonies. Clearly, the standard did not describe what laws were in effect in the colonies. Indeed, in Massachusetts Bay, a number of laws were enacted and remained in force which were entirely foreign to any laws known in England.

Equally misleading and inaccurate is the official theory of American courts that all English statutes enacted prior to the founding of Jamestown were in force in the colonies, and all statutes enacted thereafter were applicable only insofar as expressly extended. English statutes of both periods were in some instances rejected, in others adopted in whole or in part by colonial enactment or judicial decision. Whether, therefore, an English statute was part of the colony's law at a particular time is a question to be answered by research and inquiry, not by assumptions. As the Chief Justice of Pennsylvania observed in 1813:

It required time and experience to ascertain how much of the English law would be suitable to this country. By degrees, as circumstances demanded, we adopted the English usages, or substituted others better suited to our wants, till at length, before the time of the revolution, we had formed a system of our own....

The truth is that American law in the colonial period drew upon a complex legal heritage which included not only many of the English statutes and the rules applied by common-law courts but various customs of particular localities—all of which were supplemented by colonial enactments and decisions. Unquestionably, as the eighteenth century progressed, a substantial amount of English common law was absorbed into the local product as English lawbooks and reports found their way into colonial libraries and as a number of the colonists went over to the Inns of Court for legal training. Nevertheless, the extent of the reception of English law remains a fact to be proved in particular instances.

The second mistaken assumption about early American law is an extension of the first. It presupposes that, because the law of the colonies was essentially that of England, colonial law was basically the same everywhere. This assumption is wholly without foundation. There was no uniform growth of an "American" law throughout the colonies beginning with the founding of Jamestown in 1607. On the contrary, the conditions of settlement and of development within each colony meant that each evolved its own individual legal system, just as each evolved its individual social and political system. Geographical isolation, the date and character of the several settlements, the degree or absence of outside supervision or control—all had their effect in ultimately developing thirteen separate legal systems. The divergencies between English and colonial practices had become so marked by the end of the seventeenth century that an *Abridgement* was published in 1704 of the laws of several of the American settlements, including colonies on the continent of North America and in the West Indies. Even at the end of the eighteenth century, when there had been a substantial reception of much common-law doctrine, Thomas Jefferson, writing in Virginia, could properly refer to the law of Massachusetts, along with that of Bermuda and Barbados, as "Foreign Law." Whatever the impact of Blackstone's *Commentaries,* not only in accelerating the reception of English doctrines but in helping to bring about uniformity by eliminating many local divergences fostered by independent growth, the experience of the colonial period was neither jettisoned nor forgotten. That period remains the essentially formative era of the law of the several American states.

Even among scholars who have not been misled by these two assumptions but have recognized the separate and independent legal developments of the colonies, there have arisen substantial misconceptions as to the nature and sources of their laws. This has been notably true with respect to the colony of Massachusetts Bay in the seventeenth century, which has been characterized both as "a period of rude, untechnical popular law" and as an era in which "the Scriptures were an infallible guide for both judge and legislator." Neither of these positions can be sustained, and the Code of 1648 bears eloquent testimony to the developed nature of the Massachusetts legal system. Although a number of the colony's laws were based upon the Old Testament, and although several laws were enacted to meet the needs of a wilderness community, there was also a very substantial reception of various forms of English law during the early period. Yet to assert that much of the law of the colony was substantially English provides no answers to the future and vital questions: how much, of what sort, and why?

The process of importation and rejection of law and legal institutions with which the colonists had been familiar in England is illustrative of one phase of the general problem of survival and adaptation in the colonies of English patterns of thought and habits of life. . . . [T]he colonists drew upon their English experience in developing their political institutions, their family and social life, their institutions of government. In law, too, they availed themselves of their antecedent heritage, and a consideration of their reasons for accepting or rejecting or improving upon parts of that heritage enlarges our understanding of the alchemy of cultural transformation. More than any other aspect of colonial life, the Massachusetts legal system emerges as the product of tradition and of conscious design through which countless aspects of individual and social behavior were molded to comport with the conditions of settlement and, above all, to achieve the ideals which had inspired the founding of the colony.

# THE FORMATIVE ERA
# OF AMERICAN LAW  By Roscoe Pound

WHEN WE celebrate the hundredth anniversary of Livingston's[a] death [1836], we are very near to celebrating the centennial of the formative era of American law. If we think of that era as extending from independence to the time of the Civil War, it was three quarters of its way by 1836.

*The Setting.* The legal portions of our Constitutions, state and federal, were what they were to be until the amendments to the federal Constitution, after the Civil War, and substantially what they were to be till the end of the nineteenth century. [By 1836] the legislative reform movement was well under way both in England and with us. New York, for example, already had elaborate modern statutes as to corporations, wills, and administration, descent and distribution, marriage and divorce, executions against real property, real property, and criminal law. Kent's work for American equity was at an end. Marshall had died a year before. Story and Gibson had been on the bench nearly a quarter of a century. François Xavier Martin had sat for over twenty years on the Supreme Court of Louisiana. Blackford had been for a decade on the highest court of Indiana. Shaw and Ruffin were well established in their long and fruitful judicial careers. Thus, of the ten judges who must be ranked first in American judicial history, six had done their enduring work before the Civil War, and indeed had done the most of it in the first third of the one hundred and fifty years that have elapsed since the Federal Constitution.

Of the great lawyers of the period before the Civil War, Luther Martin, after two generations at the head of the profession, and William Pinkney and William Wirt, after a generation of leadership, were dead. Jeremiah Mason had been forty-five years at the bar. Daniel Webster and Horace Binney had each been a generation at the bar and Webster had already argued many of the great cases which made our constitu-

[a] Edward Livingston was responsible for the compilation of a criminal code for Louisiana, the outlook of which was well in advance of the times. His emphasis on prevention and reform, as opposed to revenge, caused Sir Henry Maine to pronounce him "the first legal genius of modern times."

---

Reprinted from *The Formative Era of American Law* (Boston: Little, Brown, 1938) by permission of the author and the publisher.

Roscoe Pound (b. 1870) was Professor of Law, and for many years Dean, of the Harvard Law School. His voluminous writings have made a lasting imprint on American law. A few of the more recent of his publications are: *New Paths of the Law* (1950), *The Ideal Element in the Law* (1958), and *Jurisprudence* (5 volumes, 1959).

tional law. Reverdy Johnson had been two decades at the bar and Rufus Choate was well established in the profession. The Litchfield Law School had come to an end and in place of the apprentice type of training for which it stood, the academic type which was to prevail had been definitely set up with the prestige of Story behind it. Also the text writing, which was to be an element of the first importance in our legal development in this period, had become well under way with the work of Kent and Story and Reeve and Gould and Tucker....

*Receiving the Common Law.* Let us recall the task of the formative era. The common law as the colonists knew it was the law of the age of Coke, not the law of the age of Mansfield. It was heavily burdened with the formalism of the strict law. Its ideals were those of the relationally organized society of the Middle Ages and so quite out of line with the needs and ideas of men who were opening up the wilderness. It spoke from an era of organization while the colonists represented an oncoming era of individualism. But there was little need for law until the economic development of the colonies and the rise of trade and commerce in the eighteenth century. Then there began to be trained lawyers practising in the courts and courts manned by trained lawyers, so that the reception of the common law and reshaping it into a law for America were well begun at the time of the Revolution.

The Revolution, however, and its results in the years immediately following, set back this development for a time and led to a critical period in the history of our law. The conservatism characteristic of lawyers led many of the strongest men at the bar to take the royalist side and decimated the profession. A deep and widespread economic depression set in. Business had been wholly deranged. The ports had been closed and trade cut off. Enormous public debts required ruinous taxation. It was an era of strict foreclosure and imprisonment for debt. For a generation after the Revolution, law and lawyers suffered from the ill effects of this period of depression. Moreover, political conditions gave rise to a general distrust of English law. Naturally the public was very hostile to England and to all that was English, and it was impossible for the common law to escape the odium of its origin. The books are full of illustrations of the hostility toward English law simply because it was English which prevailed at the end of the eighteenth and in the earlier years of the nineteenth century.

Social and geographical conditions contributed also to make the work of receiving and reshaping the common law exceptionally difficult. The idea of a profession was repugnant to the Jeffersonian era. The feeling was strong that all callings should be on the same footing. To dignify one by calling it a profession, and to prescribe qualifications for and limit access to it, seemed undemocratic and un-American. All the states came to make entrance to the profession easy with a minimum of qualification. Geographical conditions completed the process of decentralizing the law and deprofessionalizing the lawyers. In a country of long distances and a time of slow and expensive travel, the common law system of central courts and a centralized bar imposed an intolerable burden upon litigants.[b] For a time there was a veritable cult of local law.

It was the task of our formative era, in the face of these difficulties, to work out from our inherited legal materials a general body of law for what was to be a politically and economically unified land.

*Available Treatises and Reports.* A word as to these materials. We may look at them conveniently as they stood in 1774 at the time of the Declaration of Rights of the Continental Congress. In this declaration the common law of England is asserted as the measure of the rights of Americans and applicability to American conditions is declared to be the test by which English legal precepts were to be judged. But it was not easy in the colonies to find out what that law was. Of forty-eight law books listed by Dr. James as published in the colonies before 1775, thirty-six are pertinent to our subject. The rest are editions or translations of Beccaria, accounts of the trial of Zenger, and the like. Of the thirty-six, seven have to do with the rights of Englishmen (mostly on the basis of Coke's Second Institute), twelve with constables and sheriffs, five with justices of the peace, three are clerk's manuals, one treats of grand juries, one of courts martial, and one is a manual for country and town officers. Three handbooks for laymen (of the *Every Man his own Lawyer* type), an edition of Blackstone (two of book 4), and a treatise on pleading, are all that have to do with . . . the staple of the lawyer's work. For practical purposes Coke's Second Institute and Blackstone are the repositories of the law.

A like story is told by the law reports of the time. Only three reporters have cases of this period, Dallas, Jefferson, and Quincy. But 1 Dallas was published in 1790, Jefferson in 1829, and Quincy in 1865. There simply were no generally accessible reports of decisions of American courts until the nineteenth century. Moreover, the decisions themselves down to 1775 have to do with a very narrow field. Of thirty-three cases in 1 Dallas (from 1743 to 1774) seventeen are on points of evidence, three on real property, three on civil procedure, three on criminal procedure, two on pleading, and three on what English statutes were in force in Colonial Pennsylvania. One case on sales, one on equitable conversion, and two on customary modes of conveyancing in the colony, have some bearing on the law of the future. In Jefferson's reports, three-fourths of the cases have to do with slavery. The rest relate to the old law of real

[b] It will be interesting to recall at this point the factors which, according to Holdsworth (p. 44), contributed to the success of case law in England.

property or to the law of the state church. In Quincy's reports, two-thirds of the cases have to do with the technicalities of the old common-law practice and most of the rest go on the old technical land law. One case on bills and notes has to do with what we should regard today as living law. Once more we are left to Blackstone, with his complacent view of the feudal real property law, overrefined procedure, and seventeenth-century equity in which he had been brought up, as things complete and final, needing only a bit of tinkering here and there.

*Social and Economic Influences.* Trade and commerce, with resulting development of equity and of the law merchant, had done much to liberalize the common-law system by the end of the eighteenth century and the industrial revolution was to make it over in the nineteenth century. But the crystallizing of equity and absorption of the law merchant were not complete in England when we became independent and the industrial revolution was almost complete in nineteenth-century England before it began with us. In our social development we begin with a pioneer society struggling to subdue the wilderness and defend against the Indians. Then follows a time of settled agriculture, an era of small towns. Upon this follows a period of commercial progress, involving the rise of seaport cities and trade centers. Then comes industrial supremacy and the rise of great metropolitan centers. . . . Thus the pressure in our formative era came partly from the needs of a pioneer society, impatient of forms and eager to cut across technical procedural lines and modes of conveyancing and requisites of transactions, and partly from the exigencies of trade and commerce.

As to the pioneer contribution, Mr. Justice Miller is reported to have said that a prime factor in shaping the law in our western states was ignorance: The first judges "did not know enough to do the wrong thing, so they did the right thing." As to the effect of expanding trade and commerce, Plato had noted that where there is maritime commerce there must be more law. Montesquieu, observing the phenomena of his time, says that in a trading city there are more laws. Jhering, in a characteristically eloquent passage, speaks of commerce as a pathfinder in legal history. The classical period of Roman law, the no less classical period of the modern Roman law, the era of the development of equity and of the law merchant in England, and the formative period of American law all bear abundant witness to this.

*Natural Law.* In our formative era, some relied on rational overhauling of the legal materials at hand. Others urged that we make a complete legal new start; that we set up an American code out of whole cloth, just as today, in a new creative era, there are jurists who would start over again on a wholly new basis. But most lawyers sought to reshape or add to the existing stock of authoritative legal materials, just as today, for the most part, we would make over what has come down to us from the last century with the aid of a social philosophy and in the light of the social sciences. But whether they thought to make over or to build anew, the lawyers and judges and teachers of the formative era found their creating and organizing idea in the theory of natural law. This idea, at work in legislation (for in the maturity of law legislation is the chief instrument of change, and this was the time of the legislative reform movement both in England and in America), in judicial decision, and in doctrinal writing, guided the creative process of applying reason to experience which has been the life of the law. . . .

A perennial problem of the legal order is to reconcile the need of stability with the inevitableness of change. In practice, this reconciliation is achieved by means of ideals, to which lawmaking and interpretation and judicial application and doctrinal development tend to conform. These ideals give direction to change. They lead to change, but they guide it, and, as they are applied to authoritative legal materials shaped by the past, and as the ideals are of necessity largely ideal conceptions of the society and institutions and legal precepts with which lawmaker or judge or jurist is familiar, they tend to maintain stability during change. . . .

In the ferment following independence, in the finding of a law for the new world, in the working out of bodies of law for the new commonwealths which grew up so fast in the course of our westward expansion across the continent, the creative side of natural law was resorted to by legislators, judges, and text writers. The system of equity was not yet complete in England and absorption of the law merchant was still going forward. Much of the seventeenth-century law was in the condition in which it had come down from the Middle Ages. The criminal law of Blackstone's time was full of archaisms and the penal system was almost untouched by the humane ideas of the classical penologists. The legislative reform movement began here rather than in England. Our courts had to complete the development of equity and the taking over of the law merchant concurrently with the English courts. Legislatures and courts and doctrinal writers had to test the common law at every point with respect to its applicability to America. Judges and doctrinal writers had to develop an American common law, a body of judicially declared or doctrinally approved precepts suitable to America, out of the old English cases and the old English statutes. They did this, and did it thoroughly, in about three quarters of a century. No other judicial and juristic achievement may be found to compare with this. However much the last generation may have railed at the theory of natural law, no achievements of any of its theories are at all comparable. . . .

*Legislation.* Great things were expected of legislative lawmaking in the beginnings of our polity. Many looked forward to an American code which no less than our Constitution was to embody the idea upon our seal—*novus ordo seclorum*. It was not doubted that legislation would carry the chief burden of making an American law. Yet the results of our legislative reform movement fell far short of the anticipations with which it began. The latter part of the nineteenth century distrusted legislatures as profoundly as late eighteenth-century America distrusted executives. In the end judicial decision rather than legislation proved to have pulled the laboring oar and even doctrinal writing, of which the common-law tradition had no great opinion, proved to have furnished most of the power behind the courts.

American legislation began with every advantage. Despite our constitutional theory of three co-ordinate and co-equal departments of government, the hegemony of the legislative department from the beginning to the time of the Civil War is clear enough. Legislators thought of themselves as peculiarly the representatives of the sovereign people, with all the powers of the sovereign developed upon them. As late as the impeachment of Andrew Johnson it was confidently asserted that the executive was accountable to the legislative for the exercise of powers committed to the executive by the Constitution. All through the formative era legislative assemblies assumed that courts were accountable to them for the way in which they decided controversies. State legislatures summoned judges before them to be interrogated as to particular decisions exactly after the manner of the famous colloquy between James I and the judges of England. There was an idea of legislative omnicompetence. The earlier legislatures did not hesitate to enact statutes reversing judgments of the courts in particular cases. They sought to admit to probate wills rejected by the courts. They sought to dictate the details of administration of particular estates. By special laws they directed the details of local government for particular instances. They validated particular invalid marriages. They suspended the statute of limitations for a particular litigant in a particular case. They exempted a particular wrongdoer from liability for a particular wrong for which his neighbors would be held by the general law.

What was behind the extravagant faith in legislative assemblies to which such phenomena testify? Politically it grows out of the conditions of a time in which the absolute governments characteristic of the seventeenth and eighteenth centuries were giving way before a rising tide of democracy. It is reinforced by the victory of Parliament in the contests of Parliament with the Crown which culminated in the English Revolution of 1688, and by the part taken by the assembly in the French Revolution.

On its legal side many things contributed. Statesmen and lawyers of the time were deeply read in French and Dutch publicists who thought of the Roman law as a body of legislation, as it had been taught since the Middle Ages. The common law, as something English, was under a cloud after our Revolution. Roman law was taken to be embodied reason and historical scholars had not made men aware that behind the legislative form of that law was a long development of juristic opinions on detailed points in concrete cases very analogous to the development of English law by judicial decision. The Byzantine-Roman conception of law as the will of an absolute lawgiver pervaded the law books of the Continent.

Then, too, there was the idea of the lawmaker producing merely by an effort of reason a complete code, which community and judges might take as ultimate wisdom; an idea which was propagated by the law-of-nature school. There was the Rousseauist idea of law as the "expression of the general will" with the legislature as the organ of that will, and a generation of legislators drawing conclusions from the phase "representatives of the people." There was the example of the Codes, French, Prussian, and Austrian, which sprang up at the end of the eighteenth and the beginning of the nineteenth century. There was a certain momentum left over from the lawmaking urge of the Puritan Revolution which had led to a flood of lawmaking in more than one of the colonies where the Puritans were strong. There was the doctrine of separation of powers which, taken literally as late as 1915, led to a proposal in the New York Constitutional Convention of that year to forbid anything more than a mechanical judicial application of established rules.

Most of all, however, the legislative was the first of our departments of government to get its growth. It was the first to develop in the colonies and it took on an American aspect from the start. Prior to the Revolution the executive was a royal governor or proprietary governor and so could afford no model for the future. In the first century of colonial existence courts were not needed on any large scale. Magistrates, with an appeal to the legislature or to some council or to the executive, sufficed for the simpler relations of the beginnings. Legislatures on the model of the representative lower house of Parliament were set up generally from an early time and by the eighteenth century had attained strength and had obtained the confidence of the public. The English polity after 1688 made men familiar with a sovereign legislature as, in the two centuries before, Tudors and Stuarts and the old régime in France had made them familiar with a sovereign king. In more than one of our states until well after the Revolution, legislatures claimed and exercised the plenary powers over adjudication and administration which belonged to the British Parliament.

What did legislation achieve for American law in the height of legislative leadership from the Revolution to the Civil War? When we compare the permanent results with those of judicial decision in the same period and reflect on the volume of local statute making, we must admit it did relatively little. The enduring creative legislation of the time is almost entirely in constitutions and bills of rights, federal and state. Certainly legislation gave our common-law jurisdictions nothing in private law of such significance as the Code Napoléon or as the Civil Code of Louisiana. For the most part it did away with survivals in seventeenth-century English law which had not been eliminated in the wake of the Puritan Revolution, and for the rest formulated what jurists of the school of natural law and courts of equity had worked out and made ready for legislative adoption. One can number on his fingers the outstanding statutes of the era which have an enduring place in our private law. In truth, the legislative reform movement, especially in England, was chiefly taken up with repeal. It abrogated rules and institutions which had come down from feudal England. It pruned away restrictions on free individual activity which spoke from the relationally organized society of the Middle Ages and had ceased to be applicable to a society organized on the basis of free individual competitive self-assertion. What it reshaped, as for example in the Married Women's Acts, was mostly reshaped to the patterns laid out by equity.

Undoubtedly the best work of our nineteenth-century legislation was done in criminal law and penal administration. Natural law had little scope in judicial finding of law on the criminal side. The general security calls for more rule and less latitude of application here than anywhere else unless in the law of estates in land. There was little place here for creative judicial decision such as that of Lord Mansfield on quasi contract and on the law merchant. Critical natural law found one of its best fields in penal legislation and administration. But there was little scope for judicial development of that subject. What has been done for American penal administration, what has been done for American criminal law, has been mostly legislative. Except for one writer of the first magnitude at the very end of the formative era, doctrinal writers have neglected it, and law schools, which have done so much for the law in every other connection, have left this branch to take care of itself. . . . Here was *par excellence* the opportunity of legislation. Is it not significant that while notable strides have been made in every other department of law, our criminal law has been and remains relatively stagnant?

It would seem that while legislation has proved an effective agency of ridding the law of particular institutions and precepts which have come down from the past and have not been adapted or were not adaptable to the needs of the time, it has not been able, in our legal system, except in rare instances, to do much of the constructive work of change in eras of growth. So far as everyday relations and conflicts of interest are concerned, it has not been able to anticipate new demands nor to move fast enough when they made themselves felt through litigation. Judicial finding of law has a real advantage in competition with legislation in that it works with concrete cases and generalizes only after a long course of trial and error in the effort to work out a practicable principle. Legislation, when more than declaratory, when it does more than restate authoritatively what judicial experience has indicated, involves the difficulties and the perils of prophecy. But these considerations are not enough, of themselves, to explain why we, in common-law America, in comparison with the civil-law world, have been able to do so little in the way of enduring monuments of legislative lawmaking.

What are the reasons for the relative failure of American legislation of the formative era to do what was expected of it? Certainly it was not that the English-speaking world lacked leaders for legislative lawmaking. Three names among those who urged and sought to guide legislation in common-law jurisdictions are at least as great as any among contemporary judges or doctrinal writers. Put in chronological order, they are: Jeremy Bentham (1743–1832), Edward Livingston (1764–1836), and David Dudley Field (1805–1894). Each of these exceptionally gifted men labored long and devotedly to give to the English-speaking legal world the best possible legislative lawmaking. But they could not legislate directly, whereas lesser men on the bench could hand down directly legal propositions of which other judges and doctrinal writers were bound to take account. Men of lesser stature could, in the role of doctrinal writers, direct the course of judicial decision much more than these masters of the science of legislation could direct the action of parliamentary lawmakers. Thus more and more the growing point of our law came to be in judicial decision.

We can hardly say that legislative development of our law was hindered by the necessity of fitting legislation into the common law, which was traditionally unsympathetic to statutes. For it might well have happened, and an intelligent observer in the first quarter of a century after the Revolution might well have predicted, that the common law would have to fit into or adjust itself to a body of legislation. But one can see why, as the bench came to be manned by trained lawyers and their training came to be in the common-law tradition, the scope for effective legislation was sure to narrow. For one thing, the common law has never been at its best in administering justice from written texts. It has an excellent technique of finding the grounds of decision of particular cases in reported experience of the decision of other cases in the past. It has always, in comparison with the civil law, been awkward and none too effective in deciding on the basis of legislative texts. Moreover, its traditional attitude toward statutes stands in the way of making them a basis of creative development. The common law thinks of a statute as giving a rule, prescribing a detailed consequence for a detailed situation of fact, but not as a starting point for legal reasoning. While the civil law thinks of the course of judicial decision as providing a rule and turns for analogies to code or statute book, the common-law lawyer finds a rule in a statutory provision and takes his analogies from judicial decision. Nor does it stop here. He assumes that the statute is not meant to change the common law, or at least is meant to change it as little as possible, and so is prone to hold it declaratory if he can and at any rate to construe it strictly when it seeks to effect a change. He thinks of the constitutional checks upon legislation as enacting common-law limitations, and systematically develops those checks in terms of the common law. Thus the area of legislative reform of the law is restricted at the same time that effectiveness within the narrowed area is diminished.

How the common law tradition operates when a great piece of legislation is in the making is illustrated by the Sherman Anti-Trust Law. As John Sherman drew it originally it was a typical bit of Anglo-American legislation dealing specifically with a specific situation by a simple detailed rule. It provided, as he drew it, that in case of products of combinations in restraint of trade, the products of foreign competitors should come into the country free of duty. The judiciary committee of the Senate felt that this was not enough. They wished to draw a general statute as to such combinations. But they did not undertake to frame such a statute beyond a skeleton which they expected would be filled out by judicial decision. Senator Hoar tells us that they took it that by using the words of the common law they insured that the courts would take the act as a warrant for a gradual development of the common law on the subject. Instead of this, he tells us, the Supreme Court of the United States construed the words, not as at common law, but as meant to introduce a new rule, and so the statute was made to introduce a sweeping change. One cannot put the whole blame of such things upon either legislature or courts. They are the result of an attitude which has a long-taught tradition behind it and will not readily yield. But they make the path of the legislative lawmaker a rough one.

We must remember, however, that the legislators of the formative era were full of confidence. They were in no wise held back by considerations of how statutes would be received and applied by the courts, and if they had retained the confidence of the public they might have forced a better judicial attitude. Instead they gradually lost it and the courts gradually acquired it, so that in the period from the Civil War to the end of the century the hegemony of the judiciary in our policy is as marked as was that of the legislature in the earlier period. There were many reasons for this growing distrust of legislatures which became strong in the last quarter of the nineteenth century, and we must look into them in some detail for the light they throw upon the question what we may expect to achieve through legislation in another era of legal growth.

*Courts versus Legislatures.* With the development of the legal profession, the growth of confidence in the judiciary and the rise of academic legal education based on the common law, a contest between courts and legislatures began in our formative era which is comparable to the contests between courts and crown in seventeenth-century England and was in part brought about, so far as the courts are concerned, by the influence of the legal literature of the English contest, which was classical for the lawyer.

In seventeenth-century England the courts had stood for the common-law doctrine that no official action was above the law as against arbitrary rulers in an age of absolute governments. In nineteenth-century America certain grave abuses of legislation led the judges in the states to insist upon constitutional checks designed to meet those abuses and to stand for the common-law doctrine of the supremacy of the law as a doctrine that the legislature itself is subject to the Constitution as the supreme law of the land, to be interpreted and applied by the courts in the course of orderly litigation as in any other case involving finding and application of law.

One of these abuses, against which state constitutions provided every sort of drastic limitation, was involved in special legislation. The American legislator found his warrant for this type of lawmaking in Blackstone. The latter distinguishes general or public from special or private acts. He says:

> The statute 13 Eliz. c. 10, to prevent spiritual persons from making leases for longer terms than three lives or twenty-one years is a public act, it being a rule prescribed to the whole body of spiritual persons in the nation; but an act to enable the Bishop of Chester to make a lease to A.B. for sixty years is an exception to this rule; it concerns only the parties and the bishop's successors and is, therefore, a private act.

Special legislation of this sort is legislative administration rather than legislative lawmaking. It could have raised nice questions as to the constitutional separation of powers. But the volume of it and abuses to which it gave rise . . . led to provisions in state constitutions prohibiting it or limiting it, either generally or to certain subjects or classes of subjects. These provisions were often difficult to interpret and to apply and were not always easy for lawmakers to adhere to. They gave rise to much litigation and in more than one state involved important statutes in uncertainty session after session. This condition did not make for good legislation. . . .

Grave abuses grew up also with respect to riders on bills whereby surreptitious clauses were introduced as to which the public had little or no chance of making itself heard in opposition. Hence many state constitutions made strict provisions as to the title of acts and correspondence of the content with the title, or as to the number of subjects which could be included in one act, which involved quite as much confusion in application and had quite as unhappy effects upon statute lawmaking as in the cases of special legislation, amendment, and repeal.

Along with the foregoing abuses there was a tendency of legislatures to interfere with executive administration and with exercise of the judicial function. There were legislative prescribings of appointment of particular persons to particular offices by the governor. There was special legislation as to local highway improvements where today we should leave the matter to a board or commission. There were legislative prescribings as to admission to the bar, even as to the admission of a particular person or reinstatement of a particular disbarred lawyer. There were legislative prescribings that judges should do the work of law reporting by writing judicial head notes to opinions. Here difficult questions were raised as to the constitutional distribution or separation of powers. Such things go far to explain the persistence in the United States of the common-law attitude toward statutes which is admittedly an unhappy feature of our Anglo-American legal tradition. Instead of legislatures and courts working together toward the ends of law, in the last century, if they were not actually in conflict, they tended each to be suspicious of the other. Partly this was an inheritance from the seventeenth-century English polity upon which ours was built. Partly it was involved in the application to legislation of our common-law doctrine of the supremacy of the law. Partly it is a phase of the general regime of non-cooperation, of independent agencies of government pursuing their individual ways independently, which was characteristic of pioneer America on every side. It became more marked in the second half of the century as the personnel of state lawmaking bodies declined.

In many cases in the first third of the nineteenth century, state courts took Blackstone's statement that "no human laws are of any validity" if contrary to the law of nature, as a warrant for refusing to apply statutes which they considered arbitrary and unreasonable. Thus in 1822 the Supreme Court of Connecticut said that if a statute without any cause deprived a person of his property or subjected him to imprisonment, so that there was a "direct infraction of vested rights too palpable to be questioned and too unjust to admit of vindication," it would be "a violation of the social compact and within the control of the judiciary." In 1814, in passing on an act which dispensed with the provisions of the statute of limitations in favor of a particular creditor as against a particular debtor, the Supreme Court of Massachusetts said:

It is manifestly against the first principles of civil liberty and natural justice and the spirit of our constitution and laws that any one citizen should enjoy privileges and advantages which are denied to all others under like circumstances, or that any one should be subjected to losses, damages, suits or actions from which all others under like circumstances are exempted.

Likewise in 1831 the Supreme Court of Tennessee said that since there are "eternal principles of justice which no government has a right to disregard," it did not follow that "because there may be no restriction in the Constitution prohibiting a particular act of the legislature that such act is therefore constitutional." It added: "Some acts, although not expressly forbidden, may be against the plain and obvious dictates of reason." Accordingly the court refused to give effect to a retroactive statute creating a special tribunal to try certain suits by a bank against its officers.

Since the Fourteenth Amendment such statutes come within the express prohibition of the Constitution. But in our formative era there was no other check than the common-law tradition from the Middle Ages that all official action was subject to the law and was not to be arbitrary and unreasonable. This doctrine had been applied by Coke in 1610 in *Bonham's Case*, and by Hobart in 1615 in *Day* v. *Savadge*, and Holt had laid down in 1701, in *City of London* v. *Wood*, that an act of Parliament "cannot make one that lives under a government judge and party." Under the influence of the idea of popular omnicompetence and hence of legislative absolutism in the representatives of the people, and of laws as formulations of the popular will, reinforced later by ideas of law as the command of the sovereign, there was a marked tendency to arbitrariness in legislation. The memory of contests between courts and crown over the royal dispensing power was too recent to lead common-law courts to admit a like arbitrary legislative dispensing power. The taught tradition was adverse to absolute power anywhere. That was what constitutions and bills of rights sought to preclude, and things which colonial legislatures had done were among the mischiefs which our constitutional separation of powers was designed to obviate. But all power is liable to abuse and power must exist somewhere if a politically organized society is to do its work. That the line which the courts took in the end has been followed and found practicable for a century speaks for itself. On the whole the courts worked out a difficult balance well in our formative era. If natural law led to some extravagances for a time, its rationalism proved a useful guide.

Perhaps legislatures are more unmindful than courts of the limitations of effective legal action. They have to predict detailed applications where the court draws its principle from detailed applications after the event and in the light of experienced limitations. But well as judicial scrutiny of legislative action has worked, looked at as a whole, it must be admitted to have had a bad effect in lessening the sense of legislative responsibility. Observers have often remarked a tendency, in common phrase, to pass the buck to the courts, comparable to the tendency to leave it to the courts, or today to administrative agencies, to fill out a skeleton statute. Part of the relative ineffectiveness of state legislatures in matters of law reform must be attributed to this irresponsibility. . . .

*Dogmatic Teaching.* It will have been noted that in these lectures the emphasis is put on historical continuity of the taught legal tradition. This tradition, received from England, to no small extent through a few leaders in each of the colonies who had been trained in the Inns of Court, and transmitted by generations of lawyers trained under the apprentice system, likewise received from England, was taught later in law schools which preserved much of that system and continued to hand down that tradition. It was not till the present century that the academic type of law school definitely prevailed and the apprentice type ceased to train the bulk of those who came to the bar from law schools. It was not till the present generation that law-school training definitely superseded apprentice training in the offices of practitioners as preparation for the bar. The dogmatic teaching which prevailed in law offices and in the apprentice type of law school made for an obstinate legal tradition.

One might tell the story of the formulating agencies of the law in our formative era with the emphasis on change rather than continuity. If we look only at the body of legal precepts which obtains in the United States today in comparison with those obtaining in seventeenth or even eighteenth century England, we might easily feel that the change has been radical and complete. But change has been gradual, has been chiefly in details, and hence not to be understood without understanding what was changed, and has been guided by the received traditional technique, applied to received traditional materials. Thus much that has been changed has continued to furnish analogies and to serve as the basis of legal reasoning and even to affect the newer precepts in their interpretation and application. . . .

*Lay Judges and the Influence of Case-Law.* As an agency of growth in the shaping of American law, judicial decisions did not have the advantage of public confidence at the outset and a long start as legislation did. Where the English courts had stood for the rights of Englishmen against the crown, it had been the colonial legislatures which stood for the rights of the colonists against crown and royal governors. There was much distrust of judges. The time of colonization, the seventeenth century, saw the nadir of the bench in England under Charles II and James II, and a bad tradition of judges was brought to the New World. Ideas bred by experience of Whigs and dissenters in England were reinforced by experience of colonists with royal judges in America. Hence judicial organization went forward slowly and the personnel of the bench for some time was not such as to make judicial decision an active creative agency. In Massachusetts, of ten chief justices and twenty-three associates between 1692 and 1776, only one chief justice and two associate justices were lawyers. Two of the three justices of the highest court of New Jersey during the Revolution were not lawyers. Of the three justices in New Hampshire after independence, one was a clergyman and another a physician. A blacksmith sat on the highest court of Rhode Island from 1814 to 1818, and a farmer was chief justice of that state from 1819 to 1826. There are no reports of American judicial decision of any consequence till the last decade of the eighteenth century, and regular reporting begins in the nineteenth century.

But the legal materials available to courts and lawyers were English. The French and Dutch books on natural law gave them guiding ideas. But Blackstone and Coke gave usable legal precepts for everyday use. As lawyers cited and law students studied them, a taught tradition became established, and such a tradition makes enduring law. Thus the common-law technique of finding the grounds of decision in reported judicial experience became the decisive agency of law making in our formative era. Even in Louisiana, where the civil-law background might have put doctrinal writing where it then was in Continental Europe, judicial decision became controlling.

*Confidence in Reason.* There are many signs that American law has entered on a period of creative activity analogous to the two classical creative eras in our legal history—the seventeenth century which made the feudal land law of medieval England into a system which could go round the world in the nineteenth century, and the time after the Revolution when English legal institutions and doctrines and precepts were made over to conform to an ideal of American society by a criterion of applicability to American conditions. In each of these creative eras lawyers had a lively faith that they could do things by conscious effort intelligently directed. In each they were guided by a philosophical theory of natural law. In each they turned to some extent to comparative law to give concrete content to abstract ideas of natural law. In each they sought to bring the legal and the moral into accord, and thus brought into the authoritative legal materials much from outside of the law.

On every hand there are signs of a revival of this faith in the efficacy of effort, in marked contrast with the juristic pessimism of a generation ago. Interest in philosophy of law is notably reviving in all English-speaking lands. Comparative law is taking on new life. Jurists everywhere are seeking a canon of values which is in some degree restoring the old consciousness of the relation of law to morals.

History of a system of law is largely a history of borrowings of legal materials from other legal systems and of assimilation of materials from outside of the law. In the history of Anglo-American law there are successive borrowings and adaptations from Roman law (e.g., the rules as to title by occupation), from the canon law (e.g., our law and practice as to marriage and divorce and probate and administration), from the modern Roman law and Continental codes (e.g., in our law of riparian rights), and from the commercial law of Continental Europe, as Mansfield's decisions and the decisions and texts of Kent and Story make clear abundantly....

In all these cases it is the form and shape that has been made by the lawmaking agencies, not the content. The content was found. The form was given authoritatively. For except as an act of omnipotence, creation is not the making of something out of nothing. In legal history it is the reshaping of traditional legal materials, the bringing in of other materials from without and the adaptation of these materials as a whole to the securing of human claims and satisfaction of human wants under new conditions of life in civilized society. The creative process consists in going outside of the authoritative legal materials of the time and place, or even outside of the law, and selecting something which is then combined with or added to the existing materials, or the existing methods of developing and applying those materials, and is then gradually given form as a legal precept or legal doctrine or legal institution. In Jhering's apt phrase, the process is one of juristic chemistry. The chemist does not make the materials which go into his test tube. He selects them and combines them for some purpose and his purpose thus gives form to the result....

More of the creative spirit of seventeenth-century natural law is to be found in the doctrine that the common law was received only so far as applicable to the physical, political, social, and economic conditions of America, and in a later and specialized form in which legal precepts were judged by their conformity to "the nature of American government" or the "nature of American institutions." In truth, what is original in the judicial working out of American common law in the formative era comes in through these ideas. Through them courts rejected inconvenient items in what they found in the English books or in the treatises on commercial law or in comparative law. Where the other identifications of natural law were instruments of borrowing and adaptation from other legal systems, these theories were agencies of developing our indigenous political and social institutions into legal materials. But before the century was out the doctrine of applicability had done its work, and the ideas of conformity to the nature of American government and conformity to the nature of American institutions had become means of holding down social legislation by subjecting it to the test of what was suited to the rural, pioneer society of the time when our institutions were formative.

*Doctrinal Writing.* No truthful account of the development of American law in the nineteenth century can ignore the part played by text writers. While in form our law is chiefly the work of judges, in great part judges simply put the guinea stamp of the state's authority upon propositions which they found worked out for them in advance. Their creative work was often a work of intelligent selection. In this respect, as also in the part played by law teachers, American law is closer to the civil law than to the English common law. Yet doctrinal writing played in every way a very much greater part in the growth of the common law to its maturity in the last century than our juristic theory admits. . . . Certainly the most creative of judges have not made legal precepts out of their own minds, nor have they been inspired wholly by "authority." Text books have had and still have much influence. In the formative era of American law this influence was often controlling.

Indeed, the nineteenth-century text writers did much more for English law at home than appears upon the surface. Chief Baron Pollock is reported to have said that he "read no treatises" but "referred to them as collecting the authorities." However, the systematic collection of the authorities in the hands of a skillful writer involves suggestive interpretation of them and the way in which they are set forth may be and often was more than a mere indexing of them. It is true the English have or had some strict rules as to citation. The writer to be cited must have become a judge, and the living were not to be cited. Thus Byles on Bills (1829), Sugden on Vendor and Purchaser (1805) and Sugden on Powers (1808) could be cited for what had been written before the authors went upon the bench. So with Lindley on Partnership (1863) and later its outgrowth Lindley on the Law of Companies. But one would deceive himself much if he thought that Jarman on Wills (1844) or Lewin on Trust (1837) or Preston on Estates (1820) did no more than serve as collections of the authorities. Moreover, at a later date, the books from which English law students learned their law succeeded more than once in bringing into English judicial decision and thence into the American books ideas from the nineteenth-century Pandectists—sometimes ideas which were not as happy as they seemed.

We had no such rules as to citation in America. Here the judicial use of text books was general and avowed and not always discriminating. . . .

American text writing as a significant force in our legal development begins in 1816 with Reeve's, Baron, and Feme. Down to the Civil War the list of textbooks which went far to shape the law for us is impressive: Kent's Commentaries (1826–1830); Gould on Pleading (1832); Story on Bailments (1832), on the Constitution (1833), on the Conflict of Laws

(1834), on Equity Jurisprudence (1836), on Equity Pleading (1838), on Agency (1839), on Partnership (1841), on Bills of Exchange (1843), on Promissory Notes (1845); Wheaton on International Law (1836); Greenleaf on Evidence (1842–1853); Wharton on Criminal Law (1846); Sedgwick on Damages (1847) and on Interpretation of Statutory and Constitutional Law (1857); Rawle on Covenants for Title (1852); Bishop on Marriage and Divorce (1852) and on Criminal Law (1856–1858); Parsons on Contracts (1853–1855); Washburn on Real Property (1860–1862). All of these went through many editions. They were standard to the end of the century, some well into the present century, and some are standard even today. So much were they used by the profession and by the courts that an indignant practitioner is said to have demanded of a court as to one of them whether there was any statute making it an authority.

From the Civil War to the end of the century, Cooley's Constitutional Limitations (1868), Dillon on Municipal Corporations (1872) and Pomeroy's Equity Jurisprudence (1881–1883) exhaust the list of those which can stand with the great texts of the formative era. But by this time our case law had reached maturity and for a time the need of writings such as those of the earlier period had ceased.

Let us note more in detail what these doctrinal treatises of the fore part of the century were able to bring about. The most important of them were the work of law teachers—Kent, Gould, Story, Greenleaf, Parsons, and Washburn....

Not only were these books the product of teaching, they became and remained the basis of law teaching down to the present century. Thus, they became immediately the basis of a taught tradition and so got quickly a real even if not a theoretical authority. Maitland tells us that taught law is tough law. That is, it is enduring. That these books could at the same time serve practitioner and teacher insured their triumph.

First, they fixed the reception of the common law for all but one of our jurisdictions. This was still in doubt at the end of the first third of the last century. It was never in doubt thereafter....

One feature of this feeling for historical continuity was to bring to an end the agitation to supplant the common law as the basis of American legal systems. Many things had operated to retard a complete and final reception of the English common law, not the least the example of the French Civil Code, the enthusiasm for things French following the Revolution and in the era of Jeffersonian democracy, and the natural-law idea that a code could be drafted independent of the historical materials of the law and on a basis of pure reason. It is significant that Walker's American Law (1837) contains a vigorous argument for codification which is retained in later editions down to 1895. In 1833 it was still not wholly settled that we should receive the common law. . . . But Story had begun to write and under his decisive influence the struggle was substantially at an end.

Blackstone and Kent, it is true, had prepared the way, Blackstone especially being taken for an authoritative statement of the law we had received. But they did not and could not go sufficiently into detail for the everyday purposes of the courts. The courts had to turn to what they could find elsewhere, particularly as there were still few American reports. Pothier on Obligations had been translated by François Xavier Martin in 1802, but the translation was not generally accessible. Pothier's treatise on Sales was translated in 1839. Domat had been translated in 1720 and there was a second edition in 1737. These were English. There was an American edition in 1850. Pothier's treatise on partnership was not translated till 1854. It will be seen that most of these translations came too late. Between 1832 and 1845 Story had covered the whole field of commercial law as well as constitutional law and equity with books which at once came into general use.

In the meantime, however, the exigencies of commercial law, on which there was no useful material in Blackstone, had led to an increasing resort by the courts to the civilian treatises. Kent's Commentaries did not appear till 1826–1830. For over a generation after the Revolution the civilians had this field to themselves. In the first volume of Johnson's Reports, reporting decisions of the Supreme Court of New York and of the Court of Errors and Appeals of New York during the year 1806, Pothier is cited four times, Emerigon five times, Valin three times, Casaregis twice, and Azuni once. In seventh Johnson (1810–1811) Pothier is cited three times, Huberus twice, Emerigon once, Justinian's Code once, and the French Civil Code once. . . . From commercial law this tendency to rely upon the civilians spread to the private law generally. . . .

As I have said in another connection, in effect the result was a conception of an ideal of comparative law as declaratory of natural law, a conception which is especially marked in the writings and judgments of Kent and Story. It was not merely creative, it made for stability and gave direction both to judicial decision and to doctrinal writing. It was the most efficient of the instruments by which the great text writers of the formative era were able to bring it about that the English common law should be the basis of the law in all but one of the United States.

But it was not merely that for more than a generation after the Revolution there were no English treatises of consequence on commercial law. When the lawyer or judge of that time sought detailed information as to English law, he had to go to Coke's Institutes, Hale's Tracts and Pleas of the Crown, precedents of pleading, and alphabetically arranged abridgments. Not unnaturally those who could read them turned with delight to the treatises on the civil and commercial law of Continental Europe. When they compared the order and system and rational modernity of the civilian treatises with the disorder and alphabetical arrangement and scholastic medievalism of the English books of the time, they were led to think much worse of English law and much better of the law of continental Europe than the facts warranted. The high estimate of the civil law which was formed in that period lingered in this country till the end of the third quarter of the last century. But it lingered only as a traditional admiration of something not really understood. Henry Adams going to Germany in the late fifties to study the civil law is one of the last cases of what might have been such a phenomenon as the flow of Scotch students of law to the Dutch universities down to the nineteenth century. As good texts in English appeared in America and few could read the untranslated civilians, the cult of the civil law disappeared. . . .

It should be added that, except on commercial law, the great civilian treatises did not deal with the sort of thing which had to be decided in American courts of the formative era. It was hard to find in them the help which the courts and lawyers of the time required. To use them intelligently called for a training and technique quite unknown in English-speaking jurisdictions. As we look at these treatises now, without consulting them under the pressure of cases to be decided at once and with leisure to use them not as books of reference but as systematic expositions of the law as a whole, interdependent in the several parts, and thus to work out their possibilities as their authors intended, we may see that the rich civilian literature of the seventeenth and eighteenth centuries could have been made to yield abundant useful principles and analogies. But the courts needed rules. To perceive the possibilities of finding them by reasoning from the Continental treatises, one had to be a much better civilian than any one could have been at that time—than any one but Kent and Story actually was. Law, as distinguished from laws, is a taught tradition. The civil law was and is an academically taught tradition. There were no faculties of law, trained in and teaching the civil-law tradition, to give vitality to the texts of that law in this country. But if we could not use this legal literature as a whole there was much in it which we could and did use. The genius of the civilians was chiefly employed upon what may be called in a broad sense the law of contractual obligations. . . . The side of the law which called for immediate development in the formative era was the very side where the civilians could help, and it was fortunate that there were a few strong judges and well-trained, well-read doctrinal writers who knew how to avail themselves of that help and make it available for the courts.

In the second place, then, doctrinal writing gave the courts at a critical period what they could take to be authoritative statements of the received common law and so gave judges and legislators something from which to make required new starts. Take, for example, the Georgia Code of 1860. The part known as the civil code, made up of 1586 sections, is a digest of extracts from the ordinary text books of the common law in use in the United States at the time. It is not a code in the modern sense. But it furnished an authoritative text book of the common law at a time when many questions remained unsettled in that jurisdiction and libraries in which to find the materials for passing upon them were not generally at hand. Such a thing could not have been done without the textbooks. Indeed, there are gaps in that code exactly where there were gaps in the text book legal literature of the time. Courts not infrequently wrote opinions out of the text books exactly as the Georgia code commission made a code out of them.

Thirdly, the doctrinal writing of the formative era delivered us from the danger of premature crude codification. For there was a very real danger of premature crude codification during the legislative reform movement. Bentham's writings attracted wide attention. The French Civil Code had fascinated many, as it had almost every one abroad. Law discussions of American law in the first quarter of the nineteenth century abound in demands for an American code. The New York constitution of 1846 provided for a system of codes. Massachusetts had a code commission under legislative authority which made on the whole a favorable report. Georgia adopted a civil code, such as it was, on the eve of the Civil War. California adopted Field's draft codes. In a comparison of abstract systems the common law is at its worst. There was no handy compendium to show to the pioneer with his boundless faith in versatility; to assure him that with it and his common sense he could solve all the legal problems of daily life. The strength of the common law is in its treatment of concrete controversies as the strength of the civil law is in its logical development of abstract conceptions. The latter can be put in much smaller compass than the former and has much more appearance of completeness and certainty. Had such men as Kent and Story allowed their good sense to be overcome by the Continental philosophers of law, whom they undoubtedly admired, the future of American law might have been very different. I doubt if our judges would have been strong enough to withstand the movement for codification. But when the movement culminated in the draft code of David Dudley Field, English law was thoroughly received, well established, and able to resist it.[c]

Fourthly, doctrinal writing preserved unity in our law when its unity was sorely threatened. In the cult of local law which developed in the nineteenth century with the continual setting up of new commonwealths

[c] The codification movement is more fully explored in Chapter 3.

each with independent power to make law by legislation and find it by judicial decision, our American law might have lost its unity. Had it lost its unity the movement for a premature Benthamite code might well have swept the country as the French codes swept over Europe. If the flood of statutes which poured from our legislatures from the beginning had been turned upon a system of purely local rules, as the country became unified economically we should very likely be seeking relief in codes, if we had not done so long ago. An intolerable diversity of local law in a politically and economically unified land has always led to codification. The attempt of the Supreme Court of the United States to preserve unity by its doctrine as to questions of general law could achieve relatively little because the bulk of ordinary questions of private law could not come before that court as fast as they arose in the state courts. What Story the judge could not do, Story the text writer largely accomplished. More than anything else the books of our great nineteenth century text writers defeated the urge for a code which we were in no condition to frame in our formative era. In Louisiana you had the French Civil Code for a solid foundation. But in jurisdictions which had inherited English law there was no such foundation. There was nothing ripe to be codified. Codification could only come effectively after an era of legal maturity which was still well in the future. A code in the common-law states of nineteenth-century America would have required far longer to develop into a workable body of American law than it took under the leadership of our great doctrinal writers to make such a body of law from the traditional materials. If one doubts this he need only look at the California Code, which has been made to serve chiefly by assuming it to be declaratory of what has been worked out there and elsewhere by judicial experience.

Fifth, doctrinal writing was the chief agency in saving equity for us as a part of our received system. It was in equity especially that the text writer's method of comparative law was fruitful of good results. Over and above the hostility to all English law there was for historical reasons special hostility to English equity, so that the courts of Pennsylvania did not have equity jurisdiction as such till 1836 nor did the courts of Massachusetts have complete equity jurisdiction till the last quarter of the nineteenth century. Equity has never been popular in America. The Puritan has always opposed it. It acts directly upon the person. It coerces the individual will. It involves discretion in its application to concrete cases and that in the Puritan mind means that a magistrate is over us instead of with us. It means that he may judge by a personal standard instead of by the "standing laws" which the Puritan demanded in the Massachusetts Bill of Rights. He called for a universal and unyielding rule, and it was such things that equity sought to mitigate. Moreover, the pioneer was suspicious of equity because it relieved fools who had made bad bargains, whereas the self-reliant frontiersman felt that fools should be allowed and required to act freely and be held for the consequences of their folly. Nor were the methods and doctrines of equity congenial to our nineteenth-century tribunals. The text writers of the decadence of our law-book writing tried hard to reduce the principles of exercise of the chancellor's discretion to hard and fast rules as to jurisdiction.

Probably the decisive factor in our reception of English equity was Story's Equity Jurisprudence. With much art, whether conscious or unconscious, he made it seem that the precepts established by the decisions of the English Court of Chancery coincided in substance with those of the Roman law as expounded by the civilians and hence were but statements of universal principles of natural law universally accepted in civilized states. If equity had been expounded to American judges and lawyers and students in the dry and technical fashion of the contemporary English treatises, we might have been sorely hampered in the development of American law by a crippled equity. Story's sympathetic exposition of English equity, referring continually to the civilians and to the Roman law, making it appear, untruly as we know now, that the system was essentially Roman and so approved by experience of all men as a body of universal principles of justice, often comparing the development of these principles in England with that upon the Continent to the disadvantage of the latter, and all this in most readable form, with an orderly arrangement and a system which at least improved immeasurably upon what had gone before, was the one thing needed to commend equity to our American courts and to counteract the forces which were working against it.

Lastly, doctrinal writing in the formative era saved us from legislative experimentation at a time when legislatures were not well prepared to deal with the general development of an American private law. What might have happened, if our law had been forced to grow up by legislative empiricism, the New York Code of Civil Procedure, its overgrown mass in the last quarter of the nineteenth century, and the struggles to get away from it and its results in the present generation, warn us abundantly.

*Law Books as Case-Finders.* In the organizing, systematizing era after the Civil War text writing ceased to be doctrinal writing and became what Chief Baron Pollock said of English text writing, a mere key to the cases. This period was the nadir of American law-book writing. Writers assumed to find a rule for everywhere in a common-law decision anywhere. So far as possible by plausible formulation and consecutive statement they made those independent decisions read like parts of an integrated logically interdependent whole. Where this could not be done, they announced a difference of judicial view, on which they seldom ventured an opinion, for they were stating "the law as it is," and pointed out the numerical weight of authority in a list of cases in accord and to the contrary, in which very likely New York and Nevada each counted as one. In part, this resulted from the firm basis for judicial decision which had become established in the formative era. The courts could for the most part find what they wanted in the reports. But in part it resulted from the growth of the law-publishing business to large proportions. The exigencies of large-scale publication, with traveling law-book salesmen going from city to city and office to office—a system still in full vigor when I came to the bar in 1890—called for nationally marketable treatises, and the textbook which was the best index to the reports best met that requirement. An orderly presentation of all the cases in the English-speaking world in narrative form, reconciled in illusory appearance at least, so far as the writer's skill would allow, could find a publisher. Criticism of decisions threw doubt upon the proposition that American law, or even the common law, was a body of detailed rules, evidenced by reported cases, in which a decision of an appellate court in any common-law jurisdiction established a rule for every other. The law-publishing business was based upon this postulate. There might at most be cases where a writer could only set forth the "weight of authority" with an appendix of decisions establishing a "minority view." In time such books were superseded by the development of excellent systems of digests, both general and for each state, and of cyclopedias, proceeding on the same presupposition as the mechanical textbooks, but with a better mechanism.

*Influence of Doctrinal Writers.* Let us look more closely at the reasons why, in spite of the common-law tradition and with no formal authority behind them, doctrinal writers were able to become so great a factor in the shaping of American law. One reason was that in our formative era, as a result of our political history, of the tradition of masterful judges under the Stuarts in the time when the colonists emigrated, of the memory of some royal chief justices and judges before the Revolution, and as a legacy of Puritanism, there was general fear of entrusting to judges the power which the common-law polity called for. To some extent the judges of that time did not always have full confidence in themselves, as shown by the rejection of the common-law doctrine as to misdemeanors in the states of the Northwest Territory although the Ordinance of 1787 had made the common law the measure of decision in that domain. If they could not fall back on a statute for a definitely prescribed rule of decision, let them at least use a law book. As late as 1837, Walker argues that there is danger in admitting judicial empiricism as an agency of lawmaking. He says: "Although in theory precedents are binding, yet in point of fact judges do not regard precedents as absolutely imperative like statutes, but rather as lights to aid their discretion and inform their judgment. They sometimes overrule their own prior decisions, and very often the decisions of other courts, in so much that a collection of overruled cases has been published, exceeding a thousand." Obviously the prevalence of such views made for resort to the textbooks. We can understand why so many courts so often accepted textbook statements of supposed general rules of law.

Then, too, we had before us the example of a growing body of law text writing in England. Hale had begun something of the sort in the seventeenth century. In the eighteenth century there comes to be a marked departure from the alphabetical abridgment or digest type or the discursive-commentary type of law writing which had governed from the Middle Ages to Coke. Of the eighteenth-century texts much cited in America in the fore part of the nineteenth century, we may note Gilbert's treatises (1734–1758), Foster's Crown Law (1762), Fearne's Contingent Remainders (1772), Mitford's Equity Pleading (1780), Jones on Bailments (1781), Sanders on Uses and Trusts (1791), Fonblanque's Equity (1793–1794), Watson on Partnership (1794), and Chitty on Bills (1799). When American reports were only beginning and full libraries of English reports were by no means always accessible, such books were sometimes the best available repositories of the law. Some of these were by no means outstanding. But not infrequently they suggested even more insistently what was suggested in the Continental treatises on commercial law.

Also such books suggested like books to American lawyers and especially to American law teachers who needed books as the basis of teaching. It is suggestive that the Litchfield Law School, the first of our law schools in point of time, gave us two of our earliest text books of a modern type and that the first fruit of the Harvard Law School was a treatise on real actions. But much of the impetus for Anglo-American doctrinal writing came from reading the treatises of the Continental civilians. This was not merely because in the growth and absorption of the law merchant for want of other materials English as well as Americans had recourse to Continental books on commercial law. As they sought in the nineteenth century to organize and systematize the results of two centuries of growth, they looked to the civil law, upon which great systematists had been at work since Donellus in the sixteenth century, to furnish the general systematic ideas which were lacking in their own books. When Austin in 1826 was elected to the chair of jurisprudence in London, he felt bound to go to Germany, to study the civil law as a necessary preparation. He speaks of it in comparison with the common law as it stood in the English books of his time as "the realm of order and light." Such was the impression it made also on two generations of American lawyers. One can understand why our law teachers set out to write such treatises and why when written their treatises were eagerly received.

But if the civilian treatises were a stimulus to American doctrinal writers, there was a fundamental difference from the start in the concreteness of our texts, and such is the Anglo-American frame of mind that this concreteness made for the success of books which had no claim to authority in the tradition they expounded. Gray tells us that "the common-law judge neglects imaginary cases but the civil-law jurist is in danger of neglecting real cases." He goes on to say: "It is comparatively easy to frame a rule when you can frame your own examples. Putting simple extreme cases, it is not difficult to draw a line between them. But when you come to the cases which real life presents, with their complications and limitations, the theorist is apt to divert his eyes." Again he says: "The judge has his facts given to him. The text writer makes his own typical cases, and the temptation to make them such as to render easy the deduction of general doctrines is well nigh irresistible." There is much truth in this. But we must remember that Gray wrote in the nadir of American textbook writing and grew up in the time of reaction from the extravagant estimate of the civil law which governed in the earlier part of the century. The civil law is a law of the universities. Its oracles have been law teachers. The common law is a law of the courts. Its oracles have always been judges. Our doctrinal writers could not write us oracles. They had to found their texts on the judicial oracles and those oracles were pronounced on the actual controversies of life, not on the hypothetical cases of the lecture room. Thus, the quality of concreteness was assured. It is suggestive that recent Continental commentaries are making a large use of the decisions of the courts, as our texts had to do from the start.

Yet doctrinal writing was able to achieve what it did for our law in its formative era largely because the best of the texts were the work of law teachers who had been required to formulate their ideas to the exigencies of teaching and submit them to critical hearers. The doctrinal treatises of the civil law had more than the traditions of Roman law and of the medieval universities behind their success in maintaining themselves as repositories of the law for centuries. But a taught tradition is the most enduring form of law. In this country the rise of law schools was steady after the first third of the nineteenth century and textbooks were the backbone of the instruction. Indeed, we did not learn to teach from the primary authorities as had been done in the medieval Inns of Court, till the last quarter of the century. By this time the text books had done their work and they passed out of the law school curricula in the era of systematizing and organizing of the law which followed.

What may we expect of doctrinal writing in our work of creative finding and shaping of law which is before us? The need of such books as those of the formative era is quite as great now as then, but for a different reason. Then the courts had little to go on and much to bring about. Now, they have too much to go on to permit judicial working over of all that must be treated, especially under the limitations that bind judicial action. They have increasingly less time for thorough first-hand work upon the vast mass of available material. Primarily they must render just decisions in the cases before them and the increasing complexity of cases adds to this task. Their dockets are congested. The labors of counsel, with the aid of the modern apparatus of digests and cyclopedias, put before them an enormous mass of authoritative matter in which they must find starting points for reasoning or analogies or rules. They cannot give the time to oral argument which was possible in the formative era. If they are to do their work well there must be thorough working over of the law which has come down to us as only jurists and law writers can do it. And no one who has followed the history of American law can doubt that the jurists and law writers who are to do this will be law teachers. The experience of the American Law Institute confirms this.

Moreover a revival of doctrinal writing has begun in this generation. Such books as Wigmore on Evidence, Williston on Contracts, and Beale on the Conflict of Laws are permanent contributions to our law. They put the matured nineteenth-century law in form to be used in a new era of growth. So, too, of the work of the American Law Institute. For more than a generation the best energies of our law teachers have gone into the preparation of case books to be instruments of teaching. In many of these case books we may find creative work of the first order. They are necessary forerunners, under the conditions of today, of the great treatises that must come presently from the law schools. They have made possible the restatement which will be no small part of the basis of a juristic and thence a judicial new start. Whether as affording material for judicial decision or for administrative determination or for legislative lawmaking these summings up of the nineteenth-century law and placings of it in the order of reason with reference to the legal problems of the time will be invaluable. I am not in the least troubled that they have not essayed to give us an ideal body of precepts on each subject but rather have sought to present our law in its now stage of development at its best. We shall proceed more surely toward the ideal body of precepts for the future if we start from the best possible statement of what we have been able to achieve up to date. . . .

WE HAVE ALREADY BEEN INTRODUCED to the impact of equity upon the legal system. We have seen something of the contest in English law between the system of justice based on the common law writs and the intrusions of the Chancellor. In addition, Dean Pound, writing of the "formative era" of American law, has referred to the hostility of the new American states to the power of the Chancellor.

The contribution of equity to American legal development deserves closer examination. A good opportunity for analyzing the role of equity is provided by the experience in Pennsylvania, where for a hundred and fifty years the usual equity powers were denied to the courts. The consequences are examined in the following classic essay.

---

# THE ADMINISTRATION OF EQUITY THROUGH COMMON-LAW FORMS    By Sydney G. Fisher

EQUITY AND its administration have been favourite topics with law reformers. Whether the distinction between equity and law is a sound and essential one, whether equity can be administered by the same court that administers law, and whether equity can be absorbed into the common law and be administered by common law forms have been the great questions. In the solution of the last question the American State of Pennsylvania has had a long practical experience. Her system, which is correctly described as the administration of equity through common law forms, has now [1885] been in existence for more than one hundred and fifty years. No other commonwealth in the world has tried the experiment in so thorough a manner or on such an extensive scale. It is therefore fair to say that the exact value of the system, what it can and what it cannot do for the conduct of litigation, ought to be found in the experience of Pennsylvania.

The subject naturally divides itself into three parts. *First,* the various unsuccessful attempts, from the founding of the Colony in 1681 until the year 1836, to obtain courts with the usual Chancery powers. *Second,* as a consequence of these failures, the growth during the same period of the administration of equity through common law forms. *Third,* the period

---

Reprinted from the *Law Quarterly Review,* vol. 1, 1885, pp. 455–465. Sydney G. Fisher (1856–1927), a member of the Pennsylvania bar, was the author of numerous books of colonial legal history and biography, and was influential in the movement for civil service reform.

from 1836 to the present time, during which the Courts have gradually obtained from the legislature nearly all the ordinary powers of Chancery.

William Penn obtained his charter for Pennsylvania in 1681, and by its terms could have at once erected a Court of Equity. He did not do so. Apparently he was not an admirer of such courts; for he describes the Indians as "perplexed by Chancery suits," and in accordance with his Quaker belief he made arrangements for having appointed by every County Court "three peacemakers," who acted as arbitrators to prevent lawsuits.

But the General Assembly, which was created by Penn as the legislative body of the Colony, was of a different mind. In 1684 it made two provisions for introducing equity. The first made the County Courts courts of equity as well as of law. The second created a Provincial Court, which was to be a court of appeals from the County Courts, and was also to try all cases, both in law and in equity, not triable in the County Courts. Both of these provisions were repealed by the English Government in 1793. The first was re-enacted by the General Assembly the same year that it was repealed. But it is believed that very little business was transacted under either of them. It is also probable that any equity that was administered at this time was not the technical and scientific equity of lawyers, but a sort of natural equity, consisting largely of the amendment of judgments at law which were considered too harsh. The judges had great discretionary powers, and were usually laymen. In fact there were very few trained lawyers in the Colony. . . .

[I]n 1720, at the suggestion of Governor Keith, a separate Court of Equity was provided. It lasted sixteen years, and was not interfered with by the home government. It is to be observed that the other attempts were all law courts with an equity side. But this court, founded in 1720, was the first and only separate Court of Equity Pennsylvania has ever had. Considerable business was transacted by it. But unfortunately for the court's existence the Governor was its Chancellor, and the colonists were so jealous of any power exercised by the King of England, or his representative the Governor, that in 1736 they brought to an end the only real Court of Chancery they ever possessed.

For the next hundred years—that is to say, until the final grant of equity powers in 1836—the lovers of Chancery met with even less success. By the Constitution of 1776 they got for the law courts the powers of equity so far as related to perpetuation of testimony, obtaining evidence outside of the State, and the care of the persons and estates of the insane. The Legislature was at the same time allowed to grant such other Chancery powers as might be found necessary. But no other powers were granted, except a method of supplying lost deeds and writings, and a proceeding in the nature of a bill of discovery against garnishees in foreign attachment. The Constitution of 1790 mended matters by giving somewhat larger discretionary powers to the Legislature. But that conservative assembly exercised them only to the extent of letting the courts appoint and dismiss trustees, compel them to account, compel answers on oath in certain cases of execution, and when the vendor of lands had died, complete the contract of sale. The inconvenience of this meager grant was a little alleviated by the Legislature's appointing a "Committee of Grievances," which in cases of great hardship gave liberal relief.

Throughout the whole early history of Pennsylvania it appears that there was always a party which wanted Courts of Chancery, and sometimes succeeded in getting them. . . . Before and immediately after the Revolution the same party was thwarted by the jealousy which the people felt for any exercise of unusual power. And in later years they were opposed in the Legislature and throughout the State by another party. This new party took the ground that Chancery courts were contrivances of the Devil to defeat justice, and that Pennsylvania had a system of equity of her own, which was complete in itself, and would in time reform the world.

So, with the exception of the sixteen years from 1720 to 1736, the Courts of Pennsylvania were, for over a hundred and fifty years, left in this predicament—that, in an enlightened community whose trade and commerce were growing every day, they were obliged to administer justice without the aid of a Court of Equity. It is not surprising that they struck out into a new path and did something unheard of in the annals of Anglo-Saxon jurisprudence. If their action was a piece of judicial audacity, it was authorized and justified by the circumstances.

The precise time at which the courts began to administer equity through common law forms is not known. Some say it was done from the beginning. The first reported case on the subject [*Swift* v. *Hawkins*] was decided in 1768. It was an action of debt on a bond, and the defendant offered to prove failure of consideration. The court admitted the evidence, saying, "there being no Court of Chancery in this province, there is a necessity, in order to prevent a failure of justice, to let the defendants in, under the plea of payment, to prove mistake, &c." The Chief Justice added, that he had known this as the constant practice of the province for thirty-nine years. In 1783 the case of *Kennedy* v. *Fury* decided that a cestui qui trust of land could bring ejectment in his own name, the court observing that otherwise "he would be without remedy against an obstinate trustee." These decisions show very clearly how in certain plain cases, and to prevent intolerable hardship, the courts deliberately usurped the necessary powers. . . .

The next characteristic to be observed in the Pennsylvania system, is the rule which allows the defendant, in an action-at-law, to plead an equitable defence. This he may do by offering it in evidence (with notice) under the pleas of payment, non-assumpsit, or performance, which have become equitable pleas in Pennsylvania. If his defence does not properly come under one of these pleas he can set it up specially. This method of working equity through common law forms was probably adopted at a very early date. The case of *Swift* v. *Hawkins* cited above, and decided in 1768, is an instance of an equitable defence admitted under the plea of payment. The court speaks of the custom as one of long existence. It is probable that this method and that of charging the equity to the jury, were the first contrivances for obviating the lack of Chancery powers. Allowing the defendant to set up an equitable defence was soon extended by allowing the plaintiff to rebut it. By such means many opportunities were given in actions-at-law for the consideration of the principles of equity.

The next advance was to allow the plaintiff to begin proceedings by setting out in his declaration a purely equitable right, making the declaration somewhat resemble a bill in equity. This practice was apparently not introduced until a rather late period, when the advancing civilization of the State had made the position of plaintiffs unbearable; for they could make no use of an equity except to rebut one used by the defendant. The first case [*Commonwealth* v. *Coates*] was in 1791. The plaintiff sued in debt on a bond, but at the trial was unable to make *profert* because the bond had been lost. A juror was withdrawn by consent and the case went over. The plaintiff then took a rule on the defendant to show cause why the declaration should not be amended by striking out the *profert* and averring the loss of the instrument. The rule was made absolute, and the plaintiff allowed to amend. The court gave the old reason, that there was no Chancery, and there would be a failure of justice unless some such arrangement were made. This decision was followed by similar ones, until it became a settled rule, that when the common law forms were inadequate, a declaration might be framed setting out the equity of the plaintiff and suited to the circumstances of the case. It is very curious that, in 1789, only two years before this Pennsylvania case, Lord Kenyon made the same decision in England. It was the case of *Read* v. *Brookman*. Austin cites it as a rare instance of liberal-mindedness in a common-law judge, and also as showing the absurdity of the distinction between law and equity. Unlike the Pennsylvania case it remained solitary and did not become one of the starting points of a new system. So far as appears by the report the English case was not cited in the argument of *Commonwealth* v. *Coates*.

The equitable rights of the plaintiff received a further extension by the turning of certain well-known common law actions into equitable ones. Thus ejectment became an equitable action, and the plaintiff without a special declaration could recover on a purely equitable title. The exact date of this innovation is unknown; but in the first reported case (1811) it is spoken of as an old custom. The action of replevin was changed in the same way, and made to apply to every case of disputed title to goods. The writ of *estrepment* with the aid of a little tinkering supplied the place of an injunction to restrain waste on land. The foreclosing of mortgages was provided for by statute. When a judgment-at-law was obtained unfairly, instead of resorting to a bill in equity, a rule was taken to show cause why the judgment should not be opened and the party complaining let into a defence on the merits. The assignee of a right of action was always treated as the real plaintiff. To complete the system, equitable rights in land were made subject to the lien of a judgment. And finally, the Orphans Court, which may be described in a general way as a court having control of everything relating to decedents' estates, has always been, so far as its jurisdiction extends, a court with full equity powers.

Such are the methods by which the Courts of Pennsylvania tried to solve the problem that was forced upon them. They dug channels in the barriers of the common law, and through them they attempted to make the waters of equity flow. They succeeded to this extent, that in most law trials, equitable doctrines applicable to the case could be considered. But when it came to remedies, and the practical execution of the doctrines so considered, they signally failed. It is easy enough for a law court to say that it will hear equitable arguments and frame its judgments accordingly. But for carrying out those judgments, the common law method of execution offers no adequate substitute for the equitable proceedings of injunction, specific performance, *quia timet,* and discovery. It is in methods of administration that equity excels the common law, as much as, if not more than, in doctrine. The Pennsylvania law courts were daring enough to usurp the doctrine, but all their ingenuity could not obtain for them the practical remedies. Of course, in many cases where equitable principles were applied, the common law method of damages and execution was enough; and if the defendant set up an equity which defeated the plaintiff, that ended the matter. But whenever specific performance was necessary, the only way of enforcing the equity (except in the cases of ejectment and replevin already mentioned) was by conditional damages. Thus in *Clyde* v. *Clyde* (1791), the Plaintiff's right to a watercourse was disturbed by the defendant. The judge charged the jury to award large damages, and the plaintiff's attorney agreed to release them when the defendant should give a secure grant of the watercourse.

The sum of the whole matter is, that the courts contrived, by special declarations, pleas, etc., to bring up for consideration in law trials, the doctrines of equity; and they succeeded in partly administering those doctrines, in some cases by the ordinary common law methods, in others by conditional damages, and in others by such actions as ejectment, replevin, *estrepment,* rule to open judgment, etc., which they themselves invented or the Legislature invented for them. Here they stopped. They squeezed equity part way into the common law; but it would not go all the way. The whole subject of preventive justice was left outside. They never found a common law substitute for injunctions, bills *quia timet,* or discovery. Without these the administration of justice would in modern times be at a standstill. . . .

Writers on jurisprudence tell us that our distinction between law and equity is illogical and unnecessary; judged by scientific principles it should not exist; that wherever equity appears, whether in Rome or in England, it is merely an historical accident; it is unknown in France, and would be unknown to us, if it were not for certain peculiar circumstances attending the infancy of our system. But on the other hand, it must be admitted that law, though in part composed of logical reasoning, is also a thing of growth, influenced by custom and individual opinions. If it has taken for itself a certain method of formation, it is in vain that you ignore or try to eradicate that method. The experience of Pennsylvania is a proof that equity, though unscientific, is in our law necessary and vital. It may make an unreasonable distinction; but still it is a form which the law has assumed, and to try to cut it out or join it to something else, is very much like attempting similar improvements on the human body. The modern codes, which turn all forms of action into one, have not been able to abolish the distinction. No code has ever enacted an abridgment of equity's principles; but, on the contrary, they are always adopted entire. It baffled the astuteness of the Pennsylvania judges to find a substitute for the preventive remedies of equity. The codes have met with no better success, and have taken injunctions, *quia timet* and the rest, with changed names perhaps, but without diminishing or adding aught in substance. The great Mansfield thought he could amalgamate law and equity; and men not so great as he have had the same dream. But they are all alike in failure. Pennsylvania's attempt shows how far the distinction is meaningless and how far it is to be respected. The doctrines can be combined with legal forms, but not the remedies.

In 1830 the Legislature appointed a commission of three to revise the whole civil law of the State. These three men deserved well of the Commonwealth, and the eight reports they submitted to the Legislature remain as an everlasting monument to their skill. In no respect did they show themselves to better advantage than when they came to the vexed question of courts of equity. They were able lawyers and knew exactly what the Pennsylvania system was worth; and they had made up their minds that it was not equal to supplying the wants of the people. But being wise in their generation, they were careful to heap on it lavish praises, to call it a combination of all that was good; at the same time they thoroughly analyzed it, and quietly suggested that full Chancery powers be given the law courts in the following cases:

(1) trustees, (2) trusts, (3) control of private corporations, unincorporated societies and partnerships, (4) discovery of facts material to any case, (5) interpleader, (6) injunction, (7) specific performance.

This included nearly the whole jurisdiction of Chancery, and was a severe commentary on the Pennsylvania system. The Legislature could swallow only part of it. In 1836 they gave to the Courts of Philadelphia alone all the equity jurisdiction suggested by the commissioners. To the rest of the State they gave jurisdiction only in the first three cases above mentioned.

But the ice was broken. In 1840 Philadelphia got Chancery power in cases of fraud, accident, mistake and account; and the rest of the State in cases of account. In 1844 Allegheny county got the same jurisdiction as Philadelphia. In 1845 Philadelphia was given equity power in dower and partition. And so it went on from one point to another until in 1857 the equity jurisdiction was made the same throughout the State. Since then and up to the present time there have been other, but less important, grants. . . .

This legislative grant does not interfere with the administration of equity through common law forms. That system continues to exist, and is used whenever the occasion requires it. It has served and still serves a useful purpose. It was the result of hard necessity, and under the circumstances that attended the early days of the State no better arrangement could have been made. If it has failed of complete success it is a failure in attempting great things.

---

COMMENTS. *The Common Morality of Law and Equity.* The interplay between law and equity in responding to ethical and moral considerations has been a continuing problem. In Chapter 1, pages 37–43, we saw how Blackstone responded to and recorded Mansfield's attempts to enforce "equity" into the common law.

Professor Chafee opened a series of lectures as follows: "The most amusing maxim of equity is 'He who comes into Equity must come with clean hands.' It has given rise to many interesting cases and poor jokes." Chafee, *Some Problems of Equity* (1950).

In the course of these delightful lectures, Professor Chafee examined the results of numerous cases to determine whether equity decisions reflect a point of view which is different from that at law. He found, in general, that the outlook which in equity is expressed by the "clean hands" maxim has parallels in rules of law, such as failure of consideration and illegality. He concludes as follows:

> What has really happened is that equity is still ethical, though not in the oversensitive fashion of some cases, and law has also become ethical. In almost all out states the same judges may sit one day in a damage suit and another day in an injunction suit. It is impossible to believe that they can put on and take off morality at will as if it were a hat. Cardozo's decisions in damage cases are filled with ethical attitudes. I do not mean to say that law and equity are absorbing all the principles of morals. Litigation is too rough an instrument to handle all the delicate questions of conscience which arise in life. But the factors whch divide judicial action from moral judgments seem to me the same whether the particular suit resembles what used to go on in chancery or what used to go on in the courts of common law. If injunctions and specific performance ought sometimes to be refused in situations where damages are granted, this distinction is due to the nature of these specific remedies and not to the existence of different levels of morality inside the judicial system.

*Further References.* The nature of law in equity is well worth further examination. The best combination of enlightenment and delight will be found in the full text of the Chafee lectures which were cited above. The "clean hands" lectures also appear in *Michigan Law Review*, vol. 47, 1949, pp. 877–906, 1065–1096. See also Walsh, "The Growing Function of Equity in the Development of the Law," *Law: A Century of Progress*, vol. 3, 1937, pp. 139 *et seq.*; Rundell, "The Chancellor's Foot: The Nature of Equity," *University of Kansas City Law Review*, 1958, pp. 71 *et seq.* (primarily history).

A thoughtful comparison of "equity," as general principle of justice, with the rules of equity made by the Chancery court will be found in Allen, *Law in the Making*, 5th ed., chap. 5. (Oxford, Clarendon, 1958).

# LAW AND SOCIAL CHANGE
# IN THE UNITED STATES  By Carl A. Auerbach

## Law and Change in the Nineteenth Century

*Political-Constitutional Framework.* It has become more or less fashionable of late to explain the bleak prospect for democracy in underdeveloped countries on the ground that these countries, though underdeveloped, are striving to become modern and industrialized as quickly as possible—an aspiration which only some form of totalitarian government can realize. Yet it is a fact that the American democracy became firmly rooted while the United States was still an underdeveloped nation. In 1789, the United States had a population of only four million people living mostly on farms. Poverty was pretty much their lot. At this time, if I may quote Stuart Chase: "Industry was in the handicraft stage of little mills on streams, little ironmasters, little shipbuilders; and George Washington's false teeth were made of wood." Yet the leaders of this small, premodern, underdeveloped society espoused a vigorous liberalism, resorted to violent revolution to win political independence and laid the foundation of a democratic republic. I think it would be equally true to say that political democracy became rooted in Great Britain before the advent of the industrial revolution. When Karl Polanyi, in his book entitled *The Great Transformation,* tried to make us appreciate the depth of the social changes wrought by the industrial revolution in England, he asked us to think of its impact upon underdeveloped countries today.

Just as political democracy may precede industrialization, so there is no guarantee that it must follow industrialization, as the history of modern Germany woefully attests. One is tempted, therefore, to ascribe primacy to political factors in accounting for the rise of political democracy in the United States and Great Britain, as well as for the rise of totalitarianism in the Soviet Union and China.

The political fact, for example, that our federal union was based upon the Constitution of 1789 had profound consequences for the course of social change in the United States. The Constitution founded a democracy. By the middle of the nineteenth century, white manhood suffrage

---

Reprinted from *University of California L.A. Law Review,* vol. 6, 1958–59, pp. 520–532, with the permission of the author and the publisher. Carl A. Auerbach, Professor of Law, University of Minnesota, is coeditor of *The Federal Regulation of Transportation* and of *The Legal Process.* He was also a Fellow, Center for Advanced Study in the Behaviorial Sciences, 1958–59.

prevailed generally in the United States and no property qualifications for holding office were imposed. The Constitution gave the federal government ample power to deal with the exigencies of the future, yet prevented the centralization of over-all political power in the hands of the national government and of the federal government's power in the hands of any single branch within it. The Constitution created an independent judiciary to solve disputes within the federal structure peacefully and to enforce the constitutional guarantees of freedom of speech and association and against arbitrary action by the federal government. The Civil War Amendments extended these guarantees to the individual in his relations with the states.

A form of government was thus established which made peaceful change possible, yet which imposed limits upon the temporary majority's treatment of the temporary minority. It therefore gave all groups in our society a greater stake in the rules by which peaceful change was to be effected than in the particular decisions reached by the lawmaking institutions at any particular time, no matter how adverse these decisions may have been to particular group interests. Having stated this generalization, I should hasten to point to the one great exception—the Civil War.

The very establishment of the federal union had more direct economic consequences also. With the constitutional provision for the admission of new states on a basis of equality with the old, it afforded the opportunity for the creation of an internal market of sufficient size for large-scale industrial growth—the importance of which has most recently been attested to by the European common market arrangements.

*Influence of Law and Industrialization.* It is true that the advent of industrialization did not have the traumatic effect upon social and community organization in the United States which Professor Polanyi explains it had in Great Britain. English village life, ruled and protected by a hereditary landed gentry and an established clergy, and innately antagonistic to the march of industrialization, did not exist to be destroyed in the nineteenth-century United States. The abundance of land in the United States led to the early abolition of primogeniture and feudal tenures and to the enactment of a policy favoring the free alienability of land. Farming was thus commercialized before industrialization came. The Constitution, of course, prohibited the federal government from establishing any church. And by 1833, no state in the Union had an established church. The drive to use the self-regulating market as the central mechanism for improving the material conditions of life in the United States thus never came into conflict with a system of strongly held, opposing values.

*Decision-Making.* The American environment, as early as our colonial period, tended to encourage self-reliance and generate individual expectations of material improvement. Satisfaction of these expectations required the restriction of governmental power in certain areas of social life and its exercise in others.

To release the productive energies of the individual, it was necessary, first, to sweep away the reflections in law of the colonial policy of Great Britain which severely restricted the scope of private economic decision-making. Colonial laws interfering with the free alienation of land, limiting wages, regulating prices and marketing practices and fixing standards of quality and measure were repealed.

Then, to foster a self-regulating market economy, contract and criminal law doctrines were developed which safeguarded the claims to freedom of contract and the security of transactions and to private property and the security of acquisitions. The business corporation, probably the most significant legal invention of the century, enabled entrepreneurs to gather large aggregates of private capital for economic development. The accumulation of capital was further facilitated by the absence of any general federal or state income, gift, or inheritance taxes throughout the nineteenth century. The federal income tax of 1894 was declared unconstitutional by the Supreme Court.

Government also intervened during the nineteenth century in order to promote economic development. The federal government subsidized agriculture by selling the vast lands which it owned in small lots at low prices.

Government on all levels subsidized the construction of turnpikes, canals, railroads and river and harbor improvements.

Government aided the private credit facilities by delegating to them the power to issue banknotes.

Industry was sought to be aided by the protective tariff and, in many localities, by direct subsidies.

Through its policies with respect to banks, interest rates and the currency, the federal government sought indirectly to influence the allocation of scarce capital. The fact that capital was so scarce throughout the nineteenth century may explain why these policies provoked so much legal and political conflict.

To stimulate the import of capital, the Constitution embodied a number of provisions designed to protect foreign creditors. During the nineteenth century, too, the United States promoted immigration. And the states and municipalities pledged their tax revenues to back internal improvements for which it was sought to attract foreign capital.

*Social costs.* The achievements of the nineteenth-century American capitalism were great. But its social costs were very high. The law did little to curb the extravagant exploitation of our natural resources. Forests were despoiled. Soil was permitted to erode. Game was exterminated. Air and water supplies were polluted and fish life destroyed. Natural gas was burned to get oil, which was squandered. Unplanned railroad development left a heritage of problems with which we are still struggling today.

Human resources were also cruelly used. The public health was nobody's concern. The workday and workweek were very long and earnings very low, though conditions of the American worker in the nineteenth century were probably better than the conditions of the worker anywhere else. Workers and their families bore the staggering costs of industrial accidents. The business cycle, which recurred throughout the nineteenth century, victimized farmers and workers.

As the pace of industrialization increased after 1870, the competitive process, central to the concept of the self-regulating market, began to destroy the basis of the competitive order by giving rise to big business and big finance.

Social unrest grew and found expression in the protest movements of the farmers; the railroad strikes of 1877 and 1894; the Haymarket bomb throwing in 1886; the Homestead strike riot of 1892 and Coxey's army of the unemployed in 1894. This unrest found political expression in the bitter Presidential campaigns of the 1890s.

Before the close of the nineteenth century, the law began to do something about these unintended consequences of rapid industrialization based upon private economic decision-making in order to allocate, in a more just and humane fashion, the material and human costs which did not show up in the accounts of any private firm.

Ironically, the ideology of individualism and laissez-faire reached its ascendancy in the United States only late in the nineteenth century when the developing economy became incompatible with the kind of society men like William Graham Sumner were extolling. Change always seems to outrun man's contemporaneous capacity to grasp its significance.

To curb the exercise of private economic power, Congress passed the Interstate Commerce Act in 1887 and the Sherman Antitrust Law in 1890. The Sherman Act was designed to safeguard the competitive order; the 1887 Act, to regulate the exercise of monopoly power in an industry in which it was thought not possible or not desirable to attempt to restore competition. To this day, both laws continue to provoke controversies which highlight the difficulty of weighing the effect of legal factors in the process of socioeconomic development. And these controversies are carried on by economists who, of all social scientists, have been most successful in quantifying their analyses and their findings.

## Law and Social Change in 20th Century United States

*Legal Intervention.* Great effort, for example, has been expended to show that the degree of concentration of industry has not increased since 1890. But the same degree of concentration may have greater significance, from the point of view of power in society, as the scale of industry grows larger, which, of course, has happened since 1890. And even the constancy of the relative degree of concentration may be due, as Professor Galbraith has pointed out, to the appearance of new industries since 1890. It remains true that American industry is typified by a few large corporations and a fringe of small ones and that a small number of large corporations account for a very substantial proportion of industrial activity. Certainly, the antitrust laws have not restored the kind of competitive order which Justice Brandeis desired and thought it was the aim of these laws to restore.

But would there not have been greater concentration if the Sherman Act had not been enacted? It is difficult to know how one should go about trying to answer such a question. We might adopt a comparative approach and find that in countries, like England and Germany, which up to recently had no anti-trust laws and tolerated cartels, single giant corporations or combinations came to dominate whole industries. It seems generally agreed that our situation of oligopoly is preferable, because it is more conducive than monopoly to technical progress and the development of countervailing power, to cite Professor Galbraith again. And it seems plausible to say that the anti-trust laws were responsible for the development of oligopoly, rather than monopoly, in the United States.

It has also been argued that so long as the anti-trust laws do not facilitate concentration, they should be retained because they profess the ideal of a competitive order to which our people are still attached. But are they? My old boss, Leon Henderson, used to say that most businessmen clamor for competition in the things they buy but detest it when it comes to the things they themselves sell. But, more seriously, our economic strength, technical progress, our standard of living, our defense capabilities all depend upon the successful functioning of the large-scale organization of business and labor. Would our people countenance its disruption? And is it desirable to cling to a myth which hides current reality?

The Interstate Commerce Act raises similarly perplexing problems. It initiated the policy of subjecting the traditional "public utility" industries —those furnishing light, heat, power, water, transportation and communications—to legal control of the prices they charge and the quality and quantity of the services they render. The Act originally dealt with railroads, but now also covers road and water transport. Air transport and ocean shipping are subject to regulation under separate laws, as are the power, radio and television and telegraph and telephone industries. At first, regulation was justified on the ground that the industries subjected to it were monopolistic. Since the Great Depression of the 1930s, however, regulation has also been used to prevent too much or "cutthroat" competition from producing socially undesirable results. This, for example, explains the regulation not only of trucking but also of agricultural production, marketing and prices. American agriculture, in short, has become a "public utility."

How shall we assess the effects of this system of regulation? Some think it combines the worst features of both capitalism and socialism— that by divorcing authority from responsibility, it unites capitalism's lack of planning with socialism's bureaucratic rigidity. Of late—as the Goldfine-Adams case revealed—it has raised very serious problems of how to regulate the regulators.

Would we be better off without such regulation? Should we leave these industries in unregulated private hands? Or socialize them? How do we go about evaluating these alternatives? Could Congress and the states be persuaded to experiment—to try out the different alternatives in limited areas?

In any event, neither the anti-trust law nor public-utility-type regulation curbs the exercise of private economic power in many vital areas of the American economy. Should we be concerned about this fact? Whether or not our twentieth century society can be justifiably described as affluent, no one disputes the fact that the material conditions of life of our people have been greatly improved. We have also achieved a tolerable measure of social justice, distributing income about as equitably as do Great Britain and the Scandinavian countries. But the creditable performance of American capitalism in recent years cannot be attributed to the exercise of unchecked private economic power. I would agree with Galbraith that it is due, in large measure, to the development of centers of countervailing power, a process in which the law has played a most significant part.

*Private Countervailing Power.* Thus, the farmers have organized buying and selling cooperatives to enable them to attain a more equal bargaining position vis-à-vis the oligopolies from which they buy and to which they sell. But only the buying cooperatives have succeeded.

Farmers as sellers remained in a weak position until the New Deal support price programs were launched.

Independent food stores and department stores have organized cooperative buying organizations for similar reasons. The large chain retailers, which stand to gain by a policy of low prices and high sales volume, have attained sufficient power, by virtue of their size, to force large manufacturers to share the fruits of their economic power—to the consumer's ultimate benefit. Galbraith suggests that this may be the reason why consumer cooperatives have not prospered in the United States.

Twentieth-century law has encouraged the organization of farmers' cooperatives. But it has shown hostility to the large chain retailers. Efforts have been made to cripple chains by taxation. And the A&P was prosecuted for violation of the anti-trust laws. If we accept Galbraith's analysis, a change in legal policy would be called for. But the law sees the chain not only as a center of power which countervails that of the oligopolist manufacturer, but also as a center of power which can overwhelm smaller retail competitors, as well as smaller manufacturers. How to deal with institutions which countervail the power of other institutions in our society yet, at the same time, also exercise overbearing power in other areas, has become a puzzling problem in our contemporary law.

The trade union is another vital center of countervailing power. It became such only after long and arduous struggle and the history of this struggle reveals the important role political and legal factors played in overcoming powerful business resistance to unionization. But again, it is difficult to weigh the purely legal factors. The voluntary association enables large numbers of people in a democracy to combine to exert political pressure in a legal fashion. The product of its efforts may be legislation which, in turn, enhances the power of the voluntary association itself. Difficult as it is to assess the influence of legislation under these circumstances, it seems to be agreed that the NRA and the Wagner Act (and the Clayton Act of 1914 before it) and the labor legislation and administration of World Wars I and II stimulated the growth of trade unions by recognizing them as essential institutions in a democracy.

The trade unions have forced the giants of American industry to share the fruits of their economic power with their workers. Equally important, the trade union has been responsible for the evolution of a rule of law in industry which has secured the individual worker's claim to the job and thereby given him a sense of status and community and independence.

*Legal Intervention and Public-Decision-Making.* The exercise of private countervailing power does not, of course, displace private economic decision-making. It merely enlarges the number of private individuals and groups participating in such decision-making. However, twentieth-century law has also greatly enlarged the scope of public decision-making in order to protect those who are not able to take care of themselves. In these cases, the law may be said to embody countervailing power. In order to achieve its ends, this body of legislation had to limit claims regarding the use and disposition of private property and the freedom of contract.

*Minimum living standards.* So government has stepped in to assure, by law, that every individual should enjoy the material conditions necessary for a minimum decent life. Significant steps toward this goal were taken during the nineteenth century. A public school system was created by law. Factory safety legislation was passed. Conditions of labor for women and children were regulated, as were methods of wage payment generally. Laws for the relief of debtors were passed. Public care was provided for dependent and neglected children, old people and the insane and tax exemptions were granted private institutions undertaking these responsibilities.

Twentieth-century legislation took additional giant steps. Minimum wages and maximum hours were fixed. Child labor was abolished. A social security system was elaborated which now includes workmen's compensation and disability insurance, unemployment insurance, old age and survivors' insurance and programs of assistance to the old, dependent children and the needy. The losses suffered by the ordinary family as a result of illness (or accident not connected with the job) remain the major ones not covered by a universal system of insurance.

The legal institution of insurance makes it practical to spread losses incurred by individuals in the natural course of their lives over the community as a whole and, therefore, to reject the individualistic notion that these losses should be borne by the persons upon whom they happened to fall or by those who were legally at fault in causing them.

Our farm programs—price supports, federal crop insurance and rural electrification—are also part of the attempt to assure every individual a minimum decent life, as are the many state and federal laws designed to stimulate public and private housing.

I do not wish to imply that the protection of the law is so pervasive that it covers every individual in the United States whose interests are not furthered by a group having sufficient power to do so effectively. There are still more than two million hired farm workers who earn very low wages and have no strong unions to fight for them. In practically all states, these workers do not enjoy the benefits of workmen's compensation. And only in 1955 was a beginning made to bring them into the unemployment insurance system. The lot of the migratory farm worker, is of course, particularly bad. Because they are migratory, the American citizens among them cannot exert the pressure which usually accompanies the vote in a democracy. Clerks in retail and service establishments, government employees and even teachers could also use strong organization to protect their interests. In all, about 25 per cent of our families—more than 10 million families in all—had incomes in 1957 of less than $3,000 a year. There is much unfinished business to take care of here.

*Rights of Citizenship.* Legal intervention to protect the political and civil rights of women and of the Negro citizen reflects this same concern for the individual life. The wife became the equal of her husband when the law recognized her claim to hold property, enter into contracts and institute lawsuits and then liberalized the grounds for divorce. (The individuality of the child, too, has been recognized by laws requiring vaccination and compulsory school attendance and making it possible to divorce a child from parents which mistreat it.)

In the case of the Negro citizen, we are witnessing an unprecedented legal effort to change the traditional behavior patterns of whole communities spread over large areas. Most serious questions have thereby been raised about the effective limits of law as an agency of this change.

*The Individual as Consumer.* Law has also intervened to protect the individual as a consumer, in which capacity he seems unable to organize to protect the interests which tend to be ignored in our producer-minded economy. This intervention also began in the nineteenth century, with the enactment of public health legislation. It has been extended during the twentieth century to include general pure food, drug and cosmetic laws; laws prohibiting false labeling and false advertising; and laws regulating the issuance of securities and the operation of the commodity and stock exchanges and insuring bank deposits.

Nineteenth century laws required fire and life insurance policies, mortgages and contracts for transportation to contain certain standard provisions to protect the contracting natural person. These laws exemplify the swing from contract to a kind of status which Dean Pound has called "The New Feudal System." It is "new" because the relationship is entered into by contract but the law attached certain rights and obligations to it, no matter what the parties to the relationship may have agreed upon —usually in order to protect the weaker party. Legal rights and obligations now surround the relationship between insurer and insured, mortgagor and mortgagee, common carrier and ticket holder, employer and employee, wife and husband, parent and child and even automobile manufacturer and dealer.

*Natural resources.* Finally, legislation has also been enacted to conserve and develop our natural resources. To this end, we have not hesitated to resort to public ownership, as in the case of TVA and the Bonneville Power Administration.

*Employment.* I am aware that the control and offsetting of private economic power and the assurance of a minimum decent life for every individual contribute to, but do not guarantee, the maintenance of full employment and that the improvements in the general standard of life and the more equitable distribution of income to which I have alluded could not have taken place without full employment. But our government is now committed by law, the Employment Act of 1946, to maintain full employment and it seems fairly clear that neither political party will have much success unless it uses the governmental powers to tax and to spend and to regulate the banking, credit and currency system, so as to accomplish this objective.

## Some Problems Awaiting Legal Solution

... In conclusion, I should like to outline some of the major problems that still await legal solution and which I have not previously mentioned.

Since the advent of the Industrial Revolution we have been struggling, it seems to me, with the problem of determining what combination of public and private ordering of human activities is necessary to safeguard and enlarge individual freedoms and at the same time enable individuals to enjoy the potential benefits of modern science and technology. For classical liberalism, centralized political power was the principal danger to individual freedoms. So it insisted that the exercise of political power be limited by excluding economic decision-making from its scope. Classical liberalism failed to foresee that private economic power, when not checked either by private countervailing power or by political power, would itself come to endanger the freedoms of those subject to its exercise. Classical liberalism also underestimated the extent to which a modern, complex economy would require planning and coordination of private and public actions in order to make it an instrument of the general welfare. Socialism anticipated this need and because it regarded the exercise of private economic power as the principal danger to individual freedoms, it insisted upon the complete subordination of economic to political power. Thereby socialism failed to appreciate that the concentration of economic and political power in the same hands could endanger essential individual freedoms.

I do not propose, now, to enter into the controversy whether the public ownership of all the means of production and distribution will always result in tyranny, no matter how dedicated the people and its leadership may be to the maintenance of political democracy. It will suffice for present purposes to point out that our democracy has subjected, but not completely subordinated, private economic power to political power in a way Marxists did not believe to be possible. Markets—the arenas of private economic decision-making—continue to play a crucial role in reflecting consumer wants, in distributing the national income, in determining the rate of economic growth and in making possible the development of private, countervailing power. But these markets are no longer self-regulating; they are regulated by law to satisfy the claims and achieve the ends I have tried to describe.

A tolerable measure of social justice and individual freedom has thereby been achieved in our society as a result not of the pursuit of a vision of an ideal economic system but of the political struggle which individuals and groups have waged, according to the rules of democracy, to satisfy their claims.

Yet though we now have welfare corporations, (big business), welfare trade unions (big labor) and a welfare state (big government), we cannot say that we have succeeded in controlling the power through the exercise of which alone welfare can be promoted. This task, in fact, becomes more difficult as the complexity and technicality of the problems requiring legal solution tax the understanding of our people and big business, big labor and big government acquire effective means to manipulate the individual. The possibility of fuller individual participation in arriving at the decisions which affect the individual life appears to be getting remote. We seem, as a result, to be advancing from the idea of laissez-faire the individual to that of laissez-faire the group.

It is true that a minimum notion of justice requires that all claims made by individuals and groups should at least be heard and considered by the lawmaking authorities. This is why the freedom to speak and to associate with others in pursuit of common interests is so vital in a democracy dedicated to the achievement of justice. Furthermore, a larger measure of justice will be achieved if the law, as it has done, helps to assure that no single group becomes so powerful as to submerge the claims of all other groups in society, even if the law is then willing to accept the decisions reached as a result of private group conflict and adjustment.

But is this all justice should mean? Will the outcome of the struggle of groups roughly equal in power secure the interests of outsiders? Do groups always reflect the claims made by their individual members?

As we saw, we have used law directly to satisfy certain individual and social claims which could not be satisfied in any other way. So, for example, it seems generally agreed in western, democratic societies that law should intervene to make certain that every individual enjoys the material conditions necessary for a minimum decent life and to lessen the degree of inequality in the opportunities open to different individuals. Is this as far as law should go?

Thus, for example, the question may be raised as to why the corporate manager is the legitimate arbiter of the competing claims of stockholders, workers, consumers, the managers themselves and generations as yet unborn. A number of answers have been offered. Adolph Berle of late is optimistic that we can rely on the growing social conscience of the industrial manager to perform this function equitably. A more acceptable answer may be that the divorce of ownership from management of large corporate enterprise has had the consequence of divorcing the inheritance of wealth from the inheritance of economic power. So long, therefore, as there is little prospect that a hereditary managerial elite will develop and the paths to managerial position remain reasonably open, the exercise of managerial power is tolerable.

Galbraith, of course, thinks the existing situation is tolerable only because the decisions of the corporate manager are checked by the countervailing power exerted by those with whom he deals and by government. But this answer only shifts the question of legitimacy to that of the proper scope of government intervention. Why, it may be asked, should corporate management and organized labor be permitted to enter into collective agreements which have even greater impact upon the public at large than do taxes imposed by governmental power? Is greater legal intervention, via direct wage and price controls, necessary to protect the public? Is it particularly required if we are to achieve the rate of economic growth needed to meet the exigencies of the Cold War without ruinous inflation?

It also may be said in answer to the question of legitimacy that the present system of decision-making reasonably satisfies the wants of our people. But Galbraith makes the fundamental objection that consumer wants are largely created by modern advertising and do not reflect the most urgent needs of our society and that our economic system is not, in fact, satisfying urgent needs. Though he calls our society affluent, Galbraith makes us acutely aware that we are poverty-stricken when it comes to the essential services which only government can provide.

The most persuasive answer to the question of legitimacy raised may be that no alternative decision-making process has been proposed which would not create even greater difficulties for a democratic society. But the imagination of the social scientist has not exhausted all the possible alternatives which might yet prove to be acceptable.

The problem remains, too, of preventing individuals or groups within each power-wielding association—corporation or trade union—from acquiring such a preponderance of power internally that they can ignore the wishes of the individuals who make up the association and block their full participation in the life of the association. This is the problem with which the Fund For The Republic is now wrestling. As a minimum, legal intervention may be necessary to safeguard the individual claim to membership and participation in the association. Twentieth-century law already tends in this direction.

So far as the government bureaucracy is concerned, we seem more disturbed by its apparent ineffectualness than its potential power. We have not succeeded in developing a civil service of the calibre which the armed forces are creating. Apparently, the antibureaucratic bias, ever-present on the American scene, is expressed most strongly in popular attitudes toward the civil government bureaucracy (with the "labor bosses" a close second) rather than toward the business or the military bureaucracy. The difficulties which have recently afflicted our administrative agencies can be traced to these attitudes, as well as to the refusal of those regulated to accept the legitimacy of regulation.

Possibly, changes already under way, which we have not full grasped, will help to solve our difficulties. Automation and low-cost power may enable us to enjoy a still higher standard of living with an even shorter work week. This could lessen the tensions that now surround the adjustment of economic claims and make possible more humane conditions of work and the use of leisure for the fuller development of the individual personality.

Even then, all our troubles would not be over. The "paradise of our domestic security," as Reinhold Niebuhr recently said, would still be "suspended in a hell of global insecurity." But the problem of reconciling the human race is not on our agenda this evening.

CHAPTER 3

# The Codification Movement

THE MOST DISTINCTIVE FEATURE OF the common law system is, of course, the fact that its central precepts must be distilled from a mass of court decisions. One trained in a civil law system is astonished and dismayed to learn that there is no authoritative, organized formulation for the ideas which support and control the enforcement of contracts, the redress of torts and the protection of property.

Early in the eighteen-hundreds efforts were made to establish codes in the United States. In 1811 the great English scholar, Jeremy Bentham, wrote to President James Madison volunteering to codify the laws of the United States. With characteristic vigor, Bentham summed up his attack on the case-law system:

## AN OFFER TO CODIFY THE LAW OF THE UNITED STATES *By Jeremy Bentham*

THROUGHOUT THE whole extent of the territory of *the United States* (new-acquired dependencies excepted, in which matters cannot but be still worse,) what is it that, at this moment, forms the basis of the rule of action? What but an ideal and shapeless mass of *merely con-*

---

Reprinted from Bentham, *Codification and Public Instruction* (London: M'Creery, 1817), pp. 30–33. Jeremy Bentham (1748–1832), "the Great Utilitarian," came to fame in England in 1789 with the publication of his *Introduction to the Principles of Morals and Legislation*. The center of a group which included John Stuart Mill and John Austin, Bentham developed the principles of Utilitarianism and advocated numerous measures for law reform. See Morris, *The Great Legal Philosophers* (Philadelphia: U. of Pa. Press, 1959), pp. 261–288.

*jectural* and *essentially uncognoscible* matter?—*matter* without *mind*, *work* without an *author;* occupying, through the oscitancy of the legislature, a place that ought to be filled; and exercising in it the authority that ought to be exercised, by *law?*

<blockquote>
Nullis lex verbis, a nullo, nullibi, nunquam—<br>
Law, in no *words,* by no *man,* never, made:—
</blockquote>

Law which, having had for its *authors,* not the *people* themselves, nor any persons chosen by the people, but the creatures, the ever-removable and completely and perpetually dependent creatures of the *king alone* (till *the revolution* this was completely true, and even since, it has not wanted much of being so,) had, of course, for its main object, not the good of the *people,* but as far as the blindness or patience of the people would permit, the interests—the sinister and confederated interests—of the *creator,* under whose influence, and the *creatures,* by whose hands, it was spun out:—

Law, blundered out by a set of men, who—their course of operation not being at their own command, but at the command of the plaintiffs in the several causes—were all along as completely destitute of the *power* as, under the influence of sinister interest, they could not but be of the *inclination* to operate in pursuit of any clear and enlarged views of utility, public or private, or so much as upon any comprehensive and consistent plan, good or bad, in the delineation of the *rights* they were *confirming* and the *obligations* they were imposing:—and which accordingly never has been, nor, to any purpose good or bad, ever could have been, nor ever can be, the result of *antecedent* reflection, grounded on a *general* view of the nature of each case, of the exigencies belonging to it, or the analogous cases connected with it; nor, in a word, anything better than a shapeless heap of odds and ends, the pattern of which has, in each instance, been necessarily determined by the nature of the demand, put in by the plaintiff, as above:—

Law which, being, in so far as it could be said to be *made,* made at a multitude of successive periods, and for the use and governance of so many different generations of men—men, imbued with notions, habituated to modes of life, differing, more or less widely from each other, as well as from those which have place at present—would, even had it been well adapted to the circumstances and exigencies of the times, in which its parts respectively came into existence, have, to a considerable extent, been thereby rendered, not the *better* adapted, but by so much the *worse* adapted, to the notions and manners *now* prevalent, to the state of things *at present* in existence:—

Law, which, by its essential *form* and character, as above indicated, is, so long as it retains that form, altogether disabled from either giving to itself, or receiving from any other quarter, *improvements* or *correction*, upon a scale of any considerable *extent;* which, even upon the *minutest* scale, cannot give to itself any improvement in the way of *particular utility*, but at the expense of *general certainty:* nor, even at that price, but by a course of successive acts of arbitrary power—acts productive, in the first place, of a correspondent succession of particular *disappointments*, followed, each of them in proportion as it comes to be known, by those more extensively spreading *apprehensions of insecurity*, which are among the inseparable concomitants and consequences of that ever deplorable, howsoever originally necessary and unavoidable, taint of iniquity, inherent in the very essence of *ex post facto* law. . . .

PRESIDENT MADISON POLITELY DEclined the offer. (In the light of the style of Bentham's letter, should Madison have been concerned about the readability of the code which Bentham would have produced?)

The codification idea gained support in other quarters. In 1836 a commission appointed by the Massachusetts Legislature brought in a report favoring the establishment of a code to embrace the bulk of the common law.

# REPORT ON CODIFICATION TO THE HOUSE OF REPRESENTATIVES OF MASSACHUSETTS

THE COMMON law is growing every day still more cumberous, and unwieldy, by the addition of the innumerable decisions of the United States courts, and of the supreme courts of every state in the union. So that unless this work of reform shall soon commence, this world of ever varying contradictory decisions must create a jargon, a confusion more dangerous to the rights of the people, and the cause of justice, than the

---

Reprinted from Massachusetts House of Representatives, Report No. 17 (1836). Joseph Story, a member of this commission, in 1821 had developed the case for a general code in his address, "Progress of Jurisprudence," in *Miscellaneous Writings of Joseph Story*, W. W. Story, ed., (Boston: Little, Brown, 1852), pp. 237–239. See Pound, *Jurisprudence,* Vol. 3 (St. Paul, Minn.: West, 1959), p. 713.

abolition of all law, and leaving the judiciary with the power of deciding upon every case according to their own notions of equity and justice. It is said, that extremes meet, and when the laws become so multiplied, ambiguous, and contradictory, as to be beyond the power of man to understand them, the necessity is imposed upon the judges of deciding according to the best power of their own minds. . . .

It is believed, that if this great law reform can be accomplished, it will be regarded, as the commencement of a new era in the history of our government. A beginning will then be fairly made of a republican kind of jurisprudence, and the people for the first time will have it in their power to boast of living under laws made by themselves through their representatives. . . .

Let the obsolete, unconstitutional, frivolous and iniquitous parts of the common law be abolished, and whatever is good and useful be passed into statute law, and a work will be accomplished, however imperfect it may at first be, which will be remembered for ages. The constitutions and the laws would then form a volume or two, written in concise, chaste, and elegant language, fit to be introduced into our common schools, and constitute the book of reading and study for the highest class. So that while our children shall be acquiring the rudiments of an English education, and learning to read, write and speak their mother tongue, they may at the same time be acquiring a knowledge of our forms of government, constitutions and laws. Liberty and popular government will then be placed on the broad foundation of knowledge and virtue, and the superstructure will be adorned and perfected from age to age, exciting the admiration and imitation of the world. . . .

---

THE MASSACHUSETTS MOVEMENT DIED down, but in New York the cause was carried further by David Dudley Field. Field's Civil Code, although rejected in New York, was adopted in the Dakotas, California, Idaho, and Montana. It is thus a significant part of the law of America, and deserves examination.

In recent years there have been stirrings of further life in the codification movement. The Uniform Commercial Code by 1964 has been adopted in over half of the states. To be sure, the UCC is not a true "code" as we have been using that term: in spite of its breadth it is ancillary to basic, undeclared principles of contracts and torts. But this "code" does frame many rules of contract law for the sale of goods; the existence of statutory rules in this limited area is leading to inquiry as to whether such rules should be made more general.

# THE MOVEMENT LEADING TO CODES
# IN THE WEST  By *Maurice Harrison*

W<small>E</small> SHALL reach within the next few months [1922] the fiftieth anniversary of the adoption of the California Civil Code; and because this enactment was the first attempt on the part of an English-speaking community of considerable size to codify comprehensively the substantive common law, the result of our experience under it should be of interest to us, not merely as practitioners who consult it daily, but also as students of our juristic system. . . .

Usually codification has had for its chief purpose the unification of discordant elements in the law of a particular country; in France, in Napoleonic times, the reconciliation of the Roman law obtaining in the south with the customary law of the north; in the Germany of Frederick II, the assimilation of the customs and laws of the various parts of a greater Prussia; and in our own day, the commercial codes framed by the Commissioners on Uniform Laws have for their object the substitution of uniform rules for the varying laws of the several states. But our code was born of no such impulse. The primary object of its chief author and advocate, David Dudley Field, was to restate in systematic and accessible form the common law as it had been modified to suit American conditions, to settle questions upon which disputes had arisen and to introduce such reforms as might seem necessary to make the legal system harmonious and free from anachronism.

Field began his agitation for the adoption of a Civil Code in the year 1839, when the nineteenth century legislative reform movement was at its height. The New York Revised Statutes which had remodeled the law of real property, were only ten years old. Other American states had followed its example by adopting legislation which abolished common-law rules that were considered to be out of harmony with American conditions. Livingston had recently completed his task of drafting and revising the codes of Louisiana. Meanwhile, in England, the same movement for legislative reform was in full swing, and the agitation of Bentham and his followers was bearing fruit. The English law of property was being transformed by the Wills Act and the Fines and Recoveries Act and similar legislation, and the complacent attitude of Blackstone and Eldon was

---

Reprinted from "The First Half-Century of the California Civil Code," *California Law Review*, vol. 10, 1922, pp. 185–187, with permission of the publisher. Maurice Harrison was a Professor of Law (1910–1919) and Dean (1919–1924) at the Hastings School of Law, University of California.

definitely discredited. The French code had spread over the greater part of Europe and was about to penetrate the new republics of South America. Under such conditions it is not surprising that Field found a receptive attitude towards his suggestion of codification, and was able to secure the insertion in the New York constitution of 1846 of a provision calling for the reduction into a written and systematic code of the whole body of the law of the state.

One result of this constitutional provision was the first New York Code of Civil Procedure, which has been the model for the procedural system which has obtained in most American states since the Civil War period. The credit for this reform is due almost entirely to Field himself; nor should this credit be abated because of the lack of sympathy which many courts manifested towards his reform in administering the code, or because of the need of further change at the present time.

The proposed civil code did not meet with the same success. In 1850 a commission appointed by the New York legislature to draft a code of substantive law reported against the project. In 1857 a new commission was appointed, with Field as one of its members. Critics of the civil code drafted by this commission have been too ready to assume that its work was hastily done. In fact, the final draft was not published until 1865, with the ninth report of the commission, and during the eight intervening years the draft had been submitted for suggestions of change to the judges, leading members of the bar and prominent men of business of the state of New York, and many important changes had been made. Unfortunately, however, the draftsmen themselves were busy lawyers who were unable to give to their task the study and attention which it deserved. When the draft civil code was presented by Field in 1865, the legislative reform movement had, to a large extent, spent its force, and for thirteen years the New York legislature took no action upon the proposal, in spite of Field's continuous activity in its behalf. In 1878 he persuaded the legislature to adopt the civil code, but the vigorous opposition of many of the leaders of the bar caused the governor to veto it. Field continued to urge its adoption, and it was not finally rejected in New York until 1887.

Meanwhile the prophet of American codification was not without honor in states other than his own. In 1865, the very year of the submission of the Field civil code, it was adopted by the legislature of Dakota Territory. The popularity of the code in a frontier community, and its lack of popularity in the older states of the east, is not surprising. A young state, without any local legal tradition, confronted with the problems of pioneer life, would naturally welcome a legislative summary of the experience of the eastern states in reconciling the rules of the English common law to American conditions. When the Field code was published, American law had just completed the period during which judges and text writers, such as Kent and Story, had fixed the general principles of American private law. The Field code was an epitome of this reaction of a community still largely imbued with the frontier spirit to a system of law which had developed in an older civilization under different conditions. Since its drafting, it has been adopted, with minor changes, in five Western states: in North and South Dakota, in California in 1872, in Idaho in 1887, and in Montana in 1895. . . .

For the approach of the draftsman, we return to New York and to the debate that resulted from Field's proposal of a Civil Code for that state.

## FIRST REPORT OF THE COMMISSIONERS OF THE CODE (1858)

*By David Dudley Field, William Curtis Noyes, and Alexander W. Bradford*

THE COMMISSIONERS of the Code, appointed by the Act of April 6, 1857, beg leave to make this their first Report. . . .

It is known to the Legislature, that the duty which the Commissioners are performing is one of the greatest, most difficult, and most responsible.

Nothing within the range of government can exceed in magnitude the task of collecting, condensing and arranging the jurisprudence of a people. The structure of government and society, and all their complex relations, are comprehended within it. Public order, sound morals, all advancement in the arts of civilization, and all growth in true prosperity, are dependent, in a great degree, upon those rules of action, which the state prescribes for the conduct of its citizens.

---

David Dudley Field was a successful New York lawyer as well as the draftsman of codes of both substantive law (the Civil Code) and procedure. The latter was enacted in New York as the Code of Civil Procedure. He was a member of a distinguished family: one brother, Stephen J., in 1863 became a justice of the United States Supreme Court; another brother, Cyrus, laid the first transatlantic cable. Stephen J. Field was one of the draftsmen for the California Civil Code, which was based in large measure on his brother's Civil Code.

The difficulty and responsibility, in this instance, are increased by two considerations: the present state of the law, and the necessity of some modification to make a harmonious system. The condition of our law at the present time, is not unlike that of the Roman law in the time of Justinian, or of the French law in the time of Napoleon. From the date of the Twelve Tables to the age of Justinian, the polity and institutions of the Romans had so largely changed, so many new and various laws had been added, and the numerous decisions consequent upon the extension of commerce, the enlargement of the Republic and Empire, the modifications of social relations, and the conflict of laws of different provinces and nations, had become so complicated, that a Code which is a condensed and reformed Digest, was a matter of necessity. Something of the same kind is observable now.

Our law is the product of ten centuries, most of them filled with tumult and disorder; it is compounded of many incongruous elements, Saxon and Norman customs, Feudal and Roman law, provincial usages, and the decisions of various and disagreeing tribunals. We have Equity law, Admiralty law, Canon law, as the law of marriage and succession, and two kinds of Common law, one contradistinguished from Statute, and the other from Equity. Society has undergone an entire transformation. The feudal system has fallen to pieces; monarchial institutions have given place to republican; land from being almost inalienable has become an article of daily and hourly traffic; and commerce, once so narrow and timid, embraces the world. Personal rights, and personal property have assumed an importance never before known; the numberless questions arising from modern enterprise, travel, emigration, and the expansion of industry and commerce, have developed new departments of jurisprudence; while the multiplication of courts required by the necessities of an increased population, and a traffic constantly augmenting, has produced a mass of adjudications, painful for the student to contemplate, and often difficult if not impossible to reconcile. Thus we have arrived at the period of which the Roman historian complained so justly, when "the infinite variety of laws and legal opinions had filled many thousand volumes, which no fortune could purchase, and no capacity could digest."

How far, in the preparation of a Code, changes should be recommended, is a question of much delicacy. They should, without doubt, be cautiously admitted. Law is the growth of time and circumstance. An original system of jurisprudence, founded upon mere theory, without reference to national characteristics, habits, traditions and usages, would be a failure. The science of government and law is progressive; new regulations spring from necessity, or are suggested by experience, and the application of the rules of justice to human affairs is constantly modified by the changing circumstances of society. The process is easily understood. In the earlier stages of civilization, when communities are small and isolated, local customs are more distinct, in conformity with local character; but as cultivation and intercourse gradually break down provincial peculiarities, and eradicate partial customs, the tendency to assimilate enables the legislator to disregard inconvenient rules, venerable only from age and habit, and gradually to introduce changes which have the experience of other communities to recommend them, and which seem better adapted to an advanced civilization. We thus reach a stage, in which valuable improvements may be borrowed from other systems and engrafted into our own, without impairing the harmony of our laws, by the introduction of unsuitable elements. For example, the law of special or limited partnerships, the offspring of the commerce of the Middle Ages, unknown to the common law, has with a recent period been adopted into our own legislation, with manifest advantage. So we have also seen the influence of our jurisprudence reflected back upon the country from which we derived our language and our laws; and reforms, readily admitted by our plastic legislation, slowly adopted there, after having been tested by our experience; though the settled constitution and the fixed habits of England might have prevented their origination in that country.

Thus two great purposes are to be subserved in revising the jurisprudence of a nation; one, the reduction of existing laws into a more accessible form, resolving doubts, removing vexed questions, and abolishing useless distinctions; the other the introduction of such modifications as are plainly indicated by our own judgment or the experience of others. We are satisfied that this work should be performed with delicacy, caution and discrimination, that nothing should be touched, from the mere desire of change, or without great probability of solid advantage.

A Code of all the law of a commercial and opulent people can only be made after the most patient study and incessant toil. A superficial observer might, perhaps, suppose a year or two of labor sufficient for it, but he who reflects upon the infinite variety of human affairs, and that the law aims to furnish a rule for every known relation and every foreseen transaction, knows how idle it is to expect it to be hastily, if it be faithfully performed. The task should seem, indeed, to be hopeless, if it were designed to provide an express rule for every case which can possibly present itself for judicial decision. It is of course impossible to foresee all the questions which will arise in the future, or to collect and arrange all those which have arisen and been solved, so as to meet every contingency in human affairs, by a definite legal rule. That which in the judgment of the Commissioners can reasonably be attempted is to collect, condense and arrange those general and comprehensive rules of action, resting upon fundamental principles, recognized by the law or by reason, which will afford, as far as possible, a guide in regard to the rights of person and of property. There should be neither a generalization too vague nor a particularity too minute, in the Code of an enlightened and free people, whose intelligence demands that the law should be written, and brought within the knowledge of all, and whose liberty requires that no greater restraints be imposed upon their action than policy and necessity dictate. . . .

## INTRODUCTION TO THE COMPLETED CIVIL CODE (1865)

### By David Dudley Field and Alexander W. Bradford

WHETHER a general Code of the law be possible, should seem, from the nature of the subject, hardly to be doubtful. The common law of New York, like the common law of England, from which it is in great part derived, consists of a vast number of rules of property and of conduct, which have been applied by the judicial tribunals, and which had their origin either in legislative enactments, now forgotten, or in traditions from ancient times, or in the consciences of the judges, as the cases came before them. The decisions of the tribunals have been for ages preserved in writing. If there was ever a time when they were held in the memory alone, that time has long passed. All that we now know of the law, we know from written records. To make a Code of the known law is therefore but to make a complete, analytical, and authoritative compilation from these records. The records of the common law are in the reports of the decisions of the tribunals; the records of the statute law are in the volumes of legislative acts. That these records are susceptible of collation, analysis, and arrangement, might have been assumed beforehand, even if we had not the proof in our libraries, in digest upon digest, more or less perfect, to which we daily resort for convenience and instruction. The more perfect a digest becomes, the more nearly it approaches the Code contemplated by the Constitution. In other words, a complete digest of our existing law, common and statute, dissected and analyzed, avoiding repetitions and rejecting contradictions, moulded into distinct propositions, and arranged in scientific order, with proper amendments, and in this form sanctioned by the Legislature, is the Code which the organic law commanded to be made for the people of this State. That this was possible, was all but proven by what had already been done among ourselves.

It was fully proven by what had been done in respect to the law of other countries. The law of Rome in the time of Justinian was, to say the least, as difficult of reduction into a Code as is our own law at the present day. Yet it was thus reduced, though, no doubt, to the disgust and dismay of many a lawyer of that period. The concurring judgment of thirteen centuries since, has, however, pronounced the Code of Justinian one of the noblest benefactions to the human race, as it was one of the greatest achievements of human genius.

France at the beginning of her revolution, was governed partly by Roman and partly by customary law. The French Codes made one uniform system for the whole country, supplanting the former laws, and forming a model by which half of Europe has since fashioned its legislation. It should seem, therefore, to be quite beyond dispute, that a general Code of the law is possible.

Whether it is also expedient, is a different question. One of the objections made is, that it is not possible to provide for all future cases. You may, it is said, stretch your foresight to its utmost limit; you may exhaust all the sagacity and ingenuity of the human mind; the future, nevertheless, is a sealed book: you cannot look into its unopened leaves; and, therefore, attempting to provide for what they contain, is spending your strength in a vain and fruitless effort. This does not appear to be an objection of any weight whatever. Because we cannot provide for all cases, should be thought a poor reason for not providing for as many as possible. To render the existing law as accessible, and as intelligible as we can, is a rational object, though we cannot foresee what ought to be the law in cases yet unknown. To cast aside known rules which are obsolete, to correct those which are burdensome, or unsuitable to present circumstances, to reject anomalous or ill-considered cases, to bring the different branches into a more perfect order and agreement, may be of immense value, though we cannot look beyond the present, to make provision for what has never yet appeared. . . .

If a case unprovided for could not arise under the code of Civil Procedure, much less could it arise under the Code of Criminal Procedure. It may, therefore, be safely affirmed, that there is but one of the five Codes, that is to say, the Civil Code, to which, with any semblance of justice, it may be made an objection that it cannot provide for all future cases. This Code is, undoubtedly, the most important and difficult of all; and of this it is true, that it cannot provide for all possible cases which the future may disclose. It does not profess to provide for them. All that it professes is, to give the general rules upon the subjects to which it relates, which are now known and recognized, so far as they ought to be retained, with such amendments as seemed best to be made, and saving always such of the rules as may have been overlooked. In cases where the law is not declared by the Code, it is to be hoped that analogies may nevertheless be discovered which will enable the courts to decide. If, in any such case, an analogy cannot be found, nor any rule which has been overlooked and omitted, then the courts will have either to decide, as at present, without reference to any settled rule of law, or to leave the case undecided, as was done by Lord Mansfield, in *King v. Hay*, 1 W. Bl. 640, trusting to future legislation for future cases.

The language of the Code in this respect should seem to be sufficiently guarded, thus:

Sec. 2. Law is a rule of property and of conduct, prescribed by the sovereign power of the State.
Sec. 3. The will of the sovereign power is expressed:
1. By the Constitution, which is the organic act of the people;
2. By statutes, which are the acts of the Legislature, or by the ordinances of other and subordinate legislative bodies;
3. By the judgments of the tribunals enforcing those rules, which, though not enacted, form what is known as customary or common law.[1]

Sec. 4. The common law is divided into:
1. Public law, or the law of nations;
2. Domestic, or municipal law.

Sec. 5. The evidence of the common law is found in the decisions of the tribunals.
Sec. 6. In this State there is no common law, in any case, where the law is declared by the five Codes.
Sec. 2032. The rule that statutes in derogation of the common law are to be strictly construed, has no application to this Code.
Sec. 2033. All statutes laws and rules heretofore in force in this State, inconsistent with the provisions of this Code, are hereby repealed or abrogated; but such repeal or abrogation does not revive any former law heretofore repealed, nor does it affect any right already existing or accrued, or any proceeding already taken, except as in this Code provided.

Therefore, if there be an existing rule of law omitted from this Code, and not inconsistent with it, that rule will continue to exist in the same form in which it now exists; while if any new rule, now for the first time introduced, should not answer the good ends for which it is intended, which can be known only from experience, it can be amended or abrogated by the same law-giving department which made it; and if new cases arise, as they will, which have not been foreseen, they may be

[1] In the first draft of the Code (1862) there was no reference to "common law"; the unenacted rules were all embraced by the description "customary law."

decided, if decided at all, precisely as they would now be decided, that is to say, by analogy to some rule in the Code, or to some rule omitted from the Code and therefore still existing, or by the dictates of natural justice. . . .

Having thus considered the principal objections to the codification of the law, it should next be considered whether there are advantages in it. Assuming that it is possible to have a body of written law in a convenient form, and in scientific order, containing the materials and framed in the manner already described, what benefits will it confer?

In the first place, it will enable the lawyer to dispense with a great number of the books which now incumber the shelves of his library. In the next place, it will thus save a vast amount of labor, now forced upon lawyers and judges, in searching through the reports, examining and collecting cases, and drawing inferences from the decisions, and so far facilitate the dispatch of business in the courts. In the third place, it will afford an opportunity for settling, by legislative enactment, many disputed questions, which the courts have never been able to settle. In the fourth place, it will enable the Legislature to effect reforms in different branches of the law, which can only be effected by simultaneous and comprehensive legislation. Thus, for example, the closer assimilation of the law of real and personal property, and the changes in the relation of husband and wife, as to property, cannot be effected by any other means so wisely and safely, as by a General Code. The making of a Code involves a general revision of the law. It is indeed in this way alone that such a revision seems practicable. The occasion is thereby afforded to look at the law of the land, as a whole, to lop off its excrescences, reconcile its contradictions and make it uniform and harmonious. In the fifth place, the publication of a Code will diffuse among the people a more general and accurate knowledge of their rights and duties, than can be obtained in any other manner. This is an object of great importance in all countries, but more especially in ours. If every person can have before him, in an authentic form, the laws which are to affect his property, and govern his conduct, he can have an additional guaranty of his rights, and a better acquaintance with his duties. Here, more than anywhere else, all classes of citizens interfere in all the affairs of the State. They elect, directly, nearly all the officers who make, administer, or execute the laws. If in Holland or in Germany, or France, a Civil Code has been found beneficial, much more is it likely to be beneficial to us.

So far as the choice lies between law, to be made by the legislature, and law to be made by the judiciary, there cannot be a doubt that whatever may be the determination elsewhere, the people of this State prefer that theirs shall be made by those whom they elect as legislators, rather than by those whose function it is, according to the theory of the Constitution, to administer the laws as they find them. Hence, the idea of a Code has taken such hold of our people that they have made provision for it by their organic law.

## REASONS FOR CODIFICATION      By David Dudley Field

I WILL MENTION here four *reasons* for codification, and four *sophisms* against it:

*First.* There are certain propositions which have become maxims of government, one of which is that the legislative and judicial departments should be kept distinct, or, in other words, that the same person should not be both lawgiver and judge. There is no need of arguing about it. The maxim is founded on philosophy and experience. It has taken ages of struggle to establish it. And here it is. We profess to take it for absolute truth; we talk of it as one of the fundamental doctrines of modern government; we write it at the head of our Constitutions; but we violate it every hour that we allow the judges to participate in the making of the laws.

*Second.* Another of these maxims is, that they who are required to obey the laws should all have the opportunity of knowing what they are. These laws are now in sealed books, and the lawyers object to the opening of these books. They can be opened by codification and only by codification. Do not say that this is a figurative expression which proves nothing. It proves everything. The law with us is a sealed book to the masses; it is a sealed book to all but the lawyers; and it is but partly opened even as to them. It is an insult to our understanding to say that the knowledge of the law is open to everybody.

It should be open. That none can deny who has common understanding and a decent regard for truth. How can it be opened? In one way, and only one: writing it in a book of such dimensions and in such language that all can read and comprehend it. What if lawyers should say unwritten law is good enough for them? They are used to delving in it; they like it; they live by it. What then? Supposing it to be so does not mend the matter, unless it be assumed that the law is made for the lawyers and not for the people.

These two reasons for codification should of themselves be decisive.

---

Reprinted from Titus Munson Coan, ed., *Speeches, Arguments and Miscellaneous Papers of David Dudley Field,* Vol. 3 (New York: Appleton, 1884–90) p. 239.

*Third.* Another and a third reason is the lawyer's own experience; the experience, I might say, of every lawyer. What does he do when a case is brought to him, for the courts or for his private opinion? The first question he asks himself is: Has the point been decided? He looks for a decision. Where does he look? First in the volumes of his own State reports. It may be that he finds a case just decided in the highest court on all fours with his own, and he fancies that he may rely on that. Can he? We lawyers know that there is still a chance of mistake. Look at the list of "cases cited, criticized, and distinguished, or overruled." This is the very best aspect of the lawyer's position in the case supposed. But what if there be no such decision? Then he looks into the decisions of inferior courts in his own State. If he finds one that he thinks is applicable, he ventures to take it, though with less confidence, because he knows that he is to go through the ordeal of the higher court, and his chances there are uncertain. Should he happen to find no decision at home applicable to his purpose, he goes abroad into other States or across the sea. Now that he has got beyond the hundreds of volumes of his own State he resorts to the thousands of volumes of other states and countries. What "a codeless myriad of precedents" to look through! What "a wilderness of single instances" to explore! Consider the nature of the search, and what is found, after all? He peers into volumes upon volumes, and with no other guide than an index at the end of each volume, or a compilation or collection of indexes called digests, of many volumes. These are made sometimes by men of sense, and sometimes by men of no sense, without any agreement upon a plan or classification of subjects. The result is, as might have been expected, that the lawyer, with an earnest desire to get the "best opinion" or the "weight of opinion," has, after all, to make a guess. Now, if he had been asked at the outset whether he would not prefer to look for an authoritative statement of the rule for his case in a statute-book, *if he could find it there,* he would have answered yes.

*Fourth.* The fourth reason that I will mention is that no people, which has once exchanged an unwritten for a written law, has even turned back. One might as well expect the sun to return upon the dial. Even where the written law has been imposed upon a conquered people, to whom it must have been at first distasteful for that reason, it has held its place after the foreign domination has departed. The eagles of Napoleon were driven back across the Rhine, but the code which went forward with the eagles did not return with them; it remains there today. These facts are arguments worth all the theories in the world. Scholars may write as many treatises as they will; the experience of mankind is worth all the books that were ever written. You can not explain away this experience; you can not reason it down; it proves the superiority, beyond dispute or cavil, of written to unwritten law, of statute law to case law, or, as it might be better called, to guess-law.

Now for the sophisms against codification:

*First.* It is said that the law will be "cabined, cribbed, confined," if it be written. . . .

*Second.* A second sophism is that a perfect code can not be made, and therefore, inasmuch as none but an imperfect one is possible, there had better be none at all; which is much as to say, you can not have all you want, therefore you shall have nothing. . . .

*Third.* A third sophism is this one: We have grown strong and prosperous without a code, why get one now? What need is there of a change? . . .

*Fourth.* A fourth sophism is, that Legislatures are always at work changing the laws, and therefore if a code is made it will be subject to continual change, and so it is better to have none of it. . . .

# THE PROPOSED CODIFICATION
# OF OUR COMMON LAW *By James Carter*

WHOEVER GLANCES over the varying systems of law exhibited by civilized States, will perceive that in some, as in England and with us, the great body of the rules which determine the rights of men in respect to their persons and property, have never been directly *enacted* in statutory form. They have their origin in the popular standard, or ideal, of justice as applied to human action, and the usages and practices sanctioned by it. The system, therefore, rests upon an original, but ever growing, body of custom, and the rules thus established have been, through a long succession of centuries, expounded, applied, enlarged, modified and administered by a class of experts—lawyers and judges—who are supposed to devote their lives to the study of the system and to the work of adapting it to the ever shifting phases which human affairs assume. The cultivating and perfecting, of this body of rules, which is called "*the law,*" is a part, and a most important part, in the *natural growth* of the civilization in which they are found. The means of ascertaining what these rules are—in any given case, by ascertaining what the judges have

---

Reprinted from *The Proposed Codification of Our Common Law* (New York: Evening Post, 1884), pp. 1–91. James Carter was the president of the American Bar Association in 1894–95 and served as a leader in New York's municipal reform movement.

determined in like cases, and by maxims and principles which, from long adoption and frequent application, have become familiar and authoritative.

In other states, however, such as most of those on the Continent of Europe, the system of law is found to be different. There, the rules which perform the same functions in society, stand, to a large extent, in the form of positive statutes, or *Codes,* enacted by the arbitrary power of the sovereign, or by the authority of a legislative assembly, where such a body exists.

It will also be observed that the system first above described is a characteristic of States of popular origin, or in which the popular element is predominant, while the latter system is a characteristic feature in those which have a despotic origin, or in which despotic power, absolute or qualified, is, or has been predominant. Nor is this contrast accidental. It arises necessarily from the fundamental difference in the political character of the two classes of states. . . .

It is a matter for wonder that any one acquainted with the history of English jurisprudence should suggest such a total departure from the law of its growth, as is involved in the adoption of the method of codification; still more that any people of Anglo-Saxon origin should receive with favor the proposition to substitute the methods of despotic nations in the place of those through which their own system has been built up. And yet we have seen the press, the public, and even the Bar of the State of New York, viewing with comparative unconcern the endeavor of a few men, it might be said, of one man, to abrogate our system of unwritten law, to discard the principles and methods from which it has sprung, and to substitute in its place a scheme of codification borrowed from the systems of despotic nations.

Two Legislatures have been found so insensible of the magnitude of the trust confided to them as to give their assent to the passage of a scheme of legislation called "*Civil Code,*" which, confessedly, few of them had even read, none had intelligently understood, and which had been proved to contain multitudinous changes in the existing law, proceeding either from ignorance or design, which never could have received their assent, had they been made the subject of separate and independent bills. . . .

It is extremely desirable in the discussion of the important questions raised by the effort to secure the adoption of this proposed *Civil Code* that matters of a personal nature should be avoided; but this is not altogether possible. It seems necessary, in order to fully make known the nature of the forces enlisted in support of the measure, to point out that it has behind it strong personal contentions. Mr. David Dudley Field, a member of the Commission which originally reported this scheme, has long enjoyed the repute of having been its principal author, and he certainly has been for several years its chief promoter. The desire to effect an improvement in the law is, surely, in the highest degree praiseworthy; and to connect one's own name with a lasting improvement is a noble ambition. But the danger is that the gratification of the ambition or the vanity will become a motive greatly superior to the wish to effect a solid improvement—a danger to which the law has been in almost every age exposed.

The cherished passion of the gentleman referred to for the enactment of a *Civil Code* bearing his image and superscriptions has, it may be feared, survived his concern for the merits of the performance or its effect upon the public welfare. His superior mental powers, his activities, unimpaired in his venerable age and highly useful when exercised upon a matter less precious than the entire jurisprudence of a State, his ingenuity and influence, are all employed in the task of pressing the inattention, indifference or the good nature of the legislative bodies to yield an assent to the adoption of his *Civil Code*. The work has stood charged with, and convicted of, errors which if exhibited in any treatise upon the law, would confound its author; but his amazing answer is, "Adopt the Code, with all its errors, and amend it afterwards!" If the hesitancy of some reluctant member cannot otherwise be overcome, he is ready to adopt almost any amendment, or modification, which will satisfy the scruple; and the sarcasm is not all hyperbole which has said that he would consent to strike from the proposed *Civil Code* everything but its cover, if the Legislature would enact only *that!* . . .

The main question upon which the expediency of such "codification" as that with which we are dealing depends, is, not whether the law to which it relates should be arranged in a concise and orderly form—all of which may be accomplished by a *Digest*—but whether it should be reduced to *writing* and enacted in *statutory* form; in other words, whether it should be *converted* from *unwritten* to *written law*. The first inquiry, therefore, should be, in what particulars these two forms of law differ, and what consequences must flow from the conversion of the former into the latter.

The whole administration of law consists in applying the national standard or ideal of justice to human affairs. That is true whether this standard is to be found in the written statutes of a Legislature, or the unwritten rules sanctioned by the courts. When we are obliged to seek for it in the latter, the inquiry is usually satisfied without difficulty, if the particular case has before happened and been considered by the courts; but if it presents new features, different minds may differ concerning the rule which justice should apply, and the doubt can be resolved only by the voice of the tribunals. Until this has authoritatively spoken, it may be said to be uncertain what the rule is. *Uncertainty,* therefore, in this form, and in such instances, is one characteristic feature of unwritten law. If, however, a rule clearly embracing the particular case has been enacted in writing, no question of justice or injustice, which was the sole source of the uncertainty before spoken of, can be raised. It may be that the case is obviously one which the framers of the statute did not foresee, and did not make provision for, and, consequently the enforcement of the rule as written, will work gross injustice. It may be that the case is so clear as a simple question of justice or injustice that all minds would agree that a different rule *ought* to be applied, and, consequently, that, were there no statute, the rule of the unwritten law would not only be just, but free even from any form of uncertainty. It would be to no purpose to urge considerations like these. The law would be enforced as it stood written and enacted.

It is thus perceived that written law offers a means by which *certainty* may, in some cases, be better attained, though it must frequently happen at the sacrifice of *justice;* and that unwritten law offers a means by which justice may be better attained, though it must sometimes happen at the sacrifice of certainty. Now, in the constitution of human society there are many subjects, in relation to which the necessity, or the advantage, of certainty predominates over those of strict justice, and many others in relation to which the necessity or the advantage, of exact justice predominates over those of rigid certainty. . . .

The appropriate province of *unwritten law* may be described, sufficiently for the present purpose, as embracing the rights, obligations and duties in respect both of person and property which arise from the ordinary dealings and relations of men with each other, so far as it is not expedient for the considerations above stated to make them the subject of a statutory enactment. This immense field covers the general law both of contracts and torts, the law of sales, of partnership, of agencies, of corporations, of bills and notes, of shipping, insurance, and admiralty; the law governing the rights and duties springing out of particular employments, occupations, relations and engagements, as the law of carriers, of bailees, of master and servant, of husband and wife, of telegraphs, and the principal body of the law affecting the ownership and transfer of property, real or personal.

The grounds and reasons which render statutory law inadequate to deal with these subjects in the infinite variety of the conditions which different cases present need not here be pointed out. This is one of the main questions which arise upon the proposed *Civil Code,* and will hereafter be deliberately considered. It is enough for the present to say, that in our law as it now stands, and in any really scientific system of jurisprudence, these topics are left under the dominion of unwritten law. It will thus be perceived that all subjects connected with the *public administration* of a State, or which are predominating *public interest,* fall, for the most part, within the province of *written law;* while those which more immediately relate to *private* interests and business belong, with few exceptions, to the domain of *unwritten law.* The Roman writers designated the law embracing the former class of subjects by the short and appropriate term *public law;* and that embracing the latter class by the corresponding term *private law*; and these terms will, for convenience and brevity, be adopted in this discussion. . . .

If such a revolution were necessary, if the acceptance of some form of codification were inevitable, it would yet be possible to greatly reduce and mitigate the unavoidable evils which would flow and perfect a codification as the wit of man could contrive. The talents and learning which cannot be found in one man, or three men, might be enlisted in the work. The masters in each of the different branches of the law might be called to the task. The combined result of their labors might be submitted to the judges elected by the people for their suggestions and criticism; and a small, selected number of the wisest and best might be appointed for the task of final review and completion. A work might thus be produced, not, indeed, worth to replace our present system (for that, as I believe, is impossible); but one in the presence of which the crude compendium now urged for adoption would be left in the obscurity and forgetfulness from which it is now sought to rescue it. . . .

The advocates of codification either directly assert, or tacitly assume, that the rules of law pronounced by courts in their opinions are so pronounced as being absolutely and under all circumstances true; and they must stand upon this proposition, for without it, "codification," in the sense in which we are dealing with it, cannot be safely attempted. In the Introduction to the proposed *Civil Code,* understood to have been written by Mr. Field himself, this position is clearly taken. It is there said (p. xiv): "All that we know of the law we know from written records. To make a Code is therefore but to make a complete, analytical and authoritative compilation from these records. The records of the common law are in the reports of the decisions of the tribunals; the records of the statute law are in the volumes of the legislative acts." And in the Report made by the Commission to the Legislature in 1865, understood to have been penned by the same hand, and which accompanied the original measure, it is said (p. viii): "Whatever is known to the judge or the lawyer can be written, and whatever has been written in the treatises of lawyers, or the opinions of judges, can be written in a systematic Code."

The fallacy (and it is a gross one), wrapped up in these plausible assertions that whatever is known can be written, and that if a rule of law can be written by a judge in an opinion, it can be written and enacted in a Code, consists in the false assumption that courts lay down rules *absolutely*, whereas, they lay them down *provisionally* only. They do not, indeed, declare in terms that the rules pronounced are to be taken in reference to the facts which have elicited the opinions, but this is always understood; and whenever a case arises presenting different aspects, the rule is subject to modification and adaptation as justice or expediency may dictate. This, of course, cannot be done with a rule enacted in a statute. All such rules are rigid and absolute, and cannot be modified and shaped to suit the varying aspects which different cases may exhibit. If a codifier should correctly state any rule laid down by the court he would attach to it the limitation which is always understood in connection with such rules. In stating it without such limitation he omits a most essential element always belonging to it. The facts with which codification assumes to deal, and out of which it seeks to build its system are the opinions of the courts. Whence does it derive its authority to omit, in arranging these facts, one of their most essential features? . . .

I here conclude the discussion of the question whether any codification of our unwritten private law is expedient; and if I have been at all successful in the task, that question must be answered in the negative for:

*Firstly*. The scheme of codification is condemned on scientific principles;

*Secondly*. It is condemned by the teachings of actual experience; and,

*Thirdly*. It is condemned by a preponderating weight of the opinions of jurists, judges and statesmen.

I should not, however, leave this subject without setting down, in concise and orderly form, a statement of the evils which would flow from its adoption. These, or some of them, have necessarily been touched upon in the course of the preceding observations.

1. THE NECESSARY INTRODUCTION INTO THE LAW OF A GREAT MASS OF ERROR. As has been shown, a rule enunciated by a statute must be applied to all cases which fall within its scope, according to a fair interpretation of its language. Let it be supposed that language employed in it is used with the utmost accuracy, it is still impossible that its framers should *intelligently* provide for unforeseen cases. But the statutory provisions, by reason of their generality, *must* unavoidably embrace such cases, and the result necessary is that such cases must be disposed of by a statute framed without reference to them, and consequently such disposition is as likely to be wrong as right, depending as it does wholly upon chance.

2. A GREAT INCREASE OF UNCERTAINTY IN THE ADMINISTRATION OF THE LAW. The sources of this uncertainty are two fold. *Firstly*, human language is, at the best, so inaccurate an instrument, there being often numerous different senses in which the same word is understood that there are, and always will be, a multitude of doubts concerning the

meaning of the best drawn statutes. And all such doubts would be pure additions to those which now arise from other sources. *This* source of doubt does not exist in unwritten law. *Secondly,* whenever statutory law, in its application to an unknown case, is found to work injustice in consequence of the case not having been foreseen, the effort and the tendency always is to impose violently upon the statute an interpretation not in harmony with the natural meaning of its language. In every such case, it is highly *uncertain* whether the effort would succeed. And this is a source of uncertainty unknown to unwritten law.

3. INCESSANT, FREQUENT, SHARP AND OFTEN ILL-CONCEIVED CHANGES IN THE LAW. Next to absolute *right,* stability is the chief excellence in jurisprudence. This virtue never was, and never can be, secured in any high degree in the field of private law when such law is reduced to statutory form. Whenever a statute is found to work injustice, it must be changed. Society never has endured, and never will endure, except in trivial matters, any dealing by the courts with private rights not in accordance with the popular standard of justice. So, also, when uncertainty is found to exist, amendments of the statutory law must be made to remove the doubts. To effect such changes, the Legislature must be appealed to. The appeals will and must be frequent. The habit of changing the law necessarily tends to destroy that sense of the necessity of stability which is now (although unfortunately diminishing) one of the greatest safeguards for property, business and liberty. Besides, these changes are to be effected by a numerous body, for the most part wholly unskilled in the delicate science with which they are thus called upon to deal. . . .

4. THE SUBSTITUTION IN FORENSIC DEBATE OF CONTROVERSIES CONCERNING WORDS IN PLACE OF CONTROVERSIES CONCERNING PRINCIPLES. This would be a certain and serious evil. At present, when any doubt arises in any particular case as to what the true rule of the unwritten law is, it is at once assumed that the rule most in accordance with justice and sound policy is the one which must be declared to be the law. The search is for that rule. The appeal is squarely made to the highest considerations of morality and justice. These are the rallying points of the struggle. The contention is ennobling and beneficial to the advocates, to the judges, to the parties, to the auditors, and so indirectly to the whole community. The decision then made records another step in the advance of human reason towards that perfection after which it forever aspires. But when the law is conceded to be written down in a statute, and the only question is what the statute means, a contention unspeakably inferior is substituted. The dispute is about *words.* The question of what is right or wrong, just or unjust, is irrelevant and out of place. The only question is what has been written. What a wretched exchange for the manly encounter upon the elevated plane of principle!

5. THE ARREST OF THE SELF-DEVELOPMENT OF PRIVATE LAW—ITS TRUE METHOD OF GROWTH. This is, as I conceive, perhaps the gravest mischief with which codification is pregnant. It cannot too often be repeated that the practical business of administering private law consists in the application by the courts of the national standard of justice to the business and dealings of men. This national standard of justice is something which cannot be embodied in written rules, or set down in any form of words. It is the product of the combined operation of the thought, the morality, the intellectual and moral culture of the time. Under our present unwritten system of law it is ascertained and made effective by the judges, who know it and feel it because they are part of the community. . . . The question is, shall this growth, development and improvement of the law remain under the guidance of men selected by the people on account of their special qualifications for the work, or be transferred to a numerous legislative body, disqualified by the nature of their duties for the discharge of this supreme function? . . .

6. THE LOSS OF ANOTHER DISTINCT INSTRUMENTALITY FOR THE IMPROVEMENT OF THE LAW, *viz:* THAT FURNISHED BY THE WRITINGS OF PRIVATE JURISTS. As has already been shown, it was from this source that the Roman law drew its principal nutriment; and who will undertake to estimate the value of the contributions which the jurisprudence of England and America has from time to time received from the private labors of Coke, Hale, Blackstone, Hargrave, Sugden, Kent and Story? . . .

7. THE ENFORCED ABANDONMENT OF ALL HOPE OF BRINGING THE PRIVATE LAW OF ALL ENGLISH SPEAKING STATES TO A UNITY. . . .[a]

## THE FIRST HALF-CENTURY OF THE CALIFORNIA CIVIL CODE            *By Maurice Harrison*

THE CIVIL Code as originally adopted in this state, was the Field draft code, with some changes to adapt it to previous California legislation. But it was found to contain many provisions which unnecessarily conflicted with the prior statutes and decisions of the state, and in 1873 it was submitted for revision to a Board of Code Examiners, consisting of Stephen J. Field, Jackson Temple and John W. Dwinelle. This board,

[a] The American debate over codification was paralleled in Germany, and produced a classic exchange between Thibaut and Savigny. See Clarence Morris ed., *The Great Legal Philosophers* (Philadelphia: U. of Pa. Press, 1959), p. 289.

This excerpt is a continuation of the article introduced on page 104.

after calling for and receiving suggestions from California judges, lawyers, and business men, submitted an extensive series of amendments, which were adopted in 1874.

The enactment of the Civil Code presented a novel problem to the courts of California. Statutes dealing with governmental affairs and public law generally were familiar enough; statutes of a special nature, designed to correct particular abuses, had been frequently before them. But they had never had to do with a statute which purported to codify the common law of private rights. They might conceivably have treated the code as taking the place of all previous law and as furnishing by itself the sole guidance for all future decisions. This was the traditional French attitude towards the Code Napoléon, which the terms of that code attempted to impose. The code was considered to be the sole source of all rules of law. This theory involves the decision of every case by reference to the express provisions of the code; or, in case no controlling provision is found, then a rule is deduced by a purely logical process either from other provisions of the code, by analogy, or from the presumed intent of the legislature as disclosed by its arrangement, classification and legislative history; or, finally, if no controlling principle can be deduced from such a literal analysis of the code, then the case is to be determined by the judge's sense of natural justice, unhampered by any rules or principles. Upon this theory the traditional school of French jurists has built an elaborate system which, however, has been modified during the past century by two influences: first, by a partial recognition of the binding force of judicial decision, and secondly, by the rise of a school of jurists, under the leadership of Professor Gény, which insists that in the interpretation of the code the courts should not confine themselves to a system of purely logical deduction and analogy, but that, where the letter of the Code does not control, the judge should be free to base his decision upon considerations of legislative policy, including prevailing custom and social needs. But whatever variations of the general theory happened to be in vogue, it has been agreed that the primary basis of the interpretation of any of the continental codes has been and still is the terms of the code itself. This we may refer to as the continental system of interpretation.

Of course, no one has seriously urged the adoption in California of the extreme view that the code is the exclusive source of our private law; for such a theory would fall to the ground as soon as any court decision was given effect as a precedent governing the application or interpretation of our code. But the question remained as to the extent to which the code was to supersede common-law principles as the foundation of the system of private rights which were to be recognized and enforced by the courts. This question first received careful consideration in a series of articles by Professor Pomeroy, published in the third and fourth volumes of the West Coast Reporter. Pomeroy contended—and his view has now been adopted by California courts—that the continental theory of code interpretation was entirely inapplicable to a code such as ours and that the code must be treated as merely a supplement to the common-law system, altering its rules only to the extent that the intent to do so clearly appeared.

At the outset of his discussion, Pomeroy insisted that in order to avoid confusion and uncertainty some uniform rule for the interpretation of the Civil Code should be established and followed. He then proceeded to show, with a wealth of illustration, that the code departs from the terminology theretofore used by judges and text writers in stating common-law doctrines, and substitutes new and unfamiliar expressions, which have no definitely settled legal meaning. Furthermore, the Civil Code, as he states, "does not embody the whole law concerning private relations, rights and duties; it is incomplete, imperfect and partial." It does not attempt to state the mass of special rules which constitute the body of our law; but it deals with each subject by the enactment of a few general and abstract definitions, followed sometimes by a few special rules, which in most cases were plainly introduced to settle some question upon which there had been a difference of opinion or conflict of authority. He proposed as the remedy for the difficult questions of construction resulting from the novel terminology and the incompleteness of the code, that "except in the comparatively few instances where the language is so clear and unequivocal as to leave no doubt of an intention to depart from, alter or abrogate the common-law rule concerning the subject-matter, the courts should avowedly adopt and follow without deviation the uniform principle of interpreting all the definitions, statements of doctrines and rules contained in the code in complete conformity with the common-law definitions, doctrines and rules, and as to all the subordinate effects resulting from the interpretation."

The rule of interpretation thus expressed by Pomeroy is a statement, perhaps overemphatic, of the attitude which our appellate courts have generally adopted in considering various provisions of the code. In a case arising soon after Pomeroy's articles appeared, the Supreme Court referred to the code rules for the interpretation of wills as being a mere re-enactment of the rules already established by the courts. Again, the code statement of the duty of lateral support seems to be entirely different from the common-law rule upon the subject; yet the courts held, in effect, that the common-law rules were not altered, except as to the obligation to give notice of an intended excavation. Examples could be multiplied indefinitely. Although sometimes decisions have been rendered which overlooked a pertinent provision of the code, yet in most cases the courts have without discussion of the proper method of interpretation, followed the rule proposed by Pomeroy. . . .

But any method of interpretation should be a general guide rather than a fixed rule; and Pomeroy's theory is subject to some very definite qualifications. For instance, it is not applicable to the provisions of the code with regard to estates and future interests, which were taken by Field from the New York Revised Statutes of 1829. The purpose of this revision of the laws, as is clearly shown both by the comprehensiveness of its terms and the notes of the revisers, was to supersede completely the common-law system. The distinction between this and other parts of the code is recognized in the decisions dealing with the suspension of the power of alienation, which reject altogether the authority of cases from other states which enforce the common-law rule against perpetuities. In discussing a case of this kind recently, Justice Sloane said: "For the very purpose of avoiding the subtleties and technicalities of the common law as to real property, there has been enacted into our Civil Code what appears to be intended as a complete scheme or system on the subject." So it has been held that the Statute of Uses and the technical rules thereunder which still obtain in many states, although never expressly repealed, are no longer in force in California. Nor is this method of interpretation impaired by the recent New York decisions under almost identical provisions of the revised statutes, which hold that future estates must vest, as well as become alienable, within the statutory period; for these decisions are justifiable as having been based upon a legitimate interpretation of technical words used in stating the complete statutory scheme.

In the second place, Pomeroy's rule is not by its terms applicable where the code language shows a clear intent to depart from the common law. Sometimes it is a difficult question to determine whether or not this intent is shown, because mere incompleteness, or even inaccuracy in stating the common-law rule, will not suffice. In deciding this question, the courts have given remarkable weight to the annotations of the Code Commissioners of Califorina, which to a large extent are a repetition of the notes of Field himself. In his introduction to the draft Civil Code, Field stated the purpose of his notes as follows:

> The reference to adjudicated cases, which in most instances follow the sections, are intended as much to answer the purpose of illustration as to justify the text. It is a favorite idea of many that, for promoting certainty, the propositions of a Code should be accompanied by illustrative examples. Whatever advantage there may be in this method, these references, it is supposed, will afford the best kind of illustrations.

A recent and striking example of the consideration accorded by our courts to the notes of the commissioners is the case of *O'Hara* v. *Wattson*, where the Supreme Court was called upon to reconsider its holding that in suits for specific performance there must be substantial adequacy of consideration, as a condition of granting relief. It was claimed that the requirement of adequacy, as stated in the code, was no more than a partial and incomplete declaration of the equitable rule under which relief is denied only where the inadequacy is so great as to amount to evidence of fraud. But the court held that the contrary view, as stated by the Chancellor Kent in a New York decision, was adopted by the code; that upon this point the code was not declaratory of the general law and that this interpretation was "established beyond controversy" by the notes of the California Code Commissioners.

The commissioners' notes were again given controlling force in a recent case where a sub-lessee sued his immediate lessor for breach of the implied covenant of quiet enjoyment. The defendant contended that the common-law obtained; that under the common law there was no implied covenant of quiet enjoyment after the termination of the estate of the lessor; and that although section 1927 of the Code stated an unlimited liability, this was merely an imperfect and partial statement of the common-law rule. But the court said that "the notes of the commissioners who prepared the Civil Code indicate that the section was not intended to be a re-enactment of the common law, but that it was borrowed from the civil law," and it was held that a common-law rule had been changed, and the liability of the lessor thereby enlarged.

This section 1927 is only one example of the large drafts which Field made upon the French and Louisiana codes in the preparation of his draft. The whole arrangement of the code is surprisingly similar to that of the Code Napoléon. No lawyer imbued with the principles of the English common-law would classify the subjects of Trusts and Agency under the law of obligations, rather than under that of Persons or Property; and yet Field followed in this and many other respects the civil law theory, to such an extent as to deprive the code of much of the capacity for stimulating legal progress which it might otherwise have had. But the contribution of the civil law is not confined to matters of classification. The chapters on accession to personal property and accretion to real property were taken almost literally from the French code. We had already adopted the community property system before the code; but the holographic will, the extinction of obligations by deposit in bank for the creditor, the validity of a written release without consideration, and many other specific rules, were deliberately adopted from the civil law. To these provisions the Pomeroy rule has of course no application. And it is interesting to notice that California is the only common-law state of the Union which has been subjected to all three influences which have tended to infuse civil-law principles into the American common law; for although it shares with all the other states in the civil law contributions contained in the texts and opinions of Kent and Story, it shares only with the states of the southwest the effect of the Spanish and Mexican occupation and only with the Dakotas, Montana and Idaho, the civil law element in the Field codes. . . .

The question remains whether the effect of the code upon our law has been harmful or beneficial; and in this connection we may consider first the prophecies of evil which were so freely made while it was under consideration in New York. James C. Carter and his followers, who procured the rejection of the code in that state, based their opposition upon two grounds: first, that private law is incapable of conscious improvement by legislative action, and that it must develop through the enforcement of changing custom as recognized and carried into effect by the decisions of the courts; and secondly, that the adoption of a code unduly hampers the flexibility and elasticity of the common law. The first objection we may definitely reject. In spite of the huge volume of hastily prepared and ill-considered legislation, the experience of the past ten years will suffice to show that private law can be changed, and consciously and effectively changed, by legislative means. For instance, the common-law rules of contract have been altered in important respects by the Public Utilities Act. And the Workmen's Compensation Act has materially modified the common-law rule which makes liability dependent on fault, and has altered the law to make it conform to changed conditions in a manner that the courts, bound down by precedents and common-law principles, could not.

But the other objection of the opponents of codification is far more serious. The adoption of a code does unquestionably make for a less elastic system, because the very certainty which the code attempts to bring about is inconsistent with the adaptability and power of development which is one of the chief merits of the common-law system. But judicial precedents as well as legislative enactment may impede juristic progress and the extent to which a code impairs the development of the law depends to a large extent upon the character of the code and the spirit in which it is administered. In the case of our own code, we may safely venture the assertion that during the past fifty years it has not interfered with the growth of our law to any serious extent, and that the fears of the opponents of codification in this regard have proved to be without substantial justification. This peril has been largely avoided because the code deals almost exclusively with subjects as to which the rules of the common law had already been settled. It is a partial code, not only in the incompleteness of its rules, but also in the scope of its subject matter. It does not, for instance, mention the subject of rights in underground waters, and since its adoption the courts of California have developed a system of rules governing that subject in harmony with the physical conditions of the state and the needs of its people. It omits all reference to the regulation of public service as affecting the private rights of individuals, and the courts have been free to adjust claims based upon private contract with those based upon public service regulation under newer statutes without being hampered by code provisions. And so the courts have been free to develop, without any substantial code restrictions, the rules which seemed to them to be sound and just, in the law of contributory negligence and last clear chance, of trade-marks and unfair competition, and in other rapidly developing fields of law. The conservatism of the framers of the code, in thus refraining from attempting to codify those parts of the law which were likely to be the subject of judicial adaptation to changing conditions, has protected us in large measure against the primary disadvantage of the code system. . . .

We have had another corrective of the danger of inelasticity in the very method of interpretation which I have already discussed. If a code provision not clearly indicating a contrary intent is to be deemed a re-enactment of the common-law rule, then it is a re-enactment of the common-law rule with a reasonable flexibility in its application to novel conditions. An instance of the value of this point of view occurred in a recent decision where one of the parties claimed an easement over the land of another for the maintenance of a reclamation system. His opponent resisted on the ground that the easement did not come within the specific enumeration of servitudes contained in the code. But the Supreme Court held that the easement was established, and said that "the ingenuity and foresight of the legislature would be taxed in vain to name and classify all the burdens which might be imposed on land"—a declaration which not only repudiated a narrow and restrictive view of the code provision, but likewise repudiated the narrow common-law view, as announced by some judges and writers, that the common law will not recognize any novel incidents to or burdens upon the ownership of land.

Notwithstanding the favorable view which I have stated of the effect of the code on the growth of case-made law, there are several instances in which the code has fastened upon the California of 1921, rules which can be justified only by the conditions which obtained and the traditions and legal ideas which were in vogue in the New York of 1850. What could be more unsuited to the day of large business enterprise than the rule of the code that contracts in restraint of trade, though made for a legitimate object and in connection with the sale of the good will of a business, are not valid in so far they extend beyond the confines of a particular city or county? The courts of other states have been able to deal adequately with this problem in the light of business growth,

## The Codification Movement 129

whereas our courts have been held down by the explicit provision of the code. Again, the code declares that a minor's appointment of an agent, or his contract made under eighteen years of age with regard to real property, is void; and this rule has caused our courts to refuse any effect whatever, by way of estoppel or otherwise, to a minor's misrepresentation of his age, although the courts of other states have had no difficulty in reaching the contrary and juster result. A still more striking case is that of conditions in restraint of alienation. You will remember the recent decision to the effect that a condition forfeiting title in case of a transfer to a colored or Mongolian purchaser was utterly void, irrespective of the question of the reasonableness of the restraint, because the code forbade all restraints on alienation. Yet a few months later the Supreme Court held that a provision which, instead of prohibiting a transfer, forbade only the taking of possession by one of another race, was entirely free from objection. You may charge your land in perpetuity with a restriction upon the taking of possession by any class of persons, no matter how large, but you may not impose the slightest burden on the alienation of the title. If we had no code, the courts might have escaped this anomalous result. But when all is said and done, these are occasional instances of arbitrary and unreasonable rules, which cannot be said to characterize the body of our law.

So much for criticism of the code; there remains to be said what can fairly be said in its favor. Dean Pound has recently stated that the legitimate purpose of a code is to furnish a people with the premises of a new juristic start. It can hardly be claimed that the Civil Code of California has performed its full function in this regard. The decisions of our courts are usually not based on the spirit of the code, or on any deduction of the presumed legislative intent with regard to the classification of the law or the solution of problems which had not been dealt with in common-law decisions. Occasionally the Supreme Court refers to the spirit of our legislation, as it did in holding that estates by the entireties do not exist in this state, because they conflict with this spirit. But occasional references such as this can be duplicated in jurisdictions where there is no code whatever. The adoption of the rule of interpretation advocated by Pomeroy, while it has preserved our law from the dangers of too iron-clad rules, has also prevented us from realizing to the fullest extent this advantage of a restatement of the law. The imperfections of the code itself are responsible in part for our loss of this advantage. A code which declares that real property is immovable property and then defines a leasehold interest as a chattel real; a code which uses the term "property" in the double sense of the rights of ownership and the subject matter of those rights, can hardly furnish a comprehensive basis for a more accurate terminology nor for a more scientific classification of legal doctrine. The continental system of logical and analogical deduction, far from being the basis of judicial administration of the code, is practically unknown. The code has not done what could have been done in furnishing the basis for a new and sounder scheme of legal rights.

But it is not to be assumed that the code has been without value. It has done away with many a legal anachronism. Its practical convenience, the basis which it affords the legislature for drafting remedial legislation, the assistance which it has rendered in the settlement of controversies out of court—these benefits need not be dwelt upon. But beyond these more immediately practical considerations, the code has had, I believe—a profoundly beneficial effect upon the development of our local law in two ways: first, by preserving us from an artificial system of legal reasoning, and secondly, by facilitating the elimination of unreasonable distinctions between rules of common law and equity.

Fifty years ago, when our Civil Code was adopted, the legislative reform movement of the early nineteenth century had, as I have already stated, about lost its force. The period which followed was characterized by an intensive study on the part of scholars and jurists of the historical phases of the law. The writings of Maine and Maitland, and the intensive study of English case law in the university law schools, were reflected to a greater or less extent in the point of view of the better trained lawyers and judges. These historical students made contributions of the greatest value to our knowledge of the scope of common-law principles; but some of them were so carried away by the logical symmetry and historical continuity of the English common law that they lost sight of the necessity that it should conform to the life of the community which it was to regulate. The fact that a rule could be traced to the Yearbooks was for them sufficient reason for applying it to the United States at the end of the nineteenth century. The assignee's legal position as agent of the assignor, rather than owner; the purely personal nature of the right of cestui qui trust; and similar principles of the common law and equity became the bases upon which legal reasoning was artificially developed and legal problems actually solved. An instance of this attitude may be found in the opinion of the United States Supreme Court in the case of *Hart* v. *Sansom*, a case which is now thoroughly discredited—which declares that a state has not the power to enter a valid decree quieting title against a nonresident served with publication, because an equity decree can operate only on the person. This tendency has been admirably described by Dean Pound of the Harvard Law School in his recent work, *The Spirit of the Common Law*, as follows:

> The exclusive reign (of the historical school) in American juristic thought in the past fifty years brought out its worst side. For the historical school also worked a priori and gave us theories fully as absolute as those of the school of

natural law. Each deduced from and tested existing doctrines by a fixed, arbitrary and unchangeable standard. When the historical jurists overthrew the premises of the philosophical school of the preceding century they preserved the method of their predecessors, merely substituting new premises. They were sure that universal principles of jurisprudence were not to be found by deduction from the nature of the abstract individual. But they did not doubt that there were such principles and they expected to find them through historical investigations. In the United States we carried this further than elsewhere. . . . Even now, on the whole, the basis of all deduction is the classical common law. No system of natural law was ever more absolute than this natural law upon historical premises. For other systems of natural law gave ideals developed from without. With us, under the dominion of the historical school, the sole critique of the law was to be found in the law itself.

Here in California we have been almost entirely free from the artificial emphasis on the historical phase of the law which Dean Pound describes; and our freedom from this influence has been due in no small measure to the influence of the Civil Code. It has been in force during the precise period when the historical school has been most powerful. Whatever may be its defects in completeness and phraseology, it represents an earnest attempt on the part of an American lawyer of large experience to state in terms of contemporary speech the common law developed in an American state before the historical school had had its day. This code, especially after its revision by judges who had dealt at first hand with the problems of a pioneer state, was not likely to express any extreme of historical pedantry. It has been on the desk of every California judge and lawyer for fifty years; and its constant use has done us a service in preserving us from the danger of dealing with the problems of today in the spirit of the concepts of centuries ago.

If the code had rendered no other service than this, it would surely have justified its existence. But in addition, it has facilitated the elimination of unreasonable distinctions between rules which were developed in courts of law and those developed in courts of equity. The dual nature of our substantive law is due to an historical accident, and no classification or restatement of our law can be successful until the problem of the reconciliation of law and equity has been faced and solved. The Field civil code dealt with this problem in a spirit far more advanced than did the case law of its time. The terms "legal" and "equitable" are studiously avoided in the statement of rules. There is little detailed re-enactment of principles which courts of equity had developed as guides for their discretion rather than as controlling rules. The specific relief granted by way of injunction or specific performance is classified with the specific relief formerly obtained in ejectment or replevin, and equitable liens with legal liens.

The enactment of a code framed in this spirit has been followed by the development of a local law which is singular, as compared with that of other American states, in its freedom from unjustifiable distinctions with no better reason to support them than a former dual system of courts. The former distinction between the sort of fraud which justifies cancellation and the sort which furnishes a cause of action for damages has practically disappeared. Marketable title has the same meaning whether legal or equitable relief is sought. The code has enacted, as applicable to all contracts, the equitable rule that time is not of the essence unless so intended by the parties. The fiction by which the purchaser of real estate is in most states charged with the risk of loss before receiving his deed has been happily repudiated. And finally, we may call attention to the solution which we have reached, both by court decision and code amendment, of the questions involved in building restrictions and covenants enforceable in equity.

Neither the American nor the English courts have answered this question in a manner to accord with any sound and consistent theory; but within the past few years an amendment to the code, fortified by a decision of remarkable brilliance of analysis, has broadened the rigidity of the narrow legal rule so that it conforms to the needs of business transactions, and has curbed the looseness of the equitable rule by a reasonable requirement of formality. There still remain cases in which unreasonable distinctions between legal and equitable rights persist; a promise to make a gift of land, when followed by improvements, will still furnish the basis for an enforcement of the gift, although apparently no recovery can be had in damages for the breach of the promise; and it is still the rule that the vendor suing for the purchase price must or must not prove adequacy of consideration, according as the theory of his action is legal and equitable. And of course it can be said that the same process of amalgamation which I have described in this state may be observed, to some extent, in states which have no code. But when all is said and done, we may fairly claim that the California Civil Code has gone a long distance in rendering the content of our law, in this regard, more scientific and rational.

Jurists are agreed that a system of codified law requires periodical and systematic revision of the code. The rapidly increasing number of reports has caused a demand for a classification and restatement of the law. If our civil code is to be revised, we shall have the opportunity of contributing to the achievement of this ideal. Fifty years' experience and fifty years' development of our social and industrial life will reveal many incongruities in the code which have not been removed by haphazard amendment; but a successful revision should be conservative in altering the actual content of the law. And if revision is to be attempted, the task should be committed to experts with ample leisure for the task of drafting and with ample opportunity of consulting representatives of the various elements of our people. Only upon these conditions should a remodeling of the code be undertaken.

Writers who have discussed the Civil Code of California have usually emphasized its faults. Yet the fact remains that it has become a living part of our law, and in no jurisdiction where it has been enacted has its repeal been seriously advocated. And as it governs today the business and property interests of a commonwealth of three millions of souls, as it embodies a noble ambition to restate a great system of law, it stands as a fitting monument to the genius of one of the greatest American jurists—David Dudley Field.

## A STRANGE STORY

WE SURRENDER a large portion of our columns today to the report of a case which has attracted and absorbed the attention of the whole community, and created a greater excitement than any which has heretofore occurred in this section of the State. The indignation of the public generally at this disgraceful result of the careless manner in which the new codes have been gotten up is excessive; and as there is a painful suspicion that other defects as yet undeveloped may exist, the feeling is universal that the Civil Code should be at once repealed and the other codes referred to a competent commission to revise them.

The case referred to is that of the *People* v. *Oades,* just decided in the County Court of San Bernardino. Oades is an Englishman of good education, who came to that county about two years ago, and purchased and settled upon a farm in Temescal township. In January last he married Mrs. Nancy Foreland, a young widow lady of great beauty, residing in that neighborhood by whom he has since had a child, now about one month old. Both parties have always been regarded in the neighborhood as eminently respectable.

About two months ago a woman, accompanied by three children—two boys and a girl—arrived at the city of San Bernardino, and after inquiring of Oades' whereabouts proceeded to his residence, where she has since continued to reside. It afterwards transpired that this woman and Oades comported themselves towards each other as man and wife, and the neighbors, indignant at such open profligacy, laid a criminal com-

---

This story appeared in the Los Angeles *Weekly Express* of December 18, 1873 and was reprinted in the *American Law Review*, vol. 20, 1886, pp. 764–770.

plaint against them before Justice Billings, under the act of March 15th, 1872, for "open and notorious cohabitation and adultery." When the parties were brought up for trial, however, they produced a certificate of marriage, and proved by it and other authentic documents that the woman was Oades' wife—having been married to him in England about twenty years ago and moved with him to New Zealand, where their children had been born. The accused were therefore acquitted and returned to their home, where Oades continued to live with the two women as before.

Thereupon another complaint was laid before the same justice against Oades and Mrs. Oades No. 2, charging them with the same offense. On this trial it was proved that about eight years ago Oades was living in Wellington County, New Zealand, on the frontiers; when, without warning, the Maoris—a tribe with whom the English were at peace—made an inroad into the settlements. Oades was at the time temporarily absent in Victoria, and returned only to find his homestead burnt and his family disappeared. Some human remains were found in the ruins; and from this and from such information as he could gain during the ensuing two years he was gradually forced to the conviction that his wife and children were dead; and being loth to remain amid the scenes of his distress he left New Zealand and came to California. Upon this state of facts Oades claimed that this marriage with Mrs. Oades No. 2 was valid under the second subdivision of the sixty-first section of the Civil Code, which provides that the marriage of a person having a former husband or wife living is void, "unless such former husband or wife was absent and not known to such person to be living for the space of five successive years immediately preceding such subsequent marriage, in which case the subsequent marriage is void only from the time its nullity is adjudged by a tribunal." Upon an examination of the law this proposition was found too clear to be disputed, as there was no doubt that when Oades married his second wife he had been ignorant of the existence of his wife for more than five years. The complaint was therefore dismissed.

Oades still continuing in open cohabitation with the two women, a deputation was sent by the neighbors to lay the matter before Mr. Cokeman, the district attorney, who after examining the case, referred it to the grand jury, who found a true bill against Oades for bigamy. The trial, which took place last Monday, attracted a large crowd of eager spectators, among whom, the observed of all observers, appeared the two Mrs. Oades. The same state of facts was proven, and after the close of the evidence Mr. Cokeman, the district attorney, opened the case for the prosecution in an able and eloquent argument, of which we can only give a brief abstract:

"The law," he urged, "was to be construed according to its spirit and intent, and the language where contrary thereto was to be disregarded. These time-honored principles have been expressly adopted in the new code: 'Where the reason of a rule ceases, so should the rule itself. *Cessante ratione legis, cessant ipsa lex*'. And again, 'where the reason is the same, the rule should be the same. *Ubi eadem ratio ibi eadem jus.*' And again, 'he who considers merely the letter goes but skin deep into the meaning. *Qui haeret in litera haeret in cortice.*' Now, in this case," he continued, "the evident intention of the law was simply to provide against the illegitimacy of the children of the second marriage, and it certainly never could have been intended to make bigamy lawful. It is true, that at the date of the second marriage, Oades was ignorant of the existence of his first wife, but his voluntary cohabitation with both women, after learning the facts, was to be taken as conclusive proof of a guilty intention, *ab initio*. And, in support of this view, the counsel cited 'The Six Carpenters' Case.'" That case was very similar in principle to this, and it was adjudged that "the law judges by the subsequent act the *quo animo* or intent, for *acta exteriora indicant interiora secreta.*"

On the other hand, the counsel for the accused relied upon the provision of the Penal Code in relation to bigamy, which expressly provides that no person shall be held guilty of bigamy "whose husband or wife has been absent for five successive years" (prior to the second marriage), without being known to such person within that time to be living; and in reply to the argument to the district attorney, he urged upon the court that in criminal matters it would be a dangerous precedent to adopt so liberal a principle of construction as that contended for by Mr. Cokeman; and he cited in support of his position the following maxims: "*A verbis legis non est recendendum,*" "*Index animi sermo,*" and "*Maledicta est expositio quae corrumpet textum,*" the meaning of which, as he explained for the benefit of the court, was that in the interpretation of statutes "we must stick to the letter." That it is true that the intention must govern, but "the language is the evidence of the intention," and that "it is wrongly called interpretation when we alter the text."

The learned judge said that however desirable it might be to convict the prisoner, the position taken by his counsel was clearly the right one, and accordingly he instructed the jury to acquit, which was done, and Oades returned home triumphantly with his two wives.

Thereupon all the most eminent counsel of San Bernardino were retained by citizens interested in the virtue of the community, with a view of ascertaining some means of removing this terrible scandal of Oades and his two wives; and after an exhaustive examination of the case they came to the conclusion that the only method of annulling the marriage was to proceed under the second subdivision of the eighty-second section of the Civil Code, which provides that a marriage may be annulled where the "former husband or wife is living" at the time of the second marriage. But, as under the second subdivision of the eighty-third section of the Civil Code, an action for the annulment of such a marriage can be brought only by one of the parties to the second marriage, or by the husband or wife of the first marriage, it was evident that as neither Oades nor either of his wives were willing to bring the suit, the difficulty remained as great as ever.

What further steps will be taken is at present unsettled. But the people are very much excited and determined not to let the matter drop. Eminent counsel in San Francisco and Sacramento, including one of the Code Commissioners, have been written to, but as yet no answer had been received. We will keep the public informed of further developments.

This case still continues the all-absorbing subject of interest to the community. We give the latest, information upon the subject as furnished by a special correspondent, dispatched by us several days since to San Bernardino. Our correspondent interviewed Mr. Cokeman last night, from whom he learned some details not hitherto divulged. It seems that last Wednesday, Mr. John Howlett, of San Bernardino, was by advice of counsel dispatched to seek an interview with Mrs. Oades No. 1, with a view of offering her inducements to bring a suit to annul the marriage of Oades with Mrs. Oades No. 2. It was thought that she, being the party principally injured by the second marriage, might easily be persuaded to do so. After considerable difficulty and some danger—having on one occasion been run off by Oades with a shotgun—Howlett on Thursday morning managed to secure a private interview with Mrs. Oades No. 1, while Oades was out riding with his second wife. She appeared to be a mild, timid woman, but it was impossible to induce her to move in the matter—although Mr. Howlett offered her large inducements to do so. Oades, she said, had sworn that if she attempted to annul his second marriage he would not only beat her half to death, but also would never live with her any more; that she wouldn't mind the beating so much, but that she preferred to submit to the present state of circumstances rather than lose Oades altogether, especially as being married to him she couldn't marry any one else. Howlett therefore returned without affecting anything; and after consultation of counsel, was again dispatched to make the same proposition to Mrs. Oades No. 2. But neither would she accept the offer. "If there was any way," she said, "of annulling Oades' first marriage" she might be induced to move in the matter, although she really didn't mind Mrs. Oades No. 1 much; as she was getting too old to be a very formidable rival; and, besides, she found her a considerable help around the house; but as to her bringing suit to annul her own marriage there was no use talking about it, as she was perfectly well satisfied with Oades even with the incumbrance of his first wife and children.

Upon the receipt of this information the Rev. Mr. Kiggett, a minister of great and deserved influence in the community, was dispatched to expostulate with Oades himself. Oades received him courteously and discussed the matter with great frankness. Theoretically, he was a monogamist, and believed that the law should not allow a man to have more than one wife. He therefore joined with his reverend friend in saying that the aciton of the Code Commission in allowing bigamy could not be too severely condemned. "But such matters," he continued, "after all, are to be settled in each State as the legislators in their wisdom should deem best, it being now a settled principle in jurisprudence that all rights and obligations have their courses solely in legislative enactment; that all the most eminent jurisprudents, including the New York and California Code Commissioners, are agreed that right is what the legislature wills, this being the fundamental idea upon which the Civil Code is based. As to the old notion of natural right, that is entirely exploded. *Nous avons changé tout cela*," said Oades (who appears to be somewhat of a literary turn). "If there were such a thing," he continued, "the appointment of the Code Commission to reduce all law or right into a code would have been as absurd as to have appointed them to codify chemistry or mathematics—it would, in short, have been to repeal principles established by the Almighty, and to substitute in their place the shallow notions of ignorant and fallible men. For his part he didn't pretend to be wiser or more virtuous than the laws; and as the laws allowed him two wives his conscience didn't disturb him for having them; neither of his wives were willing to give him up and to tell the truth he couldn't get along very well without both of them. He loved them both so well (he added facetiously) that he was like the ass between two bundles of hay, and didn't know how to choose between them. Besides, if either marriage was annulled it would have to be the last one; and while he might possibly stand the loss of the old woman (that is, his first wife), nothing on earth would induce him to part with the last."

The reverend gentleman thereupon left in great and just indignation; which was greatly increased on Sunday at seeing Oades who had always been regular in his attendance at Church—seated in his pew with his two wives, listening complacently to the sermon.

As we stated yesterday the San Bernardino lawyers had written to one of the code commissioners. Our correspondent was shown the answer but did not have the opportunity of taking a copy. He was able, however, to send us a very full abstract of its contents.

The codifier—who appears from his letter to be a much more sensible man than one would think (judging only from the codes) wrote that it was a bad thing and that he didn't see what was to be done about it; but that the commission was not responsible for it; that all they had done was to copy the code of that eminent codifier Mr. David Dudley Field; that it was evidently the intention of the legislature that the commission should pursue this course; for if they had wanted a new code made they certainly should have known better than to refer the matter to them; that it couldn't be expected that a commission of three men, without any special training or experience of the purpose, could complete in two years a work for which Justinian had found it necessary to employ the great Tribonian and seventeen other of the most eminent lawyers in the Empire during many years; a work of such transcendent difficulty that the greatest of English jurisprudents, Austin, had thought it necessary to recommend that a large number of the ablest men should be especially educated for it and should devote their whole lives to it; a work, finally, so extensive that it had taken even Mr. David Dudley Field some time to accomplish it. As for himself, he said he never had pretended to be much of a codifier, but the position was offered to him with a good salary and he didn't feel called upon to decline it; that he made it a rule never to decline anything that was offered on account of his own incompetency— that being a matter that concerned only those who employed him; that if any one were to offer to employ him to make a piano or a steam engine— which was as much out of his line as codifying itself, he would accept the offer provided always that it was on a salary, and that he would not to be paid by the job; that in his opinion the other commissioners were no better than himself, and finally that the whole commission reminded him very forcibly of Pantagruel's opinion of the French lawyers, which he quoted as follows: "Seeing that the law is excerpted out of the very middle of moral and natural philosophy, how should these fools have understood it, who, *par Dieu,* have studied less in philosophy than my mule."

All other means failing, yesterday a mass meeting was called to deliberate about the matter, which was largely attended by the citizens of San Bernardino, and also of Los Angeles and San Diego. After much discussion it was finally proposed, as the only remedy, to petition the legislature to pass a special act dissolving Oades' last marriage. But Oades, who was present, immediately rose to address the meeting, and told them that that was no go; for by the twentieth section of the fourth article of the constitution of California it is expressly provided that "no divorce shall be granted by the legislature." As Oades produced the book itself, this argument was unanswerable. It was then proposed that the legislature should be petitioned to call a constitutional convention for the

## The Codification Movement 139

purpose of annulling one or the other of Oades' marriages; but Oades produced the constitution of the United States, and read the tenth section of the first article, which expressly provides that "no state * * * shall pass any law * * * impairing the obligation of contracts," "and marriage," he said, "was well settled to be a contract, and therefore no earthly power could deprive him of his vested right in his two wives." This brought the assembly to a stand still; for it was very evident that nothing short of an amendment of the constitution of the United States could reach his case. At length, however, the silence was relieved by a prominent citizen of Los Angeles, who proposed—as a simple and effectual means of meeting the difficulty—to hang Oades. "This," he said, "was a very common way of arranging such affairs in Los Angeles, and it had always met the public approbation except on one occasion; when, indeed, they had perhaps gone a little too far in hanging seventeen Chinamen." This suggestion took so well with the meeting that Oades took the hint and left while the Los Angeles man was explaining his views. The meeting at once broke up in pursuit, but Oades, after a close race, reached his house, where he barricaded himself and drove off the crowd with a shotgun.

After the crowd had dispersed our correspondent interviewed Oades at his house. He found him just sitting down to supper with his two wives, all in high spirits, and was cheerfully invited to join them. He had a long and interesting conversation with Oades, but this morning it had entirely escaped his memory, and our correspondent is too truthful to invent an account of what passed. He says, however, that he found Oades a very genial companion, and that they only separated at three o'clock in the morning, after the consumption of two flasks of whisky between them. The latter part of his letter is indeed a little incoherent, and were it not for the well known steadiness of his character, might give rise to a suspicion that he has himself been converted by the sight of Oades' connubial felicity—for he says that Oades is a good fellow, and that in his opinion, the whole affair has grown out of the jealousy of the people of San Bernardino; which is an old Mormon settlement; and that they are mad with envy at seeing Oades in the enjoyment of a privilege of which the laws have deprived them.

---

COMMENT. *The significance of the "strange story."* Your editor must confess that the strange case of Titus Oades is here at least as much for its humor as for any light it sheds on the problem of codification. Does it shed any light at all on the following issues: (1) The feasibility of codification; (2) The difficulty of draftsmanship and the time and care required for the preparation of a code; (3) The possibility of literal construction as contrasted with creative judicial work even after codification?

*Codes of Civil Procedure.* The Field Civil Code was adopted in only five western states. (See page 106, *supra.*) Much wider success met attempts to codify the law of procedure. The code of civil procedure which Edward Livingston drafted for Louisiana was adopted by that state in 1805, whereas his code of criminal law was rejected. A code of civil procedure drafted for New York by a commission which included David Dudley Field was promptly adopted in 1848; within twenty-five years it had been adopted in twenty-five other states and its influence has now reached nearly every state. See Hepburn, *The Historical Development of Code Pleading in America and England* (Cincinnati: Anderson, 1897); *David Dudley Field, Centenary Essays,* (New York: N.Y.U. School of Law, 1949), *passim* and esp. pp. 55 *et seq.* On the continuing reform of procedure under the influence of the Federal Rules of Civil Procedure see Barron & Holtzoff (Wright Revn.), *Federal Practice and Procedure,* chap. 1 (St. Paul: West, 1960).

## THE ADVISABILITY OF CODIFYING ANGLO-AMERICAN LAW  By Roscoe Pound

IF WE apply to common-law jurisdictions what experience has shown as to the conditions which lead to codes, it must be evident that, especially in America, we are rapidly approaching a condition in which codification is likely to be resorted to.

(1) It can hardly be questioned that our case law is by no means able to rise to new situations as it could do in the past. Practically it broke down on the important subject of employer's liability and workmen's compensation. There was clear failure in holding promoters to their duties. Development was too slow in the law of public service agencies and conspicuously too slow in labor law. In these fields legislation and administrative commissions and boards have replaced common law and adjudication. Even in legal procedure it took legislation in England, Canada, and Australia to provide a modern system, although judicial rule-making has done the most for that subject in the present century. It

---

Reprinted from *Jurisprudence,* vol. 3 (St. Paul, Minn.: West, 1959), pp. 732–738, by permission of the author and the publisher. Biographical material on Professor Pound appears on page 52.

must be admitted that the traditional element has shown signs for a time of having exhausted its possibilities.

(2) The defects of form in Anglo-American law of today are obvious. They may be summed up as five: (*a*) Want of certainty. This is very marked in jurisdictions in which questions which have been passed upon in other jurisdictions are still open. There is no certain assurance that the solution which has been adopted elsewhere will be followed. Moreover, it often happens that different solutions have been reached in other jurisdictions so that on many questions there are a number of competing rules of persuasive authority from which to choose, with respect to which the law is still open in some of our most important states. All sorts of trivial questions receive elaborate answers in the books while great and fundamental ones remain in a provoking state of uncertainty because lawyers advise clients to settle rather than pursue a doubtful litigation. Statutory changes are piecemeal and haphazard and the law has to be settled in each jurisdiction as to each controverted point by an elaborate system of judicial opinions which detracts much from thorough judicial consideration of individual cases.

(*b*) Waste of labor entailed by the unwieldy form of the law. As Chief Justice Sharswood put the matter, the difficulty is not so much to know the law as to know where to find it. Undoubtedly in the long run it is a good thing for the science of law to leave rules and principles to be worked out, in the language of Mr. Justice Miller, by a process of judicial inclusion and exclusion. But the process is hard on the community and the law and takes time away from thorough consideration of cases. Our appellate courts have often to put in so much time in finding the law that they cannot always give adequate consideration to the case. In 1885, a committee of the American Bar Association found that in one volume of New York Reports, in 79 decisions reported, the judges cited 449 cases or between five and six to each, of which 353 were from New York, 56 from England, and the rest from 16 different states. But these 449 cases cited by the court were taken from 5300 cited in the briefs of counsel. In other words, a conscientious court was expected to look at 5300 reported decisions in order to decide 79 cases. From personal experience I can testify that the labor is very heavy. The judges in important appellate courts today must have law secretaries to enable them to reduce this task to reasonable proportions.

(*c*) Lack of knowledge of the law on the part of those who amend it. It must be admitted that the fault in our sometimes crude legislation on matters of private law is not all with legislators. It is sometimes an almost impossible task in jurisdictions where many controverted questions, often fundamental, are still open, to ascertain with assurance what the law is which is to be changed or amended or abrogated.

(d) Irrationality, due to partial survival of obsolete precepts. In Illinois in 1910, the Supreme Court had to decide that contingent remainders could still be barred by merger. After that, real property lawyers in Chicago trembled for a decade. What other supposedly obsolete common-law rules must they reckon with? No one knew. In Nebraska in 1907, title to valuable lots in the business center of the capital turned on whether there were possibilities of reverter in that jurisdiction. It was not thought safe to try and a compromise was made. Anomalous rules and rules based on history only, which are out of touch with the legal system as a whole, embarrass many important fields of the law. Our analytical methods have been fast identifying these anomalies. But we do not get rid of them. Moreover, irrationality of form continually breeds irrationality of substance.

(e) Confusion. Courts are frequently led into mistakes between the two parallel lines of case law and statute law, dealing with the same subjects, the one potentially with the whole, the other unsystematically with parts here and there. No court has authority and no legislature, as a rule, undertakes to reduce any subject to systematic and complete orderly statement.

(3) Passing to the third point which we have seen in connection with the enactment of codes, we come to a matter which is likely longest to retard effective codification in the United States. Where significant codes have been enacted the growing point of the legal system had shifted to legislation and an efficient organ of legislation on matters of law had developed. Undoubtedly with us the growing point had largely shifted to legislation. But we have not developed an efficient organ of lawmaking for the ordinary civil side of the law. In England, if the government takes up a proposal for legislation it has the machinery for pushing it through Parliament. Also through the institution of parliamentary counsel England has got rid of some of the causes of crudity in legislation as to private law. But as has been said, Parliament is not interested in "lawyer's law." In the United States, both houses of Congress now have competent legislative counsel and this is true in some states. This, however, does not suffice to do more than insure the form of statutes. It seldom involves grasp of the legal difficulties at the root of a question. Moreover, there is nothing with us comparable to the taking up of a measure of detailed law reform by the cabinet in England and thus giving it the right of way in a crowded session.

(4) On the other hand, the fourth point, the need for one law, is of more importance with us today than any of the others. It is suggestive that with the economic unification of the country conflict of laws is becoming one of the most important everyday subjects in the average American practice. The demand for one law was behind the growth of

the common law. Prior to the Conquest there was no one law of England. Local customary law differed greatly. As one of the demands in Magna Carta was for one measure of corn and one measure of ale for all England, so another demand of the time was for one measure of law. Such a demand may some day lead to codification of the common law in the United States.

Our condition is much worse than that of England in respect of uncertainty, unwieldy bulk, and need of unification.

Attempt to reshape the law by judicial overruling of leading cases is no substitute for well-drawn, comprehensive legislation. The English have an advantage in that down to the nineteenth century, and indeed till the second half of that century, relatively few cases were decided by the House of Lords. Hence old cases decided by tribunals not of ultimate authority may be questioned, whereas with us the ultimate reviewing court is likely to have fixed a century ago or more the law we should like to see changed or given up. Patchwork overruling along with patchwork legislative tinkering often does at least as much harm to the legal system as it does good. Our situation calls for a ministry of justice or a code; and a code will need a ministry of justice also.

---

COMMENT. The adequacy of the legislative arm to deal with legal reform will be more fully considered in Chapter 6.

The arguments for and against codification are clearly summarized in Yntema, "The Jurisprudence of Codification"; *David Dudley Field, Centenary Essays* (New York: N.Y.U. School of Law, 1949), p. 251. Professor Yntema concludes that such codification should be based on an intensive study of modern social conditions and the experience of foreign legal systems. This latter suggestion will be explored further in Chapter 9. See also Haskins, "Codification of the Law in Colonial Massachusetts: A Study in Comparative Law," *Indiana Law Journal*, vol. 30, 1954, pp. 1–17.

CHAPTER 4

# Codes Without Legislation: the Restatements

THE URGE TO BRING ORDER AND UNIformity out of the ever-increasing mass of case law, which led to the codification movement, also produced the American Law Institute and the Restatements. As we shall see, opinions clashed over the question whether Restatements have been beneficial or baleful.

We turn first to the story of the development of the Restatements—a remarkable illustration of the power of a man with an idea and of adroit techniques for launching a great enterprise.

In 1922 William Draper Lewis, Professor and later Dean at the Law School of the University of Pennsylvania, developed an idea—which had grown out of papers presented at a meeting of the Association of American Law Schools—for a "Permanent Organization for the Improvement of the Law." It was clear to Lewis that if the plan was to be executed "the initiative must come from Elihu Root," then "dean" of the American bar. In March 1922, Lewis carried the idea to Root. Lewis reports: "Mr. Root grasped the possibilities of the Institute and the importance of the work proposed and before the interview ended all the necessary organization steps had been planned. At that the Restatement was born."

The next necessary step was to enlist the support of the leaders of the bar. To this end, Lewis prepared the following Report on behalf of a "Committee on the Establishment of a Permanent Organization for the Improvement of the Law." The report, outlining the problems to be discussed at a meeting in Washington in 1923, was sent to four hundred judges, law professors, and practitioners throughout the country.

In following the further evolution of the project it will be instructive to see how the initial plan was transmuted by the interplay between scholars and practitioners.

For an informative account of this project see Goodrich and Wolkin, *The Story of the American Law Institute* (St. Paul, Minn.: American Law Institute, 1961).

# REPORT OF THE COMMITTEE ON THE ESTABLISHMENT OF A PERMANENT ORGANIZATION FOR THE IMPROVEMENT OF THE LAW

*Introduction.* There is today general dissatisfaction with the administration of justice. The feeling of dissatisfaction is not confined to that radical section of the community which would overthrow existing social, economic and political institutions. If it were, we as lawyers could afford to ignore it. But the opinion that the law is unnecessarily uncertain and complex, that many of its rules do not work well in practice, and that its administration often results not in justice, but in injustice, is general among all classes and among persons of widely divergent political and social opinions.

It is unnecessary to emphasize here the danger from this general dissatisfaction. It breeds disrespect for law, and disrespect for law is the cornerstone of revolution. The danger would be real, even though the feeling that much is wrong with our law and its administration had no foundation in fact. There are, however, just causes for complaint. Rightly we are proud of our legal system considered as a whole, but as lawyers we also know that parts of our law are uncertain and unnecessarily complex, that there are rules of law which are not working well in practice, and that much of our legal procedure and court organization needs revision.

With the knowledge of the need for improvement in the administration of justice has come a consciousness of the obligation which rests upon the profession to take informed action to better existing conditions. . . . The American Bar Association . . . and state and local bar associations have been increasingly active in endeavoring to maintain high standards of legal ethics and to promote the simplification of procedure, the uniformity of law among the several states, and the improvement of legal education. But the possible scope of the activity of such associations in the improvement of the law is limited. They are without endowment and moreover they are not organized for that patient legal scientific and scholastic work which must precede all real improvement of our substantive and procedural law. . . .

*Two Chief Defects in American Law.* Two chief defects in American

---

Reprinted from *American Law Institute Proceedings,* vol. 1, 1923, pp. 1 *et seq.,* with the permission of the publisher.

law are its uncertainty and its complexity. These defects cause useless litigation, prevent resort to the courts to enforce just rights, make it often impossible to advise persons of their rights, and when litigation is begun, create delay and expense.

When the law is doubtful most persons are inclined to adopt the view most favorable to their own interests; and many are willing if necessary to test the matter in court while those willing to overreach their neighbors are encouraged to delay performing their obligations until some court has passed on all the novel legal theories which skilled ingenuity can invent to show that they need not be performed. In either case litigation is carried on, which but for the law's uncertainty would be avoided. Again, the present degree of uncertainty in many parts of the law tends to create the feeling that the outcome of all court proceedings is uncertain no matter how just the claim, the result being that many whose legal rights are clear indirectly encourage a failure of justice by compromising with opponents who are conscious of the lack of merit of their own contentions.

Furthermore, injuries caused by uncertainty in the law are not confined to situations in which controversies have arisen so that rights claimed must be either compromised or referred to the courts for their decision. Though one function of law is to provide rules by which disputes may be settled, its other equally important function is to provide rules of action. Because of the existing uncertainty in the law those who turn to it for guidance in conduct often find that it speaks with a doubtful voice. For example, the lawyer who assists in the combination of commercial enterprises, or the lawyer who draws a will with provisions suggestive of the rule against perpetuities, will often find that he cannot positively inform his clients of the legal consequences of their acts.

The same bad effects, though in a less degree, result from the law's complexity. Besides which, complex law tends to make the administration of justice a game in which knowledge and skill are more important for obtaining victory than a just cause.

The time consumed by the courts in disposing of cases is an obvious fact which all persons may note and criticize. Furthermore, everyone realizes that long-drawn-out litigation is, on account of the expense, a greater hardship on those of relatively small means than on the litigant with a long purse. It is therefore natural that the delays of the law rather than its uncertainties or complexities is the defect on which those who criticize the administration of justice usually lay stress; and yet, the most of these delays are due to uncertainties and complexities.

Perhaps, however, the most serious result of these defects is that they create a lack of respect for law. Their effect is the same as the effect of clear, certain but unjust law, and for the same reason; law to perform its functions must be adapted to the needs of life, and no such need was ever satisfied by uncertain and complex rules. Lack of respect for law, whether it has its origin in the law's uncertainty or in the injustice of its provisions, undermines the moral fibre of the community. In itself it becomes a cause of antisocial conduct; the rich are more apt to use their wealth to oppress; the business man is more apt to cheat; those in immediate want are more apt to steal. In our opinion the most important task that the bar can undertake is to reduce the amount of the uncertainty and complexity of the law. It is essential if an adequate administration of justice is to be had that lawyers awaken to the extent to which the law should be and may be simplified and clarified.

At the outset we realized that it was useless to attempt to come to any final conclusion in regard to the right way to reduce the present uncertainty and complexity of our law until we had made a thorough analysis of the principal forces now operating to make our law more or less certain or more or less complex. . . .

All [the] causes of the law's uncertainty would continue to exist were the Federal Constitution repealed and the United States made one state. The fact, however, that the nation is composed of forty-eight states, each of which as well as the Federal government is an independent source of law, means that the law on any subject in any one jurisdiction may differ from the law of one or more or all of the other jurisdictions. These variations in law are themselves a potent cause of uncertainty and complexity, and because of this and for other reasons do much injury, not only where transactions are carried on in two or more states, but also where transactions are carried on wholly within one state.

Any practical plan devised and carried out by lawyers to promote certainty and simplicity in the law must meet those conditions causing uncertainty and complexity which it is possible for the profession to modify or eliminate. It is manifest that some of the causes are beyond the power of the bar to remedy. The number and nature of novel legal questions, and those differences in the law of different states due to differences in economic or social conditions, are entirely outside the control of the bar. Furthermore, the great volume of the annual increase to the already overwhelming mass of reported cases, which is another cause of the law's uncertainty, cannot be directly checked by any action which may be taken by the profession. As lawyers, our instinct to regard as an authority the prior decision of any court on a matter pertinent to the case under consideration is too strong to be arbitrarily limited to the decisions of particular courts or to the particular decisions of any one or more courts. Should only a few selected cases appear in the officially printed reports, the enterprise of private publishers would soon result in the printing of "Cases Omitted from the Official Reports," and consequently in their continued citation and use by lawyers and judges.

On the other hand, many causes of the existing uncertainty and complexity are more or less within the power of the legal profession to control by intelligent united action. Bar associations have done and are now doing much to improve legal education and thereby create conditions which will tend to reduce one cause of the law's uncertainty—the ignorance of judges and lawyers. . . .

Finally, . . . lack of agreement among lawyers concerning the fundamental principles of the common law is the most potent cause of uncertainty. The bad effect of this lack of agreement is not confined to creating uncertainty in the law of each state. To it is due much of the unnecessary and harmful variation in the law of the different states. Closely interwoven with this cause is the lack of precision in the use of legal terms.

Fortunately these two causes of uncertainty and complexity are precisely those over which the legal profession has the greatest control. The people through the legislatures are theoretically responsible for the uncertainties and complications of statutory enactments. The common law and its terminology, however, have been developed solely by lawyers. To say that the system of developing and applying law is primarily responsible for the lack of agreement on legal principles and the lack of precision in the use of legal terms does not excuse the profession which through the centuries of English history has evolved the system with all its great merits and also with all its defects. As the common law has been developed under the guidance of the legal profession, that profession has the power and the duty to reduce its principal defects. At present chief among them is this lack of agreement among lawyers concerning the principles of the law and lack of precision in the use of legal terms. The fact that lawyers have so far failed to appreciate the extent of the resulting evil or to recognize the responsibility of the profession to try to improve conditions is the sole reason that today these defects loom so large.

*Need for a Restatement of the Law.* . . . [O]ur examination of the causes of the present uncertainty of the law shows conclusively the need of a restatement of the law that will have an authority much greater than that now accorded to any existing encyclopedia or treatise. We are convinced therefore that the specific work which any organization created by the legal profession to improve the law should undertake on its formation is the production of such a "Restatement of the Law."

We speak of the work which the organization should undertake as a restatement; its object should not only be to help make certain much that is now uncertain and to simplify unnecessary complexities, but also to promote those changes which will tend better to adapt the laws to the needs of life. The character of the restatement which we have in mind can be best described by saying that it should be at once analytical, critical, and constructive.[a]

The statement must be analytical because there should be a division of topics based on a definite classification of the law the result of thorough study by a group composed of persons qualified by their studies and their intellectual attainments. Each topic also should be treated analytically, not historically. Those who state the law must, of course, do so with full understanding of its development, but the primary object of the restatement is to set forth the law, not to give an account of its growth.

The restatement should be critical, because it must be more than a collection and comparison of statutes and decisions, more than an improved encyclopedia of law, more than an exposition of the existing law, even though such exposition were an accurate photograph of all the law's existing certainties and uncertainties. There should be a thorough examination of legal theory. The reason for the law as it is should be set forth, or where it is uncertain, the reasons in support of each suggested solution of the problem should be carefully considered.

The restatement should be constructive. In the first place, while necessarily largely based on the two official sources of the law, statutes and decisions, it should not be confined to examining and setting forth the law applicable to those situations which have been the subject of court action or statutory regulation, but should also take account of situations not yet discussed by courts or dealt with by legislatures but which are likely to cause litigation in the future.

Again, where the law is uncertain or where differences in the law of different jurisdictions exist not due to differences in economic and social conditions, the restatement, while setting forth the existing uncertainty, should make clear what is believed the proper rule of law. The degree of existing uncertainty in the law would not necessarily be reduced by a mere explanation of rival legal theories. Indeed, a restatement which confined itself to such an explanation would reduce the degree of existing uncertainty only in those instances where but one line of decisions was supported by reasons worthy of consideration. Where the uncertainty is due, as it often is, to the existence of situations presenting legal problems on the proper solution of which trained lawyers may differ, the courts can best be helped by support given to one definite answer to the problem.

Furthermore, there can be little doubt that the law is not always well adapted to promote what the preponderating thought of the community regards as the needs of life. The limitation on the character of any ref-

[a] It will be interesting in following the evolution of the Restatement operation to see whether this objective was met.

ormation of the law by an organization formed to carry out the public obligation of the legal profession to improve the law is reasonably definite. Changes in the law which are, or which would, if proposed, become a matter of general public concern and discussion should not be considered, much less set forth, in any restatement of the law such as we have in mind. Changes which do not fall under the ban of this limitation, and which will carry out more efficiently ends generally accepted as desirable are within the province of the restatement to suggest. . . .

In view of the limitation just suggested, the changes proposed would be either in the direction of simplifying the law where it is unnecessarily complex or in the direction of the better adaptation of the details of the law to the accomplishment of ends generally admitted to be desirable. . . .

---

THE FOLLOWING ARTICLE SHOWS what transpired during and following the 1923 meeting in Washington to discuss the above Report.

---

## HOW WE DID IT  By William Draper Lewis

THE MEETING was well attended. Chief Justice Taft and Justices Holmes and Sanford were present from the Supreme Court. There were also five judges of the Circuit Courts of Appeals and twenty-eight judges of the highest courts of their respective states, as well as special representives of the American Bar Association, and the National Conference of Commissioners on Uniform State Laws. Mr. Root was chairman, and made an address summarizing the reasons for the meeting.

On motion of George W. Wickersham it was unanimously resolved:

That we approve the formation of the American Law Institute, the object of which shall be to promote the clarification and simplification of the law and its better adaptation to social needs, to secure the better administration of justice, and to encourage and carry on scholarly and scientific legal work.

The next day, February 24th, the first meeting of the Council was held. It was the unanimous desire that Mr. Root should be President; but he was firm in his position that his age made such a step unwise. He con-

---

Reprinted from, Lewis, "How We Did It," *History of the American Law Institute and the First Restatement of the Law* (Philadelphia: American Law Institute, 1945), with the permission of the Publisher.

sented to become Honorary President and gave us essential help until his death in February, 1937. The Council elected George W. Wickersham the first President. I resigned from the Council and was appointed Director. Mr. Wickersham held the office of President until his death in January, 1936. He was not only a good lawyer but an able executive, capable of loyalties to the organizations with which he was identified and above all to the Institute. After his death on January 25, 1936 he was succeeded by our present President, George Wharton Pepper.

*Planning the Work on the Restatement.* The spring of 1923 was spent in planning the subjects which should be first undertaken and the organization of the work. First, however, the necessary money had to be obtained. We had no idea how long the work would take but thought that adequate financing for some ten years would be sufficient to demonstrate conclusively the practicability of the project. Furthermore, we had analyzed the work sufficiently to know that we would have to spend something over $100,000 a year. At the first interview between Mr. Root and myself nothing was said about possible sources of donations; but I realized, as subsequently did the Committee submitting the report to the organization meeting, that there was a well-founded hope that with Mr. Root's active interest, the Carnegie Corporation might give the financial cooperation needed. Indeed, Dr. Henry Smith Pritchett, the then President of the Corporation, attended the meeting on May 10, 1922, and thereafter took a keen interest in the Committee's report and the organization of the Institute. . . . At the Executive Committee meeting held on April 21st I was able to read to them a letter from the Corporation, dated April 17th, notifying us that it had granted us $1,075,000, approximately the sum requested, payment to be made over a ten year period.

Subsequent donations of the Corporation increased this generous initial donation to the Restatement work to a total of $2,419,196.90. . . .

At the meeting of the Executive Committee of the Council held on May 5, 1923, I submitted a Plan on Organization of Work and Budget which was approved and reported to the second meeting of the Council on the 19th. The "Plan of Work" with little change has been followed in all our work on the Restatement of the Law. The main features have also been adopted, not only by the Institute in the drafting of Model Codes and Statutes, but by other public and private organizations in the prosecution of serious legal drafting work.

The plan involves four steps:

1. The appointment of a Reporter for each subject undertaken. This Reporter prepares all drafts.

2. The appointment of a Committee of Advisers presided over by the Director as Chief of the Editorial Staff. The Committee with the Reporter for the subject considers all preliminary drafts and in a series of meetings each usually

lasting from three to five days develops a final preliminary draft for the consideration of the Council; the Committee also reconsiders in the same manner any draft referred back to it by the Council or a meeting of the members. The Reporter is obliged to incorporate into a draft any statements of law adopted by the Committee of Advisers or by the Council or by a meeting of the Members of the Institute; but except in the preparation for the printer of the text finally adopted by the Institute as the official draft the Reporter registers his own dissent, if any, and on the request of any member of the Committee or the Council the dissent of such member.

3. The final preliminary draft is considered by the Council, the Reporter being present. The Council returns the draft for further consideration to the Committee of Advisers, or, as amended by them, submits it to the Annual Meeting of the Institute either as a tentative or as a proposed final draft.

4. The consideration of the tentative drafts by a meeting of the Institute and their return to the Council and the Committee of Advisers with any amendments adopted by the meeting for further study; the consideration of the proposed final drafts and their final adoption, with any amendments made, or their return for further consideration to the Council and the Committee of Advisers.

When a proposed final draft is amended by the meeting it is resubmitted to the Council which either agrees with the meeting or asks it to reconsider its action. When both the Council and the meeting of members approve the same text, it is printed and promulgated as an "official draft."

The result of the operations of the plan is that the official draft is the successive composite work of the three groups; first, the advisers who have special knowledge of the subject; second, the Council, a body of some thirty-three eminent lawyers consisting mainly of judges and practicing attorneys, and, finally, a meeting of the members of the Institute. In relation to any subject of the Restatement the most important person is the Reporter. The ultimate result is his work as discussed, changed and developed by group consideration. It is this careful group study and development that is the significant feature of the plan. The fact that the Restatement is the final product of highly competent group scholarship subjected to a searching criticism of equally learned and experienced members of bench and bar justifies both the time and large financial expenditure.

*Changes in Scope and Form of the Restatement During its Execution.* . . . [T]he original intention . . . that the Restatement should be accompanied by treatises citing and discussing case authority had to be abandoned, although not until after a fair trial had been made. About a year after work on the Restatement of the Conflict of Laws was begun, Mr. Beale, as Reporter, submitted to his group of experts text sections of a treatise pertaining to corresponding sections in the proposed Restatement. The group, already trained to feel responsibility, considered the tentative text of the treatise as carefully as they considered the text of the Restatement. This meant that every sentence was examined and very often became the subject of debate. Several conferences were held without really any progress being made. It became clear that a group development of the text of the treatise was impossible in any reasonable time or by the expenditure of any funds then or likely to become available. A good treatise discussing decisions might be written by an individual, but could not be produced by a group; the attempt to do so would have forced us to abandon the whole Restatement project as impossible. . . .

In view of the abandonment of the production of treatises, the second question to be decided by the Council was whether comment or other notes to the Restatement should discuss case and other authorities. For several years this question recurred, sometimes at the suggestion of a Reporter, more often at the suggestion of a member of Council. In Volume II of the Restatement of Property, the Reporter, Richard R. Powell, was allowed to publish in an Appendix notes written by him on certain questions which had been much discussed by his group, the notes containing citations of authorities. The experiment was not repeated. It became clear that it was not necessary to add individual opinion to support the official statements of the Institute, and that the professional position of the Institute and the known care with which the Restatements were prepared in the light of existing authorities permits it to speak with authority on the general law in the United States. The omission of the citation of case or other authority is practicable only because the Institute has attained an influence far greater than at the start of the work was thought possible. The Institute in its Restatement has become like the Courts an agency for the statement of the law.

*Subjects Included in the Restatement.* The first subjects undertaken were Contracts, Torts and Conflict of Laws. Work on these subjects started in June, 1923; Agency followed in the fall of that year. The reason for this selection in each instance was the existence of an outstanding member of a notable law school faculty who had spent years of work on the subject and was generally recognized by the profession as the leading expert. Samuel W. Williston, in Contracts, Francis H. Bohlen, in Torts, Joseph H. Beale, in Conflict of Laws and Floyd R. Mechem, in Agency, were all in this class. . . .[a]

[a] Following is a list of the restatements, followed by the dates of commencement and completion, and the names of the principal reporters. See Table No. 8 of the *History, supra*.
Agency (1923–1933): F. R. Mechem, W. A. Seavey.
Conflict of Laws (1923–1934): J. H. Beale, H. F. Goodrich
Contracts (1923–1932): S. W. Williston, A. L. Corbin
Torts (1923–1938): F. H. Bohlen, *et al.*
Property (1927–1936): R. R. B. Powell, *et al.*
Trusts (1927–1935): A. W. Scott
Restitution (1933–1937): W. A. Seavey, A. W. Scott
Security (1936–1941): J. Hanna
Judgments (1940–1942): A. W. Scott, W. A. Seavey, E. N. Griswold

*Results of the Restatement.* The first Restatement of the Law is done. We started with the belief that out of the mass of case authority and legal literature could be made clear statements of the rules of the common law today operative in the great majority of our States, expressed as simply as the character of our complex civilization admits. The result shows that this belief was justified. The Restatement of each subject expresses as nearly as may be the rules which our courts will today apply. These rules cover not merely situations which have already arisen in our courts but by analogy rules applicable to situations likely to arise. The Restatement of a subject is thus more than a picture of what has been decided; it is a picture of present law expressed by foremost members of the profession. As a result of the way in which the work has been done and the persons who have labored on it, the Restatement has acquired an authority far greater than those of us who organized the Institute to do the work anticipated. Though the rules are expressed in the form of a code, except in sporadic instances, there never has been any desire to give them statutory authority. The Restatement is an agency tending to promote the clarification and the unification of the law in a form similar to a Code. But it is not a Code or statute. It is designed to help preserve not to change the common system of expressing law and adapting it to changing conditions in a changing world. . . .

## WHAT SHOULD THE AMERICAN LAW INSTITUTE DO?

*By Hessel E. Yntema*

THE INITIAL conception of the work of the Institute as outlined in the original report, subject to certain qualifications somewhat incidental which may be noticed in a moment, furnishes an admirable standard by which to measure the adequacy of the actual Restatement of the Law. It is not possible to read this document justifying the creation of the Institute without being impressed by the cogent analysis of the defects in the system of American law therein portrayed and by the appropriateness of the objective thereby defined for the American Law

---

Reprinted from *Michigan Law Review*, vol. 34, 1936, pp. 461, 465–467, with the permission of the author and the publisher. The author, Professor of Law Emeritus at the University of Michigan, has written widely in the field of Comparative Law and is Editor in Chief of the *American Journal of Comparative Law*. For an appreciation of Dr. Yntema's work see *Twentieth Century Comparative and Conflicts Law* (Leyden: Sythoff, 1961), pp. 535–544.

Institute. Measured by this yardstick, the work of the Institute has been incompletely accomplished in a number of significant respects.

1. The initial plan contemplated an ideal statement of law, analytical, critical, and constructive, embodying whatever improvements in the law itself might be recommended by exhaustive study. The actual Restatement of the Law purports to be, and is substantially limited to, a statement of the law as it is. This departure from the original conception, it need not be emphasized, is a material nullification of the major objective of the Institute.

2. The initial plan definitely prescribed that a complete citation and critical discussion of all relevant legal materials to support the Restatement would be essential to its success. The present Restatement contains no citation and no critical discussion of any specific legal sources. The sole relief to this situation is that the several Restatements are being supplemented by state annotations, which are, however, necessarily inadequate, because localized and for the most part uncritical.

3. The initial plan explicitly anticipated that studies of the field of legal procedure and of the administration of justice might form a part of the Restatement of the Law. Thus far, the work of the Institute in these basic fields has been limited to criminal procedure, and the product has been put forth not as a part of the Restatement itself but as a model law.

4. The initial plan supposed that the law in the books would provide inadequate information with respect to certain legal questions and therefore contemplated that the activities of the Institute should necessarily include factual surveys. For reasons which are not entirely apparent, no such endeavor to obtain factual information on vital issues has been made by the Institute as such.

In addition to these limitations of the Restatement of the Law revealed by comparison with the initial plan, there are two further limitations, which derive from imperfections in the plan itself.

5. The initial plan did not prescribe a clear and satisfactory position as to the value which should be attributed, in the work of restatement of the law, to modern statutory trends as contrasted with currents of judicial decision. This ambiguity is reflected in the actual Restatement, which exhibits no definite policy as to either the inclusion or the exclusion of statutory materials as a basis for the restatement of the law. Even to a restatement of the law as it is, it might be thought, such statutory materials are relevant.

6. The initial plan made no specific provision for the comparative study of foreign experience or even for the consideration of data accumulated in other sciences, in connection with the Restatement, and it does not ap-

pear that such data have systematically been employed in the actual work.

Of course, this method of ascertaining the aspects in which the actual Restatement of the Law needs to be supplemented, amended, or repealed by reference to the initial plan for the Institute, is not necessarily conclusive. The ultimate question is whether the Restatement is an effective remedy for those defects in the system of justice to which the American Law Institute has been addressed. This is a question which it is doubtless premature to estimate at the present time. Nevertheless, it is to be remarked that the affirmative evidence as to the influence of the Restatement of the Law in alleviating the defects in the legal system thus far is negligible. Assuredly, the burden of the mass of the law has been increased rather than lessened to date by the Restatement and the related legal literature. The flow of judicial decisions continues unabated. The complexities of legislation have magnified rather than diminished during the past decade. There are more law reviews to be examined than ever before. The stream of jurisprudence has not been stopped by adding to its waters. It is to be anticipated that many of the tributaries will be affected, if not illuminated, by the Restatement of the Law, but whether the total result will be to clarify uncertainty, to eliminate diversity, to create greater precision in legal terminology, or to enlighten the ignorance of judges and lawyers, is, in view of the limited scope of the Restatement, the generality of its rules, and the absence of a critical explanation of the authorities, disputable, to say the least. No significant evidence to that effect has yet appeared. In the absence of cogent evidence as to results, the adequacy of the Restatement of the Law as hitherto conceived has to be tested by general considerations.

For this reason, the preceding remarks have suggested that the initial plan of the Institute, envisaging a thoroughly scientific, thoroughly documented, and forward-looking study as a basis for the improvement of the law, furnishes an acceptable standard of reference. In the interests of clarity, the first thing to be recognized in this discussion is that the limited scope of the present Restatement of the Law necessarily reduces it to a partial, or let us rather say, a preliminary contribution to such a study. . . .

# THE RESTATEMENT OF
# THE LAW OF CONTRACTS     By Charles E. Clark

THE PUBLICATION of the completed Restatement of the Law Contracts makes officially available the first fruit of the gigantic project to "clarify, unify and simplify our common law" undertaken ten years ago by the leading figures of the American bar, organized in a wholly unique and original manner into "The American Law Institute." Beautifully bound in red leather in two volumes of clear type on a small page with 609 sections and 1,129 pages, exclusive of index and table of contents, and with a price appropriate to its sumptuous setting, the "restatement" has been given every advantage which mechanical skill can afford. It appears with the acclaim of bench and bar, an acclaim justified by the ambitious nature of the project and the devoted labors which have gone into its making.

Its appearance is an important event in our law, deserving of the most careful and intelligent appraisal of which the profession is capable. The very magnitude of the project and the number and professional standing of its protagonists do, however, tend to prevent such appraisal. One is tempted either to embalm it in words of general and fulsome praise or to indulge in humor at the expense of its more ponderous phases depending upon one's previous emotional stimuli.

In what follows I shall pay the endeavor the sincerest compliment in my power by giving it the best thought that is in me. Particularly am I anxious to approach it in this spirit because the first official volumes confirm a sincerely held opinion which I have shared with others, that in spite of significant accomplishments (of which the Chief Justice of the United States rightly selects as the most important collaboration of all members of the profession in joint endeavor for law improvement) the Institute, by reason of the narrow limits of an artificial formula of expression which it has chosen to respect, is rendering its main product of less value than its many important by-products and of less significance than its careful fabrication deserves. . . .

---

Reprinted from *Yale Law Journal*, vol. 42, 1933, pp. 643–644, 650–652, 654–655, 658–662, with the permission of the author and the publisher. When he wrote this article, Charles E. Clark (1889–1963) was Dean of the Yale Law School. In 1939 he became a Judge (later Chief Judge) of the Court of Appeals for the Second Circuit. He was also Reporter for the Advisory Committee of the United States Supreme Court on Rules of Civil Procedure.

From the beginning, the plan seems to have suffered from a vacillation between the two positions that the restatement should announce a more or less binding and final rule of law and that it should be an informed and informing statement of actual legal realities. On the former plan it is subject to the defects of a code with an added question as to the nature of the sovereign authority behind it, but at least it then has the opportunity of boldly forcing reform. On the latter plane it is bound by conditions as they are, but it is realistic and actual. The plan has swung more and more to the former position, but with the important limitation that the *now* law must be stated. In result this has meant the assumption of the chief defects of each position—the rigidity of a code (with the added unreality that it is a declaration unsupported either by a sovereign or by past precedent) and without the opportunity for reform and advance which a code affords. . . .

The subordination of everything else to the black-letter Principles seems to have come from a complete absorption of the Institute activities in their preparation, and this in turn from the steady emphasis by its officials on the necessity of *simplification* of the law by an *authoritative* statement of it. If time and thought were to be devoted almost exclusively to the perfection of the black letter, it seems natural that other matters should be subordinated or neglected. Soon we find the Director complaining of the difficulty and expense of providing Commentaries and the apparent lack of interest in them by the members of the Institute.[1] . . .

The draft now officially presented is apparently the final answer that the Word alone counts, and the long and tortuous way by which the Word was ascertained is to be forgotten. We have only the statement of the distinguished Reporter on Contracts, Professor Williston, that the Council "ultimately decided that increased clearness, brevity, consistency, uniformity and accessibility could best be achieved by putting the Restatement in the form of concise rules analogous to those in a carefully drawn statute." . . .

Simplification as an end in itself is false. Simplification as a clarification and orderly statement of intellectual processes and conclusions is desirable. The idea that there is "the law"—the "common" *nonstatutory* law—of our forty-eight states, our territories and our federal system, which can be stated, is the former kind of simplification. Actually the resulting statement is the law nowhere and in its unreality only deludes and misleads. It is either a generality so obvious as immediately to be

---

[1] [*The Proceedings of the American Law Institute*], pp. 47–50 (1926), contain this illuminating statement, "If I may express a personal opinion, the impression which the Commentaries distributed, taken as a whole, make on me is that matters of doubt and difficulty are not always discussed with sufficient fullness."

accepted, or so vague as not to offend, or of such antiquity as to be unchallenged as a statement of past history.

The other part of the ideal, namely, the securing of authority (i.e., the authority of the Institute) to back up statements, seems equally fallacious. The Institute seems constantly to be seeking the force of a statute without statutory enactment. Bitter experience with code-making in this country should have warned us of the dangers inherent even in statutes. So far as statutes can be made to say something quite definite (for example, to set a rate of interest) they may at least be understood though they may then be too inflexible for general use. When, however, they try to formulate rules which must apply to varying situations, difficulties are many. The code reform of procedure in this country is an outstanding example. Thus the attempt to state rules of joinder of parties in abstract general terms was a failure, and modern reform is in the direction of stating merely a standard and leaving its application to the discretion of the courts. But after all a statute must mean something because the state stands behind it. Therefore the courts must construe it, and a body of statutory interpretation grows up, which is more important than the original wording of the statute. To this the restatements ought not and cannot look forward. There is no sovereign power behind them to compel the courts to breathe meaning into them. If they do not seem to have meaning the courts should turn to something else and are doing so.

The process of statutory interpretation, though inevitable, is difficult and full of pitfalls. The restatement interpretation is an unreality. And without interpretation, or *background* against which meaning can be discovered, the black-letter statements are not understandable. The idea that words speak for themselves, without interpretation in the light of the circumstance under which they were composed or arranged, has been too often exploded with reference to wills, contracts and written instruments generally, to be believed again with respect to the restatements.

A restatement then can have no other authority than as the product of men learned in the subject who have studied and deliberated over it. It needs no other, and what could be higher? Given freedom of expression to such men, it will stand or fall of its own strength or lack thereof. In such event, I would have no doubt of its survival. I would have such doubt, however, if their studies and deliberations are to be concealed as they are under the present plan. It seems designed to take away the intellectual strength which a collaboration of this kind should present. . . .

[The problem] . . . of stating ancient history as modern law is strikingly illustrated by an example from the Restatement of Property. In the first section of actual restatement—after the two chapters of definition of terms—the old common law rule in all its fierceness is stated—that an estate in fee simple can be created by deed only if words of general inheritance ("and his heirs") are used, and the statement is clamped down by illustrations that grants "to B forever" and "to B in fee simple" create only life estates in B. From special notes both to this section and to an equivocal black-letter, thirty pages on, dealing with statutes (special notes, I believe, do not survive to permanent publication) it appears that this rule has been abrogated in all but seven jurisdictions by statute and in three of these seven by judicial decision. This leaves at most only four jurisdictions to which the dogmatic black-letter can apply. Now this is not a result which the Property group desired. They all supported the statement of the Reporter: "That such a rule is at the present time a socially undesirable one, that it represents a survivorship of the formalism of the earlier days of the common law, is of course undisputed." A majority of them, however, felt themselves forced by the rules of the Institute to the stated conclusion—a conclusion, it is submitted, patently absurd.

Such a problem could hardly arise in this stark manner, anyhow, because it would be affected by other facts and circumstances such as entry in possession, payment of consideration, and the like. Moreover, the law now offers facilities for carrying out the obvious intent of the parties even where imperfectly or mistakenly expressed; and it is not conceivable that a deed would not now be reformed if necessary to achieve the purpose of both parties to it. In fact the Property advisers did insert a section stating that such a deed "may be reformed to carry out the intention of the parties"; but this was stricken out by the Council on the ground that this was Equity *and not* Property! . . .

Perhaps even more important as showing the direction of the wind are the judicial citations of the various restatements. Parts of the published material have been in existence in printed form since early in 1925, and the personnel of the membership is such as to call it to the attention of courts at once. There has already been a substantial number of citations to the several restatements, although not as many as one might suppose from the nature of the project. But there have been enough to disclose the very definite trend. It is that the restatements *are furnishing the impeccable judicial citation* with which to garnish an opinion and that they are not affecting the course of decision in any material way, nor in a way comparable to texts and articles of law professors.

The use of the citation is apparently of two forms. The first is the general reference as a jumping off point for the opinion. It is here that the obvious and bromidic sections seem to come to their own. The second is as the last of a string of citations, usually of local cases, thus showing that the local rule has outside support. It is interesting, however, in these contract cases to see the use made of other authorities, notably of Williston on Contracts. It does not seem too much to say that while the courts cite the restatement, they quote, discuss and follow Williston. One cannot read these cases without seeing the demonstration that the courts, *for the difficult points,* need and look to discussion and analysis, not formal statements. . . .

## A REVIEW OF THE PROPERTY RESTATEMENT  By Myres S. McDougal

IN A world where funds and capacity for and interest in legal scholarship are limited it seems not unfair to criticize a great research organization for its choice of aims—especially when the announced aim is a will-o'-the-wisp that can lead only to subsidized snark hunting. To assume that the judicial handling of property problems in contemporary America can be made more predictable by an authoritative canonization and rationalization of ancient, feudal-conditioned concepts and doctrines . . . is little short of fantastic. If the investigations of fact indispensable to reform "cost a lot of money and take a lot of time" there is all the more reason why an institute embodying the best resources of the nation should undertake such studies. . . .

It is only when the Restatement of Property is measured by what needed to have been done that its shortcomings become oppressive. . . . What students, young and old, of the subject need is a comprehensive, genetic history of the ancient concepts, a delineation of how they came to be what they are, both their literary history and the social conditions that brought them forth, and a careful, informed assay of their adequacy to achieve certain commonly accepted social ends of our day. . . .

Recognition of this need appears in various comments throughout the Restatement. Perhaps it is not too much to hope that the *Restatement* may be but a prelude to more penetrating studies and to more effective social action. A few years ago the then President of the Institute stated a novel conception of its function. "It may be very helpful," Mr. Wickersham said, "to state what is a recognized principle of law in such clear and distinct form that its bad nature becomes apparent." More recently

---

Reprinted from *Illinois Law Review*, vol. 32, 1938, pp. 513–515, with the permission of the author and the publisher. Myres S. McDougal, Professor of Law at Yale Law School, has written widely on Property and International Law. Two of his more recent publications are: McDougal and Associates, *Studies in World Public Order* (1960); and McDougal and Feliciano, *Law and Minimum World Public Order* (1961).

Professor Shimes has written: "If this statement of obscure and complicated rules is to be of social value, it should be followed by legislation correcting the difficulties which have been discovered." Through its efforts to effect certainty the Institute may—strange fate—find itself initiating a movement to promote change.

# THE RESTATEMENTS AS THEY WERE IN THE BEGINNING, ARE NOW, AND PERHAPS HENCEFORTH SHALL BE    By W. Barton Leach

[AFTER SOME LIGHTHEARTED COMment on the ways in which the Restatement enterprise had helped professors to see the country, Professor Leach continued in a slightly more serious vein.]

My worthwhile thought No. 2 is along a somewhat different line. It may perhaps be best expressed by the statement that the finest thing about the Restatement as it now stands is how different it is from what it started out to be.

In the first fresh flush of enthusiasm the accepted notion was that the Restatement would stand on its own authority. It would give no reasons; it would cite no authority; it would state no history; it would concede no doubt or divergence. There was to be no law but law, and the Institute was to be the prophet of law. The black-letter was to be law because we said so, and that was that. There were two precedents for this general attitude toward things and they had varying degrees of success. The first was in the Book of Genesis. Someone said, "Let there be light"; and this went off very well, or so it is reported. The second was the familiar case of King Canute—and in this instance command and dogmatic assertion were not so successful. If the Institute had persisted in merely saying "Let this be law," history would have repeated itself one way or the other —and, loving the Institute as I do, I am just as glad that we never found out which way. Of course, it was one thing in the Restatement of Contracts and quite another thing thereafter. Williston could say "This is

---

Professor Barton Leach, of Harvard Law School, delivered this speech at the Annual Dinner of the American Law Institute. It is reprinted from the *American Bar Association Journal*, vol. 23, 1937, pp. 517–521 with the permission of the author and the publisher. Professor Leach is the editor of several casebooks on Wills, Property, and Future Interests, and is coauthor of the *American Law of Property* (1952).

law" and everyone outside the walls of the law building at New Haven would believe it. But it was not clearly foreseen in those early lush days that the supply of Willistons was distinctly limited—that sooner or later it would be necessary for the Institute to appoint X as Reporter for this and Y as Reporter for that, finally getting down to Leach as a Reporter for Property.

So, little by little, it became visible to the naked eye that something more than dogma was requisite.

(1) First came the Explanatory Notes—the first suggestion that what appeared in the black-letter was not carved in marble above the clouds of Mt. Sinai but was the resolution of some very human conflicts arising from very human sources. Of course these were to be read only by the chaste eyes of the members of the Institute; but sooner or later it was inevitable that someone would think they were pretty useful and argue that they should pass into the Restatement. This inevitability came to pass in what I shall later refer to as the Battle of Explanatory Notes.

(2) Next came the Special and Statutory Notes—reminders that what the Institute said wasn't so in many places—indeed, with reference to one section of the Property Restatement, wasn't so anywhere except in South Carolina. These got into the printed volumes, not without struggle, but at least without bloodshed.

(3) By this time the camel was obviously getting substantial portions of his anatomy into the tent. So it was no great surprise when the Introductory Notes were approved. There was no particular limitation to the function of an Introductory Note except that it be introductory—and a liberal constructionist could crowd quite a bit into that word. So, as things turned out, these amorphous organisms proved to be great instruments of progress in the hands of so inflexible a pursuer of flexibility as Professor [Richard R. B.] Powell [of Columbia, a principal reporter for the Restatement of Property].

(4) Then came the Rationale comments—where the Institute concluded that it was not *infra dignitatem* to give the reasoning upon which the rule of the black-letter was adopted. This was a great step; for it changed the Restatement from a dogmatic to a rational basis. The Institute undertook to persuade rather than command, and thus made itself a part of the process that has always been the foundation of the common law and its greatest safeguard against perpetuated error. This was the great change; though it was somewhat less dramatic than the next.

(5) This was the pronouncement that the historical comment was kosher. In the historical comment—*mirabile dictu*—it became permissible to cite cases, provided only that they were very, very old cases. The Yearbooks would slide through without a murmur; Coke's Reports were

considered respectable; Vesey, Jr., was suspect; but decisions since 1850 were definitely taboo.

(6) Finally came the Battle of the Explanatory Notes. Nearly all of the Restatements had had Explanatory Notes, containing citations of conflicting authorities on doubtful points; but up to the Property Restatement there had been no serious attempt to issue these to the public in the published volume. Dick Powell, however, thought the Explanatory Notes should be included; the Director thought otherwise. After a long series of sit-down strikes by Powell and lockouts by the Director, they finally got together in a room for a definitive negotiation and closed the door. The privacy of this conference is one of the great tragedies of all time; for it must have been something to observe. Joe Humphreys ought to have been there to start it off; "In this corner, William Draper Lewis, the mildest man that ever murdered an adjective or scuttled a noun, that world-famous genius at saying offensive things inoffensively. He is not to be confused with the Detroit Bomber; he comes from the Philadelphia branch of the Lewis family. In that corner Richard R. B. Powell, that—what shall I say—that hesitant, deferential, retiring, obsequious, soft-spoken master of the art of understatement." Well, after a tense period they emerged from the room, looking rather like John L. Lewis and Walter P. Chrysler; and they had with them a formula. The formula was this:

Clause 1. No Explanatory Notes were to be published.

Clause 2. About 99 44/100 per cent of what was in the Explanatory Notes was to be published under other forms. Most of it was bootlegged into the text directly in the shape of historical comments, with names of cases, citations of cases and quotations from Blackstone, complete with wheels. Some went into Special Notes, also with case references. And the rest went into what were known as Monographs at the end of each volume. These looked like Explanatory Notes, smelled like Explanatory Notes, acted like Explanatory Notes—but were not Explanatory Notes because they were Monographs. The way you could tell was that they appeared in the printed volume after the Index, rather than before it. They were in the Restatement but not of it.

Practically all this development has taken place within the last five years. Simultaneously with it there was progressing a work whose usefulness and importance cannot be overestimated—and by this I refer to the State annotations. State decisions were being collected and correlated to the Restatement, so that lawyers, taking the Restatement as a starting point, could find the local cases the necessity for which no Restatement lacking legislative force could obviate. So now we have in increasing quantity, linked directly to the Restatement, the case authority which the

Restatement shunned for ten years and now lets into the official volume only grudgingly through a few side doors.

So the Institute has traveled a long road since 1923. And it is right that it should. The early hope that dogmatic assertion by the Institute might replace history, authority and reason as the basis upon which American law is built has never been realized. As things developed it became clear that what was originally referred to corporatively as the statements of the Institute were really statements by groups of school teachers; for by necessity the basic work of the Institute has to be done by the Reporters and the Advisory groups. And while school teachers are a good deal better in the field of politics, I as one of them do not deplore the fact that the American Bar seems not to be ready to substitute decisions by professors arrived at *in abstracto* in the retirement of the conference room for decisions by judges arrived at *ad hoc* in the presence of the contending vital forces of the court room. We have our appropriate and very useful functions; but they are in aid of the traditional processes of the common law, not in substitution for them. Privileged as we are to devote large portions of our time to the study of a single field of the law, we are in a position to suggest the applicability and, what is often more important, the limitations of history, to indicate the impact of analogies and to point out the distinction between reason and fallacy from the longer perspective of a view of the subject matter as a whole. Auxiliary functions these, not substitutional functions—functions in which you, as the body of the Institute, participate by checking our natural tendencies to become hyperacademic and by giving the weight of your authority to the conclusions which we reach and you approve.

From the austerity of the Contracts Restatement to the varied forms and expanded substance of the current Restatements has been an evolutional process. Introductory Notes, Special Notes, Statutory Notes, Rationale Comments, Historical Comments and Monographs—all these have crept into the picture without much fanfare of trumpets. The rule of the Contracts Restatement has been whittled away here, distinguished there, but never reversed. Of course, this is all in ancient tradition of lawyers; but we are not forced to be thus traditional. If the Supreme Court of the United States can frankly overrule the Adkins Case we can frankly overrule the Williston Case. I may say that no one is more in favor of such a reversal than Mr. Williston himself.

A fair question presents itself: Would such an express reversal of Institute policy be a futile gesture in view of the fact that the policy has already been in effect reversed by devious and indirect means? My answer is, No. For if it were once frankly recognized that the Institute now is offering a Restatement which is visibly supported by history, reason and authority, certain action would be obviously indicated.

In the first place some residual corollaries of the older notion would be abolished.

One of these is the extremely irritating bylaw that we can never adversely criticize a rule which we find we have to state. Such a bylaw presents a very unpleasant dilemma to a Reporter. He must either state a good rule which he knows perfectly well is not the law; or he must state a bad rule and by his very statement entrench it further.

The choice between these disagreeable alternatives is made now one way, now the other. For example, in § 160 of the Property Restatement the Institute has taken the position that when a person attempts to transfer a right of entry for condition broken (of course, those of you who are loyal members of the Institute won't know what that is until I tell you that it's the same thing as a power of termination) the right of entry is destroyed—a senseless rule for which there never was a justification. And this is put forth in the same language and with the same apparent approbation as the rule that a contract must have consideration or a seal. There she stands, sanctified for all time as far as the Institute has the power of sanctification. On the other hand there is § 240 which states as the common law that a legal contingent remainder in land is valid though it fails to vest before the termination of the preceding estate—a statement which ranks with the declaration in the New Republic by the eminent dean of Northwestern Law School that the sit-down strike is legal. A hope of his, perhaps, as the contingent remainder rule is a hope of ours; but sheerest bunkum as a judgment. The vice of such statements by Dean Green in the New Republic and by ourselves in the Restatement is that some trusting soul may believe it, rely on it and find himself on the wrong end of a criminal prosecution in the one case or an action of ejectment in the other. I don't feel qualified to tell Dean Green what he could have done instead. But I can tell the Institute: state the rule as we know it to be; state that it's a bad rule; state that courts which have adopted it have overlooked its inapplicability to American institutions; and point out the grounds upon which a court would be justified in ignoring it. When the essence of the Restatement was dogma, it was plainly a contradiction in terms to declare that our dogma was bad dogma. But with the passing of the dogmatic basis, we can freely admit that law is not perfect just because it is still law.

Perhaps another way of expressing this same idea is to say that the abolition of this corollary bylaw will allow the Restatement to depict the law as dynamic rather than static. To state on a dogmatic basis rules of law which are in a state of flux is just as realistic, and no more realistic, than a still photograph of a horse race. The picture may show the horse with all four feet in the air and his nose just a foot short of the wire; but when you see this picture in the Sunday sports section you have a pretty good hunch that the horse isn't still in the same position. So with the Restatement. It began by showing the law as completely static—"stopped" as the news photographers say. Then the historical comments were introduced, showing the evolutionary processes of the past out of which the present rule arose. It is too obvious for argument that the companion to the historical comment, and perhaps the most useful thing the Institute can produce, is the critical comment indicating the probable and desirable evolutionary processes of the future.

It is true that the statutes amending the common law which the Institute is preparing in cooperation with the Commissioners on Uniform State Laws are designed to meet this difficulty. But they can succeed only in part and in a rather small part. Most of the situations in which it is desirable that the Institute should express its disapproval of existing rules are those in which the rule is either a small one, not important enough to justify legislation, or in which the rule is less a rule than a constructional tendency, not appropriate to remedy by legislation. To rely on such statutory projects alone is to ignore the great potentialities for flexibility and progress which exist within the framework of the common law. It will be an evil thing if the Restatement tends to retard those processes. It will be a splendid thing if the Restatement accelerates them along desirable lines.

You will observe that the bylaw whose repeal I have just been advocating, and which would necessarily be repealed if there were a frank avowal that the credo of the Institute has been amended, is a bylaw which applies to the reverse situation—that is, where we are stating a rule which we believe to be sound but which is opposed by a substantial body of authority. The current official position is that we cannot recognize the existence of the opposing view and therefore, of course, cannot discuss means by which its application can be minimized so that the preferred result will be reached in most cases. Here is another corollary to the old dogma of Institute infallibility that we should joyously push off the Tarpeian Rock.

Let me point out how the present bylaw works. We have declared in the Property Restatement that legal contingent remainders in land are indestructible. Without treading on any controversial ground concerning this matter I can say that there are several things upon which everyone is agreed:

1. That the rule as we have stated it is the preferable rule as a matter of principle;
2. That the opposite rule exists in many states;
3. That where the opposite rule exists there are six or eight ways in which the operation of the rule can be so minimized that there is precious little left

of it when competent counsel, aware of these devices of minimization, are on the job.

Certainly one of the most useful things we could have done was to point out what these devices were and thus reduce to a minimum the cases where the opposite rule actually produced an opposite result. Mr. Powell had done this very expertly in an Explanatory Note; but this material was one of the casualties in the Battle of the Explanatory Notes. So the reader of the Restatement in whose state it is settled that the opposite rule applies, finds a statement that is completely untrue in his jurisdiction and obtains no help in solving the problem which his local law presents. Of course the *reductio ad absurdum* of this Institute bylaw comes when we deal with some subject where all states have taken a position and where there are two or three views about equally well supported—as in the case of the division of dividends between life tenant and remainderman in the Trusts Restatement. We select one of the positions, elaborate it fully; but give no indication as to what the other positions are or how they are applied.

We do this, too, in the face of the long-established practice that if the opposing rule is only statutory we can state what it is in Comment and cite the statute with some discussion of cases construing it in a Statutory Note or a Special Note. Why judge-made law should be thus discriminated against is beyond my powers of comprehension.

Naturally the aspects of a frank avowal of a change in Institute policy which loom large to me are those which are of particular importance to a reporter and adviser. Beyond this I do not presume to speculate in detail. I suppose that, for one thing, Restatements already published would be implemented with the rational, historical and authoritative materials which have been approved in later Restatements—and I understand from the Director that this is contemplated at such time as reprinting becomes necessary. I suppose also that there would arise in a new form the question whether the extensive and unique memoranda of law prepared by the Reporters should be published by the Institute or whether the Institute should collect all state annotations into a single volume for the use of the profession.

To me the essential aspect of the present situation is that we are well on the road to recovery from a pretty serious institutional Jehovah complex; and the important thing for us to do is to admit it, nay proclaim it, to ourselves and to the world. Nothing but good can come from such frankness with ourselves and with those whom we serve.

# NEW LAW IN THE RESTATEMENTS  *By Harrison Tweed*

[AT THE 1957 ANNUAL MEETING OF the American Law Institute, Harrison Tweed, Esq., President of the Institute, made the following statement.]

I have said that the effort of the Institute is to state the law as it has been laid down by the Courts, and not to state the law as the Institute thinks it ought to be. I find that the original organizers of the Institute dreamed dreams of stating what the law ought to be, and of really going ahead and telling the courts what they ought to do. But apparently the more conservative minds joined the group, and the decision was that that should not be attempted.

I must admit that when two years ago we started in on the Second Restatement there were those who had a little adventure in their souls and they thought that perhaps it would be interesting to branch out and make a little new law. But we restrained ourselves; we felt that, after all, the record of the past when the First Restatement was brought out was such that we had better not take any chances on new methods of procedure, and that we would continue in the old tradition.

I think it is very much to the credit of those who work for the Institute, particularly of the Reporters, that they have adhered to that tradition; that they do not state law unless they can find that law in the decided cases.

I have noticed that there have been several instances in which the advisers to the Reporters have urged the statement of a principle of law when there were no cases to support it. I don't mean that they have urged that that be done when there were cases against it, but merely that in the absence of cases the advisers to the Reporters were disposed to break new ground and state their own concept of what the law should be. The Reporters have been very conscientious and have refused to do this.

---

WILLIAM DRAPER LEWIS' ACCOUNT of "How We Did It," *supra*, brought the story of the American Law Institute up to 1945. After that date the activities of A.L.I. continued and expanded; this further activity included the preparation of important

Reprinted from *American Law Institute Proceedings: 34th Annual Meeting*, 1957, pp. 39–40, with the permission of the publisher. Harrison Tweed, Esq., is a partner of the New York law firm of Milbank, Tweed, Hadley, and McCloy.

uniform statutes and revision of certain of the Restatements. This further development is outlined, and some of the criticisms of the Restatement process are answered, by Judge Herbert F. Goodrich, who became director of A.L.I. in 1947.

# RESTATEMENT AND CODIFICATION

By Herbert F. Goodrich

IT IS interesting to speculate upon the answers which the enthusiastic David Dudley Field and his withering critic, Mr. James Carter, would have made in 1923 to the American Law Institute's proposal to restate the common law. Would Mr. Field have thought the proposal for restatement a pale and bloodless substitute for his plan of codification of the law? Would Mr. Carter have asserted that an attempt at restatement, so far as it succeeded, carried with it all the evils which he felt inherent in codification, or, as an alternative, that the plan was a futile gesture destined for failure? The answers we can never know. Certain it is that the elder statesmen in the Institute, like Mr. Root, Mr. Milburn, Mr. Wickersham, were alert to dispel the suggestion, which was not infrequently offered, that the proposed restatement was a plan for codification under another name. Perhaps they heard the echoes of the nineteenth century controversy still ringing in their ears and wanted to avoid the reopening of that battle. At any rate, the position they took was clear in their minds; they were not going to codify the common law. They were to improve and clarify it by restatement but what was to be done was not and did not look to codification. That proposition was iterated and reiterated for more than the score of years which passed between the beginning of the work in 1923 until the appearance of the last volume of the Restatement in 1944.

*Restatement of the Law Versus Codification.* This same desire to avoid even the appearance of codification showed itself in the great concern expressed by some, both on the floor of the general meeting and in the council, when they felt that a reportorial group had gone further in the statement of a given rule than the decided cases warranted. "We are not restating the law as we would like to make it, but as it is," was the

---

Reprinted from *David Dudley Field, Centenary Essays*, edited by Alison Reppy (New York: N.Y.U. School of Law, 1949), pp. 241–250, with the permission of the author and the publisher. Herbert F. Goodrich (1889–1962) was Dean of the Law School of the University of Pennsylvania and in 1940 became a judge of the United States Court of Appeals for the Third Circuit.

shibboleth. It was not always realized that even the acceptance of this criterion left a good sized area for the exercise of judgment. Anyone who works in the law knows the difficulty often encountered in determining just what a decision or a line of decisions does establish in terms of a generalized rule. Even more problematical is the implication of the decisions to related but distinguishable sets of facts. And when confronted with opposing lines of authority upon one question, it was obvious to the most timid that here a choice had to be made. The law could hardly be clarified by stating it two ways. The restatement of the law "as is" presented a standard for guidance, but a standard the limits of which were, in the nature of things, somewhat elastic.

*Methods Used in Producing the Restatement.* Whatever the theory, the work of restatement went on. The services of leading scholars from the law schools were enlisted as reporters. They called to their assistance as advisers groups of interested and learned men from the schools, the bench, the bar. Drafts were written, worked over, criticized and amended by the conscientious and experienced members of the Institute's Council, debated with interest and vigor by the membership of the whole body in meeting assembled. Funds to finance the work were provided by the generosity and highly competent understanding of the trustees of the Carnegie Corporation. Volume by volume the finished product appeared and was duly published and distributed to the legal profession throughout the country.

*Acceptance of the Restatement by Bar and Bench, and in Legal Education.* That the undertaking has been a success is no longer a matter of debate. The work has found acceptance. It is used by lawyers in briefs and office memoranda. It has found favor with the courts—if use is a test. And what other test can one offer for the acceptance of a work which was intended for the use of the profession in its day-to-day work? The forthcoming supplement to the volume on the Restatement in the Courts shows 15,197 citations to the Restatement in the various subjects by the courts whose decisions appear in the National Reporter System. How many more there are in judicial opinions not so reported we have no facilities to discover.

The Restatement has likewise found its place as a useful tool in legal education. Law teachers have used it in classrooms as a supplement to the presentation of law problems through their casebooks. Law students have studied its black-letter text, its comments and its illustrations. Law students are critical people and the result of their years of analysis and judgment have benefited those responsible for the reexamination of the product which was finished last year.

Thus the venture which seemed to everyone a bold one at the time of its inception and to some persons a futile, if not a foolish one, has proved a success. The organization which undertook it has become a powerful and beneficent force for public service in the law. Many distinguished lawyers have taken part in it, important contributions have been made by scores of them. For whatever has been accomplished, the enterprise and those benefited by it must always be appreciative of the vision, courage and industry of William Draper Lewis, Samuel Williston, and Joseph H. Beale.

*Relationship of Restatement to Field Codes.* Just how far apart is this Restatement of the common law from the code proposed by Mr. Field? The question raised now is not the accuracy of the substantive rules contained in the Field Code as contrasted with the Restatement, but the theory or principle behind the job to be done. A code has been described as "an orderly and authoritative statement of the leading rules of law on a given subject." (Ilbert). The object of the Restatement one may find stated by the then director, Dr. Lewis, in the preface he wrote to the first volume of Contracts, which was also the first volume offered as a finished product. It is there said: ". . . in order to clarify and simplify the law and render it more certain, the first step must be the preparation of an orderly restatement of the common law. . . . The function of the Institute is to state clearly and precisely in the light of the decisions the principles and rules of the common law."

Note that there are at least two common assumptions made by codifiers and the Institute.

One is that there are such things as rules of law. There are those who deny this, or at least give the impression that they deny it, and insist, or give the impression that they insist, that lawsuits are decided *ad hoc*, and that the mouthings of the judges are but the ritual intoned while the real business is done on considerations wholly apart from ritual. For such persons either codification or restatement could be regarded as a harmless if tiresome form of intellectual exercise, as far away from the business of life as the logic of medieval scholasticism. This is not the place or occasion to thresh over this well seasoned straw. In law, as in life generally, either some assumptions must be made, or some questions once critically considered and answered must stay answered for a while at least. One cannot examine all the basic premises of life or law every day and have time for anything else. We may, for purposes of discussion here, assume the existence of general rules of law. If that assumption is erroneous, it is at least a common basis of error for one who would restate as well as for him who would codify.

*Second,* codification assumes that some rules are more important than others. It is, according to our definition, the "leading" rules which are to be reduced to statement. The general principle that mental tranquility is to be protected against intentional invasion in the form of threatened bodily contact may find expression as a code principle. The rule that one may be liable for pointing an empty gun at a victim who does not know the thing is unloaded may be left to the common sense of the court which is informed of the general principle.

The same distinction will be found, in varying degrees of sharpness, in the various volumes of the *Restatement*. Principles or general rules (choose whichever term seems preferable if there is a difference) may be found in black-letter statement; comment gives the explanation of why and how far they go; illustrations give the answer in concrete illustrative cases.

Now let us go back again to our definition. Codification is an "orderly and authoritative statement." The adjective "orderly" need give us no concern. It may not, with regard to a room in a home, mean the same thing to a sixteen-year-old girl as it does to her mother, but it is not likely to raise differences among those who would arrange the rules of law in systematic order.

The dividing word between the processes is of course "authoritative." Upon whose authority is code or restatement to rest? It would be taken for granted, would it not, that a code has the force of government behind it, whether that force be exercised by the emperor Napoleon or the legislature of the state of Idaho. The authoritative source of the code is that of the lawmaking body of the state where it is promulgated. The *Restatement* has no such backing. It was submitted to the legal profession on its own merits as a good piece of work, the merit vouched for by the professional standing of those who did it. If an advocate thinks the Restatement was wrong as applied to his case, he can urge the court not to follow it, but to apply some other rule. If the court agrees, it will do so, but it will do so with the knowledge that the rule which it rejects has been written by the people who by training and reputation are supposed to be eminently learned in the particular subject and that the specialists' conclusions have been discussed and defended before a body of very able critics. The presumption is in favor of the Restatement and the course of decision since its appearance shows that the presumption is very seldom overthrown. Yet it can be overthrown and that fact leaves Restatement acceptance to persuasion. It is common law "persuasive authority" with a high degree of persuasion.

*Knowledge of Common Law as Acquired by Work on Restatement— Prevalence of a Common Law Throughout the United States.* We have learned a great deal about the common law in our experience with restating it. Some of what we have found is directly contrary to the premises of the nineteenth-century codifiers and contrary also to certain assumptions made by the promoters of the Restatement at the inception of the work. The most important modification we have had to make was that which had to do with inconsistencies and contradictions as to rules of law among the courts of the various states. Nearly everyone thought such contradictions existed; even in advisers' meetings there was frequent talk by members to the effect that the rule in their states differed from the statement proposed, however accurate the rule as drafted might be as a general proposition.

An analysis of state annotations tested the truth of the inconsistency notion. The Institute suggested to state and city bar associations that they analyze their local decisions with a view to ascertaining in what instances the local decisions were in accord with the Restatement, in what opposed, and how large was the area in which there were no local decisions one way or the other. The response to the suggestions that such annotations be prepared was generous. Research men in many states went to work; finished annotations duly appeared. When a good-sized batch of them were published we looked them over to learn the score. There were a surprising number of gaps in the decisional law in every state. By this is meant that there were many propositions in the law of a given subject which were considered important enough for black-letter statement upon which there was no local authority. This was unexpectedly true even in a state with a long judicial history, as in Pennsylvania, and in such a much litigated subject as Contracts.

The next thing the survey showed was the deviations from the common law as expressed in the Restatement were very infrequent indeed. In general agreement ran between 95 and 98 per cent. The following table shows the [percentage] breakdown in more detail:

|  | Accord | Contra | No Local Authority | Doubtful |
|---|---|---|---|---|
| Agency | 61.9 | 1.4 | 35.8 | 0.9 |
| Conflict of Laws | 48.8 | 2.6 | 47 | 1.6 |
| Contracts | 69.3 | 2.6 | 26.4 | 1.7 |
| Property | 47.9 | 2 | 49.2 | 0.9 |
| Torts | 50.1 | 2.5 | 46.4 | 1.0 |
| Trusts | 60.3 | 1.7 | 37.1 | 0.9 |

The conclusion reached following this study is that there is in fact a common law which prevails throughout the United States. The legal principles are sometimes buried under a mass of verbiage and inaccurate language. After all the lawyers who put on black robes and sit on judicial benches cannot oftener than now and then transcend the limitations of their own abilities and training. A careful restatement, which is the kind of restatement all of us hope that this one is, will clear away that verbiage and bring the accepted principles and rules to the easy understanding of those whose business it is to know and apply them. That the Restatement does. It is more important to find that we have a country-wide common law and to put it in understandable and usable form than to find that we do not have such law and try by a *tour de force* to create it.

There is one more item to mention relative to this point before one passes on to something else. The statement has been made that deviations from the consensus of common-law rules in any one state would not run more than five and probably would average 2 or 3 per cent. That is small. But every navigator and every surveyor knows how a course or a line which varies that much from accuracy will bring him out if the erroneous course is carried a considerable distance. So here. Confusion and lack of uniformity can grow and develop as further instances present themselves. Departure from accustomed common-law principles can grow wider and wider, just as common law itself develops doctrine in its growth from precedent. It may well be that a restatement can and will have the effect of smoothing out accidental variations which in the future might become the means of confusion and uncertainty.

*The Restatement in Retrospect—Reexamination of Original Conclusions—Rejection of Theory that Restatement Would Restrict Future Growth of its Law.* In 1946 and 1947 the Institute looked back over the material covered in the Restatement. It had been fourteen years since the first volume of Contracts had appeared. What, if anything, had happened in the course of decision since that time which called for a change in or addition to what had been said when the Restatement in each subject was published? The original Reporters, so far as they were available, were called back into service. If they were no longer living, as in the case of Professor Beale and Professor Bohlen, one of the advisory group was asked to take the laboring oar. The correctness of original conclusions was assumed. The new question was whether, in the view of the course of decision since, prior conclusions must now be modified, or new propositions added. The method of work was the same as before. The decisions were examined and reexamined. The advisory groups, largely composed of the same persons as before, met and threshed over the proposed changes suggested by the reporter. These amendments and additions were in turn worked over by the Council and the membership of the Institute. Some of the proposals were adopted, others rejected. But through the changes which were adopted, the Institute expresses its view of the law as of now.

This re-examination was illuminating in many ways. It gives light on the interesting question: how fast does the law change. In three subjects of the Restatement the course of decision was not thought to call for any changes, even by way of addition. These were Agency, Restitution and Security. In all of Contracts but two changes were required. In Trusts it was necessary to amend only two of the black-letter statements and in

Property five; there were other modifications of the comments and illustrations, some by way of amplification of stated principles because of new decisions but interestingly enough many, if not most, were prompted by legislation and governmental regulations since the appearance of these two Restatements.

Torts brought some changes and additions. This subject is, perhaps, the most rapidly developing area in the common law. Emotional disturbance without impact, the liability of the seller or manufacturer of chattels; these and other questions growing out of urban mechanized life are constantly before courts. The rapid growth in a decade and a half called for additions to a statement correct at the time but incomplete later. Such changes were made.

In Conflict of Laws and in Judgments we also have growing changing law. But we also have the effect of the decisions of the Supreme Court when the questions involve the application, most often of the due process and full faith and credit, or less frequently, of other clauses of the Constitution. A fair-sized number of changes were offered and adopted in Conflict of Laws, several in Judgments. Of the former only one was a common law question. It was the legal capacity of a wife to acquire a separate domicil regardless of the marital propriety of her conduct. The other additions and changes come from constitutional-law decisions, involving in the main problems of jurisdiction of courts over both individuals and corporations. There is rapid development here with new decisions, court rules and statutes constantly being checked for their constitutional validity. Jurisdiction for divorce as every lawyer and some laymen know (or at least a man named Williams does) has been reexamined and rewritten. The decisions bind all courts and certainly a restatement is inaccurate if it does not show their effect. So, too, with regard to judgments—*res judicata* as to jurisdictional facts, the effect of a workmen's compensation award upon the assertion of the subsequent claim. All this is Conflict of Laws, yes, but also constitutional law by a court whose word may change, but until it does we are all bound by it. It seems too clear for argument that a restatement which is to reflect the law of the land must bring in such changes as these. They were of course included. The finished product will be available this fall.

This process of revision has showed the conclusive answer to those who said that restating the law would constrict it and prevent future growth. Some of us always thought this fear was fantastic. Courts find their way out of the bonds of restrictive statutes; witness the development of the law under the statute of frauds or the penalities against usury. If that is what happens to rules backed by legislative sanction, is it not to be expected that those declared unofficially by fellow judges and lawyers should be given less finality? It was always said by those responsible for the Restatement that all they hoped to do was to give the profession the correct rules up to time of publication. The Restatement said "This far." It did not say "This far and no farther." And courts, whose members really do have a fair amount of common sense, have not felt there was any implication of "no farther" either. Places where the law is alive and rules are developing continue to abound in new growth. That is as it should be. Examination of the course of recent decisions shows that what should be and what is are the same; a rare phenomenon in an imperfect world. The Restatement provides the fertile field for new growth; it does not impede it.

The Restatement venture has come out very well. It has provided an orderly statement of the law with emphasis on principles. This statement has not had to wait for legislative action to make it effective. Indeed its authority was able to work into the law even while the drafts were still in tentative form. But the authority being persuasive, not imperative, there is no feeling of constriction. The way is open for growth and the courts have followed it. Perhaps Mr. Field would be content.

One more point and the comment upon the Institute and codification can be concluded. All the discussion hitherto has been about the Restatement and common law. The bulk of it is acceptable and satisfactory. It grows slowly but it grows fast enough to keep up with the needs it fills. What we need to do here is to understand it, keep it in order and encourage its growth and change where needed.

*Collateral Benefits Resulting From the Restatement—The Code of Criminal Procedure—The Code of Evidence—The Code of Commercial Law.* But by sticking to restatement for the bulk of the common law the Institute has certainly not taken the position that codification which includes a large measure of change is not desirable elsewhere. Simultaneously with the preparation of the Restatement there was drafted a Code of Criminal Procedure. It picked up reform legislation from statutes throughout the country and with additions combined the current thinking into an orderly statement of rules from a modern point of view. It is now included, in whole or in part, in the legislation of many states and was a valuable source of assistance to the draftsmen of the federal rules who carried simplification even further.

The Institute has written a Code of Evidence. It was felt that restatement here was futile; this body of law did not need a tonic but a surgeon's knife. This it got. What will happen to the patient we do not yet know. But the operation was a highly successful one. Whether this Code will receive wide adoption we cannot yet foretell. But it is serving as the pattern for many, many law students of what the law of evidence ought to be. It is going to have great influence upon the law whether it is adopted or not.

At the present time the Institute is drafting, along with the National Conference of Commissioners on Uniform State Laws, a Code of Commercial Law.[a] Why? There are several reasons. The subject is one where the courts have had to have legislative help. We all remember that it took the Statute of Anne to force negotiability for promissory notes. We have had codification here ever since the English Bills of Exchange Act, which was followed in turn, by the Negotiable Instruments Law. Finally, even with the adoption of modern rules hastened by the swifter process of codification over case law development, the new rules themselves tend to become inadequate or obsolete. Business changes as communication becomes more rapid, goods more plentiful. Commercial law must expand and where necessary change to provide the rules for the new ways by which business is done. That is what the Institute and the Commissioners seek to do through the proposed Code.

*Conclusion.* An unfriendly critic perhaps could say on the basis of this, that the Institute does not know what it is doing. One day it opposes codification, the next it makes friends with the other side and helps write a code. Can it not make up its collective mind, or is it that it does not know what it is doing? So could the criticism run.

The answer is as clearly right as the criticism is unsound. It is all summed up in that famous Holmes dictum that the life of the law is not logic but experience. Common law judges and common law lawyers are practical men. If common law rules are adequate and work, they leave them alone. If they do not keep up, resort is had to legislation to supply the defects. The change from one to the other does not involve a discussion of grave philosophical considerations. It is made because it is thought necessary. It is continued so long as it produces desirable results. This has been the method of the Anglo-American law. In following the same course the Institute has been true to its common law ancestry.

---

COMMENT. *Continued Activity.* In the twelve years following the foregoing review by Judge Goodrich of the American Law Institute's history and principles, the Institute has opened up new fields for further work. As Judge Goodrich noted, in 1946 and 1947 the creators of the Restatements looked upon their work and saw that it was good—subject only to the need for a few supplements and corrections which were to be completed by 1948.

But a different point of view soon prevailed, and in 1952 the Institute began a full-scale revision of the old restatements so they could retain

[a] Later called the Uniform Commercial Code. An initial version was completed in 1952 and promptly was adopted in Pennsylvania, effective July 1, 1954. By 1964, revised versions of the Code had been adopted in over half the states.

"the characteristics of living law"; the new product will be called Restatement, Second. The Institute began with the Restatements of Trusts, Agency, and Conflict of Laws. In view of some of the criticism of the dogmatic flavor of the Restatements which has appeared in the preceding pages, one significant change must be noted: following the black-letter rules, the completed editions of Trusts and Agency contain references in a separate volume to A.L.I. annotations and to the key numbers of the American Digest System. Work continues on Restatements, Second, for Conflict of Laws, Torts, and, most recently, Contracts. The Institute has also begun an entirely new project to restate the Foreign Relations Law of the United States, with the help of foreign legal experts.

In recent years, a larger share of the work of the A.L.I. has been directed to projects with legislative potential: the drafting of uniform or model laws, and studies which could lead to legislative action. Of the model codes and statutes, the Model Youth Correction Authority Act has been adopted by Congress and by five states; legislative activity has lagged since 1951. The Model Code of Evidence is continuing to play the academic role that Judge Goodrich foresaw in the foregoing essay. The Uniform Commercial Code has been adopted in over half the states. The Model Penal Code was completed in 1962. Some parts of the tentative drafts are already successful, having been either cited by courts or embodied in state legislation. The Institute and the tax liaison committee of the American Bar Association have combined into a study group to consider legislative reform of the tax statutes. Since 1952 they have completed reports on the Income, Estate, and Gift taxes, the Income Tax Problems of the Corporation and Shareholders, and a study of Capital Gains. The newest A.L.I. project is a study of appropriate distribution of jurisdiction between federal and state courts and of proposals for federal legislative change.

Other cooperative efforts of the A.L.I. and the A.B.A. have resulted in a program of Continuing Legal Education which encourages and assists in creating national, state, and local groups to conduct regular planned educational projects for members of the bar. The organization also publishes and sells handbooks on practical legal problems and procedures.

*Further References.* Debate over the restatement phenomenon has produced delightful polemic writing, as vigorous as it is instructive, which limitations of space have unhappily excluded from these materials.

Judge (then Dean) Goodrich opened one lively round with an article entitled "Institute Bards and Yale Reviewers," *University of Pennsylvania Law Review,* vol. 84, 1936, pp. 449–466; Thurman Arnold replied in kind with "Institute Priests and Yale Observers—A Reply to Dean Goodrich," *University of Pennsylvania Law Review,* vol. 84, 1936, pp. 811–824.

Other materials on the Restatements and the American Law Institute include the following: Clark, "The American Law Institute's Law of Real Covenants," *Yale Law Journal*, vol. 52, 1943, pp. 699–738; Wickersham, "The American Law Institute and the Projected Restatement of the Common Law in America," *Law Quarterly Review*, vol. 43, 1927, pp. 449–474; Lewis, "The American Law Institute," *Journal of Comparative Legislation and International Law* (3rd series, part III), 1943, pp. 25–30; Yntema, "The American Law Institute," *Canadian Bar Review*, vol. 12, 1934, pp. 319–350; Goodrich and Wolkin, *The Story of the American Law Institute* (St. Paul, Minnesota: A.L.I., 1961); Franklin, "The Historic Function of The American Law Institute: Restatement as a Transition to Codification," *Harvard Law Review*, Vol. 47, 1934, pp. 1367–1394; Milner, "Restatement: The Failure of a Legal Experiment," *University of Pittsburgh Law Review*, vol. 20, 1959, pp. 795–826.

Too irreverent for inclusion even in such a book as this is a mock "Restatement of the Law of Constitutional Law—Proposed Tentative Draft No. 1" by the late Professor Thomas Reed Powell, "Reporter." This "Restatement" was printed in the Harvard Law Revue [sic], vol. 1, no. 1 (1932), pp. 5–12.

*Part Two*

# LAWMAKING INSTITUTIONS

CHAPTER 5

# The Judge

WE HAVE ALREADY SEEN SOME OF THE forces which led to the peculiar importance of judges in the development of Anglo-American law; this phenomenon will be the more striking after the examination in Chapter 9 of the role of judges in continental civil-law systems. To be sure, there are signs of a trend in this country toward reliance by judges upon scholarly works organizing and criticizing the law, a development which suggests the tone of our judicial work early in the nineteenth century as well as of continental law. (Compare pages 68 and 78, with Chapter 9.) But even if this trend enlarges, the judge will retain his crucial position in our legal system. It is he who chooses between tradition and change, and in introducing change determines its direction and speed. The most intricate statutory structure can be mangled by inept judicial hands. Perhaps most important, the trial judge's ability and personality shape the determination of the "facts" to which the rules are applied, and finally decide the rules themselves in the multitude of cases which cannot be appealed.

Everyone agrees that we should have "good" judges. But what are our criteria of quality? In reading the materials which follow it may be helpful to consider the relative importance of the following: (1) *Intellectual ability:* The capacity to read a statute or opinion with understanding, and to apply facts accurately to principles; (2) *Integrity:* Character such that a judge's decision is his own and not the response to a bribe or to pressure from a political organization; (3) *Social and judicial outlook:* The judge's response to the competing appeals of property and poverty, and his view of the propriety of judicially reshaping the law in the light of such preferences.

This chapter opens with the story of a dramatic change in the American outlook toward the judiciary, a development which produced attitudes and procedures which are of large importance today.

# THE DEMOCRATIC REVOLUTION IN
# AMERICA, 1830–1850          By Evan Haynes

IT HAS been the opinion of most of the world for a very long time that judges must be selected by some person or group capable of making an intelligent choice; that the exigencies of the judicial function require the judge to be free to perform his duties without fear of reprisal; and that this latter requirement is best fulfilled by giving the judge tenure of office during good behavior.

As presently shown in more detail, this view prevailed in America until about the middle of the last century, when, within a short twenty years, the states of this Union, taken as a whole, abandoned the practice of the rest of the civilized world, and amended their constitutions so as to provide for popular election of judges, to hold office for short terms of years.

Any serious and dispassionate reconsideration of the question how judges should be selected must attempt to determine whether this sweeping adoption of popular election of judges—effected independently in many states under very different conditions and adhered to almost unanimously ever since—was the result of failure of the methods thus replaced, or was the result of other forces, having little or nothing to do with specific problem of the technique of judicial selection.

Consideration of this question makes a brief digression unavoidable: a brief (and perforce inadequate) survey of the struggle for popular control of government that reached a climax all over the western world, in the second quarter of the nineteenth century.

During the Napoleonic Wars, the whole of continental Europe was introduced by force to the radical social and political ideas and institutions of the French revolution; and they have pervaded the development of political institutions ever since. Those ideas, moreover, were not newly invented out of whole cloth by the revolutionists in France, but were the result of some centuries of development. . . .

[T]he forces of change proved stronger than those of reaction; and in 1830 a whole series of revolutions broke out. In France the last of the Bourbons was in that year removed by violence. Belgium, which had

---

The foregoing selection is reprinted from Haynes, *The Selection and Tenure of Judges* (Newark, N.J.: National Conference of Judicial Councils, 1944), pp. 80–101, with the permission of the publisher. Professor Haynes (1875–1955) was a Professor of Law at the School of Jurisprudence of the University of California and was an active member of the bar of California.

been annexed to Holland in 1815, revolted in 1830 and the Powers recognized her independence the following year. Revolutions broke out in several of the smaller German states: Brunswick, Saxony, Hanover, Hesse-Cassel; and constitutional reforms were granted. A number of revolutions broke out in the small states of northern and central Italy in 1831, but these were successfully suppressed by Austria. Poland had been partitioned among Russia, Prussia and Austria; and Russian Poland revolted in 1830, but was defeated.

In England, the impulse for revolt against the old order manifested itself in the reform bill of 1832. Up to that time representation in Parliament had grossly favored the old land-owning aristocracy at the expense of the commercial, financial and industrial classes in the cities. By the reform bill material improvements were made. The cities were given relatively adequate representation and the franchise was somewhat extended, although universal manhood suffrage did not come until later extensions, the final one being in 1918.

The revolutions of 1830, although temporarily successful, were (except in France, Belgium and some of the German states) soon undone. But in 1848, the revolutionary spirit broke out again. In France there had been considerable reaction and withdrawal of the reforms of 1830. Violence broke out early in 1848 and Louis Philippe, who had succeeded the Bourbons as a liberal and constitutional king, was forced to abdicate. Even in Austria trouble arose: revolts in various parts of the empire so weakened the home government that it was compelled to grant a number of liberal reforms at home. In Hungary, after rioting and bloodshed, some of the fundamental principles of liberalism such as freedom of the press and trial by jury were proclaimed, and virtual independence from Austria was demanded and for the time being granted. Bohemia also demanded and was granted a considerable degree of autonomy and a number of the Austrian states were temporarily successful. In a number of the small states of Germany further reforms were demanded and granted; and even in Prussia there were barricades and bloodshed.

In England, where the purposes of the continental revolutionaries had long since been accomplished, the radical movement of 1848 went deeper, taking the essential character of demands for betterment by the laboring class, who on the Continent, were not yet making demands on their own behalf. There was a good deal of armed violence.

Radical ideas which are now familiar but were then new or little known, began to take definite form in this period. The word "socialism" seems to have first appeared in print in 1827, in a publication of the London Co-operative Society, which appropriately was the earliest socialist organization, founded in 1824. In the same year Robert Owen, an Englishman who had made a fortune in cotton manufacturing, bought

30,000 acres of land in Indiana and founded a colony there (which soon failed), organized on what we would call thoroughly communistic principles. In 1819, in his *New Principles of Political Economy*, Adam Smith anticipated the ideas that were elaborated thirty years later by Karl Marx in *Das Kapital*. During the decade following Owen's venture in Indiana, a number of similar communities were established in England.

Returning now to developments in America, the wave of democratic fervor that was sweeping over Europe was felt and responded to by a large part of the American population. To many, the events in Europe seemed the first steps toward adoption by the whole world of the American model of government by the people. There were, moreover, additional factors operating on this side of the water. It was now clear that the American colonies had been successful in their own revolution. They had adopted the ideas of liberty and equality and had made them work. Moreover, they were beginning to realize the unlimited resources of the country of which they found themselves masters. The Mississippi Valley was, after 1815, in their secure control; an area three times that of the original colonies was open to their exploitation. Unlimited development, economic well-being for all, seemed to be just over the horizon. And all this could be attributed to the democratic ideas which had been the justification for the revolution.

But politically the country was still in the hands of a small aristocracy. The war of independence had won political sovereignty, but the essentially aristocratic society that had developed in America during the latter years of the colonial period continued. . . . And this aristocracy had kept a monopoly of political office for generations, and continued to do so after the revolution.

All this contradicted the democratic ideas which the mass of the people had been taught during the revolution to accept as the gospel of America.

Moreover, the creation of new frontier states not only permitted, but forced, the common people to enter into politics, both state and national. By 1830 nine new states had been added to the Union, and by 1850 sixteen had been admitted, all (except Maine and Vermont) on the western frontier. And the population of these new states consisted entirely, or nearly so, of poor and uneducated pioneers. The aristocratic traditions of the old communities on the seaboard simply could not exist, and political offices, both state and national, passed in these communities to men who were indistinguishable from the mass of their fellow citizens.

The West, during this period, was rapidly outgrowing the East in population. Between 1830 and 1850, the population of the country nearly doubled, but the population of the Atlantic seaboard increased by less than one-half, whereas that of the Mississippi Valley and the gulf states increased to approximately two and one-half times what it was in 1830.

One of the most important factors that have determined the speed and direction of all movements in American history is undoubtedly the circumstance that the country was peopled by immigrants who were dissatisfied with the state of affairs in the lands of their fathers, and had sufficient enterprise and courage to take radical and irrevocable action. And more specifically, the activity of English, Irish and Scotch judges was a very prominent part of the cause for the three great waves of immigration from the British Isles. The prosecution of Whigs and dissenters in England in the time of Charles II and James II, the prosecution of Whigs in Scotland in the late eighteenth century, and the prosecutions that arose out of the first movements for Irish freedom in the first half of the nineteenth century, each led to a flood of immigration to America. . . .

It was inevitable that there should be an assault everywhere on the political monopoly of the old upper class. The assault can be said to have begun with the election of Jefferson in 1801. In the years after 1815 substantial progress had been made in New York and Pennsylvania; and in 1829 the new democratic spirit swept into national power with Andrew Jackson.

Another important factor in the victory was the extension of the suffrage and the removal of property qualifications for public office. During colonial times, the requirement that an elector be a freeholder disfranchised few; but as time went on, more and more people did not own land, or did not own enough to meet the suffrage requirements; and agitation for manhood suffrage began almost immediately after the revolution. In 1800 only three states had adopted manhood suffrage, but by 1820 it had been provided for by the constitution of seven other states; and by the time of Jackson's election in 1828, very liberal although not quite universal manhood suffrage existed in all of the states except two of the original thirteen. The new states, as they came into the Union, adopted manhood suffrage as a matter of course.

At the same time that the franchise was being extended, property qualifications for holding office, which existed in nearly all of the original thirteen states (and were very high in some), were one after another materially reduced or removed altogether. Only a few, notably Delaware and Massachusetts, kept even the remnants of such qualifications.

The extension of the suffrage was, to be sure, accomplished only over the vehement objections of most of the ablest men, who defended property qualifications both for voters and for the holders of public office. John Adams, Daniel Webster and Joseph Story of Massachusetts, Chancellor Kent in New York, and Madison, Monroe, Marshall, and Randolph in Virginia, all objected to the change. Daniel Webster urged as obvious, that equality of suffrage and inequality of property were necessarily inconsistent institutions. All of them saw grave dangers in extension of the suffrage; but their protests were almost completely without avail.

The original state constitutions were on the whole rather conservative documents. Only two of them had been submitted to the people, the others being adopted by conventions; but between 1830 and 1850 all but two (Delaware and Arkansas) were required to be approved at the polls before going into effect.

During the period in question the sweep of change to popular election of judges was a mere item in a long list of other democratic and humanitarian changes. Maine abolished capital punishment in 1837, and Vermont in 1842. A number of states abolished public executions, and others the old practice of flogging. Twelve abolished imprisonment for debt, and four abolished it where the debtor surrendered all his property. Seven states established hospitals for the insane before 1850. Maryland abolished forfeiture of estates for capital crimes.

Along with these changes, nearly all public offices were either made elective, or provided with shorter terms, or both; the long ballot became a fact. In the very constitutions whereby judges were made elective, some, and generally many, other public officers, formerly appointed by the governor or by the legislature, were made subject to popular election; and similarly with respect to provisions shortening terms of office. In short, the wave of democratic fervor that was sweeping over the world tended in America to bring nearly all public officers under direct popular control, the judges among the rest.

There were, to be sure, considerations affecting the judges in particular. In the first place, the popular party was able to capture the executive and legislative branches of the government by the ballot alone. As to the judges, however, most of them in 1830 held their offices during good behavior; and other means for gaining control of these offices were necessary. Many of the incumbents were Federalists, and as such both unfriendly and obnoxious to the leaders of the popular movement.

In the constitutional debates and public discussions of proposals to change the selection and tenure of judges there were, of course, particular reasons advanced for the particular change. For example, in Alabama in 1830 and in Maine in 1839, complaint was made that they were enforcing (as of course they were bound to) claims of creditors bearing high interest against needy debtors.

The doctrine of nullification, although it related directly to the federal courts, must have affected people's ideas about courts generally.[a] This doctrine was emphatically stated by a chief justice of Pennsylvania in

[a] It will be interesting to read this account of the nullification controversy in the light of the attacks on the United States Supreme Court after the segregation and redistricting decisions of the 1950s and 1960s.

connection with the case of *State* v. *Cobbett*. The Federal Constitution, he said, is "a treaty made by individual States, as one party, and all the States, as another party"; and as with any other treaty, where parties differ as to its meaning, the dispute must be settled by negotiation, arbitration, or war. He denied, therefore, the power of the federal courts to decide disputes impairing what the state contended were its sovereign rights. The familiar Kentucky and Virginia resolves of 1798 announced the same doctrine. The state of Georgia made it a felony to attempt to enforce the judgment of the Supreme Court of the United States in *Chisholm* v. *Georgia*. The Embargo Act of 1807 roused New England to assert the nullification doctrine, and even to threaten secession if this supposed encroachment on the sovereign rights of the states was enforced. In the same year the Pennsylvania legislature passed a resolution concerning a federal court decision affecting public lands, denying the court's power to adjudicate the controversy. Pennsylvania continued to defy the federal courts for some years concerning other supposed encroachments on its sovereign rights. In one case the United States marshal, seeking to serve process on a federal decree, was met by the state militia called out by the Governor of Pennsylvania.

The Virginia legislature, in dealing with the tariff question in 1829, resolved that "There is no common arbitrator to construe the Constitution of the United States, the Constitution being a federal compact between sovereign states, each state has the right to construe the compact for itself." The nullification argument was again urged in debate . . . on other occasions down to the Civil War.

A striking example of how this controversy led to dissatisfaction with long tenure for state court judges is furnished by the "old court-new court controversy" in Kentucky. In 1821 a case went to the Supreme Court of the United States in which the constitutionality of a Kentucky statute was questioned. The Kentucky legislature resolved that adjudication of such a question by the federal court was "incompatible with the constitutional powers of this state," and did "solemnly remonstrate and protest against any such adjudication." A delegation was sent to Washington to protest to the Court directly. The statute was nevertheless held void.

The Kentucky legislature then proceeded to take up certain Kentucky decisions in which the state supreme court had set aside state legislation enacted for the benefit of debtors; and having resolved that such decisions were "subversive of their, the people's, dearest and most valuable political rights," decided that the justices who had decided the cases in question should be removed. But they held office by appointment for life; and the two-thirds legislative majority necessary to remove them could not be mustered. The legislature, therefore, enacted a statute purporting to abolish the court; and created a new one in its place. But the "old court" refused to submit; and for some years there was hopeless confusion, both courts attempting to function as the *de jure* court of last resort. The controversy became an issue at the next election; the new court advocates had lost ground, and the House was won by the conservatives, but the Senate was still dominated by new court advocates; so the confusion continued. Finally, in 1826, the matter was settled by the passage, over the Governor's veto, of an act declaring that the "people" had decided the statute abolishing the old court was invalid; wherefore it was repealed.

The great name of Thomas Jefferson contributed materially to distrust of the judiciary, and to the idea that popular election of judges for short terms was feasible and desirable. Before he became President, Jefferson strongly favored the appointment of judges, to hold office during good behavior:

The judges . . . should not be dependent upon any man or body of men. To these ends they should hold estates for life in their offices, or, in other words, their commissions should be during good behavior.

But after the decision of *Marbury* v. *Madison,* and his public and personal feud with Marshall which followed, he became convinced that the power thus given to the judges to nullify legislation agreed upon by the Congress and the President, without fear of losing their posts if their action was disapproved, was inconsistent with democratic principles:

It is a misnomer to call a government republican in which a branch of the supreme power is independent of the nation.

After trial and failure of impeachment as a means of removing politically undesirable judges, he decided that the constitution should be amended so as to limit the judges to six-year terms:

A better remedy, I think, (than making the Senate a court of Appeal on constitutional questions) would be to give future commissions to judges for six years (the senatorial term) with a re-appointment by the president with the approbation of *both houses.* If this would not be independent enough, I know not what would be such, short of the total irresponsibility under which they are acting and serving now.

He expressed his views frequently and at length; and undoubtedly did much to turn the tide in favor of the democratic changes in the judiciary already brewing in the states.

He even expressed the view (although without much conviction), that perhaps popular election of judges might be satisfactory:

It has been thought that the people are not competent electors of judges *learned in the law.* But I do not know that this is true, and, if doubtful, we should follow principle.

His savage attack on Marshall also undoubtedly focused attention on and promoted resentment against state judges who held acts of the legislatures void. In a letter of September 28, 1820, he wrote:

You seem to consider the judges as the ultimate arbiters of all constitutional questions; a very dangerous doctrine indeed, and one which would place us under the despotism of an oligarchy. Our judges are as honest as other men, and not more so. They have, with others the same passions for party, for power, and the privilege of their corps. . . . The constitution . . . has made all the departments coequal and sovereign within themselves. . . . When the legislative or executive functionaries act unconstitutionally, they are responsible to the people in their elective capacity. The exemption of the judges, from that is quite dangerous enough. . . . The true corrective of abuses of constitutional power is to educate the people.

A few months later in another letter:

The judiciary of the United States is the subtle corps of sappers and miners constantly working underground to undermine the foundations of our confederated fabric. . . . This will lay all things at their feet. . . . Having found from experience, that impeachment is an impractical thing, a mere scarecrow, they consider themselves secure for life. . . . An opinion is huddled up in conclave, perhaps by a majority of one, delivered as if unanimous . . . by a crafty chief judge.

Removal of politically obnoxious judges by impeachment had been tried in the states also, and a number of such proceedings followed Jefferson's advocacy of this device with respect to the federal judges.

Attempts were made in Ohio in 1808, in Kentucky in 1822 and in New York in the same year, to remove judges for holding statutes unconstitutional. Although all were unsuccessful, impeachment proceedings in Ohio failed in the state Senate by only one vote: nine were for acquittal against fifteen for conviction.

It is said that in one state the legislature, enraged at a decision of the supreme court, reduced the judges' annual salaries to twenty-five cents.

Another factor of some consequence in the movement to bring the judges under popular control, seems to have been the idea that American judges, much more than judges generally, were invested with legislative functions. This idea doubtless arose out of the fact that the common law was, in many states, looked upon as an alien system, which, far from being binding upon the courts, was to be regarded with suspicion. And there being no considerable body of statute law, and very little local precedent, the courts of necessity acted frequently without the aid of controlling authority of any kind. Hostility toward the common law occasionally found formal expression. New Jersey and Kentucky passed statutes forbidding the citation of common law authorities. The judges of the supreme court of Pennsylvania were impeached on the ground, among others, that they had invoked the common law as authority for imposing fines and imprisonment for contempt of court. It is said that toasts like the following were frequently proposed:

The common law of England: May wholesale statutes soon root out this engine of oppression from America.

To the extent that the courts were thought of as entrusted with powers which we should now regard as purely legislative, it was not unnatural to argue that they should somehow be subject to popular control.

Still another important circumstance was the prevailing attitude toward the law and lawyers generally. Immediately after the Revolution, a strong feeling of hostility arose among large numbers of people toward the whole machinery of judicial administration. Although most of the attacks were directed at the lawyers rather than at the judges, the latter also were affected. This wave of hostility appears to have been due to a number of causes. For one thing, a considerable proportion of the more substantial members of the bar had been Loyalists, and had left the country or retired from practice before the end of the Revolution. In the whole of Massachusetts, for example, there were only ten lawyers in 1779 who had been lawyers before the Revolution. The result was that in many communities the level of ability at the bar was not high. Distressed conditions which followed the war led to a great number of actions to collect debts and to foreclose mortgages, against debtors who could not pay. Shays' Rebellion, in Massachusetts in 1777, arose largely out of these conditions, and was directed largely against the courts and the lawyers. Rioters set fire to courthouses in Vermont, and nailed up courthouse doors in New Jersey. In many states there were demands for laws permitting litigants to represent themselves in court; in others complete abolition of the legal profession was demanded.

With respect to the judges, it was alleged, apparently with good reason, that the legislators had used their power to favor their friends and supporters, quite without reference to fitness for office. It was charged in several states that judicial appointments were made in caucus by the legislators of the dominant party; this both in states where the legislature elected the judges directly, and in states where judges were appointed by the governor subject to legislative confirmation.

The growing class-consciousness of industrial laborers undoubtedly contributed to the spreading demand that judges be brought directly under popular control. Up until about 1850, the courts held rather commonly that a combination of laborers to raise their wages was a criminal conspiracy. Following such a decision by a New York court in 1835, the judges were burned in effigy at an open air meeting attended, it is said, by 27,000 workers.

Needless to say there were strong protests against the drift to popular election of judges and abandonment of secure judicial tenure. One of the most eloquent was an address by Mr. Justice Story before the Suffolk Bar in 1821. . . . But the triumphant advance of the popular movement was too strong; and only a handful of states escaped the deluge.

The provisions for judges in the first constitutions varied a good deal in detail, but conformed to one or the other of two types. Since the local assemblies had been the principal champions of the colonial cause during the years before the Revolution, and since the Royal governors had been the principal points of attack, it was natural that the legislatures should be made the dominant element in the new state governments; and in eight of the thirteen states, the judges were elected by the legislature. In the remaining five, they were appointed by the governor, who was himself named by the legislature in a number of states.

Most of the judges held office during good behavior; although in Connecticut they were dependent for continuance in office on the annual legislatures; and in Pennsylvania and New Jersey, held only for short terms of years.

Vermont (which, although not admitted as a state until 1791, adopted a constitution in 1777) has the distinction of being the first to provide for the popular election of judges above the rank of justices of the peace: her constitution of 1777 (modeled in most respects on that of Pennsylvania) provided that the judges of the inferior court of Common Pleas, and the judges of Probate, should be elected by the people, to hold office, however, during good behavior.

In 1802 the inhabitants of Ohio, the pioneer state of the old Northwest Territory, adopted a constitution providing that the judges be elected by the legislature for seven year terms. In 1812 the constitution of Georgia was amended, and the judges of certain inferior courts, formerly elected by the legislature to hold during good behavior, were made elective by the people for four year terms.

In 1816, the constitution of the new state of Indiana was drawn to provide that the associate justices of the circuit courts (the principal trial court) be elected by the people for seven year terms. In 1821 some of the New York judges were for the first time limited to terms of a few years instead of during good behavior; and a few years later similar changes from tenure during good behavior to rather short terms were made in Alabama and Tennessee applicable to all the judges.

By 1845, Mississippi, Michigan and Georgia had each made provision for popular election of some of their judges, in addition to Vermont and Indiana.

But election by the legislature or appointment by the governor still prevailed in most of the states. Only Mississippi had completely gone over (1832) to popular election of judges for terms of years.

In 1846, however, the great state of New York, after prolonged debates, followed Mississippi in providing for the popular election of all judges for short terms.

Within ten years, fifteen of the twenty-nine states existing in 1846 had by constitutional amendment provided for the popular election of judges; and of the states which have entered the Union since 1846, every one has provided that most or all judges shall be popularly elected for terms of years.

In the year 1850 alone, seven states changed to popular election of judges; and thereafter, year by year until the Civil War, others followed.

Immediately following the Civil War, the exigencies of Reconstruction led some of the Confederate states to turn temporarily to gubernatorial appointment of judges, but later they returned to popular election.

In this chapter, an attempt has been made to describe, so far as space permitted, the background of conditions and events and ideas which must be taken account of in appraising the significance of the sudden and radical constitutional changes during this period which produced our system of electing judges and limiting their tenure to terms of years.

It seems reasonable to say that the fundamental causes of that change had very little to do with the relative merits of this or that system of judicial selection and tenure, but were rather the ideas and impulses of a violent swing toward the democratization of government generally. The more mature and seasoned countries of Europe, who experienced the same revolution in government, preserved the idea that judges should be competently selected, and free of political pressure; but in America, the ebullient enthusiasm and intemperance of youth and inexperience carried all before it. Whatever may be the best provision for the judiciary, it seems safe to say that solution of that problem which was adopted in the United States a century ago was arrived at almost completely without regard for the particular considerations of policy and principle which arise out of the nature and functions of the judicial arm of the government.

# COURTS AND POLITICS
# IN NEW YORK CITY  By *Wallace S. Sayre and Herbert Kaufman*

LIKE ALL other governmental officials and employees engaged in the quest for the stakes of political contest, judges and their staffs are both claimants and distributors. The special character of the judicial process sets them apart from those whose primary functions are the formulation and management of government programs, so they are most conveniently treated separately. Nevertheless, they are participants in the political contest, involved as fully as all the others who take part in it. Many individuals and groups expend a great deal of energy trying to influence court personnel (from judges down); judges and other court personnel, in turn, exert all the influence they can bring to bear upon some other contestants when certain questions are to be decided. Judges and their staffs are not without their modes of exercising influence, nor are they invulnerable to the pressures of others. . . .

## Judges As Distributors of Prizes

*As Umpires.* In particular, judges settle disputes—disputes involving money, services, office, reputations, and even life and liberty, disputes between litigants invoking governmental powers to implement their claims upon each other, upon the parties, and upon governmental officials and employees. Judicial decisions thus determine, in part, who gets what. Private citizens and nongovernmental groups may be contending with one another, or they may contest the action, or inaction, of officials or employees at any level of government.

Government officials often bring suit against one another, or, when this is precluded by existing law (the city, for example, is unable to sue the state), may achieve the same effect by staging taxpayer suits. Law enforcement officers of all kinds represent the state in litigation with alleged law violators. Public officials and employees sometimes bring actions against their employers; the city, being a corporation rather than a "sovereign" power, is especially vulnerable to attacks of this kind. Voters,

---

Reprinted from Sayre and Kaufman, *Governing New York City* (New York: Russell Sage Foundation, 1960), pp. 522, 528–34, with the permission of the authors and publisher. Professor Sayre is a member of the Department of Public Law and Government at Columbia University. Professor Kaufman is a member of Yale University's Department of Political Science.

candidates, and party members frequently challenge party leaders—sometimes within their own parties, sometimes in other parties—in the courts. At one time or another, virtually every possible combination of those identified as contestants for the rewards of governmental action appears in the courts. And the judges, in deciding the questions at issue, in effect employ governmental authority in such a way as to allocate some of the prizes. Most of the time, judges are umpires rather than players. But, after all, how a contest comes out depends in large measure on what the umpires do.

*As Interpreters of the Rules.* Judicial decisions often do much more than settle the immediate question in litigation. They often determine the content and scope of the constitutional and statutory provisions earlier characterized as "the rules of the game," and they may sometimes upset state legislation, local legislation (far more frequently), or administrative rules and regulations, instead of merely invalidating a specific governmental act under a particular rule. The way in which judges dispose of election cases has far-reaching effects on the relationships among the parties and especially among the factions within parties. Judicial attitudes and actions of both kinds generally strengthen the positions of some contestants seeking to influence governmental policy and reduce the leverage of others—rarely does an interpretation of the rules of the game affect equally all who are concerned with them—sometimes regardless of what the judges intend or prefer, but effectively just the same. Thus, for example, when the courts construe narrowly the meaning of the phrase "government, property, and affairs of the city" in the Home Rule Act, the Home Rule Law, and the home rule provisions of the constitution. . . . they permit state officers to intervene more extensively in the governance of the city than a different construction of the language would allow. When they ruled that the principle of separation of powers does not apply to governments of cities, they denied to the Mayor powers and immunities associated with the chief executives in Albany and Washington, particularly in his relations with the City Council. When they refused to invalidate inequalities of representation growing out of failure to reapportion the lines of the old aldermanic districts, they buttressed the Democratic majority that benefited from the prevailing situation; when, on the other hand, they refused to hold proportional representation unconstitutional, they strengthened the hands of the minority parties in the city. When they upheld the power of the city, under permissive state legislation, to enact rent control laws, they won the plaudits of the tenants and the condemnation of the landlords, and the net result was to increase the popularity of the Democratic officers who were responsible for the measure. When they declared municipal employees were subject to the federal income tax, the result from the point of view of these persons was a reduction in salary. It has been said the law is what the judges say it is; while this assertion, without qualification, is unquestionably an exaggeration, it reflects the fundamental truth of the proposition that the distribution of rewards among the contestants striving to influence governmental decisions is shaped to a large extent by what judges say the rules are.

*As Appointing Officers.* The 315 judges in or from the city are the formal appointing officers for several thousand employees constituting the nonjudicial staffs of the court system. The exact number of such appointees outside the competitive civil service is difficult to ascertain, but it apparently amounts to some four or five hundred. A relatively small number of appointees, in turn, are themselves appointing officers who formally name staffs of their own.

From the standpoint of salary, prestige, responsibility, and prominence, the most important of the judicial appointees are the County Clerks and the Public Administrators. The County Clerks, appointed and removable by the Appellate Division of the Supreme Court, receive $15,000 a year, except in Richmond, where the County Clerk gets $10,500; as custodians of all the books, records, and papers of their respective counties, and as clerks of their respective County Courts and of the Supreme Court when it sits in their counties, they have substantial staffs of their own. The Public Administrators are appointed by the Surrogates; they administer estates for which, for one reason or another, no other executor is available, and they have employees to assist them. The Public Administrator in New York County is paid $15,000; in Kings, $10,750; in Queens, $8,750; in Bronx, $4,000 and fees; in Richmond, $5,925.

Even the less visible positions, however, are frequently highly remunerative. The Chief Clerks of some of the courts receive as much as $20,000, while many fall in the range from $9,500 to $11,500, and their deputies normally are not far behind. Individual judges frequently have clerks who earn as much as $10,500, and some have confidential attendants in addition who get from $5,000 to $7,000. Three courts have Commissioners of Records in the same salary bracket as the clerks, and the Commissioners' deputies are proportionately well paid. There are also secretaries and law assistants who may be paid from $5,000 to $15,000. At the lower levels stand the clerks to the Justices of the Municipal Court, whose salaries are about $3,800 a year for each, and some courtroom personnel. Many of these salaries are set by the judges themselves, and are mandated upon the city by state legislation. Furthermore, there are numerous appointments as commissioners in mortgage foreclosure which yield substantial fees, as administrators of the estates of persons who die intestate, as guardians, and as referees, all of these quite apart from the appointments to positions on the public payrolls. The judges are thus formal dispensers of jobs and benefits, many of them highly rewarding.

Not all the appointments to public positions are wholly at the discretion of the judges. Most are under the jurisdiction of the city or state personnel agencies, and the appointments must be made from lists of the names of people who have passed a competitive, or at least a qualifying, examination. Party considerations play significant parts in the selection of personnel for some posts. And the necessity of having competent personnel to perform many of the duties incidental to the judicial process is an imperative which cannot be ignored; hence, as a matter of common practice, law clerks in the federal courts, the Court of Appeals, the Appellate Division, and many parts of the State Supreme Court are selected by the judges from the top law school graduates without reference to political recommendations. So the judges are not without restrictions, both legal and practical, on their range of choice. But they are the formal appointing officers in all these instances, and their discretion, if not unlimited, is still quite broad. Their appointing authority places them squarely and prominently in the political struggle.

## Judges As Contestants: The Rewards of Judicial Office

*Honorific Rewards.* Judges do not merely distribute the rewards of politics, however; they also share in them. They occupy places of great prestige; both in the courtroom and outside, they are deferred to by their legal colleagues, by the social groups in which they move, and by the rest of officialdom. Attorneys engaged in trial work constantly feel the weight of the authority of the jurists who sit on the bench above them, ruling on their efforts, controlling the procedure, and occasionally subjecting them to criticism and caustic comments to which they are in no position to reply. Even the most prominent lawyers appearing before the most obscure judges cannot escape the fact that the latter are their superiors in the courtroom. And the habits—indeed, the obligations—of deference accorded by tradition to those who sit in the highest positions in an old and esteemed profession carry over; in court and out, judges are automatically part of the legal élite, and it is not surprising that so many lawyers yearn to sit on the bench. The sense of the majesty of the law and of the judges who represent it is even more impressive to laymen involved in judicial proceedings, even for nothing more important than traffic violations; the robes, the formalities, the authority of these men elevate them to something apart from ordinary human beings. Judges, like physicians, are surrounded by an honorific aura that to many is both awesome and wonderful.

*Salary and Working Conditions.* So, too, are the material rewards. Of the 380 judgeships treated in this analysis, none brings a salary of less than $16,000 a year, and one—the Chief Judge of the State Court of Appeals—earns (including a $5,000 allowance for expenses) $40,000. More specifically, 163 are paid $16,000 or over, but less than $20,000; 59 receive $20,000 or more, but less than $25,000; 38 have salaries of $25,000 or more, but less than $30,000; 91 get $30,000 or over, but less than $35,000; 29 are paid over $35,000. This puts virtually all of them in the highest income brackets in American officialdom, and many of them well above federal cabinet officers, Representatives, and Senators. Moreover, constitutional provisions forbid reductions in the salaries of judges while they are completing a term of office (not at all, therefore, for lifetime appointees while they continue to serve). Finally, many of them are covered by rather liberal pension plans.

Working conditions are relatively pleasant. The work is taxing, it is true, for the strain of intense concentration and heavy responsibility in the courtroom is wearing. Moreover, work in the courtroom is only part of the job; many additional hours are spent pouring over briefs, perusing legal literature, and trying to achieve agreement between litigants in informal sessions in judges' chambers. Still, judges have greater freedom in allocating their time than many other officials. Court sessions do not normally begin until ten o'clock, and are commonly recessed by four in the afternoon. During the summer months, some courts virtually suspend operations, and some have only abbreviated sessions presided over by a small percentage of the full judicial staffs. Vacation periods are generous. Most judges have comfortable offices, adequate professional assistance, and ample secretarial help.

Finally, to a larger extent than most other public officials, judges may be said to be their own bosses. To be sure, there are administrative and procedural requirements they must observe. And they may be assigned by their chief judge to categories of adjudication they find not especially attractive. Most important of all, the opinions of virtually every judge are subject to review by higher courts, and no judge likes to be reversed. Nevertheless, each judge is in full command of his own courtroom, sets his own pace, and is insulated from many of the external pressures and imperatives that sometimes come to control the public lives of other public officials. In an increasingly frenetic, bureaucratized world, this feature of judicial positions is probably sometimes even more alluring than the unusually favorable salaries, hours, and working conditions.

*Tenure and Advancement.* Judges have exceptionally long terms of office compared with other public officials. Just under 50 per cent of the 380 treated here have ten-year terms; over 29 per cent have fourteen-year terms; more than 15 per cent have life tenure. Four per cent have twelve-year terms. Only 2 per cent have terms of less than ten years; the eight judges of the State Court of Claims are appointed for nine years. Thus many judges span several administrations, enjoying a degree of security unmatched by few other elective or appointive officials of comparable salary and stature. Not even the so-called permanent civil servants, few of whom ever attain to salaries even approaching judicial compensation, are, in practice, more secure in their jobs.

A number of informal practices tend to lengthen the already impressive duration of judges' formal terms. The Mayor and the Governor frequently reappoint judges who have satisfactorily completed their terms of service; and both major parties customarily endorse sitting judges running for reelection without regard to party, except in the most unusual circumstances. Consequently, anyone who enters the judicial hierarchy knows there is a very high probability that he can remain as long as he wants. Furthermore, the ranks of the higher courts are to a substantial extent filled by advancement of the incumbents of lower judicial posts; this is true of the patterns of both appointments and nominations. Thus, although the number of vacancies filled each year exceeds what would be expected if every judge served out his full term, this does not mean the position of the judges is fraught with uncertainties. Many vacancies are created by the resignations of judges moving up to higher courts, the retirement of judges who have reached the (state) mandatory retirement age after long years on the bench, and by the illness and death of men who have grown old in the judicial branch. In practice, men and women who enter the judiciary frequently remain there as long as they are able to function and would like to stay. There are, of course, exceptions to this generalization, but it applies to a large number of the judges considered in this chapter.

For some, judicial office is the capstone of a political career. Among the judges sitting in 1958, not only were there individuals who once occupied comparatively minor posts in one or another of the branches and levels of government, but there are also former congressmen, an ex-Mayor, former District Attorneys, a former Borough President, a former Deputy Mayor, and at least two former city department heads. For others, the courts have been primarily safe way-stations on the road to other political offices. In recent years two judges have left the bench to run for Mayor, and others have resigned to accept other appointive offices, or to seek other elective offices. Six of the fourteen men who have been Mayor or Acting Mayor of the Greater City since its formation in 1898 were judges at some point in their prior careers, and several moved directly from the bench to City Hall. Judicial office thus functions as both a fitting climax to a life in politics and as a snug niche in which to bide one's time.

*Bargaining Position.* A further reward of judicial office is the bargaining leverage it affords its incumbents. As referees between other contestants, as interpreters of the rules, and as appointing officers—in short, as distributors of prizes—judges are often in a position to give other people what they want, and they can presumably employ this opportunity to obtain in exchange what they, the judges, want for themselves. Actually, there is little probative evidence that judicial prerogatives and privileges are used for this purpose, although the Seabury Investigation of the Magistrates' Courts in New York in 1932, as well as the exposure of some individual judges in other courts in the past, demonstrate that this was not always the case. Today, however, although surveillance of the courts by professional associations of lawyers and by civic groups has grown more thorough and more stringent than ever before, one only occasionally hears the charge that a judge conducted a trial or decided a case on the basis of a favor done him by one of the litigants or because of a request denied him by one of the parties at suit. There is reason to suspect that practices of this kind occur, but the supposition is unproved.

In the matter of nonjudicial court appointments, things are quite different. There can be little question that (excepting the federal courts and the higher state courts, as noted above) most of the jobs over which judges have broad discretion are filled not so much on the basis of the competence of the candidates as for the value of particular appointments in paying political debts to the party leaders responsible for the judges' election or appointment and in position to affect their future careers. The same is true of the appointment of referees in foreclosures, special guardians, commissioners in incompetency proceedings, and referees to hold hearings. Indeed, it appears likely that many more nonjudicial positions in the court system have been created than are necessary to perform the work of the courts, that many of those who occupy these positions have little idea of their responsibilities, and that some of them never actually report to their duty stations except on payday. Naturally, some of these discretionary appointees are highly competent and hard working, or the judicial system would break down; this is perhaps especially true of merit system appointees under the supervision of the state or city personnel departments. (In the federal courts, where there is a well-developed centralized institution for judicial administration, the standards are particularly high.)

Prominent among the rewards of judicial office, then, stand the opportunities for bargaining that accompany elevation to the bench. Although the powers of judicial decision are not often employed for this purpose, the powers of appointment are, and it will become apparent in later discussion that the use of this bargaining implement is one of the factors accounting for the high rewards in the judicial branch.

## Differences Between Judges and Other Contestants

While judges, since they share in the distribution of the stakes of politics and can use their control over the distribution of other prizes to buttress their own claims and those of their allies, may thus be treated in much the same fashion as other governmental participants in the contest for these stakes, the distinguishing features of the judicial process and judicial institutions must not be overlooked. On the whole, the distinctions between the courts and other governmental institutions and practices are differences in degree rather than in kind. But the differences are sufficiently pronounced to warrant particular attention.

Take, for instance, the Anglo-Saxon juridical principal of judicial independence. This tradition is reflected in the deliberate insulation of judges from many types of control exercised by legislatures and chief executives over other public officers and employees; hence, the security of tenure, the unusually strong safeguards against suspension or removal, the constitutional and statutory bans on reductions in the salaries of sitting judges, and the weakness of overhead agency controls upon the courts. The procedures that keep the other agencies of government responsive and "accountable" to elected legislators and executives have purposely been rendered inapplicable to the courts; they contravene the principle of judicial independence. Some administrative agencies, it is true, achieve substantial autonomy, sometimes by the way they are structured (as, for example, in the case of regulatory commissions, public corporations, and public authorities), sometimes by accident, and sometimes by virtue of the personalities and strategic skills of their leaders. But no other agencies are shielded as are the courts by so many built-in protections, by such strong constitutional and statutory and traditional bulwarks. Even judges are not totally immune to pressure and retaliation, but successful assaults on their redoubt are less frequent. Figuratively speaking, they can follow the dictates of conscience almost to the extent of thumbing their noses with impunity at those outside the judicial hierarchy. Other things discussed in this chapter make it most improbable that they will feel so inclined, but the fact that they could conceivably do so sets them apart from most of their governmental colleagues.

In addition, the formality of judicial procedure, the weight of legal traditions, the ethical norms instilled through professional training and policed in a general way by professional organizations, and supervision of lower courts by higher ones appointed by other chief executives or elected from other constituencies, all combine to restrict the avenues of access to judges and to limit both their opportunities and their willingness to use their decision-making powers for bargaining purposes. Again, this is only a relative proposition; it is not impossible to negotiate with, or bring pressure to bear upon, a judge, but it is rather more difficult to reach a judge this way than to reach other public officials who are regarded, and who regard themselves, as having a primarily "representative" function in contrast with the emphasis on judicial independence.

Taking account of these qualifications (which apply primarily only to the processes of judicial decision and less to appointments by judges), it may be said that the factors identified in the foregoing paragraphs tend to reduce the vulnerability of judges to the pressures of other claimants on the prizes of politics, and to limit (but by no means to eliminate, particularly in the lower courts) the responsiveness of judges to some influences from outside the courts and the legal profession.

The distinctions between judges and other participants in the contest for the rewards of politics can easily be overdrawn. All the participants have much in common, and judges are participants. But it is important to bear in mind that the independence of the judiciary is one of the central values around which our court system is organized, and that judicial procedure is less flexible, less hidden from scrutiny, more circumscribed by expectations of neutrality and impartiality and by the traditions of the legal profession, than most of the other institutions involved in the governmental process.

## Courts and The Parties

*Incentives to Party Workers.* The court system provides much of the fuel for party engines. It is true, as noted in an earlier chapter, that many party workers are satisfied with relatively nominal material rewards. But almost invariably, predominant among the ranks of those who give unstintingly of their time and energy and money to their party are lawyers striving for positions on the bench, and both lawyers and nonlawyers endeavoring to establish claims on other court posts. On the one hand, this enables the parties to recruit, hold, and motivate a large body of willing, industrious, and often able workers in their cause. On the other hand, it helps the parties maintain a measure of discipline in their ranks and among officeholders who owe their positions to their respective parties.

Positions in the court system are not the only ones furnishing motivations for party workers, of course. But one must climb to the highest echelons of the executive branch in any level of government before the scale of remuneration begins to approach that which obtains for even minor judgeships. In the legislative branch, with the exception of Congress, salaries do not compare at all (although the pay of city councilmen, relative to the time and effort their jobs require, is exceedingly generous though less than half in absolute figures of the pay of a city magistrate). At the same time, judges need not be concerned, except at long intervals, about the ordinary vicissitudes of politics or the recurrent financial crises and economy drives that sometimes sweep other public officials and employees from office or result in cuts in pay. Furthermore, as noted earlier, even many nonjudicial employees of the court system—County Clerks, court clerks, judges' clerks, and Public Administrators, for example—commonly receive salaries rivaling those of bureau chiefs and Deputy Commissioners and far exceeding the pay of local and state legislators. For jobs of this kind, people are willing to work and wait, to accept the onerous chores of party activity, to fill for a time less prized posts and less rewarding ones, and to follow their leaders. The unusual attractiveness of court system emoluments thus plays a large part in the maintenance of party organizations.

Not only does the judicial system provide strong incentives, and in relative abundance, but it does so on a continuing basis. In the first place, 322 of the entire 380 judgeships (and 286 of the 315 occupied by New York City residents) have fixed terms, and the terms are staggered so that part of the membership of each such court comes up for reappointment or reelection annually; each year, therefore, some vacancies are sure to occur. In the second place, despite efforts to keep the number of expirations roughly equal each year, retirements, deaths, resignations, and the intermittent addition of new posts disrupt the regularity of the cycle and increase the actual number of vacancies to more than the expected number. (Retirement at the end of the year in which a judge turns seventy is mandatory under the state constitution. Furthermore, elevation to the bench often comes relatively late in life. Still further, since judgeships are, as observed earlier, convenient positions from which to wait for still greater opportunities, there are voluntary resignations.) Thus, from 1947 to 1957, a total of 500 vacancies—a figure far in excess of mathematical prediction—were filled in the 380 places. With as many as 40 to almost 50 openings a year, it is not difficult to advance many judges to higher courts and simultaneously to introduce 15 or more deserving and qualified party workers into the judiciary. In any four-year period, this source of high-level jobs is likely to prove richer than any other; the legislative and executive branches help keep the parties going with many lesser rewards, but they provide fewer big prizes. The plenitude of choice jobs in the courts increases enormously the ability of party leaders to reinvigorate the loyalties of the congeries of Assembly District and clubhouse organizations of which the parties are composed. District Leaders play key parts in the accession to office of both appointed and elected judges, and they work hard for their parties in order to justify their claims to as many of these positions for their followers as they can. One factor holding the parties together despite powerful centrifugal tendencies is the number of judicial offices available, which helps the County Leaders placate every area and every unit of their parties in the long run.

The profusion of court positions also facilitates the satisfaction of many demands by religious, ethnic, and national elements in every party in the city. Dealings of this kind are neither clandestine nor unconscious. Party officers have testified to seeking out Irish or Italian or Jewish candidates for appointment or election to judicial office, and, more recently, Negroes and Puerto Ricans have begun to take their place in the judiciary. The demands are overt; ethnic groups have high regard for the prestige of the courts, and for the opportunities for professional and social advancement offered by judicial offices. The efforts to satisfy these demands are candid. This does not mean there is any formula for the automatic partitioning of the prizes, or that there is any mathematical balance among the claimant groups. On the contrary, the calculus of adjustment is intricate, so that one or two high judicial offices allocated to one group may offset the nomination of a member of another group for executive or legislative office, or the appointment of a member of another group to an administrative position. The number of judgeships thus permits the parties to diversify the basis of their electoral strength.

It also enables the parties to reconcile individuals politically eligible for high office, who, denied a top spot on a ticket, might decide to run independently or negotiate with the opposition. And it gives party leaders a chance to repay the loyal party workers who cannot easily be given more prominent positions. (Thus, for example, two former Mayors—Hylan and Impellitteri—accepted judicial posts after being denied renomination for the mayoralty.) Moreover, a judgeship is sometimes a convenient way of neutralizing a District Attorney or other law enforcement officer whose zeal in his enforcement practices offends important party supporters.

The attraction and the number of judicial offices is probably one reason for the abundance of lawyers in politics. Even without the stimulus of positions on the court, politics would probably become the vocation of many lawyers. Their skills equip them to perform the legal services of which the political clubs and their members seems always to stand in need, their profession often allows them to allocate their time as they see fit, and their training tends to encourage the versatility needed for negotiations among contending and competing individuals. If they are partners in large law firms, they may continue to share in the profits of the firm although they direct the major part of their energies to their political pursuits (partly because these often work to the financial benefit of the firm). When to all of this is added the allurement of numerous, highly valued judgeships for which only lawyers are eligible, the magnetism apparently becomes almost irresistible. So lawyers come eagerly to politics. Except for the general requirement that every judge be an attorney admitted (from three to ten years earlier, depending on the judgeship) to the bar of the state, the statutes are virtually silent on the professional qualifications of judges. Nevertheless, professional legal standing is always requisite, thereby removing nonlawyers from competition for many of the best positions the political system can offer, and putting on this occupation a premium that brings its practitioners to the parties.

Added to the judgeships themselves are the remunerative appointments as referees, guardians, administrators, and executors of estates mentioned above. There are enough rewards of this kind—particularly in the hands of the Surrogates—to make working for the parties worthwhile.[1] Even lawyers with small hopes of becoming judges themselves are thus drawn to the parties. But, it must be added, the hope of becoming a judge does not die easily in those who once set their sights that high.

While the incentives of judicial office appeal particularly to lawyers, they are important also to nonlawyers in the parties. As noted earlier, the courts employ, in addition to judges, several thousand individuals to perform the work of the judicial system. All but several hundred of these are in the competitive civil service. These hundreds add substantially to the reservoir of rewards party leaders can use to attract and motivate followers, and it is not unlikely that at least a portion of the classified positions are filled by the party faithful through manipulation of the provisions of the Civil Service Law. Some of this patronage is used by some judges to provide employment for relatives and personal friends. By and large, however, the judges accept the recommendations of District Leaders in filling the choicer posts. Indeed, many District Leaders and County Chairmen themselves have found well-paid judicial clerkships a convenient source of income to sustain them while they perform their demanding party services. The New York State Crime Commission reported that in 1952, 29 per cent of the 199 District Leaders of both major parties in the city were employed in the court system, and that 38 per cent of them were either serving at that time or had served there in the past. Al-

---

[1] Indeed, it has been said that control of the Surrogates in New York County sustained the Democratic party in the county during the lean years of the thirties. The long terms of the Democratic Surrogates elected prior to the accession of Mayor La Guardia saved these positions for Tammany Hall in the defeats it suffered at the polls in that period. With the rewards thus available to its supporters, it was able to hold itself together despite the fact that it was displaced in City Hall, cut off from federal support by President Roosevelt (whose nomination Tammany fought in the 1932 Democratic National Convention), who favored Edward J. Flynn's Bronx organization, and was treated coldly by Governor Lehman (who identified with the Roosevelt-Flynn alliance).

though most of the jobs entailed legal work, almost three quarters of the District Leaders holding them were not lawyers. A more recent study by the Citizens Union of the clerks to the resident Justices of the Supreme Court alone revealed that more than one third are District Leaders or County Chairmen, with both parties being well represented. District Leaders are not the only party functionaries to find sources of personal income in the court system; Captains and other organization workers are also frequently employed here. However, the fact that so many District Leaders are employed by the judiciary is a rough indication of the importance to the parties of nonjudicial posts in the court system, and the District Leaders constitute only the visible segments of the iceberg, no studies having yet been made that penetrate much below this level. But there is little doubt that the grip of the parties on judicial patronage is quite firm. Indeed, there are instances on record of judges submitting to demands by some party leaders that they discharge the secretaries in their employ and replace them with appointees suggested by the faction in ascendancy. So it is not just the judiciary per se that makes the court system important to the parties; rather, it is all that goes with the judgeships as well as the judgeships themselves that helps the parties build and maintain their organizations.

*The Judicial System as a Source of Party Revenue.* A man who wants to be a judge must normally be a party insider, and, in addition, must be prepared in many cases to donate substantial sums of money to the organization of the appropriate party leader whose influence will be the chief factor in his nomination for appointment or election. This practice obtains even when the aspirant has worked long and hard for his party and is well qualified for the post. And he is expected, once in office, to contribute generously to his party in its fund-raising campaigns.

Some District Leaders can apparently extract as much as a year's salary plus an additional "campaign fund" of several thousand dollars.[2] For *elective* office, the amount is frequently set on the basis of a fixed sum (from $50 to $100) for each Election District in the judicial area. The smallest of these territories, Municipal Court Districts, normally encompass between 145 and 180 Election Districts, and the prospective candidate is therefore expected to furnish up to $20,000 over all. The charges are higher for judgeships on higher courts having larger constituencies. Practically no reliable evidence is available on the finances underlying judicial *appointments*, but since it is demonstrable that the appointing chief executives tend to rely very heavily upon their party functionaries to supply them with the names of men to be appointed to fill judicial vacancies, it is possible, if not probable, that similar practices prevail.

[2] It is rumored among lawyers that there is a "going rate" for judgeships, currently the equivalent of two years' salary for that office.

Not much is known, either, about what happens to payments of this kind. By and large, it would appear that the District Leaders take a substantial part of it themselves for their own and party uses, and divide the remainder among their workers in the Election Districts. This is apparently regarded in party circles as an ordinary part of the revenues of the District Leader and of the party workers in the field; presumably, for shouldering the burdens of party work, and for their services to their parties and to their candidates, the members of the party hierarchies are widely regarded as entitled to this form of party resource and personal compensation. Most candidates for elective office, and even for appointive office, outside the judiciary as well as in it, give money to their respective party units for putting forth their names and assisting them in their quests; in addition, some of the money donated by the general public for election campaigns ends up in the hands of local party personnel. In this fashion, the party organizations manage to "pay" their regular "staffs." A substantial part of this recompense comes from those who would like to be judges.

Moreover, since those who attain the bench or nonjudicial court posts generally seek to strengthen their chances for advancement and to ensure that, if they are not promoted, they will at least be renominated or reappointed at the expiration of their term, they can almost always be counted upon to contribute generously to all fund-raising efforts and to heed the advice of their party mentors in matters of appointment and perhaps even of decision.

Like all organizations of the modern world, parties need money to operate. Clearly, one of the primary reasons the court system is of such profound concern to the parties is that this is where a part of their money comes from.

*Protection of Party Interests.* In one additional and final respect, the court system is important to the parties. In the Supreme Court, where many decisions about electoral conduct and procedure are in practice decided (though subject to appeal which infrequently materializes), judges who are beholden to party organizations will probably be less sympathetic to challengers to party discipline and authority than would critics of "machine politics." The method of selecting judges greatly reduces (if it does not preclude altogether) the likelihood that party organizations will often be confronted with hostile judges. The pattern of judicial rulings interpreting Election Law provisions governing designating and nominating procedures and the use of party names by insurgent groups in any of the parties seem to bear out this inference. So, too, do other more isolated decisions in other courts—as, for example, a magistrate's dismissal of the charges against members of a Democratic club who were arrested for gambling and for using loud and boisterous language. The magistrate ruled that "political organizations are to be allowed to meet without interference." Admittedly, the evidence that the party obligations of the judges are controlling in these cases is far from conclusive, and there are certainly important judgments one would not anticipate on the basis of party loyalty. Many other elements, which the judges themselves do not control (such as the working of statutes), are operative here. Nevertheless, one reason the parties display such deep interest in the judiciary is that their own organizational security rests to a significant extent in the hands of the judges.

*Parties and Judicial Selection.* Except perhaps for the highly skilled court jobs, such as court stenographer, nobody gets one of the better judicial or nonjudicial positions in the court system without going through party channels.

When a judicial appointment, whether for a full term, the remainder of a term, or until the next election, is to be made by a chief executive, the usual procedure is for the County Leader in whose territory the court sits (or who is acknowledged by other County Leaders as a result of some earlier bargain to have first claim on the filling of the next vacancy) to determine which of his District Leaders is entitled to nominate the appointee for this post. An able County Leader generally succeeds in balancing the distribution of these prizes among his constituent units so that his decisions are accepted by his party subordinates. While most County Leaders manage well enough in this regard, even the best of them may run into strong objections from clubs that feel they have been victims of discrimination or neglect. When this happens the County Leader may relieve the tension by promising future openings to the offended groups, or by reallocating the existing vacancy to the plaintiffs and mollifying the deprived groups with a lesser prize, or with the promise of a better one in the future. Occasionally a group of District Leaders may get together and agree among themselves on the distribution of nominations and appointments; in such cases, their County Leader commonly endorses their decision. Once agreement is reached in one fashion or another, the name of the candidate is put before the appointing executive, who, in most cases, promptly appoints the organization choice. The procedure is roughly the same in each of the major parties, whenever it has captured the office of the chief executive at City Hall, in Albany, or in Washington, while the third parties can hope at best to be granted one or two places (for which their own party hierarchies, like those of the major parties, select the candidates) in return for their support in the elections—particularly in close elections. (Only the highest federal positions seem to be more or less exempt from these practices.)

The hold of the inner cores of the parties on nominations for elective judgeships is, as was noted in the discussion of the nominating process, equally strong, if not stronger. Almost all the nominations made by the rank and file of the parties in direct primaries are dominated by the Assembly District Leaders in each jurisdiction; the primaries are little more than ratifications of the individuals the Leaders select. For Municipal Court nominations it is primarily the Leaders whose Assembly Districts fall within each Municipal Court District who bargain with each other and arrive at decisions on their slate of nominees. For the County Courts (including the Court of General Sessions in New York County), the City Court, and the Surrogates, it is the County Executive Committees, made up of all the Assembly District Leaders in each county, negotiating with each other and with their County Leaders (who are occasionally overruled by coalitions of their District Leaders), who are chiefly responsible for the choices. The county committeemen routinely go along with the Leaders, and the voters in the parties are seldom offered alternatives in the primaries, although the contests are usually energetically fought when they do occur.

Similarly, the nomination of candidates for the Supreme Court by party conventions in each of the Judicial Districts of the state is controlled by the County Leaders in those areas; the convention delegates almost invariably accept the names presented by them. Even the nominees for the Court of Appeals, selected by the state conventions of the several parties, are chosen largely by bargaining among County Leaders from all parts of the state. (As a result, at least three or four of the justices are virtually certain to come from New York City, the remainder from upstate and suburban sections.) In short, no part of the judiciary, however high, is divorced from the parties.

The parties are important, too, to those who seek to or do occupy nonjudicial offices in the court system as well as to judges. Most judges maintain amicable relations with their party sponsors (past, present, and future) by employing their discretion in making appointments to install in office people recommended by District Leaders, which, as noted above, frequently means appointing the District Leaders and County Chairmen themselves, among others. Indeed, one judge is reported to have been so assiduous in satisfying claims made upon him by a District Leader that he accepted the Leader's recommendation for every appointment without regard to the qualifications of the candidates, and then found himself compelled to engage competent assistants at his own expense. Appointed court officers with appointive powers of their own adopt in the same manner and for the same reason their party organizations' suggestions as to whom to select. It may therefore be said that nearly everybody in a more important position in the court system owes his position in good part to the support of some party functionary, and that even some holding lesser posts (probably including a number of posts nominally protected by Civil Service Law and regulations) are similarly indebted.

Few are the aspects of government in which the influence of the parties is never felt at all. Nowhere in government, however, is that influence more pervasive and profound than in the court system.

*Judicial Election Campaigns.* Candidates for elective judgeships find the parties especially important to them because of the character of judicial electoral campaigns. For one thing, campaigning has somehow come to be considered inconsistent with the dignity and the duties of judicial office—a rather strange myth in the light of the way judicial candidates are chosen, but one that helps obscure the realities of judicial politics from the eyes of many voters and that is therefore scrupulously observed. Candidates for judicial office do not ordinarily make "political" speeches, do not appear regularly at campaign rallies and demonstrations, or engage in the usual campaign practices designed to bring candidates into personal contact with as much of the electorate as possible; indeed, the statements of campaign expenditures by judicial candidates generally (and, in a technical sense, no doubt accurately) show no personal outlays. Barred from the opportunity of applying their own energies and talents and personalities to their own election, the candidates for judgeships are forced, even more than colleagues running for places in the other branches of government, to rely on the established party machinery for vote-getting. The "citizens' committees" that spring up to promote the election of a particular candidate are occasionally made up of persons who for professional or personal reasons are willing to work for his victory. Far more frequently, these are merely the parties in other guises, establishing these auxiliary associations to avoid legal limitations on campaign expenses, to obtain donations from people reluctant to give money to political parties themselves, and to exploit the myth that their judicial candidates have independent rather than merely partisan support. Organizing in this fashion is not by itself sufficient to guarantee election, but lack of it is enough to make defeat virtually certain in a close contest.

In the second place, nominees for judicial office commonly enjoy the endorsements of both major parties; this is one of the reasons for their security of tenure. Originally, the custom of joint nomination apparently applied only to judges who had completed a full term on the bench. Judges appointed to fill vacancies in an elective court until the next election, and candidates running for judicial office without any prior service in the positions at stake, ordinarily encountered an opposing candidate from the other major party. Over the years, however, the parties began to make bargains with each other involving temporarily appointed incumbents and even nonincumbents, so that many more candidates for judicial office make their runs uncontested than the "sitting-judge" tradition would lead one to anticipate. For example, twice since the end of World War II, more than 80 per cent of the judicial seats to be filled by election were won by candidates having both Republican and Democratic nominations. On the other hand, there is nothing fixed about this ratio, the number of joint endorsements by the major parties having fallen as low as 2 out of 14 elective judgeships in 1952. Indeed, in one case in 1955, another in 1956, and two in 1957, one or the other of the major parties refused to endorse an elected sitting judge renominated by the other party and instead put up a candidate of its own. The number of dual nominations clearly depends on a great many delicate adjustments. This point is underscored by the bipartisan deals behind the creation of new judicial posts. In 1931, 12 new court positions were created in the Second Judicial District. None of them, however, was contested in the election. Democratic leaders agreed to endorse Republican candidates for 5 of the 12 new seats in return for Republican support in getting the Republican-dominated state legislature to establish the positions, and the Republicans in the Judicial District completed the bargain by endorsing seven Democrats for the remaining seven vacancies. A similar understanding underlay the passage of bills in 1956 creating new seats on the Supreme Court in the First, Second, and Tenth Judicial Districts. This measure was opposed by Mayor Wagner (allegedly on the grounds that the city would be unable to finance its share of the additional costs) and Governor Harriman vetoed it, but a new agreement between the parties dividing the seats (by joint endorsement) resulted in the establishment of seven additional seats in the Tenth District in 1958. Since bipartisan endorsement makes election a certainty, and since it also depends upon agreements reached by the County and District Leaders of the regular party organizations, every judicial candidate doubtless awaits tensely the outcome of negotiations regarding his own situation. He cannot help being aware that the decision is his party's and not his to make. Candidates from districts that are strongholds of their own party need not, of course, worry about this phase of the electoral process. In doubtful districts, and in districts where the opposition party is in firm control, what the party functionaries do is of deep concern to the candidates.

In sum, aspirants to elective judicial posts, after having surmounted the obstacles to nomination, are not freed from dependence on the parties for the attainment of their objectives.

*The Emoluments of Office.* Since World War II, judicial salaries have risen rapidly. In large measure, this must be ascribed to inflation and to the widespread consensus that levels of judicial compensation should keep pace with the rest of the economy. To a lesser extent, it must be attributed to the skill of the judges themselves. Although the traditions and public expectations of dignity and reserve have somewhat hampered their quest for higher pay, they have managed to press their claims quietly and discreetly through their own groupings (such as Magistrates' Associations, the County Judges' Association, and others). They have had some assistance from professional associations of lawyers and civic groups, but the initiative has not come from this quarter. The real thrust, the driving force, and the strategies behind increases in the compensation of judges have originated to a large degree in the party hierarchies, which have strong incentives to elevate salary levels, and which (as was noted earlier) have the influence in the legislature and the Executive Mansion to attain their objectives.

The interest of the parties in judicial salaries is clear. The better the pay, the more attractive the office; the easier it is to get willing workers, to get generous contributions from office seekers and officeholders. So bills providing increases for the judges of now one court, now another, are introduced virtually every year. This is not to say, on the one hand, that judges do not welcome these raises, or, on the other, that they do not deserve them. But they get many of them because party leaders, for reasons of their own, fight for them. In a sense, the benefits to sitting judges are more or less incidental. Just the same, their debt to party leaders is real.

Similarly, judges on the bench enjoy the advantages accruing from increases in the number of seats in the higher courts. For them, it means additional possibilities of advancement. But this is not the principal benefit to party leaders; for party leaders, new judgeships mean more rewards to distribute to party workers and, therefore, more compliant party units. To be sure, most courts of civil jurisdiction have been swamped by litigation, and some cases take several years to come to trial; under these conditions, there are reasons other than pure partisanship and sources other than party leaders behind proposals for additional judgeships. The main drive, however, seems to originate with County and District Leaders; the incidental benefits are more or less accidental. To judges, these incidental benefits are often important, and so, consequently, are the party organizations responsible for them.

*Mutual Accommodation.* The relationship between courts and parties —as, indeed, between the parties and all elected or politically appointed government officials and employees—is thus one of mutual benefit and accommodation. The court system is important to the parties; the parties are important to the judiciary. As things are now constituted, this is an inevitable and an indissoluble bond.

## Courts and Chief Executives

The power of appointment is useful to the appointing officer in two ways. He may employ it to install in office individuals of his own choosing. He may also use it to install in office someone favored by somebody else in return for a favor or a series of favors by that "somebody else."

The appointment of judges by chief executives is more widely used for the second purpose—bargaining—than for the first. For chief executives are generally not in a position to *direct* their legislative bodies to do what they, the executives, want. Nor can they easily *compel* party organizations to do their bidding. Nor, for that matter, are they always able to *command* all administrative agencies; many of these are quite autonomous. So the executives, lacking adequate sticks, must employ carrots whenever they can. Hence, they make appointments recommended by legislators or party leaders in return for support for their programs or candidacies, and they move administrators into choice jobs if the administrators are faithful to the chief executives. But the programs of chief executives are more dependent on the actions of administrative officers than of judges (although there are important exceptions). Executives, as a result, seem more inclined to try to induct the persons they individually prefer into many high administrative positions and to use judicial office to bargain with legislatures, parties, and with administrators hoping for seats on the bench eventually. The two purposes often merge, but they are distinguishable.

The President, the Governor, and the Mayor are equipped to bargain with varying degree of effectiveness in the political contest in New York City. From this special point of view, the Mayor may well be in the strongest formal position of the three. The President appoints to vacancies in all of the federal judgeships whose respective jurisdictions include New York City, but the names he proposes must win the consent of the Senate. Because of the practice of senatorial courtesy, he is obliged to come to terms with the Senators of the states affected when he appoints men to United States District Courts, and he must reach agreement with the Senate committee on the judiciary and other senatorial leaders when filling vacancies on higher courts. As for the Governor, the only court appointed by him is the State Court of Claims, and he, like the President, must obtain the consent of the upper house of his legislature before his appointments to vacancies take effect. . . .

The chief executives freely use their powers of judicial appointment as currency in political negotiations. This enables them to do many of the things they were presumably elected to do. It also enables party leaders to exert great influence over the choice of appointed judges. The executives thus gain some control over policy; the parties thus get jobs for their people.

## Courts and Other Contestants

Besides the party leaders and chief executives, only professional associations of lawyers, the Citizens Union, and the press exert any significant, visible influence on the composition of the court system. Insofar as the claims of ethnic, national, and religious groups and of neighborhood consciousness affect the courts, they make themselves felt through the party hierarchies, or, in a general way, through the voting behavior of the electorates, both discussed earlier. The impacts of the lawyers, the press, and the Citizens Union are more direct and distinct.

There are many professional associations of lawyers in New York City. Especially prominent is the Association of the Bar of the City of New York, which is a citywide organization. In addition, there is a bar association in each of the five counties (the New York County Lawyers' Association being the largest in the metropolitan region and second in size in the country only to the American Bar Association). Each year the Association of the Bar rates all the candidates for judicial office, after their nomination, as "outstandingly qualified," "qualified" or "unqualified." Each of the county bar associations does the same most of the time for all judicial nominees within their respective areas. These findings are printed in moderate quantities and distributed to the membership of the organizations and to the press, ordinarily receiving something more than routine attention but less than front-page coverage from the latter. . . .

The actions of the bar associations have had little, if any, effect on the choice of nominees for judicial office. Indeed, until 1956 the parties made only sporadic efforts to solicit the opinions of the bar associations regarding prospective nominees; the bar associations were thus in no position to bring any weight to bear on the selection of candidates. In that year, in response to the persistent urging of the Association of the Bar and of the *New York Times,* the New York County Leaders of both major parties pledged themselves to seek systematically the opinions of the bar associations about all prospective candidates prior to nomination. Whether this will have any discernible effect, and whether the party organizations in the other counties will follow suit, remains to be seen; the complaints that led to the adoption of this policy constitute convincing evidence that the professional legal associations have heretofore been largely ineffective in their efforts to influence the nominating process.

Their impact on elections also appears to be limited. Were this not the case, they would not feel compelled to try to intervene at an earlier stage; they would be content, if they could assure the defeat of a candidate by withholding their approval, to punish the parties in this fashion if the parties put forth unqualified candidates. But their ratings apparently do not sway electorates (perhaps because almost all the candidates are called "qualified"). Consequently, if they are to influence the composition and caliber of the judiciary to a larger extent than they have managed to affect in the past, the bar associations must somehow manage to intervene in the selection of nominees. Otherwise, they become little more than helpless bystanders.

If their role in nominations should become more prominent, the lawyers in the parties would probably move in to take over the leadership of the bar associations. The charge has already been leveled that the Bronx and Kings (Brooklyn) County Bar Associations are dominated by Democrats, and that the New York County (Manhattan) Lawyers' Association is controlled by Republicans, with the alleged result that the endorsements more closely reflect political preferences than professional judgments. If party domination is not the case now, it is likely to develop should the bar associations become more influential. Thus the prevailing situation is unlikely to change significantly in the immediate future.

The Citizens Union operates in much the same way as the bar associations, except that it uses a four-category rating scale ranging from "unqualified" through "qualified," "qualified and preferred" to "endorsed." Its influence on the nomination and election of judges, however, is no greater than that of the bar associations, particularly since it tends to follow the lead of the Association of the Bar.

Some of the daily newspapers grumble editorially about the process of judicial selection, and all of them express editorial preferences for judicial along with other candidates, but their recommendations sometimes cancel each other out. Anyway, it is doubtful that they control the voting behavior of their readers. Consequently there are no indications that the parties vie for their support when choosing nominees for judicial office.

Thus the dominance of the party hierarchies over the selection of elected judges is virtually uncontested by the only respectable nongovernmental groups in the community that consistently pay any attention to this phase of politics. The ascendancy of the inner cores of the parties over the selection of appointed judges is even more complete, for there is customarily no evaluation by nongovernmental groups at any stage of the appointive process, and only the most egregious incompetence or dishonesty is likely to attract any significant attention from them at all.

The control of the party leaders over judicial *machinery* is shared with a great many other contestants in the political arena. It is in the naming of court *personnel* that their ascendancy is all but unchallenged in practice.

Clandestinely, however, one element of the population outside the parties in New York City plays a role in the selection of some judges: the underworld. The extent of underworld influence is difficult to assess and is probably limited, but it is unquestionably present and probably extends to both elective and appointive posts. Both the New York State Crime Commission (the Proskauer Commission) and the Special United States Senate Committee to Investigate Organized Crime in Interstate Commerce (the Kefauver Committee) elicited testimony from witnesses about the connections between known gangsters and racketeers on the one hand and some judges on the other. The leaders of large-scale unlawful enterprises—gambling, prostitution, narcotics handling, and extortion through counterfeit labor unions and spurious trade and industrial associations—generally have a good deal of cash on hand, and, since some of it finds its way into units of each party, it occasionally influences some choices of nominees and finances part of some campaigns.

Yet the underworld, like the other nongovernmental and nonparty groups interested in the judiciary, stands on the periphery of the arena. At the center are the party hierarchies and the judges and other court personnel. The roles of all the others in the staffing of the court system are secondary by comparison.

## Conclusion: The Courts and Public Policy

Judicial decisions, like the decisions of other governmental institutions, are vehicles of public policy. Inevitably, therefore, judges are targets of influence exerted by other contestants in the struggle for the stakes of politics. The strategies of the contestants are the same as they are with respect to other policy-forming institutions: (1) efforts to determine the choice of policy-making personnel, and (2) attempts to sway the decisions of the personnel who actually come to occupy office.

The methods of influencing policy decision made by judges are somewhat different from those applied to other organs of government. Tenure, tradition, procedure, and myth render them less susceptible than other officials to many of the standard techniques of political pressure. They are, to be sure, not impervious to pressure, but they are in especially favored positions to resist if they choose, and find fewer imperatives to bargain or cultivate support than the members of the other governmental branches. Policy decisions of judges are thus made in a field of forces in which many contestants are of limited effectiveness at best, and from which many are excluded for all practical purposes. This probably tends to skew their decisions in a different direction from the decisions of officials who face competitive elections far more frequently, or who depend on alliances with a functional constituency for strength. At any rate, the influences on judicial decisions are not obvious.

One natural channel of influence of this kind would be the parties. The bonds between courts and the parties are numerous and strong. The willingness of party leaders to transmit to the courts the requests of constituents is widely recognized; except when the interests of the parties themselves are at stake, party leaders tend to be more concerned with the jobs, the revenues, and the loyalty supplied by the men they put in office than by the substance of court decisions and, as far as policy goes, are apparently as happy to press one way as another as a favor to a supporter. To what extent party hierarchies actually employ their dominance over selection of court personnel for such purposes is not known, but the opportunities certainly exist, and the temptations must be very strong.

Thus, whereas much of the maneuvering and negotiation elsewhere in government are overtly and explicitly oriented toward shaping the substance of decisions, the visible foci of judicial politics are selection of personnel and design of organization and procedures. The forces concerned with the substantive aspects of political questions are hampered; the forces with the greatest influence are commonly neutral with respect to content. Professional associations of lawyers and civic organizations must be content to direct their attention to raising the general professional standards of appointment and to improving judicial machinery. Public policy is often affected or formed by judicial decisions, but the policy questions are rarely highly perceptible or widely discussed. In appearance, at least, judicial politics is a politics of personnel and procedure rather than of program. Although policy flows out of it, the policy seems often to be an unwitting by-product of other considerations, and sometimes to be the work of contestants who see in the special processes of the judicial world opportunities to escape from the competition in the other branches of government. The full significance of the courts in the formulation of public policy still remains to be explored.

---

COMMENT. *The Seabury Investigation.* The foregoing selection referred briefly to the revelations of the 1932 Seabury Report—one of the important milestones on the long road toward judicial reform. As a court-appointed Referee, Samuel Seabury conducted an exhaustive examination of the Magistrates' Courts of the First Judicial Department (Manhattan); the investigation led to widespread resignations and dismissals of magistrates and other court officials. His book-length report, *Final Report of Samuel Seabury, Referee, In the Matter of The Investigation of the Magistrates' Courts: New York Supreme Court Appellate Division—First Judicial Department* (1932), unrolled, with lurid detail, a picture of corruption and incompetence in the lower courts. The Report noted that after the revelations in 1909 of the findings of the Page Commission, the Magistrates' Courts were reorganized by the Inferior Criminal Courts Act. The Report continued:

... The reason why we are no better off today under the Inferior Criminal Courts Act than we were prior to its enactment is that the Inferior Criminal Courts Act left unimpaired and free to flourish the basic vice in the Magistrates' Courts, i.e., their administration as a part of the political spoils system. It left the Magistrates to be appointed by a political agency, the Mayor, upon the recommendation of the district leaders within his political party—and these men, as we know, have regarded the places to be filled as plums to be distributed as rewards for services rendered by faithful party workers. The Courts are directed by these Magistrates in cooperation with the Court clerks, who are not Civil Service employees and who are appointed without the slightest regard to fitness or qualification, but solely through political agencies and because of political influences. The assistant clerks and attendants, though nominally taken from the Civil Service List, are still, in almost all instances, faithful party workers who, despite Civil Service provisions, have secured their places through political influence as a recompense for services performed for the Party. The insidious auspices under which the Magistrates, the clerks, the assistant clerks and the attendants are appointed are bad enough; the conditions under which they retain their appointments are infinitely worse, because they involve the subserviency in office to district leaders and other politicians. It is a byword in the corridors of the Magistrates' Courts of the City of New York that the intervention of a friend in the district political club is much more potent in the disposition of cases than the merits of the cause or the services of the best lawyer and, unfortunately, the truth of the statement alone prevents it from being a slander upon the good name of the City.

Much, if not all, of the hideous caricature which parades as justice in these courts is avoidable; complaisance, unconcern and corruption are alone responsible for it—and these causes, in turn, are the product of the system which permits what was intended to be a great instrument of justice to remain a part of a political system, the purpose of which is to retain and control the jobs and perquisites relating to government. As long as appointments to office in these courts are permitted to rest in the hands of a politically controlled agency, just so long must we expect the appointees to be recruited from the ranks of those whose only claim to appointment is their subserviency to their political party, and as long as this remains the yardstick by which candidates for these places are to be measured and selected, there is no justification for expecting any substantial improvement in the administration of these courts.

Detailed accounts of the disclosures of the Seabury investigation appear in Moley, *Tribunes of the People* (New Haven: Yale, 1932). A more recent report on the seamy side of justice is Borkin, *The Corrupt Judge* (New York: Potter, 1962).

MOST PEOPLE LEARN ABOUT JUSTICE and law from the minor judiciary, commonly called justices of the peace, aldermen, or magistrates. The picture that emerges from the following report on the Magistrates' Courts of Philadelphia is, unhappily, to be found in many urban centers. In Philadelphia, as other portions of this Report explain, magistrates are elected and need not have legal training.

# MAGISTRATES' COURTS IN OPERATION: THE PHILADELPHIA STORY

## Environment and Conduct

THE MAGISTRATES conduct hearings in forty-two courtrooms consisting of thirteen police courts, twenty-eight magistrates' courts, and the traffic court. In addition, magistrates conduct criminal hearings in special circumstances in other public buildings, such as Philadelphia General Hospital, the prisons, or the Board of Education building.

*Condition of Courtrooms.* Few of the courtrooms used by the magistrates in 1957 expressed the dignity and majesty of the law in their physical appearance; many of the police courts were extremely poor examples of judicial facilities.

Of the thirteen police courts, one was in City Hall, eleven were in police stations, and the thirteenth was a station of the Fairmount Park police. The central police court in City Hall was eminently fitted as a courtroom, with suitable appointments and facilities for the presiding magistrate, the stenographer, the district attorney, witnesses, and spectators.

All of the courtrooms located in the police stations, however, had defects as suitable chambers for the judiciary. Half of the police courts were in buildings of recent construction which were adequately lighted and ventilated. The remaining courtrooms were in older buildings and the lighting and ventilation generally were poor. But none of the courtrooms had separate witness stands, none had seating facilities for witnesses, attorneys or spectators. In some of the courtrooms, the layout of the rooms permitted persons to stand behind the magistrate, the prose-

---

Reprinted from *The Magistrates' Courts of Philadelphia* (Bureau of Municipal Research and Pennsylvania Economy League, rev. ed., 1960), pp. 1–18, 67–97, with the permission of the publisher. The report is based on a study which was financed in part by a grant from the Thomas Skelton Harrison Foundation.

cutor, and the clerks while court was in session. Another serious defect in some of the police courts—both new and old—was the fact that the courtroom was part of the main avenue of entry and egress from the station house, magnifying problems of noise and disorder.

Of the twenty-eight magistrates' courts, only one was located in a public building. The others were housed in rented quarters—for example, the first floor of a row house, the second floor of a corner store—indistinguishable from the private dwellings among which they are located. The interiors of the courts, while usually neatly furnished with the basic court facilities, generally were too cramped to impart any feeling of dignity to the proceedings.

The central traffic court, which went into operation in September 1957, had excellent facilities.

*Conduct.* Given the physical facilities of the courtrooms in which they must work, only optimum conduct on the part of the magistrates would serve to promote a judicial atmosphere. Unfortunately, the conduct of many of the magistrates is such that even in the best of surroundings the proceedings would leave much to be desired. Among the specific deficiencies noted by observers ... were the following: ...

ORDER. Noise and confusion were continuous in many of the police courts. Although this was in large part the fault of the physical facilities, few of the magistrates made any serious effort to maintain order.

RUDENESS. The defendants, and often the witnesses and spectators, were frequently treated with rudeness or familiarity. This was particularly noticeable in cases involving nonwhites.

LEVITY. A sense of humor is as desirable in a judicial officer as in anyone else, but there is a difference between its legitimate expression and conduct which makes a joke of justice. A few of the magistrates (three of twenty-six observed) engaged in buffoonery at the hearings, while a number of others punctuated the hearings with uncalled-for humorous or sarcastic remarks.

INTERRUPTIONS. In some courts, people talked privately to the magistrate or his clerk while court was in session.

SOLICITING VOTES. Two of twenty-six magistrates solicited votes in open court during the course of the hearings.

*Legal Wrangles.* Although most magistrates are laymen (e.g., twenty-six of twenty-eight in office in 1958), they are often called upon to referee legal arguments between the assistant district attorney and a defense attorney. On these occasions, the magistrates' lengthy experience or their "common sense" often proves no match for the importunities of some attorneys, regardless of which side they represent. Thus, unseemly wrangles, seldom seen in higher courts, marred many of the magistrates' hearings observed. ...

Many of these legal arguments concerned the admissability of evidence or permissability of lines of questioning. In resolving these arguments, "there is a definite magisterial tendency to accept without question the assistant district attorney's contentions as to what the proper rules of evidence are."

In the absence of the assistant district attorney, the magistrates generally appear to rely on the police witness for their "law." Only on very rare occasions did observers . . . note that the magistrate himself checked on a point of law stated either by the assistant district attorney or in his absence by the police witness.

*Inadequate Consideration.* Whether in the police court or in the magistrates' own courts, cases often received inadequate consideration because of the desire for speed. Many of the magistrates impatiently interrupted explanations of a witness or defendants; few attempted to ascertain more fully the facts of a case. With the exception of those few magistrates who appear to give adequate consideration to all cases, the magistrates generally entered into a full hearing only when the case involved a very serious charge or when the defendant was represented by a lawyer.

Many magistrates undoubtedly believe that their long experience enables them to grasp the truth of the matter after listening to only a few moments of testimony. To that contention, two things may be said. First, it is important not only to arrive at a just result, but to follow procedures which leave the impression that justice has been done. Secondly, when orderly procedures are not followed, even the most experienced magistrate may be mistaken in an unusual case.

### The Preliminary Hearing

Each year, the magistrates sitting in police courts give preliminary hearings to about 15,000 to 25,000 persons arrested by the police and charged with committing indictable offenses. In the first six months of 1957, for example, the magistrates gave preliminary hearings to about 13,500 persons; 52 per cent of the defendants were held for the action of the grand jury, 13 per cent were held for further hearing, and 35 per cent were discharged. . . .

*Complaints on Dispositions.* In the great majority of cases, the magistrates' dispositions in the preliminary hearings appear to be the proper ones. However, there have been complaints that in a small proportion of cases the magistrates' dispositions have been improper: discharging when the defendant should be held, holding when the defendant should be discharged, and sentencing where the magistrate had no legal power of summary conviction.

TOO MANY DISCHARGED. Over the years, the police and the district attorney have complained that some magistrates discharge defendants even though prima facie cases are established. Almost invariably, the discharges involve vice cases, particularly gambling and liquor violations.

In 1948, the head of the police vice squad refused to take his cases to the central police court while a certain magistrate was presiding, because the magistrate, in his view, improperly discharged defendants again whom prima facie cases had been established.

The district attorney in his annual reports for 1952 and 1953 wrote that "racketeers and those engaged in the numbers racket, are still discharged by some few magistrates in the teeth of the evidence. This is intolerable, since these men, unlike most criminals, have deliberately set out to break the law."

The author of a study of vice cases heard by the magistrates in 1956 and 1957 concluded that "in lottery and perhaps in prostitution cases there appear to be frequent improper dismissals."

A measure of the frequency of improper discharges is the number of rearrests requested by the police and the district attorney. To overcome the improper decisions of the magistrates, the police and the district attorney developed the practice of rearresting the defendants and bringing them before a quarter sessions judge sitting as committing magistrates.

In 1956, the police requested rearrests in 177 cases heard by the magistrates (about 1 per cent of those heard). Of these cases, 78 were approved by the district attorney for rearrest. . . .

[T]he statistics on rearrests clearly indicate that in a small percentage of cases some magistrates improperly discharge defendants.

TOO MANY HELD. As a converse to the complaint that some magistrates improperly discharge, is the complaint that some magistrates hold defendants for court when they ought not to be held. In his report for 1952, the district attorney wrote: "If a case sufficient to warrant holding the defendant for later trial in criminal court is not proved, it is recommended (by the assistant district attorney present) that the defendant be discharged. The dead weight of decades of practice is a burden in this respect and it cannot be said with candor that Magistrates have desisted from the old practice of sending cases to court which should never go there."

The district attorney reported that the grand jury in 1956 "refused to hold some 700 defendants for court action after the magistrates had bound them over for grand jury action. . . . Where a bill of indictment is ignored by the grand jury it is usually because the evidence presented to the grand jury is insufficient to make out a prima facie case on the charges returned by the magistrate's transcript." . . .

PRIVATE WARRANT CASES. Complaint is frequently made that some magistrates improperly hold some of the defendants in the hearings conducted in their courtrooms. It will be recalled that these cases are initiated by private prosecutors, and eventuate in defendants being brought before the magistrate by a constable. The hearings are held without an assistant district attorney being present. This led to the observation by the district attorney in his 1953 annual report that as a result of these private warrant hearings, "persons who ought not to be held for the grand jury are held without our having a say in the matter." The district attorney added: "for this no one can blame the magistrates who must act without guidance in such cases," without stating why judicial officers should need guidance from other agencies in making judicial decisions.

A later district attorney pinpointed the criticism, in his statement made at the end of 1956, when he reported that the magistrates often improperly held defendants on the criminal charge of false pretenses where the remedy to the prosecutor should be civil. "Too often a defendant is held for action by the grand jury on what amounts to nothing more than a breach of contract where a civil suit is the sole remedy. Many lawyers attempt to use the criminal courts as added pressure in order to collect a debt or other moneys to which they believe their clients are entitled. It would be most difficult to fully set forth the case law on false pretenses. . . . The magistrate should not be confused by what he will be told by the attorney for the prosecutor. The defendant usually has no attorney present in this type of case."

It should be noted in passing that these criminal proceedings by private warrant are private proceedings in which defendants are processed without necessary notice beforehand to the district attorney as the public prosecutor or notice at any time to the police department which is the city's public or "official" law enforcement agency. It is possible for a criminal to develop a substantial "police" record at least for summary offenses in Philadelphia without the city's police department necessarily becoming aware of it. This may come about through magistrate's hearings on private warrants.

ILLEGAL SENTENCING. At the preliminary hearing of indictable offenses, the magistrate may either hold the defendant for court or discharge him; the magistrate does not have the power to find a defendant guilty of an indictable offense and sentence him to pay a fine or serve a period of imprisonment. However, observations . . . indicate that some magistrates occasionally fine or imprison in indictable offenses. Such dispositions have been noted in gambling cases and in assault and battery cases. . . .

Assault and battery is a crime for which a person may be legally punished only after trial in a court of record. However, observers noted several instances where magistrates summarily sentenced defendants to three months' imprisonment in assault and battery cases arising out of marital disputes. That Philadelphia magistrates sometimes assume summary jurisdiction in marital disputes which culminate in the indictable offense of assault and battery, was also reported in a study in the Harvard *Law Review:* "The magistrate may hold the husband under detention to give the wife time to move out of the house, or may give the husband a choice between leaving his wife and spending six months in jail. *Such orders are beyond the authority of the magistrate,* but the defendant, who is always unrepresented, is unaware of this fact."

*Setting Bail.* When the magistrate has found that a prima facie case exists, he must determine the amount of bail required, if the offense is bailable by him. The Constitution of Pennsylvania forbids "excessive bail," which would appear to mean that the amount of bail may not exceed a sum which is sufficient to ensure the defendant's presence at the trial. As guides for determining the amount of bail, the nature and circumstances of the offense charged, the weight of the evidence, the financial ability of the defendant to give bail, and the character of the defendant are some of the pertinent elements.

Despite these individuating factors, it appeared to observers . . . that most magistrates fixed "standard" amounts of bail for most common offenses; the "standard," however, varied from offense to offense and from magistrate to magistrate.

The authors of a 1954 bail study also found that there was no basic pattern. They concluded: "the amount of bail for each crime depended . . . on the particular magistrate before whom the defendant appeared, for each magistrate develops his own intuitive pattern."

In the majority of preliminary hearings—where the accused did not have counsel—there was usually no discussion of the relative responsibility of the accused: his employment, home ownership, financial status, character or reputation. However, in the minority of cases where the accused was represented by counsel, the amount of bail was often the subject of a hot debate, during the course of which the magistrate, the assistant district attorney, and the defendant's attorney did explore the defendant's status for purpose of setting bail.

Occasionally, the magistrate set such low bail that the assistant district attorney challenged it; then the magistrate explored the accused's status by means of leading questions which indicated that the magistrate was acting on information other than that educed in the open hearing.

HIGH BAIL AS PUNISHMENT. Occasionally, the magistrate's purpose in setting high bail appeared to be to punish the defendant rather than ensure his appearance in court. The following colloquy, recorded by the authors of the bail study, illustrates this practice:

One case inspired the magistrate to exclaim: "Anybody that hits their mother with a blackjack, there is sure something wrong, lady." When the assistant district attorney objected to the bail of $1,000 by saying that $500 would be sufficient, the magistrate replied: "I disagree with you, Mr. District Attorney. I feel that the man should be punished and I don't feel that $500 bail is sufficient." When the defendant's attorney protested the use of bail as punishment, the magistrate denied such an intention and reduced bail to $800.

RELEASE WITHOUT ADEQUATE SECURITY. For certain serious offenses, the 1937 Magistrates' Act provides that the magistrate may release a defendant on bail only if the bail is secured by adequate real estate, by the bond of a corporate surety, or by cash. For all other offenses, the magistrate may release on a personal recognizance (allow the defendant to sign his own bail bond) or require adequate security, depending on his judgment of the defendant's reliability.

According to the reports of the controller, some magistrates violate these provisions. For example, in his audit for the year 1955, the controller wrote: "Throughout the year, we have observed serious irregularities concerning bail. Various criminal charges require a magistrate to accept good and adequate bail to release a defendant held for court. Notwithstanding this, there are some cases where only a personal recognizance is accepted."

### Trial of Summary Offenses

By far the largest number of persons who appear before the magistrate, whether in the police court or in the magistrate's own court, are charged with committing summary offense, i.e., offenses which the magistrate may himself try, determine guilt or innocence, and impose a sentence. . . .

[I]n exercising his powers of summary conviction, the magistrate must follow the basic elements of procedure which the courts have held to be prerequisites of a valid summary conviction.

*Summary Offense Tried in Police Courts.* In 1956, about 66,000 of the 84,000 persons given hearings in the police courts were charged with committing summary offenses. The summary offenses included drunkenness (47,592 arrests), disorderly conduct (8,205 arrests), vagrancy, gambling on the highway, failure to pay cab fare, possession of untaxed liquor, shoplifting, and a host of miscellaneous offenses.

As to dispositions, the great majority were discharged, with only a relatively small percentage convicted and sentenced. Available statistics show that about 95 to 97 per cent of those arrested for drunkenness were discharged; about 60 to 65 per cent of those arrested for other summary offenses were discharged. (However, as noted below, many of those formally discharged either contributed to a "kitty" or were assigned to a work squad for a few hours.)

LACK OF DUE PROCESS. Those who are convicted by the magistrates are convicted in a proceeding which generally lacks many of the elements considered basic to a summary conviction by the higher courts.

For example, in hundreds of cases of summary convictions . . . the defendant was rarely charged with the commission of a particular offense. In most cases, the defendant was expected to learn of the nature of the charge from the arresting officer's narration of the details of the arrest. As noted below, in some cases, even this element was missing.

In very few cases observed was the defendant asked to plead guilty or not guilty to the charge. And in no case observed, did the magistrate state explicitly that he found the defendant guilty or not guilty; rather he concluded the hearing with the sentencing or discharge of the defendant.

In hearings of cases of drunkenness and vagrancy the procedure was especially inadequate, and "deprived defendants of the most elementary requirements of a fair hearing."

Most of those accused of vagrancy and drunkenness had been imprisoned overnight in the police station, and were brought out in a group for disposition by the magistrate. The procedure varied. In its most detailed form, it included (1) a reading of the defendant's name by the magistrate, his clerk, or the police clerk; (2) a question or two addressed to the prisoner; and (3) disposition by the magistrate. In its most summary form, the prisoners were brought in and disposed of in groups.

The actual procedure varied from magistrate to magistrate, and with individual magistrates, it varied from hearing to hearing, tending to become briefer as the hour got later.

As noted previously the great majority of those arrested for drunkenness were discharged. However, a few were committed to prison, for terms ranging from three months to two years. In the cases of conviction, the proof in most cases consisted of the mere exhibition of the defendant with no prosecutor—public or private—testifying. (It should be noted that the assistant district attorney constitutes himself a protector of the accused's rights only in indictable offenses. When all of those accused of indictable offenses are heard, the assistant district attorney and the court stenographer usually leave.)

Where a person was convicted of habitual drunkenness, there was rarely evidence of habitualness presented, "unless the magistrate's unsubstantiated memory and/or opinion or a policeman's unsworn comments be so considered." And even when a policeman stated that the defendant had been arrested numerous times, never did he state specifically on what dates and under what circumstances the previous arrests had been made. Except in the alcoholic court, no records were available to the magistrates at the time of trial to show prior convictions.

In many vagrancy cases, despite undisputed testimony that the defendants were Pennsylvania residents, convictions were found under a statute that applies only to those who come from "without this Commonwealth."

This lack of the elements of a fair trial does much to account for the many abuses found in a 1953 study of commitments to the House of Correction. "In some instances a person committed for H.D. [habitual drunkenness] had no record of a previous arrest or commitment. . . . A few persons committed for vagrancy had property and a job. Some feeble old people who had become confused and were unable to find their way home were committed by a magistrate for H.D. or vagrancy even though they were not intoxicated."

JUSTICE NOT ACCORDING TO LAW. Many of the defendants brought before the magistrates are changed with the summary offense of "disorderly conduct." In the Pennsylvania Penal Code, the offense of disorderly conduct is defined as follows:

Whoever willfully makes or causes to be made any loud boisterous and unseemly noise or disturbance to the annoyance of the peaceable residents nearby, or near to any public highway, road, street, lane, ally, park, square, or common, whereby the public peace is broken or disturbed, or the travelling public annoyed, is guilty of the offense of disorderly conduct, and upon conviction thereof in a summary proceeding, shall be sentenced to pay the costs of prosecution and to pay a fine not exceeding ten dollars ($10), and in default of the payment thereof, shall be imprisoned for a period not exceeding thirty (30) days.

Despite the clear statutory mandate (1) that there must be a noise or a disturbance and (2) that this must cause annoyance to the public to make up the offense of disorderly conduct, often the magistrates modify other more serious offenses to that of disorderly conduct and then summarily dispose of them. The magistrates, for example, dispose summarily of persons actually arrested as corner loungers, as prostitutes, or as frequenters of disorderly, bawdy or gambling houses. Observers have also noted that exchanges within the confines of the home between husband and wife, father and son or daughter, or landlady and roomer or boarder are dealt with summarily as disorderly conduct.

In these cases, the defendants were punished for actions which the complainant, the police, the magistrate, and perhaps, even the public, believe should be punishable. Nevertheless such magisterial dispositions violate the principle of "justice according to law." Summary convictions to be valid, must conform precisely to the *statutory* definition of the crime to be punished, as "there is no such thing as an offense punishable in a summary proceeding at common law."

LENIENCY IN GAMBLING OFFENSES. The magistrates have summary jurisdiction over the offense of playing "at cards, dice, billiards, bowls, shuffleboard, or any game of hazard or address, for money, or other valuable thing." The penalty specified is a three-dollar fine.

Many defendants are arrested each year for violating this statute, particularly for "gambling on the highway." However, despite eye-witness police evidence regarding the commission of the offense, the magistrates rarely impose the statutory penalty. In the years 1954 and 1955, for example, 2,871 persons were charged with this offense, according to statistics compiled by the police department, but only 214 defendants (3 per cent of the total) were fined, with the other 97 per cent discharged.

ILLEGALLY REDUCING PENALTIES. Some laws defining summary offenses, notably the Vehicle Code, specify the fines and costs which the magistrate must mandatorily impose when he finds the defendant guilty. Some magistrates do not abide by these legal requirements and impose fines or costs which are different from those specified. The controller has noted: "magistrates have frequently disregarded these laws by waiving, lowering, or remitting fines or costs."

Further, it is "unlawful for any magistrate to . . . review, alter, modify or remit any sentence of fine or imprisonment imposed by him. . . ." The controller notes in his audit for 1955. "in police cases where the fine is discretionary, it may not be reduced or remitted other than in open court; however, we have noted instances of fines reduced or remitted in violation of the above." Reductions or remissions of penalties after the individual hearings and after the court sessions were completed were also noted by observers. . . .

EXCESSIVE PENALTIES. The statutes and ordinances providing for convictions in summary proceedings specify the maximum penalties which may be imposed. It was observed that some magistrates imposed penalties in excess of the maximums. For example, although the maximum sentence of imprisonment for disorderly conduct is 30 days' imprisonment, sentences to the House of Correction for periods of three months and six months were noted; and although the maximum fine for gambling is $3, fines of $5 were occasionally imposed.

UNAUTHORIZED PENALTIES. Although the majority of persons arrested and tried for committing summary offenses are discharged as a matter of record, some of the magistrates impose unauthorized penalties upon those discharged in certain types of cases.

In drunkenness cases, about half of the magistrates observed required defendants before they were released to contribute a small sum (usually $1 or "any change you have"), to a designated charity, or in default, to join a squad to do custodial work around the police station after the hearing. (This latter penalty was not applied to women defendants nor to men who were either well-dressed or who appeared physically incapacitated.)

The charitable contribution was either in the form of the purchase of a ticket to a benefit performance or, more commonly, in the form of a cash contribution to a "kitty," a glass jar or box provided by charities for collecting purposes.

In cases involving gambling, "corner lounging," disorderly conduct or frequenting a disorderly house, a smaller number of magistrates (about one-third of those observed) require the defendants to contribute a sum to the "kitty" or purchase tickets for a benefit, but these exactions were usually larger than those in drunkenness cases, with many of the contributions $5 or more.

One newspaper has commented on this practice in an editorial entitled "Judicial Extortion":

In the courtroom this passes as charity. Elsewhere it would be called extortion, all the more obnoxious because an official who should be protecting people from extortion is himself engaging in it.

When a person in judicial position has trouble keeping separate his charitable impulses and his judicial duties, somebody gets cheated. If the accused has done something for which he should be fined, his fine should go into the public treasury. If he is not legally liable for a fine, he shouldn't have to pay anybody.

It may be noted parenthetically that while some magistrates supply their own "kitties," some appear to be provided for them by the police stations in which they sit.

*Leniency in City Cases.* One of the most important functions of the magistrates is to try and dispose of violations against laws and ordinances which are prosecuted by the city solicitor on the behalf of the City. These are the offenses in which the City as the local government has an especial interest: the violations against the housing, building, fire, and health codes and the other ordinances and statutes, the enforcement of which is a peculiar municipal concern. In form, most of the proceedings are those of a civil suit for a penalty, but some are criminal proceedings in the nature of summary convictions.

A frequent criticism which is directed against those magistrates who handle City cases is their reluctance to impose fines on violators. In 1956, for example, the City's law department instituted about 9,900 original cases, excluding tax cases, in the magistrates' courts. As to dispositions, about 400 cases were discharged without the imposition of fines or costs, about 7,500 were discharged on the payment of costs, and only 2,000 (20 per cent of total) were required to pay fine and costs, that is, found guilty as charged. The total fines collected were about $56,000, an average of about $28 a fine.

These criticisms of magisterial leniency have been especially prevalent as they involved the enforcement of the zoning, building, housing, and fire codes by the department of licenses and inspections. . . .

The magistrates take the view that compliance with the law is their first concern and that punishment is to be imposed only if compliance cannot be secured in any other way. Some fault may rest with the inspectional agencies in delaying their resort to the magistrate to secure compliance on substantial violations, or in resorting to the magistrate to secure compliance on technical (not to say, trivial) violations of the codes.

But in view of the records of some violators, it appears that some fault rests with the magistrates in being too ready to accept the statements of the violators as to their willingness to comply and in being too lenient in fining flagrant violators. Apparently, some violators will comply only when they receive notices from the magistrates. It seems reasonable that fining these is the proper remedy, rather than discharging them on payment of costs if they make a promise to comply. Some of the violations marked "law complied with" (and discharged) later reappear before the magistrate when a reinspection proves that not all of the violations are remedied. While this situation obtains, some revision of "ground rules" both in the inspectional agencies and in the magistrates' courts would be in order, so that generally earlier resort may be made to the magistrates' courts.

### Trial of Civil Cases

In 1956, approximately 12,500 to 14,000 civil suits were instituted in the 28 magistrates' courts, with the bulk of the cases—about 75 per cent—instituted in the courts of four magistrates. Although no statistics are published concerning the disposition of cases, available information indicates that the overwhelming majority of the suits result in a judgment for plaintiff.

*Default Judgments.* It appears that in most civil suits instituted in the magistrates' courts the plaintiff obtains judgment by default—that is, the defendant does not contest the action. An analysis of 1,577 cases in the docket of one magistrate, for example, showed that in 1,409 cases (90 per cent of the total) plaintiff obtained judgment by default.

According to attorneys who practice in the magistrates' courts, many magistrates enter default judgments without requiring the plaintiff to appear to prove his claim. This is permissible in contract cases where the plaintiff has filed an affidavit of claim and the defendant has not filed an affidavit of defense; however, the finding of default judgments without hearing plaintiff's testimony would appear improper in contract cases where no affidavit of claim has been filed, as well as in all actions of trespass.

According to attorneys who practice in the magistrates' courts, many magistrates permit the plaintiff to institute a suit by telephoning or writing the magistrate or one of his constables; thus, when a default judgment is entered, the magistrate has neither seen the plaintiff (nor his attorney) nor heard any of his testimony.

*Favoring Plaintiff.* In many magistrates' courts, even if the defendant does appear, his case receives scant consideration. In some courts, if a defense is offered, the counsel for the plaintiff will be called on the telephone to come to the hearing. When he arrives, if he cannot arrange a settlement, the hearing is frequently continued because of the absence of plaintiff. This may happen again and again until the defendant is tried out or unavoidably absent, whereupon judgment is entered for the plaintiff.

In other magistrates' courts, if both parties appear, the magistrate urges them to settle the case between themselves. If they are unable to reach a settlement, the magistrate frequently gives judgment for plaintiff for the full amount of the claim without hearing testimony.

In many courts, the magistrate takes the position that if there is a dispute the defendant is not prejudiced by the entry of judgment for the plaintiff, as the defendant may appeal. But this involves additional costs and delay, and tends to produce unjust settlements. It is an evasion of responsibility. And the first skirmish has been decided for plaintiff.

This propensity of the magistrates to give judgment for plaintiff even if a good defense is offered is one of the reasons so few defendants appear to contest the action. Many lawyers believe it is a waste of time to defend a suit in the magistrates' courts and advise their clients not to appear at the hearing but to appeal the decision to the municipal court.

This does not mean that it is impossible for a defendant to obtain a judgment in his favor in a magistrate's court. Such judgments are given in rare instances (e.g., in one of 1,577 cases heard by one magistrate).

*Improper Criminal Actions.* It has been noted earlier in this chapter that the district attorney has complained of the number of persons held—improperly, in his view—for the grand jury on the criminal charge of false pretense. Some magistrates, in order to aid a plaintiff in a civil suit against a "judgment-proof" defendant, are said to threaten the defendant with arrest if he does not pay the amount claimed, although no evidence of obtaining money under false pretenses is present. Other magistrates, apparently unable by themselves to determine whether or not the crime of obtaining money under false pretenses has been committed, are willing to accept the authority of the plaintiff-prosecutor. . . .

## Political Influence

Were justice administered by the magistrates according to their best idea of the law, it would not be especially satisfactory, but it would have the merit of impartiality. The public, however, suspects the impartiality of the magistrates, partly because of the absence among them of the tradition of impartiality which operates so powerfully among the "regular" judges and is kept alive by the members of the bar, and partly because of the close connection of the magistrates with local politics and politicians.

A former Philadelphia magistrate wrote the following regarding political influence in magistrates' decisions:

The great majority of citizens who receive notices to appear and answer for minor violations of the law, instead of courageously facing the charges at an open hearing, importune their committeeman to 'fix it' for them, under the threat, expressed or implied, of voting against his ticket at the next election. . . . Needing their cooperation at election time, and also desiring to be regarded as influential, the committeeman refers the matter to his ward leader to 'take care of' for him. The ward leader, who must face re-election by the committeeman of his ward every year, presents the matter to the magistrate or other official in authority, for extension of 'leniency.' Each refusal by the official to cooperate correspondingly lessens his chances for re-election or reappointment. . . .

*Politics Observed in Courtroom.* Some evidences of political influence were seen in the observations of courts in session. . . . A few magistrates, upon discharging defendants, were heard to mention to the defendant that someone had "put in a good word for you." Two magistrates asked defendants in minor cases to vote for them as a condition of discharge. Many a time, a committeeman appeared in open court to represent a defendant. . . .

## Conclusion

We have now reviewed complaints, criticisms, and charges concerning the manner and place of hearings before the magistrates; improper disposition of criminal cases; inadequate consideration of civil cases;

political influence in decisions; late and faulty records and returns; poor money-handling practices; and failure to abide by the requirements of the magistrates' court acts. The picture of the courts in operation has been built up largely by a recital of deficiencies. This picture shows a system of administering justice in which illegal or improper practices are strikingly prevalent. The dignity and learned tradition, the impartiality, of judicial office seem largely wanting.

By necessity, much of the description of the system was based upon the observations of specific magistrates in action. It is often said, when complaints are made about the magistrates, that they are complaints against men, and not against the system, the inference being that such complaints raise no question of the inadequacy of the system. We are, of course, primarily interested in the system, but the answer to the viewpoint expressed is that so many complaints against a part of the system convict the system itself. Any system, however good, will fail in some cases and, however bad, will succeed in some. But there is something definitely wrong with a system in which so many personal delinquencies occur.

With three more thoughts we close. . . . First, the complaints catalogued do not apply to all of the magistrates in office at the time of writing. As noted in the individual sections, some of the complaints apply to only a few of the magistrates; others, to a large majority of them. Therefore, it would be an injustice to conclude from the description . . . that there are no magistrates who handle their work competently and judiciously, as far as the system permits.

Second, the complaints made against the magisterial system as it operates in the late 1950s are not new. Similar complaints on a broad scale were made in the first edition of this work which was published in 1931, after a statutory revision in 1927, and . . . in the report of the special grand jury of 1935 and the subsequent commission, which resulted in the statutory revisions of 1937. Similar complains on a smaller scale have been made and reported in newspaper stories, editorials and other media throughout the years. The men who administer the system have changed; the system itself has undergone some modifications, particularly in 1937 and in 1949; and yet its deficiencies and inadequacies remain remarkably consistent and, unhappily, large.

A final thought is that whatever the merits of the magistrates—and some of them are excellent within the system—the complaints against them and their administration of justice has generally put the system in disrepute. There is, and can be, no public confidence in a part of a judicial system which is constantly pictured as the magistrates' courts are pictured and which is held so generally by the public in such low esteem. It is a grave question whether once a system has lost public confidence it can ever be useful and again deserving of that confidence without being thoroughly overhauled and established on a basis to command public respect.

---

MORE RECENT EVIDENCE ON CONDItions in the Philadelphia Magistrates' courts was gathered in a field study by Mr. Richard Frey for the Greater Philadelphia Branch of the American Civil Liberties Union. See 9 Civil Liberties Record No. 6, page 1 (Dec. 1960).

An earlier thorough field study in a specialized setting is reported by Professor Caleb Foote: "Vagrancy-Type Law and its Administration," *University of Pennsylvania Law Review*, vol. 104, pp. 603 *et seq.*, 1956. The effects of one attempt at reform are examined in: "The Philadelphia Traffic Court," *University of Pennsylvania Law Review*, vol. 109, pp. 848 *et seq.*, 1961.

---

## JUDICIAL SELECTION  By Sidney Schulman

JUDGES IN Pennsylvania, from the lowest Justice of the Peace to the Justices of the Supreme Court, are presently, with the exception of Police Magistrates in Pittsburgh, who are appointed by the Mayor of that city, nominated and elected in partisan primaries and general elections. None enjoys life tenure. Supreme Court Justices serve a 21-year term and are not eligible for re-election. All other judges serve for 10 years or less and are eligible for re-election. The law judges of courts of record serve for 10 years, associate lay judges for 5 years, justices of the peace, aldermen and magistrates for 6 years, Pittsburgh police magistrates for 4 years subject to removal at the pleasure of the mayor.

Life tenure appointment by the Governor, provided by Penn's Frame of Government for the Province of Pennsylvania and the Constitutions of 1790 and 1838, succumbed in 1850 to the fervor of the "Jacksonian Revolution" for popular direct electoral control of public officials. Attempts to restore the appointive system in the Constitutional Convention

---

Reprinted from *Toward Judicial Reform in Pennsylvania* (Philadelphia: Institute of Legal Research, U. of Pennsylvania, 1962), pp. 19–58, with the permission of the author and the publisher. (Copyright 1962, by University of Pennsylvania.) Sidney Schulman is a member of the Philadelphia Bar.

of 1873 which drafted the present Constitution of 1874 failed. Life tenure appointment of judges, which still prevails in practically all other countries now prevails only in the Federal judiciary and a few states.[1]

The elective system has however in practice been converted into a combination appointive-elective system, since the great majority of judges first reach the Bench by interim appointment of the Governor to fill a vacancy or a newly created judgeship. Thereafter, they submit themselves to the party primary and general election process.

Former Chief Justice Vanderbilt has asserted that were it not for the interim appointment practice, the elective system would long since have proved unworkable in practice. It may be true that the executive-appointing power . . . is more responsive to the high needs of the judicial system than the invisible party structure which controls the nominations, yet in practice, Governors of Pennsylvania have most always accommodated their appointments to the wishes of the party leaders. The Governor, by virtue of his position of power, prestige, and titular party leadership, may and often does make what are known as personal appointments usually to the Supreme or Superior Appellate Courts. He may on occasion choose men for these courts simply because he knows and respects them. This kind of choice is rarely exercised on the county level. Where his personal appointments run counter to the demands of party leadership, as was recently the case, party leaders have not hesitated to overrule him through their control of the subsequent party primary.[2] . . .

Political selection of judges is inevitable from the nature of the party machinery which places the nomination of judges in the hands of a small group of political leaders acting in caucus. County political leaders acting as the State Committee slate the judges for statewide judicial offices. The county committees consisting of ward or district leaders slate the

[1] *Book of the States,* 1958–59, Table I, Classification of Courts and Terms of Judges. Massachusetts and New Hampshire are the only remaining two states with life tenure. Although Rhode Island is listed as a life tenure state, a judge of the Supreme Court holds office "until his place be declared vacant by a resolution of the General Assembly to that effect."

In New Jersey, following a seven-year appointive term, the judges may be reappointed for life with retirement at age 70. New Jersey Constitution, Article VI, Section 6(3).

[2] In 1958, Governor Leader, a Democrat, appointed his Attorney General, a distinguished lawyer, to the Supreme Court, although claim was laid to the office by a distinguished Common Pleas judge who had recently been defeated as the party's candidate for a previous vacancy on the Court. The Democratic State Committee refused to support Governor Leader's appointee in the primary and slated their previous candidate, who was successful in both the primary and the general election. Governor Leader's lack of influence in the party caucus was undoubtedly caused by the fact that he was a "lame duck" governor, unable to succeed himself under the State Constitution. Although the public interest may not have suffered since both the deposed judge and his successor were well qualified, the public was aroused by the control and manipulation of judicial office by political party leaders.

county judges. Control of the caucus usually gravitates to the chairman and a few allies who, through the power of withholding or dispensing patronage, can influence the other members of the caucus. Thereafter, the slated candidates become the parties' official candidates in the party primaries.

Independent voter interest is difficult to arouse in most primaries and the cost of campaigning is prohibitive. This discourages many highly qualified aspirants for judicial office from "bucking" the party. If there is intraparty warfare, one set of party bosses and their judicial candidates are often replaced by another. Judicial candidates must seek the favor of one group or the other. Where one party predominates in the county or state, nomination is tantamount to election. If there are two vigorous parties the voters' choice is limited to the candidates of rival political leaders. If both parties agree to support the same judicial candidates in a bipartisan judicial deal, which is often the consideration for creation of new judgeships, or new courts, or antiraiding agreements, the voters can be said to have little real choice at all.

Most often in national or state elections straight party lines or national or state issues rather than discriminating choice between judicial candidates governs the voters' selection of judges, so that even if real choice were possible, it is in practice rarely exercised.

With the power of judicial selection thus concentrated in the hands of a few political leaders, the criterion of selection they employ becomes of the utmost importance.

Political leaders today are rarely as blatant in their partisanship as was Governor Tener of Pennsylvania in 1913 when he announced that four of the five new Common Pleas judges in Philadelphia, authorized by the legislature, would be Republicans, and that one would be a Democrat, as "a sop to the minority of the state."

Political leaders today profess the need for high professional qualifications in judicial selection. This attitude even if sincere is often negated by the demands of party organization and discipline. The party leaders in selecting candidates for appointment and nomination are faced with the need of presenting "a balanced ticket," of rewarding political service, of recognizing the claims of powerful political chieftains who for reasons of prestige and power demand the right to fill the office. Substantial contributors often interject their own suggestions. Coupled with these factors is the practical consideration of assuring party loyalty by the judicial candidates in the dispensation of judical patronage available to the courts once they are elected. This ordinarily precludes candidates of superior attainments but with independent political proclivities. . . .

Political or party service which may be rewarded by judicial office ranges from service within the political organization itself to the higher realms of distinguished public service in the executive, legislative and judicial branches of government.

Public life, which can usually only be achieved within the framework of the political party system, is a stepping stone to judicial office. A review of the biographical material available on all the judges of the courts of record in Pennsylvania as of January 1, 1958, reveals that of the last ten Attorney Generals (excluding an Acting Attorney General for a thirty-day period), six were subsequently appointed to the Pennsylvania Supreme Court, one to the Superior Court, one to the U.S. District Court and two declined judicial appointment. This background of high public service is not to be deprecated. When coupled with high judicial qualifications it brings to the Bench valuable attributes which any system of selection should seek to encourage.

When we come to the lower courts, we find that on the magistrate, alderman and justice of the peace level, especially in the metropolitan areas, service in the party vineyards is the common criterion for selection. The reason is that the office has been so demeaned that it is considered beneath the dignity of men who occupy positions of any importance in public life. A Philadelphia Inquirer news story of September 21, 1958, is typical of the public recognition of these political facts of life:

> Governor David Lawrence, Monday named three Democratic ward leaders as magistrates to fill existing vacancies . . . Lawrence made the appointments on recommendation of the Chairman of the Philadelphia Democratic organization.

The rewards of party service are not so blatantly publicized in appointments to the county trial courts of record, but there has been a tendency to reward county or district party leaders who are lawyers by elevation to the bench.

A review of the biographical material publicly available on the county trial courts of record in Pennsylvania reveals that the best road to judicial office is through the District Attorney's office and the legislative branches of government. Excluding Philadelphia and Pittsburgh, almost 44 per cent of the Common Pleas judges and 50 per cent of the Orphans' Court judges had prior service as District or Assistant District Attorneys. In Philadelphia and Allegheny Counties the figures are somewhat lower. In Allegheny County, a recent survey disclosed that all the 26 judges of the Common Pleas and County Court had records of public service, 15 to elective office and 11 to some appointive public office. In Philadelphia County, our survey reveals that apparently only two judges have no record of prior public service in the legislative, executive or administrative branches of government. Throughout the state, only nine judges had no record of prior public service.

No contention is made that prior political activities should disqualify aspirants to the judiciary from consideration. It is necessary, however, that the field of opportunity for candidates without political background be widened. Justice David W. Peck, formerly of the New York Supreme Court, has defended political considerations in the selection of judges:

> Political considerations are fair considerations in the nomination and election of judges ... not as a reward for party service, but as recognition of the requisite interest in public affairs carried to the point of political effectiveness. ... The real trouble with the political selection of judges is not that political considerations enter, but that professional considerations may be disregarded or minimized. ... There is nothing mutually exclusive between political activity and professional qualifications ... and if as a result of giving recognition to political activity in judicial selection we give some encouragement to lawyers to participate in politics, the development will be a healthy one.

Justice Peck's argument overlooks several basic considerations. Although he recognizes the need for professional qualifications, he offers no solution to the present incompatibility between political party organization and this objective. He completely ignores the fate of the independent in politics, who cannot hope to see his interest in public affairs recognized by judicial appointment.

Justice Peck also confuses political activity with public service. They are not necessarily interchangeable. The public service rendered by those active in politics must not be minimized, but there are other types of public service which might be equally rewarded. The public spirited lawyer of independent political inclinations usually must wait until a time of crisis in party fortunes when political leaders often accept as judicial candidates men of outstanding reputation, ability and independence as an attraction to the independent voter or to dispel the public image of boss domination. This factor, however, is the exception rather than the rule and lawyers with no claims of their own to party favor must look to powerful sponsors within the parties.

Another political consideration openly reported in other jurisdictions, particularly New York City, and periodically revived by innuendo and rumor in Pennsylvania, is that judgeships can be purchased by substantial political contributions by a candidate or his sponsor.[3] There is no evidence whatsoever in Pennsylvania to support this thesis. There is no doubt, however, that judges in Pennsylvania are expected to and do contribute to their own campaigns and that many often contribute to campaigns other than their own. The need for political contributions and for political campaigning by judicial candidates discourages many highly

---

[3] Canon 20 of the Canons of Judicial Ethics urges the judge to avoid making or soliciting contributions, but recognizing the political realities involved was amended to permit contributions where "it is necessary for a judge to be nominated and elected as candidate of a political party."

qualified aspirants and should be prohibited. Contributions should be prohibited and the American Bar Association plan does this.

Considering all the factors that political leaders take into consideration in selection of judges the amazing part about the present system of selection in Pennsylvania, imperfect as it is, is that it has produced many good judges and so few venal judges. Its shortcomings, however, lower the general level of qualification. Its vice is that it undermines the degree of judicial independence necessary to resist the patronage and other demands of political party leaders. Only security of tenure and a system of selection which will release judges from obligation to political leaders for their appointment and nomination can really make our judges free.

## Pennsylvania Contributes the Sitting Judge Principle

Once appointed, nominated and elected, the obligations of an elected judge to political leaders are not over. The need for re-election is an ever present consideration. The judge's record of able, conscientious service is not in itself, under our present elective system, a guarantee of tenure. During the judge's term in office he must be conscious that for renomination his record of party loyalty may count as much with his party leaders as an unimpeachable record on the bench. Many of the county leaders who sit in judgment are themselves lawyers, constantly appearing before the court, and perhaps themselves ambitious for judicial office. Even if acceptable to his own party his record may count for nothing with the opposition party. Where the political balance of power in the county between the two parties has changed in the intervening years, even if the judge's own party supports him, the rival party will usually not hesitate to claim his office for itself. In the ensuing election the fate of the sitting judge becomes intertwined with the fate of his party; and national, state and sometimes local issues having nothing to do with judicial qualifications often determine the course of the election.

The desirability of protecting competent incumbent judges from electioneering and the vicissitudes of primary and general elections has led to what is known as the "Sitting Judge Principle" in Pennsylvania. This principle contemplates that a judge found qualified should receive bipartisan primary and general election support from the bar, the political parties and the public, thus insuring his re-election. The privilege of determining qualification has been assumed by the bar.

Claims have been made that the wide application of the sitting judge principle in Pennsylvania obviates the need for the American Bar Association nonpartisan selection plan. To determine the extent to which the principle is followed in the 67 counties of Pennsylvania we communicated with the Presidents of the local bar associations of each county.

Of 54 local bar associations reporting none, except Philadelphia, applies the sitting judge principle to the statewide Supreme and Superior Appellate Courts.

No bar association applies the principle to the minor judiciary.

No bar association except Philadelphia applies it to interim appointees seeking their first term.

Only 12 bar associations embrace the principle as to judges seeking re-election after a full term, and of these only Philadelphia has adopted the same by a formal vote of its Board of Governors and the membership of the Association.

Only 6 of the 12 associations accepting the principle have ever implemented it by a bar poll or plebiscite.

In 21 of the 42 reporting counties not recognizing the principle, sitting judges have, however, from time to time received bipartisan support, and in 8 counties, despite the absence of the principle, interim appointees have on occasion received bipartisan support. In some instances this seems to be motivated by the fact that the opposition parties were so weak that they had no hope of obtaining the office for themselves. In most counties, except Philadelphia County, it was reported that judgeships involved "bitter fights," either in the party primary in counties where party domination of the county makes nomination tantamount to election, or in the general election.

In discussions with judges throughout the smaller counties of the state, a number have stated that in their counties "a good judge has nothing to fear," and that even if unsupported by his party leaders, an incumbent may be able to win popular support. There is no doubt that in local elections, a well known sitting judge in the smaller counties enjoys a definite advantage over rivals and this factor is, in some cases, sufficient to swing the balance of victory. But it means a bitter and expensive campaign, to which a judge seeking re-election on the basis of a demonstrated record of ability should not be subjected. The American Bar Association nonpartisan plan resolves this difficulty by providing that a judge seeking re-election will run only on his record and not against political rivals.

In Philadelphia County, the sitting judge principle may be said to have had moderate success. In recent years, the rival political leaders have in most cases, but not all, accepted it even as to interim appointees.[4]

---

[4] In 1937, both parties tried unsuccessfully to unseat each other's judges, particularly the 6 interim Democratic appointees to the Philadelphia Common Pleas Court, whom the Bar considered sitting judges. In 1949 both parties joined in bipartisan nomination and election of a judge found unqualified by the Bar. He was elected. In

This is due to a number of reasons. One is that public sentiment looks with disfavor upon political manipulation of selection of judges, and the parties have found that unseating judges is an unpopular issue. Second, the present bipartisan nature of the Bench in Philadelphia represents an uneasy accommodation of the two parties to the spoils system and distribution of judicial patronage, an accommodation which the parties deem it expedient to preserve on the theory that the "outs" may in the future be in and the "ins" out.

Recognizing the vulnerability of the minority party to raiding of judicial office, the initiative was taken by the leader of the Philadelphia Republican party in asking the Bar Association to endorse unanimously for re-election all sitting judges coming up for re-election in the 1961 Municipal election. Since 4 of the 5 incumbents were Republicans and Philadelphia is considered a "Democratic" city as evidenced by sweeping Democratic victory in the 1960 presidential election, the importance of the sitting judge principle to a minority party becomes self-evident. The Democratic leaders agreed to support the Republican incumbents. The *quid pro quo* was said to have been the agreement of the Republican judges who controlled the board of judges to appoint the nominee of the Democratic City Committee as interim district attorney. On the state level they denied the sitting judge principle and swept a Republican incumbent on the Superior Court from the bench in the Democratic landslide in the November 1960 elections.

### The Bar Fails to Influence Judicial Selection

Political leaders in Pennsylvania, although they appeal to the organized Bar to support the sitting judge principle when it serves party purposes, completely ignore the Bar in the initial selection of judges. The organized Bar has thus far not found the means to make itself an effective force in raising the quality of judicial appointment. The lack of an integrated bar with a dedicated unity of purpose is undoubtedly a contributing cause, but equally important is the failure of the state and local bar associations to insist upon a working relationship with the Governor and the political leaders. The bar also lacks militancy in protesting poor appointments.

---

1951, the Democrats unseated a Republican Common Pleas judge, with the Bar failing to conduct a plebiscite. In 1953, the Democrats tried unsuccessfully to unseat Republican incumbents, and suffered their first defeat since 1949. In 1954, the Republicans opposed Democratic incumbents on the State Superior Court. In 1957, Judge Kun, found "unqualified" in a Bar Association poll, was replaced by a Democratic nominee. In 1959 and 1961 both parties joined in bipartisan nomination of sitting judges.

The Pennsylvania Bar Association is a voluntary statewide group of individual lawyers with a membership of 6,440 of the state's 10,000 lawyers. Unlike other states, lawyers in Pennsylvania can practice only in the county in which they maintain their principal office. Membership in the State Bar confers no state wide privileges. This insularity is claimed to be a matter of economic self-defense against the big city lawyers and lawyers from populous surrounding counties who, it is felt, would gobble up the business of the smaller counties. The insularity of law practice has reflected itself in 67 completely independent, voluntary, local bar associations in the 67 counties.

Membership in most local bar associations is fairly small. Forrest, Fulton and Sullivan have three active lawyers and members each; Cameron and Pike counties, six and seven. Except for Philadelphia's bar of 4,500 lawyers and an association of 3,000, and Allegheny's 2,500 lawyers and 1,000 members, no other county has over 300 lawyers.

Twenty-six states, Puerto Rico and the Virgin Islands have state and territory-wide integrated bars, in which membership is compulsory as a condition for practicing law.

Attempts at statewide integration of the Pennsylvania bar have resulted in dismal failure. Attempts at integration on the local county level in Philadelphia have also failed.

The Pennsylvania Bar Association has never taken an active part in judicial selection. Its Judiciary Committee, unlike its counterpart in the American Bar Association, has failed to establish an influential advisory role with the appointing power and the legislature. It has in the past confined its efforts to an occasional approval or disapproval of nominees to the Federal Bench, but left to the American Bar Association the disagreeable task of actually appearing before the United States Senate Judiciary Committee in opposition to the confirmation of nominees of obviously inferior qualifications....

The local bar associations have been unable to establish a similar relationship of either power, trust, or influence with the Governor as the appointing power, or with the state and county political leaders. Attempts of the Philadelphia and Allegheny County Bar to pattern its procedure after the American Bar Association have met with blunt rejection by the Governors of Pennsylvania. The ... Governor [incumbent until 1963, David Lawrence] has been particularly emphatic in his rejection of the suggestion that prospective appointees be cleared through the bar associations, considering it as a surrender of the prerogatives and responsibilities of office to a body which, in his opinion, is just as political in its own way as the political parties themselves. The Philadelphia and Allegheny County Bars have been equally unsuccessful in obtaining pledges from the local county political leaders to submit in advance their candidates for appointment or nomination. Other jurisdictions have had some limited success with local leaders, the most recent being New York City.[5]

In the absence of cooperation from the Governor and local political leaders, the bar associations in Philadelphia and Allegheny have attempted to take the initiative by presenting their own panels of "qualified" nominees to the Governor when a vacancy is to be filled by appointment.

The Philadelphia system is administered by a 21-man, elected Judiciary Committee. That Committee has refused to consider preferential ratings of the candidates as a delicate and difficult task bound to arouse antagonisms among its members and the bar generally. Some of its members believe that under our democratic elective system their function is only to exclude those obviously unfit. Others seek service on the Committee with the frank intention of advancing the hopes of particular candidates. This they can do by voting for only their own candidates, thus preventing others from obtaining the necessary majority of votes. A dedicated minority is unable to weld the Committee into a unanimity of purpose so as to substantially improve its procedures.

The term "qualified," used by the Committee, has been such a broad umbrella that its list of recommended candidates almost invariably includes not only those most highly qualified, but also those who a majority of the Committee would agree are mediocre. The list also invariably includes those reputed to be the favorite candidates of the political leaders, and who are invariably appointed. The result is that the imprimatur of bar association approval is often bestowed upon mediocre and obviously political appointees. This constitutes a fraud upon the public.

No attempt is made by the Committee or the bar generally to encourage or press the candidacy of men of superior qualifications. This plays directly into the hands of the political leaders who run so little risk that their candidates will be rejected or opposed by the bar that they can pay lip service to the need for bar approval. Bar association blessing thus becomes a valuable campaign asset obtained at no cost whatever to the party power of selection.

The Association of the Bar of the City of New York last year for this reason abolished the use of the term "qualified" as meaningless and as one which stultified the Association. The Association now has only one category of approval, "well qualified and approved," which is bestowed only upon lawyers and judges with qualifications "well above the average." The host of mediocre candidates who formerly were designated as "qualified" are given no rating whatsoever. Where candidates are obviously

[5] Mayor Wagner, in redemption of a campaign pledge appointed a committee of 25 lawyers and civic leaders to screen all judicial aspirants and make recommendations to him for appointment. (*New York Times*, Feb. 18, 1962.)

unfit for judicial office, it has courageously agreed to designate them as "not qualified." Their hope is that the new method will "encourage political leaders to select candidates deserving the designation well qualified and approved."

The Allegheny County Bar Association has likewise had little success in improving judicial selection. Under their system, nominees of an appointed Judiciary Committee together with additional nominees made by the Bar at large are voted on in a bar plebiscite, each member voting for three candidates for each vacancy, indicating first, second, and third choice.

In past years these polls have had occasional success in influencing public opinion in primary fights, the most notable being the campaign of 1927, when 8 Bar-supported plebiscite candidates, some opposed by the political organization, were victorious. Ten years later most of these same judges were defeated for re-election.

Leaders of the Allegheny County Bar report that in recent years the plebiscite plan has not been effective, since as a practical matter most vacancies are filled by appointment and their elaborate bar procedures are largely a waste of time because of lack of cooperation by the Governors.

Aside from Philadelphia, which uses the bar plebiscite only in sitting judge polls, and Allegheny County, only four other counties have apparently resorted to bar plebiscites and polls. In Montgomery County, in 1957, the bar association attempted to obtain agreement among the judicial candidates that they would abide by the results of a bar poll and eliminate themselves from the primary election. The poll was taken, the losers refused to abide, and such ill feeling was engendered that the idea of bar polls has been abandoned.

Bar polls used in connection with open primaries or panels of prospective appointees have been assailed as mere popularity polls which encourage electioneering. It is true that considerations other than judicial qualifications may enter the vote, but the bar presently has no other forum in which to express its opinion.

Bar associations in other states have refined the sitting judge questionnaire used in par polls. Instead of the single question "is judge X qualified?" used in Philadelphia, various weighted counts are assigned to itemized categories such as judicial temperament, ability, promptness in dispatch of duties, impartiality, independence, integrity, with the proviso that if the candidate does not score at least 70 per cent, he will not be supported.[6]

[6] For a discussion of the Cleveland, Ohio, Bar Association procedure, see "Judicial Candidates. The Bar's Endorsement Role," *Cleveland Bar*, vol. 30, 1959, p. 167. For the recently revised Chicago plan, see *Journal of the American Judicature Society* vol. 43, 1959, p. 27.

One of the main weaknesses of the Bar Association procedure has been its failure to involve citizen support "so as to bring about concentration of electoral power on the most desirable candidates." The Philadelphia Bar has in recent years conducted two public campaigns for support of sitting judges, but has never engaged in attempts to influence open primaries or elections. . . .

## Three Methods of Minimizing Political Influence in Judicial Selection

There has been a constant concern in Pennsylvania and elsewhere with minimizing political influence in judicial selection. . . . Constitutional and legislative devices in Pennsylvania to achieve this end have, in the past, taken a number of forms, among them the separate judicial nominating conventions to replace the partisan party primary; the nonpartisan primary and election system and bipartisanship in appointment and election, which still has limited application in Pennsylvania.

A. *The Judicial Nominating Convention.* The Judicial Nominating Convention, abolished in Pennsylvania, still has its supporters. The late former Chief Justice Schaeffer of the Pennsylvania Supreme Court, speaking in opposition to the Pennsylvania version of the American Bar Association plan for selection of judges, stated:

I think, furthermore, the way to select judges, the way to nominate them, and that is where the thing starts, the way to nominate them is by judicial convention, statewide and districtwide. I think the convention sysem of all nominations is the best system we have ever had (applause). Because it is a representative system. This is a representative republic, and you start in the precincts to select delegates, and if you want to adopt what in the old days we knew as the Crawford County system, the voters can indicate who they want . . . the delegates to vote for, and in that way it becomes a more popular choice.

The Judicial Nominating Convention in practice fell prey to the same party forces which control the party primary system. In New York State, where the separate judicial nominating district convention is still in force, the convention, in effect, consists of no more than a slate of delegates put up by the district party leaders, and the nominations are still dominated by the party bosses. The system prevails in only three states, Illinois, Iowa and New York, and no serious student of judicial selection urges it as a solution to the problem. Iowa and Nebraska have already taken the first step towards constitutional approval of the American Bar Plan.

B. *The Nonpartisan Primary.* The nonpartisan primary and election of judges, on the other hand, still has great appeal and is used in eleven states. It was part of the reform movement which swept over the country after the exposures of the muckraking era of the early 1900s, which bared the low standards of morality of the political machines. Utah adopted it to implement the high principles enunciated in its constitution which was amended in 1945 to provide that judicial selection "shall be based solely upon consideration of fitness for office, without regard to any partisan political consideration, and free from influence of any person whomsoever." In 1913, Pennsylvania adopted a nonpartisan plan for the selection of judges. The first judicial election to which the nonpartisan system applied was to the new Municipal Court of Philadelphia, created in 1913. There were over 40 candidates in the primary for the then 6 judges of the court. The dominant political party, then the Republican Party, had no difficulty in adjusting itself to the new situation. The late former Chief Justice Schaeffer of the Pennsylvania Supreme Court described the situation:

> We had a nonpartisan act for the selection of judges, and when that act was in force, the first Municipal Court of Philadelphia had to be selected, and I came into the hotel two or three nights before the primary, and a then very potent figure in Philadelphia politics was sitting in the dining room. I knew him well. He called me over and he said, "I am selecting here in this room the entire Municipal Court of Philadelphia, because the names that I mark on this long list of candidates will go out on the sample ballots to be voted for tomorrow and these men will be the men who are selected."

The prediction of Justice Schaeffer's informant was substantially correct. Despite the wave of reform then sweeping the City which carried the Blankenburg Administration into office, all independent candidates were defeated except one, a Democrat who had joined the reform group as a marriage of convenience.

The Pennsylvania Nonpartisan Election Act was repealed in 1921, apparently without great regret by anyone. Although we have no documented record of its effect on judicial selection, the power of the party, from conversations with those still familiar with its operation, was never seriously affected.

The candidates on the nonpartisan ballot were plunged more than ever into politics, for, deprived of open party support, they were required to create their own campaign organization or to seek clandestine support within the party. The open primary also encouraged a plethora of publicity-seeking candidates, whose cheap antics in campaigns in some states seem almost unbelievable.

The success of the nonpartisan primary depends in a large measure on the political traditions of the state. Some of the Midwestern states, with a tradition of independent voters and liberal political crusaders, have undoubtedly used the nonpartisan device to weaken the hold of the old line party organizations on the electoral process. However, Pennsylvania, which was not ready for a nonpartisan primary system in 1913, is perhaps less prepared today from the viewpoint of voter militancy, independent political organizations and a sense of liberal tradition to effectively utilize the limited benefits available from a nonpartisan primary system.

C. *Bipartisanship.* Bipartisan division of judicial office as a means of minimizing political influences in the selection of judges, has been extolled by former Chief Justice Vanderbilt:

> There is much to be said for requiring, under any plan, the appointment of all judges on a bipartisan basis. Justice, on principle, should be bipartisan. Its administration should not be vested in a single party. Bipartisan appointments are the best way of proving to the public that one party does not control the courts, and that the courts are not in politics. The matter is of essential importance in the decision of highly controversial political issues. If all the judges in a bipartisan court, regardless of party affiliations, concur in the decision of such an issue, as they frequently do, then decision carries a weight with the public, that an opinion from a partisan bench could not possibly do.

A number of states, by constitution, legislation, and tradition, have established bipartisanship in the selection of judges. The Delaware constitution requires appointments to be equally balanced between the two major political parties. In New Jersey, an unwritten tradition of bipartisan selection of Justices of the Supreme Court was gradually extended by law to all courts. In Connecticut, the reorganization of the Justice of the Peace system into a new 44-judge statewide Circuit Court provided for equal division of judicial office between the two parties. In New York State, a tradition of forty years' standing, which calls for bipartisan support for promotion of the senior Associate Judge regardless of his party, was recently observed in the appointment of a new Chief Justice.

In Pennsylvania, the only judicial office to which bipartisanship directly applies is the Police Magistrate system of the City of Pittsburgh. The statute creating the court provides that the judges may not all be of the same political party, and of the seven judges, a token appointment is given to the minority party.

Magistrates in Philadelphia are also divided by law between the two parties for no voter may, under the Constitution, vote for more than two-thirds of the number of judges to be elected, thus indirectly giving the minority party representation. The Governor, however, in filling vacancies is not required to follow bipartisan lines so as to preserve the division of offices between the parties. Bipartisanship in the election of magistrates has proven a complete failure in improving the quality of that bench or of its administration, as documentation by the Philadelphia Bureau of Municipal Research has conclusively demonstrated. . . .

Bipartisanship is in practice little more than a division of the spoils between the two major political parties. . . .

## Plans for Selection and Tenure

The approach which comes nearest to solving the problems of selection and tenure is, as we have already indicated, the American Bar Association Plan for the nonpartisan selection and tenure of judges. Proposed by Professor Albert Kales in 1914 as a compromise system of selection, embodying elements of both the appointive and elective system, it was approved in 1937 by the American Bar Association. Missouri in 1940 became the first state to adopt the Plan, although California in 1934 had adopted an earlier version which operates in reverse of the American Bar Plan in that the California Governor first appoints and then submits the name for approval to a commission on qualifications. Kansas and Alaska have recently adopted the Plan. Iowa and Nebraska have taken the necessary legislative steps towards constitutional amendment, and numerous other states are engaged in campaigns for its adoption.

*The Missouri Plan.* The details of the Missouri Plan, whose general outlines have already been referred to, provide:

1. The Governor appoints from a list of three names submitted by a judicial Selection Commission.

2. The Selection Commission for the Appellate Courts consists of the Chief Justice, three lawyers elected by the State bar, and three laymen appointed by the Governor. Other than the Chief Justice, they cannot hold public office, are appointed for six-year, staggered terms, and are ineligible to succeed themselves. The Selection Commission for the lower courts has five members consisting of the presiding judge of the Court of Appeals in the judicial district, two lawyers and two laymen. They also have staggered, six-year terms, except for the presiding judge, and are ineligible to succeed themselves, and cannot hold public or party office.

3. After appointment from the list submitted, the appointee serves for a year and then submits himself for continuation in office for a full term to the electorate at the next general election. The judges' names are on a separate judicial ballot, without party designation, and the only question is, "Should Judge X of the ——— Court be returned to office?" There are no opponents on the ballot.

In the Pennsylvania Plan, each judge appointed serves for a term ending the first Monday of January following the next election appropriate for his election. In Pennsylvania local judges are elected in Municipal elections held in May in odd numbered years. Statewide judges are elected in either statewide elections held in even years or in Municipal elections. Thus the trial period of service can vary from about six months to over a year depending on the date of appointment.

4. At the expiration of his full term the judge under the Missouri and Pennsylvania Plans may file a notice of intention to succeed himself and his

name then appears on a separate judicial ballot at the next election for confirmation or rejection by the voters.

5. The judges are prohibited from making any contribution to or holding office in a political party or organization, or taking part in any political campaign. The Pennsylvania plan also so provides.

The Missouri Plan in operation demonstrated that a hostile Governor may attempt to reject panels unpalatable from a political point of view. In 1953, Governor Donnelly of Missouri refused to make any appointments from three panels to fill three vacancies because the nominees included not only members of the opposite party, but members of his own party who had politically opposed him. This he felt was rubbing salt in the wounds. The Commission refused to submit new names, claiming it had no constitutional authority to do so. Even though the Supreme Court revised its Rules of Procedure to permit the Commission, if it desired, to rearrange the panels or submit new names when any were withdrawn "for cause," the impasse carried on until the next year when, after rearrangement of the panels, the Governor quickly made the appointments. This isolated instance, which has not recurred in Missouri, has given rise to the claim by the minority of the 1958 Pennsylvania Constitutional Revision Commission that the plan fosters delay in appointment. This is not so. The incident was merely part of the growing pains of the new system.

*The Pennsylvania Plan.* The Pennsylvania Plan, like the Missouri Plan, is not statewide. Both plans are mandatory only as to the appellate courts and the lower courts of the major cities; they are optional with the voters as to the courts of other counties. In Missouri it applies only to St. Louis and Jackson County (Kansas City). The Pennsylvania Plan applies only as to the appellate courts and courts of record of Philadelphia and Allegheny Counties. As to all other counties, it is optional. This is, frankly, a concession intended to diminish the opposition of rural legislators, who under the banner of home rule would probably otherwise defeat the Plan in its entirety.

The Pennsylvania Plan also differs from the Missouri Plan in that it expressly provides that the Governor may reject the panels of nominees and demand new panels until an appointment is made. This is considered by the proponents of the Plan as a minor administrative difference. Others consider it a major weakness. It was, frankly, a concession to soften the blow to the political parties and the present prerogatives of the Governor. There is no doubt that in effect it changes the character of the judicial nominating commission into an advisory committee and that the commission's effectiveness will depend upon its prestige, the quality of its nominees and the pressures of public opinion upon the Governor.

The Pennsylvania Plan gives both the State and local commission members only three-year, unstaggered terms; also the local commissions have seven members, one judge who may be chosen from another judicial district, three lawyers from the district selected in accordance with rules prescribed by the Supreme Court and three lay members, appointed by the Governor. . . .

*Experience in Missouri.* Although volumes have been written concerning the Missouri Plan and testimonials to its success are legion, there are unfortunately no recent definitive studies in depth, such as the early University of Missouri study made after the plan was in operation only for a few years. However, public opinion gives it impressive endorsement. It has been praised and actively supported by every leader of the bar in the State of Missouri. The majority of the rank and file of the bar, even those apathetic in originally supporting it, joined the public and the media of information in rallying to its support on the occasions when, since its adoption, it came under attack. Attempts to repeal the Plan in the Missouri Constitutional Convention of 1943–44 were not only defeated, but the plan was, in fact, expanded under the new Missouri Constitution of 1945 extending it to other courts.

Many of the old doubters, including former Governor Phil N. Donnelly, who made twenty appointments under the Plan in two nonconsecutive terms and was bitterly opposed to it, no longer favor a return to the old elective method of selection. Former Governor Forrest Smith, who made 14 appointments under the Plan, although still not committed to it, grudgingly agreed that the quality of the judges has improved.

The Plan still has active opponents. Among them is the present Governor James T. Blair, who thus far has made four appointments under the Plan and hopes for a return to the old interim appointive and elective system. Public sentiment, from all that can be gathered, does not support him, and the political leaders apparently have no thought at the moment of testing public opinion on the issue. All this speaks rather well for a Plan which its opponents in Missouri, in Pennsylvania and elsewhere call an attack on the democratic right of the people to elect their own judges and on democracy itself. The cry of lack of democracy is an overworked shibboleth. The Plan is democratic; the people do elect and re-elect judicial candidates, and in a more effective manner than under the present appointive elective system in Pennsylvania. The election is concerned solely with the qualifications of the candidate and the electorate is unrestricted in its judgment. It may reject a judge on the ground that he is competent or incompetent, too liberal or too conservative, prolabor or antilabor. These have been issues in Missouri.[7] Even political

[7] In 1956, the Teamsters Union in St. Louis urged that all seven members of the Supreme Court be rejected, although only three were to be voted on for re-election, on the ground that the court had been antilabor in some recent decisions. The incumbent judges, one Republican and two Democrats, were retained in office.

considerations are conceivable, though the ballot carries no party designation.

But whatever the reasons for or against the judicial candidate, the campaign for acceptance or rejection under the Plan is clearcut. It is not confused by party labels or public issues having no relevancy to the judiciary. It directs the attention of the electorate to the point at issue, namely, the judicial officer and his right to continue in office. A judicial candidate is no longer a tail to a political kite.

The opponents of the Plan and the minority of the Pennsylvania Constitutional Revision Commission claim that only an election which offers a choice of rival candidates in primary and general elections satisfies the requirements of democracy and that an election in which an incumbent judicial candidate runs against his record is a mockery "since you can't lick somebody with nobody."

And, should the idea behind *judicial* elections be to encourage a party or group within a party to lick an incumbent in office? Should a judge be required to continually defend his tenure of office against self-seekers, against party displeasure, against political factions? Should not the only question be his qualifications and conduct in office?

The claim of the Pennsylvania minority that the abandonment of the open primary limits the field of opportunity to seek judicial office fails to take cognizance of the facts of political life, for as already pointed out, it is only on rare occasions that the choice of the party leaders can be prevailed against in the primary, and then without assurance that the successful candidate is any better qualified than his defeated opponent. Under the Plan, the field of opportunity for judicial office is in reality widened, for the nonpartisan commission of judges, lawyers and laymen are free to explore the entire range of the bar in their selection, unrestricted by party lines and by the political considerations in "slating" which so often minimize judicial qualifications.

### The Missouri Plan Proves Itself

Summarizing the twenty years' experience under the Missouri Plan, the consensus of informed observers is that it has (1) raised perceptibly the quality of judicial appointment, (2) promoted security of tenure, so essential for independence from political pressures, (3) promoted nonpartisanship in selection, gradually resulting in a bipartisan bench, (4) removed the judges from the political arena by prohibiting political activity and contributions, (5) continued to give recognition as under the present elective system to the racial, ethnic and religious groups in the community, but on a basis of higher qualification, (6) continued to give recognition, as under the present elective system, to public service in the legislative, executive and other departments of government as one road to judicial office, but on the basis of higher qualifications, (7) encouraged the meager beginning of a career service by promotion from within the judicial system, and (8) restored the confidence of the public in the courts of Missouri.

Outstanding men, such as Justice Laurance Hyde of the Missouri Supreme Court, who under the old system could not, in the opinion of most members of the Missouri Bar, conceivably have been slated by political leaders because of political independence, have done much to improve judicial administration in Missouri. Lawyers, who under the old system would not have given up their practices for the hazards of primary and general elections, are now willing to accept appointments.

The fear of some Pennsylvania legislators, expressed to the writer that the Plan will favor "appointment of blue bloods of the bar" and will stifle the ambitions of men of humble origin, has not been borne out in practice. This is confirmed by our conversations and correspondence with leaders of the Missouri Bar and examination of the published biographical material of the 44 Missouri judges appointed under the Plan. They come from all walks of life and from all races, colors and creeds. The ethnic, religious and racial groups of the community are represented. There is no "big office" domination of the selections.

Lawyers with backgrounds of service in the legislative and executive branches of government have not been discriminated against under the Plan. This has disenchanted some who expected the Plan to rip out root and branch appointment of judges with political backgrounds. A review of biographical material indicates that as in Pennsylvania the public prosecutor's office is still a stepping stone to judicial office in Missouri, but the concentration of former prosecutors in judicial office is much less marked than in Pennsylvania.[8]

An interesting development is taking place, in that outstanding lawyers who have served the Supreme and Circuit Courts of Appeals as appointed Commissioners under the Missouri judicial system have been nominated and appointed to the Supreme Court and the Circuit Court.

---

[8] William Crowdus, former President of the St. Louis and the Missouri State Bar, in a recent speech commenting on the political background of recent appointees, frankly stated, "The last two judges appointed to the Circuit Court of Jackson County had been very active in political organizations and there was some comment that it would have been better if non-politicians, as it were, received the appointments. However, everyone agrees that both these judges are capable and honest men." (Crowdus, "20 Years of the Missouri Plan," 31 *Okla. Bar J.* 2270, 1960.

This is a form of career promotion, which has brought criticism from some members of the bar that the Court is perpetuating itself. However, the high qualifications of the Commissioners have never been challenged and their selection has injected into the bloodstream of the judicial system first class practicing lawyers of wide experience with a quasi-judicial background and helped provide an experienced and balanced bench.

No Missouri judge appointed under the Plan since 1940 has been rejected. Had the old elective system been followed, Missouri judges would undoubtedly, as in the past, been swept in and out of office by party swings. In the 1942 election, when Missouri went Republican, two Supreme Court Justices, previously elected as Democrats, were nevertheless retained in office. In St. Louis, six Democratic judges were retained despite a Republican sweep. In the November 1944 election, all four Republican judges seeking re-election were retained in office despite a Democratic landslide.

The security of tenure enjoyed by the judges under the Missouri Plan has been used by the minority of the Pennsylvania Constitutional Revision Commission as an argument against the Plan on the ground that it freezes into office at the time of its adoption many incompetent sitting judges who probably could not have been nominated and appointed originally under the Plan.

There is no doubt that the bar polls in Missouri which found these judges qualified were probably too tender in their judgment and that Pennsylvania lawyers will do likewise. However, one holdover judge, who had previously been re-elected by the political machine, despite universal condemnation by the bar and public press, was defeated for re-election under the Plan. Because the judge was voted on by a separate judicial ballot solely on the basis of qualification, the public was made aware of the issue and acted accordingly. Time has cured the problem of the holdover judges, for in the 20 years since the adoption of the Plan, retirement or death has paved the way for new appointees and the same will happen in Pennsylvania if the Plan is adopted here.

Security of tenure in Missouri has been achieved without the need for political campaigning and contributions which are prohibited. The campaigns for the sitting judges have been conducted by the bar associations and the public at minimum cost, usually a few hundred dollars, and in a dignified manner. The judge is not compelled to neglect his judicial duties during elections. The bar has assumed an important responsibility under the Plan, for its plebiscites as to whether the judge is qualified carry great weight with the public. There is no reason to doubt that, if the Plan is adopted in Pennsylvania, the bar, even though not integrated, will rise to its new responsibilities.

### The Pennsylvania Plan Hangs Fire

The Pennsylvania Plan, approved by the Pennsylvania Bar Association in 1947, remains unimplemented.[a] Despite the dedicated devotion of a succession of chairmen of the Pennsylvania Bar Association Special Committee on the Pennsylvania Plan, it is paid but lip service by the bar. . . .

There seems little hope that the 1963 Session of the Legislature will act differently than its predecessors. A 1957 survey by Professor William J. Keefe of Chatham College, under a grant from the Citizenship Clearing House of Pennsylvania, revealed that a clear majority of the legislators in both parties favored the continuance of partisan election of judges. Of the 29 lawyer-members of the legislature responding to the survey, almost 95 per cent were against the Plan, with the hard core of opposition centered in Philadelphia and Pittsburgh. Surprisingly, in the suburban areas and some of the rural areas many of the legislators, although opposed to the Pennsylvania Plan, expressed a desire for nonpartisan elections. The survey concluded with the observation that proponents of the Plan are faced with three blunt political facts: "(1) institutional forms and partisan loyalties in the United States have an extraordinary tenacity, (2) reform movements are hindered where there is virtually no public opinion on the issue . . . , (3) political change is wrought by people organized and insistent."

## FEDERAL JUDICIAL SELECTION — THE ROLE OF THE AMERICAN BAR ASSOCIATION

*By Bernard G. Segal*

THE ROLE of the American Bar Association in the matter of the appointment of Federal judges commenced in 1945. In that year, the Association created for the first time, a Special Committee on Federal Judiciary. This Committee was successful in quickly establishing a cor-

---

[a] In 1964 Governor Scranton by executive order established a commission to nominate candidates for the judiciary in Philadelphia and promised to make appointments from names so designated.

---

Reprinted from an address delivered March 28, 1961 to the American College of Trial Lawyers with the permission of the author. Bernard G. Segal, Esq., until 1962 was Chairman of the Standing Committee on Federal Judiciary of the American Bar Association, and is a partner of the Philadelphia law firm of Schnader, Harrison, Segal, and Lewis.

dial relationship with the Judiciary Committee of the United States Senate. The Chairman of the Senate Committee made it a practice, which succeeding Chairmen have continued, to notify the Chairman of the ABA Committee whenever there was to be a hearing on a judicial nomination. The ABA Committee was thus afforded an opportunity to advise the Senate Committee of its collective opinion on the nominee's qualifications.

In two notable instances in those days, the strong objections of the ABA Committee, backed by evidence vigorously presented at public hearings of the Senate Subcommittee, resulted in President's withdrawing the nominations and submitting other more qualified nominees instead. . . .

From 1945 to 1952, the ABA Committee made repeated efforts to establish a similar relationship with the Attorney General, but it was completely unsuccessful. The channels of communication from the Attorney General to the Committee were practically nonexistent. Under these circumstances, the Committee followed the only procedure available to it. When it knew of a vacancy, it canvassed the judges and lawyers of the particular community and sent to the Attorney General a list of qualified persons available for appointment. Often, however, before the Committee had an opportunity to complete its canvass, the nomination had already been made. And in numerous other cases, the Committee's first information of the existence of a vacancy came from the public announcement that the President had sent a nominee's name to the Senate. It hardly seems possible that this was the situation as recently as eight years ago.

In August, 1952, a notable step forward was taken. Ross L. Malone . . . had just been appointed the Deputy Attorney General of the United States. Promptly thereafter, he entered into an agreement with the ABA Committee that he would submit to the ABA Committee for its investigation, report, and recommendation, the name of each prospective judicial nominee. This was to be done simultaneously with the submission to the Federal Bureau of Investigation, which traditionally had conducted investigations prior to any nomination. As it happened, there were no judicial nominations during the short period of President Truman's term which remained, but Mr. Malone's agreement represented an important principle, officially pronounced, and a blueprint for future development.

Attorney General Brownell and Deputy Attorney General Rogers, with President Eisenhower's approval, put the system into effect immediately after they assumed office in 1953. There was one modification. Mr. Brownell suggested that the Committee's influence would be more persuasive and its reports less suspect of partisanship in behalf of any individual, if it discontinued its practice of proposing names of individuals when vacancies occurred. The Committee readily adopted Mr. Brownell's recommendation, and since then, the ABA has scrupulously avoided initiating any nominations.

Step by step, appointment by appointment, the program developed during Mr. Brownell's tenure as Attorney General, and later during Mr. Rogers' when Judge Walsh became the Deputy Attorney General.

During the eight years, there were of course many problems and numerous difficulties, but there were remarkably rapid advances, too.

A word about the ABA Standing Committee on Federal Judiciary. It consists of 11 members, one from each of the Federal circuits. . . .

The primary sources of the Committee's information on a prospective nominee's qualifications are the opinions of the judges and the lawyers of the community involved. We endeavor to secure the views of a fair cross section of the Bench and Bar there, always including ABA, State, and local bar association officials, and Fellows [of the American College of Trial Lawyers]. In a very real sense, our Committee is the conduit through which the informed opinion of the Bench and the Bar in a given area, sifted and weighed, is objectively conveyed to the President, through the Attorney General.

To us as lawyers it seems clear that the opinions of lawyers, through the Organized Bar, should be sought and should carry weight with the President in the appointment of judges. Government seeking a scientist for highly skilled work in a critical scientific area would be expected to solicit the advice of the professional community of scientists. In the process of judicial appointments, government is seeking a lawyer for highly skilled work in the critical areas of litigation and justice; it would seem equally appropriate that it officially solicit the recommendation of the professional community of lawyers. . . .

From the beginning, a problem with which the Committee has constantly grappled is the definition of qualified. Some standards must be applied in determining whether an individual is "qualified" to be a Federal judge. But the Committee's work is collecting the opinions of the profession—of lawyers and judges—and these opinions come to us in all varieties of expression, a whole range of information and reflections. We dare not impose standards in advance of our canvass; we must, however, apply objective standards in collating all the data and the opinions we receive.

Everyone would readily agree that every person appointed to a Federal judgeship should be possessed of character, judgment, industry, experience, judicial temperament, professional ability. This is axiomatic. But to apply this principle to any given case is sometimes difficult. Long ago, a great practicing lawyer, Alexander Hamilton, observing how difficult it would be in the new government to secure able judges, commented on the difficulty of accurately appraising in advance whether an individual would be a good judge. "Science," he observed, "had discovered no way of measuring the faculties of the mind." It hasn't even yet.

All of us as lawyers have observed the metamorphosis which that thin, black robe can cause in a man. But dare we count on it? The office can make, has made, its holder, on occasion. On more occasions, however, the holder has reduced the office to his own level. Normally, we can rely on a lawyer's past record as a reliable guide to his future performance. We have little else to rely on; it is his past record which our canvass of professional opinion reveals.

Sometimes, as I have said, the record reveals facts which oblige the Committee to report adversely on a prospective nominee. There is no more difficult or unpleasant task for any group of lawyers, than to report to executive authority, that an individual is deemed by his professional colleagues Not Qualified for a post to which he has probably aspired during the whole of his career. Unfortunately, our Committee has had to make many such unfavorable reports—as many as twenty-seven in a single year. I assure you, we have never made an unfavorable report that was not based on especially intensive investigation, particular thoroughness, the most careful scrutiny and weighing of testimony, and a very deep searching of our own collective soul.

Many reasons may contribute to the judgment Not Qualified. Two in particular have caused a great deal of controversy before we were able to establish them as accepted principles, at least in so far as the President, the Attorney General, and the Deputy Attorney General were concerned.

One is the matter of age. It is only three years since it has become firmly established that no lawyer 60 years or over, should be appointed to a lifetime judgeship for the first time, unless he is regarded by professional opinion as Well Qualified or Exceptionally Well Qualified, and is in excellent health. This rule has not been applied to a Federal judge under consideration for elevation to an appellate court, but the rule has been that in no event, should anyone, even a judge being elevated to an appellate court, be appointed if he has passed his sixty-fourth birthday. Congress itself has decreed that a Federal judge, with the requisite years of service, may retire at age 65 with full pay for life. Surely this is not the age at which a person should be tendered a new appointment.

One other qualification—really disqualification—has aroused even more dispute. This is the question whether a lawyer should be required to have trial experience before he is considered qualified for appointment to the Federal bench. In England, of course, no one but a barrister is eligible for appointment to the bench. Our Committee has not adopted the rigid view that only trial lawyers should be considered, but we have taken the position, from which we have refused to recede, that in the case of a vacancy in a United States District Court—a trial bench called upon to conduct the most complex and varied litigation—a lawyer to be considered must have a reasonable amount of trial experience, preferably at least some of it in the Federal courts. We have stood firm in this position, even though it has resulted in delaying appointment of needed judges for a year and a half in two cases and for more than a year in a third. In two of the cases, the individuals were incumbent United States Attorneys. Nevertheless, the President and the Attorney General supported the Committee's position and the appointments were not made.

A measure of the usefulness of the Committee to public authority may be found in the increased use of the Committee in the past few years. For example, during the first years of the Eisenhower Administration, the Committee was not consulted respecting appointments to the Supreme Court of the United States. But a change came beginning with the nomination of Mr. Justice Brennan, when President Eisenhower announced that he wished to have the report and recommendation of the ABA Committee before considering the nomination. And from that time on, by virtue of the President's decision, the Committee's role respecting Supreme Court nominations has been the same as for all other courts.

A serious complaint, proved by our experience over several years' appointments, was that the Committee's views were being sought too late in the nominating process. Usually, we received only a single name per vacancy—the person who had virtually been decided upon for the vacancy, most often with the knowledge of the prospective nominee and his Senatorial sponsor. Under these circumstances, only clearest evidence of the most glaring lack of qualification could stop the nomination.

Three years ago [1958] in a step of the utmost importance, Judge Walsh agreed to use the Committee at a much earlier point in the selective process—to request of us an informal investigation and report on every individual whose name was submitted to the President or the Attorney General by any responsible source, and who therefore was likely to be seriously considered for the nomination. This preliminary screening, conducted by the Chairman and the member of the Committee from the particular Circuit in which the vacancy exists, has provided the Attorney General with information concerning the comparative qualifications, early in the appointive process, of all probable candidates. It has in numerous cases enabled the President to hold out for the better or the best of a number of qualified candidates.

The informal requests did not eliminate formal reports. In every case, the Committee is still asked, at the same time as the FBI, for a formal report on the qualifications of the person who finally appears most likely to be nominated.

To accommodate the procedures of the Committee to this significant new function, the Committee no longer uses only the word Qualified in affirmative reports. It now distinguishes among those whom professional opinion deems Qualified, Well Qualified, or Exceptionally Well Qualified.

These changes have brought singularly beneficial results, even though the informal reports have vastly increased the Committee's responsibilities and the volume of its work. In a single year, the Committee has been called upon to investigate and report on the qualifications of 127 judges and lawyers, as many as 19 in connection with a single vacancy. If they were evenly spaced, that would mean a report every two and a half working days, if the Committee worked six days a week. This gives some indication of the high level of the liaison which had developed between the Department of Justice and the Committee. It could not have been improved upon. . . .

By the end of the Eisenhower Administration—eight years after the Attorney General's arrangement with the ABA Committee had first been put into effect—certain statements of the utmost significance could be made with complete assurance. It could be said that no person would be considered by the President for nomination to a lifetime judgeship without first, a preliminary screening, later, a formal report to the Attorney General, by the American Bar Association's Standing Committee on Federal Judiciary. It could be said that the President would not nominate to any Federal court, including the Supreme Court, any person whom the Committee, for valid reasons stated in detail to the Deputy Attorney General, had reported as "Not Qualified." Indeed, during the last three years of the Administration [1958–60] no nomination had been made without a prior favorable report from the Committee; during these three years, two out of every three appointees to the United States courts had been rated by the Committee, not merely as Qualified, but as Well Qualified or Exceptionally Well Qualified—designations reserved for the best qualified among those available.

In one respect, however, the record was not improved. Appointments during the past eight years have been made, as before, primarily from members of the political party of the administration in office. Invariably, Presidents have appointed judges from the ranks of their own party. Criticism on this score goes back as far the presidencies of John Adams and Thomas Jefferson. Judicial appointments by Democratic Presidents Cleveland, Wilson, Franklin D. Roosevelt, and Truman ranged from 92 per cent Democratic by President Truman to 99 per cent Democratic by President Wilson. Judicial appointments of Republican Presidents Theodore Roosevelt, Taft, Harding, Coolidge, Hoover, and Eisenhower ranged from 86 per cent Republican by President Hoover to 98 per cent Republican by President Harding.

The implication of this is not at all to suggest that political bias or partisanship is an issue in the courtroom. . . . [W]ith remarkably few exceptions in our history, Federal judges, secure in life tenure, have left political affiliations behind them when they mounted the bench, and have conducted the judicial function without consideration of previous party associations.

And, of course, there is nothing inherently wrong about political activity prior to a lawyers appointment to the bench. Lawyers traditionally are leaders in politics. One of the strongest positions the ABA Committee has taken on any question is that political activity should not bar a lawyer from appointment as a Federal judge—any more than it should be his primary qualification.

But certainly we cannot expect to have full citizen respect for law and our courts, so long as members of the public have their present cynicism about "judicial appointments and politics." Citizens have, not unjustly, come to regard judicial appointments as matters of political patronage, just like appointments of local postmasters.

Under these circumstances, the American Bar Association has long contended for the austere objective that only the best qualified lawyers or judges available should be appointed Federal judges, without regard for political affiliation. We recognize we are a long way from achieving this objective, but we shall continue to strive for it nevertheless.

In the meantime, we seek bipartisanship in appointments as an intermediate step. This is controversial, too. There are those who argue that in bipartisan appointments, politics would continue to be as much of a factor as before. I do not think so. As Judge Walsh has aptly remarked, bipartisan appointments would "reduce the impact of partisan politics on judicial selection." It would create a wholesome atmosphere around the whole issue of judicial appointments, and would be a long step toward establishing in the public mind, "the difference between a Federal judgeship and Federal patronage."

When President Eisenhower assumed office, approximately 84 per cent of the Federal judges had been Democrats when appointed. He announced his determination to make appointments on a bipartisan basis as promptly as possible. Four years later, when the balance of judgeships was approaching more nearly toward equality between the two parties, Attorney General Rogers stated that it would be desirable as a matter of national policy "to prevent a gross imbalance from ever occurring again." He urged both political parties, in the public interest, to arrange "appropriate safeguards" to this end.

Last summer, for the first time in the history of either political party, the ABA Standing Committee and an ABA Special Committee . . . were successful in having included in the Republican Platform, a plank calling for Federal judges to be "appointed on the basis of highest qualifications and without limitation to a single political party." (Possibly, in an oral presentation, the ABA representative might have persuaded the Democratic Platform Committee to recede from its rejection of the ABA proposal, but an unfortunate plane cancellation resulted in our representative's arriving at Los Angeles just after the meeting of the Committee had been adjourned.)

In a letter to . . . John Randall, then President of the American Bar Association, Vice-President Nixon said last August: ". . . I believe it is essential . . . that the best qualified lawyers and judges available be appointed to judicial office, and . . . that the number of judges in federal courts from each of the major political parties be approximately equal. . . ."

Editorial writers throughout the country hailed these statements at the time, and urged their implementation at the earliest possible moment. Undoubtedly, the stage was set for a major step forward in the substantial reduction of political considerations in judicial appointments.

That was the situation as a new Administration took over the reins on January 20, 1961. . . .

# THE BAR REVIEWS
# THE JUDICIAL APPOINTMENTS
# OF PRESIDENT KENNEDY *By Bernard G. Segal*

IN THE matter of judicial appointments, the year which has elapsed since this House last met is without precedent in American history. And it has been far and away, the most difficult and demanding year that the Standing Committee on Federal Judiciary has ever had.

*The Volume of Appointments.* Since President Kennedy assumed office, he has nominated 128 persons to the Federal bench, 113 of them to lifetime judgeships and all but ten since this House last met. Thus, during the past twelve months, the President has been nominating Federal judges at a rate of almost ten per month.

There are nineteen vacancies, for which nominations have not yet been made, of which sixteen are lifetime judgeships.

Accordingly, there have been 147 judicial vacancies in the Kennedy

---

This selection is part of the oral presentation of the *1962 Report of the Standing Committee of the Federal Judiciary of the American Bar Association to the Association's House of Delegates,* August 7, 1962. Mr. Segal presented the Report on behalf of the Committee as its Chairman. Reprinted with the permission of the author. (See biographical note, p. 255.)

administration thus far—almost 40 per cent of all the judgeships in the Federal system at the time President Kennedy came into office. Except for Presidents Truman and Eisenhower, this is more vacancies than any President of the United States has had to fill in two entire terms of office.

Since the Kennedy Administration began, your Committee has been requested to investigate and report informally to the Attorney General on the qualifications of 463 persons for lifetime judgeships, and to submit in addition 147 Formal Reports, or an aggregate of 610 reports. The Committee has rendered, in a little over one year, almost double the number of reports it made in the eight years of the two Eisenhower administrations. Since the enactment of the Omnibus Judgeship bill on May 19, 1961, these reports have averaged almost 10 per week....

*Quality.* So much for the quantity of appointments. What of their quality?

Of the 100 nominations or recess appointments to lifetime judgeships made by President Kennedy since the last Annual Report of this Committee, sixteen were reported by your Committee as Exceptionally Well Qualified, forty-five as Well Qualified, thirty-one as Qualified, and eight as Not Qualified. This means that 61 per cent of the nominees during the past year—those rated Exceptionally Well Qualified or Well Qualified—were among the best qualified judges and lawyers available for the particular position. On the other hand, for the first time in several years, nominations were made of individuals whom your Committee—and in some cases State and local Bar Associations as well—had reported as Not Qualified.

Your Committee has greatly improved its procedures in the past few years and has introduced important innovations to make its work more effective. We recognize the possibility of error, and we are therefore scrupulously careful before we report any individual as Not Qualified. We have never made such an adverse report until after an especially intensive investigation, particular thoroughness, a most careful scrutiny and weighing of the testimony, and a very deep searching of our own collective soul.

*Appointment of Persons Rated Not Qualified.* It is therefore, most disappointing that eight, indeed that any, nominations should have been made of persons who, after exhaustive investigation of the views of Bench and Bar, your Committee, unanimously and with regret—and in some cases, State and local Bar associations as well—had concluded were Not Qualified for reasons fully stated to the Attorney General or the Deputy Attorney General. Of these eight, one was found to be Not Qualified because of having passed the age of 65 years. This has occasioned inquiries as to whether the present Administration had abandoned the rule that it would not appoint any person who had reached his sixty-fifth year. Our Committee is confident that this one departure from the rule may be regarded as the proverbial exception proving the rule, rather than as evidence of a decision by the present Administration to abandon it.

There is one thing I believe I should make clear. Our Committee is entirely convinced that the objectives of the President, the Attorney General, and the Deputy Attorney General do not differ essentially from our own, insofar as the *quality* of judicial appointments is concerned. We are fully aware that political pressures are great on any President, and of course, this is all the more so at the start of a new Administration when there has been a change from one Party to another. The need for confirmation by the Senate continues to be a major consideration in the making of nominations. Inevitably, the cumulative pressures resulting from the unprecedently large number of appointments in so short a period, have been greater than ever before; and a time urgency created by the desperate need for appointments in courts laboring under heavy backlogs and tremendous delays in litigation, have substantially aggravated the situation.

Parenthetically, it is worth repeating and emphasizing that the task has not been made easier for the Attorney General or his Staff by the fact that many lawyers, and even judges, are unable to resist, and they therefore comply, with the importunings of even clearly unqualified candidates or their sponsors, by writing strong letters of endorsement or commendation. Thus, they arm poor candidates and their supporters with what appears to be substantiation from highly reputable sources of claims that the candidates are men of the highest qualifications, when the contrary is the fact. . . .

[Y]our Committee believes that it is of the utmost importance that we do not permit our disappointment at the fact that the President has appointed to the Federal Court, 8 individuals whom the Committee unanimously voted to be Not Qualified, to make us lose sight of the very significant grounds for satisfaction which presently exist. Let me state a few of them.

First, of course, is the excellent liaison between the Department of Justice and your Committee, which President Kennedy publicly acclaimed and supported in a telegram addressed to Whitney North Seymour as President at the Annual Meeting last August. The present relationship of your Committee with Attorney General Kennedy and Deputy Attorney General Katzenbach could not be improved upon.

Second, is the fact that it may be said with complete confidence that today the Attorney General would not make a recommendation for an appointment to a lifetime judgeship, and the President would not make the appointment, until after receiving and studying the Committee's report on the candidate's qualifications and affording the Committee opportunity for fullest discussion. As long as this relationship continues in its present strength, your Committee hopes that in the more normal period of appointments which lies ahead, and with the experience the Administration has acquired, there will be no more appointments of persons who must be rated as Not Qualified.

Third, is the fact that, by and large, the 105 nominees for lifetime judgeships upon whom your Committee has reported favorably since President Kennedy came into office add a very good quality of judges to the Federal Bench. Many of them are highly able and among the best qualified judges and lawyers available for appointment. Of these 105, our Committee rated almost 70 per cent as Well Qualified or Exceptionally Well Qualified. These nominees meet very high standards of judicial selection. Many of these appointments came only after determined perseverance by the President and by the Attorney General and his Staff.

Fourth, consider these facts. Of the hundreds of persons that we were requested by the Attorney General to screen and report on informally, we reported 158 as Not Qualified, and 150 of them were not nominated. While the fact that the Attorney General refers a name to the Committee for preliminary investigation and an Informal Report does not necessarily mean that he considers the person to be qualified, or even that he has as yet conducted any investigation of his own, nevertheless, many of these persons who were not nominated had strong political sponsorship and support. Under conditions existing not so many years ago, at least some of them, probably a substantial number, would have been appointed.

Finally, it is most significant that a very high percentage of persons whom your Committee, in its Informal Reports, found to be Well Qualified or Exceptionally Well Qualified, were ultimately nominated by President Kennedy. It is apparent that where a highly qualified candidate is put forward by a responsible source, the Attorney General and his Staff are becoming increasingly successful in eliminating less worthy competitors, who in many cases were the first preferences of the same sponsors. And there are several instances of men rated as Exceptionally Well Qualified or in the top range of Well Qualified, who have been nominated although they had no political sponsorship whatever.

This spotlights an important challenge to the organized Bar of the nation. If the Record is to be improved in the future, a primary task is to insure that the roster of persons submitted to the President include predominantly, if not exclusively, persons of the first rank. Plainly, this calls for action by State and local Bar Associations, which can best exert local pressures on the United States Senators and other political powers in State and local communities. The Resolution adopted last August by the

Assembly of this Association, and concurred in by this House calling upon State and local Bar Associations (1) to recruit and persuade the best qualified judges and lawyers to accept appointment if tendered and (2) to establish liaison and work with the United States Senators and other responsible sources who propose persons to the President and the Attorney General for appointment as judges, has as yet produced no significant results. It may well be that once again this Association will have to provide the active leadership to get the ball rolling.

*Political Complexion of Appointees.* I come now to the subject of bipartisanship.

On January 20, 1961, when President Kennedy was inaugurated, the Judges sitting in the Federal Courts were for the first time in more than a generation, just about evenly divided as to their preappointment political party affiliation—160 Democrats and 161 Republicans. It is true that as far back as the Presidencies of John Adams and Thomas Jefferson, judicial appointments by Presidents have been primarily from the ranks of their own party, and this has continued up to the present time with only President Hoover (whose appointments were 83 per cent Republican) falling below the 91 per cent mark for appointments from his own party. Nevertheless, we had hoped that with so many appointments to be made for the first time in the Country's history, and with no imbalance to redress for the first time in a generation, President Kennedy would break new ground and introduce a more substantial degree of bipartisanship into his appointments than any President in the past.

When this House met last February, we expressed great disappointment that except for two recess appointees of President Eisenhower confirmed by the present Congress at President Kennedy's request, and one member of the Liberal Party in New York appointed by President Kennedy, every other appointee of the Kennedy Administration up to that time had been a Democrat at the time of his selection. The Kennedy nominations, therefore, then stood at 84 Democrats, 1 Liberal Party member, and no Republicans.

We stated that we believed a great opportunity had been lost, but hopefully added first, that this result had not been without effort in the other direction by the Administration, and second, that a number of Republicans were then under consideration with the likelihood that some of them would be appointed. We affirmed our intention to continue to hope and strive, intermediately for bipartisanship in judicial appointments, eventually for nonpartisanship.

Today, the disparity is once again substantial. In place of the even division between the two parties at the beginning of the Administration, there are now on the Federal Bench, 223 Democrats, 158 Republicans, 1 Liberal Party member, and one unaffiliated with any political party.

Nevertheless, we take heart from the developments which have occurred since the last meeting of this House. On March 12, 1962, President Kennedy made his first nomination of a Republican for a judgeship; and of the 21 nominees for lifetime Federal judgeships starting with March 12, 1962, 8 were Republicans and 13 were Democrats. Thus, more than one-third of the nominations since March 12 have gone to members of the opposition Party.

The reaction of news media and editorial writers to the partisan character of the appointments, after the February meeting of this House, was widespread and vehement, and came from all parts of the Country. We have quoted typical editorials in the Committee Report which is in your hands.[a] Similarly, the appointments of Republicans by the President more recently, have been widely hailed by some of the very same news media and editorial writers.

While there has been no official public statement by any Administration spokesman, your Committee applauds the bipartisan character of the nominations by President Kennedy since March 12 and continues to hope that for the future, we may anticipate an increase in the degree of bipartisanship in Federal judicial appointments. We are not unmindful of the obstacles which will be thrown in the President's path by some Senators and by others of great political power in his own Party. But we are convinced that once an Administration is firmly committed to the goal of a reasonable degree of bipartisanship, public confidence and commendation will be so strong and the support of newspapers and other mass media will be so enthusiastic, the Administration will prevail. Thereby, the cause of justice will be greatly enhanced, not because better judges will necessarily result from bipartisanship, but because citizen respect for our courts will be greatly increased when members of the public come to realize that judicial appointments are no longer matters of political patronage like appointments of local postmasters. The fight will not be easily won, but the cause is worth the battle, and the President who fights and wins it, will merit the acclaim and the gratitude of the nation. He will have made our generation's greatest contribution to the preservation of an independent judiciary. . . .

Countless mountains, large and small, remain to be conquered. Not the least of them is the problem of finding a way to persuade top-flight lawyers to consider judicial office, and to galvanize support for such men in a form cognizable by the Senators and other political leaders of the communities involved.

[a] Among others, the Report quoted this excerpt from the *Christian Science Monitor* of February 24, 1962: But doesn't it seem a little peculiar that out of all the lawyers in the United States who are regarded as Republicans the administration could not find seven whose juristic abilities would warrant their appointment ahead of the seven whom a bar association committee considers Not Qualified?

We have previously taken notice of Chief Justice Vanderbilt's famous utterance, that judicial reform is no sport for the short-winded. It is also no sport for the skeptic. Ten years ago, few would have predicted the accomplishments of the American Bar Association in the field of judicial selection today. These accomplishments, here as elsewhere, are never brought about by men of little faith. I have every confidence that the march forward will continue unchecked, and that the high goals of this Association will eventually be achieved.

## THE SELECTION OF JUDGES IN ENGLAND: A STANDARD FOR COMPARISON By Morse Erskine

NO ONE can doubt that our judges, state and federal, should be men of the highest quality. Dean Pound has said that the fact that our polity is a legal polity, operating according to law, not according to the personal will or judgment or inclination of any man, is its outstanding feature, the thing which distinguishes our system from the authoritarian regimes now existing in the world and which is most vital to the preservation of our freedom. "Laws," he says, "may be the instruments of the autocrat; law is incompatible with absolute power; law is the arch enemy of autocracy." And then he says: "Law, as distinguished from laws, calls for judges. A polity carried on according to law calls for judges of the highest order of character, ability and professional competence."

It is likewise obvious that as society becomes more complex the necessity for good government becomes more imperative. Efficient and incorruptible courts, interpreting and applying the law and doing justice, are a vital part of good government. It is an essential means of maintaining a society which is fairly united and it is the best refutation of the cynical claim, as old as Plato, that in the last analysis justice is the rule of the strongest. Whether a society is to have such courts rest upon the quality of its judges. As Justice Cardozo said in *The Nature of the Judicial Process*, "In the long run there is no guaranty of justice except the personality of the judge."

In view of the great importance of the subject, it seemed to the writer worthwhile to investigate when he was in London how the English select their judges and especially the part which politics and political influence play in their selection. It seemed particularly important to make

---

Reprinted from *American Bar Association Journal*, vol. 39, 1953, pp. 279 *et seq.*, with the permission of the publisher. The author is a member of the California bar.

an investigation in England because it is generally conceded that the English courts and administration of the law are among the best in the world.

It is first necessary to have in mind the English courts and the officials who under the law appoint the judges to these courts. The highest courts in England are the House of Lords and the Privy Council. Next below is the Court of Appeal. Then comes the High Court having general jurisdiction. Lastly there are the county courts which are courts of limited jurisdiction. The judges of the courts above the county courts are all appointed by the Crown on the nomination of either the Prime Minister or the Lord Chancellor. As the Crown is bound to accept the advice of the minister making the nomination, the minister in effect makes the appointment. In cases of the judges who sit in the House of Lords, the Privy Council and the Court of Appeal, the Prime Minister makes the submission to the sovereign, whereas, in the cases of the judges of the High Court, the Lord Chancellor makes the submission. There is, however, little substance to this distinction because the Lord Chancellor is far more able to form an opinion with respect to who should be appointed and in practice the Prime Minister in making his submission seeks and follows the advice of the Lord Chancellor. The Lord Chancellor appoints all the judges of the county courts without any formal submission to the Crown.

## The Lord Chancellor

There is no office in our federal or state governments like that of the Lord Chancellor. As everyone knows, the members of an English cabinet are also members either of the House of Commons or the House of Lords. The extraordinary thing about the Lord Chancellor is that he is not only part of the executive and legislative branches of the government (as a member of the Cabinet he takes part in executive functions and as a member of the government in the House of Lords, he explains and defends the government's position respecting legislation), but he is also a judge; he can sit on appeals to the House of Lords and the Privy Council, and he is president of the High Court, the Court of Appeal and the Chancery Division.

Lord Jowitt was Lord Chancellor for the six and a half years during which the Labour Party was in office. When in the election of October 25, 1951, the Conservative Party was returned to power, Lord Jowitt ceased to occupy that office. The writer, in mailing Lord Jowitt a letter of introduction, accompanied it by a letter stating that he was interested in finding out how in practice English judges were appointed, particularly to what extent politics and political influence played a part in their appointment. Lord Jowitt's reply stated:

I think that I can fairly say that we have established a tradition in which "politics" and "influence" [in the appointment of judges] are now completely disregarded. The Lord Chancellor selects the man whom he believes to be the best able to fill the position. In my own case I had an unusually large number of appointments, and I can only recall appointing two men who were members of my own party.

You must remember these facts which help in establishing the tradition. The Inns of Courts are completely independent of any governmental control. The Lord Chancellor has always been a barrister, and must therefore be a member of one of the Inns. He is in close touch with all that goes on in his Inn of Court. How should I have felt if I had made a lot of unworthy appointments, when I noticed the cold looks that I should have received when next I went to lunch at the Inn.

Secondly, in practice, the Lord Chancellor would always consult with the Head of the Division to which he was called upon to appoint a judge. If I had to appoint a judge to the Queen's Bench Division, I should, in practice, always consult with the Chief Justice; if to the Divorce Division, with the President; if to the Chancery Division, with the senior Judge. In all my many appointments, I never in fact made one without the approbation of such a person. When it came to the Court of Appeal, I should consult the Master of the Rolls as to who was the most suitable person. . . .

Sir Albert Napier, the permanent secretary of the office of Lord Chancellor, recently prepared a paper describing that office in which he said much the same thing as Lord Jowitt as follows:

The Lord Chancellor is the most appropriate Minister to advise on appointments and promotions for the very reason that he is a Judge and is qualified for that position by actual practice at the Bar. He knows by experience as an advocate, the nature and degree of the knowledge and kind of character and temperament which go to make the best judges. When he sits he hears eminent Barristers arguing before him. He is in almost daily touch as a Law Lord and a Bencher of his Inn, with the Lord of Appeal and other Judges and members of the Bar. The Bench of an Inn is a society where all are equal, and talk is free, and so far as precedence is necessary, it goes by date of election and not by rank. In such a society a bad appointment could not escape criticism, and if it were ever suggested to a Lord Chancellor that he should appoint or promote the wrong man for the wrong motive, he would know not only where his duty lay but that if he were to accede he would lose the respect of the whole profession.

As stated in Lord Jowitt's letter, he did have an unusually large number of appointments, eighty-one in all. At the time he ceased to be Lord Chancellor there were seventy judges in office who owed their selection to him. These seventy were the following: he had appointed (or it would be more accurate to say that he advised the Prime Minister to submit to the sovereign for appointment) seven out of a total of nine judges of the House of Lords and the Privy Council who are called Lords of Appeal in Ordinary, all of the eight judges of the Court of Appeal who are called Lords Justices, and the Lord Chief Justice, and the Master of the Rolls; and he had also appointed (that is, he directly submitted to the sovereign for appointment) twenty-five out of a total of thirty-seven judges of the High Court as well as appointing directly (without any submission) twenty-eight out of a total of sixty-three judges of the County Courts. In addition to these seventy he during his term of office had also appointed eleven judges who had retired, died or been promoted before he went out of office, thus making the total of eighty-one.

Something should be said in explanation of the remark made by Lord Jowitt in his letter that he could recall that only two out of his eighty-one appointments were members of his own party. In England they have nothing comparable to our primary elections and therefore there is no need for a man when registering to vote to declare his party affiliation. So when Lord Jowitt made this remark he did not mean what an American might infer he meant, that is that according to his recollection only two of his appointments were registered to vote as members of his party while all the others were registered as members of the Conservative Party; but he meant that only two of his appointments were members of the Labour Party in the sense of being active in its party politics (as for example representing the Party in Parliament or acting on committees of the Party organization) and that the remaining seventy-nine were either members of the Conservative Party in the same sense or what can be called nonpolitical men who do not declare their politics and are free to vote for either party as they see fit. It is safe to say that the great majority of the seventy-nine belonged to the latter group.

### Use of "Influence"

Sir Albert Napier, in response to a question, said that letters from influential people supporting a candidate for a place on one of the appellate courts or High Court, are simply not written, and, if by chance the Chancellor does receive such a letter, it has quite the opposite effect from the one intended. The Chancellor knows the men who are qualified; he has, of course, many ways in which he can supplement his knowledge of them; and, as pointed out by Lord Jowitt, he consults with the chief judge of the division of the court to which the appointment is to be made; but he has the responsibility of making the appointment and an effort to influence him is strongly disapproved. In the case of appointments to the courts of limited jurisdiction, the County Courts, the Chancellor frequently does not know the men available for the places and so he seeks information from those who do know them; but he seeks the information; it is not given him by persons seeking to bring pressure to bear on him. But in the United States a candidate for an appointment to judicial office ordinarily mobilizes all the influence and pressure he can exert on the official making the appointment; and as part of his campaign he usually asks everyone he knows who he believes might have some influence to write or speak to such official in support of his candidacy.

The English barristers with whom the writer talked were unanimously of the opinion that there is a firmly established tradition in England that the men best qualified by character, temperament and learning should be made judges; that politics and political influence should play no part in their selection; and that a violation of this tradition would be violently resented not only by the profession but also by the public generally. However, as we are considering a human institution, controlled by human beings with all of their passions and frailties, we should not expect a perfect adherence to this tradition or that those familiar with its operation should be in entire agreement with respect to departures from it.

For example, a very well-informed barrister said that when the Earl of Halsbury, a man of strong Conservative convictions, was Lord Chancellor (he occupied that office from 1886 to 1892 and from 1895 to 1905) he tended to appoint judges who were strong Conservatives; but another barrister equally well informed stated that although the Earl of Halsbury did appoint as judges men who shared his economic and social views, he is usually criticized because two of his appointments turned out to be bad judges in different ways, one irascible and undignified and the other stupid and rather prejudiced. . . .

The writer was likewise told that when a vacancy in a high judicial office occurs, it is quite usual to appoint the Attorney General of the party then in power to the place. It could be claimed that this practice, to the extent to which it has been followed, seems like the rewarding of a political figure for his services to his party. But the writer was also informed that no one would be appointed Attorney General unless he was a man of high character and great experience and fit in every way to occupy one of the highest judicial offices, and that consequently it is entirely logical and proper that he be given a high judicial office if he can be spared from the government.

It is likewise true that the tradition that political influence shall play no part in the appointment of English judges and that only the best men shall be selected is not one that was established without a struggle or has existed for a long period. Mr. Evan Haynes, of the San Francisco Bar, in his excellent book, *Selection and Tenure of Judges,* says that more than a century ago Lord Brougham in a speech on the state of the law, lamented the custom by which only the adherents to the party of the Ministry of the day were considered for judicial appointments; that when Lord Oxford and Asquith was Prime Minister from 1907–1916 he did a great deal to remove political considerations from the selection of judges; and that even after the day of Lord Oxford and Asquith complaints were heard that political favor was playing its part in their selection.

However, it can be said with confidence that the English, despite an occasional failure to adhere strictly to the tradition, have now succeeded in firmly establishing it as part of their system. The appointments made by Lord Jowitt are cogent proof of its existence.

## Role of the Inns of Court

As pointed out by both Lord Jowitt and Sir Albert Napier in their statements quoted above, the English Inns of Court were and are a potent influence in establishing and maintaining the tradition. These Inns of Court are extraordinary and typically English institutions. There are four of them, the Inner Temple, the Middle Temple, Gray's Inn and Lincoln's Inn. Every English barrister must be a member of one of the Inns of Court. Each Inn admits to practice the barristers belonging to it and disciplines or disbars any of its members found guilty by it of any violation of the law or ethics. Each Inn is governed by its Benchers; and the Benchers fill any vacancy occurring among their members. If any judge of an Appellate Court or the High Court is not a Bencher of his Inn at the time of his appointment, he is made a Bencher at the first opportunity. The Lord Chancellor is a Bencher of his Inn.

This incident which recently occurred illustrates the control of the Inns over their members. It appears that two of the judges of the High Court were considering resigning to return to practice to increase their incomes; but that they were advised by the Benchers of their Inn that they could resign if they pleased but that they could not resume practicing law because the fact that they had been judges might give them an unfair advantage in practice and so would be contrary to a sound administration of the law. Nothing exists in America which would prevent or influence a resigned judge from resuming practice, but such are the powers of the Inns over their members. The extraordinary fact is that their powers do not rest upon any statute but only on custom and that they are not subject to any governmental control. Only in England where customs and tradition acquire the force of law could such institutions exist.

The statements of Lord Jowitt and Sir Albert Napier which have been quoted make it clear that the Inns of Court exercise their strong influence in maintaining the tradition by what can be called social pressure. It will be remembered that Lord Jowitt said in effect that if he had made unworthy appointments, he could have been made to feel the strong displeasure of his fellow Benchers of his Inn; and Sir Albert Napier stated that the Bench of the Inn would not hesitate to let the Bencher who happened to be Lord Chancellor know that if he made a bad appointment "he would lose the respect of the whole profession." Luncheon with the Benchers of the Middle Temple showed how sound these statements were. There were at the luncheon barristers who had grown old in the practice of the law and there were younger men at the height of their powers. Lord Jowitt, who as already stated, was the Lord Chancellor of the Labour Government, was there; and so was the Attorney General of the present Conservative Government, and so were several judges. The atmosphere was entirely informal and friendly. There was no sign of any special deference to any one because of his rank or position; and, to use Sir Albert Napier's expression, talk was free. There could be no doubt that these men would strongly resent the appointment to the Bench for political or other unworthy reasons of a man not fully qualified. It was equally clear that they knew one another well and respected and liked one another; that they would not hesitate to criticize any one of their number who happened to be Lord Chancellor if he made a bad judicial appointment; and that the Lord Chancellor would value the esteem of his fellow Benchers and would hesitate a long time before offending them by making such an appointment.

Although the Inns of Court, by their strong influence on their members, do much to sustain the tradition, it is doubtless true that the tradition would not be effective for any long period of time without the support of public opinion. Such support is given wholeheartedly and with deep conviction. It can be said of the English that they do more than understand intellectually that the stability and freedom of their society demand that their judges be men of high character and be appointed without regard to politics; that they have an emotional conviction that this is so. They have "in their hearts recognized the bonds of law and society."

We have a great deal to learn from the English so far as the selection of judges is concerned. One thing which we can learn from them is that judicial and professional opinion should be given weight in the selection of judges because no one knows better whether a lawyer possesses the character, learning and temperament to be a judge than the judges before whom he practices and his colleagues at the Bar. But the most important thing we can learn from them is that a society can create standards, a tradition, requiring the appointment of qualified men to judicial office without regard to politics or political influence, which a politician possessing the appointing power will disregard at his peril. . . .

COMMENT. *Further References on the Selection of Judges in Other Countries:* Goddard, "Politics and the British Bench," *Journal of the American Judicature Society,* vol. 43, 1959, p. 124 (an informal and somewhat anecdotal account by a former Lord Chief Justice); Coldstream, "Judicial Appointments in England," *Id.*, p. 41 (a firsthand report by the Clerk of the Lord Chancellor); Kilmuir, "Individual Freedom under an Unwritten Constitution," *Virginia Law Review,* vol. 45, 1959, p. 629 (a discussion by the Lord High Chancellor of Great Britain on the relationship between individual liberty and the independence of the judiciary); Stason, "Judicial Selection Around the World," *Journal of the American Judicature Society,* vol. 41, 1958, p. 134; Vanderbilt, *Judges and Jurors* (Boston: Boston U.P., 1956), pp. 32–35. The selection and role of the judges outside the Anglo-American orbit will be considered in Chapter 9 on the civil law systems.

*Further Discussion of Current Proposals on Judicial Appointments:* A thorough and favorable report on the objectives and results of the Missouri Plan is presented in Douglas, "Judicial Selection and Tenure," *American Bar Association Journal,* vol. 33, 1948, p. 1169. See also Hemker, "Experience Under the Missouri Non-Partisan Court Plan," *Journal of the American Judicature Society,* vol. 43, 1960, p. 159; Leflar, "The Quality of Judges," *Indiana Law Journal,* vol. 35, 1960, p. 289 (a report on the frustrating unsuccessful attempt to secure adoption of a new system of judicial selection in Arkansas); Teller, "The Selection of Judges: The Faults of the Pennsylvania Plan," *American Bar Association Journal,* vol. 41, 1955, p. 137; Harris, "The Virtue of the Pennsylvania Plan," *American Bar Association Journal,* vol. 41, 1955, p. 142; Hyde, "The Missouri Method," *Journal of the American Judicature Society,* vol. 41, 1957, p. 74 (a report by a justice of the Supreme Court of Missouri); Crowdus, "The Operation of the Missouri Plan," *Nebraska Law Review,* vol. 23, 1947, p. 177; and Vanderbilt, *The Challenge of Law Reform* (Princeton: Princeton U.P., 1955), pp. 30–33. The Report of the Pennsylvania Commission on Constitutional Revision (1959) by a close vote (8–7) recommended the adoption of a system for the selection of judges based on the ABA-Missouri Plan. See the Report pp. 37, 214–216.

*The Federal Judiciary.* Although the independence of federal judges is, on appointment, protected by the constitutional provision for life tenure, political influences are far from absent from the processes of selection. See Evans, "Political Influences in the Selection of Federal Judges," *Wisconsin Law Review*, 1948, p. 330 (a delightful speech, with significant personal reminiscences, by a judge of the United States Court of Appeals for the Seventh Circuit); Miller, "Federal Judicial Appointments," *American Bar Association Journal*, vol. 41, 1955, p. 125; Miller, "The Selection of the Federal Judiciary," *American Bar Association Journal*, vol. 45, 1959, p. 445. *Cf.* Frank, "The Appointment of Supreme Court Justices: Prestige, Principles and Politics," *Wisconsin Law Review*, 1941, pp. 172, 343, 461.

## POLITICS, THE BAR, AND THE SELECTION OF JUDGES    By Francis D. Wormuth and S. Grover Rich, Jr.

OUR POLITICAL institutions are no doubt susceptible of improvement, and proposals for innovation should be welcomed for whatever of merit can be winnowed from them. On the other hand, they should also be scrutinized with care, and measured against the teachings of experience and established principles of political science.

Two proposals for the selection of judges have attracted attention in Utah recently: the so-called Missouri plan, which was defeated by a gubernatorial veto in 1949, and nonpartisan election, which was enacted by the legislature in 1951. Both plans are based on the assumption that the judicial function is nonpolitical, and that the selection of judges should also be nonpolitical; they therefore undertake to remove the influence of parties and political considerations in the choice of judges. The political scientist's criticism of both plans rests on his conviction that the judicial function is necessarily political, and that parties are essential to democratic government. If this is true, judges should be chosen in a partisan manner. The traditional methods of executive appointment and partisan election meet this test; the issue between these two is not canvassed here. . . .

---

Excerpts reprinted from *Utah Law Review*, vol. 3, 1953, pp. 459 *et seq.* with the permission of the authors and the publisher. Both authors are professors of Political Science at the University of Utah.

## The Missouri Plan

The Missouri plan is said to share with nonpartisan election the virtue of taking the judiciary "out of politics." It is supposed to have the additional virtue of providing a superior method of nomination. The commission is composed of outstanding lawyers who are able to nominate to the governor a panel of candidates all possessed of integrity, technical competence, and judicial balance. Put together, of course, these two arguments are the arguments for aristocracy. The people are not qualified to choose their own governors, nor are the officers they elect qualified to do so for them. Rather, their judges would be chosen for them by the wise, the virtuous, and the well-born. In this case, the wise, virtuous, and well-born will be the lawyers of the state, and more particularly the leaders of the state bar association. Having secured the adoption of the "integrated bar" in most states, and thus having legislated all lawyers into the state bar association and having secured control of admission to practice, the legal profession is now reaching out to control the courts. One advocate of the Missouri plan states flatly that if it is adopted, "[M]embers of the bar can have the kind of judges they want. . . ."

Inescapably judges are vested with political powers. In Holmes' words, "Judges do, and must, legislate." And in so doing, it may be added, they inevitably are influenced by their personal views. Mr. Justice Brandeis, in the words of his biographers, was "like his conservative colleagues . . . inclined to translate his economic and social views into the constitution." But can any judge do otherwise? No amount of mumbo-jumbo about "objectivity" can conceal the facts. . . .

Inevitably judges formulate public policy. It is a commonplace of political science that policy-forming officers should be in sympathy with the official formulators of policy. Judges should be lions, said Francis Bacon, but lions under the throne. In a democracy they should execute the policies of the people. This is a simple condition of orderly and efficient government. There is no practical means by which the people can formulate policy in a democracy except through the machinery of partisan politics. There is no means of insuring that judges will carry out the policies of the people except partisan choice of judges—whether by executive appointment or by popular election.

So little are these matters understood that the very word "partisan" has a bad odor. It connotes jobbery and corruption, while the word "nonpartisan" is equated with "virtue." But jobbery and corruption are by no means synonymous with a party system. They can occur under any governmental form. On the other hand, practical experience has shown that democracy and a party system are synonymous. Only through a party system can issues be formulated and presented to the voters; only through a party system can the majority of the voters choose policy-forming officers committed to executing the program they have indorsed. It is late in the day to insist that judges stand above politics, that their decisions are dictated by abstract rules, that their views on public issues play no part. Their views on public issues are bound to play a part.

The significant question, then, is whether the judges are to implement the views indorsed by a majority of the voters. If a court is able to frustrate the popular desire for long, "The people will," as Abraham Lincoln said, "have ceased to be their own rulers, having . . . resigned their government into the hands of that eminent tribunal." One suspects that this is a covert purpose of at least some of those who desire nonpartisan selection of judges.

From what has been said it should be clear that the political choice of judges should not be confused with the sale of public office; that the political qualities of the good judge are not partisan qualities of the ward boss; that judges should be chosen not merely because their views on policy agree with those of the majority of the voters but for their competence, their training, and their judicial temperament. The political qualifications of a judge are no substitute for the nonpolitical qualifications. But the political qualifications equally with the others must be met; they are indispensable in a democracy. Neither is it intended to suggest that the popular will should prevail over constitutional prohibitions by any other means than the orderly process of constitutional amendment. This is an entirely distinct issue. Distortions of constitutions can be carried out as effectively by "nonpartisan" judges—judges who represent minority views—as by partisan judges who represent majority views. The history of judicial interpretation of the Fourteenth Amendment is too well known to require rehearsal here. Nor is it intended to suggest that the constitutional ideals of the separation of powers and the independence of the judiciary should be ignored. Certainly judges should no more improvise rules to promote than to thwart the popular will. All that is intended is to argue that judges should reflect settled public opinion; that is, they should have enough sympathy with popular programs to prevent them from sabotaging such programs. Anyone who is familiar with the tortuous course of interpretation of constitutional provisions and social legislation in the period 1890–1937 will agree that sabotage is not too strong a word to describe what judges entertaining minority views have done in the past. . . .

Under the Missouri plan the participation of the voters in the strictest sense is meaningless. The choice of the governor in appointment is limited to the three names proposed to him by the commission. Complete power over the judiciary rests in the hands of this anonymous and politically irresponsible group of seven men, three of whom—and surely the most influential three—are directly chosen by the state bar association. The hand is the hand of Esau, but the voice is the voice of Jacob.

One can hardly take seriously, then, the assertion that the Missouri plan is "democratic" or that it "insures popular control" over the selection of judges. On the contrary, it represents no more than the pseudo-democratic device of plebiscitary ratification, and its real purpose is the prevention, rather than the strengthening, of popular control.

### Evaluation

Certainly discretionary executive appointment and partisan election of judges have their weaknesses. But they are not fatal weaknesses; nor do the newer methods overcome these weaknesses. The evils of election are not removed by making elections nonpartisan; the evils of appointment are hardly avoided by entrusting the power of appointment to an irresponsible committee. It is not even true that these methods accomplish their announced objective of taking "politics" out of the choice of judges. The determination of policy is politics. Whenever men are to be selected for positions which involve the determination of public policy, there will always be persons and groups interested in the selection of certain candidates and the defeat of others. Nonpartisan choice does not mean that a policy-forming position has suddenly become politically neutral. It merely means that the people are deprived of the only instrument—admittedly a weak and erratic instrument—for insuring that policy determination responds to majority sentiment. This instrument is political parties.

No good can come from the legal profession's lulling itself into a belief which denies the political role of the judiciary, or from the sponsoring of proposals which hinder effective party government. Its proposals become all the more suspect when it is realized that they would absolve the bench of ultimate responsibility to the public and place it under the control of the bar. The traditional methods of judicial selection no doubt have their faults, but these remedies are worse than the disease.

---

COMMENT. *"Political" Judges.* The view that judges make law and therefore should be subject to popular control deserves careful examination. How much of the creative work of judges involves the choice between "left" and "right"? How much calls for the intelligent development of general principles accepted by the electorate? See Mishkin and Morris,

*On Law in Courts* (temp. ed., 1961) Chapters 2 and 3. What outlook toward the role of judges would one expect in the Soviet Union? (See Chapter 9.)

A recent study concludes that British judges too rigidly hold to prior decisions. See Davis, "The Future of Judge-Made Public Law in England," *Colorado Law Review*, vol. 61, 1961, pp. 201 *et seq.* Can strict adherence to precedent be expected of judges selected from among the most successful barristers? Do other forces of English legal history provide a more plausible explanation? See Maitland on the Inns of Court, *supra*, at 25–26. (See also pages 27–28 and 46–47.)

*Regretted Omissions.* This chapter of course fails to live up to its name, for a complete study of the judge and his work would cover a substantial part of the law.

The corner of the field which we have seen is both incomplete and unpleasant. The chapter has been directed toward some of the current realities of the judiciary rather than toward the ideal judge, not through disinterest in the ideal, but because most readers have probably already thought more about what judges *should* be and do than about practical considerations which affect the quality of the judicial corps.

Thus, your editor assumes that you have read Cardozo, *The Nature of the Judicial Process* (New Haven: Yale U. P., 1922). If not, this deficiency should be remedied immediately! Most libraries have a copy and a paperback edition has recently been published.

An important study of judging in action, recently published, is Llewellyn, *The Common Law Tradition: Deciding Appeals* (New York: Little, Brown, 1960). A very useful view from a different angle is provided in Wyzanski, "A Trial Judge's Freedom and Responsibility," *Harvard Law Review*, vol. 65, 1962, p. 1281. Interesting also is Peltason, *Fifty-Eight Lonely Men: Southern Federal Judges and School Desegregation* (New York: Harcourt, 1961).

*Delay.* Limitations of space have forced us to exclude important problems of judicial administration, of which the most serious is the problem of delay resulting from overcrowded dockets and inefficient handling of the business of the courts. See Levin & Wooley, *Dispatch and Delay: A Field Study of Judicial Administration in Pennsylvania* (Philadelphia: Institute of Legal Research, 1961); Zeisel, Kalven, and Buchholz, *Delay in the Court* (Boston: Little, Brown, 1959); "Lagging Justice," *The Annals*, vol. 328, March 1960; and Vanderbilt, *The Challenge of Law Reform* (1955), pp. 36–133.

*The Jury as Lawmaker.* Important and interesting writing on the role of the jury may be found in Frank, *Courts on Trial* (Princeton: Princeton U. P., 1949); Devlin, *Trial by Jury* (London: Stevens, 1956); Joiner, *Civil Justice and the Jury* (Englewood Cliffs, N.J.: Prentice-Hall,

1962); Kalven, "The Jury, the Law, and the Personal Injury Damage Award," *Ohio State Law Journal*, vol. 19, 1958, p. 158; Botein and Gordon, *The Trial of the Future: Challenge to the Law* (New York: Simon and Schuster, 1963). Valuable additional material is in the course of preparation by the Jury Project at the University of Chicago Law School.

CHAPTER 6

# The Legislature

IMPORTANT AS IS THE JUDGE IN THE administration of justice, it is the legislature which to an ever-increasing extent determines the shape of the law. The judge, it has been well said, dispenses law at retail; the legislature makes it wholesale.

Legislation intrudes at crucial points even into the "common law" of contracts, torts, and property; legislation dominates the law of crimes, procedure, corporations, sales, negotiable instruments, bankruptcy, and taxation. And, of course, legislation establishes the framework for modern public controls over a multitude of areas—labor relations, restraints of trade, the issuance of securities, to mention only a few examples. It is important to consider some of the factors which influence the quality of law which emerges.

Lawyers share with their fellow citizens a concern for the wisdom and responsiveness of basic legislative choices on social and economic problems, but these materials cannot embrace this mighty theme. Writing in this area is seldom of the requisite quality, and the exceptions are too bulky for inclusion.[1]

This chapter is concerned primarily with tools and workmanship. We here deal with the adequacy of legislative equipment to do work (such as the correction of recognized common law absurdities) the need for which is accepted by the lawmakers or, more realistically, would readily be accepted if the point were called effectively to their attention. What

---

[1] A classic example is Dicey, *Lectures on the Relation between Law and Opinion in England during the Nineteenth Century* (New York: Macmillan, 1905); a sequel is given in *Law and Opinion in England in the Twentieth Century*, edited by Morris Ginsburg (Berkeley: U. of California P. 1959).

For book-length analyses of the American scene, see Hurst, *Law and the Conditions of Freedom in the Nineteenth-Century United States* (Madison: U. of Wisconsin P. 1956); Hurst, *Law and Social Process in United States History* (Ann Arbor: U. of Michigan Law School, 1960). Worthwhile material on the way in which public opinion is (and is not) reflected in legislation may be found in D. B. Truman, *The Governmental Process* (New York: Knopf, 1951) (see especially "The Dynamics of Access in the Legislative Process," p. 321); Wahlke and Eulau, *Legislative Behavior* (New York: Free Press, 1959).

factors decide whether the legislative job will get done and, if something is done, whether it will be done well?

Answers to these questions are relevant not only to the further development of legislative institutions, but also to the role of the judge in lawmaking. Courts often say: "The traditional rule of law is out of keeping with current need, but correction must be left to the legislature." But is it always realistic to assume that the legislature will face the problem?

To help resolve these questions we shall examine the adequacy of the legislature's equipment to deal not only with the clamoring controversies of the day but also with those quieter problems which reach the attention only of scattered citizens and their puzzled attorneys. We open with a landmark both in legal literature and in the development of the law.

A MINISTRY OF JUSTICE          By Benjamin N. Cardozo

THE COURTS are not helped as they could and ought to be in the adaptation of law to justice. The reason they are not helped is because there is no one whose business it is to give warning that help is needed. Time was when the remedial agencies, though inadequate, were at least in our own hands. Fiction and equity were tools which we could apply and fashion ourselves. The artifice was clumsy, but the clumsiness was in some measure atoned for by the skill of the artificer. Legislation, supplanting fiction and equity, has multiplied a thousand fold the power and capacity of the tool, but has taken the use out of our hands and put it in the hands of others. The means of rescue are near for the worker in the mine. Little will the means avail unless lines of communication are established between the miner and his rescuer. We must have a courier who will carry the tidings of distress to those who are there to save when signals reach their ears. Today courts and legislature work in separation and aloofness. The penalty is paid both in the wasted effort of production and in the lowered quality of the product. On the one side, the judges, left to fight against anachronism and injustice by the methods of judge-made law, are distracted by the conflicting promptings of justice

---

Reprinted from *Harvard Law Review*, vol. 35, 1921, pp. 113–126, with the permission of the publisher. (Copyright 1921, by Harvard Law Review Association.) Benjamin N. Cardozo (1870–1938) practiced law in New York before his appointment in 1913 to the New York Court of Appeals, where he later became chief judge. In 1932 he became Associate Justice of the Supreme Court of the United States, succeeding Mr. Justice Holmes. His works include *The Nature of the Judicial Process* (1921), *The Growth of the Law* (1924), *The Paradoxes of Legal Science* (1928), and *Law and Literature* (1931).

and logic, of consistency and mercy, and the output of their labors bears the tokens of the strain. On the other side, the legislature, informed only casually and intermittently of the needs and problems of the courts, without expert or responsible or disinterested or systematic advice as to the workings of one rule or another, patches the fabric here and there, and mars often when it would mend. Legislature and courts move on in proud and silent isolation. Some agency must be found to mediate between them.

This task of mediation is that of a ministry of justice. The duty must be cast on some man or group of men to watch the law in action, observe the manner of its functioning, and report the changes needed when function is deranged. The thought is not a new one. Among our own scholars, it has been developed by Dean Pound with fertility and power. Others before him, as he reminds us, had seen the need, and urged it. Bentham made provision for such a ministry in his draft of a Constitutional Code. Lord Westbury renewed the plea. Only recently, Lord Haldane has brought it to the fore again.[1] "There is no functionary at present who can properly be called a minister responsible for the subject of Justice." "We are impressed by the representations made by men of great experience, such as the President of the Incorporated Law Society, as to the difficulty of getting the attention of the government to legal reform, and as to the want of contact between those who are responsible for the administration of the work of the Commercial Courts and the mercantile community, and by the evidence adduced that the latter are, in consequence and progressively, withdrawing their disputes from the jurisdiction of the Courts." In countries of continental Europe, the project has passed into the realm of settled practice. Apart from these precedents and without thought of them, the need of such a ministry, of some one to observe and classify and criticize and report, has been driven home to me with steadily growing force through my own work in an appellate court. I have seen a body of judges applying a system of case law, with powers of innovation cabined and confined. The main lines are fixed by precedents. New lines may, indeed, be run, new courses followed, when precedents are lacking. Even then, distance and direction are guided by mingled considerations of logic and analogy and history and tradition which moderate and temper the promptings of policy and justice. I say this, not to criticize, but merely to describe. I have seen another body, a legislature, free from these restraints, its powers of innovation adequate to any need, preoccupied, however, with many issues more clamorous than those of courts, viewing with hasty and partial glimpses the things that should be viewed both steadily and whole. I have contrasted the

[1] Report of Lord Haldane's Committee on the Machinery of Government (1918). [The quotations are from pages 63 and 64 of the Report.]

quick response whenever the interest affected by a ruling untoward in results had some accredited representative, especially some public officer, through whom its needs were rendered vocal. A case involving, let us say, the construction of the Workmen's Compensation Law, exhibits a defect in the statutory scheme. We find the Attorney General at once before the legislature with the request for an amendment. We cannot make a decision construing the tax law or otherwise affecting the finances of the state without inviting like results. That is because in these departments of the law, there is a public officer whose duty prompts him to criticism and action. Seeing these things, I have marveled and lamented that the great fields of private law, where justice is distributed between man and man, should be left without a caretaker. A word would bring relief. There is nobody to speak it.

For there are times when deliverance, if we are to have it—at least, if we are to have it with reasonable speed—must come to us, not from within, but from without. Those who know best the nature of the judicial process, know best how easy it is to arrive at an impasse. Some judge, a century or more ago, struck out upon a path. The course seemed to be directed by logic and analogy. No milestone of public policy or justice gave warning at the moment that the course was wrong, or that danger lay ahead. Logic and analogy beckoned another judge still farther. Even yet there was no hint of opposing or deflecting forces. Perhaps the forces were not in being. At all events, they were not felt. The path went deeper and deeper into the forest. Gradually there were rumblings and stirrings of hesitation and distrust, anxious glances were directed to the right and to the left, but the starting point was far behind, and there was no other path in sight.

Thus, again and again, the processes of judge-made law bring judges to a stand that they would be glad to abandon if an outlet could be gained. It is too late to retrace their steps. At all events, whether really too late or not, so many judges think it is that the result is the same as if it were. Distinctions may, indeed, supply for a brief distance an avenue of escape. The point is at length reached when their power is exhausted. All the usual devices of competitive analogies have finally been employed without avail. The ugly or antiquated or unjust rule is there. It will not budge unless uprooted. Execration is abundant, but execration, if followed by submission, is devoid of motive power. There is need of a fresh start; and nothing short of a statute, unless it be the erosive work of years, will supply the missing energy. But the evil of injustice and anachronism is not limited to cases where the judicial process, unaided, is incompetent to gain the mastery. Mastery, even when attained, is the outcome of a constant struggle in which logic and symmetry are sacrificed at times to equity and justice. The gain may justify the sacrifice; yet it is not gain without deduction. There is an attendant loss of that certainty which is itself a social asset. There is a loss too of simplicity and directness, an increasing aspect of unreality, of something artificial and fictitious, when judges mask a change of substance, or gloss over its importance, by the suggestion of a consistency that is merely verbal and scholastic. Even when these evils are surmounted, a struggle, of which the outcome is long doubtful, is still the price of triumph. The result is to subject the courts and the judicial process to a strain as needless as it is wearing. The machinery is driven to the breaking point; yet we permit ourselves to be surprised that at times there is a break. Is it not an extraordinary omission that no one is charged with the duty to watch machinery or output, and to notify the master of the works when there is need of replacement or repair?

In all this, I have no thought to paint the failings of our law in lurid colors of detraction. I have little doubt that its body is for the most part sound and pure. Not even its most zealous advocate, however, will assert that it is perfect. I do not seek to paralyze the inward forces, the "indwelling and creative" energies, that make for its development and growth. My wish is rather to release them, to give them room and outlet for healthy and unhampered action. The statute that will do this, first in one field and then in others, is something different from a code, though, as statute follows statute, the material may be given from which in time, a code will come. Codification is, in the main, restatement. What we need, when we have gone astray, is change. Codification is a slow and toilsome process, which, if hurried, is destructive. What we need is some relief that will not wait upon the lagging years. Indeed, a code, if completed, would not dispense with mediation between legislature and judges, for code is followed by commentary and commentary by revision, and thus the task is never done. "As in other sciences, so in politics, it is impossible that all things should be precisely set down in writing; for enactments must be universal, but actions are concerned with particulars."[2] Something less ambitious, in any event, is the requirement of the hour. Legislation is needed, not to repress the forces through which judge-made law develops, but to stimulate and free them. Often a dozen lines or less will be enough for our deliverance. The rule that is to emancipate is not to imprison in particulars. It is to speak the language of general principles, which, once declared, will be developed and expanded as analogy and custom and utility and justice, when weighed by judges in the balance, may prescribe the mode of application and the limits of extension. The judicial process is to be set in motion again, but with a new point of departure, a new impetus and direction. In breaking one set

[2] Aristotle, Politics, Bk. II (Jowett's translation).

of shackles, we are not to substitute another. We are to set the judges free.

I have spoken in generalities, but instances will leap to view. There are fields, known to us all, where the workers in the law are hampered by rules that are outworn and unjust. How many judges, if they felt free to change the ancient rule, would be ready to hold to-day that a contract under seal may not be modified or discharged by another and later agreement resting in parol? How many would hold that a deed, if it is to be the subject of escrow, must be delivered to a third person, and not to the grantee? How many would hold that a surety is released, irrespective of resulting damage, if by agreement between principal and creditor the time of payment of the debt is extended for a single day? How many would hold that a release of one joint tortfeasor is a release also of the others? How many would not prefer, instead of drawing some unreal distinction between releases under seal and covenants not to sue, to extirpate, root and branch, a rule which is to-day an incumbrance and a snare? How long would Pinnel's case survive if its antiquity were not supposed to command the tribute of respect? How long would Dumpor's case maintain a ghostly and disquieting existence in the ancient byways of the law?

I have chosen extreme illustrations as most likely to command assent. I do not say that judges are without competence to effect some changes of that kind themselves. The inquiry, if pursued, would bring us into a field of controversy which it is unnecessary to enter. Whatever the limit of power, the fact stares us in the face that changes are not made. But short of these extreme illustrations are others, less glaring and insistent, where speedy change is hopeless unless effected from without. Sometimes the inroads upon justice are subtle and insidious. A spirit or a tendency, revealing itself in a multitude of little things, is the evil to be remedied. No one of its manifestations is enough, when viewed alone, to spur the conscience to revolt. The mischief is the work of a long series of encroachments. Examples are many in the law of practice and procedure. At other times, the rule, though wrong, has become the cornerstone of past transactions. Men have accepted it as law, and have acted on the faith of it. At least, the possibility that some have done so, makes change unjust, if it were practicable, without saving vested rights. Illustrations again may be found in many fields. A rule for the construction of wills established a presumption that a gift to issue is to be divided, not *per stirpes,* but *per capita.* The courts denounced and distinguished, but were unwilling to abandon. In New York, a statute has at last released us from our bonds, and we face the future unashamed. Still more common are the cases where the evil is less obvious, where there is room for difference of opinion, where some of the judges believe that the existing rules are right, at all events where there is no such shock to conscience that precedents will be abandoned, and what was right declared as wrong. At such times there is need of the detached observer, the skilful and impartial critic, who will view the field in its entirety, and not, as judges view it, in isolated sections, who will watch the rule in its working, and not, as judges watch it, in its making, and who viewing and watching and classifying and comparing, will be ready, under the responsibility of office, with warning and suggestion....

We are sometimes slow, I fear, while absorbed in the practice of our profession, to find inequity and hardship in rules that laymen view with indignation and surprise. One can understand why this is so. We learned the rules in youth when we were students in the law schools. We have seen them reiterated and applied as truths that are fundamental and almost axiomatic. We have sometimes even won our cases by invoking them. We end by accepting them without question as part of the existing order. They no longer have the vividness and shock of revelation and discovery. There is need of conscious effort, of introspective moods and moments, before their moral quality addresses itself to us with the same force as it does to others. This is at least one reason why the bar has at times been backward in the task of furthering reform. A recent study of the Carnegie Foundation for the Advancement of Teaching deals with the subject of training for the public profession of the law. Dr. Pritchett says in his preface:

> There is a widespread impression in the public mind that the members of the legal profession have not, through their organizations, contributed either to the betterment of legal education or to the improvement of justice to that extent which society has the right to expect.

The Centennial Memorial Volume of Indiana University contains a paper by the Dean of the Harvard Law School [Roscoe Pound] on the Future of Legal Education.

> So long as the leaders of the bar, he says, do nothing to make the materials of our legal tradition available for the needs of the twentieth century, and our legislative lawmakers, more zealous than well instructed in the work they have to do, continue to justify the words of the chronicler—'the more they spake of law the more they did unlaw'—so long the public will seek refuge in specious projects of reforming the outward machinery of our legal order in the vain hope of curing its inward spirit.

Such reproaches are not uncommon. We do not need to consider either their justification or their causes. Enough for us that they exist. Our duty is to devise the agencies and stimulate the forces that will make them impossible hereafter.

What, then, is the remedy? Surely not to leave to fitful chance the things that method and system and science should order and adjust. Responsibility must be centered somewhere. The only doubt, it seems to me, is where. The attorneys-general, the law officers of the states, are overwhelmed with other duties. They hold their places by a tenure that has little continuity, or permanence. Many are able lawyers, but a task so delicate exacts the scholar and philosopher, and scholarship and philosophy find precarious and doubtful nurture in the contentions of the bar. Even those qualities, however, are inadequate unless reinforced by others. There must go with them experience of life and knowledge of affairs. No one man is likely to combine in himself attainments so diverse. We shall reach the best results if we lodge power in a group, where there may be interchange of views, and where different types of thought and training will have a chance to have their say. I do not forget, of course, the work that is done by Bar Associations, state and national, as well as local, and other voluntary bodies. The work has not risen to the needs of the occasion. Much of it has been critical rather than constructive. Even when constructive, it has been desultory and sporadic. No attempt has been made to cover with systematic and comprehensive vision the entire field of law. Discharge of such a task requires an expenditure of time and energy, a single-hearted consecration, not reasonably to be expected of men in active practice. It exacts, too, a scholarship and a habit of research not often to be found in those immersed in varied duties. Even if these objections were inadequate, the task ought not to be left to a number of voluntary committees, working at cross purposes. Recommendations would come with much greater authority, would command more general acquiescence on the part of legislative bodies, if those who made them were charged with the responsibilities of office. A single committee should be organized as a ministry of justice. Certain at least it is that we must come to some official agency unless the agencies that are voluntary give proof of their capacity and will to watch and warn and purge—unless the bar awakes to its opportunity and power.

How the committee should be constituted, is, of course, not of the essence of the project. My own notion is that the ministers should be not less than five in number. There should be representatives, not less than two, perhaps even as many as three, of the faculties of law or political science in institutes of learning. Hardly elsewhere shall we find the scholarship on which the ministry must be able to draw if its work is to stand the test. There should be, if possible, a representative of the bench; and there should be a representative or representatives of the bar.

Such a board would not only observe for itself the workings of the law as administered day by day. It would enlighten itself constantly through all available sources of guidance and instruction; through consultation with scholars; through study of the law reviews, the journals of social science, the publications of the learned generally; and through investigations of remedies and methods in other jurisdictions, foreign and domestic. A project was sketched not long ago by Professor John Bassett Moore, now judge of the International Court, for an Institute of Jurisprudence. It was to do for law what the Rockefeller Institute is doing for medicine. Such an institute, if founded, would be at the service of the ministers. The Commonwealth Fund has established a Committee for Legal Research which is initiating studies in branches of jurisprudence where reform may be desirable. The results of its labors will be available for guidance. Professors in the universities are pointing the way daily to changes that will help. Professor Borchard of Yale by a series of articles on the Declaratory Judgment gave the impetus to a movement which has brought us in many states a reform long waited for by the law. Dean Stone of Columbia has disclosed inconsistencies and weaknesses in decisions that deal with the requirement of mutuality of remedy in cases of specific performance. Professor Chafee in a recent article has emphasized the need of reform in the remedy of interpleader. In the field of conflict of laws, Professor Lorenzen has shown disorder to the point of chaos in the rules that are supposed to regulate the validity and effect of contracts. The archaic law of arbitration, amended not long ago in New York through the efforts of the Chamber of Commerce, remains in its archaic state in many other jurisdictions, despite requests for change. A ministry of justice will be in a position to gather these and like recommendations together, and report where change is needed. Reforms that now get themselves made by chance or after long and vexatious agitation, will have the assurance of considerate and speedy hearing. Scattered and uncoordinated forces will have a rallying point and focus. System and method will be substituted for favor and caprice. Doubtless, there will be need to guard against the twin dangers of overzeal on the one hand and of inertia on the other—of the attempt to do too much and of the willingness to do too little. In the end, of course, the recommendations of the ministry will be recommendations and nothing more. The public will be informed of them. The bar and others interested will debate them. The legislature may reject them. But at least the lines of communication will be open. The long silence will be broken. The spaces between the planets will at last be bridged.

The time is ripe for betterment. "Le droit a ses époques," says Pascal in words which Professor Hazeltine has recently recalled to us. The law has "its epochs of ebb and flow." One of the flood seasons is upon us. Men are insisting, as perhaps never before, that law shall be made true to its ideal of justice. Let us gather up the driftwood, and leave the waters pure.

# LEGAL RESEARCH TRANSLATED INTO LEGISLATIVE ACTION: THE NEW YORK LAW REVISION COMMISSION 1934-1963

By John W. MacDonald

IN 1921, Benjamin N. Cardozo published his article "A Ministry of Justice" (see *supra*). He had given it as an address before the Association of the Bar of the City of New York. This paper summarizes the experience of an agency consciously created in response to that proposal, an experience dating back to 1934.

### The Need for Information in the Legislative Process

A thoughtful and scholarly participant in the legislative process [Moffat] has characterized it as being "in its essence, a judicial process" in which the "burden of proof is on the plaintiff." "Very little legislation ever originates within the legislature itself," he wrote. "The legislature is the tribunal to which are brought proposed changes in the rules governing our lives. That tribunal, weighing the arguments for and against, renders judgment by the adoption or rejection of the proposed amendment to the laws."

This may be oversimplification. The premise, however, is sound that in the exercise of its functions the legislature must be informed. "No parliament can fulfill its basic duties intelligently without ascertainment of the facts."

Information is necessary with respect to the existence of a problem, the desirability of legislation as a solution as compared with other possible solutions, the alternative courses which the legislation might take, the experience acquired in other places and perhaps at other times, and the relative advantages and disadvantages of one decision over the other. Presumably, with this information, the legislature is ready to decide and to act.

---

Reprinted from "Legal Research Translated Into Legislative Action," *Cornell Law Quarterly*, vol. 48, 1963, pp. 401-454 (Copyright 1963 by Cornell University) with the permission of the author and publisher. The author is Professor of Law at Cornell Law School and coauthor (with Read and Fordham) of *Cases and Materials on Legislation* (2d ed., 1959). He was Executive Secretary and Director of Research for the New York Law Revision Commission and was made Chairman of the Commission in 1958.

Is this information available and where does the legislature get it?

An obvious source is the Executive. Perhaps in great questions of public policy, this is the major source. The President of the United States "shall from time to time give to the Congress Information of the State of the Union and recommend to their Consideration such Measures as he shall judge necessary and expedient." The Governor of New York "shall communicate by message to the legislature at every session the condition of the state, and shall recommend such matters to it as he shall judge expedient." In addition to the Chief Executive, the President or the Governor as the case may be, information and recommendations also come to the legislature from the various executive departments. . . .

Another obvious source of information and demand is from interests outside of the legislature, those with very special interests of their own, those who are acting pro bono publico and those—most of them—running in the large middle area from one extreme to the other. Moffat has justified the existence of the "lobbyist," the individual who presents these positions to the legislature.

Despite all these sources, and because of some of them, the need is such that from early days British and American legislatures sought to inform themselves not only with respect to the need for legislation, but also with respect to the execution and administration of existing legislation.

One kind of legislative inquiry has so occupied the news spotlight as to make it seem as if there were no other. This type of legislative investigation is based on the use of the subpoena and the forced testimony of witnesses. It involves the full panoply of power. It has caused controversies which have racked public opinion and caused much trouble to the courts.

That there is an effective means by which a legislature may itself obtain information required for intelligent action, other than use of the legislative investigation based on sanction and power, is the thesis of this paper. There are areas, even areas with strong conflicts of interest and policy, in which this other effective means of investigation may well be, and has been used. This has been particularly true in New York. This statement is not meant to be provincial. It is a fact that in New York the process is older, more continuous, and more highly organized than in most other common law jurisdictions. The basic tool of this kind of legislative investigation is pure research, the kind of research which goes into preparation of theses, articles and treatises—done by professional people with an intellectual bent for this kind of activity, some of whom make it their life work. It is not ivory tower research, with publication and sharing with scholars the sole goal. It is research which looks to a decision, statute or no statute, as the goal, with the final place of contention the legislative floor itself. The scope of the research will be determined by the scope of the problem, the imagination and skill of the researcher and of those to whom he reports, and the active nature of the decision which will ultimately be required. Publication of the results of the research is only an incidental objective (historically, perhaps, it is accidental that there is publication); publication is part of a forensic process to accomplish a result, and when the result is accomplished, either positive (enactment) or negative (rejection), the purpose of publication is explanation of legislative intent.

### The Proposal of a Ministry of Justice

In 1921, Judge Benjamin N. Cardozo, addressing the Association of the Bar of the City of New York, proposed the establishment of an agency —he called it a Ministry of Justice—"to mediate between [courts and legislatures]." . . .

And it is not in the area of public law where information is lacking; the judge marvels and laments "that the great fields of private law, where justice is distributed between man and man, should be left without a caretaker." . . .

In 1923, two years after the publication of this most influential law review article, the State of New York created the Commission to Investigate Defects in the Law and its Administration. Cardozo's Ministry would have had at least five members; the Commission had seventeen. Cardozo would have had "if possible" a representative of the bench, and a representative or representatives of the bar; the Commission had five judges to be designated by the Governor, two from the Court of Appeals, two from the appellate divisions, and one a trial judge. Cardozo mentioned nothing about legislators or the attorney-general; the Commission had four legislators and also that executive officer. Cardozo would have had two or even three law faculty men; the Commission had seven men to be appointed by the Governor with no specific qualifications other than that they must have been admitted to the bar. So far as can be ascertained, the 1923 Commission had no legislative program except perhaps a bill to transform this "heavy commission with judges on it, into a straight commission of five."

Independent of this agency created in response to Judge Cardozo's suggestion, in 1931 the Legislature created a temporary legislative Commission on the Administration of Justice in New York State. The proposal for this Commission was first made by Governor Roosevelt. The basis of the proposal was quite different from that of Cardozo's. That

Commission, however, in its 1934 report recommended the creation of a permanent agency, the Law Revision Commission, a recommendation accepted by the Legislature. . . .[1] In recommending the creation of the Law Revision Commission, the Commission on the Administration of Justice wrote as follows: . . .

In our Preliminary Report we pointed out the distinction between a Ministry of Justice and the bodies which have come to be known as Judicial Councils. The former was powerfully advocated by Mr. Justice (then Judge) Cardozo in 1921. In the time that has elapsed since Mr. Justice Cardozo's article first appeared, a Judicial Council has come to be known as a group, composed, at least in part, of judges, vested with authority to collect information and make recommendations to the Legislature on matters chiefly concerned with the administration of the courts and methods of practice and procedure. Such bodies have been established in twenty states. On the other hand, a Ministry of Justice, or, as we have called it, a Law Revision Commission, has come to be thought of as a group of students of the law, vested with the responsibility of considering particularly the substantive statutory law with a view to scientific revision in the light of modern conditions, and acting as a link between the courts and the Legislature. So far as we are aware, no state has yet adopted the idea of such a commission, although the suggestion has received wide support from legal scholars, leaders of the bar and students of govern-

[1] At least five states have functioning groups similar to the New York Revision Commission. . . .

New York created its Commission to Investigate Defects in the Law and its Administration in 1923, two years after the Cardozo address . . . a similar agency was created in New Jersey in 1925. . . . In 1939 the Commission on Statutes was created, . . . with authority to conduct substantive law revision. This Commission was abolished in 1944 and the Law Revision and Bill Drafting Commission established in its stead. . . . "A study of the annual reports of the Law Revision and Bill Drafting Commission and its predecessor make clear that substantive law revision has been sacrificed because of pressure for the performance of the other auxiliary legislative services for which the Commission is responsible." This comment, however, was made in 1948. . . .

The Louisiana State Law Inst. was created in 1938. . . . The provision with respect to its duties is similar to New York's. . . .

The California Law Revision Commission is the one most recently created and most like New York's, since it is patterned on the New York Commission. It came into being in 1953. . . . For its manner of functioning see Government Code §§ 10300–340; also 1 Cal. Law Revision Comm'n Rep. 7 (1957). . . .

A North Carolina agency, now defunct, was called the "North Carolina Commission for Improvement of Laws." By 1940 it had recommended ten bills, of which four became law. Stone & Pettee, "Revision of Private Law," 54 Harv. L. Rev. 221, 231 n.22 (1940). . . . It was succeeded by the General Statutes Commission created in 1945, which was assigned the task of substantive law revision in 1951. . . .

In 1959, the duty of substantive law revision was assigned to the Legislative Counsel Committee in Oregon . . . That Committee had been created in 1953 (Ore. Rev. Stat. § 173.150) and assigned the task of bill drafting and publishing new editions of the Oregon Revised Statutes. . . .

For a collection of proposals with respect to law revision activities and proposals for establishment in other states, see Goodrum & Gordon, "Substantive Law Revision in Texas," 37 Texas L. Rev. 740, 759–63, particularly nn.125, 128, 129, 131, 132; Stern, "A Law Revision Commission for Pennsylvania," 29 Penn. B.A.Q. 180 (1958). . . .

ment. However, according to Judge Cardozo, "in countries of continental Europe the project has passed into the realm of settled practice" . . .

Your Committee therefore advises that the Commission recommend to the Legislature the formulation of a permanent agency or commission for the amendment and correction of the law as it is administered in the courts. . . . The members . . . should not be more than five in number. We are strongly persuaded that at least two of the five should be members of the law faculties of some university of the State or of some institute of learning of like standing and authority. Scattered amendments of the law are likely to prove a snare and an evil unless effected with scientific understanding of the law as a whole. Correction at one spot may produce abnormalities and inconsistencies at another unless the relation between the parts is remembered and perceived. The scholarship essential to so delicate a task can be found in the law schools more readily than elsewhere. On the other hand, the practising lawyer, too busy often to arm himself with the scientific equipment of the scholar, must contribute his knowledge of affairs, his experience of the practical workings of the law, his readiness of resource, his skill in administration, his sagacity and wisdom. Representation of both these elements of strength with their diverse points of view is likely to bring us in the end to the level of the best results.

Governor Smith in his Annual Message of 1925 said:

I am thoroughly in accord with the report of the Commission and I recommend that you enact suitable legislation to create such a permanent agency. . . .

This paper studies the work of the New York Law Revision Commission as an agency which, from the time of its organization, has depended solely on research as its tool for investigation and report to the legislature. . . .

The Law Revision Commission held its organizational meeting on July 31, 1934. On February 21, 1935, the first bills recommended by it were introduced in the Legislature. In the twenty-eight legislative sessions between 1935 and 1962, bills on 327 different subjects were recommended by it to the Legislature. During three years of this period, 1954–56, the Commission, on direction of the Governor, was exclusively occupied with one study, the Uniform Commercial Code, and no bills were recommended by it. Of these 327 bills, 243 were enacted into law. This is a study of the techniques employed in the transition from research by the Commission to legislative action, especially to the favorable action disclosed by this record.

Perhaps, to a participant in this process, any one factor can be overemphasized. Was the Commission's research the key to its success? This, I suppose, is the major question posed by this paper.

It cannot be denied that there are problems which are peculiar to an official agency whose sole purpose and function is to "root out many antiquated and unjust rules of law" by recommending legislation to one of the great political branches of the government, concerned as it is with many problems far removed from law reform in "the great fields of private law, where justice is distributed between man and man." An examination of those problems, disclosed over the years, will be helpful in showing the background of the research and the recommendations of this agency and the pattern within which they are made. . . .

## Organization of Research Within the Law Revision Commission

*The Plan of Research.* With the headquarters of the Commission organized and its staff provided for, a fundamental question facing the new agency was the planning of a research program for the members of the Commission itself. It was necessary to decide how the Director of Research and his staff would function in relation to the Commission members and how research tasks would be distributed within the membership. Obviously, a distinction had to be made from the first between the appointed members of the Commission and the ex officio members. Their positions differ. The ex officio members, of course, are neither appointed nor paid. Their membership results from their position in the Legislature. For them, regular attendance at meetings and definite assignments could not be planned. Their presence at working sessions of the Commission would be appreciated, but could not be required. All members present at meetings are of course entitled to vote; ex officio members should be able to exercise this right without being bound when the same matter later came up for consideration in the Legislature, either before a committee or in the deliberative body itself.

The appointed members, therefore, became the active group. Immediately, a decision had to be made as to how they would function: would each member of the Commission participating in research himself conduct his own research, reporting to the full Commission his findings and his recommendations? Or would research be conducted under the general supervision of the Director of Research, for the Commission as a whole, with the results reported directly or indirectly to the full group for its decision? It was decided that instead of members of the staff being assigned to each individual Commissioner, with duties comparable to those of law secretaries to judges, the Director of Research himself would be responsible to the organization as a unit and would direct the entire research program of the Commission.

*Selection of Projects.* From whence comes the grist for the Commission's mill? It comes from the project suggestions sent to the Commission by outside individuals or groups, and from its own study of New York law.

Outside suggestions follow no particular pattern. They may be detailed or merely briefly stated. Usually, they gave no more than a mere idea of the nature of the desired change—an unbriefed, unresearched idea. This is true no matter whether the suggestion comes from the courts, from the Governor, from the Legislature, from public officials, from lawyers, or from the public.

Although a suggestion from a court may go no further than, "We must read statutes as they are written and, if the consequence seems unwise, unreasonable or undesirable, the argument for change is to be addressed to the Legislature, not to the courts." It may be more succinctly stated in an opinion which makes specific reference to the Commission, as was done by Judge Moule in the case of *Germain v. Germain*.

The court believes that consideration should be given to amending the New York State law to provide for the appointment by the court of a conservator of the property of one who disappears voluntarily or involuntarily and cannot be proved dead, seen or heard of. . . . This court, by sending copies of this opinion to the New York State Law Revision Commission, New York State Bar Association and Erie County Bar Association, is suggesting that remedial legislation be enacted.

The suggestion for change may be contained in a letter from the Court directed to a particular case, which if followed leads to an undesirable result. . . .

At times, the Governor may transmit a specific suggestion for study by the Commission, as has been done respecting several matters: the desirability of changes in the Penal Law and in the Code of Criminal Procedure with regard to the establishment of commissions to examine the sanity of persons accused of crime; the need for changes in the Uniform Criminal Extradition Act and the Correction Law; the question of what should be done respecting the law of felony murder and second degree rape; and, notably, the study of the Uniform Commercial Code.

The Legislature may, itself, direct the Commission to undertake a particular study. Most recently, this was done as the result of a bill introduced in the Legislature in 1961, duly enacted into law, which "authorized and directed" the Law Revision Commission to make a thorough study and examination of all laws of the State relating to the offices of coroner and medical examiner. And in 1962, by concurrent resolution, the Legislature directed the Commission to study the desirability and feasibility of an Administrative Procedure Act for the State.

Suggestions have come to the Commission from other executive departments of the State. For instance, the Comptroller wrote that the abolition of the distinction between sealed and unsealed instruments had had some unexpected results affecting bonds of the state and of some municipalities, so far as the statute of limitations was concerned, and that correction was needed.

Proposals indicating a need for change in the law quite frequently come from lawyers, with respect to problems disclosed in counseling or in advocacy, or with respect to problems which have been noted without particular professional interest.

When the project suggestion comes from within the Commission itself —from one of the members or from the staff—it usually has been very carefully considered before being proposed. This is the source of most topics for consideration.[2] . . .

*Organization of Research.* We have seen the participation of the Commissioners in the selection of projects and the formulation of the Calendar. Once the Director of Research has determined which subjects are to be studied during a given year, a committee of the Commission, usually consisting of two members—sometimes in a simple case of one member, rarely of three members—is appointed to undertake the preliminary study. A research assistant or a research consultant is then assigned to the topic and he makes the basic study under the supervision of the Director of Research. Sometimes, particularly in the case of a large exploratory subject, the Committee holds a preliminary meeting with the person assigned to the research. Thereafter the research assistant or consultant proceeds to make the basic study (to be later discussed) culminating in a lengthy report which concludes with his personal recommendations for action. Upon completion of this report and its submission to the Committee, a meeting or a series of meetings of the Committee is held at which all of the research materials are considered. Minutes are kept of each meeting. The Committee then meets with the full Commission and presents its plan of action. All the material considered by the Committee, including the conclusions of the research assistant or Consultant, however tentative and even if overruled by the Committee, goes to the full Commission. The Committee's submission may or may not include a proposed recommendation and draft statute, depending upon whether or not there is agreement respecting the need for legislation. The Commission considers the subject from every angle. There is debate. If no decision can be reached the matter may be referred back to the Committee for further study and the whole process is repeated. If the Commission decides to recommend legislation, consideration is at once given to the drafting of a suitable statute, which may not, in its final form, be approved until a later meeting.

*Research Assistants and Consultants.* The basic research of the Com-

---

[2] Since 1934, approximately three thousand suggestions for study have been received from all sources; approximately half of these have come from outside the Commission itself and its staff.

mission is carried on by research assistants, who are members of its regular staff, and by research consultants, who are engaged only for a particular topic. The consultants may be law professors or lawyers with offices remote from the Commission's headquarters. . . .

The use of assistants and consultants has shifted over the years. In the early years there were as many as nine research assistants, with relatively fewer consultants. In later years, the Director's staff has included as few as two, or even one assistant. This shift began when the war and draft made it nearly impossible to recruit and keep a regular staff. It was accelerated after the war by the great increase in the beginning salaries paid by metropolitan law offices to young lawyers who would be considered eligible for appointment as research assistants. One assistant today costs as much as three or more in 1934, and the appropriation for the Commission has not been increased proportionately. There has been no comparable increase in the sum paid to consultants. . . . The smaller number of research assistants reflects this more attractive beginning salary in law offices generally, and also the increased opportunities for top law graduates, as well as the increasingly satisfactory experience with a smaller staff and reliance on the consultant system.

For the most part, a typical research assistant is a high-ranking recent law-school graduate who takes the job with the idea that it is a temporary step (one year or two) in obtaining experience and prestige. The research consultant, on the other hand, is usually a member of a law school faculty, sometimes of outstanding prestige and authority, or, as is equally possible, a young professor who desires to supplement his income and to obtain the professional prestige that attaches to an appointment as consultant to the commission. It is an experience which consultants often repeat year after year, partly due, perhaps, to the satisfactions inherent in being a participant in reform of the law—of having a part in this forward movement. . . .

*The Research Study.* This brings us to the research study, the heart of the research process. The Commission has drawn up general standards which apply to all such work and which serve as a guide to research assistants and research consultants alike. They are in line with the exposition that follows.

The basis upon which a study is undertaken is that it is to provide the Commission with a thorough review of the problem, in all its varied and related aspects, so that a correct conclusion can be reached as to whether or not legislative action is required, and if such action is to be recommended, how it is to be formulated. Any study must include an analysis of the New York law, a comparison of it with the law in other jurisdictions, sometimes even including foreign law, and a consideration of the policy questions involved. Statutory as well as decisional law is to be examined, and the thinking of jurists, textwriters and eminent authorities consulted. All available pertinent legal literature is to be considered—treatises, periodicals, restatements, model or uniform laws, etc. The search for relevant authorities and the recognition of a sufficient quantum of authority is, of course, the professional responsibility of the researcher. Factual investigations are seldom called for, since the studies made by the Commission are legal studies. However, where factual data is needed, or where it may be deemed helpful to obtain the opinion of the bar in specialized fields of practice, this may be done, but the manner in which it takes place is always a matter to be decided by the Commission. Neither the assistant nor consultant is expected to conduct any such inquiry upon his own initiative, but he may recommend to the Commission that such inquiry be made. . . .

The studies made for the Commission are published in its annual reports. But this normally occurs only if a recommendation or communication to the Legislature results. If no action whatever is taken, the study is simply filed. All studies are reviewed by the Director of Research for the purpose of editing. Since they are frequently consulted by the bar, it is important to exclude any passages, originally written to convey to the Commission the Consultant's own opinion, that could be erroneously relied on as expressing views of the Commission, especially as to matters of policy or as to possible interpretations of the recommended statute. It is advisable, also, in some cases, to withhold from publication passages dealing with matters on which the Commission is reserving action.

*Steps After Approval of Study.* With the research study completed, the next step, assuming the Commission has reached a decision that legislative action is desirable, is the drafting of the proposed statute. This will be submitted in bill form to the Legislature, and is accompanied by an explanatory "statutory note," a short statement of what the bill accomplishes. The "statutory note" is printed with the bill as a kind of footnote. Along with the proposed legislation goes a separate and distinct document known as the "Recommendation," which is particularly helpful since it explains the reason for the proposed legislation and reviews concisely but fully the entire problem as presented in the research study. The legislation proposed is the product of the joint considerations of all members of the Commission, and has been fully passed upon and agreed to by them before it is submitted to the Legislature.

The proposal, however, is not yet ready for submission to the Legislature. There are some preliminary steps. The most important of these bears upon the relation of the Commission with the organized bar of the State. From the beginning there has been cooperation between these two groups. It is perhaps sufficient to state here that the voice of the organized bar is heard through a standing committee of the New York

State Bar Association especially created in 1935 to cooperate with the Law Revision Commission. Consultation with this group is deemed by the Commission to be an essential part of the research process before its recommendations and proposed statutes are formally presented to the Legislature.

The Cooperating Committee of the State Bar Association meets annually with the Law Revision Commission, usually at the completion of the year's work of the Commission, and shortly before the Commission makes its report to the Legislature, which it is required to do "on or before" February 1st, each year. But the Cooperating Committee has been apprised much earlier of the Commission's planned program. Early in the Fall, the Director of Research advises the Chairman of the Committee of those projects which seem likely to be completed for submission to the next legislative session, and the Chairman, in turn, advises the Commission of his designation of subcommittees of the Cooperating Committee to report on each of the topics. Materials showing the tentative recommendations of the Commission on each topic are sent to the entire membership of the Cooperating Committee. Copies of the research materials which were before the Commission are also lent to the members of the subcommittees. Each subcommittee later reports to a full meeting of the Cooperating Committee, at which the conclusions that have been reached are either approved (with possible suggested changes) or rejected. In many instances, perhaps more often than not, the Cooperating Committee approves the Recommendations proposed by the Commission. There then follows a joint meeting of the Committee and the full Commission and all the proposals are reviewed in round-table discussion. The full Commission, at a subsequent meeting, determines what action it should take respecting the suggestions of the Cooperating Committee.

The legislative program has now been finally determined and bills to carry out the Commission's recommendations are prepared for introduction in the Legislature. The *ex officio* members of the Commission—the Chairmen of the Judiciary and Codes Committees of both houses—introduce the bills or arrange for their introduction by other legislators.

*The Bills in the Legislature.* An attempt is made, and it is nearly always successful, to have the bills ready for introduction during the first week of the legislative session. Simultaneously, a complete set of the Recommendations of the Commission, in multilithed form, is delivered to the post office box of each member of the Legislature, to the Governor's Counsel and to the clerks of each house.

Following their introduction, the bills are referred to the appropriate legislative committees, usually Judiciary and Codes, and preparations are made for a joint legislative hearing before those Committees, usually held, at their convenience, in mid-February.

Also, soon after the Commission's bills have been introduced, copies are distributed to other groups—to the appropriate committees of the different bar associations located in metropolitan New York; to local bar associations upon a current mailing list furnished by the Executive Director of the New York State Bar Association; to the State Library and to several court libraries and other law libraries; and to such legal reference services as the Legislative Index and the New York Legislative Service, Inc. A substantial number of the Recommendations are also distributed in response to requests received from lawyers and other interested persons while the bills are before the Legislature. Thus the Commission disseminates information about its proposals to interested groups throughout the State. The Legislative Reporter of the New York State Bar Association usually devotes the first three issues of his weekly report to discussion of the Commission's bills.

In the period that elapses between the introduction of the Commission's bills and the joint legislative hearing, the Commission is busy keeping itself informed of the sentiment regarding its proposals. An "objections" file is made up for each bill before the Legislature. In many cases a very satisfactory liaison has been established between bar committees and other legally oriented groups. For example, the Director of Research keeps in touch, either by correspondence or telephone, with the legislative committee members of the two major metropolitan bar associations. Comparable liaison has been established with the legislative committees of various other organizations such as the Executive Committee of the New York State Surrogates' Association, the Committee on Law Reform of the Supreme Court Justices, the Association of County Clerks, of District Attorneys, etc.

Once again the Commission holds a full meeting, before the legislative hearing is scheduled to take place, and examines all the accumulated data. It reconsiders its previous action in the light of this material—the objections and the approvals—and either reaffirms its prior stand or may propose that certain of its pending bills be amended, or even, in some instances, that they be withdrawn for further study.

The full Commission attends the joint legislative hearing and each Commissioner in turn presents those measures which were assigned to him and which have been his responsibility. He explains them and answers any questions raised concerning them.

It sometimes happens that the Legislature itself amends the Commission's bills. The Commission may approve this action, but if it does not, its objections are made known to the Governor at the time the bill comes before him for signature. It is noteworthy that all Commission bills that go before the Governor are accompanied by a full memorandum, directed to his legal counsel, which supplements the formal "Recommendation" already previously supplied by the Commission, and analyzes all comments on the proposal, whether they be for or against.

## Problems Peculiar to an Official Agency Engaged in Law Reform

*Political Aspects.* The operations of the Law Revision Commission are divorced from politics, but the question of partisan influences may arise, so it may be well to examine the Commission's legislative record in this light. This seems particularly pertinent since the Commission is part of the legislative branch of the government, with an appointive power in the Governor and with four ex officio members from the Legislature (chairmen of legislative committees) whose identity is determined by the control in the Legislature.

There is an obvious connection between the political affiliation of the appointing officer and the nature of his appointments. In the twenty-eight years that the Commission has been functioning, the Governorship has been held almost an equal number of years by the Democrats and the Republicans. For thirteen years a Democratic Governor appointed the salaried members; for fifteen years, a Republican Governor. One might expect to find that the political association of the appointees accorded with that of the Governor, but this has not always been the case. Significantly often, the Governor ignored political hue, and either permitted the incumbent to hold over or reappointed him despite his different political affiliation. This accounts in part for the remarkable continuity of service among the appointed members of the Commission, a continuity found also, as it happens, among the ex officio members. The possible influence of these facts on the legislative record of the Commission is later discussed. . . .

*Fear of a "Super-Legislature."* On several occasions, early in the Commission's history, fear was expressed that it would become a "super-legislature," and the agency was scrupulous to avoid any practices which would point in that direction. Even before its creation, when the idea of a Law Revision Commission was first proposed in 1923, a somewhat similar fear was expressed. This was the concern lest it become a "super-court." But the point was apparently never raised again.

The "super-legislature" fear has long since died, but it may be well to consider just what is meant by it. How it manifests itself is not wholly clear, but it would seem that if the Commission had ever sought to make its bills "must" legislation; if it had lobbied for its bills, or its "program," then it might have been regarded as striving to override the Legislature and to assert its own dominance. But this has never been the case. The Commission not only has never thought in terms of "must" legislation— an incredible position to the early Commission—but has refrained from even referring to its "program" until it had been established for many years, and the phrase became one of common parlance. The Commission, it is true, does more than merely "suggest"—it recommends. But it attempts to give to its "Recommendations" a truly integral and distinctive status comparable to a judicial opinion. The Legislature is not expected to take the Commission's proposals on faith, nor does it do so. There is little danger that the Legislature will abdicate its function here. It has, on the other hand, come to rely on the Commission's proposals, being fully aware of the careful and complete study and consideration that has been given to each bill recommended.

Another possible manifestation of a "third house" or "super-legislature" would be if the Commission attempted to defeat proposals made in the Legislature under the sponsorship of others; or if it attempted to secure a veto by the Governor of bills coming from other sources. But such action would never be taken by the Commission, for it would be deemed beyond its competence.

The experience of the Commission . . . may serve to illustrate this problem: . . .

*Competing Bills.* In May, 1948, the Commission had added to the Immediate Study List of its Calendar the general topic "Revision of Law Relating to Trade Marks and Trade Names," which was reached for study about two years later. Professor Milton Handler of the Columbia Law School was retained as research consultant. After this study was initiated, the National Association of Secretaries of State approved a so-called Model Uniform State Trade Mark bill. That Association had been assisted by the United States Trade Mark Association, which also worked with a committee of the Council of State Governments. Prior to the completion of the Commission's study of the subject a bill was introduced into the New York Legislature in 1952 which would, if passed, enact the Model Act. It bore the sponsorship of the New York Department of State and of the Joint Legislative Committee on Interstate Cooperation. It passed both Houses, but was vetoed by Governor Dewey for the reason that it had been introduced late in the session and a substantial number of business and trade associations as well as the practicing bar had not had sufficient opportunity to examine its provisions.

Meanwhile, the Commission had concluded its study in 1952, following a conference with representatives of interested groups, held on October 29, 1952. It recommended its own bill in 1953.

There were significant differences between the Model Act and the Commission bill. Another conference was held on January 7, 1953, this time with the sponsors of the Model Act. Both bills went to the Legislature.

In the meantime, a bill on which the Commission took no position, dealing with the related subject of marking receptacles, came before the Legislature. To enable this measure to stand on its own feet, without technical objection, the Commission introduced a revision bill amending its own bill to avoid any inconsistency with the receptacle bill if it were to pass the Legislature.

All the bills passed the Legislature, leaving the choice to the Governor. He vetoed them on April 17, 1953, obviously hoping that the conflicting points of view could be resolved. They were resolved by events. The Law Revision Commission on February 8, 1953, was assigned by the Governor the task of studying and reporting on the Uniform Commercial Code. No bills were introduced in the Legislature for the next three years on the Commission's recommendation. In 1954 the Model Act became law. . . .

Case histories show how the Commission is sometimes faced with bills before the Legislature, introduced from another source and inconsistent with a pending Recommendation of its own. Absent such a Recommendation, the Commission would not oppose any other pending bill. This is a standing policy which has obtained since the formation of the Commission. However, with respect to a proposal which competes with its own Recommendation, the Commission necessarily takes a position but acts with complete respect for legislative supremacy.

*Impingement on Another Agency.* The several trademark bills just discussed present another interesting facet—that of the respective competence or jurisdiction of state agencies. The Model Act was recommended by the Department of State and by the Joint Legislative Commission on Interstate Cooperation. The Commission bill was its own product, drafted after its own study and recommended by it alone. The two were in conflict. The matter happened to resolve itself. In line with this attitude, the Commission refrains from entering an area within the province, or the scope of interest, of another department of the government. Likewise it declines to undertake matters involving primarily a question of policy. This avoidance cannot be stated in terms of an absolute rule. It has become a practice rather than a rule.

On the other hand, there are always bills within the area of private law, the area of the Commission's own special competency, in which other departments of government definitely have some interest. Such other departments, not subject to the problems of this agency, do not hesitate to oppose such measures as seem to them undesirable. . . .

*The Uniform Commercial Code.* In 1953, the Law Revision Commission was directed by the Governor to study the Uniform Commercial Code. This direction was the result of the joint urging of the New York State Bar Association and the Association of the Bar of the City of New York that a publicly sponsored and financed study be made of the Code as proposed by the National Conference of Commissioners on Uniform State Laws and the American Law Institute in 1952 (hereinafter called the sponsors or the sponsoring organizations). What was envisaged was a detailed study and critical analysis of the provisions of the Code and the changes in New York law that would result if it were enacted. It was expected that such a study would make possible an informed decision as to whether the Code was satisfactory in its present form or whether it would need to be revised.

The Commission's study of the Uniform Commercial Code was a major undertaking, engaging its attention to the exclusion of all other work until its completion some three years later. During this period the Commission not only increased its regular staff in order to handle all aspects of the problem, but as well engaged law teachers and legal practitioners conversant with this particular field of knowledge—some twenty in number—to make special studies of various aspects of the Code. A series of public hearings was held, as a consequence of which a considerable number of memoranda were received. A large volume of correspondence was carried on. Ultimately, all these materials were studied and debated by the Commission itself, which considered each section of the Code in detail.

The Commission's Report to the Legislature was submitted in March, 1956. It discussed significant aspects of the Code and commented briefly on a number of provisions. The conclusion reached was that the Uniform Commercial Code as promulgated by the sponsoring organizations in 1952 was not suitable for adoption in New York without making changes so extensive as to require comprehensive re-examination.

The Commission believes that it is clear, from the criticisms indicated in this Report, that the Uniform Commercial Code is not satisfactory without comprehensive re-examination and revision in the light of all critical comment obtainable.

Criticisms of the Uniform Commercial Code advanced at public hearings which the Commission held in the course of its study led the sponsors to reconsider its draft and a revised text was published in 1954. Throughout its study the Commission kept in touch with the sponsors and transmitted to its various subcommittees copies of all studies prepared for the Commission by its consultants and staff, and also materials which indicated criticisms and questions raised in the Commission's own discussions. The subcommittees, in turn, furnished to the Commission the reports of their discussions, including comment on questions raised in the Commission's materials and comment as well on other problems arising in their own discussions or coming to them from studies that were going on in other states.

In 1957 the recreated Editorial Board of the sponsors recommended the adoption of many amendments to the Code to meet criticisms and suggestions. Some of the amendments arose out of the studies going on in other states, or originated within the various subcommittees. A very large number of them, however, were responsive, directly or indirectly, to comments of the New York Law Revision Commission. These amendments were approved by the National Conference of Commissioners on Uniform State Laws, the American Law Institute and the American Bar Association, with the result that a revised Code was published as the 1957 Official Edition, and after a number of further changes approved in 1958, an Official Text was published in that year, which is the current text.

Thus the work of the Law Revision Commission has played a part in the history of the Code since 1952 and has had an influence on the provisions of the Code as it exists at this time.

Study of the Uniform Commercial Code has continued in New York under the direction and sponsorship of the New York Commissioners on Uniform State Laws, resulting in the publication of New York Annotations and a recommendation for the enactment of the Code in New York. A bill to this effect went before the 1962 Legislature, sponsored by the New York Joint Legislative Committees on Interstate Cooperation and on Commerce and Economic Development and by the New York Commissioners on Uniform State Laws. The text of the bill proposed some changes from the 1958 official version of the Uniform Commercial Code. On April 18, 1962, the Governor signed this bill, with a memorandum.... The effect of the Commission's study is extensively discussed in the memorandum of approval. This study is discussed herein in the next section.

## The Influence of Research Upon Legislative Action

To paraphrase a question posed at the beginning: Is it possible to evaluate the influence of research by the Commission's staff and its consultants, and by the Commissioners themselves, in the legislative record achieved in enactment or rejection of bills recommended by the Commission in the legislative process?

To attempt an answer to this question is the prime purpose of this paper. The answer, such as it will be, comes from an active participant in the history. Perhaps it is therefore a biased answer, one colored by preconceptions, hopes, and misconceptions of results. Perhaps the answer should be given by one of those to whom the recommendations were directed, or by a disinterested observer of the legislative scene. Before any answer is attempted, I will try to name other influences which could have been present and indeed some of which certainly were present.

In any evaluation of influences on the Legislature, no one can fail to include the one popularly supposed to be omnipresent: lobbying. I have testified that "the Commission will not lobby for one of its bills." I do not know whether this statement has been publicly challenged; it certainly has been privately—by direct inquiry or by a quizzical and sometimes incredulous glance. Does this mean that the Commission is so disinterested a participant in the legislative process that it recommends as if in a moot court of mythical jurisdiction, with no interest whatever in result? Indeed it does not so recommend, nor is the agency that disinterested. What it does mean is that the Commission will not attempt, in any way or manner, to enlist support or invoke pressure from sources outside the Legislature for enactment of its bills or any of them or for rejection of any proposal before the Legislature from any other source.

On the other hand, the Commission is highly sensitive to criticism of and objections to its proposals, from whatever source they may come. Perhaps the best illustration of this attitude is expressed in the consideration by the Commission of actions by the New York State Bar Association Committee to Cooperate with the Law Revision Commission. Not only does the Commission receive the reported action of the Committee, it also receives the individual memoranda which the Committee debated and on which it acted. And not only does the Commission consider the reported actions, it considers scrupulously the individual suggestions which may have been rejected by the full Committee.

This certainly is not hypersensitivity to the possibility of individual objection or pressure on the Legislature. It is a manifestation of the overwhelming motive to be right, to have a good solution, one which will not cause as many problems as it solves. This Commission was specifically suggested because it was said that the Legislature acting "without expert or responsible or disinterested or systematic advice . . . patches the fabric here and there and mars often when it would mend." Those were serious words to a Commission set up to give that kind of advice and to avoid marring of the fabric of the law. It is a rare rule which cannot remain for a few years until the right change is made, if any change is to be made. Rightness, in such changes, is a matter of study and consideration, of logic, and experience—and it does not necessarily depend on a majority vote in a committee.

Of course, when the Commission finally does recommend legislation, it attempts in all ways possible, as a messenger to the Legislature to convince that body of the correctness of its position. How does it act in this regard? First and primarily, it submits its full Recommendation to each member of the Legislature individually. Second, it appends to each of its bills a short statutory note as an exposition of the change, and conscientiously not argumentative for the change. Argument is reserved for the Recommendation to which the note refers. Third, the Commission attempts to identify every serious objection made to its proposal, and it attempts seriously to consider them, accept or reject them and if rejected to answer them. Fourth, it maintains contact with the legislative committees considering its bills, and with their clerks, and later with the Office of the Counsel to the Governor, for these purposes and for the purpose of avoiding merely procedural difficulties in the advancement of its proposals. Fifth, it presents orally both explanation and argument at a joint hearing of all the legislative committees considering its bills during each session. Finally it sends its Executive Secretary weekly to the Capitol during the course of the session for the purpose of obtaining such information as it may require with respect to all of these matters, and for the purpose of transmitting to the legislative committees such actions as the Commission itself has taken relative to measures which are before them. More than this, it does not do. This much is simply not in my definition of lobbying.

Certainly some of the success which the Commission has had with its program is attributable to the extraordinary continuity of service of its members. . . . The continuity of service on the Commission is matched by the length of the service of the membership and the chairmen of the New York State Bar Association Committee to cooperate with the Law Revision Commission. In twenty-seven years there have been only five chairmen, one of whom served as chairman for thirteen years and the previous three years as a member, and left the post to become president of the association.

So relatively few people being together so long is bound to have had notable effects.

Within the Commission itself traditions had a chance to develop and to grow. The selection of projects, the balancing of the annual program, the number of recommendations annually, the style of the recommendations, the form of statutory notes, the use of various kinds of drafting techniques, saving clauses, communications to the Legislature and many other methods and activities of the Commission were greatly influenced by the long experience of some of its members and by their being with each other so long. In the solution of new and difficult problems, someone would remember how a comparable earlier problem was solved. The use of precedents is not entirely a technique of the judicial process. . . .

There have been other influences in the extraordinary success of the legislative program. It is notable that in all of the recommendations made there has never been a "dissenting opinion" submitted. This does not mean that there have been no disagreements within the Commission itself. It does mean that an attempt is made to hammer out conflicting views as to policy and drafting to the point that the solution is quite acceptable to all. From the very first it became a principle to make no recommendation whatever if there was substantial—even if not a majority—opposition to the proposal within the Commission itself. What is substantial opposition in this connection varies from case to case. In large measure it depends on a majority's recognition of the validity of the minority's opposition. In some measure, compromise obviously plays a role as it does in all of the legislative process. . . .

My strong belief is that the fact that the state pays the appointed members of the Commission a substantial salary is extremely important. This salary is on an annual rather than on a per diem basis. In the original statute the salary was fixed at five thousand dollars; the present salary is in excess of nine thousand dollars, and the item of Commissioners' salaries is about one-third of the annual budget. In an individual case, the amount of the salary provided emphasizes the part-time nature of the work, as is implicit also in the statutory provisions regarding qualifications of the appointed members. But the amount also emphasizes the fact that membership on the Commission is definitely not merely honorary but involves work of a substantial amount. The Commission is a working group. And work is more than attendance at meetings. It is more than the making of decisions. It involves individual homework. Four men will tell a newcomer so, as each of the four was in his own time told. This has a definite effect on the staff and on the quality of the research submitted to this working group of Commissioners. The product is to be tested by experienced lawyers and law teachers, questioned, checked, doubted and discussed. The study—no matter if it comes from one of the great authorities in the field—goes before professionals who keenly feel their responsibility to the legislature and to their own reputations, group and individual. The kind of work expected of and done by the membership of the Commission has an effect on the chief executive officers of the staff. They obviously participate in the discussional and in the decisional process, but neither of them individually decides. If the Executive Secretary in the course of discussion with a legislative committee chairman, member or clerk discovers that a change in a bill, however minor it may be, will bring the bill out of committee for a vote, he never himself gives the go-ahead, if the amendment is to bear a Commission recommendation. He reports back and gets a vote, and a minute is made. A few incidents of this sort in the Legislature provide understanding to the legislator involved. And it brings respect and prestige to the agency of which the head of the staff is only a messenger. So also with the Director of Research in her relationships with the Commission. It is the Commission which decides and which recommends.

I seriously doubt that any honorary membership guarantees in every case the quality of every commissioner's work. It was the 1923 Commission which never submitted a bill and which ultimately disappeared. It was not a salaried group. I think that fact is highly significant.

Another influence on the success of the Commission before the Legislature is the selection of a program to be presented. A basic question concerns the scope of projects. Should the work undertaken be one study of great magnitude which might last well over the years, session by session? Cardozo certainly had less in mind: "The statute that will do this, first in one field and then in others, is something different from a code," he wrote. And, again, "something less ambitious . . . is the requirement of the hour." Sometimes the choice is not the Commission's own. Sometimes, as in the study of the Uniform Commercial Code, or in the current study of the desirability of a State Administrative Procedure Act, the direction comes from higher authority. The Commission, however, is not available to study everything. It is not a complete, always-ready substitute for the temporary joint legislative committee or commission set up to study a particular field of law. Currently there are important legislative committees or commissions in New York investigating very basic and very large areas of law: for instance, all the laws, substantive and procedural, relating to crimes and offenses; all of the laws, substantive and procedural, relative to decedents' estates; all of the corporation laws; the laws relative to domestic relations and the family. Some of these investigations may take longer than five years to make. Some of them will be expensive, and substantial appropriations are made to the committees and commissions charged with the responsibility. Each topic could have been assigned to the Law Revision Commission, some of them might well have been so assigned. No one of them in its entirety would the Commission undertake without direction so to do.

Nor does it seem wise for such legislative directions to be made wholesale. A large scale study takes the Commission out of the business which Cardozo thought so important to undertake, the correction of the rules of private law between man and man. It takes the Commission for long periods out of the Legislature. It concerns itself with one product only, submitted after years in which no other Commission bills were considered by the Legislature. It stakes the Commission's influence and prestige, and perhaps its ultimate existence, on the acceptance or rejection of one study which was spread out over years of effort.

The Commission has believed it more in line with its function to undertake the narrower studies which are illustrated by its record of recommendations to the Legislature. If a broader project is later to come, it comes by natural evolution of the greater from the less. Future undertakings presently being considered by the Commission are good examples of this possibility. Is the time ripe for a general obligations law in New York? Is it possible to consolidate the real and personal property laws into a general property law, and then to consolidate—from the combined material—new chapters dealing with trusts and fiduciaries, actions and proceedings, and landlord and tenant? Cardozo had this development in mind when he wrote "as statute follows statute, the material may be given from which in time, a code will come."

Within this framework, it has been the practice of the Commission to have about twenty to twenty-five projects being studied at one time, some short, and others long-term—the test being "is this to be ready for the next Legislature?" They will be in the area of private law, with policy questions subordinate to legal. They will not be in the special jurisdiction—or skill and competence—of another state agency, whether it be an executive department or a legislative committee specifically constituted. They will be balanced, so as to provide a grist for succeeding legislative sessions. About fifteen bills must be ready for the next Legislature. Without regard to the importance of the project, they should relate to a variety of subjects, some controversial, some not. It is not advisable to have them all directed toward one special group interest. All of this, and more, is involved in having a balanced program both in relation to studies and bills. And without a balanced program, failure is inevitable—and with repeated failures the existence of the agency is at stake.

In summary, consideration has been given to certain influences which have either had or not had part in the Commission's successful legislative record. Lobbying, at least as defined herein, simply does not take place. The continuity of service of its members, the fact that the Commission is salaried and is a working group, and the selection of a balanced program have been presented as positive influences in the record.

We are finally at the question of the influence of the research process.

How can any influence be measured? Why was the Commission's budget drastically cut in 1939 and in 1942? Would the quality of research have saved it from these cuts? The quality of research—and, indeed, a good legislative record—did not save the Judicial Council from abolition.

Withal, it must be concluded that the hard core reason for the Commission's success, undoubted prestige and continued existence as a law reform agency is the quality and character of the research which goes into the resolution of the projects which it undertakes and which composes the grist of its legislative mill. Both in the selection of subjects and in their solution, it is the all-important factor. The Commission will not take any action—for anyone—directed or not—on a subject it has not itself studied. Time and again, a particular solution is rejected because in the final discussion a problem is disclosed on which there was no study. Repeatedly, also, a narrow proposal is made reserving other matters for future study. Elaborate proposals have been withdrawn because the Commission concluded that its own study was inadequate or incomplete.

All of these propositions were thoroughly tested in the three-year period in which the sole matter before the agency was the Uniform Commercial Code. This was the only time the Commission ever had to pass specifically on another's product, completely finished and unified. It would have been impossible to undertake the job, section by section, studying independently so as to have results come out without any regard whatever to what the sponsors of the Code had originally proposed. In the beginning of the Commission's study, this was really the attitude which motivated certain of the individual Commissioners. Each section was a new project for individual study and for an ideal solution, no matter what the Code said. This was the danger which the Commission had to overcome if the study was to have any merit at all.

And, on the other hand, the sponsors had to come to realize, as they ultimately did, that study is basic to the Commission's work, and that it would study on its own and without regard to how much study others had concededly made. In view of the Commission's consideration of its own general function it simply was impossible to have the Code accepted without change. The Commission undertook independent and uncontrolled research. And it had had twenty-two years' experience in legal research as it relates to legislation and to a very active Legislature. . . .[a]

The notable record of recommendations which have been accepted by the Legislature is matched by another factor quite likely to be overlooked. In some instances where recommendations have been made and there has been no enactment, the research of the Commission in identifying the problem may have been influential in the change of the rule when the problem is met again by the courts. Sometimes, the Legislature itself has accepted an alternative solution. And, in one instance at least, a federal court, in applying New York law, used the recommendation

[a] Omitted at this point is a discussion of the part played by the Commission in the review and revision of the Uniform Commercial Code. Readers interested in the evolution of the Code should consult the original text of the article.

and Commission research to determine in an uncharted field the further course of New York decision.

Attention has already been called to the great amount of statutory revision and reconsolidation, and codification, which has recently taken place or is now taking place in New York. The ferment in the law indicated by these changes is very great. In 1921, Cardozo, from Professor Hazeltine, and through him from Pascal, quoted "Le droit a ses époques." The law has "its epochs of ebbs and flow," and then he observed "One of the flood seasons is upon us." If this statement were true in New York in 1921, it was true legislatively only by adoption of the Civil Practice Act as against the Code of Civil Procedure. It was true prospectively in the demand for change witnessed by the very article itself. Forty years later, the demand has been realized, and is being realized annually. In the number of studies made and projected, the experience and advice of the New York Law Revision Commission as a research agency in law reform through legislation is first sought and freely given. The staff of one legislative committee after another has been patterned on that developed within the Commission itself. The first grist of suggestions to these committees have come from the vast number of specialized suggestions accumulated over twenty-nine years by the Commission, partially or fully researched. The method of work adopted by the Commission has been utilized by these temporary groups with special jurisdiction: The identification of the problem is the first job; the relation of the problem to existing law in New York is the second; the various solutions to the problem disclosed by other experiences is the third; the possibilities of solution which come from analogies, experience, imagination and creation is the fourth; the testing of the solution by logic, experience and available data, legal or non-legal, is next; the testing of the solution in the vast body of remaining law, written and unwritten, is the last. In the process, research in the library, by questionnaire, by factual investigation by qualified personnel and by voluntary conference and hearings are the only tools employed. A good filing system, cross-referencing and all the other periphery of research are required. The availability of excellent general and law library facilities is absolutely essential. The process differs from merely bill drafting as it is practiced by legislative draftsmen. It is drafting not to accomplish an already determined result. This is research to determine the result and drafting only to accomplish it. Has this kind of research been translated into legislative action? The result speaks for itself, for fundamentally research is the only real weapon in the armory of the Law Revision Commission. Other factors favorably influencing the long legislative record are themselves products of the quality of the research itself.

As the preceding study shows, a law revision commission can deal with only a narrow category of legal problems comprising a small share of the grist for the legislative mill. Thus, even if adequate commissions on the New York model were widely established—and this, unhappily, has not occurred—there would be need to examine the adequacy of the state legislative process.

---

# THE MAKERS OF OUR LAWS:
# THE STATE LEGISLATURE        By S. Gale Lowrie

NEXT WINTER state legislatures will be in session in nearly all of our states. Some 7,000 lawmakers will go into action, and 60,000 bills may be introduced. The average cost in a typical state may be $1,500 for each bill introduced, and $5,000 for each law passed. The cost of this legislation to the people, and the business interests of the state in litigation, and in adjustments to changed conditions has not been computed. But for all this enormous expense the result seems to satisfy nobody. We lament the decline of our representative institutions, the lawmaking functions of the court, the growth of bureaucracy, the decline of the state governments in favor of federal power. But the greatest single cause of these tendencies is the failure of our American legislatures to properly perform their work.

Let us view a legislature from the inside and watch the career of a member of the House of Representatives who has been chosen in the November elections. The constitution of his state, like the constitutions of all but four of the states, provides for biennial sessions. Our member is a lawyer and goes to the capital with ambition to be a faithful public servant and to represent the interests of his constituents and the interests of the state at large. He has often heard and he has often repeated the statement, that we have too many laws. He is in favor of a few necessary changes, a short businesslike session, and an early adjournment. He is something of a stylist and proposes to study carefully the draft of each bill he will introduce as well as the bills of others. He knows that the lack of gratitude in republics is proverbial, but he dares hope that faithful, outstanding performance of his public duties will open the door to a career of larger usefulness.

Reprinted from *University of Cincinnati Law Review*, vol. 17, 1948, pp. 144–158, with permission of the publisher. The late S. Gale Lowrie was Professor of Political Science at the University of Cincinnati.

He finds the majority of his fellow members in the House are, like himself, new to their duties and that only one-fourth of them have served more than one term. This change in the personnel of the legislature makes organization somewhat slow. Several candidates have announced themselves for the office of Speaker. Both parties proceed to choose floor leaders. There is talk of appointments, deals, and trades of various sorts. There is a contest for membership on the more important committees. There is a certain amount of patronage at his disposal. He had thought little about this before election, but soon after the results of the November balloting were known, the matter was brought to his attention by a number of his friends whose acquaintance he had made during the campaign. It now appears that he has the appointment of a doorkeeper. Some of his fellow members prefer the appointment of stenographers. He thinks, however, that it would be a pleasant experience to have a friendly nod each morning at the main entrance and he submits the name of a member from his district. It turns out, however, that this faithful worker was in hope of a position as sergeant-at-arms and feels somewhat aggrieved because of the lowly position assigned him. Our legislator decides to use the other door.

The Governor's message has been read. It suggests quite a program for the legislature. Newspapers comment favorably upon it. New acquaintances appear within the legislature and without, particularly without. He thinks of bills he had intended to introduce and tries to get some drafted. Quite a number of important measures have been called to his attention since that important day last November. He goes home for the weekend. It is a busy time. He hardly had time to arrange his private affairs before the sessions began. Private matters and public matters crowd in upon him. Perhaps it would have been easier to have spent the weekend at the capital.

The second and third weeks arrive. Bills begin to pour in—seventy-five by the end of the second, and one hundred and fifty by the end of the third week. Long since he has given up his resolution to read every bill which appears, but he now tries to read those that have been acted upon favorably by the committees. Committee meetings are taking time. He hardly has time to read any of the bills. The inner politics of the legislature seem to command his time and strength. Constituents, lobbyists, committee members of the House, committee members of the Senate, more lobbyists, a conference with the Governor, a matter of patronage, engross his attention. He tries to study the bills which have been referred to his committee. Fifty have been referred already and there will be ninety of them before the session is over. They need further consideration. They need to be redrafted. Many seem to affect practices of long standing. There is a disagreement respecting them and proponents are not entirely disinterested.

There is the talk of a closure rule. After the sixth week no bill is to be introduced without special permission. Some of his bills are not yet ready. He decides to introduce them as they are, hoping to correct them at a later stage. There is a perfect avalanche of bills. Before the rule goes into effect, six hundred and fifty have been introduced; fifty or seventy-five more will appear later by special permission. The legislature is talking of meeting on Saturday and Monday mornings. They have been working on a four-day schedule, but the weekends have been crowded. A few trips of inspection, conferences with his party leaders, telephone calls, and some attention to his private affairs—have tended to make the weekends something of an orgy. Telegrams and mail appear. He has a form postcard prepared which he sends his constituents when they write about pending legislation. It simplifies procedure considerably. All he has to do is to write the address on one side of the card and the number of the bill on the other. His constituents should know that he is a busy man. At least the card will keep them from writing again.

The legislature is in a jam over tax bills and school legislation, but not too busy to debate for two days on a fish and game law. At the end of this time they decide to extend the hunting season for certain animals from the last day of November to the first day of December, and permit fish of certain varieties to constitute legal catch if they measure eight inches not to the tip of the tail, but to a point somewhat short of this.

Uncomplimentary editorials and newspaper stories begin to appear. They are calling this the "do-nothing legislature." They are urging them to pass the appropriations and adjourn.

A few of his local bills are taking more and more of his attention. He finds it necessary to make some concessions—to promise to support the bill to provide hog serum (he is not much interested in this anyway); to revamp several local municipal courts; to provide back pay for the sergeant-at-arms; to give additional pay to the legislative employees after adjournment. One bill he has introduced is now out of committee. It is not perfect but perhaps it is an improvement. Floor amendments crowd in; some are defeated; some are passed over his protest. They make a sorry mess of his bill, but he urges the House to vote for it in the hope that these unfortunate features can be eliminated in the Senate. If not, he will try to get the Governor to veto it.

He notices in the newspaper that the legislature of Wyoming has adjourned. The constitution of that state allows but forty days for the legislative session. He wonders whether they completed their work—or whether they just adjourned.

The legislature has now determined upon a date for adjournment. The sessions are longer. The most important bills are being considered by the committee of the whole. The legislative halls are hardly ever empty, day or night. The ventilation system is primitive. The lights glare as brilliantly as those of a Greek candy merchant. There is a constant drone from the clerk's desk—reading bills at length and calling the roll. Hours could be saved if the House would install a system for recording votes electrically, and would dispense with the useless reading of the bills, but the droning goes on. All day and much of the night there are committee meetings and sessions of the legislature. Nervous tension is affecting him and his fellow members. The last day is a hub-bub. The clock says twelve. The legislature should have adjourned at noon, but it actually continues until three-thirty the next morning.

The session is over. He goes home and in a few weeks receives copies of the bills which have been passed. How many errors have crept in! He starts to make notes and then recalls that his legislative days are over, unless perchance he should be again elected a year from the following November, and have another opportunity to try it all over again.

### Problems of Legislative Structure

If Americans have a genius for organization, this has not as yet been evidenced in the structure or operation of our legislative bodies. The greatest trouble is that there is too much of a rush—a rush to get bills drafted; to get them introduced; to hold committee hearings; to get them out of committee; to get them voted upon before the legislature can adjourn; to do the same in the other House; to get the Governor to consider them. We elect our state legislators for two-year terms, but their activities are normally confined to a few months. The real problems of legislation are rarely sensed until developed in the legislature itself, particularly in the committee hearings. By this time, the session may well be on its way with adjournment in the offing. This gives undue power to certain individuals in strategic positions to advance or retard legislation, particularly the committee chairmen and those in charge of formulating the legislative calendar.

There are too many steps to be taken. The theory of checks and balances has been carried to an absurdity. It may be questioned whether the theory is a sound one under any circumstances. The most valuable check is perhaps the knowledge of an official or board of officials that everything depends upon careful scrutiny of proposals. But as it is, each body passes measures it knows to be faulty in the hope that errors will be detected and corrected further on. The House passes bills in the belief they will be amended in the Senate. The Senate passes them, because they believe that the House has scrutinized them, or that the Governor will examine them; and the Governor signs them in belief that both Houses have become convinced of their wisdom. But the path of the bill is so intricate that the issues become confused rather than clarified.

Our present legislative sessions require too long an absence from private affairs to secure the type of legislator we wish to attract. Conditions are very different from those existing when our legislative agencies took their form. In those days many of our occupations were seasonal. The winter was a time of comparative inactivity, and many of our representative citizens could go to the capital in December and complete the legislative program before February was well along. The public bills to be considered were few in number, and usually those which were enacted could be printed in a little pamphlet of modest proportions. Today the measures are far more complicated and the members are usually unable to complete their work before the spring is far advanced. In many states they are subject to frequent demands for attendance upon special sessions of the legislature.

There is little chance for a career except by winning party favor, or by making political acquaintances which may prove useful later on. Party favor depends very largely upon the vote-getting capacity the member displays in November, before his term begins, rather than upon his record as a legislator, providing, however, he displays party regularity.

There is very little opportunity for conference with one's constituents. Comparatively few of our people know the members of the legislatures personally. There is little time to get acquainted with them between the elections and the legislative sessions and then, the legislators are too busy to give matters adequate consideration until the legislature has adjourned. Thereafter, their power to be of assistance to their constituents has passed.

The present confusing system increases the power of the lobby. In fact, the lobbyist has become an almost essential go-between for the citizens and the legislature. The members of the legislature cannot give the interests of their constituents the attention they need, and the constituents must depend upon hired representatives. The opportunity of actually creating the situation which will result in their employment, has not been overlooked by the astute lobbyists.

It would be interesting to note the result were the legislature to stay in session until its work were not only done but done well, if this were possible under our present organization. The great bulk of the measures introduced at each session are either bills which were introduced at an earlier time and failed to receive consideration, or are bills to correct badly drafted measures. Both Houses are accustomed to pass bills and amendments they do not understand in the vain hope that the other House will correct their error. A floor leader of a recent legislature testifies on this subject. He is reported to have said with reference to a tax bill intoduced late in the session, "Many members were not provided with copies of the bills, consequently they did not know what they were voting on. After passage many members admitted they did not know that they had voted for certain provisions. The printed copies of the bills were not available until Wednesday and were rushed through on Thursday." The Governor is reported as saying with reference to the same legislation that it was full of errors and contradictions which the Senate would have to take out. And those were bills to collect and distribute $80,000,000! Every man, woman, and child in the state is affected. So are business interests!

What is needed first of all is more opportunity for deliberation. This in itself would reduce the number of bills introduced to those which seem to have a fair chance of serious consideration and approval. If haste were eliminated the measures might be better written. Dr. William E. Britton, Professor of Law at the University of Illinois, speaking on the bankruptcy laws, says: "Statutes drafted in this vague and cumbersome style often defeat their own ends. Not only that, but carelessly drafted statutes generate unnecessary litigation. It is a deplorable waste of public and private funds and precious time, to say nothing of the primary matter—the uncertainty of rights created. There is no excuse for it. We often hear the criticism that we have too many laws enacted. Most of this is amendatory legislation and much of it is due to careless work done in the original act. The quantity of legislation is not nearly so disturbing as its quality. And I am not referring to the major objects of the legislation, but only to the skill, or lack of skill, shown in fitting means to ends. There is reason to believe that the time is not far distant when we shall have to pay marked attention to this matter in all departments or our laws will engulf us and democracy will find itself crippled at a vital spot."

A slower tempo would also enable the legislators to keep in close touch with their constituents. No legislators are wise enough to enact statutes without the advice and help of those who must operate under them. The people of the state are entitled to have copies of all measures under consideration by the legislature. That is the theory of the procedure today, but these rights are violated at every session.

Lastly, deliberation would remove the greatest single cause for the confused statutes which we now have, and that is the hastily prepared floor amendment, which often becomes incorporated in the bill upon the instigation of those who have not fully studied its implications.

How can this be secured without unduly protracting the legislative sessions? First of all, the legislators should meet periodically, perhaps quarterly, throughout the life of the legislature. This alone would obviate many of the difficulties we now experience such as the closure rule, the calendar committee, the failure to keep in touch with the constituents, the rush to introduce bills before the temper of the legislature is ascertained. It would obviate the orgies of the closing days of the sessions. It would give the members of the legislature time to consider and pass with some intelligence upon the measures submitted to them.

Secondly, the people of the state would be better represented by a small legislature. It is the theory of the larger House that with fewer constituents each member may know his constituents better and ascertain their views and needs. But as we have already pointed out, this acquaintance does not develop until the legislative session has come to a close, and the legislator's opportunity for good or evil is gone for the remainder of his term. A member of the legislature too busy to do anything but write the number of a bill on a postcard and the address of the constituent on the other side can hardly be said to be an adequate representative. There is dictum in *The Federalist* that "in all legislative assemblies the greater the number composing them may be, the fewer will be the men who in fact direct their proceedings."

Lastly, the second chamber should be abolished because with the changes suggested it is not only useless but confusing. A single chamber of moderate size, meeting quarterly or monthly, would give the people adequate representation, more careful consideration to measures, reduce the anxiety which now goes over the state every biennium, give opportunities for careers of public service, and would reduce measurably the million dollar expense of holding regular sessions of the legislature. If one House must pass measures in the haste we have described, perhaps something can be said for a second chamber which can at least throw the legislature into a deadlock and keep us in status quo. But the multiplicity of checks is not what we want. The more checks we have, the less effective will each one of them become, and the more confusing will be the process of government.

One state, Nebraska, has now a unicameral legislature since the constitution of that state was amended in November, 1934, to effect the change. The new Nebraska legislature was sponsored by the late Senator Norris, but his original plan was departed from in some respects. Unfortunately, the suggestion for a well-paid legislature meeting in frequent sessions was not followed, but as additional sessions may be provided by law, the way may be open for this needed amendment.

The courts are not concerned so much with changing the policies laid down by the legislatures, as with trying to find out what those policies are as expressed in bewildering and contradictory language. And the turn to bureaucracy, commissions, and executive officials has been brought about in a large measure by the failure of our lawmaking bodies to function. The reason these commissions have as a rule served us better than have the legislatures is not because bureaucracy is preferable to democracy, but because these bureaus and commissions are relieved of the necessity for hasty action, and because those who make the rules have had some opportunity to acquaint themselves with the problems with which they are attempting to deal. But let those who have observed the constant increase in the number of federal agencies pause to consider whether their interests and rights are better protected by an enormous bureaucracy than they would be by state and local governments properly organized to conduct such affairs as are essentially local in character.

## TWENTIETH-CENTURY LEGISLATURES FOR TWENTIETH-CENTURY PROBLEMS

*By Richard L. Neuberger*

BECAUSE I am so recently "sprung" from a state legislature, people invariably ask me about the difference between service in the U.S. Senate and a typical state senate. If there is any one dividing characteristic, it is in the vastly superior information and assistance which are available to a United States Senator. State senators are on their own. United States Senators have the advantage of extensive and well-trained committee staffs, of the reference facilities of the Library of Congress, of the vigilant majority and minority conferences of their respective political parties.

When I first entered the Senate, I was shocked to see bills gaveled to passage like pickets flashing past on a fence. "Without objection, the bill is passed," intoned the presiding officer with monotonous regularity. Then I began to realize that all such bills had been carefully screened prior to reaching the unanimous-consent calendar. This was the result of elaborate staff work. It probably could not be risked in a state legislature, with so relatively few aides and researchers.

When legislation comes before a committee of the U.S. Senate, I find expert committee assistance readily available. For example, the Senate

---

Reprinted from Stanley Scott, *Streamlining State Legislatures* (Berkeley, Calif.: Howell-North, 1956), pp. 68–70, with the permission of the editor and the publisher. The author was the late Senator from Oregon.

Public Works Committee, on which I serve, can provide me speedily with engineering or legal data on any bill. I also have discovered that the two parties study bills thoroughly, through their respective conferences. On the closing day of the first session of the Eighty-fourth Congress, I was desperately eager to secure enactment of a bill allowing a generous family in my state to bring eight Korean war orphans to America. Yet, because of slow departmental work in the Immigration Service, the bill had been inexcusably delayed. I went to Senator William F. Knowland of California, the minority leader, to see if Republican approval could not be secured for a Democrat's bill at this eleventh hour. When he understood the humanitarian nature of the legislation, he dropped everything to have the minority conference "clear" my bill. This was done in less than an hour. Staff work of this kind rarely is available in state legislatures.

Because no legislature of one of the forty-eight states can be provided with staffs comparable to that of the national Congress, I would suggest that state universities and other institutions of higher education in each state might somehow close this gap. They have libraries and trained faculties of economists, political scientists, engineers, foresters, etc. Where the university is in the same city as the state capital building—as at Madison, Wisconsin, or Columbus, Ohio, for example—contiguity would make such a service readily accessible. The stationing of skeleton staffs away from the university might be necessary in states like California, Oregon or Washington, to cite a few, where the university campus is located in a different community than the seat of government.

But I would recommend that our universities could well furnish state legislatures with the detailed information and background that are so essential to an understanding of complex issues. President Franklin D. Roosevelt is supposed to have told a friend that he could trust himself to reach a sound decision if he were "not licked on the facts." This is likewise true of thousands of conscientious state legislators throughout the nation. They will do right, provided they have the knowledge and facts necessary to know right from wrong on the particular question at stake. The providing of these facts could be the task of our universities, if only they will set themselves to it.

*Public Records Needed for Effectiveness and Responsibility.* In addition to staff work, one of the great differences between the Congress and the typical state legislature is the completeness and wide public distribution of the records made at committee hearings and during floor debate, and of committee reports. The committees of the state legislature of Oregon, the one with which I am most familiar, for instance cannot begin to fill the public role in the legislative process which congressional committees play on the national level. True, they hold hearings and do preliminary work on legislation pending before them. But the testimony developed at these hearings is not published and made available to other members of the Senate or House and to the public at large before voting, nor are committee reports. And the committees do not engage in investigations comparable to those of congressional committees, with the power to compel truthful testimony.

Finally, no verbatim record is kept of statements in floor debate itself. In the Congress, hearing transcripts, committee reports and the *Congressional Record* permit a legislator to study an issue upon which he will have to vote and to base the reasons for his action upon the public record. Under the conditions prevailing in state legislatures, on the other hand, important votes must often be cast in ignorance of any considerations except those brought out in floor debate, and perhaps in reliance upon actual—but unrecorded—misstatements of fact.

# THE NATIONAL CONFERENCE OF COMMISSIONERS ON UNIFORM STATE LAWS

By James W. Day

THE DESIRABILITY of uniformity in certain phases of the law of the various jurisdictions of the United States has long been recognized. The need for uniformity is greatest, of course, in those fields in which the steps leading to the completion of a transaction or project are frequently so taken in two or more jurisdictions as to necessitate the consideration of more than one set of relevant laws or to present difficult questions of conflict of laws that are avoided when the laws of the jurisdictions do not differ. This need for uniformity received recognition at the time of the formation of the American Bar Association in 1878 through the inclusion of a statement in the original constitution of that body that one of its objectives was "to promote . . . uniformity of legislation throughout the nation."

In 1881, a committee of the Alabama Bar Association brought to the attention of the American Bar Association and the bar associations of other states the desirability of efforts to attain uniformity in certain fields

---

Reprinted from *University of Florida Law Review*, vol. 8, 1955, pp. 276–286, with the permission of the publisher. James W. Day has been Professor of Law at the University of Florida, Gainesville, and has served as a Commissioner from Florida to the National Conference on Uniform State Laws.

of the law. In 1889, the American Bar Association appointed a Committee on Uniform State Laws consisting of one member from each state.

The New York Legislature on April 28, 1890, authorized the governor to appoint by and with the consent of the senate three commissioners who should have the duty

> ... to examine the subjects of marriage and divorce, insolvency, the form of notarial certificates and other subjects; to ascertain the best means to effect ... uniformity in the laws of the states, and especially to consider whether it would be wise ... for the state of New York to invite the other states ... to send representatives to a convention to draft uniform laws to be submitted for the approval and adoption of the several states. ...

On August 21, 1890, the American Bar Association, at the instance of its committee on uniform state laws, adopted a resolution recommending the passage by each state, and by the Congress of the United States for the District of Columbia and the territories, of an act similar to that of New York. In New Jersey and Pennsylvania acts were passed respectively on April 14, 1891, and April 15, 1891, providing for the appointment of commissioners on uniform state laws; and on August 28, 1891, the Committee on Uniform State Laws of the American Bar Association reported to that body that legislation of this type was then in effect also in Delaware, Massachusetts, and Michigan. On March 29, 1892, a similar statute was enacted in Mississippi, and at about the same time a Commission on Uniformity of Legislation was established by Georgia. In 1895, it was provided by statute in Florida that three commissioners for the promotion of uniformity of legislation in the United States should be appointed by the governor with the consent of the senate and that they should cooperate and advise with similar commissions appointed in other states.

The first general meeting of the commissioners was held at Saratoga, New York, on August 24, 25, and 26, 1892, at the time and place of the annual meeting of the American Bar Association. Commissioners were present from each of the eight states mentioned in the preceding paragraph with the exception of Mississippi. Commissions on Uniformity of Legislation were established by eleven additional jurisdictions in 1893, by three in 1894, and by seven in 1895. Florida was one of the last-named group. The organization of commissioners from the participating states and territories in 1896 was named the National Conference of Commissioners on Uniform State Laws, the title by which the group continues to be designated. Since 1912, all of the states and territories and the District of Columbia have been officially represented in the Conference.

A second meeting of the commissioners was held in 1892 in New York City on November 15 and 16. Since that time, there has been a meeting every year, with the exception of 1945 when war conditions made it impracticable for the commissioners to assemble.

## Organization and Procedure of the National Conference

The National Conference is composed of commissioners, usually three in number, from each of the states, the District of Columbia, the territories of Alaska and Hawaii, and the Commonwealth of Puerto Rico. A few states appoint more than three commissioners. They do not, however, thereby increase their voting strength, since the vote on the adoption of proposed acts is taken by states; and any commissioner can demand such a vote on other matters coming before the Conference. The number of commissioners is further augmented by the fact that since August 21, 1943, a commissioner who has served for twenty years may be, and usually is, elected to life membership in the Conference by that body. The principal administrative officer of each state legislative reference bureau or other agency charged by law with the duty of drafting legislation at the request of the legislative or executive officers of the state is ex officio an associate member of the Conference. As such he has the privileges of the floor and is eligible to serve on committees but does not have the right to vote in the Conference. As of 1953, there were twenty-five life members and twenty associate members of the Conference.

In most jurisdictions the commissioners are appointed by the chief executive acting under express legislative authority, and in the other jurisdictions the appointments are made by virtue of the general executive authority. The commissioners serve without compensation, but from the beginning many states have made an appropriation to cover their necessary expenses. As early as 1894 and 1895, the Committee on Uniform State Laws of the American Bar Association recommended that no state appoint commissioners without providing for such expenses. Probably a majority of the states now defray these expenses, including those connected with the attendance of their commissioners at the annual meeting of the Conference. The constitution of the Conference places on the commissioners from each state the duty "to secure the passage of acts . . . providing for . . . the expenses of the Commissioners from such state in attending the Annual Conference." The commissioners from Florida have been either derelict or unsuccessful with reference to this duty.

The Conference and its members have been described in the following terms:

> The Conference itself is an organization of great inherent strength. Its personnel, recruited from the bench, bar, and classrooms of the 53 jurisdictions, encompasses the social, economic, and political experience of rural and urban societies and the contrasting viewpoints of a geographically diverse nation. The personal scholarship, industry, and integrity of the Commissioners have produced an informal legislative body of unmatched competence. In-

dividually and collectively the Commissioners have performed their duties with a responsibility which assures not only a quality product but also reflects a high sense of public duty in its manufacture.

Included among those who have participated in the work of the Conference are James Barr Ames, Louis D. Brandeis, John W. Davis, William Draper Lewis, Roscoe Pound, Wiley Rutledge, John H. Wigmore, Samuel Williston, and Woodrow Wilson.

The Conference is formally organized under a Constitution and by-laws. It convenes each year at the site of the annual meeting of the American Bar Association and remains in session for the week immediately preceding that meeting. It maintains its headquarters office and a permanent staff in the new American Bar Center in Chicago. Much of its preliminary work is done there and elsewhere between annual meetings by individuals and by committees through correspondence and in special meetings.

The Conference is divided by its president into seven sections, and no commissioner serves as a member of more than one section at the same time. For each contemplated new act, the president appoints a special committee, usually from the members of one of the sections, to investigate and, if deemed desirable, to draft the act under consideration. In the case of the more important acts, an expert draftsman is sometimes employed to work with the committee. During the preparation of the act, the committee consults with the appropriate committee of the American Bar Association or, if there is no such committee or section, with the secretary of that organization. In appropriate situations, it confers also with officers of the Council of State Governments and the Interstate Commission on Crime, with representatives of trade, financial, labor, and similar organizations, and with individuals who are conversant with the field in which the proposed act lies. The contributions of those who are called upon in this fashion are frequently of inestimable value.

The chairman of the committee in charge of the act presents his draft section by section before a meeting of the section of the Conference to which his committee is assigned. At this meeting, designated individuals not members of the Conference and representatives of appropriate organizations are frequently invited to participate in the consideration of the act. Extensive revision often is made in this meeting. After the act is approved by the section, it is referred to the Conference Committee on Style for revision as to phraseology and similar matters.

The act is then mimeographed and submitted for tentative approval to a meeting of the Conference. Here, too, selected individuals and representatives of associations not affiliated with the Conference are frequently invited to participate in the discussion. The committee that has prepared the act sits facing the assembly, and its chairman presents the act section by section. The consideration given by the Conference to each section is deliberate, painstaking, and thorough. Each commissioner evaluates the various provisions generally and from the legal, economic, and social background of his own jurisdiction and suggests such changes as he deems desirable. The committee in charge of the act often accepts these suggestions at once. In other instances, a vote is taken on formally proposed alterations. The Conference can refer the act back to the committee for further work. Sometimes this procedure is repeated in several annual meetings before the tentative approval of the Conference is obtained.

After an act has been tentatively approved at one annual meeting of the Conference, copies as amended and with such further revision as the committee in charge of it may desire are printed and distributed to the members of the Conference; and it is again presented to the Conference at the next annual meeting. When an act receives the final approval of the Conference and the sanction of the House of Delegates of the American Bar Association, it is recommended to the various jurisdictions for adoption.

Uniform acts are acts promulgated by the Conference in fields of law in which it feels that uniformity among the various jurisdictions is desirable. Model acts are acts drafted by it that cover subject matter concerning which, while there is no pressing need for uniformity, there seems to be a demand for legislation in a substantial number of states. Uniform acts are recommended to all jurisdictions for adoption. Model acts are prepared merely for the convenience of such legislative bodies as may be interested in them. Opinions sometimes differ as to how a particular act should be classified in this respect. When the question is close, the Conference tends to designate the act as a uniform act.

In order to attain the goal of uniformity in a field of law, it is essential not only that the relevant statutory law of the jurisdictions be in accord but also that identical or similar provisions of that law be construed in the same manner by the various courts which interpret it. In order to call to the attention of courts and individuals the fact that an act is a uniform act, it is customary to embody in it a short-title provision reading, "This act may be cited as the Uniform . . . Act." In a further effort to obtain uniformity of interpretation, the Conference has since about 1912 included in most uniform acts a provision that "this act shall be so interpreted as to effectuate its purpose to make uniform the law of those states or jurisdictions which enact it."

It should be noted, however, that the inclusion by a legislature of the word *uniform* in the title of an act does not necessarily indicate that the act has the sanction of the Conference. Thus chapter 691 of Florida Statutes 1953 is entitled the "Uniform Trust Administration Law," and section 691.01 provides that the chapter may be cited by that name. The act has, however, never been approved by the Conference. Similarly, when the Conference withdraws a previously approved act from its active list, a jurisdiction that has theretofore adopted it is likely to continue it in effect under its former designation as a uniform act. The Uniform Mechanics' Lien Act, for example, which was adopted by Florida in 1935, was withdrawn as a uniform act by the Conference in August, 1943; but it remains in effect in Florida under its original title as the "Uniform Mechanics' Lien Law."

The funds necessary for carrying on the activities of the Conference are derived from small appropriations made by a majority of the states and contributions from the American Bar Association and many of the state bar associations. Occasionally, too, grants are obtained for special projects from foundations and other sources. For the preparation of the Uniform Commercial Code by the Conference and the American Law Institute, for example, $250,000 was made available by the Maurice and Laura Falk Foundation of Pittsburgh; and an additional $100,000 was contributed by the Beaumont Foundation of Cleveland and ninety-eight business, industrial, financial and transportation concerns and law firms. It is not suggested, of course, that the donations made in connection with this enterprise, which is by far the most stupendous in which the Conference has participated, are typical.

## Achievements of the Conference

Forty-eight uniform acts promulgated by the Conference are at present recommended by it for adoption by all jurisdictions. These acts and the dates as of which they were respectively first approved by the Conference are as follows: Acknowledgment Act, 1949 (amended 1955); Act to Secure the Attendance of Witnesses from Without a State in Criminal Proceedings, 1936; Adoption Act, 1953; Ancillary Administration of Estates Act, 1949 (amended 1953); Aircraft Financial Responsibility Act, 1954; Arbitration Act, 1955; Business Records as Evidence Act, 1936; Act on Blood Tests to Determine Paternity, 1952; Civil Liability for Support Act, 1954; Commercial Code, 1951 (amended 1953); Common Trust Fund Act, 1938 (amended 1952); Contribution Among Tortfeasors Act, 1955; Criminal Extradition Act, 1936; Rules of Criminal Procedure, 1952; Disposition of Unclaimed Property Act, 1954; Declaratory Judgments Act, 1922; Divorce Recognition Act, 1947; Enforcement of Foreign Judgments Act, 1948; Rules of Evidence Act, 1953; Federal Tax Lien Registration Act, 1926; Fiduciaries Act, 1922; Flag Act, 1917; Foreign Depositions Act, 1920; Fraudulent Conveyances Act, 1918; Insurers Liquidation Act,

1939; Interstate Arbitration of Death Taxes Act, 1943; Interstate Compromise of Death Taxes Act, 1943; Judicial Notice of Foreign Law Act, 1936; Limited Partnership Act, 1916; Marriage License Application Act, 1950; Motor Vehicle Certificate of Title and Anti-Theft Act, 1955; Narcotic Drug Act, 1932 (amended 1942 and 1952); Partnership Act, 1914; Photographic Copies of Business and Public Records as Evidence Act, 1949; Post-Conviction Procedure Act, 1955; Prenatal Blood Test Act, 1950; Preservation of Private Business Records Act, 1954; Principal and Income Act, 1931; Probate of Foreign Wills Act, 1950; Proof of Statutes Act, 1920; Reciprocal Enforcement of Support Act, 1952; Reciprocal Transfer Tax Act, 1928; Simultaneous Death Act, 1940 (amended 1953); Single Publication Act, 1952; Small Estates Act, 1951; Supervision of Trustees for Charitable Purposes Act, 1954; Veterans' Guardianship Act, 1942; and Vital Statistics Act, 1942.

The ten model acts drafted by the Conference that remain on its active list are as follows: Act to Provide for the Appointment of Commissioners, 1944; Anti-Gambling Act, 1952; Court Administrator Act, 1948; Crime Investigating Commission Act, 1952; Department of Justice Act, 1952; Act on Perjury, 1952; Police Council Act, 1952; Post-Mortem Examinations Act, 1954; State Administrative Procedure Act, 1944; and State Witness Immunity Act, 1952.

The Conference has at various times promulgated eighty-seven other uniform or model acts. It subsequently has declared thirty-three of these to be obsolete, has substituted newer acts for twenty-four, and has placed four on the inactive list pending further study. It has not removed the remaining twenty-six of these acts from its active list. Due to existing coverage of the respective fields, however, or to opposition to the acts in question, they have not received wide adoption and are retained on the list of the Conference primarily for consideration in jurisdictions having a need for such legislation.

New uniform and model acts approved by the Conference in any year are published, together with appropriate comments, in the *Handbook* of the Conference for that year. The *Handbook* also contains drafts of acts that have been tentatively approved that year subject to further action at a subsequent annual meeting. Uniform and model acts that have been enacted in at least one jurisdiction are set forth in a fifteen-volume set entitled *Uniform Laws Annotated*. This work shows under each section of every act any deviations from the original that have been made in enacting the section in the various jurisdictions. It also annotates under each section all decisions that construe the section. The set is kept up to date by cumulative annual pocket parts and occasional new volumes.

Certainly everyone connected with the Conference is aware that its work is not perfect. Particularly is it impossible in drafting an act to foresee subsequent changes of conditions that may affect its desirability at a future period. Many of the instances in which a uniform or model act has later been amended, superseded by a new act or declared obsolete are attributable to this factor.

At times, too, the functioning of an act after its adoption in one or more jurisdictions focuses attention upon matters that were overlooked in its preparation and leads the Conference to amend the act or to replace it with a more perfect version. The Reciprocal Enforcement of Support Act, for example, was promulgated in 1950 and was adopted in forty jurisdictions within a very short period. Experience with the act in these jurisdictions brought to light so many needed additions and changes that the Conference replaced it in 1952 with a new act of the same name.

In general, however, the results of the deliberations of the Conference are excellent. Codification and partial codification are always difficult; and the very fact that the Conference never permits pride of authorship to interfere with subsequent modernization, improvement or even repudiation of acts previously approved further augments the confidence that can be placed in its recommendations. The necessity for occasional later modifications of this type is attributable to the fluidity that must be maintained in the law in an ever-changing environment and to the difficulty, which only too frequently is brought home to lawyers, of always attaining perfection in matters pertaining to the law.

It would indeed be difficult to devise a system that would ensure the subjection of proposed acts to a more careful scrutiny than they receive under the procedure established by the Conference. Acts approved by it, therefore, merit consideration by legislative bodies.

## THE BRITISH SYSTEM                                       By Herman Finer

IT IS probably true to say that since the early part of the nineteenth century hardly a social, economic, or political statute of any importance has been drafted and introduced into Parliament otherwise than as the result of recommendations of a Royal Commission of Inquiry. This is the form of inquiry used in Great Britain to cover the investigation of facts and the exploration of policy in political problems of first class importance.

A Royal Commission of Inquiry is usually set up when parliamentary

Reprinted from *University of Chicago Law Review*, vol. 18, 1951, pp. 554–561, with the permission of the publisher. Herman Finer is Professor of Political Science at the University of Chicago.

opinion or the convictions of the government or of any single department of the government within whose purview the subject falls, have matured to the point where more information and guidance of an immediate sort upon policy are regarded as essential and no longer postponable. It may be that a government which has been advocating a reform for years, (especially while in Opposition) suddenly realizes that if it is to present a blueprint of legislation or is to undertake a departure in administrative policy, it must have before it the results of a deep and at the same time extensive inquiry into the factual bases and the contending opinions concerning the action it seeks. Nor is this the only origin of Royal Commissions. In a democracy where the basic assumption of government is that all men are equal, the opportunity is given to those who, by reason of their interest in public affairs and their superior knowledge and sensitivity to the need for action, wish some reform to take place. The number of leaders in a democracy is potentially equal to the total number of voters or to the total number of those who have a right to vote; but only a few hundred thousand, perhaps only a few thousand, are sensitive leaders of public opinion. When, by a long and mysterious process, such leaders become pervaded with the idea that something ought to be done or at least preparations, by improvement of the mind, should be undertaken, the Government, at the instance of Parliament or letters to the great newspapers, or prompted thereto by its friends who are not in the Government, may establish a Royal Commission of Inquiry into the subject.

A Royal Commission is, in legal form, a command by the Crown, on the initiative and responsibility of ministers or a minister, requiring that certain persons named shall examine into a subject of inquiry, which is then stated in what are called the Terms of Reference. Thus, in its legal form the Royal Commission is an executive instrument which establishes, through the executive, a body of men and women who are to make an inquiry into a subject whose bounds and scope are stated in the commission. This at once distinguishes the Royal Commission of Inquiry from the parliamentary committees of all kinds—which are set up by the House of Commons and manned by members of the House. The Royal Commissions of Inquiry are manned by people who are not members of Parliament. Parliament rarely intervenes in the process of the establishment of a Royal Commission excepting to make rather humble suggestions as to the establishment of a Commission and even more rarely suggestions that different regions of the country should be represented, that women as well as men shall be appointed; it practically never suggests names. It is understood that since all parties desire that a Royal Commission shall render an impartial report, Parliament itself ought to remain impartial in its choice, leaving to the Government the responsibility of objectivity and competence. It is rare that any of the parties to such an understanding are disappointed in their hopes. The actual establishment of the Commission occurs by means of the issue of a document as letter patent or a warrant of appointment by one of the departments of state. The authorization is, in fact, that of the whole Cabinet.

The Commission is sharply distinguished from the committee investigations undertaken within the body of the House of Commons itself by the fact that no time limit is set upon their proceedings. Royal Commissions last as long as is necessary to conduct and conclude their investigation and submit their report. Some Commissions, therefore, are of extremely short duration; others quite long. Some have reported within a few months, others have taken years to fulfill the task imposed. Each Royal Commission constitutes a problem and an opportunity in itself. Its problem sets the stage for its scope, its personnel, its term and its procedure.

The problem before the Commission determines the choice of its personnel. Commissions may be divided into the three main groupings of representative, expert, and general civic. In the first category are those Royal Commissions which are faced with a problem that must be settled fairly immediately and where great existing and traditional interests are in conflict, for example, reform of local government or reform of liquor licensing. In the second category are those whose problems are a little more remote, which do not call for immediate legislation, and where the issues of fact are more important than the discovery of a practical compromise which may be implemented in government policy or through a statute, and where expert knowledge is needed in the conduct of what is virtually a social-scientific research. The Royal Commission on Population is an example. In the third group, all the qualities of truth discovery are needed, but general civic ability and culture are required, as, for example, on the Royal Commission on the Press. It is exceedingly rare to find a member of Parliament appointed to a Royal Commission, though it has occasionally occurred....

Usually the chairman calls together his commissioners. He is assisted by a secretary with assistants provided by one of the departments of the civil service. By this time, and even a considerable time earlier, the fact that a Royal Commission is about to commence its sessions is well known throughout the country, more especially to the special interests and experts. The chairman and the members of the commission draw up the lines of the inquiry and consider and decide on the persons and bodies who ought to be questioned by them. At this particular stage the secretary (usually one of the more promising of the administrative class in the civil service) is of great value, since he has presumably been allocated to the Commission because of a special interest and special knowledge acquired in the course of his departmental duties. Almost invariably the

Commission announces that it is prepared to receive evidence and to invite the submission of memoranda from interested persons and civic organizations. The secretary will, at the request of the Commission, or by taking the initiative with suggestions, make connection with people who are prepared to give evidence and to submit memoranda in advance. Some Commissions inform themselves by questionnaires. The use of memoranda of evidence preceding the appearance of the writers or of their colleagues and spokesmen before the Commission for cross-examination has been recognized as a particularly desirable procedure because, while it does not prevent the commissioners from asking questions outside the scope of the memorandum submitted, it focuses the minds of witnesses on the written formulation, and is both stimulating and guiding to the commissioners, some of whom may not be familiar with this special section of the evidence. In some cases, research workers have been employed to make field investigations, in others, to do documentary research.

The evidence on the subject (fact, opinions and recommendations of policy) is then elicited by the practice of public hearings. The Commission may find it necessary from time to time to conduct hearings in closed session; it is exceedingly rare. There then appear before the governmental officials any witnesses the Commission may find useful in its investigation, men and women who come forward in their own right as acknowledged experts on the subject, and the regular representatives, the secretaries, and spokesmen of various economic, political and social groups whether these are of a "lobbying" type or not, the academic experts and specialists of established repute. The chairmen and the various commissioners ask their questions according to their intelligence and their understanding of the subject, and also, sometimes, by the private prompting of their secretary, or of their personal friends. What is missing in this procedure, which might enable the truth of fact or policy the better to be adumbrated, is the cross-examination of witnesses by each other where the evidence severally rendered to the commissioners might be probed in order that the obscured spots might be opened up by witnesses who may understand the situation as it virtually is better than do the commissioners.

It is very noticeable that the Commissions are more severely selective of their witnesses than it would appear that congressional investigating committees are. It appears to the onlooker of long years of observation that almost anybody may appear before a congressional committee to give evidence, however insignificant and irrelevant. It is rare, indeed, that witnesses come before a Royal Commission without some substantial contribution of facts or policy as a recompense for the time the committee spends on them.

In marked contrast with congressional committees of investigation, the Royal Commissions are not provided with the legal counsel (e.g., Francis Biddle at the TVA Committee of 1938) or the publicly paid investigator who asks questions in cross-examination of the witnesses as though he were prosecuting or a defending attorney. The process of questioning and hearing is extremely quiet, sober and decorous—and truth-finding. . . .

It is worthwhile now to consider briefly one or two problems relating to this method of investigation. First, could the procedure be improved? Second, ought Commissions be expert or representative, and thirdly, should one press for a unanimous report or be satisfied if the Commission decides to fall into segments of opinion?

Time has taught the Royal Commissioners how best to get at the answer or answers to the problems set them: there is an acute consciousness of the apt use of research, questionnaires, memoranda of evidence, questioning of witnesses, and so forth—this is obvious from the concern of each Commission with this question and their public explanations. The duration, being dependent on the work to be accomplished, is usually adequate. The scope of the problem always needs the closest attention, since any fuzziness about it can be a hindrance to the Commission in its procedure, in its questions, and in its deliberations within its own executive sessions, and can lead to a split report. For this reason, a certain proximity to the date of necessary action is desirable, as this necessity has already stressed and sifted the important from the unimportant. There may be something in the suggestion that the Commissions employ research staffs of their own as distinct from reliance on the experts from the civil service; and the appointment of committees of experts by the Commission on Population offers a fruitful idea.

Shall the Commissions be representative or expert? The answer depends on the nature of the problem. If a problem in practical policy is posed in a field where organized groups, whether employers, trade unionists, local authorities, and so forth are well established with acquired interests, and if the administration of any solution is to depend on their cooperation and goodwill, then, to reduce the area of coercion, it is desirable to have a representative commission. It will in any case be obliged to meet and contend with the evidence, given in public of a cross section of national interests other than their own, and ministers, representing the whole nation, are finally sovereign—or they make the law, resting on a popular majority. But it may be argued, if the vested interests compromise with each other, they will stop short of the discovery of truth, which the student needs, which the public needs, and of the policy that is first-best for the nation as a whole. These criticisms are valid: and yet they have no fully persuasive relevance. The path of advance cannot but take account of the vehicles which are to carry the reforms. It is, of course, most desirable where a problem is of the pure-truth variety, as for example, in the problem of declining population (I do not mean it has no practical bearing—far from it); then the experts are needed: they may see beyond the generations and beyond local, class, and dysgenic boundaries. If pure-truthers were put on the Commissions that are handed a practical and awkward problem, encrusted with long-housed inveterate interests, what would be the result? From the standpoint of reform, we should have an academically perfect answer—and yet, more possibly than not, several answers by a split Commission. As it is in practice, the representative Commission, by the admixture of impartial men and women, cannot help but evoke the facts—and these give them no rest in the long run, whatever the compromise in the short.

Ought the Commission to aim at a unanimous report? It has been highly recommended by a Commission on Commissions! It argued that unanimity was convincing to political leadership and to the public, and that action was all the more liable to follow. A divided report, on the other hand, would be inconclusive as to action. But, is not the question, thus posed, nonsense? If there is no spontaneous consensus emergent from the enlightened goodwill of public-spirited men and women, is it worth having an artificially induced one? After all, the ultimate unifier is Government, Parliament, and the public. Let the Commissioners be faithful to their views of the public good and true, in their own light and to the common body of evidence. If they are then divided there is still a valuable contribution to the principles of what shape a law should take.

---

COMMENTS. *Selection of an Appropriate Lawmaking Agency.* As the materials in the foregoing chapters suggest, different tools are needed for different types of legislative jobs. The point can be driven home by considering which agency is appropriate to deal with the following problems: (1) Reshaping the rules on assignment of contracts; (2) Revision of state constitutional provisions on the judiciary; (3) Preparation of a Model Penal Code; (4) Preparation of a state sales tax.

*Further References.* Fordham, *The State Legislative Institution* (Philadelphia: U. of Pa. Press, 1959), "The Legislative Process," Chapter 2; Hurst, *The Growth of American Law: The Law Makers* (Boston: Little, Brown, 1950), "The Uses of the Legislature," Chapter 3; Fuld, "The Commission and the Courts," *Cornell Law Quarterly,* vol. 40, 1955, pp. 646–666 (a Justice of the New York Court of Appeals reports on the work of the New York State Law Revision Commission); Stern, "A Law Revision Commission for Pennsylvania," *Pennsylvania Bar Association Quarterly,* vol. 29, 1958, pp. 180–184 (immediate past Chief Justice of the Supreme Court of Pennsylvania urges adoption of a commission on the New York model, with examples of problems needing attention); *State of California, Report of the California Code Commission* (1950) (the report which led to the creation in 1953 of the California Law Revision Commission); "Proceedings of the 1960 Annual Meeting, American Foreign Law Association," *American Journal of Comparative Law*, vol. 9 (1960) p. 335 *et seq.*, and 370–371 (the need for ministries of justice to work on the international unification of law).

For material on current developments in Britain see "Law Reform—A Symposium," *Modern Law Review*, vol. 24, January 1961; Lord Kilmuir, "Law Reform," *Journal of the Society of Public Teachers of Law*, Vol. 4, New Series, December 1957, pp. 75–85.

---

# THE GAP IN LAWMAKING—
# JUDGES WHO CAN'T
# AND LEGISLATORS WHO WON'T   By Henry J. Friendly

I TAKE AS my text a sentence from a little book by a great English judge, Lord Devlin's *Samples of Lawmaking*. Here is the sentence:

The work done by the Judges of England is not now as glorious as it was.

Lord Devlin's remark is not just the usual middle-aged lament over the old grey mare. There is a reason why the work of the judges of England is not what it used to be. The reason is that others are doing the work—the judges of England, poor souls, have had no union leaders to protect their jobs. The usurper has not been automation—at least not yet; it has been the legislature. "I doubt," writes Lord Devlin ruefully, "if judges will now of their own motion contribute much more to the development of the law. Statute is a more powerful and flexible instrument for the alteration of the law than any that a judge can wield." And again, "Parliament has of its own volition superseded judges as lawmakers and the judges have accepted the subordination. They could not do other-

Reprinted from *Columbia Law Review*, vol. 63, 1963, pp. 787–807, with the permission of the author and the publisher. (Copyright 1963, Columbia Law Review Association.) Before appointment to the Court of Appeals, Judge Friendly was a partner in the New York firm of Root, Clark, Buckner, and Ballantine, and later of Cleary, Gottlieb, Friendly, and Hamilton.

wise." This resigned attitude is hardly what would be expected of a man with the fighting name of Patrick Devlin; yet there it stands.

I am not here to solicit your sympathy for having forsaken the not unpleasant fleshpots and the other attractions of practice in favor of a trade whose future is painted thus dimly by one of its master craftsmen. My purpose is rather to examine how far Lord Devlin's analysis runs also on these shores, particularly as to the federal scene, and, to the extent that it does, what problems arise from it.

We must begin with a qualification. The judges of England, Lord Devlin notes with a touch of regret, have "no great constitutional questions . . . to decide such as still have to be considered by the Supreme Court of a Federation"; one might say, rather, by the courts of any state whose constitution is the supreme law of the land. Yes, Virginia, there still are great constitutional questions to be decided; we, who have witnessed *Brown* v. *Board of Education* and *Baker* v. *Carr* within a decade, scarcely require more by way of chapter and verse. There seems to be a kind of spontaneous generation about the federal constitution; the more questions about it are answered, the more there are to be answered. Although this was hardly their prime purpose, the framers of our constitutions did stake out a preserve where American judges need not accept the subordination to the legislature that is the lot of their counterparts in England; perhaps here lie the seeds of a Freudian explanation of judicial activism in constitutional law. So I leave to one side the role of American judges and especially of the *novem sancti* on constitutional issues.

In contrast, "inferior" federal judges, as Judge Learned Hand liked to call us, and in many areas the Justices of the Supreme Court as well, have suffered since the birth of the federal judicial system from the malaise that, in Lord Devlin's view, has now afflicted the judges of England. Federal law has always been mostly statute law. As early as 1812, it was decided that the federal courts had no common law criminal jurisdiction. Surprisingly, they were not given general federal question jurisdiction for nearly a century; when they were, the juridiction of necessity concerned the Constitution, federal statutes, and treaties. Most of the so-called "federal specialties"—patents, copyrights, bankruptcy, and, more recently, antitrust—are statutory. Even the broad waters of the admiralty have latterly been confined by statute. . . . More dramatically, as the result of the encounter between an Erie freight train and the not otherwise illustrious Tompkins in Hughestown, Pennsylvania, in the early hours of a July morning in 1934, what was thought for a century to be a happy hunting ground for the creative effort of federal judges was abruptly fenced off, and their activity denounced as poaching on the preserves of others. What would Lord Devlin think of an appellate judge who, in important areas of adjudication in which no legislative interloper has trespassed, must look solely to what has been said by judges of a cognate judicial system—even quite lowly ones—so that he is only the little dog seeking to make out his master's voice?

As against this, we must note a few areas in which federal judges have recently been dispatched on new quests for "federal law" outside the constitutional field. The great cases are *Clearfield Trust Co.* v. *United States*, dealing with Government commercial paper, which fixed the principle, and *Textile Workers* v. *Lincoln Mills*, which launched the federal courts, under the colors of Section 301 of the Taft-Hartley Act, on what bids fair to be a long voyage in labor law. A historical philosopher might see the Hegelian dialectic at work in this development, with *Swift* v. *Tyson* the thesis, *Erie R.R.* v. *Tompkins* the antithesis, and *Clearfield* and *Lincoln Mills* the synthesis. Indeed, it is wryly amusing that, despite all that Mr. Justice Brandeis said on the score of unconstitutionality, *Erie R. R.* v. *Tompkins* itself, concerning the liability of an interstate railroad to a trespasser, was the kind of case that could be easily swept into the mid-twentieth century style of "federal law"—not limited to cases of diverse citizenship in the federal courts as was *Swift* v. *Tyson*, but a truly uniform law on a subject within federal power, created by federal judges because of some hint that Congress wants them to do so, and enjoying the prerogatives of the supremacy clause. This unifying principle, I am bold enough to predict, is a young man with a future.

Federal judges have thus had many years to adjust themselves to the rather low estate to which Lord Devlin finds the judges of England have now descended. I cannot speak with assurance as to our state brethren, but I suspect the trend with them is the same, although it has not gone quite so far. Max Radin wrote more than thirty years ago:

> Anglo-American law is in a fair way of becoming statutory, not by a great act of summation like the *Bürgerliches Gesetzbuch* or the Swiss Code, but piecemeal by the relentless annual or biennial grinding of more than fifty legislative machines.

Vast areas once the province of the judges have been enclosed by the legislature. Procedure, the quondam delight of the common law pleader or the chancery practitioner, has been taken over either by statute or, with better results, by rule; in one way or another, David Dudley Field has had his way. Criminal law is now as much a creature of statute in the states as it has always been for the United States. Here, as in England, legislators have made deep incursions into property law; the Personal Property Law and the Real Property Law are not the end of the road for the New York judge, but they are at least the beginning. Decedents' estates, always in some degree a creature of legislation, are regulated in every detail today. Corporations are the children of statute, and partnerships are governed in most states by the Uniform Partnership Act. Beginning with the Negotiable Instruments Law and the Uniform Sales Act, great portions of contract law have been taken over by legislation; if we were searching for a twentieth-century American counterpart of Lord Mansfield, we would find him not in any judge but in the lamented draftsman of the Uniform Commercial Code, Professor Karl Llewellyn. The equity receivership has been largely superseded by the variety of reorganization and composition opportunities offered by the Bankruptcy Act. Tort law likewise has not resisted the legislative invasion —workmen's compensation acts, wrongful death acts, family automobile acts, automobile guests acts, laws prescribing safety standards for factories, mines, construction, explosives, drugs, and other dangerous articles, legislative protection of trademarks, and statutes as to contribution among joint tortfeasors, are only a few examples. The increased scope of legislation could hardly be better evidenced than by the fact that the conflict of laws, once exclusively a judge-made subject, has become in considerable degree a matter of statutory interpretation. Finally, there are wide areas in which the courts have been wholly removed from firsthand contact in favor of administrative agencies operating under statutes—not only the traditional public utilities and their modern counterparts but many aspects of insurance, labor relations, land use, and the sale of securities—so that even the most significant decisions in these fields simply open, or occasionally close, problems to administrative action. This is by no means the end of the development; in Sir Winston Churchill's phrase, it is not even the beginning of the end although it may be more than the end of the beginning.

I should not want anyone to gather from this catalogue of the ships that I am a spiritual descendant of those mid-Victorian judges who looked askance at statutes, regarding legislation, in Mr. Justice Frankfurter's phrase, "as wilful and arbitrary interference with the harmony of the common law and with its rational unfolding by judges." *Au contraire*, I would not even join Lord Devlin's nostalgic pronouncement: "At its best the common law is, I think, better than any statute could be"; my vote is rather for the remark I previously quoted: "Statute is a more powerful and flexible instrument . . . than any that a judge can wield." Some months ago, I called attention to the peculiar need for legislation to deal with problems concerning which judges lack adequate factual data and as to which the so-called "arbitrary" rule that statute can furnish will provide surely a surer and perhaps a juster justice than the best a judge can give. . . . Of course, we must not go overboard in our enthusiasm. As Cardozo warned: "Substitute statute for decision, and you shift the center of authority, but add no quota of inspired wisdom." Still, the legislature's superior resources for fact gathering; its ability to act without awaiting an adventitious concatenation of the determined party, the right set of facts, the persuasive lawyer, and the perceptive court; its power to frame pragmatic rules departing from strict logic, and to fashion a broad new regime or to bring new facts within an existing one; its practice of changing law solely for the future in contrast to the general judicial reluctance so to proceed; and, finally, the greater assurance that a legislative solution is not likely to run counter to the popular will: all these give the legislature a position of decided advantage, if only it will use it.

I thus do not at all lament the diminished role of the judge vis-à-vis the legislator as a maker of law. What I do lament is that the legislator has diminished the role of the judge by occupying vast fields and then has failed to keep them ploughed. It matters not very much, Lord Devlin wrote, whether the law "is made by Parliament or by judges or even by ministers; what matters is the law of England." But it matters very much if legislators, having gone so far as to stunt the law-creating role of judges, fail to keep on creating law themselves. That would have mattered even in the more nearly static and laissez-faire era in which our fathers lived; it may be fatal in an age of automation, supersonic airplanes, atomic power, and pervasive governmental concern with the affairs of men.

My criticism is not leveled at instances, such as the Sherman Act or much of our labor legislation, in which the legislature has spoken with what some may consider undue generality. There may be good reason for such broadly framed statutes, especially when the legislature is dealing with novel subjects; and these statutes leave the courts, or in some cases administrative agencies, free to perform their historic role of formulating more definite standards within the general mandate. My criticism is directed rather at cases in which the legislature has said enough to deprive the judges of power to make law even in such subordinate respects but has given them guidance that is defective in one way or another, and then does nothing by way of remedy when the problem comes to light.

I begin with the occasional statute in which the legislature has succeeded in literally saying something it probably did not mean. The solution here, some may think, is easy—the courts should give effect to what they believe the legislature meant rather than to what it rather plainly said. Yet this encounters the rival claims that courts ought not rewrite statutes—at least not too much—and that citizens ought be able to rely on what they read in the statute book, especially in areas in which citizens make plans on the basis of what they read. Some legislative errors of this sort are inevitable; even the best draftsman is likely to have experienced the occasional shock of finding that what he wrote was not at all what he meant. My criticism is not of Congress's fallibility, but of its failure to move promptly to correction. Why, when such situations come to light, does not the legislature act speedily to express what it meant, rather than let years go by while judges try to puzzle out what to do and citizens are left in doubt? If the legislature repaired the damage as soon as the defect was discovered, the problem would at least be confined to small compass and short duration. But such rectification of error does not appear to enjoy a high priority on congressional calendars.

More frequent are the statutes—and here again I am speaking of rather detailed statutes—that are ambiguous and are left so for decades. Indeed, ambiguous is too modest a word—often more than two meanings are possible.

Examples of such long-continued ambiguity in statutes are so numerous that the only problem is selection. The leading text on admiralty stated six years ago: "the Limitation Act is one of those statutes which Congress tinkers with every generation or two, adding a patch here and mending a leak there, but never rebuilding from the ground-up"; the act "has been due for a general overhaul for the past seventy-five years; seventy-five years from now that statement will be still true, except that the overhaul will then be one hundred and fifty years overdue." Yet most of the questions involved, although debatable, are not of the sort as to which the opposing forces are so evenly balanced as to prevent legislative change; the problem is rather lack of time and attention. Anyone who has had to deal with the Copyright Act of 1909 must stand in awe of the ability of the framers to toss off a sentence that can have any number of meanings. The need for revision is widely recognized; yet nothing happens, and litigants and judges are left to make such shift as they can, often in areas in which the judges could have done better if the statute had been altogether silent. The purpose of the Robinson-Patman Act was to make more definite and specific a principle that had been stated more generally before. From the outset, it was recognized to be a badly drafted statute which would impose serious interpretive problems on industry, the Federal Trade Commission, and the courts. The expectation has been amply fulfilled—Mr. Justice Harlan has just called it "a singularly opaque and elusive statute"—but in twenty-six years not a word has been altered. The tiniest fraction of the time spent by lawyers, legal writers, administrators, and judges in an unsuccessful endeavor to elucidate the obscurities of this statute would have sufficed to put the house in order once the problems were revealed; but that time has not been spent. . . .

Let me turn from imperfections and ambiguities to a different area, in which the statute may be clear enough but is clearly wrong. Here the picture is even more dismal. Nine years ago, Professor Keeffe wrote an article provocatively entitled "Twenty-Nine Distinct Damnations of the

Federal Practice—and a National Ministry of Justice."[1] Almost all the damnations were statutory or at least correctible by statute. Not everyone would agree that each of the twenty-nine was a damnation or, if so, just what should be done to create a beatitude in its place. But few would deny that a good half of the twenty-nine damnations shrieked for reform. Not one has had it. A similar article could be written as to the manifold damnations in the veritable jungle of review of action by federal agencies. Some orders are reviewable by a single district judge with appeal to a court of appeals, some by a "statutory" district court of three judges—one of whom must be a circuit judge—with direct appeal to the Supreme Court, some by a court of appeals of appropriate venue, some only in the Court of Appeals for the District of Columbia; in other cases, no method of review is provided. The periods in which review may be sought are even more variegated, fifteen, twenty, thirty, sixty, and ninety days, three months, six months, and no limits at all. Sometimes the period starts with the entry of the order, sometimes with its mailing, sometimes with the giving of public notice. In some cases, rehearing must first be sought, in others not. Some orders are immediately effective unless stayed, others have no effect until enforced, still others will be effective save for a petition to review which works an automatic stay. These differences create pitfalls for the unwary practitioner and undue interpretive burdens for the courts. Whatever the historical reasons for this efflorescence of variety, its continuation is unworthy of an ordered legal system. No vital interests are at stake here; these weeds have grown simply for lack of a gardener.

You may well have guessed that if the picture is this bad with respect to changes in matters of procedure, it is ever so much worse as to issues of substance. I have written elsewhere of the sorry contrast between Congress's willingness to make necessary amendments of public utility regulatory statutes in earlier days and the more recent legislative paralysis. I have remarked also how the paralysis not only concerns issues for which the conflicting pressures are great, such as the battle over newspaper ownership of radio or television stations, or the struggle among rail, water, and motor carriers as to minimum rate regulation, but extends to matters that are quite uncontroversial. For many years the Civil Aeronautics Board had been recommending that the civil penalty provision of the Civil Aeronautics Act be broadened to include violation of the economic as well as the safety provisions, the former being sub-

[1] The title comes from Browning's *Soliloquy of the Spanish Cloister:*
>There's a great text in Galatians,
>Once you trip on it, entails
>Twenty-nine distinct damnations,
>One sure, if another fails.

ject only to penal sanctions. So far as I know, no one opposed this utterly reasonable suggestion; yet the Board's proposal was not enacted, not even in 1958 when the entire act was repealed and reenacted as the Federal Aviation Act. Day after day the courts are dredging up problems that call for new statutes or changes in existing ones. . . .

Who would want to contradict Judge Learned Hand?

When a judge tries to find out what the government would have intended which it did not say, he puts into its mouth things which he thinks it ought to have said, and that is very close to substituting what he himself thinks right. . . . Nobody does this exactly right; great judges do it better than the rest of us. It is necessary that someone shall do it, if we are to realize the hope that we can collectively rule ourselves.

Indeed, Lord Devlin's pessimism as to the role of the judges of England may, to a degree, reflect the exceedingly wooden attitude English judges have needlessly imposed upon themselves as to questions of statutory construction—a sad retrogression from the sixteenth century wisdom of the Barons of the Exchequer. But the lawmaking incident even to such labors as Judge Hand described lies in a narrow range. The restriction on the lawmaking ability of a judge in the 1960s, hemmed in by statutes, is far more drastic than that which prevented the common law judge from saying, in Mr. Justice Holmes's famous phrase, "I think the doctrine of consideration a bit of historical nonsense and shall not enforce it in my court," but still left him free to legislate "interstitially." No *Slade's Case*, no *MacPherson v. Buick Motor Co.*, lurks in the interstices of statutes other than those of the most general type. Sometimes, when the ambiguity is confined, a court's construction of a statute can set matters right for good and all. But generally, the best the judge can do is to keep the ship afloat, in better shape or worse, in the hope that rescue will arrive. The job must be done, and will always have to be, and the judges are the men to do it; but we should not suppose that even if we do it well, we will have done more than a small fraction of what needs to be done.

Let me put one more and rather different situation before I turn to the cause of the difficulty and a possible remedy. The problem is not always a defect in a statute, be this ambiguity, the *casus omissus*, the case included that ought not to have been, or the statute that time has proved to be a poor solution to a problem. Often the difficulty is a veritable rash of doctrine, some made by judges, some by legislators, all perhaps well-conceived at the outset, but ending in what can only be described, to plagiarize from a former law clerk, as "the Devil's own mess." I take as an instance the law governing liability for injury to workers in various forms of transportation. If an airline pilot or an interstate truck or bus driver is injured, he recovers a fixed amount, under a state workmen's compensation act, without having to prove fault or, usually, anything beyond the fact of injury. Their counterparts on an interstate railroad, governed by a quite different statute, recover an amount that is unlimited, but only after proving negligence, at least in theory—unless the accident is due to faulty appliances on rolling stock, when even less need be proved, or to defects in a locomotive or tender, when practically nothing need be. Although the proverbial visitor from Mars might think this sufficiently irrational, in the colloquial phrase he "wouldn't have seen nothing yet"; the maze of rules governing maritime workers awaits him. In addition to the ancient remedy of maintenance and cure, which many render a shipowner liable for the illness of a seaman completely unrelated to the latter's activity, our visitor would discover one regime of liability for fault, provided in the Jones Act, and another of liability without fault, provided by the doctrine of unseaworthiness. At some times, these two regimes are concurrent; at others, because of the restricted applicability of the Jones Act, they are not. Still more baffling than the seaman would be the harbor worker, covered by a federal compensation act passed to place him on a parity with similar workers covered by state compensation statutes, yet also given the judge-made remedy for unseaworthiness against the ship because he is doing work traditionally done by the ship's crew. One wonders whether even if the Martian visitor had followed up to this point, he would understand the next steps—that unseaworthiness of the ship and consequent recovery from it may flow from a defective appliance brought on board by the injured stevedore himself, and that after the stevedore has recovered from the ship for the injury from the defective equipment furnished by his employer, the ship can then recover from the employer what it has paid the stevedore although the stevedore's direct recovery from his employer would have been limited by the Longshoremen's and Harbor Workers' Compensation Act. Finally, these legal doctrines as to a seaman or stevedore who has been injured are of the starkest simplicity as compared to those concerning one who has been killed.

How, in the last half of the twentieth century, can we defend such a complex and disparate set of regimes of liability for injuries to transport workers within the sphere of federal legislative power? I do not say at all that injured railway workers, seamen, or stevedores now receive too much; for aught that I know their net receipts may be too little. I am sure they are too long delayed, and I am shocked at the occasional case when a seaman or a railroad worker receives no compensation for an injury in the course of his employment although almost any other worker would be protected by a compensation act. I do not profess to know which of these regimes produces the most just results; I do know there can be no valid reason for having so many, with the attendant uncertainties, high costs on litigants, burdens on the courts, and wild differences in results as between workmen whose need and employers whose conduct is the same. It is, I think, quite revolting that twentieth century judges should be obliged to determine the future of an injured seaman and his family on the basis of distinctions so fine that a thirteenth century theologian would have regarded them as undue hairsplitting. Yet this is not a situation that can be cured through more jerry-built improvisations by judges; those, however well intended, have helped to get us where we are. The need is for the thoroughgoing reform which only the legislature can accomplish.

What is the reason for the failure of Congress to perform its legislative task in these areas? The examples I have chosen, with the exception of the last, are not in those highly controversial areas in which lack of action may reflect not lack of interest or activity but equivalence of conflicting pressures—in which the chessmen have been moved and moved but the game has been a draw. The instances I have put before you, as countless others could have been, are rather what Dean Pound once called "the petty tinkering of the legal system which is necessary to keep it in running order." No Congressman would lose a vote if orders of the Interstate Commerce Commission were made reviewable by courts of appeals rather than by a district court of three judges, a proposal made by Chief Justice Stone over twenty years ago and recently revived by the Administrative Conference. Neither can the inertia be explained by the stereotype that most Congressmen are indolent and unintelligent creatures. I doubt that ever was true; I know it has not been during the thirty-five years as to which I can give testimony. The difficulty is rather that Congressmen are too driven to be able to attend to such matters, save occasionally, and then under the pressure of a special force. Some studies of Congress "have indicated that it is not unusual for a member to devote up to 80 per cent of his time to his dealings with constituents," very little of which, I should suppose, relates to legislation. I would guess that figure to be too high as an average; I certainly hope it is. But fifty per cent would hardly be so, and the demands on the balance of a member's time are staggering. . . . Many days must be given to appropriation bills; foreign affairs and the national defense make demands undreamed of before World War II; and every session has a half-dozen measures of prime political importance. It is thus not strange that there is neglect of the undramatic type of legislative activity I have depicted.

What is strange is that although the ailment and the cure have been known for well over a century, the patient, at least on the federal scene, has gone without remedy. In this country, the diagnosis and the prescription were written out at least as early as Dean Pound's address to the delegates of the American Bar Association at Saratoga in 1917. "Our legislative organization and legislative methods," he said, "are devised for appropriations and political legislation, not for legislation on legal matters"; what is needed is "a ministry of justice, charged with the responsibility of making the legal system an effective instrument of justice." Even then the idea was old—it goes back to Lord Brougham's speech of 1828 on law reform, to Bentham's provision for a ministry of justice in his draft of a constitutional code, and to the resolution, offered in the House of Commons in 1856, that "provision should be made for an efficient and responsible Department of Public Justice with a view to secure the skilful preparation and proper structure of Parliamentary Bills and promote the progressive amendment of the Laws of the United Kingdom." In this country, Cardozo continued the development of the idea with, if I may borrow the felicitous phrase he applied to Dean Pound's efforts, "fertility and power," and, in our own state of New York, eventually with success. His paper, "A Ministry of Justice," led Governor Alfred E. Smith to appoint him to a commission to consider the problem; its report, in 1925, recommended—in language so different from the usual legislative report that the authorship can hardly be doubtful—that "a disinterested agency should exist to survey the body of our laws patiently and calmly and deliberately, attempting no sudden transformation, not cutting at the roots and growths of centuries, the products of a people's life in its gradual evolution, but pruning and transplanting here and there with careful and loving hands." Nine years later—rather a record for speed in the light of the English experience—the New York legislature, under the spur of Governor Lehman, brother of a deeply respected judge, created the Law Revision Commission. Now that we have it, we must surely wonder how we could have done so long without it; in its first twenty-three years, the commission submitted the impressive total of 315 bills dealing with 245 subjects, 181 of which were enacted. A plea calling expressly for a national ministry of justice was made by Professor Keeffe in 1954, but without result. Some useful work has been done by the Judicial Conference of the United States through its Committee of Revision of the Laws, but its aims have been largely procedural, its members are fully occupied with other tasks, and for these and other reasons the results have have been too small in scope and too slow in coming. The same reasons for a permanent establishment devoted to critical study that have recently been emphasized as to the administrative agencies demand the creation of a group whose prime business it is to see that federal statutory law becomes what it ought to be. . . .

Although one hesitates to say even a word in criticism of the endeavors of Dean Pound and Judge Cardozo, I shall venture a minor one. It was, I think, a mistake to baptize the proposed new agency a "Ministry of Justice." Perhaps the word "Ministry" was apt in Great Britain, where legislation so generally originates with the administration; but even there a different term was used, when the idea finally took somewhat modest root, after a century. Here the overtones, suggesting an executive department and, in the federal area, association with law enforcement, are unfortunate. It would seem elementary that an agency whose task is to formulate legislation and secure its enactment should be attached to the legislature. That has been one of the strengths of the New York Law Revision Commission; four of its nine members are legislators, serving ex officio, along with five private citizens appointed by the governor. The legislature thus does not regard the commission as an alien usurper; the bills the commission recommends are introduced by the ex officio members who have worked on them and are in a position to forward their enactment. Since words are so important, I would also like to avoid "commission," a term whose suggestions of size, and of independence of the legislature, seem inappropriate. For the federal government, I would prefer "committee," if that would permit the appointment of persons who are not members of Congress; otherwise, "conference" or "bureau" or even "office" might do. "Justice" is not quite the right word either; it is too embracing and, on the federal scene, misleading, in view of the executive department already so named. Even "law reform" or "law revision" seems a bit pretentious; amendment or re-examination or legislative development of the laws might be better.

Ideas as to the membership of such an agency will differ. Let me send up a trial balloon. The agency should include the chairman and the ranking minority member of the Judiciary Committees of the Senate and the House, with each having the right to appoint another committee member of his own party as his standing alternate. Its chairman should be a federal judge, selected by the Chief Justice from judges who have availed themselves of the privilege of retirement from active service. Such a man would bring to the task unrivaled knowledge of the problems, personal distinction, and the prestige of his office; as examples, I need only cite Judge Prettyman's work as chairman of the Administrative Conference, and Judge Maris's as chairman of the Judicial Conference's Standing Committee on Rules of Practice and Procedure. I would add another four or six part time members, appointed by the President, with the advice and consent of the Senate, for terms of say six years—with the caveat that the "part" should be a large part, of the order of 50 per cent. They should be drawn from the ranks of legal scholars, retired judges, and lawyers who have attained the age when such public service is more attractive than continued professional success. The permanent staff would be small; but the agency should have an appropriation sufficient to enable it to call on the outside resources most useful for whatever task is at hand. It should work closely with the law schools and the American Law Institute, and use the aid now available in the American Bar Foundation, with its new Director of Research, Professor Harry W. Jones—most appropriately, the former Cardozo Professor of Jurisprudence at the Columbia Law School.

The success of such an agency will depend not only on the reputation, ability, objectivity, and devotion of its members, staff, and advisers, but on the skill with which it chooses its subjects and the relations it establishes with the committees of Congress. A critic might fairly ask whether, since the agency would be doing work with which the committees and their staffs are already charged, resentment, rivalry, and ultimate frustration are not inevitable. The answer starts from the point that whatever the committees and their staffs may be bound to do with respect to the undramatic kind of lawmaking we have been discussing, they are not doing it, nor, with certain possible exceptions, is there any real prospect that they will. Leadership of the congressional committee lies in its chairman and a few other senior members who are pressed with other tasks. The committee staff can do little on its own account, and membership on such staffs is a long way from being the kind of career that will attract the talent needed here. The time that committees devote to legislation is likely to be in the highly controversial areas—not to speak of investigations and the publicity attractions these afford; such attention-getting areas are exactly what the new agency should eschew. The committees, if handled with tact and understanding, ought to welcome an agency that would aid them in the politically unrewarding areas here considered. I have suggested elsewhere that the Legislative Reorganization Act be amended so that each standing committee would be obliged to render a comprehensive report every ten or fifteen years on each major piece of legislation subject to its jurisdiction, either with specific proposals for amendment or with a considered statement that none is required; if that were to be done, the new agency could cut its cloth accordingly. At least until the new agency was well established, its watchwords should be deliberation rather than speed, discretion rather than valor; its objective would not be to formulate a Wagner Act or an Atomic Energy Act, but to attend, if I may repeat Dean Pound's phrase, to "the petty tinkering of the legal system which is necessary to keep it in running order." It should have a passion, if not for anonymity, at least for the background; it should be happiest when committees reap where it has sown. If it is convinced that certain committees are so well staffed and so abreast of their subjects that effort on its part is not likely to be useful—as ought to be true, for example, with respect to taxation—it should have the grace to say so. Should experience prove that some committees simply cannot be worked with, it could turn its energies elsewhere; it will have plenty to do. Current examination of all decisions of the Supreme Court and the courts of appeals construing federal statutes would start it on its way—a routine task, perhaps, but not one to be performed in a routine fashion. When it had proved its worth in remedying ambiguities and imperfections turned up by the courts and by critics in the law schools, it would move on to larger tasks, like the ones I have suggested as to interstate defamation or personal injuries to transport workers in interstate or foreign commerce, for which a completely new look is required and which cross committee lines.

No one can guarantee that an agency organized and proceeding somewhat as I have outlined will succeed in closing the existing gap in federal lawmaking. But we can hardly approach the third millennium without some effort to that end. Forty years have already passed since Cardozo preached to us, "The time is ripe for betterment. . . . Let us gather up the driftwood, and leave the waters pure."

CHAPTER 7

# The Administrator

IN THE TWENTIETH CENTURY, A LEGAL institution of ever-increasing importance is the administrator, who appears in a multitude of manifestations in governmental bureaus and administrative tribunals. His importance to society and to lawyers, and some of the problems which he poses, will emerge from the following material. One will note the recurrence here of themes which we have encountered in examining other legal institutions: the tension between "the rule of law" and flexibility that we met in the conflict between common law and equity; political control *versus* independence as a determinant of the quality of judging; the adequacy of staff and expertness as measures of the capacity of legislatures for lawmaking.

## THE DEVELOPMENT AND ROLE OF THE ADMINISTRATIVE PROCESS

*By Kenneth Culp Davis*

MR. JUSTICE Jackson asserted in a formal opinion in 1952: "The rise of administrative bodies probably has been the most significant legal trend of the last century and perhaps more values today are affected by their decisions than by those of all the courts, review of administrative decisions apart."

A statistical measure of the place of administrative law in Supreme Court litigation has recently been set forth by Mr. Justice Frankfurter, on

---

Reprinted from *Administrative Law Text* (St. Paul, Minn.: West, 1959), pp. 3–27, with the permission of the author and the publisher. The author is Professor of Law at the University of Chicago. His works include *Administrative Law Treatise* (1958) and *Administrative Law and Government* (1960).

the basis of analysis of cases of two recent terms of the Supreme Court (348–351 U.S.): "Review of administrative action, mainly reflecting enforcement of federal regulatory statutes, constitutes the largest category of the Court's work, comprising one-third of the total cases decided on the merits." Constitutional law, including "cases with constitutional undertones," was in second place, with less than one-fourth of the cases.

The average person is much more directly and much more frequently affected by the administrative process than by the judicial process. The ordinary person probably regards the judicial process as somewhat remote from his own problems; a large portion of all people go through life without ever being a party to a lawsuit. But the administrative process affects nearly everyone in many ways nearly every day. The pervasiveness of the effects of the administrative process on the average person can quickly be appreciated by running over a few samples of what the administrative process protects against: excessive prices of electricity, gas, telephone, and other utility services; unreasonableness in rates, schedules, and services of airlines, railroads, street cars, and buses; disregard for the public interest in radio and television and chaotic conditions for broadcasting; unwholesome meat and poultry; adulteration in food; fraud or inadequate disclosure in sale of securities; physically unsafe locomotives, ships, airplanes, bridges, elevators; unfair labor practices by either employers or unions; false advertising and other unfair or deceptive practices; inadequate safety appliances; uncompensated injuries related to employment; cessation of income during temporary unemployment; subminimum wages; poverty in old age; industrial plants in residential areas; loss of bank deposits; and (perhaps) undue inflation or deflation. Probably the list could be expanded to a thousand or more items that we are accustomed to take for granted.

The volume of the legislative output of federal agencies far exceeds the volume of the legislative output of Congress. The Code of Federal Regulations is considerably larger than the United States Code. The Federal Register, the accumulation of less than one-quarter of a century, fills much more shelf space than the Statutes at Large, the accumulation of nearly a century and three-quarters. The quantity of state and local administrative regulations is hard to estimate, but the administrative codes of the states that codify their regulations seem to approach in size the unannotated statutes.

The quantity of adjudication in federal agencies is probably many times the quantity of adjudication in federal courts. Statements of responsible people to this effect have become very common, but the statements are typically about as vague as the one just made. A rare statement having some degree of precision is that "There are now between three and four times [as many] matters coming before the administrative agencies

[as] are presented in our Federal courts today, and they are of great importance to the country and to the Nation." The Director of the Office of Administrative Procedure is more cautious: "It is estimated that the administrative business today may exceed in volume the civil business in all of our courts."

Why not count the cases and turn all this customary vagueness into precise statistics? The answer is that administrative and judicial business are to such an extent lacking in comparability that precision has to give way to many imponderables.

Limited comparisons can of course be easily made, and some such comparisons may be meaningful. For instance, during one year 1,644 cases were docketed in the Supreme Court of the United States, and the number of written opinions of the Court was 82, filling 1,165 pages. During the same year, the NLRB received a total of 13,388 cases of all types, and the number of written opinions of the Board was 747, filling 4,791 pages. The Board receives more than eight times as many cases as the Supreme Court; the Board writes opinions in nine times as many cases; and the Board's opinions fill more than four times as many pages.

The bulk of judicial business, of course, is in the district courts. During 1956, the total number of civil cases filed in all federal district courts was 62,394, and the number of civil cases that went to trial was 7,341. A "trial" for this purpose is "a contested proceeding . . . in which evidence is introduced and a final judgment sought." Why not use this definition and count the number of administrative trials and make the comparison?

One type of answer is found in the Bureau of Customs. In one year duties were collected on more than two and a half million merchandise entries. Importers filed 30,074 protests. Of the cases in which collectors denied protests, 15,003 appeals for reappraisement were filed. Each appeal seems to fit the definition of "trial." But the cases are not comparable to cases in district courts, for the process is one of appraisal and reappraisal, not of submission of evidence subject to cross-examination and rebuttal.

One of the nine units of the Department of Health, Education, and Welfare is the Social Security Administration, in which one of four units is the Bureau of Old Age and Survivors Insurance. The Bureau handles about two million claims annually. If each claim is a "case" then this one Bureau receives thirty times as many cases as all the federal courts. The Bureau does not report the number of contested cases.

A claims agency that keeps statistics on the number of contested cases is the Administrator of Veterans Affairs. Out of the millions of claims presented by the twenty-two million veterans, appeals were taken during one year to the Board of Veterans Appeals in 54,791 appellate actions. During the year, 15,158 hearings were disposed of by the Board of Veterans Appeals. This one appellate Board thus held twice as many hearings as all the federal district courts held in civil cases during the year.

Possibly a more meaningful measure of quantity of business is the number of people who work full-time on it. The ICC has a staff of 1,822. All federal courts other than the Supreme Court have 249 district judges, 66 circuit judges, 19 judges of special courts, 12 judges of territorial courts, and 57 retired judges, assisted by 312 secretaries, 226 law clerks, 5 secretary-law clerks, and 1,214 total personnel for clerks' offices—a grand total personnel in all courts except the Supreme Court of 2,160. Although a breakdown of district courts as against other courts is lacking, the total personnel of the district courts seems to be less than the personnel of the one regulatory agency, the ICC. Of course, members of the ICC staff work on much business in addition to adjudication. But the ICC is only one of many federal agencies. . . .

The average state probably has more than one hundred agencies with powers of adjudication or rule making or both. A count of the agencies in Mississippi, one of our least industrial states, shows at least seventy-five. Nearly all states have major agencies such as public service commissions, insurance commissioners, workmen's compensation tribunals, zoning agencies, unemployment compensation commissions, departments of agriculture, departments of labor, and many others. Every state has a large and growing number of occupational licensing agencies.

No one knows how many administrative agencies have been created by municipalities and other units of local government. The number may be in the tens of thousands. Anyone who tries to count them in a single city will quickly discover the insuperable problems of classification.

### What Political Groups Are Hurt or Helped?

The administrative process is a governmental tool. It is no more conservative or liberal than the elevator in the Senate Office Building. It is used to promote pro-business policies, antibusiness policies, and policies having little or nothing to do with business. It has often been used as an instrument of law reform, but it is also used as a means of protecting vested interests. During the 1950s, the public has been made frequently aware of the administrative process in connection with the loyalty-security program; the criticisms of the administrative process as thus used have come largely from the political left. During the 1930s, when the focus was upon the New Deal's use of the administrative process as an instrument for a new degree of regulation of business, the criticisms naturally came almost entirely from the political right.

Although the administrative process is politically colorless in that it has no distinctive political character of its own, it does have a peculiar chameleonic quality of taking on the color of the substantive program to which it is attached, and it is always attached to a substantive program. During the 1930s when the focus was upon the administrative process as the instrument for carrying out New Deal policies, many observers took one glance at the administrative process and were sure it was either red or pink. When it is attached to programs of paying subsidies to private business, or of protecting railroads against too much motor carrier competition, some can see in it the purple hues of economic royalists. More commonly, it seems to have grayish or neutral tones of varying shades, as when it is used for getting benefits to veterans, collecting taxes, admitting or excluding aliens, inspecting meat, or licensing the use of fissionable materials.

The administrative process does of course have independent characteristics of its own, just as a chameleon does. A chameleon does not become an elephant or a kangaroo when its background changes, and the administrative process cannot become an instrument for laissez-faire by attaching it to a program of opposition to positive government. Even though it is only a tool, and even though it has a wide range of flexibility and adaptability, the administrative process is always a tool for positive government, never a tool for laissez-faire.

But the all-too-prevalent assumption that positive government is contrary to the interests either of business or of big business is false about as often as it is true. Even though the Interstate Commerce Act of 1887 was designed to protect the public against abuses by railroads, even though the Federal Trade Commission Act of 1914 was enacted to prevent abuses by business, and even though the principal thrusts of both the Securities Act of 1933 and the National Labor Relations Act of 1935 were undeniably antibusiness, many of our major regulatory programs have been sponsored by the biggest business interests affected. Radio broadcasters brought about the regulation of radio broadcasting; some system of assignment of frequencies was indispensable to the prevention of chaos in broadcasting. Pioneer airlines in need of subsidies helped promote the establishment of an administrative authority to dispense subsidies and to supervise the development of an orderly system of routes. Both the railroads and the largest truckers joined in sponsoring the Motor Carrier Act of 1935. When corporations gained the political power to enact antiunion legislation in 1947, they did not destroy the NLRB but they added to its powers; they authorized the Board to administer a system for preventing labor unions from engaging in unfair labor practices. The major oil companies initiated the most drastic system of regulation administered by a state agency—oil proration in Texas; they wanted the regulation because their only hope for profit was to limit production so that the price of oil would not again sink to ten cents a barrel. Nearly all the occupational licensing agencies set up by state legislation, averaging perhaps thirty or forty in each state, have been brought into being at the instance of the regulated groups.

On the occasion when the Senate was considering the Investment Company Act of 1940 and Investment Advisers Act of 1940, Senator Robert A. Taft made some especially discerning remarks: "I dislike very much the practice of giving infinite and all kinds of discretionary power to the Securities and Exchange Commission, power to tell a man how he shall conduct his business, what kind of directors he shall have, how his business generally shall be operated in detail. . . . I may say that one of the great difficulties of the Congress in attempting to avoid the detailed regulation of business, with indefinite power in a Federal bureau, is the fact that in many cases the businessmen themselves seem to want that kind of regulation. It is so in this case, and so it has been in other cases. So it was in the case of the NRA. Much of the demand for that regulation came from businessmen themselves. . . ."

The widespread assumption that the administrative process is necessarily antibusiness is mistaken not only to the extent that business has sponsored the creation of many of our regulatory agencies but it is also mistaken to the extent that agencies which were created as a result of antibusiness political movements are often controlled in some degree by the regulated groups. Even though the ICC was created to protect the public against railroad abuses, no voice can be heard today crying out against antirailroad regulation of the railroads, but many voices are crying out against an alleged "railroad mindedness" of the ICC. Representatives of carriers typically commend ICC policies; a former president of the ICC Practitioner's Association has written: "I have a great deal of sympathy for the ICC as well as a long standing affection for it. I regard it as the finest regulatory agency that ever existed in this country or in any other country." In 1892 the Attorney General wrote to the president of a railroad, in response to a proposal to abolish the ICC: "The Commission . . . is, or can be made, of great use to the railroads. It satisfies the popular clamor for a government supervision of railroads, at the same time that the supervision is almost entirely nominal. Further, the older such a commission gets to be, the more inclined it will be found to take the business and railroad view of things. It thus becomes a sort of barrier between the railroad corporations and the people and a sort of protection against hasty and crude legislation hostile to railroad interests. . . . The part of wisdom is not to destroy the Commission, but to utilize it."[1]

A reminder that the political attitude which led to the creation of an agency is not necessarily the attitude which governs the agency's operations is the Federal Trade Commission of the 1920s, which for a time was dominated by William E. Humphrey, whose policy "directed attention from the Clayton Act and problems of monopoly to relatively minor questions of trade practice." Senator George Norris asserted that the Commission was "imbued with reactionary sentiment," and President Roosevelt before removing Humphrey wrote him that "I do not feel that your mind and my mind go along together on either the policies or the administering of the Federal Trade Commission. . . ."

Even in very recent times the principal criticism of the FTC has not been that it is doing too much but that it is doing too little. A recent staff report to a congressional committee undertakes to refute assertions by the Commission and its officers that a "revitalized" FTC "has become an increasingly effective instrument for antitrust enforcement and the preservation of competitive vigor." The staff undertakes to show that during a recent period the companies charged by the FTC with antitrust violations were, on the average, about one-eighth the size of companies so charged during an earlier period. With other statistics, the staff tries to show that the Commission's recent policies have tended to protect the larger business interests. The assertions of the staff are hotly disputed and may or may not be valid, but the location of the battleground seems significant.

Not all statutes administered by the regulatory agencies are designed primarily to cut into interests of regulated groups in order to further a general public interest; only a portion of them are, and even then the purposes are often mixed or unclear. The Interstate Commerce Act of 1887 may have been so designed, but in the many amendments Congress itself has often shown a pro-railroad disposition.

The key to effective administrative resistance to pressures of regulated groups is probably continued congressional and presidential support for administrative aggressiveness. The outstanding instance during the present century of an aggressive program sustained over powerful opposition of regulated parties is the administration of the National Labor Relations Act from the time it was held constitutional in 1937 until it was amended by the Taft-Hartley Act in 1947. This probably would not have been possible without strong support from both Congress and the President.

[1] Letter from Richard Olney, Attorney General under President Cleveland, to Charles E. Perkins, President of the Chicago, Burlington & Quincy Railroad.

About one-third of federal peacetime agencies were created before 1900, and another third before 1930. The first was established by the Act of July 31, 1789, to "estimate the duties payable" on imports and to perform other related duties. The second agency to be given the power of adjudication was established by the President, pursuant to a statute of September 29, 1789, providing for military pensions for "invalids who were wounded and disabled during the late war," to be paid "under such regulations as the President of the United States may direct." From that day to this, Congress has been grinding out legislation creating new agencies and adding to their powers.

Administrative law existed long before the term "administrative law" came into use. The first federal administrative law was embodied in the 1789 statutes. Further enactments, interpretations, and practices gradually produced a whole body of administrative law, until in 1893 Frank J. Goodnow published a book on Comparative Administrative Law, and in 1905 another book on Principles of the Administrative Law of the United States. In the first book Goodnow said that "the general failure in England and the United States to recognize an administrative law is really due, not to the nonexistence in these countries of this branch of the law but rather to the well-known failure of English law writers to classify the law. For . . . there [has] always existed in England, as well as in this country, an administrative law. . . ." In 1911 Ernst Freund brought out a casebook on administrative law. But, as Mr. Justice Frankfurter has pointed out, the work of Goodnow and Freund "was for many years unheeded by bench and bar."

In 1916 Elihu Root in an address as President of the American Bar Association made a statement that could hardly be improved upon with the hindsight of nearly a half century later: "There is one special field of law development which has manifestly become inevitable. We are entering upon the creation of a body of administrative law quite different in its machinery, its remedies, and its necessary safeguards from the old methods of regulation by specific statutes enforced by the courts. . . . The necessities of our situation have already led to an extensive employment of that method. . . . Before these agencies the old doctrine prohibiting the delegation of legislative power has virtually retired from the field and given up the fight. There will be no withdrawal from these experiments. We shall go on; we shall expand them, whether we approve theoretically or not, because such agencies furnish protection to rights and obstacles to wrong doing which under our new social and industrial conditions cannot be practically accomplished by the old and simple procedure of legislatures and courts as in the last generation." In his clarity of perception, Elihu Root may have been a generation or more ahead of other leaders of the bar. At the same time he uttered important words of caution: "If we are to continue a government of limited powers, these agencies of regulation must themselves be regulated. . . . The rights of the citizen against them must be made plain. A system of administrative law must be developed, and that with us is still in its infancy, crude and imperfect." Unfortunately, leaders of the bar for the most part rejected this wise counsel. Emotional resentment against the rise of administrative power gradually welled up. The desire was to kill the agencies, using whatever weapon would most effectively get the deed done—invoke the separation of powers theory to forbid combination of legislative, judicial, and executive functions, or use the nondelegation doctrine to prevent a grant of power to the agencies, or require by statute a de novo judicial review of administrative action. The growing antagonism of the bar toward the administrative process was unmistakable. But Congress and the state legislatures went right on increasing administrative power.

In 1929 Lord Hewart's book, *The New Despotism,* gave emphatic and emotional expression to the concern shared by most lawyers both in England and in the United States. But the British Committee on Ministers' Powers investigated and reported "no ground for public fear, if the right precautions are taken." James N. Beck, a former Solicitor General of the United States, published in 1932 a book entitled *Our Wonderland of Bureaucracy:* "Uncle Sam has not yet awakened from his dream of government by bureaucracy, but ever wanders further afield in crazy experiments in state socialism. Possibly some day he may awaken from his irrational dreams, and return again to the old conceptions of government, as wisely defined in the Constitution of the United States." Beck's book was poor scholarship, but it may have been effective politics. The antibureaucracy slogan became popular with all parties.

Then came the New Deal. New agencies flew thick and fast. General Hugh Johnson's NRA seemingly regulated all economic life. The new SEC, according to some of the legal advisers of corporations, made impossible the issuance or sale of corporate securities, except at the risk of huge personal liabilities. The NLRB seemed to many lawyers to decide every issue against the employer, stepping in to assure that labor organizers would win victories over employers who were only trying to live peacefully and keep their employees satisfied without outside interference. A host of other agencies were thorns in the sides of businessmen. If before the New Deal the antagonism toward bureaucracy was fast reaching the breaking point, the reasons for alarm had now been multiplied many times.

Opponents of the administrative process usually paid little heed to the view that the agencies were administering constructive programs. Many of them did not care whether the investor was now for the first time effectively protected against fraud in the sale of securities, or whether the workingman was enjoying something in the nature of an equality of bargaining power; indeed, animosity toward the NLRB was usually intertwined with a belief that the workingman had been given a superiority of bargaining position. The agencies—especially the SEC and the NLRB—were for most lawyers becoming the symbol of an obnoxious political philosophy which was fast destroying freedom.

The American Bar Association went into action. In 1933 it appointed a special committee on administrative law, which in 1934 began a series of annual reports: "The judicial branch of the federal government is being rapidly and seriously undermined. . . . The committee naturally concludes that, so far as possible, the decision of controversies of a judicial character must be brought back into the judicial system." In 1938 the committee, this time headed by Dean Roscoe Pound, reported "ten tendencies" of administrative agencies—to decide without a hearing, to hear only one side, to decide on evidence not produced, to make decisions on the basis of preformed opinions and prejudices. . . .

President Roosevelt on February 16, 1939, requested the Attorney General to appoint a committee to investigate the "need for procedural reform in the field of administrative law." A committee of distinguished practitioners, judges, and professors was appointed, which set about its tasks in scholarly fashion. It went after the facts. Its staff interviewed administrative officers, subordinates in the agencies, and practitioners who had had cases before the agencies. A detailed monograph was written on each agency, submitted in tentative form to the agency, and the committee and the agency then discussed the problems raised. Thereafter the committee held public hearings to receive opinions concerning the descriptions of procedures and the criticisms in the monographs. An elaborate report was finally prepared, which, with its appendices, fills 474 printed pages. This report, together with the monographs on which it is based, is still a primary source of information about the federal administrative process; even though it is out of date, no new comprehensive study has penetrated so far.

While the committee was investigating, the Walter-Logan bill, sponsored by the American Bar Association, came before Congress. James M. Landis demonstrated that it would "cut off here a foot and there a head, leaving broken and bleeding the processes of administrative law." Its proponents seemed fully aware of its devastating character, for they exempted from its provisions the agencies whose work they were anxious to protect. The bill was passed by both Houses, but the President's veto was upheld.

On some points the Attorney General's Committee rendered majority and minority reports, both of which proposed legislation. Several bills embodying these proposals were introduced in the congressional session of 1941, and hearings were held. The war cut off further efforts until 1944, when new bills were introduced and new hearings held. The Administration and the American Bar Association forces finally compromised, and the result was the enactment in 1946, by a unanimous vote in both Houses, of the Administrative Procedure Act (APA).

The major effects of the Act were to satisfy the political will for reform, to improve and strengthen the administrative process, and to preserve the basic limits upon judicial review of administrative action. The American Bar Association had fought for the propositions that "the decision of controversies must be brought back into the judicial system," that "life tenure should be assured to all who are to exercise judicial functions," that "administrative absolutism" stems from Marxism, and that the administrative process should be crippled through the Walter-Logan measure; but the Association was apparently reasonably satisfied with the APA, even though it transferred no power back to the courts, did not substantially increase judicial review, continued the system of adjudication by those enjoying no life tenure, improved the administrative process instead of weakening or crippling it, and in general gave assurance that further efforts to cripple the power of the agencies would be unlikely to succeed. The battle over fundamentals has ceased. The federal administrative process seemed secure.

After the enactment of the APA a period of relative tranquillity set in. Judicial interpretations of the APA were generally sympathetic to its purposes, and the Act's middle positions seemed to satisfy the former partisans on both sides. The courts kept on grinding out refinements of administrative law, both under the Act and apart from it. The pace of law development seemed to be decelerating. The 1949 report of the Task Force on Regulatory Commissions, of the first Hoover Commission, was based upon careful investigation but led to no recommendations for drastic changes in adjudication, rule making, or related activities: "The independent regulatory commission is a useful and desirable agency. . . ." In 1955 came the report of the President's Conference on Administrative Procedure, which had been appointed in 1953 to inquire into the narrow subject of "unnecessary delay, expense and volume of records in some adjudicatory and rule-making proceedings." The report was mild and helpful and, except for the troublesome problem of status of hearing officers, mostly noncontroversial.

In the post-APA period, the calm waters were first stirred by the Task Force of the second Hoover Commission, which reported in 1955. The point of view was one of consistent distrust of the agencies; many of the recommendations were extreme and some of them seemed ill-considered. The Hoover Commission itself refused to adopt the sweeping recommendations of its Task Force; only three members of the twelve-man Commission gave unqualified support to the recommendations to amend the APA, and six members said: "We did not vote for these recommendations because of their possible consequences and possible increase in the expenditures of the Government." The ICC Practitioners' Association appointed a Committee of One Hundred, which brought in an elaborate report adversely criticizing nearly every recommendation of the Task Force.

Attorney General Herbert Brownell said of the Task Force recommendations to amend the APA: "These changes would substantially 'judicialize' the administrative process, with disastrous results to efficient and effective government. . . . [T]hese proposals are unsound, unworkable, and so costly that they should be rejected. . . . To summarize, it seems plain to me from my study of this group of Commission and Task Force proposals that, far from achieving the Commission's objectives of attaining economy, efficiency, and improved service in the transaction of public business, these proposals would do exactly the contrary."

The position of the chief legal officer of the conservative administration seemed to doom the Task Force proposals. But the American Bar Association's Special Committee on Legal Services and Procedure stepped in. During 1956 it proposed a new Code of Administrative Procedure, adopting some of the Task Force recommendations and rejecting or toning down others. The proposed Code was much more carefully drafted than the Task Force recommendations, and at this writing the question of adoption, rejection, or modification is an open one. The proposals are numerous and complex; some of the major ones include: (1) a prohibition of off-the-record consultation of deciding officers with technical advisers or assistants; (2) a provision that an agency member or hearing commissioner who presides at the taking of evidence shall be disqualified to participate in agency review of an initial decision; (3) a requirement for most adjudication that rules of evidence "shall conform, to the extent practicable, with those in civil nonjury cases in the United States district courts"; (4) a provision making a presiding officer's findings of fact final unless the agency deems them clearly erroneous on the whole record; (5) judicial review of "every final agency action for which there is no other adequate remedy in any court"; and (6) with respect to judicial review of findings of fact, substitution of the "clearly erroneous" rule for the "substantial evidence" rule.

In general, developments in state and local governments have been somewhat slower than those in the federal government. As long ago as 1930 the Governor of New York appointed Robert M. Benjamin as a commissioner "to study, examine and investigate the exercise of quasi-judicial functions" by administrative agencies. The report, *Administrative Adjudication in the State of New York,* came in 1942. It was to New York State what the report of the Attorney General's Committee was to the federal government—a thorough, painstaking, detailed examination of the manner in which administrative power was being exercised, and an inquiry into possible alternative methods. Other states sponsored investigations, the American Bar Association through its committees studied state administrative law, and finally the National Conference of Commissioners on Uniform State Laws promulgated a Model State Administrative Procedure Act. By 1957 at least thirty-two states had enacted legislation dealing with one or more of the three main subjects of adjudication, rule making, and judicial review. Yet only about eleven states had comprehensive legislation covering all three subjects. Most of the state legislation is limited to the state level and does not reach municipal and other local administrative action. Much constructive work remains to be done. Federal administrative law, whose development in general is much more refined than that of the states, furnishes a useful guide and much facilitates the solution of state and local problems. In addition, various studies of individual states should be useful for all states.

In 1957 came the report of the British Committee on Administrative Tribunals and Enquiries, known as the Franks Committee. The report is based upon unusually careful investigation and study, and deserves to have considerable effect on both sides of the Atlantic. The underlying attitude of the report can be gleaned from a few excerpts: "In recent years most other western Governments have been called upon to govern more extensively and more intensively. . . . Reflection on the general social and economic changes of recent decades convinces us that tribunals as a system for adjudication have come to stay. . . . Our general conclusion regarding tribunals is that, despite the haphazard way in which they have developed, this method of decision making works reasonably well. . . . We regard both tribunals and administrative procedures as essential to our society."

## Reasons for Growth of the Administrative Process

The fundamental reason for resort to the administrative process is the undertaking by government of tasks which from a strictly practical standpoint can best be performed through that process. When the predecessor agency of the present Veterans' Administration was created in 1789 the fundamental pattern was set that has been followed ever since;

the job of determining which claimants were entitled to be paid was assigned to an agency other than the courts because what was needed was a staff of low-paid clerks, not a few high-paid judges with all the cumbersome trappings of the courtroom. Similar reasons explain the establishment of collectors of customs in 1789, a forerunner of the Patent Office in 1790, the Office of Indian Affairs in 1796, and the General Land Office in 1812. No one was thinking in terms of judiciary versus bureaucracy, capitalism versus socialism, or laissez-faire versus governmental interference. The early agencies were created because practical men were seeking practical answers to immediate problems.

Precisely the same approach was dominant in 1887 when the Interstate Commerce Commission, the first great regulatory agency, was created. The railroads before 1870 had been free from governmental interference, except for statutory prohibitions enforceable through prosecuting attorneys and courts, and except for common-law actions by shippers for refund of unreasonable charges. But as abuses multiplied—discriminations and preferences, exorbitant rates, irresponsible financial manipulation—the realization grew that legislatures and courts were inadequate. What was needed was a governmental authority having power not merely to adjudicate but to initiate proceedings, to investigate, to prosecute, to issue regulations having force of law, to supervise. Between 1871 and 1875, the legislatures of Iowa, Michigan, Minnesota, Missouri, and Wisconsin, spurred by aroused farmers, established regulatory commissions. Then the Supreme Court in 1886 held the states without power to regulate interstate rates, and the creation of a federal commission became inevitable, since three-fourths of railroad tonnage was interstate, and since Congress and the courts could not themselves accomplish what the state commissions had been accomplishing.

The political will to regulate railroads was not a mere passing fancy of the Congress of 1887. Frequently thereafter the need for expanded regulation has been felt, and Congress down through the years, whether conservative or liberal, whether Republican or Democratic, has voted to strengthen the Commission. By the time of the Transportation Act of 1920, as the Supreme Court soon acknowledged, the purpose of the regulatory program had changed from mere correction of abuses to the affirmative responsibility for maintaining an adequate system of transportation. How far this objective has been accomplished is debatable, but no responsible voice has been heard for decades to advocate abolition of the ICC.

In enlarging ICC powers the conservative Congress of 1920 was hardly intent on furthering socialism, or boosting bureaucracy, or providing government regulation for its own sake! Administrative control was intensified for the simple reason that those who were close to the problems knew that increasing the Commission's power was the best available means of maintaining an adequate system of transportation, with a decent protection for the interests of all concerned. The impetus came, not from philosophers or theorists, not from abstractions like those about separation of powers and supremacy of law, but from such people as leaders of the Grange movement, down-to-earth men who were seeking workable machinery for stamping out particular evils.

Similar reasons explained resort to administrative regulation of other utilities—electricity, gas, water, telephones, telegraphs, ships, street cars, trucks and buses, airplanes. For such enterprises some degree of monopoly was usually desirable, but experience quickly proved that unregulated monopoly was intolerable. In 1914 the need was felt for greater protection against improper banking practices and against unfair methods of competition, and Congress created the Board of Governors of the Federal Reserve System and the Federal Trade Commission. By 1933 the old common-law method of letting a defrauded buyer of securities sue the seller had proved itself thoroughly unsatisfactory, alternative methods were studied, and the result was the invention of methods of prevention —administrative supervision of the reporting of facts in detailed registration statements. As radio broadcasting developed, someone had to assign frequencies to prevent chaos, and the assumption went unchallenged that a federal administrative agency should be given the job. When unemployment compensation and old age insurance were provided, the natural course was to establish administrative agencies to administer the programs—what good alternative was available? Labor unions in 1935 finally won their political battle for collective bargaining and for protection against unfair labor practices; no one knew a better way—no one yet knows a better way—to translate the statutory rights into economic realities, than to establish a specialized tribunal equipped with the requisite powers. When in 1947 the decision was made in favor of regulation of the unions as well as the employers, a conservative Congress did not hesitate to expand the powers of the National Labor Relations Board. . . .

The legislative process and the judicial process, which are the principal alternatives to the administrative process, frequently fall far short of providing what is needed. A legislative body is at its best in determining the direction of major policy, and in checking and supervising administration. It is ill-suited for handling masses of detail, or for applying to shifting and continuing problems the ideas supplied by scientists or other professional advisers. Experience early proved the inability of Congress to prescribe detailed schedules of rates for railroads, or to keep abreast of changing needs concerning the levels of import duties. Gradually our legislative bodies developed the system of legislating only the main outlines of programs requiring constant attention, and leaving to administrative agencies the tasks of working out subsidiary policies. This system facilitated not merely the promulgation of law through rules and regulations but the correlation of rule making with such other necessary activities as adjudication, investigating, prosecuting, and supervising.

Somewhat less compelling are the reasons for developing systems of administrative adjudication instead of transferring cases to the courts whenever specific issues are crystallized which call for the finding of facts and the application of law or policy. Even if an ICC is needed which will make rules, supervise, investigate, administer, and do other things courts cannot do, why should not the courts still decide individual controversies? Even if a social security administration must use a staff of nearly eighteen thousand to pay two million claims annually for old age and survivors insurance, why should not the courts step in whenever an issue arises for adjudication? The same question is pertinent for every other agency.

The reasons are numerous and variable. Some apply to some agencies and some to others. Some are convincing, some are not, and some may be in need of reexamination.

Perhaps the most important reason why, as a matter of historical fact, we have not sent all controversies to the courts, is that adjudication of issues naturally grows directly out of the administrative handling of cases. For instance, ninety-nine veterans are admitted to a veterans' hospital, and only in the hundredth case does a controversy arise. Even if a hearing or something like a hearing is called for, the hospital officials or members of their immediate organization may most conveniently conduct the proceeding; the adjudication is virtually a part of the administrative work of admitting the hundred veterans. This is so, even if the issues when isolated from the administrative work are entirely appropriate for judicial determination. The reasons are often about the same whether the subject matter is the award of a benefit, the granting of a license, the approval of a rate, or the issuance of a cease and desist order. Thus, even when courts are well qualified to adjudicate some classes of controversies, administrative adjudication has often been preferred mostly for reasons of convenience.

But much of the substance of administrative adjudication is, or at the crucial time has been thought to be, outside the area of judicial competence. Courts are not qualified to fix rates or to determine what practices related to rates are to be preferred. Even a simple process of granting or denying licenses, on the basis of a record of evidence, has been held so far beyond the competence of courts that a statute requiring courts to perform this task is held unconstitutional. Judges rather obviously cannot furnish the skills in law, accounting, and engineering supplied by the staff of a relatively simple agency like the FCC, to say nothing of a more complex agency like the ICC, which requires the assistance of rate men, locomotive inspectors, railroad reorganization specialists, explosives experts, valuation engineers, tariff interpreters, accountants, specialists in long-and-short-haul problems, and experts on problems of rail traffic congestion. With all the specialized personnel available on the Commission's staff, it would be odd, even when specific issues are fully crystallized, to transfer a case to a court made up of judges who are not expected to have the needed specialized experience and who are not advised by specialists.

Even when issues are of a type that courts can competently handle, such as claims for old age insurance, the advantages of specialization may be a crucial consideration. Among the eighteen thousand government workers who handle such claims are units which specialize in particular types of problems; even when the subject matter is of a type on which judges are especially well qualified, such as questions of law—say, marriage and divorce law—the specialized unit in the Bureau of Old Age and Survivors Insurance may best handle the case; the specialized unit may dispose of hundreds of such cases a week, whereas it might take a judge a week for a handful of such cases.

Even for adjudication of workmen's compensation cases, widespread experience has shown that the courts are not the appropriate tribunals. The main reason may be that administration and adjudication cannot be efficiently separated.

Where attempted in the United States, it may safely be said that court administration of workmen's compensation has failed. This has not been because of inefficiency in the courts, but because the judicial machinery is not, and cannot be, adapted to the new problems of administration presented by the system of workmen's compensation. . . . Workmen's compensation, if properly administered, presents many problems of continuous supervision for which the courts are ill adapted.

The courts may be qualified for adjudication of workmen's compensation, but not for handling whole problems.

Another major reason for the legislative preference for the administrative process has been the belief that the judicial process is unduly awkward, slow, and expensive. The public demanded a speedy, cheap, and simple procedure, a procedure which keeps the role of the lawyers to a minimum. Of course, the administrative process is by no means always fast and inexpensive, but the prevailing belief has been that it is.

Perhaps nowhere is this prevailing belief about the comparative efficiency of the judicial and administrative processes more effectively expressed than in President Roosevelt's veto message on the Walter-Logan bill in 1940:

Court procedure is adapted to the intensive investigation of individual controversies. But it is impossible to subject the daily routine of fact finding in many of our agencies to court procedure. Litigation has become costly beyond the ability of the average person to bear. Its technical rules of procedure are often traps for the unwary and technical rules of evidence often prevent common-sense determinations on information which would be regarded as adequate for any business decision. The increasing cost of competent legal advice and the necessity for relying upon lawyers to conduct court proceedings have made all laymen and most lawyers recognize the inappropriateness of entrusting routine processes of government to the outcome of never-ending lawsuits.

The administrative tribunal or agency has been evolved in order to handle controversies arising under particular statutes. It is characteristic of these tribunals that simple and nontechnical hearings take the place of court trials and informal proceedings supersede rigid and formal pleadings and processes. A common-sense resort to usual and practical sources of information takes the place of archaic and technical application of rules of evidence, and an informed and expert tribunal renders its decisions with an eye that looks forward to results rather than backward to precedent and to the leading case.

Another significant reason for using agencies instead of courts for some types of adjudications has to do with the traditional passiveness of courts, which typically have no machinery for initiating proceedings or for taking other action in absence of a moving party. This characteristic of courts has combined with the recognized need for public representation of large numbers of little people—consumers, usually—none of whom is sufficiently affected to assert his own interests in a judicial proceeding. President Roosevelt made this point in his veto message: "Where ever a continuing series of controversies exist between a powerful and concentrated interest on one side and a diversified mass of individuals, each of whose separate interests may be small, on the other side, the only means of obtaining equality before the law has been to place the controversy in an administrative tribunal." Another way, of course, would be to have courts do the adjudicating, and to have sufficiently alert prosecutors to represent the public interest.

Another major reason for resort to the administrative process has been the widespread belief, whether or not justifiable, that the biases of the judges disqualify them to administer the new programs that have been committed to administrative agencies. Whatever the proper interpretation of the facts might be, the opinion was often dominant among sponsors of reform legislation that judges during the first third of the twentieth century frequently construed away sound and necessary reform legislation. In many of the regulatory programs the fundamental cleavage was believed to be between private rights and social objectives. The assumptions were that the primary business of courts was to decide controversies involving private rights and not to further legislative policies, that judges have been typically influenced by legal training toward conservative attitudes and accustomed through experience as advocates at the bar to favoring the interests of property, and that judges were therefore biased in favor of protection of private rights against governmental interference.[2] When the primary purpose of the sponsors of regulatory legislation was to alter what was regarded as the accustomed judicial protection of private rights, the choice was naturally made in favor of tribunals other than courts to administer the regulatory programs.

A good example of the political point of view that led to rejection of the courts for administering new legislation is a 1914 statement of a Senate Committee, recommending establishment of the Federal Trade Commission because: "The people of this country will not permit the courts to declare a policy for them with respect to this subject." Of course, this attitude outrages those who are inclined to emphasize the desirability of protecting established rights from bureaucratic interference. But, right or wrong, this attitude is historically one of the prime reasons for the growth of the administrative process.

Of course, reasons for the growth of the administrative process must include not only reasons for establishment of the agencies but also reasons for keeping them once they have been established. The record here is especially impressive. Although much shifting of functions from one agency to another has occurred, probably no federal peacetime agency having significant powers of adjudication or rule making has ever been abolished. Professor Willard Hurst, in a context of discussion of state agencies, pointed out in 1950: "No important administrative agency seems ever to have been destroyed because of objections to its distinctive characteristics as an administrative agency."

The reasons, however, for the retention of agencies are by no means entirely favorable to the administrative process. That many agencies are continued because they successfully do the jobs assigned to them is clear, as probably nearly everyone would agree with respect to, say, the Internal Revenue Service, the Veterans' Administration, and perhaps most local zoning boards. But some of the most important regulatory agencies may be kept, not because of their success, but because the degree of their failure is approved by politically powerful interests that are regulated. An ineffective regulatory agency often goes through the motions of regulating, thereby silencing the sponsors of the legislation that brought the agency into existence, but at the same time the agency is careful for the most part to regulate in the interest of the regulated, thereby silencing

---

[2] Learned Hand, "The Speech of Justice," *Harvard Law Review*, vol. 29, 1916, p. 617: ". . . the profession is still drawn, and so far as we can see will always be drawn from the propertied class, but other classes have awakened to conscious control of their fate. . . . But the profession has not yet learned to adapt itself to the change; that most difficult of adjustments has not been made, an understanding of and sympathy with the purposes and ideals of those parts of the common society whose interests are discordant with its own."

them. And we go on and on with our mixture of regulatory agencies, all of them varying somewhat from time to time in their effectiveness, some rather fully dominated most of the time by regulated parties, others semi-effective some of the time or much of the time, and hardly any fully effective over sustained periods.

All in all, the political outlook is for a long-term continued growth of the administrative process. Few informed people of any political persuasion are likely to disagree with a 1955 statement by the Attorney General for the most conservative national administration we have had since 1933: "Administrative agencies have become an established part of our constitutional government, accepted by Congress, the judiciary and the people as an essential part of the governmental structure. They were created as a necessary means for protecting public interests which could not be suitably protected by the courts or other means.... Administrative agencies must be enabled and permitted to function efficiently and effectively if the public interest, which is their primary concern, is to be preserved."

## Reasons for Opposition to the Administrative Process

If attitudes of lawyers toward the administrative process were charted on a graph, with enthusiastic approval on the left and complete condemnation on the right, the bunching near the center would be pronounced, but the peak would probably be well to the right of center. Let us invent a mythical character by the name of Mr. Practitioner, whose views place him at or near the peak, and look at the administrative process through his eyes. What he sees, of course, is a mixture of what a wholly objective observer—equally mythical—could see, and what his experience and his biases contribute. He has been at the bar twenty-five years and has not systematically studied administrative law. He has a sound background of education and experience in the system of administration of justice by courts. He is aware of imperfections but by and large he has full confidence in the judicial process. He is familiar with its intricate ways, he makes his living through use of his special knowledge and skill, he feels at home in the system, and he serves his clients well. With this background, his response in 1955 to the report of the second Hoover Commission's Task Force on Legal Services and Procedure was one of warm approval, for he gathered that the main push was to try to do about all that can be done to "judicialize" the administrative process.

Mr. Practitioner has never had occasion to study the reasons why the domain of adjudication of controversies has been invaded by hordes of bureaucrats, whose administrative process is foreign and perplexing to him. Instinctively he agrees with an American Bar Association committee which put first among the evils of bureaucracy the "confusion" and "bewildering multiplicity" of the agencies. He is convinced that the fundamental structure of the agencies violates many of the most basic principles of sound government. The typical agency exercises both legislative and judicial functions, contrary to the theory of separation of powers, which, as he has understood ever since he studied political science in college, was one of the fundamental principles upon which the American government was founded. Furthermore, he deeply believes in a government of laws and not of men, and he readily accepts the view of a good many bar association speakers that the bureaucrats are conniving to destroy the basic and essential principle of supremacy of law.

When Mr. Practitioner tries to handle a case in the field of an administrative agency, he is uncomfortable and unhappy, for the usual guides, the digests, the judicial rules, the familiar methods of practice seem to afford little help. Should he file an answer to a complaint, as in a judicial proceeding? How does one find these rules and regulations that are supposed to have force of law? Why does the index of the Federal Register lack any of the titles that might lead to the relevant subject matter? What an outrage that rules of most state agencies are generally unpublished and unavailable except at the state capitol! His resentment at the widescale rejection of the tried and tested methods of conducting judicial proceedings grows deep and abiding.

Everywhere he turns, the methods are not only unfamiliar but seem to sacrifice the most precious values. The same agencies serve as investigator, prosecutor, judge, jury, and executioner; he strongly prefers the judicial process, which follows the elementary principle that no man may judge his own cause. The agencies often act on evidence that has not even been presented; reliance on extra-record specialized knowledge seems to him abominable. When witnesses testify, the rules of evidence are disregarded. Some examiners have never even studied those rules, do not know the meaning of the hearsay rule, have never heard of the opinion rule, and have to be told about the attorney-client privilege. Although an examiner presides at the hearing, the commissioners make the decision, and Mr. Practitioner has heard that the commissioners seldom read the records. Reviewers or review attorneys, behind the scenes, probably have a good deal of influence in decision-making, but they neither hear the witnesses testify nor are known to be present when counsel argue orally before the Commission. For all that a party or his counsel knows, the reason he loses his case is that an anonymous young man who has never met a payroll but pretends to be an "expert" has given erroneous advice —advice that the losing lawyer never has a chance to know or to correct.

In the judicial process, when expert opinion is needed, the so-called experts are required to take the witness stand and to subject themselves to cross-examination. In Mr. Practitioner's opinion, that is the only fair arrangement.

Furthermore, the administrators of many of the agencies seem to Mr. Practitioner to be biased. Many of them have obviously been appointed to carry out a particular program, not to see that justice is done, not to keep the scales in even balance. He is sure, as are most of his fellow lawyers, that the bias of the NLRB in its early years was disgraceful. He acknowledges that judges of the regular courts occasionally manifest an unfortunate bias—he has lost a few cases—but he also firmly believes that judges are never crusaders who are so intent upon carrying out a program that they have lost capacity to see the facts as they are. No one denies—not even the bureaucrats—that it is still the courts to which the community looks for even-handed, impartial justice. As Chief Justice Hughes once pointed out: "Legislative agencies, with varying qualifications, work in a field peculiarly exposed to political demands. Some may be expert and impartial, others subservient." Congressmen who would refuse to consider an attempt to influence a court will usually as a matter of course get in touch with administrators to help constituents with their cases. How can a lawyer fight that kind of political abuse, and why should he have to? Many administrators can be fired at the will of the President, or at the will of a department head or other political officer. The insecurity of tenure stands in contrast with the independence of federal judges, who are protected by life tenure and even by a constitutional prohibition against diminution of their salaries while in office.

Mr. Practitioner is aghast at the extent of the discretionary power which administrative agencies are exercising. Courts, as he well knows, are guided by law; their chief function is to find facts and to apply previously existing law to the findings. But the essence of administrative power lies in determination of policy. The law made by legislatures and by courts is readily accessible and relatively certain. But one can only guess at the manner in which bureaucrats will exercise discretion or determine policy. Yet a large portion of administrative action is retroactive. This is why Mr. Justice Jackson, with the concurrence of Mr. Justice Frankfurter, vehemently protested in 1947 against "administrative authoritarianism" and "conscious lawlessness."

The agencies are obnoxious not merely in the methods they use, but they are inextricably tied up with substantive programs deliberately designed to interfere with the freedom of business and the rights of property. The administrative process, Mr. Practitioner has heard and is inclined to believe, is the tool of those who are trying to destroy private initiative and establish a slave state in which all human activities are directed by government fiat. The rapid shift of power from business to government, with the increasing centralization in Washington, contributes to what may easily become an uncontrollable force pulling the nation irresistibly into dictatorship. Regulation breeds more regulation. Did not the OPA experience prove that selective price control was impossible, that a little bit led to more and more until all prices and wages and salaries had to be controlled?

The administrative process is said to be the tool of socialism, and Mr. Practitioner wishes that the rest of the community could only understand, as the lawyers do, the seriousness of the gradually developing socialism. "It's later than you think," he tells his friends. Even as early as 1932, before the New Deal, Mr. James M. Beck, a former Solicitor General of the United States, said that the United States had already succumbed to socialism: "Few States are more socialistic. . . . There is no better illustration of the pernicious effects of excessive interference by government in business than is afforded by the example of the Interstate Commerce Commission." Mr. Practitioner is a little confused by the assertion that the ICC is socialistic, for he remembers how vehemently the ICC Practitioners' Association in 1955 attacked the proposals to judicialize the administrative process; maybe the ICC is not so socialistic if the practitioners before it respond so strongly in protecting it against its attackers. But Mr. Practitioner has not relinquished his view that he developed during the 1930s that the SEC and NLRB are socialistic; still, he is a bit puzzled that Wall Street no longer condemns the basic SEC program, and that employers in 1947 supported the measure that augmented the powers of the NLRB. Even so, the agencies in general must be socialistic, for that is the view of Dean Roscoe Pound, who in 1938 as chairman of an American Bar Association committee on administrative law pointed out that the proponents of "administrative absolutism" expect a disappearance of law in the sense of a body of authoritative guides to decision, and that "This is a Marxian idea much in vogue just now among a type of American writers."

Some of Mr. Practitioner's clients tell him that they are subject to the jurisdiction of twenty or more federal agencies, with overlapping powers —that they are so harassed by the red tape of regulation that they seriously contemplate quitting business.

The excessive government interference with business, coupled with all the reckless spending, extravagance and waste, makes taxes unbearable. Expense alone seems to him a sufficient reason for cutting back administrative power. He is fond of pointing out to his friends that one of the prime objectives of government executives is to enlarge their staffs of subordinates so that little bureaucrats will become big ones, and so that big ones will become bigger.

During the late 1940s Mr. Practitioner used to tell his friends: "Just wait until we win a national election; a lot of obnoxious agencies will disappear." But now the failure of the Eisenhower administration to abolish any peacetime agency with regulatory powers gives him the uncomfortable feeling that maybe the administrative process is here to stay after all. When he comforts himself with the reflection that even if it is, maybe it can be judicialized, as the Task Force of the second Hoover Commission recommended, he gets to wondering why even the conservative Hoover Commission itself withheld its approval of that idea. And the state legislatures, many of them under conservative control, keep on adding to the numbers of agencies and adding to their powers.

"Oh, well," he says, "the world has lots of problems besides the creeping bureaucracy. And many of them are easier to understand and more pleasant to contemplate." He'll still cast his vote for the politician who promises to cut back governmental power.

### Appraisal of Reasons for Opposition to Administrative Process

We have just re-examined the reasons impelling a typical practitioner of law to resist the growth of the administrative process. Probably most members of the bar tend to agree with him, more or less, for reasons similar to those that impress him.

But the undeniable fact still remains that the community as a whole, expressing itself through repeated legislative action, federal, state, and local, steadfastly rejects those conclusions. Indeed, the long battle over the fundamental desirability or undesirability of establishing administrative agencies and of continuing to rely upon their processes is rapidly diminishing and may be about ended. Even though politicians still win votes by making broadside attacks upon the evils of bureaucracy, the day is probably past when responsible leaders will again attempt to abolish or to paralyze the principal agencies.

### Who Is Right—the Bar or the Legislative Bodies?

Any satisfying answer must distinguish those elements that seem to yield to efforts toward objective scholarship from those aspects of the problem that necessarily depend upon political philosophy. We must exclude as beyond the scope of administrative law such overshadowing questions as the soundness or unsoundness of the substantive programs and the asserted tendency toward totalitarianism, and therefore we shall attempt no overall answer. Yet we shall inquire into some of the objections in great detail; five full chapters will be devoted to the five principal objections concerning institutional decisions, bias, combination of functions, rejection of exclusionary rules of evidence, and use of extra-record information. In general, these chapters lead to mixed conclusions—that conscientious men who understand both sides believe the picture to be quite different from the one our practitioner sees, that many of the weaknesses of the administrative process are very real and remain uncured, that the judicial process should copy and is beginning to copy some features of the administrative process, and that administrative safeguards often fall far short of the high standards of the judicial process.

We shall deal later in this chapter with separation of powers and supremacy of law, and in a later chapter with what Mr. Justice Jackson called "conscious lawlessness." This leaves the antibusiness attitude, the "bewildering multiplicity" of agencies, political subservience and insecurity of tenure, and high taxes.

Utterly mistaken is the widespread impression that administrative programs are invariably sponsored by political groups antagonistic to business. The initiative in the creation of regulatory agencies is often taken by businessmen. Some of the salient historical facts implementing this observation have already been set forth above in this chapter.

The view of James M. Beck and Roscoe Pound that such agencies as the ICC are "socialistic" or "Marxian" is an absurdity to nearly every lawyer who has had enough practice before the agencies to become thoroughly familiar with their functions and with their processes.

Indeed, when he is in a reflective mood, Mr. Practitioner might agree that his animosity toward bureaucrats stems much more from his dislike for some of the substantive programs than from knowledge of and disagreement with administrative methods. Else why was he in favor of the expansion of administrative power by the Taft-Hartley Act? Why do so many lawyers join in Mr. LaRoe's expression of "affection" for the ICC? Why has Mr. Practitioner attacked agencies, whose procedures provide the best safeguards—the NLRB, SEC, and FCC—but not the ones whose procedures are relatively slipshod or questionable—the Immigration Service, the Post Office Department, the loyalty-security tribunals?

What the American Bar Association committee called "bewildering multiplicity" helps explain lawyers' antagonism toward the administrative process, but it is not a substantive evil. Those who have been brought up on admiration for the judicial process could hardly be expected to receive cordially the many administrative innovations that depart even from the fundamentals of judicial traditions. Such cordiality could result only from sympathetic study of reasons that explain the growth of the administrative process. Not many lawyers, except the younger ones through formal legal education, have made such a study. The multiplicity of agencies is neither confusing nor bewildering to those who take time to understand. And enduring evils from overlapping jurisdictions are almost entirely the figments of demagogues.

Political subservience and insecurity of tenure are facets of a single problem. How far do the agencies in fact depart from the ideal of an independent judiciary? The answer is of course various. During 1958 a congressional committee brought out facts showing some substantial departures, thereby creating a public impression that regulatory agencies are shot through with influence peddling and its consequences. Yet the number of federal judges sent to jail for corruption during the past two decades is larger than the number of federal adminstrators sent to jail for corruption during the same period. The seven independent regulatory agencies—ICC, FTC, FPC, SEC, FCC, NLRB, and CAB—serve for terms ranging from five to fourteen years. "So far as our staff reports and the comments of others have revealed, the independent commissions have largely achieved freedom from direct partisan influence in the administration of their statutes. With few exceptions, the actions of the commissions appear to be above suspicion of favoritism or partiality." This statement may still be true even if 1958 revelations make the exceptions seem rather important.

The idea that high taxes result from the regulatory process is ludicrously false. The aggregate number of employees in all seven of the independent federal regulatory agencies in 1955 was 7,089. The total civilian employees of the government was 2,397,268. The employees of the seven regulatory agencies made up three-tenths of one per cent of all civilian employees; if the seven agencies were abolished, 99.7 per cent of the civilian employees would remain. The saving in government expenditures would be even a smaller proportion, for it would be less than one tenth of one per cent. Out of every thousand dollars, more than $999 would still be spent. Seventy billion dollars would be cut to $69,954,000,000.

## Supremacy of Law or Rule of Law

Although the terms "rule of law" and "supremacy of law" are probably interchangeable, their meaning is far from clear. The terms are more often used to express a political or emotional belief than a legal meaning. We shall discuss seven principal meanings.

(1) *Law and Order.* The proposition that a system of rule by law is

to be preferred to a system of private use of force is likely to find few opponents. Aristotle said that "The rule of the law is preferable to that of any individual." As the term is often used, it means no more. An outstanding example is a statement by Mr. Justice Frankfurter: "But from their own experience and their deep reading in history, the Founders knew that Law alone saves a society from being rent by internecine strife or ruled by mere brute power however disguised. 'Civilization involves subjection of force to reason, and the agency of this subjection is law!'"

Resistance to the rule of law in this sense crops out from time to time in all parts of the United States. An example is a statement of Senator James O. Eastland at Senatobia, Mississippi, August 12, 1955: "You are not required to obey any court which passes out such a ruling. In fact, you are obligated to defy it." Another example is a public statement by the Mayor of Philadelphia in late 1956 encouraging violation of a Pennsylvania statute forbidding Sunday basketball games.

(2) *Fixed Rules.* Exponents of the rule of law often mean merely that they prefer fixed rules to discretion, that is, what the Massachusetts Constitution calls "a government of laws and not of men." Of course, no one argues for a system resembling that of the oriental potentate who metes out justice without any better guide than his own whims of the moment. The problem of the proper proportion of rules and discretion is obviously a central problem in our entire legal system. Although many abstract discussions of this problem are helpful, the fact is that most of our practical solutions are worked out in concrete contexts, not in the abstract. Solutions we reach in practice vary from one context to another, and that is probably as it should be.

Even when specific precedents are lacking, the administrative process is not necessarily dependent upon wholly unguided discretion. Judge Charles E. Wyzanski has convincingly argued that "the nominal discretion with which an officer or legislator is vested is in fact controlled by more than constitutions, statutes and self-imposed discipline. It is controlled by technical norms which have been developed for each subject and also by general norms which are basic to the society in which he lives. These 'norms' . . . are among the important sources and materials of which the law is made; they are limiting factors in the exercise of such discretionary powers. . . . After one has worked for any length of time in a particular field he acquires a sense of what considerations have a legitimate bearing upon problems in that field. . . . He comes to have an appreciation of the history and grammar of his specific topic; to understand which objectives in that field public opinion over a long term of years has sought to promote, and which to discourage; to foresee the probable evolution of his subject; and to grasp the values which inhere in that process of growth."

Of course, sizable areas of largely unguided administrative discretion continue and are likely to continue far into the future. But no way has yet been discovered for carrying out modern governmental functions without discretionary power. "If it is contrary to the rule of law that discretionary authority should be given to government departments or public officers, then the rule of law is inapplicable to any modern constitution." That discretionary power is preferable to fixed rules for the performance of some functions seems unquestionable. Even Dean Pound once asserted this in a very provocative passage: "No one can deny that there are dangers involved in committing the application of legal standards to administrative bodies. One danger is that they will do what the courts have done before them: crystallize particular applications to particular cases into rules and thus destroy the standard. More than one court attempted this in the law of negligence and American courts of equity in the nineteenth century did much toward turning experience in the exercise of the chancellor's discretion into hard and fast rules of jurisdiction. But from the very nature of these administrative tribunals they are less likely to fall into such an error than the courts."

(3) *Elimination of Discretion.* The rule of law sometimes means elimination of all discretion from governmental processes. That some influential writers are willing to take such an extreme position seems almost unbelievable. Outstanding among such writers is Friedrich A. Hayek, who in his much-acclaimed book *On the Road to Serfdom* refers to "the great principles known as the Rule of Law" and says: "Stripped of all technicalities, this means that government in all its actions is bound by rules fixed and announced beforehand—rules which make it possible to foresee with fair certainty how the authority will use its coercive powers in given circumstances and to plan one's individual affairs on the basis of this knowledge." When Congress decides whether or not to enact or to expand the Social Security Act, it is not bound by "rules fixed and announced beforehand" which determine which conclusion it will reach. Nor is the President in deciding how to reply to a note from the Russian government. Nor is a chemist in deciding whether or not the government may safely allow the amount of poison spray on fruits to be increased. Nor is an officer in choosing between two sites for a government building. Nor is a state highway engineer in planning a network of highways. Nor is a prosecutor in deciding whether his office has time for prosecution of a marginal offense.

For that matter, the Supreme Court is not "bound by rules fixed and announced beforehand" when it decides whether or not to overrule a batch of precedents, as it has often done. If the Hayek view had prevailed, equity courts would never have been allowed to escape from rigidities that were once characteristic of the common law. Indeed, if the Hayek view had prevailed, the common law never could have been developed, for the common law is the product of the exercise of discretion by judges in individual cases.

(4) *Due Process or Fairness.* The Attorney General of England has recently asserted that the rule of law is "the reverse of tyranny . . . a state of affairs in which there are legal barriers to governmental arbitrariness and legal safeguards for the protection of the individual. Where the rule of law does not reign . . . it is replaced by the rule of fear or anarchy." A tyranny through an administrative process is not only conceivable but would be a practical danger, in absence of such usual protections as legislative oversight of administration, procedural safeguards, and effective judicial review.

The antithesis of application of known principles or laws is not necessarily arbitrariness; it may be reasonable exercise of discretionary power. When the Supreme Court decides whether to overrule a precedent, it is not necessarily applying known principles or laws, but neither is it necessarily acting arbitrarily. Nor is an administrative agency necessarily acting arbitrarily when it considers whether or not to make a change in an announced policy.

(5) *Natural Law.* The rule of law sometimes means due process, natural law, or higher law. An example is the following passage from a judicial opinion: "For, if the constitutional provision, 'due process of law,' or, as it is sometimes called, 'the law of the land,' or, as the English phrase it, 'the rule of law,' means anything, it should mean equality in the determination of the rights of those affected."

A careful writer gives the concept plural meanings in the following passage: "The Rule of Law . . . is that principle of our Western tradition which teaches that ours is a government of laws and not of men . . .; that not even a king is above the law; that there is a higher law against which laws and ordinances must be measured if they are to be treated as legitimate. It is a law which governs the governors. . . ." The concept of "a higher law" and of "a law which governs the governors" is a useful one. But as a matter of terminology, the concepts of due process and of constitutional law are more precise and less confusing than rule of law.

(6) *Preference for Judges.* The rule of law sometimes means a preference for decisions by judges of the regular courts rather than decisions by administrators. The outstanding exponent of this view is John Dickinson, who in his book on Administrative Justice and the Supremacy of Law explains what he calls supremacy of law: "In short, every citizen is entitled, first, to have his rights adjudicated in a regular common-law court, and, secondly, to call into question in such a court the legality of any act done by an administrative official."

Both agencies and courts use both rules and discretion; some administrative action involves less discretion than much judicial action. Even though the aggregate of all administrative action probably involves a larger element of discretion than the aggregate of all judicial action, a condemnation of discretion would reach a large portion of all judicial action and would fail to reach a large portion of all administrative action. For instance, the proportion of discretion in most workmen's compensation tribunals is probably less than the proportion of discretion in most automobile accident cases tried in courts. Probably no judge has such a small proportion of discretionary power as the adjudicators who pass upon claims for old age and survivors insurance under the social security program.

The Dickinson position is pushed so far as to border on absurdity when he says that "the law ought to be applied by an agency whose main business is to know the law, rather than to enforce some part of it." This would mean that a judge, not an inspector of hulls and boilers, should decide whether a ship is seaworthy.

(7) *Judicial Review.* Another meaning of supremacy of law is that some or all administrative action should be judicially reviewable in some degree. Thus, Mr. Justice Brandeis once said in a concurring opinion: "The supremacy of law demands that there shall be opportunity to have some court decide whether an erroneous rule of law was applied; and whether the proceeding in which facts were adjudicated was conducted regularly."

The Brandeis statement seems clearly at variance with what the Supreme Court holds. More reliable is a statement by Mr. Justice Frankfurter, speaking for the Supreme Court: "But courts are not charged with general guardianship against all potential mischief in the complicated tasks of government." Holdings preventing the courts from reviewing even questions of law are not at all uncommon. Either we do not have supremacy of law, or supremacy of law does not require judicial review of all questions of law.

Possibly something that can be called the rule of law should require some minimum of judicial review when constitutional rights are at stake. But even when the Supreme Court recognizes a constitutional minimum of review, it does not customarily speak the language of supremacy of law or rule of law.

# CHANGING ATTITUDES TOWARD THE ADMINISTRATIVE PROCESS

By Walter Gellhorn

VESTIGES OF the savage remain in all of us. Everyone experiences occasional nostalgia for the good old primitive days, free from government. We groan in concert about the price we have to pay for civilization—though, in the end, only the anarchists at one extreme and, at the other, the advocates of repealing the Sixteenth Amendment really appear convinced that taxes are unbearable. We also groan, though as a rule not in concert, about other aspects of government, whose inescapable function it is at times to prevent and at times to compel conduct far from the wishes of governed individuals. Our necks fit into yokes less readily than do the oxen's, and we bellow more loudly when the yokes are felt. That is why, so long as vocal cords have not been paralyzed by terror, cries of concern or outrage usually provide the unharmonious accompaniment of new governmental measures.

If the American administrative process, which has had its most noteworthy growth during the past quarter century, had developed without a background of determined grumbling by vigorous viewers with alarm, the future historian would have been perplexed by the abnormality of silence. But no one need be worried in behalf of the distant scholar who seeks to interpret our age. A full quota of attacks on governmental theory and practice will satisfy him that American adrenal glands were functioning at capacity during these significant years.

While our contemporary period differs from no other in respect of expressed distaste for governmental exertions, this moment in history nevertheless does have a feature that distinguishes it from the rest. Within this brief span of years the defenders and detractors of the administrative process have all but exchanged roles, and have done so with almost unbelievable abruptness. The chorus of concern about the administrative process peals forth today with no abatement of yesteryear's volume; but the choristers are different, and those who formerly joined most lustily in the singing now seek to still it. As a matter of fact, they

---

Reprinted from Chapter I, Gellhorn, *Individual Freedom and Governmental Restraints* (Baton Rouge: Louisiana State U. P., 1956), pp. 3–22, with the permission of the author and publisher. Dr. Gellhorn, Professor of Law at Columbia University, was the Director of the Attorney General's Committee on Administrative Procedure from 1939 to 1940. His works include *Security, Loyalty, and Science* (1950); *The State and Subversion* (1952); *American Rights; the Constitution in Action* (1960).

sometimes even urge Congress to investigate daring critics of procedures they themselves so recently denounced.

The transfer of adjudicatory responsibilities from the traditional courts to the as yet untraditionalized administrative agencies aroused anxious debate from the first, and the debate continues today. The methods of the new adjudicators have been praised and blamed—praised for being functional without unfairness, blamed for being incautiously careless of litigants' rights in ways that fairminded judges would have avoided. I should like to speculate about why the praisers and blamers have recently switched sides.

Conceivably, of course, there is nothing more to the problem than discovering whether one likes or dislikes the results reached by the administrators. In this view all the pother about administration is a delusion—of oneself or of others. All that counts is whether one approves the end product. There is undoubtedly a great deal to be said for this explanation. Some of those who formerly inveighed against administrative proceedings were at bottom concerned with the governmental policies committed to the administrators rather than with the administrators themselves—though, like a bull infuriated by banderillas, they may have only partly identified the source of their irritation. On the other hand many who in the mid-thirties were cheering the newly created agencies of the New Deal were making essentially the same error as their opponents. They imagined that the administrative agency had a sort of built-in point of view. They, like those who were perturbed on the other side, believed that some inner current ineluctably made the administrative agency an instrument of social and economic progressivism—with which they vaguely sympathized. Of course neither the supporters nor the attackers of administrative agencies were accurate in their perceptions. Both groups learned as the years passed that the administrative process is not a stream running always in the same direction, but, rather, a mechanism capable of being steered.

### The Early Battle Lines

To recognize the maneuverability of the administrative process is not to detract from the positive achievements of the administrators of the midthirties. A shattering depression had damaged the nation's morale as well as its business. Resentments ran deep in a population rightly or wrongly convinced that their economic lives were effectively in the power of too few and too unenlightened hands. Elsewhere in the world men were exhibiting an alarmingly ready willingness to exchange political liberty for promises of material welfare. Even in this country the corrosives of discontent had begun to lodge in the crannies of our political structure. Cracks might have widened into fissures if the acids of that difficult period had not soon been somewhat diluted by the legislation of the early Roosevelt years. The administrative agencies of that time, said James M. Landis, a former Harvard Law School dean who had himself become a government official, reflected "an effort to grant protection to the common man in the realization of new liberties born of a new economic order. The continuity of the common man's radio programs, the security of his bank deposits, his protection against unfair discrimination in employment, his right to have light and power at reasonable rates, his protection against fraud and chicanery in our securities markets, his right to cheap railroad travel—to mention only a few of the necessities of modern life—these are some of the new liberties which make up the right of today's common man to the pursuit of happiness, and these liberties for their protection today seek the administrative and not the judicial process."

These economic "liberties" were indeed more actively recognized than in the years immediately before. Recognition was reinforced by administrators many of whom, at least in the beginning, were convinced that they were shaping a new and better society. In fact, new shapes did emerge. None can deny, for example, that the vast strengthening of labor organizations was facilitated if not made possible by legal safeguards of collective bargaining; and, while there may yet be disagreement about the desirability of the result, there can be no disagreement that American society has been profoundly altered.

Nor can one ignore the changes in American financial mores that the mid-thirties wrought. We have but recently seen their fruit. What had threatened for a moment to be The Depression of 1954 turned out to be a mere squiggle on the economic graphs; a Republican administration and a financial community that had once been bitterly hostile to "governmental interference" joined in assuring the public that the Securities and Exchange Commission, the Federal Deposit Insurance Corporation, and the unemployment insurance authorities would see to it that nobody was seriously hurt when the business boom began to show signs of deflating. And, in truth, few people were. Bank depositors remained tranquil; there were no bank closings. The stock market trembled; but it was not shoved toward disaster by the ruthless manipulative practices that were common until so recently. The ranks of the jobless increased; but unemployment insurance payments cushioned the shock of reducing purchasing power, so that credit withdrawals led to no chain reaction of insolvency.

Events thus gave substantial support to Kenneth Davis' view that the developments of "positive government"—that is, of governmental action taken affirmatively to fend off the pitilessness of life—have confounded the Marxists. "Marx failed to foresee that government could protect against the abuses of free enterprise, that government could intervene to prevent extreme maldistribution. Marx failed to foresee the potentialities of taxing and spending to provide for the general welfare. *Marx failed to foresee the modern regulatory agency.*"

But if the Marxists failed accurately to estimate the dynamics of the democratic system functioning through appointed officials, so too did some of the enthusiasts over official accomplishments fail accurately to estimate their limitations. Many believed that administrators, selflessly devoted to the general welfare and scientifically equipped to make the pertinent decisions, would ultimately assume the role of economic planners for the public good. This belief was widely shared, though with quite different emotions, by friends and enemies of the administrative process alike. Time has shown that "both the thrill and the chill failed to take into account basic factors limiting the managing and 'planning' potentialities of the administrative process." Indeed, there is much evidence that even in the avowedly "planned economies" of the totalitarian countries there has been a quiet abandonment of any notion that industrial production can desirably be planned centrally.

In any event, whether or not the thrill and the chill were entirely justified, the line between "liberals" and "reactionaries" could be charted not long ago with adequate precision in terms of their professed attitudes toward administrative bodies. By and large the liberals believed that administrators could be relied upon for wise and just decisions, and that, as a corollary, they should as far as possible be free from judicial supervision that might rigidify administrative procedures or supplant the informed administrative conclusions. Of course, friends of the administrative process did not believe that administrators were always at their best or that their procedures left no room for improvement. Quite to the contrary, substantial exertions were undertaken toward the end, as Robert Jackson put it, of "adapting the administrative process to the magnitude of its task." But the liberals did at least have general faith that the process was perfectible. Meanwhile, they confidently believed that no serious harm was being done to offset the good wrought by dispassionate specialists.

Those who disliked the policies the administrators enforced did not share this confidence. Nor were all convinced that de-emphasis of judicial power was wise. The judges, after all, had valiantly stricken down a number of statutes and had shown little enthusiasm about the efforts of "reformers" to tinker with the American way of life. Few of them as yet owed their appointments to the Roosevelt administration. They represented the ideals and values that had proved their worth in the past, and they, more than a newly created corps of administrators—composed of zealots, politicians, and, worst of all, wild-eyed professors—could be counted on to preserve the citizen's rights. From the first days of the New Deal the organized bar declaimed against "the evils notoriously prevalent" in administrative tribunals, and warned that "the judicial branch of the federal government is being rapidly and seriously undermined"—a warning to which was added the gloomy prediction that unless existing tendencies were somehow checked, the courts were "in danger of meeting a measure of the fate of the Merovingian kings." While perhaps only a few lawyers were erudite enough to know exactly what the fate had been, they were confident that it was a sorry one. The "right wing" drew together to save the courts and to stem the encroaching tide of administration. Their early efforts to "improve" the administrative process took the form of legislation that would have virtually disemboweled it.

Support for these efforts came from somewhat unexpected quarters. The greatly respected Roscoe Pound, shedding the scholarly methods that had brought him fame, declared without first investigating the matter very closely that ten unfortunate tendencies could be discerned in administrative action. These included "a tendency to decide without a hearing, or without hearing one of the parties," "a tendency to decide on the basis of . . . evidence not produced," and "a tendency to make decisions on the basis of preformed opinions and prejudices." Ignoring other scholars' detailed studies of actualities in the regulatory areas, Professor Pound repeatedly emphasized his unflattering characterization of public administration; and though his views were subjected to severe criticism, because they reflected the very tendencies he ascribed to others, they undoubtedly helped to color the legal profession's attitude towards the newer agencies of government.

As late as 1944, when cannonading was ominously heavy on a somewhat more urgent front, the firing continued against the administrative process. "Justice cannot stand half free and half enslaved," declared a prominent Ohio lawyer. "We cannot have, in this country, two systems of dispensing justice—one . . . safeguarded by restrictions and limitations and privileges which have been found to be wise and necessary through centuries of experience, and another system administered largely in disregard of our principles of jurisprudence, largely in disregard of the limitations, restrictions and privileges which our courts have found it wise and necessary to observe." And as soon as World War II was at an end dominant elements of the Congress, under the special leadership of Senator Pat McCarran and Representatives Hatton W. Sumners and Francis E. Walter, moved quickly to limit administrative authority while expanding judicial review. Their efforts led to enactment of the Federal Administrative Procedure Act of 1946.

## The Turning Tide

Almost at the moment when the administrative process was supposedly being put in its place once and for all, attitudes toward it began to change. Consider one example. The National Labor Relations Board, long an object of execration, had complained in 1947 that while its work load had increased by some 60 per cent, its appropriation had been decreased by 25 per cent, so that it was being strangulated by unmasticated business. Soon afterward the elements of Congress that had expressed the greatest fears about such agencies as the NLRB greatly expanded the Board's jurisdiction by giving it power to proceed against unions as well as employers. Thereupon its operating funds mounted quickly. By 1953 it was receiving from Congress an appropriation three times larger than it had been given a decade earlier.

Other administrative agencies had similar experiences. Having been damned roundly the night before, they awoke the next morning to find themselves apparently once more in favor. As time went on the few senators who could remember the palmy days made speeches about the "subversion of the administrative process." They complained particularly that personnel and policy changes had transformed the agencies into old lions, perhaps noble in appearance but in fact toothless, tired, and impotent—or, if still potent, using their potency to wrong purposes. Among the previously administration-minded professors a certain disenchantment became manifest. Within the academic groves could be heard mutterings that perhaps the courts were abdicating their responsibilities, and should stand readier than in the past to review administrative acts, while diminishing their deference to the supposed administrative expertness.

The reversal of attitudes toward administrative proceedings is strikingly reflected in Congressional reaction to *Wong Yang Sung v. McGrath*, decided by the Supreme Court in 1950. Wong, a Chinese seaman, had been ordered deported after a hearing that concededly fell below the standards of the Administrative Procedure Act of 1946. The single question before the Supreme Court was whether administrative hearings in deportation cases must conform to the statute's requirements.

One of the most earnestly declared purposes of the Administrative Procedure Act had been to curtail what its sponsors believed was a widespread practice of embodying in one person the inconsistent duties of prosecutor and judge. The then supporters of the administrative process regarded this as a vastly overblown issue, but rarely did the backers of the proposed legislation fail to inveigh against the "combination of functions" that they thought was usual. As a matter of fact, this practice was never as general as the critics of the administrative agencies supposed;

five years before the 1946 statute was enacted a search of the whole field of federal administration had brought to light only four minor examples of commingling of functions. Until a short while previously, it is true, the Immigration and Naturalization Service had been one of the offenders, for it had indulged the objectionable practice of merging the duties of judge and prosecutor in the single person of the officer assigned to conduct a deportation hearing. But even that agency had mended its ways after a critical investigation by a special committee appointed by the Secretary of Labor, within whose jurisdiction the Service was then lodged. In June of 1940, however, the Service was transferred from the Department of Labor to the Department of Justice, and thus came under the direction of the Attorney General. Then, growing tougher, it had reverted to its former methods. In the hearing of Seaman Wong the Supreme Court discovered "a perfect exemplification" of the very practices that had been so vigorously condemned in earlier years.

The duality of functions found to have occurred in Wong's case, the Court said in an opinion by Mr. Justice Jackson, "if objectionable anywhere, would seem to be particularly so in the deportation proceeding, where we frequently meet with a voteless class of litigants who not only lack the influence of citizens, but who are strangers to the laws and customs in which they find themselves involved and who often do not even understand the tongue in which they are accused. Nothing in the nature of the parties or proceedings suggests that we should strain to exempt deportation proceedings from reforms in administrative procedure applicable generally to federal agencies." And so the Court held that the public authorities had used illegal methods in finding poor Wong deportable.

The decision was noted with interested satisfaction in the professional periodicals. The *Notre Dame Lawyer* thought that the Supreme Court had acquired some of Senator McCarran's spirit; the *Ohio State Law Journal* was confident that the "intent of the framers" had been followed by the judges; and other law review editors joined in the congratulatory refrain. But those who had ostensibly been intent on safeguarding individuals from the dangers of administrative abuse did not greet Wong's triumph over "bureaucratic despotism" with the rejoicing one might have expected. The Supreme Court spoke on February 20, 1950. The Congress spoke back on September 27, 1950. It enacted a rider to an Appropriation Act that in terms exempted "exclusion or expulsion of aliens" from the provisions of the Administrative Procedure Act. Then, in the Immigration and Nationality Act of 1952, popularly known as the McCarran-Walter Act after its chief sponsors (who were also, it will be recalled, chief sponsors of the Administrative Procedure Act), the exemption was copper-riveted by providing that exclusion and deportation hearings could from now on be held by any immigration officer the Attorney General might care to designate, who could also simultaneously discharge whatever other duties the Attorney General might prescribe. Thus was *Wong Yang Sung v. McGrath* overruled.

The legislative aftermath of that case lays a shadow of doubt upon the genuineness of some noisily expressed fears of administrative injustice. The shadow would perhaps not be heavy if this episode stood alone. After all, a substantial segment of the Congress has traditionally shown symptoms of xenophobia, reflected in a stiffly unsympathetic attitude toward the problems of aliens. Despite the Supreme Court's repeated comments in the 1920's that administrative proceedings involving the foreign born were lacking in the security associated with judicial proceedings, and despite the notorious insensitivity with which the Immigration and Naturalization Service at times discharged its duties, the would-be revisionists of the administrative process never focused their attention on this running sore. They preferred instead to concentrate on administrators whose conduct was positively Chesterfieldian compared with that of the alien-hunters. So if the erstwhile antiadministrators had done no more than express anew their confidence in immigration officers, they would merely have been consistently inconsistent.

In recent years, however, the old time foes of "the bureaucracy" have gone much farther. They have cheerfully thrust into administrative hands a vastly enlarged responsibility for decisions of utmost delicacy. Even a partial catalog is impressive:

1. Censorial powers have been exercised with scanty adverse reaction from those who once fulminated against the dangers of administrative despotism;
2. The withholding of governmental information from the public affected by it has come to be taken virtually for granted, confidence being reposed in the administrators who will decide what it is safe for the public to know;
3. The individual's "loyalty" and his possible riskiness to the nation's security have been adjudged by administrators with slight attention to the procedural norms thought essential in other sorts of adjudications;
4. Detention of political deviants in times of crisis has been authorized, not on the basis of proof that they have committed an offense but on the basis of an administrator's ex parte decision that perhaps they might do so in future;
5. The Attorney General has been empowered to prescribe regulations for the registration of printing presses and mimeograph machines of Communist organizations—a measure that prompted a leading news-

paper executive to exclaim, "This is the nearest thing to press licensing that has existed on this continent since colonial times. Not only is it a departure from principles established for three centuries in the English speaking world; it is, inferentially, a tribute to the efficacy of Communist propaganda that no American ought to make";

6. A board has been created to determine the Communist orientation of organizations whose activities are in no way challenged as unlawful, with the consequence that administrators may supervise the labeling not only of drugs and foodstuffs (as in the past) but also of labor unions, old-age pension groups, and lawyers guilds;
7. The Department of State, controlling the issuance of passports to those who have desired to leave and of visas to those who have desired to enter the United States, has decisively affected human lives; and, despite its habitual disregard of the allegedly essential procedural safeguards, the Department of State has yet to incur the wrath of the former antiadministrationists on this score;
8. The Department of Justice has had power to affect human lives even more decisively, indeed one might be tempted to say definitively, through exercising or failing to exercise its power to withhold deportation of an individual who might be killed or imprisoned in the country of his origin; but "the bureaucrats" have been little censured for choosing to decide these life-and-death issues on the basis of informal procedures and undisclosed evidence;
9. Illegal wiretapping, notorious though little rebuked, has jeopardized the citizen's privacy; and those who formerly foresaw possible abuses of administrative discretion now join in supporting persistent legislative efforts to authorize discreet wiretapping;
10. The Post Office Department has coolly decided whether or not to deliver foreign periodicals and other printed materials to addressees in this country, acting upon its own judgment of the reader's "legitimate needs" for the publications in question; and it has done so without criticism from those who used to declaim against "bureaucratic despots" and "administrative absolutists."

During the period in which these and other new powers have been granted or old ones fortified, the former friends and the former detractors of the administrative process have been circumnavigating the globe of government, traveling in opposite directions. The friends, starting from a point on the globe that might be labeled extreme support, have now traveled all the way to the station of extreme fear. The detractors, starting from extreme fear, have seemingly reached the point from which the friends had so recently departed.

## The New "Radicals"

This exchange of attitudes may facilely be explained in terms of concern over national security. The needs of security are indeed acutely sensed by many persons of good will and sober judgment. Those needs render palatable many measures that might otherwise offend. Alexander Hamilton observed that external threats are the most powerful molders of national conduct, bending after a time "even the ardent love of liberty." Continual danger, he said, "will compel nations the most attached to liberty to resort for repose and security to institutions which have a tendency to destroy their civil and political rights. To be more safe, they, at length, become willing to run the risk of being less free." As in Hamilton's day, so also in ours; the tremors foreseen in 1788 are felt realities now. Many endorse with great sincerity steps that may conceivably strengthen national safety, even when those steps may entail some loss of freedom or occasional injustice to individuals. We face today not a sharply drawn choice between an absolute good and an absolute evil, but between one good and another—what "the Greeks thousands of years ago recognized as a tragic issue, namely, the clash of rights, not the clash of wrongs"; and we have perfected no calculus for resolving that clash.

But the facile explanation does not fit all the facts. In the first place, many who deplore entrusting the administrator with the powers catalogued above, do so precisely because they fear that the nation's security has thus been jeopardized rather than buttressed. In the second place, some who have willingly enlarged administrative authority in new realms while deploring its existence in old, may have been moved chiefly by impulses wholly unrelated to their doubtlessly genuine concern about national security. Some supporters of the more recent forms of official repressivism may be the very persons who in earlier years, when national security was no issue at all, were utterly unmoved by abusiveness in the immigration service or by obtuseness among the postal censors. They may, in short, be repression-minded as a matter of taste rather than need.

The fact is, of course, that a persuasive reason for repressivism can always be found, and, indeed, always has been found, by those who seek it. Well before Soviet imperialism threatened this country there were men who, in the name of defending traditional American values and institutions, were ready (consciously or not) to abolish them. Know-Nothingism and Ku-Kluxism in earlier times were mass manifestations of this curious coalescing of defense and surrender, of purported preservation and actual destruction; every generation has produced similar phenomena. I do not for an instant mean to impugn the true patriotism of the many devoted Americans who think that today's new administrative look is a badly needed response to unprecedented perils. Among those who are seemingly fired by patriotic passion, however, are some to whom the term "pseudo-conservative" has been usefully applied—persons who talk "conservatively" but act otherwise; persons who talk, for example, about the desperate dangers of "big government" while simultaneously urging that governmental power be extended farther and farther into zones previously deemed inappropriate.

It is the pseudo-conservative rather than the genuinely conservative element that remains blind to the possibility of "allegiance through principled recalcitrance," and is carefree about the risk that measures aimed at "subversion" may conceivably suppress mere dissidence. "All discussion, all debate, all dissidence," Judge Learned Hand has said, "tends to question, and in consequence to upset, existing convictions"—which, he adds, is precisely its purpose and its justification. But to an authoritarian-minded person, the upsetting of existing convictions is far from a "justification" of discussion; it is, rather, a reason for its suppression. Though very few people outspokenly condemn variety of opinion or originality of thought, many believe inwardly that society is better off without it. Today, as in Mill's day, "originality is the one thing which unoriginal minds cannot feel the use of."

This is by no means a peculiarly American quality. To intimate that it is would be harsh and unfair. Walter Bagehot remarked sardonically in 1874 that persecution of those who were different might almost be said to exist as a fundamental rule of life: "It is so congenial to human nature, that it has arisen everywhere in past times, as history shows; that the cessation of it is a matter of recent times in England; that even now, taking the world as a whole, the practice and theory of it are in a triumphant majority. Most men have always much preferred persecution, and do so still; and it is therefore only natural that it should continually reappear in discussion and argument." Strands of suspicion and hostility and resentment have run through the fabrics of all countries in all ages, though of course the strands are always given color and emphasis by local factors. In our own time and in our own country the atmosphere of international tension has tinted the strands—but, I suggest, some of the strands were there beforehand.

## The New "Reactionaries"

It is not the purpose of this essay, however, to criticize or to characterize those who now find elements of safety in governmental methods they formerly condemned. Its purpose, rather, is to sketch why some of the former upholders of the administrative process (I was undoubtedly among them) now feel that what were mainly imaginary dangers have become real—and frightening.

*Unfitness Coupled with Unreviewability.* During the years of major contention about the administrative process, the great bulk of administrative decisions involved either the ascertainment of past occurrences or the enunciation of informed judgments about future economic or technological developments. The "facts" were to be found in the light of objective evidence about specific nonrepetitive events—as, for example, when determining whether an allegedly injured employee had in fact been injured in the course of his employment; or whether an employer had discriminatorily discharged employees who sought to organize for collective bargaining; or whether farmers had been victimized by a commission agent at a distant stockyard to which they had shipped cattle for sale.

Still under the guise of finding facts, the administrative agencies were also sometimes called upon to make "guesstimates" about the future—as, for example, when they decided whether or not integration of public utility companies would be functionally useful in rendering service; or whether the issuance of a radio broadcasting station license to one rather than another applicant would assure better service for the public; or whether a schedule of rates would be adequate to compensate a railroad without unduly burdening the shipper in times to come; or whether a certificate of public convenience and necessity should be granted to an air carrier. In these matters, the agencies of necessity dealt in forecasts or opinions about future events, and they exercised a judgment quite different from that involved in evaluating evidence bearing upon a past or present occurrence. Nevertheless, as Judge Barrett Prettyman insisted, these estimates of the future could not be "fashioned from pure fantasy, speculation devoid of factual premise." Mere subjectivism did not suffice as a basis of action. The administrative judgments were required to have "a hard core of factual possibility, which can be ascertained and evaluated only upon the basis of present and past events and conditions," so that the rationality of the agencies' guesstimates could be demonstrated even though others might conceivably have reached different conclusions.

Finally, many agencies had the power to make rules and regulations —"sublegislation," as it has sometimes been called—that had the same effect as statutes. But those rules were not immune from later challenge. They were subject to precisely the same examination in court as though enacted by the legislature itself; and, moreover, they were valid only when within the scope of the power the legislature had delegated.

These various powers were indeed vastly important. Note, however, that they had two common characteristics. First, they dealt for the most part with essentially economic issues. Second, they almost invariably involved factual judgments that could be made with presumably greater skill by specialists than by persons who had less continuous contact with the sorts of issues to be decided. The same cannot be said about the matters that now stir the concern of the "liberals" who formerly viewed administrative proceedings with complacency or active approval.

Sheer specialization of work does not inevitably make for expertness. Some specialization is nothing more than a convenience, as when minor adjudicatory functions are assigned to administrators rather than judges, lest the regular business of the courts be overborne by petty affairs—as would happen, for example, if federal judges instead of employees of the Bureau of Old Age and Survivors Insurance had to pass on the nearly two million pension claims that are adjudicated annually. The administrators who perform that work become specialists without being able to claim any particular expertness. Similarly, administrators who make decisions concerning such abstractions as "obscenity," "security," and "loyalty," which bulk so large in the newer realms of administration, are not experts though they may sometimes be specialists. No well defined educational process or routinized training has equipped them, as distinct from judges and jurors, to determine the delicate issues of philosophy, aesthetics, psychology, or political theory that arise in contemporary administration. It is precisely here that administrative judgment is most subject to miscalculations, distortions, and delusions.

With the benefit of hindsight all of us console ourselves with thoughts of our intellectual superiority over those who made mistakes in earlier days. Unlike them, we do not believe in witches; we do not think that religious differences merit burning at the stake, either for the benefit of the burned or the burners; we marvel that two generations ago President Noah Porter of Yale demanded that William Graham Sumner discontinue using as a textbook the supposedly too radical *Study of Sociology* by Herbert Spencer, whom we now think of as a doctrinaire apostle of self-reliance and laissez faire; and we find ourselves amused that in 1940 Bertrand Russell was barred from teaching mathematics and logic in the College of the City of New York lest he demoralize its sheltered student body, after his writings had been attacked by a taxpayer as "lecherous, salacious, libidinous, hurtful, venerous, erotomaniac, aphrodisiac, atheistic, irreverent, narrow-minded, untruthful, and bereft of moral fibre."

If we feel superior to those who went before, we are probably deluded by our own self confidence. The men who made the decisions of yesterday at which we scoff today were for the most part as well intentioned and as intelligent as are we ourselves, or our administrative officials, and, with allowances for differences in time and space, just about as learned. "Orthodox Christians who are tempted to think that those who stoned to death the first martyrs must have been worse men than they themselves are, ought to remember that one of those persecutors was Saint Paul."

The point need not be further belabored. Human understanding is a chancy thing. That is why entrusting to any person the power, through censorship in any form, to shut off communication at its source is to run a great risk. Nowadays that risk is being taken with gay abandon by persons who used to be fearful of administrative errors. The censors they support are unlikely to have an expertise warranting special deference toward their findings. Yet, as will be shown more fully in a later chapter, their determinations are often dispositive of what can be read. Especially in matters of taste, where so little can be established objectively, real danger exists that an entirely fictitious expertness may limit the review of administrative rulings in a way that to all intents and purposes gives sanction to administrative fiat. Here, much more than in the areas of economic and social adjustment, there may be true need for judicial supercession of administrative commands.*

*COMMENT. Quality and integrity of the administrator.* One question, closely related to that explored in the chapter on the judiciary, is becoming increasingly insistent: What kind of man is the administrator?

The issue has been well put by Warner W. Gardner, based on experience in administration and in private practice before the agencies. Speaking in 1958, after referring to the high reputation of the British civil servant, Mr. Gardner added:[1]

I do not, in all candor, believe that we are moving very rapidly toward top-notch agency personnel. My judgment is, of course, as worthless as that of everyone who has deplored the deficiencies of the present generation as compared to his own. Still, it seems to me to be true that we have, ever since the

---

\* Professor Louis Schwartz of Pennsylvania has made a strong plea that judges rather than administrators should shape the large outlines of national *economic* policy where Congress has not itself marked them but has left policy development to others. He maintains, in this connection, that there is a sense "in which judges have more 'expertise' than commissioners. If the latter are expert in their special fields, the former are experts in synthesis. Daily confronted with the entire range of social conflict, the judges acquire perspective, become aware, as no commissioner can, of all the conflicting goals towards which a society struggles." Louis B. Schwartz, Legal Restrictions of Competition in the Regulated Industries, 67 *Harv. L. Rev.* 436, pp. 473–474 (1954). In my estimation, the asserted superiority of a judge's perspective is even more clearly present where the permissible limits of expression are in issue.

[1] "The Administrative Process," in M. Paulsen, ed., *Legal Institutions Today and Tomorrow* (New York: Columbia U. P., 1959), pp. 144–145, reprinted with the permission of the publisher.

close of the Second World War, done everything possible to make government service unattractive to men of talent. We have hounded government servants to distraction about their personal beliefs; we have made recruitment near to impossible by having months of field investigations interposed between offer and employment; we have, for a brief but catastrophic period, driven out of government service men who were appointed without a thought to their politics but who served under a defeated party; we have steadfastly refused to reward superior talent by superior pay; we have persisted in leaving the Civil Service Commission classification clerk in charge of the destinies of men whose work he does not understand; and—probably most compelling of all—we have afforded consistently brighter opportunities in industry than was done in the days of the Great Depression.

I do not mean to say that the administrative agencies are staffed by incompetents or by hacks. Their level of capacity is astonishingly high, when all things are considered, and every agency of any size will have a few men of unusual talent who have given their lives to government service either because of a sense of public service or because of the challenge of the extraordinarily large responsibilities that are theirs. With that recognition, my judgment remains that the general level of agency competence is substantially lower than it was prewar, and a great deal lower than it ought to be to achieve the most effective government.

Scandals involving extracurricular benefits to government officials, ranging from freezers to yachting vacations, have drawn attention to the problem of conflicts of interest in government. The report by a presidential commission, composed of Judge Calvert Magruder, Dean Jefferson Fordham, and Professor Bayless Manning, was employed by the President in framing his message to Congress of April 27, 1961. This message, recommending revised legislation dealing with conflicts of interest, also observed that the basic factor controlling public officials was "the moral tone of the society in which they live." The problem of quality in personnel was also one of the issues raised by James M. Landis in his "Report on Regulatory Agencies to the President-Elect" (December 1960).

*Further References.* An early study significant in the development of administrative law was Dickinson, *Administrative Justice and the Supremacy of Law in the United States* (New York: Russell & Russell, 1929). An illuminating study of the administrative arm of the federal government is summed up in *U.S. Attorney General's Committee on Administrative Procedure, Final Report* (1941). Recommendations from a more general point of view were set forth by the Second Hoover Commission: Commission on Organization of the Executive Branch of the Government, *Task Force on Legal Services and Procedures* (1955).

A vivid (and influential) report to the general public on one unhappy aspect of the administrative process is Louis. L. Jaffe's "The Scandal in TV Licensing," *Harper's Magazine*, vol. 215, p. 77 (September 1957). See also Jaffe, "The Effective Limits of the Administrative Process," *Harvard Law Review*, vol. 67, 1954, p. 1,105.

Those who would like a first-hand picture of private practice before federal administrative agencies will enjoy reading Horsky, *The Washington Lawyer* (Boston: Little, Brown, 1952), especially Chapter 2.

CHAPTER 8

# The Bar

THIS PART OF THE BOOK ON LAWMAKing Institutions has looked at the judge, the legislature, and the administrator; it closes with an examination of the work of the legal profession in the engineering of the legal structure.

The landscape here is uneven, and the view is markedly different from varying vantage points. Lawyers, from one point of view, are seen as individuals helping to shape the law as influential citizens, as legislators, and as government officials. A second aspect, easily overlooked, is the lawyer's work as advocate, assembling and shaping the materials for decision by courts. Two instances alone—the development of the cases on the power of the President to seize the steel mills and on the legality of racial segregation—dramatize this side of the lawyer's work; but isolated examples cannot expose the steady accretion to legal development which flows from daily appearances by advocates before thousands of courts and administrative tribunals. Closely related is the work of the lawyer in preparing contracts, corporate charters, union bylaws, and other documents which structure legal institutions, and in drafting legislation. Still another, and markedly different, aspect emerges from activities in professional organizations at the local level and, most especially, at national conclaves, when lawyers purport to speak for the bar on public questions.

The picture also changes with the passage of time. Writing in 1933, A. A. Berle presented a grim view of the decline of the bar from an earlier position of leadership in the public interest. We open the chapter by this critical appraisal, which will be followed by a more pleasing report.

# THE MODERN LEGAL PROFESSION  By A. A. Berle

THE POSITION of the legal profession in American life illustrates in clearest relief the consequences for the profession of the rapid industrial and financial growth of the community.

One of the results of capitalistic organization in the United States lay in the transfer some time toward the end of the nineteenth century of the responsible leadership in social development from the lawyer to the business man; at the same time the position of the lawyer had an even greater appeal than before. It remained one of the careers through which a man could attain influence and wealth even without having capital at the start; and the fortunes accumulated by a few men at the bar were taken as an index of its normal possibilities. Since the prevalent democratic philosophy made entrance to a profession not the privilege of a small group but the right of any individual, subject only to minimum standards of education and training, the number of those who entered upon the study of law increased enormously.

This coincided with the period of great industrial development and rapid exploitation of resources. The manipulations of the railroad builders, the oil pioneers, the utilities and traction magnates, and the accompanying political corruption were tolerated by the community because they seemed to be connected with an unparalleled rise of the mechanisms of industry, transportation and urban life. In defending, legalizing and maintaining this exploitative development the legal profession found its principal function. Many of the great American law firms of today, recognized as the leaders of the bar, owe their origin to the safe navigation of clients through some scandal of the latter part of the nineteenth century: the defense of the Tweed ring, the safeguarding of the interests of Jay Gould in Erie, the wreck of the Père Marquette railroad and the violences of the Harriman administration, the wreck of the Rock Island railroad. The impression grew that the lawyer existed to serve and not to counsel his clients.

The law firm became virtually an annex to some group of financial

---

Reprinted from *Encyclopaedia of the Social Sciences*, Vol. 9 (New York: Macmillan, 1933), pp. 340–345, with the permission of the author and the publisher. (Copyright 1933, 1961 by The Macmillan Co.) The author, Professor of Law at Columbia University, has engaged in private practice and has held numerous important government positions, including that of Assistant Secretary of State. His books include *The Modern Corporation and Private Property* (with G. C. Means, 1932), *The Twentieth Century Capitalistic Revolution* (1954), and *The American Economic Republic* (1963).

promoters, manipulators or industrialists; and such firms have dominated the organized profession, although they have contributed little of thought, less of philosophy and nothing at all of responsibility or idealism.

What they have contributed, however, is the creation of a legal framework for the new economic system, built largely around the modern corporation, the division of ownership of industrial property from control and the increasing concentration of economic power in the industrial east in the hands of a few individuals....

The rise of the business, or corporation, lawyer in the United States as the fine flower of the profession almost of necessity produced its reaction. Some men, like Justice Brandeis, after attaining primacy in that branch of the profession revolted from the cynicism of its views, developed a philosophy of the protection of individual rights and made their national reputations in pleading, often without pay, causes which turned on the protection of the public against exploitation by private groups. This revolt indicated that the problem was as much economic and philosophical as legal: the law can do little more than reflect and bring into order the current mores and aggregated desires of individuals.

To make action effective the lawyer who had public interests was forced either to turn to his books and become a scholar or to turn to public life and go on the bench or into political life. But political participation was a two-edged instrument. The forces of financial concentration needed political influence quite as much as they did legal ability; and the lawyer who was successful in public life was all the more valuable to them. The common result was that after a relatively brief period of public office the lawyer returned to his profession with enhanced reputation and became a more effective servant of the evolving industrial scheme. The lawyer as statesman or public officer too readily yielded to the temptations of the lawyer as practitioner and interpreted or served the business groups instead of furnishing a statesmanlike leadership. He conceived of himself as a technician rather than an originator of policy.

A third and more recent tendency is illustrated by those lawyers who seek rather to be scholars at the bar than great commercialists and who aim to mold legal doctrines through study, research, writing and teaching, translating them into legal reality through practise either private or for various public bodies. The mere technicians leave little trace behind; but the lawyer-scholars may exercise a real influence on the legal profession. The literature of the law falls very largely to them and to teachers and judges.

A cross section of the legal profession of today would show a hierarchy of activities. At the top is the "legal factory"—the great corporation offices of New York and Chicago, having thirty or forty partners and perhaps two hundred or more associated attorneys, and doing a volume of business of several millions a year. The tremendous overhead requires the assurance of a steady flow of a large volume of business; these institutions are therefore largely adjuncts to the great commercial and investment banks; and they use that connection to divert to themselves a portion of the funds flowing through the banking system. To some extent also their profits are due to the use of cheap labor in the form of young lawyers recently graduated, of whom a new crop is available every year.

Such offices are not distinguished in the courts; they act chiefly as financial experts and draftsmen of financial papers. They have contributed little to legal literature, social responsibility or public leadership; but they have been highly profitable and have safeguarded the position of the new business organizations. Not infrequently they have used political connections to procure or defeat legislation—flagrantly in the case of the Delaware Corporation Act of 1929—and in large measure they dominate the bar associations and professional organizations. Below them are the smaller offices, also in the cities, composed of from three to fifteen or twenty lawyers. These men are more often found in the courts; they are lawyers rather than solicitors and have contributed considerably more than have the "law factories" to business life and to community development. Particularly in the smaller cities and towns they divide their activities between the practise of law and participation in politics. It is from this group that the scholars at the bar are largely recruited.

Below this group are the vast majority of lawyers, practising alone or in partnership with another, primarily handling the affairs of individuals and small businesses. They run the entire gamut from the lawyer who seeks chiefly to be a human being to the marching lawyer, who finds it necessary to make his living by dubious means, chasing ambulances or carrying on doubtful litigation for revenue only. While the upper limits of this class frequently produce unexceptionable individuals, the lower limits in the great cities lie dangerously close to the criminal class. . . .

On the continent the educational system, although widely different in detail, has much the same effect on the character of the profession. In France, for example, the recognized competitive examinations of the universities, the careful examination by the technical schools, the virtual impossibility of establishing a practise except through relationship with an already established lawyer or the purchase of his clientele, tend to limit the legal group to a hereditary or carefully selected class.

In the United States, on the other hand, where the idea of equality of opportunity has called for freedom of professional choice, the raising of standards of admission to the bar has been a long, slow process opposed at every turn. The fact that a large part of American practise is made up of common sense negotiations rather than extreme technical skill has tended to favor this view. ... It cannot be said as yet ... that the gradually rising standards for admission to the bar have tended to produce a small coherent group as in England or France. Actually the confinement of the profession to men who are both able and qualified is most likely to take place through sheer economic pressure. The fact that great numbers of lawyers without considerable educational preparation find it difficult to make a living will do much to make the profession again a restricted and more or less privileged group. ...

The historic view was that a lawyer was an officer of the court and therefore an integral part of the scheme of justice. But the conception of the lawyer now obtaining is that he is the paid servant of his client, justified in using any technical lever that the law supplies in order to forward the latter's interest. Reliance is placed on the fact that the opposing interest may pull an opposite set of levers and that in the resulting equilibrium approximate justice will be performed. In the field of the large corporations, with their great concentration of power in the hands of a few men, this point of view has been disastrous for professional standards and public welfare. The financial interests are amply represented by legal skill, while the vast disorganized public, composed of investors, workers and consumers, is not represented at all.

The complete commercialization of the American bar has stripped it of any social functions it might have performed for individuals without wealth. The great law office either does not care to or cannot profitably handle cases which, while of great importance to individuals, have only limited financial significance. The smaller offices and individual practitioners, especially if they are struggling for survival, will extract the maximum compensation from their clients, whether the service is worth it or not. Criminal cases are not infrequently prolonged for the sole purpose of procuring fees. One of the worst abuses has grown up in the administration of property left in trust: a lawyer who acts as attorney for the trustee or who has some other connection with the estate will often create litigation wherever possible, delaying the fulfillment of the trust and taking advantage of every technical obstacle in order to create work for himself, and ultimately dissipate the estate in fees.

Thus the importance and influence of the bar in American life have been distinctly modified by its changing standards. In the early history of the United States there was a tradition that lawyers were fit material for politics or statesmanship. They occupied a dominant ethical position analogous to that of clergymen and received a social recognition not given to the business classes. Their services in the formation of the early state are exemplified by men like Chief Justice Marshall on the bench and Daniel Webster at the bar and in politics, who could and did mold the economic and political institutions of the country.

With the rise of the industrial system and the tremendous drive for economic development occasioned by the opening up of the west leadership was shifted to the captains of industry and finance; and the influential leaders of the bar became adjunct to this group rather than an independent influence. Traditions of public service, such as are found in the medical profession, insensibly disappeared; the specialized learning of the lawyer was his private stock in trade to be exploited for his private benefit.

This is roughly the position of the profession today. Intellectually the profession commanded and still commands respect, but it is the respect for an intellectual jobber and contractor rather than for a moral force. The leading lawyers, especially those who are the heads of the great law factories, must be able to please or serve the large economic groups and they become therefore extremely skilled technicians. They rarely dare and usually do not wish to attempt to influence either the development of the law or the activity of their clients, except along the line which the commercial interests of their clients may dictate. In this respect the American bar suffers in comparison with either the English or the continental system. The British barrister and the French or German advocate retain their liberty of action; they are not usually under permanent retainer from a series of economic interests whose economic and commercial ideals they are almost bound to assume.

The popular attitude toward the legal profession, never particularly favorable, has recently grown even more cynical. The general futility of litigation has given rise to the view that the principal benefit derived from a lawsuit is that the controversy is ended rather than that justice is done. The declaration required of the candidate for admission to the New York State bar, "I will never . . . delay any man's cause for lucre or malice," is not seriously regarded by the public. Despite this there is a public respect for the mental versatility and ability of the bar; its genius for getting results and its peculiar facility for tackling and untangling complex situations are almost summed up in the popular assumption that a lawyer can do anything, although the process is expensive. . . .

The legal profession has been regarded as the intellectual tie between functioning economic and social institutions on the one hand and organized legal administration on the other. This relation admits of two possibilities. One is that the profession merely does what the institutional set up appears to demand. The other is that it can assist in transforming the underlying potentialities in ethical and economic attitudes into actual results in the form of social and legal organization. In the United States the profession has tended strongly to the former function; in England and on the continent, to the latter. Signs are not wanting, however, that even in the United States the direction of the new economic trends indicates the need for a stronger intellectual guidance from the legal profession.

## THE BAR AS LAWMAKER  By Whitney North Seymour

IT IS proper that the bar be included in a review of law-making agencies. This is especially true when law is defined broadly to include not only judicial decisions and statutes but also administrative regulations and those customs and traditions which gradually become a part of institutions. Inherent in this definition is the wise admonition that the measure of a civilization is the extent of its obedience to the unenforceable. In this broadly defined area of law the organized bar has played, in recent years, an increasingly more important role. In fact, it is through bar associations and other professional organizations, rather than through efforts of individual lawyers, that the legal profession has made its greatest contribution to lawmaking. Of course, this is not to say that individual lawyers have not made important contributions as judges, legislative draftsmen, and advocates. For example, the advocate has played a part in the lawmaking process through the persuading of judges to decide cases in particular ways. Thus, in any treatment of Marshall's contribution to American constitutional law, it would be wrong to omit reference to Webster and the other great advocates whose arguments were accepted and became a part of the ultimate warp and woof of the law. However, this subject and the other contributions made by individual lawyers are beyond the scope of this paper.

Perhaps it would be well to be a little more specific about the nature of the lawmaking which will be discussed. Lawmaking has been primarily an educational activity on the part of the bar. A need for change has become apparent to the bar; it has then usually educated its brethren, the public, and the proper authorities as to the need for reform. It has then often, usually on their request, placed its talents at the disposal of the authorities to do the technical drafting or other work necessary to accomplishment. It has not been engaged in propaganda but in the broadest

Reprinted from M. Paulsen, ed., *Conference Marking the Centennial of the Columbia Law School—Legal Institutions Today and Tomorrow* (New York: Columbia U. P., 1959), pp. 174–201, with the permission of the author and the publisher. The author was president of the American Bar Association in 1961 and is a partner in Simpson, Thacher, and Bartlett, New York City.

sort of public service of an educational nature. And the profession can take pride in the fact that with few exceptions all of these things have not been primarily for the benefit of the bar but of the public, with the bar benefiting only as a part of the community.

*Development of the Organized Bar.* Before turning to some of the specific contributions that the organized bar has made to the process of lawmaking, it is well to sketch in a little of its development. First must be the historical background from which the organized bar emerged in this country. This has been so thoroughly covered by Dean Pound in *The Lawyer From Antiquity to Modern Times* that it need only be given the briefest treatment here. Prior to the Revolution most of the young men who studied law were trained in the Inns of Court. These English-trained lawyers became the leaders in their respective communities and owing to their influence, the caliber of the American Bar was kept at a fairly high level following the Revolution. However, after the turn of the nineteenth century, the spread of democratic notions resulted in a growing hostility toward special privileges granted by government, which, in turn, led to a lowering of the standards for admission to the bar. In Indiana, for example, any voter of good moral character was entitled to practice law in any of the courts of that state, and this remained so until, within the present generation, its constitution was amended to permit the adoption of higher standards. During this period the very loosely organized local bar groups, as such, had little influence, as the bar was subject to widespread suspicion as a sort of secret trade union of a privileged class. The result was a thorough deprofessionalizing of the bar and the advent of what has been called an "Era of Decadence," which was to last until about 1870. Dean Pound has said "there had come to be, not a bar, but so many hundred or so many thousand lawyers, each a law unto himself, accountable only to God and his conscience—if any."

The formation of The Association of the Bar of the City of New York in 1870 marked the end of the decline and has been recognized as the beginning of the "revival of professional organization for promoting the practice of a learned art in the spirit of a public service and advancing the administration of justice according to law." This great Association, which was originally formed by a small group of leading New York lawyers, principally to combat the Tweed Ring's corruption of the New York courts, has throughout its history provided leadership for the organized bar. Its purpose is set forth with great clarity in its constitution, which has formed the pattern for those of most later associations:

The Association is established for the purpose of cultivating the science of jurisprudence, promoting reforms in the law, facilitating the administration of justice, elevating the standards of integrity, honor and courtesy in the legal profession, and cherishing the spirit of brotherhood among the members thereof.

The revitalization of the organized bar was given impetus as a country-wide movement by the formation of the American Bar Association in 1878. This Association has grown from an original complement of seventy-five members, enjoying the Saratoga waters and related pleasures, to its present membership of approximately 95,000, and it is today [1959] twice the size it was ten years ago. By 1923 there was an active state bar association in every state and territory of the Union. In addition, many local bar associations were organized. Of course, these associations are of varying strength and effectiveness. Some are purely social, meeting annually for purposes of comradeship. Others, however, like The Association of the Bar, today have fifty or more active committees vigorously dealing with problems of law reform, discipline, reviews of legislation, quality of judges, and so forth. In a city like New York, a lawyer feeling some obligation to participate in the activities of the organized bar would ordinarily belong to the American Bar Association, the New York State Bar Association, The Association of the Bar of the City of New York, the New York County Lawyers' Association, The American Judicature Society, and probably several other professional organizations. Thus the individual lawyer now participates in many choruses of professional opinion and the organized bar speaks with increasing frequency and authority. . . .

The organized bar has participated in lawmaking in a wide variety of fields. I will attempt to touch upon most of the major fields, but they will not exhaust the list of these activities.

It is appropriate to touch first upon these activities which most intimately concern the quality of the bar itself. Incidentally, it is impressive to note that, here as elsewhere, almost all of the activities in which the organized bar engages are in the direction of insuring greater responsibility on the part of the bar to the public rather than merely adding new advantages to those now enjoyed by members of the legal profession. Where the latter is arguably the case, as in the growing movement to suppress unlawful practice by laymen, there is nevertheless the important factor of insuring to the public the benefit of responsible professional help in place of nonprofessional help operating without the protection of required training or ethical standards.

The development of legal education to its present high state has resulted from the cooperative effort of the organized bar and the law teachers. Very shortly after the foundation of the American Bar Association, it created in 1893 a Section on Legal Education, which since that time has been its principal arm for improving American legal education.

This Section was active from the beginning and, as previously noted, successfully carried forward a program of sharp improvement in educational standards. The Association of American Law Schools, the teaching profession's complementary organization to the Section on Legal Education, was formed under the aegis of the American Bar Association in 1900. Ever since, it has worked in close cooperation with the organized bar. Improvements in legal education have in some instances been embodied in court rule, in others they have been made the subject of statute; but all have been important in building a strong bar, increasingly willing to shoulder its obligations to the public.

The statement and enforcement of explicit ethical standards has been and is of primary concern to the organized bar. The first Code of Ethics in the United States was formulated and adopted by the Alabama State Bar Association in 1887. By 1908 this Code, which was based on Sharswood's *Professional Ethics* and Hoffman's Resolutions, had been adopted with slight changes in ten other states. In that same year, the American Bar Association promulgated its Canons of Ethics, which by 1914 had been adopted by thirty-one of the forty-four existing state bar associations. Since 1914 many additional states have adopted the Association's Canons, substantially intact. Thus, this code serves as the controlling guide on matters of ethics in practically all jurisdictions. It is the keystone of disciplinary action, and the subject of appeal where lawyers are in doubt as to the propriety of their conduct and desire advice.

The organized bar did not stop with laying down a code of ethics for the practicing lawyer, but in addition, promulgated Canons of Judicial Ethics. These Canons were prepared in 1922 by a committee headed by Chief Justice Taft, and were adopted by the American Bar Association in 1924. Since they have been subject to occasional amendments to keep them abreast of modern developments. For example, in 1952 the American Bar Association adopted the report of a Special Committee headed by the late John W. Davis that the Canons be amended to provide that the "telecasting of court proceedings are calculated to detract from the essential dignity of the proceedings, degrade the court and create misconceptions with respect thereto in the minds of the public." This Canon is now the subject of widespread discussion between the bar and some of the media. But generally this amendment as well as the other Canons are accepted by the bar, and furnish a guide to conduct where formerly guides were lacking.

Along with the Canons of Professional and Judicial Ethics came the development of examinations into character and fitness. Originally bar examinations were entirely inadequate, and there was no semblance of uniformity in the several states. The following story, which is probably not apocryphal in origin, is related in Professor Hurst's notable book about *American Law Makers,* concerning an examination conducted by Abraham Lincoln while reclining in a bathtub:

> Motioning me to be seated, he [Lincoln] began his interrogatories at once, without looking at me a second time to be sure of the identity of his caller. "How long have you been studying?" he asked. "Almost two years," was my response. "By this time, it seems to me," he said laughingly, "you ought to be able to determine whether you have in you the kind of stuff out of which a good lawyer can be made. What books have you read?" I told him, and he said it was more than he read before he was admitted to the bar.
>
> He asked me in a desultory way the definition of a contract, and two or three fundamental questions, all of which I answered readily, and I thought, correctly. Beyond these meager inquiries, as I now recall the incident, he asked nothing more. As he continued his toilet, he entertained me with recollections —many of them characteristically vivid and racy—of his early practice and the various incidents and adventures that attended his start in the profession. The whole proceeding was so unusual and queer, if not grotesque, that I was at a loss to determine whether I was really being examined at all or not. After he had dressed we went downstairs and over to the clerk's office in the courthouse, where he wrote a few lines on a sheet paper, and, inclosing it in an envelope directed me to report with it to Judge Logan, another member of the examining committee, at Springfield.
>
> The next day I went to Springfield, where I delivered the letter as directed. On reading it, Judge Logan smiled, and, much to my surprise, gave me the required certificate without asking a question beyond my age and residence, and the correct way of spelling my name. The note from Lincoln read: "My dear Judge:—The bearer of this is a young man who thinks he can be a lawyer. Examine him, if you want to. I have done so, and am satisfied. He's a good deal smarter than he looks to be."

In 1931, the organized bar led the way to the creation of a National Conference of Bar Examiners. This organization has steadily improved the quality and uniformity of bar examinations. While a perhaps excessive tolerance for repeaters sometimes permits a candidate, whose outstanding quality is persistence, to slip through after failing many examinations, the reasonable effectiveness of the modern testing procedure is generally recognized.

The bar has also been concerned with trying to screen out candidates whose character (aside from educational training) makes them unfit for the profession. Today, such examinations are generally conducted after graduation from law school and just before admission. While some character committees are equipped with adequate investigatory staffs, others are not so fortunate. There is a general feeling that improvement in these character examinations is possible and desirable. Furthermore, there is a growing feeling that character should be screened earlier than after graduation from law school. There is a tendency to deal overtolerantly with the possible deficiencies of those who have already invested three years in law school study. Many of the law schools are now using questionnaires intended to facilitate the early detection of those whose character records may present problems. This is a matter which is now under careful study by the law schools and the bar, and everyone recognizes the difficulties of the problem. If it were possible to devise a foolproof character examination before law school study begins, it would be of great advantage to the public, the schools, and the bar.

Closely related to these problems has been the movement for an integrated bar, which has been successful in a number of states. Such bars provide more effective control over admission and better disciplinary supervision, and undoubtedly give the organized bar a larger voice in public affairs within their special competence. Consideration of the creation of funds to indemnify the public against losses due to the occasional cases of lawyers' misconduct, which exist in England and most Canadian provinces, is now underway and seems particularly appropriate in integrated bar states.

The organized bar everywhere is deeply concerned with these problems. It is evident that the recalcitrance of a few members of the bar reflects on the balance, and adversely affects the public's acceptance of the positions of the organized bar on many questions. The fullest and most comprehensive enforcement of standards at every stage of professional study and practice is recognized as essential to fullest acceptance of the authority of the bar. The progress in the last couple of generations has been very notable.

One of the difficulties with all discussions of these serious matters is that they tend to chill and obscure consideration of the equally important spirit of comradeship which has always been one of the traditional joys of the profession. In the old circuit-riding days in America, the bar of the circuit had such an intimate relationship that professional ostracism as a penalty for misconduct was easy to invoke. Undoubtedly the traditionally high standards of conduct of the English bar are still maintained in part by the intimate associations of the assize messes and meals at the Inns of Court. Concern for the good opinion of one's professional brethren to whom one is sufficiently exposed may be as effective a regulator of conduct as enforced rules of ethics. One of the problems of the organized bar as it grows in size and scope is to maintain the spirit of comradeship while enforcing standards against those who refuse to recognize their obligations to their brethren and their clients.

Occasionally in America a period of public hysteria and failure of the bar to conduct necessary public education has seemed to lead to some brief decline in the independence and courage of the bar. It has been a tradition of the American bar, as of the English bar, that the most hated individual could procure adequate representation. Memories of Andrew Hamilton and Peter Zenger, Erskine and Tom Paine, John Adams and the English soldiers remind American lawyers of the duty to be bold in defense of unpopular individuals and causes. Occasionally public detestation of defendants or their views has led some members of the public and press to attribute to lawyers their clients' misdeeds. Lawyers have then been subject to economic and social penalties for courageous representation. This has caused deep concern to the organized bar. In 1953, at its annual meeting in Boston, the American Bar Association adopted the following resolution:

1. That the American Bar Association reaffirms the principles that the right of defendants to the benefit of assistance of counsel and the duty of the bar to provide such aid even to the most unpopular defendants involves public acceptance of the correlative right of a lawyer to represent and defend, in accordance with the standards of the legal profession, any client without being penalized by having imputed to him his client's reputation, views or character.
2. That the Association will support any lawyer against criticism or attack in connection with such representation, when, in its judgment, he has behaved in accordance with the standards of the bar.
3. That the Association will continue to educate the profession and the public on the rights and duties of a lawyer in representing any client, regardless of the unpopularity of either the client or his cause.
4. That the Association request all state and local associations to cooperate fully in implementing these declarations of principles.

Following that resolution, the organized bars of Philadelphia, Cleveland, Denver, and other cities provided counsel in some Smith Act cases, and the general applause which greeted the recognition by the bar of its duty to assure defense of the unpopular shows that the public actually understands and supports the tradition of the bar in this regard. . . .[a]

Improvement in the administration of the courts has been of prime concern to the organized bar. This concern brought the bar to grips with questions relating to the character of the judiciary, the organization of the courts, and the procedure used in the courts.

It was concern for the character of the judiciary that brought about the modern development of the organized bar. The Tweed Ring had corrupted judges in New York City to the point where leaders of an outraged profession in 1870 formed The Association of the Bar primarily to drive out judicial corruption. Eventually it was successful and went on to many other things. Throughout its history the organized bar has been concerned not only with the removal of unfit judges but with the improvement of standards of judicial selection. This has run all the way

---

[a] Mr. Seymour also discussed the need for legal aid services for the indigent and steps taken by the bar to deal with the problem. This subject is developed by Orison S. Marden, Esq., p. 427.

from pious observations about the importance of character and learning on the bench to detailed proposals for methods of insuring that desirable result. . . .

The bar has been concerned with the need for improved organization of the courts. The courts in most of our states were set up early in the nineteenth century, many of them in a patchwork manner. It was clear that in most states the structure could be improved by streamlining, and that most, if not all, required some centralized administration to assure efficient housekeeping. The Section of Judicial Administration of the American Bar Association brought forward a so-called "American Bar Association plan" in 1938. The essential suggestions for the managing of the business of the courts were: (1) a unified judicial system with the power and responsibility in one of the judges to assign other judges to particular tasks which would relieve docket congestion and utilize the available judges to the best advantage; (2) the strengthening of the judicial councils with representation accorded to the bar and the judiciary committees of the legislatures; and (3) the compiling of quarterly judicial statistics.

In New Jersey, under the driving leadership of Arthur Vanderbilt, which required the mobilization of the entire community over a period of some fifteen years, a constitutional amendment ultimately insured streamlining of the courts. In New York, under the leadership of the organized bar, the legislature in 1953 created a Temporary Commission on the Courts (the so-called "Tweed Commission"), of which I had the honor to be a member, to recommend improvement in the organization of the New York courts. After careful study the Commission recommended a reorganization plan; however, political, judicial, and some professional opposition persuaded the legislature to kill the plan and the Commission. Further substantial progress will require a fresh mobilization of public opinion. Progress has been made in Illinois, Pennsylvania, and other states toward the streamlining of their judicial machinery. Where the bar has been bold enough to take a look at the problem, it has generally been forthright in advocating the need for improvement.

In connection with the federal judiciary, the organized bar has made contributions of a negative sort which have helped to preserve the independence of those courts. Thus at the time of the so-called "court-packing" plan, the bar led the fight against such devices for changing judicial decisions. This was a valuable form of public education. While there are those who say, like the witty English correspondent, that "a switch in time, saved nine," there is no doubt that the bar's fight was significant. Some ten years ago the bar pressed for adoption of the so-called "Butler Amendment" to the Federal Constitution, which would have prevented

Congress from tampering with the Supreme Court's power of review in cases arising under the Constitution. Most recently, opposition to the Jenner-Butler proposals to restrict review by the Court in some areas has been led by the bar, and indeed it is not too much to say that its opposition has been decisive.

Inundation of the courts by accident cases is a universal phenomenon. Everywhere it has resulted in some delay. In some courts the delays have become so critical as almost to paralyze the judicial machinery. Friends of the courts have asserted that unless the bar and the judges find a way to overcome the consequences of this new flood, some other system of adjudication will be demanded by the public. Here is an area which challenges the best thought and devotion of the organized bar. Mr. Chief Justice Warren issued a call to mobilize the bar to deal with delay in the courts in his notable address to the American Bar Association meeting in Los Angeles in August, 1958.

At the instance of the organized bar in Pennsylvania, that state has been conducting an interesting experiment dealing with the compulsory arbitration of trivial cases. In many of the counties the courts may transfer minor cases to arbitrators, preserving the ultimate right of trial by jury if the litigants are dissatisfied with an award. Hundreds of cases are now so dealt with and apparently with general satisfaction. Similar ingenuity in relieving courts should in time commend itself to consideration elsewhere.

The organized bar has always played an important role in the development of methods of centralized judicial administration. Much progress has been and is being made in this area. A federal administrative office has functioned in the federal courts for two decades. The present head of that office has recently said that its creation was largely due to the advocacy of the organized bar, particularly The American Judicature Society....

Along with proposals for the improvement of court organization and administration have come proposals for the improvement of procedure. The federal rules, both civil and criminal, were prepared by distinguished committees with the cooperation of the organized bar, and have paved the way for procedural simplification and reform elsewhere. Procedure in some of the state systems has also been simplified. In New York a complete overhaul of the unduly complicated Civil Practice Act was begun under the aegis of the Temporary Commission on the Courts with the aid of Professor Jack Weinstein of the Columbia Law School and an outstanding Advisory Committee. It is now being carried on as an independent project under the continued supervision of Professor Weinstein and others. The federal rules have taught that simplification of procedure and broadened discovery increase the opportunity for pretrial disposition of cases and shortened trials. While the legal profession does not universally accept these developments and there is some nostalgia for the good old days when lawsuits were more like games of skill, substantial leadership for reform has always come from the organized bar. Judicial Councils in many of the states make substantial contributions to procedural and other reforms and the movement for such councils stemmed from the efforts of the organized bar.

The movement for uniform state laws on a variety of subjects has also been fostered by the organized bar. Here the American Bar Association has made an outstanding contribution in the field of substantive law revision. Its work in this area dates back to the appointment of an Association Committee in 1889. This Committee's work led directly to the creation of the Conference of Commissioners on Uniform State Laws.

Concurrently with the activities of the Commissioners on uniform state laws has progressed the enormously fruitful work of the American Law Institute, created in 1923 as a device to bring together the skills of judges, lawyers, and law teachers in restating important parts of the law. The Institute continues as a vast cooperative effort which is now channeling its energies into such new fields as the restatement of foreign relations law and tax law. The character of the Institute's debates and discussions and the scholarly contributions of its many participants amply demonstrate the kind of constructive lawmaking which the profession can produce when its best minds work together.

In various states, like New York, the need for continued study of additional areas for reform of the substantive law has given rise to the creation of such organizations as the Law Revision Commission. Here, generally on a part-time basis, leading scholars and lawyers keep the body of the law of the state under continuous scrutiny. Where there is an apparent anachronism or some ancient principle appears to have outlived its usefulness, a study is conducted and legislation recommended. In all such efforts, the organized bar has had a part in staffing the Commission, studying its work, and recommending the adoption of its proposals.

The organized bar has recognized that its responsibility for contributing to procedural reforms is by no means limited to the courts. Observing abuses in other areas of government, the bar has studied the need for reform and contributed to public education as to the desirability of improvement in a number of fields of governmental activity. The importance of fair procedure, of inclusion of the essential elements of due process in all operations of the three great branches of government is gospel with most lawyers and therefore with the organized bar.

Perhaps the bar's most notable single accomplishment in these other areas has been its contribution to reforms in the procedure employed by administrative agencies. With the expansion of governmental activities there has been a concurrent expansion of administrative bodies, both at the federal and at local levels. There are some who believe that these agencies should, in general, be left free of procedural restraints. A few zealous advocates even suggest that the administrative agencies cannot properly function unless they are left unfettered and administrators given the widest possible discretion as to all aspects of procedure. But it became evident at an early stage in this proliferation of administrative activity that the usual consequences of exercise of unfettered power by the new and vast bureaucracies were leading to abuses of the rights of many citizens. The absence of rules encouraged an absence of the basic elements of fair trial and due process. Recognizing that all of the rules applicable to courts might not apply to the conduct of administrative hearings, the bar nevertheless felt that many of them could be remolded to protect the new machinery from abuse. Accordingly, the Administrative Procedure Act was ultimately adopted as a result of the insistence of the organized bar, and improvements in administration have been the subject of steady consideration ever since.[6]

The bar has, in recent years, become concerned with the absence of rules of fair procedure in congressional investigations. Recognizing the importance of the investigative power of Congress, the bar observed that some investigations bore little, if any, relationship to legislative objectives. In others, the rights of individuals were disregarded and congressional committees sometimes behaved as if they were also charged with the duties of grand juries and criminal courts. Following a preliminary study by the Association of the Bar, a Special Committee of the American Bar Association, in a comprehensive study of congressional investigations since the foundation of the republic, recommended the adoption of a code of fair procedure for all congressional committees. This would have assimilated the procedure of the many committees which have functioned with fairness with that of the comparatively few which have not, and would have added some improvements, such as effective right to counsel, which are dear to lawyers' hearts. The recommendation was made at about the same time that a general revulsion of feeling against the worst abuses of such committees took place. While no general code has been adopted, particular committees have adopted rules and the general tenor of procedure has improved.

Widespread criticism of the operation of the government's loyalty and security programs led to a careful study of that subject by a Special

---

[6] For a somewhat different appraisal of this contribution see the comments of Professor K. C. Davis in Chapter 7, p. 351.

Committee of The Association of the Bar, headed by its present President, Dudley B. Bonsal. The report of that Committee, although not yet acted upon by the Executive Branch of the government, was recognized as a thoughtful and valuable contribution to this difficult subject. Very recently another special committee has been studying the passport problem, and its report represents another valuable contribution by the organized bar to the puzzling problem of government administration and the balance of the needs of liberty and security.

While the foregoing constitutes a fair sampling of the major areas of what may be loosely considered lawmaking in which the organized bar plays an important role, a full treatment would require a listing of the actual committees of many active bar associations. Taking The Association of the Bar as an example, such a listing would show that the organized bar concerns itself with consideration and education as to the need for improvement of the law in almost every major field. Thus, committees on admiralty, aeronautics, arbitration, Bill of Rights, various courts, copyright, criminal law, domestic relations, federal and state legislation, insurance, international law, labor and social security legislation, medical jurisprudence, municipal affairs, patents, real property, surrogates' courts, taxation, trade regulations, and trademarks show a catholicity of interest which is not only remarkable but also productive.

Any such summary would be inadequate if it did not mention the growing concern of the organized bar with the concept of the "rule of law" in all areas of the relationship between citizens and government and among governments. This concept, vague though it is, is steadily becoming the rallying point for American lawyers and indeed for lawyers of the free world. A chair on the subject has just been established at the law school of Duke University. It is devotion to this concept which has led American lawyers to advocate the limitation of possible arbitrary action by various branches of our government through the adoption of identifiable rules in such areas as administrative law, congressional investigations, and so forth. And there is also a growing feeling that the principle is the key to appraising the conduct of other governments and their dealings with their own people and with other states.

One of the great developments of the last few years has been the creation and activity of the International Commission of Jurists. Formed originally in Berlin under Dr. Friedenau, the Commission is now functioning at The Hague as an international body concerned with the rule of law everywhere. The bar of the United States has been interested in this organization from the beginning. It has participated in meetings and in support of the work of the Commission. The Commission has reviewed activities in occupied countries which have violated the municipal law of those countries. It has instituted an examination of the meaning of the "rule of law" in all countries of the free world. A committee of the American Bar Association, under the chairmanship of Ernest Angell, has conducted a most fruitful study of that question in the United States. Similar analyses have been prepared in other countries. Out of this should come a general agreement on the meaning of the "rule of law" by which the conduct of governments may be judged. The entire matter is to be reviewed at a conference in Delhi in January, 1959, conducted under the aegis of the Commission.

Recent presidents of the American Bar Association have repeatedly emphasized the importance of the "rule of law" in international affairs. The treatment of that subject by Grenville Clark and Professor Sohn in *World Peace Through World Law* constitutes a major contribution to the discussion. This whole matter is a challenge to the organized bar, not only of this country but of the entire free world. If lawmaking is to continue over any long period of time, it is evident that assurance of general adherence to the "rule of law" will be essential to the survival of the agencies that further the process.

## COMMENT                                       By Harry W. Jones

THE RANGE of ideas in Mr. Seymour's fine paper suggests to me that this discussion, on the role of the bar, is a kind of meeting place for the three that have preceded it. There is, indeed, an element of truth in the old gibe that our American tradition guarantees "a government of lawyers and not of men"; this, first and foremost, because the bar is the main source from which the state recruits its official power-holders: three fourths of its elected legislators, the lion's share of its top administrators, all of its judges. These are figures to which we lawyers point with pride, but there are sobering overtones for the law schools and for the organized bar. Lawyers, to be sure, are the dominant occupational group in Congress and the state legislatures, but are they, by and large, the lawyers we would think of as the better lawyers, the stars of our profession? To be local about it, how many Whitney Seymours, Louis Loebs, and Harry Tweeds do you find in the typical state legislature? And what can the organized bar do to get some of them there? With the candor appropriate to a serious discussion, I ask the same question about our judges. Our

---

Harry W. Jones is Cardozo Professor of Jurisprudence at Columbia University School of Law.

Traynors, Fulds, Breitels, and Schaefers would be stars in any league, but how many such genuinely superior men are there on appellate courts and trial courts of general jurisdiction, and what can we do to see that the bar offers not of its average but of its best—and that the offer is taken up by those in political power?

My comments, however, are not directed chiefly to the work of lawyers who have become official lawmakers, and not even to the matter, so admirably treated by Mr. Seymour, of the lawmaking influences of the organized bar. I will address myself instead to lawyers participating in the processes of lawmaking as representatives of private clients. Some of my ground is familiar and builds on earlier discussions presented in this Conference. In this country, we have an adversary system of adjudication, and we follow, within workable limits, a policy of stare decisis. These two institutions, taken together, make the practicing lawyer a full participant in lawmaking. The effectiveness and fairness of the lawyer's adversary argument affects not only the outcome of the particular case but also the future of the law's development. . . . To the layman it is a paradox to say that the lawyer, as a professional partisan, makes an indispensable contribution to equal and impartial justice. Those of us who believe, as I do, in the adversary system see the matter differently and regret the decline of the art of advocacy, the bar's widespread neglect of opportunities for effective professional representation before legislative committees, and the siphoning off of much of the bar's best talent from litigation to various other professional functions.

But, in a larger view of things, the shift in the bar's center of gravity from courtroom work to law office work represents no net decline in the lawmaking influence of the bar. For we cannot appraise the role of the bar as lawmaker without taking full account of the work lawyers do, in their offices, in devising institutional structures and arrangements for private enterprises and associations. This, I am convinced, is the most important work performed by lawyers in our society today, and we must not lose sight of it.

Our American system makes no effort to extend the enacted law to every phase of industrial, business, and cultural life. Wide latitude is left for autonomous development through agreement, trade practice, and private regulation. The lawyer is the person who must, as Lon Fuller puts it, "design the framework of voluntary collaborative effort." This is the area of private lawmaking, where the office lawyer is legislator. Trust receipts and letters of credit, pension trusts and executive incentive plans—even the power structure of today's corporation and trade union—are all constructions of the lawyer's art.

In this aspect of its work as lawmaker, the bar encounters moral problems of which few of its leaders are sufficiently conscious. My concern here reflects my service, for several years now, on the Joint Conference on Professional Responsibility of the American Bar Association and the Association of American Law Schools. The lawyer drafting a standard "take-it-or-leave-it" contract clause, or preparing the constitutional documents for a great enterprise, is inclined by tradition to think in terms of the interests of the clients who retained him. But these arrangements will have the effect of law—for most practical purposes—on the vital interests of many persons not then present in the lawyer's office. These "outsiders" are not themselves represented, as they would be in courts or in legislative committee hearings. In his ex parte work as office lawmaker, the lawyer must rise above the pressures that urge him toward complete identification with his client's view of things. For he will be judged, in the long run of it, less by his success as a client caretaker than by the durability and essential fairness of the institutional arrangements which are his contribution to law in society.

Mr. Seymour, in his closing paragraphs, says some important and challenging things about the organized bar and the rule of law. I have lately been privileged, in Chicago and Warsaw, to discuss the rule of law with lawyers and judges from every country of Western Europe and every principality on the Eastern side of the Iron Curtain. This much I have learned. The rule of law, government under law, is not a common man's concept. Lawyers are its only accredited custodians. But we are uncomfortably aware that our professional brothers have not always been faithful to their trust. The German bench and bar were the very first bastion to fall, surrendered nolo contendere, in Hitler's revolution against the idea of law. Everywhere on the other side of the Curtain, save only for a few in Poland and Yugoslavia, the legal profession, more than any other, reflects the ideology of the governing class. On this great issue of our time, we American lawyers are doubtless more dedicated to the rule of law than any other group in our society, but not remotely so dedicated as we ought to be.

A lawyer—a real lawyer—should react to unfairness, inequality, or abuse of procedure as a bishop reacts to heresy or a painter to a meretricious composition. What our bar needs is a capacity for indignation—indignation against congested dockets and unregulated contingent fees that threaten substantial justice in half of the civil cases filed in our courts; indignation against universities, including the best ones, that take the lawyer's role in society so lightly that they train doctors in clinical groups of two or three but support legal education only on a low-cost, mass production basis; indignation against political deals that put third-rate lawyers on first-grade courts and tempt bar associations to stamp "qualified" on judicial candidates who are, at best "pretty good" but not really good enough.

If we are to have a living rule of law in which the world's new countries can find inspiration, the organized bar must combine the physicists' dedication to objective inquiry with the single-minded zeal of the old Anti-Saloon League. The task of the bar is greater than we think. Our bar associations need less part-time committee work and more reforming passion. For, when we talk seriously today about the rule of law, "We stand at Armageddon, and we battle for the Lord."

## TOO LITTLE PROGRESS                      *By Morris L. Ernst*

A FEW MONTHS ago the firm of which I have been a partner from is inception celebrated its birth in May 1915. I thought it would be amusing to look at the *New York Times* for May 1915, to recall the kind of world which existed when I started practicing law. I found many interesting tidbits, but I was both shocked and bemused to read a headline castigating the horrible congestion of court calendars. I thought: "This is where I came in." I then wondered if all else was the same with the bar or if our noble profession had made some advances during the past forty or fifty years, and, if so, of what nature.

### The Bar and Reform

Obviously, there occurred to me the mass of social legislation such as minimum wage, child labor, social security, and other statutory innovations enacted for the fixation or transfer of the rights and obligations of the people of our republic. Then I recalled that most of those statutes had been passed despite the bitter opposition of the bar, or, at least, the opposition of the so-called leaders of the bar. Undaunted, I went further in my inquiry because it seemed quite improbable that the bar had made no contributions to our society during the last half-century. I became so desperate that I even looked for any change in our professional function, whether the change was for better or worse, that is, judged by my standard of values.

---

Reprinted from *Journal of Public Law*, vol. 5, 1956, pp. 283–293, with permission of the author and Emory University Law School. The author, a partner in the New York law firm of Greenbaum, Wolff, and Ernst, is best known for his legal work and writing in the field of civil liberties.

In this area of inquiry, I concluded that the function of leading lawyers has changed. In 1787, the leaders of the bar were trial lawyers. Surely in the metropolitan centers, the "leading" members of our profession now have become business advisors, far removed from the search for truth in the trial courtrooms of the nation. Moreover, as an incident to this change, the defense of liberty has lost its prestige in the eyes of our leaders. The defense of property pays off better, not only in dollars, but also in public esteem. We have gone a long way since lawyers John and Quincy Adams in 1770 appeared for the defendants in the *Boston Massacre Case*. In my youth, it was still fairly easy to obtain the services of leaders of the bar without compensation in cases involving civil liberties and civil rights. Now the leaders of our profession hesitate to represent an unpopular defendant without substantial compensation for fear that the public will think they believe in the cause which they advocate.

Another change in our professional function, this one more laudable than the one just mentioned, becomes apparent in retrospect. As our life and law became more complicated, the desire for certainty increased, and this impulse toward sureness naturally resisted change even though resistance creates more uncertainty. This dichotomy may contribute to the fact that the profession is less litigious and probably less inclined to advocacy. We have become, for better or worse, a profession of hand-holders, advisors and negotiators, and I rather surmise that out of such arts, if they be arts, there has been nourished a wholesome accent on what might be termed preventive law. I do not mean preventive law in any fundamental social sense, as pronounced by Nehru, but rather in terms of avoidance of public controversy or litigation. Judge Vanderbilt's remarkable book, *The Challenge of Law Reform*, illumines this problem.

The exaltation of things as they were and the associated urge toward the avoidance of litigation stem in part, no doubt, from the great expense and delays involved in court proceedings. Another manifestation of this professional revolt against the excessive delays and costs of litigation appears in the growing objection of the bar to the jury system. This drive of our profession against the jury concept is of recent origin, and I have not been able to evaluate its effect. The drive is valid only, I suggest, because the bar has failed to come to grips with the delays and costs of the jury system. It is noteworthy in this light that we have not appraised our jury system as two separate systems. Jurors in our towns and hamlets continue their historic function of familiarity with the parties and witnesses from the vicinage, while, on the other hand, the jurors in large metropolitan centers are probably more thoughtful and more objective triers of fact than they were decades ago. Likewise, in the drive against elected judges, the impact of gargantuan metropolises is appraised on a par with the smaller center of population.

Still a third change in the function of lawyers is manifested by the inception, spread and growth of the giant law firm. The growth of the big law shop—50 or 100 lawyers—has aggravated the public treatment of the profession as just one more type of big business. I surmise we are just learning that these giant offices turn out no better work, garner no more take-home pay after taxes and bring the lawyers no more joy than the moderate size offices. Moreover, as indicated by federal judges, the big monopoly law shops contribute mightily to calendar delays and congestion.

### Signs of Progress

In spite of these not too heartening first impressions, with my born optimism I continued to hope that I would find some valued advances made by our profession for the benefit of the communities we serve. I find only six items worthy of mention.

(1) In the federal jurisdiction particularly, we have aided the search for truth by various forms of discovery proceedings. Such disclosure reduces the game of lawmanship in civil controversies and surely helps move the search for truth some slight degree away from the mere game of matching wits. It should be recorded that sporadic valiant efforts have been made to carry over the discovery concept into the field of criminal procedure, but all such efforts have failed even though it may be said that early disclosure as to state of mental health and alibis is closer to universal acceptance than at the turn of the century. We are still far from the British system under which the pursuit of the prosecutor is justice rather than victory.

(2) I think that another important contribution made by our profession is the advance of organized legal aid to those who cannot afford to be adequately represented. This generous concept has no doubt fed on feelings of guilt as we lost our societal leadership status. Free aid is unfortunately undercut because the leaders of the bar, having withdrawn from courtroom practice, relegate to those possessing less than prestige symbols the representation of indigent parties. On the other hand, free service has gained respectability as our highest court has insisted in a few dire cases that the right to counsel was a duty of the state, if not of the bar. . . .

(3) Maybe our outstanding contribution in terms of community service rests on the growing acceptance of arbitration. In my *Utopia*

*1976* I am brash enough to prophesy that arbitration clauses will become universally imbedded in all business contracts. To be sure, enforceable arbitration was fought and greatly retarded in its adoption and growth by the bar. It was a small offbeat group of lawyers which finally overwhelmed the bar associations' plea that enforceable arbitration was unconstitutional in that it ousted the court of its jurisdiction. The bar still does not cotton to arbitration of marital disputes or the guidance to children in divorced homes.

(4) During the past half-century the training of lawyers took a violent shift from learning by living to the case system. I am happy to see a trend away from the dogmatic case theory of pedagogy. I say this because the case system seemed to encourage an emotional preference for status quo and stare decisis. We are now bending back again toward learning from life itself, using the past to appraise, not fixate, the present. The use of law students to try minor cases in court is a cheerful direction marker. To be sure, lawyers whose sons are studying law appear in favor of this type of experience education. Those who have no law student progeny seem to oppose it. The difference is explicable in glandular terms only.

(5) There have been some valued pilot experiments in specialized courts: children's, matrimonial, etc. Also, after the finding of innocence or guilt, there has been a slight advance in the accumulation of specialized knowledge on which sentence might more wisely be predicated. I hear some rumblings which would indicate that judges competent to search for truth and trained in the rules of law to be applied by jurors to facts are not necessarily possessors of the skill needed to determine the cure for antisocial behavior patterns. With the growth of psychiatry and penology, it may well be that this slight trend today may eventually take out of the hands of all judges the imposition of all sentences, transferring such difficult functions to some new skill or discipline. Even today our law schools have no wealth of knowledge to hand on to students with respect to types of incarceration or parole in relation to types of personalities.

(6) In the past fifty years there has been a radical change in the legal and social relationships of men and women. A fundamental upset has been made in this area of the law. I doubt very much if the bar can take any credit for it, however, since the bar was particularly laggard in admitting women to practice, accepting women as law sudents or even, in the case of the New York City Bar Association, admitting them to membership. The Association of the Bar of New York put up such a fight against female membership that it finally resorted to the argument that the toilet facilities in the bar building were inadequate. I remember I was willing

to raise funds for a special toilet for women and suggested that it be called the Texas Guinan Room.

Some will hold that the foregoing six praiseworthy items are too limited.

Perhaps in failing to list others I minimize the correctives seen in the reduction of technical hangovers in pleading, the reduction in the need of guessing between equity and law, injunction and mandamus, etc. Others may value these changes higher than I do. Also, although the shift to administrative law, a fourth department of our government, has been far-reaching and necessary to cope with the complexities of the government-citizen relationships, I doubt if the bar has made any great contribution to its expedition or decentralization, or the creation of an informed public on which all weighing of rights must depend in fundamental terms.

Nor do I overlook the fact that the tremendous growth of the mass of the law over the past century has created an almost intolerable burden for the profession. A hundred years ago, a cultured lawyer could possess a high proportion of all legal knowledge existing in our culture. In 1750, the time of Blackstone and Mansfield, there were 10,000 written opinions —and now we have over two million. In the last century and, more particularly, half-century, the quantity of knowledge in all fields has increased at an amazing pace. Today, no one can be informed. This is not only true of law, but in all fields of human knowledge. As a result, a lawyer of 1956 can possess only a minute fraction of the total of legal knowledge. With the increasing flood of knowledge (30,000 new statutes per annum), the fraction will be further greatly reduced by 1976. This societal trend should have induced the development of popularizers of law, since popularization is the needed new tool of mankind. I find little use of this instrument over the last fifty years by the bar even though newspaper columnists and uninformed editors have popularized in inaccurate terms the most dramatic but not the most significant developments in the law.

If I am right in my guess as to trends, the bar should consider a move toward the British practice under which not every case results in a printed opinion. We now have 300,000 additional printed opinions each year in our land while England has a grand total of under 400,000 opinions. I find no intelligent comments in the journals of our profession over the last decades, discussing the impact of such comparison. The bar cannot keep abreast of the law even in specialized sectors, thousands of the opinions make no contribution to our jurisprudence, and much of the legal writing derives from the ego satisfaction of judges to find their writings in print. Obviously, I am much in favor of dissenting opinions in appellate courts since they act as requisite springboards for later reconsideration of the issues involved.

## Lawyers and Changing Values

I would be less than frank if I did not say that the last fifty years have been a tough period for lawyers, tough in the sense that the changes in our economy and society have proceeded at a violent pace. To the extent that the pace is accelerated, our profession, which has the unique function of stabilizing our culture and resisting change, carries a quite unbearable burden. The conflict between the need of stabilization and the pace of change in any culture devitalizes to a substantial extent the status of the profession, creates confusion in the public eye, and reduces the profession's leadership in a society. This is particularly true in our culture as compared to practically all other present civilizations. We, and we alone, adopted the unique experiment of a just society under which our ideal was pronounced that any boy could be president of a company, college or nation. Our society is predicated on change. Ours is a culture quite different from the caste and class systems of other lands. Ours is a cruel culture since those who dream and fail must to a substantial extent look inside themselves for the reasons for failure, whereas in a caste system there are fewer hopes and fewer frustrations and fewer changes. Lawyers function in the pastures of hope and defeat.

I trust that other members of the bar will enumerate many advances which I have overlooked or which I have appraised in negative terms. No matter what changes have occurred, a mid-century stocktaking such as I am proposing is peculiarly needed. We are entering into the next twenty years where, with new sources of energy and greatly increased creative joys found in our new leisure occupations, our entire social structure will change more violently than during the entire past century. Where and how do lawyers, the holders of the social brakes, the enemies of whim, chance and adventure, function in a society shifting from an audience to a participating culture, in communities aware of the dullness of orthodoxy and where wealth (the present main res of the law) is increasingly viewed as a means instead of an end?

As we move toward the full belly and away from the tyranny of things, will lawyers maintain their ancient symbol of stabilizers? Will we become assimilated with the Madison Avenue boys, those hucksters of orthodoxy and manipulation of people? Or will we be able to reassert and deserve the role of leadership in a fast moving world where clients nevertheless will want to be counselled about rights of the day and of the foreseeable future? We need new leaders in order to discern the future trends of the newly developing environment of our republic. Change demands an adjustor like a governor on an engine, instead of a brake on a moving vehicle.

Whereas I can find little to point to with pride for our profession in the past forty or fifty years, others may be more illuminating or note trends I have overlooked, or ideas which carry for me no enthusiasm. I trust this symposium will not bog down into the boredom of agreement, but rather the search for truth by disagreement with good will.

## COMMENTS                                          By Arthur T. Vanderbilt

MY GOOD friend, Morris Ernst, does not paint a glowing picture of the contributions of the bar to the progress of the law in the last half-century, and yet who can truthfully say he is wrong? The questions linger unanswered. Why has the bar failed in so many states to relieve congestion in the courts? Why has it failed to suppress surprise and technicalities in the trial of cases? Why has it stood by and permitted the wholesale fixing of traffic tickets, every instance of which gives rise to the inference that the traffic court is subject to improper influence? Why does it permit its judges to be chosen as they are, at least in the large cities, by political bosses who dictate the nominees for whom the people are permitted to vote? Why is it that many of our American states, along with Russia and its satellites, alone elect their judges? Why do we tolerate complicated codes of procedure in many of the states when we are familiar through the federal courts with a far more simple and efficient system of pleading and practice? Why have we failed to institute in every state at least the rudiments of orderly business administration in the courts? Lawyers are often made the chief executives of big corporations, largely because of their capacity for efficiency; why cannot part of this recognized ability be applied to the fundamental tasks of improving the administration of justice, civil and criminal?

Certainly the failure of the bar to make the administration of justice workable cannot be laid to the unique function of the legal profession in stabilizing our culture and resisting change, and I am sure Mr. Ernst would not so contend. The delinquency rests first on our self-centered resistance to any change in the rules of *our* game. We do not like to learn or practice new adjective rules, however good they may be. Inertia is our best excuse, and it is not a good one. Even more discreditable is the all too general kowtowing to the wishes of an elected judiciary. For these

---

The author (1888–1957) was Chief Justice of the Supreme Court of New Jersey. His work and writings have strongly influenced the reform of judicial administration. See, e.g., *The Challenge of Law Reform* (1955).

reasons, when fundamental reforms in the administration of justice have come, it has been, as in England a century ago and in New Jersey within the past decade, by reason of the influence largely of laymen, led, it is gratifying to say, by a few enlightened judges and lawyers.

It is disgraceful to a great profession that this should be so. I venture to suggest that if the law schools would approach the organization of the courts, the recruitment of judges, the selection of jurors, the search for truth in trials and appeals, the expedition as well as the individualization of litigation, not from the standpoint of what *is* but from the standpoint of what *ought* to be, a generation of enlightened students would soon be trained who would do for the courts what the bar should long since have done.

*By Charles E. Clark*

Morris Ernst's paper is vastly stimulating and commands wide, though not complete, agreement from me. I share his general feeling of pessimism, for I think the legal profession has failed in leadership where most needed. It has been depressing to see our country tending more and more to rigid intellectual conformity, to fear of the future and of change, to loss of that tolerance for individualism and deviation from the norm which has contributed so much to our country's greatness. True, the lawyers here have been little different from the rest of the community. But that is just the reason for despondency. For they should have provided the leaders who could bring us back to reality, as did a Holmes or a Hughes in past crises. Now we have longed in vain for clear voices among our greats of the bar to force renewed recognition of the truly precious heritage we have in the Bill of Rights.

But on other levels I think there has been gain. Although courtroom performance has deteriorated, it is my impression that law office practice, as it has become more complex and more sophisticated, has become also more technically skillful and adept. Naturally as a judge I regret that the leaders of the bar tend no longer to appear in courtrooms such as mine; but I recognize the economic trends which compel this result, and am not disposed to fight against what seems to be economic progress. And in a correlative aspect of technical proficiency and creative effort, that of professional concern for improvement in law administration and the processes of justice, I am sure that there has been a decided change and a

---

See the biographical note at p. 157, *supra.*

change for the better. Here is where I part company with Mr. Ernst, who tends to decry, if not belittle, these aspects of good professional achievement.

Time was not so long ago, and in England at that, that reform in the courts and in their procedure had to be sparked by laymen; the famous hundred years' battle for procedural reform in the English courts was lay inspired and lay led. Now we have pretty much gotten away from this; lawyers and judges are showing the way for court integration and simplified procedure. It is still probably true that a poll would show more practitioners allergic to court reform than for it. But one effective leader outweighs many negative followers; and now the stimulus, as well as the expert development, is professional. It is producing results. The movement for court reorganization and integration is still in its infancy, although some substantial results have occurred or are occurring. Simplified procedure is however becoming reasonably general. But these are efforts still capable of withering away if discouraged by liberal thinkers; and consequently I am somewhat disturbed by Mr. Ernst's denigrating comments. Even his hearty approval of discovery proceedings worries me. Though I have worked for the extension of discovery, it is but as a component part of a comprehensive plan for simple pleading and speedy uncovering of the merits in issue between litigants. I hate to see it singled out and perhaps overemphasized as a sort of trick gadget to confound the enemy.

Perhaps the question of jury trial affords the best illustration for my thought. I would here stress for special praise the need "to come to grips with the delays and costs of the jury system" did I not realize—partly from his other writings—that he expects and looks for support of the existing system, with perhaps an added gadget or two tending toward increased awards. Certainly I do not find a call for that scientific exploration and unbiased study of this most overwhelming feature of modern trials which the importance of the subject and the present needs of the automobile age in my judgment require. I suggest that nothing is more illustrative of the present-day anti-intellectualism I have deplored than the recent hue and cry against carefully controlled university and judicial studies of that venerable institution—just as though that part of our court system most requiring study and indeed most likely to be rehabilitated thereby is quite untouchable, too sacred for even scholarly hands. I do hope, for my part, that Mr. Ernst can be induced to cherish and foster these good elements in our profession, for we do need them.

There are other fine things in what he says, such as that judges talk too much, even though goaded thereto by lawyers. But I do not need to stress points of agreement.

COMMENT. *The history and accomplishments of the Bar.* The foregoing excerpts can serve only as an introduction to the more extensive literature on the legal profession. Useful material may be found in Hurst, *The Growth of American Law: The Law Makers* (Boston: Little, Brown, 1950) Chapters 12 and 13. An intensive account of the development of the bar up to the Civil War will be found in Charles Warren's *A History of the American Bar* (Boston: Little, Brown, 1911); the current scene is surveyed in Blaustein and Porter, *The American Lawyer* (Chicago: U. of Chicago P., 1954). This latter book summarizes reports which have emerged from the Survey of the Legal Profession, a massive self-study project launched by the American Bar Association.

*Challenge and Response.* At the 1906 annual meeting of the American Bar Association, Roscoe Pound delivered a historic address on "The Causes of Popular Dissatisfaction with the Administration of Justice." The hostile reaction of the meeting was vividly described by Wigmore in the *Journal of the American Judicature Society,* vol. 20, 1937, p. 176.

Further challenges to the bar to assume leadership in the public interest include Harlan Fisk Stone, "The Public Influence of the Bar," *Harvard Law Review,* vol. 48, 1934, p. 1; Jefferson B. Fordham, *The Legal Profession and American Constitutionalism* (Assn. of Bar of Cy. of N.Y., 1957); Woodrow Wilson, "The Lawyer and the Community," *Reports of the American Bar Association,* vol. 35, 1910, p. 419.

EQUAL ACCESS TO JUSTICE:
THE CHALLENGE
AND THE OPPORTUNITY                    By Orison S. Marden

THE SPECIFIC problem which I venture to discuss is how best to assure competent legal advice and representation for the millions among us—and there are millions—who need the services of a lawyer but cannot pay his reasonable charges. The importance of filling this need is obvious to lawyers, for we know full well that our services are essential to assure equal opportunity for a just result. This is true in matters which never

Reprinted from *Washington and Lee Law Review,* vol. 19, 1962, pp. 153–163, with permission of the publisher. The author is a partner in the New York firm of White and Case and was President of the Association of the Bar of the City of New York.

reach a court but involve legal questions, as well as of proceedings in court....

In a society which becomes more complex and sophisticated each day, the need for legal advice and representation becomes ever greater. In the simpler days of our forebears legal problems arose less frequently and they were easier of solution. The average lawyer was able to and in fact did handle legal matters for the neighbor who could pay little, if anything, for his services. This is true today in many places, particularly in rural areas; but in the more populous cities and counties, for a variety of reasons, many who need legal advice or representation, in civil and criminal matters, are not able to enlist the unpaid services of a lawyer.

This is not because lawyers are less public spirited today; there are few indeed who do not in practice serve needy clients and even strangers without fee or at a token rate; but the great mass of those who need the help of lawyers in the more populous areas do not know lawyers as friends and neighbors. It is natural that they should hesitate to wait on a strange lawyer, hat in hand, and ask for free representation. Moreover, lawyers have obligations to their families and regular clients and there is a limit to the amount of free time they can give.

In civil matters, a survey conducted some years ago by the National Legal Aid and Defender Association among legal aid offices, showed that a national average of at least seven persons out of every 1,000 need a lawyer's help each year but cannot afford, or think they cannot afford, to hire a lawyer. The percentage will, of course, vary from state to state, from city to city, but it is probably higher today. In criminal matters, the national average is approximately one-half of all those accused of a criminal act.

The leaders of our profession have long been alive to the difficult problems involved. Entrusted by the people with a monopoly to practice law, the profession recognizes that hand in hand with this exclusive license goes the obligation to provide the services that only licensed lawyers can lawfully render, to all those who need these services, whether or not they can be paid for.

We have attempted to meet our professional obligation to indigent persons on a collective basis, through the so-called Legal Aid Movement which began some eighty-five years ago in this country. The central idea is to supply legal advice and representation for the poor through a community law office manned by lawyers who are employed by the organization or volunteer their services. The size of the office and staff and the method of operation will of course vary with the requirements of the community served. Generally, offices offering advice and representation in civil matters are known as Legal Aid offices and those supplying legal services in criminal matters, as Defender offices.

There are now 224 Legal Aid offices and 98 Defender services in this country. Together they handle over 500,000 cases a year, at a cost to the American people—mostly through Community Chest, United Fund and tax funds—of nearly $5,000,000 a year. About two-thirds of these community law offices have been opened within the past fifteen years, largely through the efforts of the organized bar, at national, state and local levels, with the expert assistance of the National Legal Aid and Defender Association.

Despite the substantial progress already made we are very far indeed from meeting the actual need. On the civil side, there are still nine central cities in this country of 100,000 or more population which are without any organized Legal Aid facilities whatsoever. Some twenty cities of 75,000 to 100,000 population have no Legal Aid service. The existing Legal Aid facilities in twenty-four cities of 100,000 or more population do not meet even the *minimum* requirements established by the American Bar Association and the National Legal Aid and Defender Association. All too few of the existing Legal Aid offices are actually covering the requirements of their own localities. Many are hampered by poorly paid and inadequate staff; others are badly directed by disinterested or inactive boards of directors.

On the criminal side, as Judge Prettyman has emphasized, the need for competent defense counsel who will be available in court when and as they are required is very great indeed. The Uniform Crime Reports issued by the Federal Bureau of Investigation show that city and rural law enforcement agencies reported a rate of 3,640 arrests per 100,000 persons for all criminal offenses during 1960 (a total of 3,959,559). City arrest rates were almost three times higher than rural rates. Yet there are now some thirty-one counties of 400,000 population or more where no Defender office or other organized service exists. In the federal courts, with few exceptions, there is no organized service.

Moreover, the trend of judicial decisions, both federal and state, indicates that the need for defense counsel in criminal cases is likely to increase sharply in the future. [In 1963 the United States Supreme Court in *Gideon* v. *Wainwright* overruled earlier decisions to hold that, in state as well as federal courts, the Constitution requires that legal service be supplied to indigent persons prosecuted for serious crimes.]

No greater challenge faces our profession today than this: millions of our people will need lawyers in the years ahead but cannot pay for the service they must have to be assured of equal access to justice. These services will be needed in and out of court—in civil and criminal matters

—as legal advice, negotiation in legal matters and representation in court.

Organized facilities are unavailable in many places and they are inadequate, in varying degrees, in most cities and counties where they now exist. Individual practitioners cannot be expected to provide the services needed; such a burden would be unfair to all concerned and is impractical except in rural areas and the smaller towns and counties. This is a community problem not unlike that involved in providing medical and surgical services for the poor. Community law offices must be provided, just as we accept and support community hospitals and medical clinics.

There is no need to draw a picture of the great dangers to our way of life which can flow from denial of this fundamental right of every citizen. "Nothing rankles more in the human heart than a brooding sense of injustice. Illness we can put up with; but injustice makes us want to pull things down." This wise observation by the Legal Aid pioneer, Reginald Heber Smith, was put even more bluntly by Judge Learned Hand when he said: "If we are to keep our democracy, there must be one commandment: 'THOU SHALL NOT RATION JUSTICE.'"

But the distressing fact is that justice *is* being rationed because of the unavailability in many instances and in many places of legal services for those who cannot pay. When this occurs, as the immediate past president of the American Bar Association, Whitney North Seymour, observed just a year ago: "poverty and not the judge, may be deciding the case." . . .

I have attempted to sketch the outlines of a challenge which our profession must face and meet with understanding, intelligence and courage. The problems raised are continuing ones and they can only be evaluated through frequent reexamination of local conditions by the bar. . . .

## The Opportunity

The encouraging fact is that we know how to solve the great problem of providing legal counsel for the poor—in both civil and criminal matters—in cities large and small. Over the past fifteen years the Legal Aid and Defender movement has established with certainty that at very reasonable cost it is possible to establish community law offices which have the manpower and competence to handle the needs of most indigent persons in the community for legal advice and representation in civil and criminal matters.

Fifty years ago fewer than 50,000 persons were served by Legal Aid officers, and less than $90,000 was spent in providing this service. There was no Legal Aid Committee of the American Bar Association nor of any state or local bar association. Not until 1921 did the organized bar bestir itself—but the movement could have had no better sponsors at the bar than Charles Evans Hughes, Elihu Root and Reginald Heber Smith.

Beginning in 1946, under the leadership of Harrison Tweed and Emery A. Brownell, and the continual prodding of Reginald Heber Smith, the movement took on a new and dramatic impetus. The American Bar Association, in partnership with the National Legal Aid and Defender Association, undertook to provide promotional leadership at the national level. With funds supplied by the bar, by industry and labor, and the Ford Foundation, a national campaign to establish new Legal Aid and Defender offices, and to strengthen existing services, was under way.

Today—a bare fifteen years later—224 Legal Aid offices and 98 Defender services, three times as many as in 1945, handle over 500,000 cases a year. The rejuvenated National Legal Aid and Defender Association has assumed its rightful stature and is affiliated with the American Bar Association. An interesting statistic is that from 1949 through 1959 Legal Aid and Defender offices handled nearly half as many cases (3,740,144) as were handled in the preceding 71 years.

On the civil side, over 130 Legal Aid offices with a paid staff of attorneys are now rendering service in 126 cities having a combined population of approximately 63,500,000 people. In 77 other cities there are Legal Aid offices operating with volunteer legal staffs serving a combined population of 16,500,000 people. Volunteer panels of lawyers are available to over 23,000,000 people in 128 other communities, large and small, throughout the country.

The most dramatic fact is the rate of growth in the last decade. In the three decades 1920 to 1950 the rate for both Legal Aid and Defender facilities had been roughly 40 per cent for each ten-year period. From 1950 to 1960, however, the rate was over 250 per cent.

If we can maintain this momentum in providing new facilities and if we can at the same time strengthen the inadequate facilities which now exist, it is entirely possible to meet the challenge in a relatively short period of time.

Experience throughout the country has shown that in organizing a new Legal Aid office it is generally desirable to establish it as a separate entity. The most practical form is that of a charitable corporation which will be eligible for tax-exempt gifts and will maintain continuity of sevice and uniform records. A board of directors of some fifteen leading members of the community has been found to be effective and efficient. It is desirable to have representation from civic and business interests and the social service field but the bar should retain control. . . .

Most Legal Aid Societies in cities which have a Community Chest or United Fund receive their support from this source. Some are financed jointly by the municipality and Community Chest. The Legal Aid office should be considered as a legal clinic for the poor, to be integrated into the community pattern of social services in much the same way as health and welfare services. There is no more reason for lawyers to be the sole support of the legal clinic than for doctors to finance the hospital and medical clinics.

The legal problems of poor people fall generally into well defined channels: debt claims, family problems, installment contracts, landlord and tenant cases, and the like. Such matters can be handled far more efficiently in the community law office than if spread around among individual lawyers. Greater efficiency is possible because of the similarity of cases and the expert knowledge of the Legal Aid lawyer as to how they can best be handled. The Legal Aid lawyer's knowledge of community resources usually exceeds that of the private practitioner. The effect of efficiency and special knowledge is shown by the fact that the costs of a case range from $7 to just over $11 on the average. . . .

These simple acts of justice—petty as they may seem in individual cases—add up to many dollars saved for people who need the money desperately; they keep families together and renew their faith in American justice; they enable people to retain their self-respect, understand their rights and so become better citizens.

Legal Aid and Defender offices do not compete with the private lawyer in the slightest degree. On the contrary, they relieve the bar of a substantial burden and through the referral of ineligible cases to practicing lawyers through a Lawyer Referral Service or bar association, actually build new business for lawyers.

It should be emphasized that the mere existence of Legal Aid and Defender offices in a particular city does not mean that the needs of that community are being served. In most cities the services provided are probably incomplete in some degree. In too many places the service is totally inadequate. Our objective of equal access to justice will not be achieved until each local agency is organized and financed and administered so as to provide full service to the community. . . .

On the criminal side the development of organized Defender services has been disappointingly slow. Nevertheless, twice as many indigent persons have the services of a Defender office today as was the case a decade ago. Most Defender services are operated as a public office, entirely through tax support. There are, however, excellent voluntary services which receive financial support from private sources. . . .

An interesting variant, and one believed to be promising for the future, is the privately incorporated Defender service, with a Board of Directors composed of community leaders, but deriving its financial support partly from private sources and partly from the municipality. In this way the Defender himself is under the supervision of the Board of Directors of a private organization and is not subject to political or judicial direction in the performance of his duties.

Experience has shown that in the more populous cities and counties the Defender office is far superior to the haphazard assignment of counsel on an ad hoc basis. The organized service is better because *experienced attorneys are available in court when and as they are needed.* Representation is given at less cost and the private bar is relieved of the burden of handling assigned cases. This is not to suggest that the assignment system does not work well in some places. But an organized service is far better in the larger cities and counties. . . .

Some have asked whether the Legal Aid movement is a step towards "socialization" of the profession. On the contrary, the movement represents the thoughtful effort of the organized bar to preserve the independence of the profession. If we can properly implement these plans—and do so with dispatch—the threat to our independence will be greatly reduced. Fortunately, the choice is still ours—to provide, with comparatively little cost and effort, community law offices which serve to assure equality before the law and, at the same time, to preserve the moral and political strength of our heritage. . . .


# THE PEOPLE BEHIND LEGAL AID STATISTICS

EVERY YEAR The Legal Aid Society publishes a report giving the number and types of cases handled by its Civil and Criminal Branches. What do these figures mean in human terms?

The *Legal Aid Review* in this issue gives examples of some of the cases handled by the Civil Branch in 1959. None of them are extraordinary or dramatic—just run of the mill and taken more or less at random—but they are typical of the great mass—40,478—that came to this Branch last year.

### Welfare and Social Security—1,908 Cases in 1959

A woman came to us because she had no proof of age, which she needed in order to become eligible for social security retirement benefits.

She wasn't able to locate any records and had long since lost contact

Introductory note and case histories reprinted from *The Legal Aid Review*, vol. 58, 1960, p. 16; vol. 60, 1962, pp. 40–42, with the permission of the publisher.

with any friends or members of her family who might have given evidence as to how old she was.

To make it worse, she had been a beautiful girl and very early had begun taking five, ten and then as much as thirty years off her age.

I questioned her at length, querying her about any possible early document—that is to say any early event in her life which could have resulted in a public record.

Because of my questions, she finally remembered an event she had long since "forgotten"—an early marriage at age thirteen in a far back mountain area of Upper Canada.

After considerable international correspondence, we located this marriage record and it was accepted as indicating that she must have been at least thirteen years old at the time the marriage took place—she couldn't reasonably have been younger. With this document, she was able to get a ruling that her present age must be at least sixty-five and "Social Security" was obtained.

### Casey at the Bat

Joe C., fifty-three years old, was arrested in Central Park, on a hot Sunday in June, and charged with violating the Alcoholic Beverages Control law which forbids the selling of liquor without a license. He was arraigned at Week-End Court and held for Special Sessions. Bail was set at five hundred dollars which he could not possibly pay. He went to jail.

Four long days later he appeared in court, still dressed in his baseball uniform. A lawyer from The Legal Aid Society represented him and explained the following facts to the judge. The team was thirsty; Joe was not at bat; he bought the beer with his own money and distributed it to his friends at cost. With the consent of the District Attorney, Joe, who had no prior criminal record and had never been arrested before, was immediately discharged and the case was dismissed.

### The Marriage Broker

The Legal Aid Society, recently won a case for a seventy-year-old woman and her granddaughter. They were being sued by a matrimonial agency for two hundred dollars. The woman's worry—that her granddaughter, an attractive "spinster" of eighteen, would never marry caused her to get in touch with the agency. She told no one of her plans, supplied the agency with a picture of the girl, arranged to have her name added to the list of available brides and paid ninety dollars as a down payment. Soon the telephone began to ring for the granddaughter with calls from "friends of friends" and she went out a good deal and, eventually, married a pleasant young man. Some time later, she had a miscarriage, and shortly afterwards, her husband developed acute appendicitis.

In due time, the matrimonial agency wanted the remainder of its fee but the grandmother would not pay, and so the agency instituted a suit against her and the girl. Unintimidated, the grandmother went to The Legal Aid Society claiming that there had been a breach of contract: obviously, the young husband had not measured up to specifications. The New York University law students, who gain experience working in the Legal Aid's office, were asked to prepare a memorandum of law. Research was done covering cases running back into antiquity showing that marriage brokers had not only been denied their fees but had received twenty lashes as additional compensation. Minus the lashes, the law remains the same today: such contracts are not enforceable and are against public policy. When confronted with the memorandum, the plaintiff's lawyer withdrew.

Subsequently, the grandmother sent the following letter with a contribution of twenty dollars:

Dear Mr. S. Barrack and Mr. Katz here is a donation to your Society I prishate very much what you don for me. you are very nice. you should have happiness and success all your life.
I is wonderful to have people lik you and to be able to help thos who nede help.
I thank you again and again

### Drunk and Disorderly

On leave from the army and celebrating somewhat prematurely his imminent retirement, Sergeant L. got deplorably drunk. Passing a liquor store and seeing an enticing array, he broke the plate-glass window and was arrested with a bottle in his hand.

The next day Sergeant L. found himself in jail and was overcome with shame and remorse. While conferring with his Legal Aid Attorney, he said that he had fought in World War II and in Korea; that he had served in the army for nineteen years and that in two months he would be eligible for an honorable discharge and pension. With despair he realized the consequences of his "little fling"—a dishonorable discharge and no pension.

His lawyer asked the Court to dismiss the charges. He argued that a defendant so enormously intoxicated could not have intended to commit a felony; indeed, the arresting policeman admitted that the defendant had been insanely drunk. He argued in addition that one transgression should not be permitted to ruin a man's life, and he arranged for two M.P.s to appear in court to testify to the Sergeant's outstanding war record and to his general reliability. Legal Aid succeeded in persuading the Judge to dismiss the charges. Full restitution was made for the damaged window, and the complaining witness was completely satisfied.

## The Scofflaw

In early September a young woman came into the Legal Aid Office in the Criminal Courts Building with her two-year-old child and twins, nine months old. The woman was desperate and on the verge of hysterics. She had eight cents in her pocket-book and the children were screaming from hunger. A Legal Aid attorney quickly ordered milk and food for the famished children and encouraged the woman to tell her story. Her husband had accumulated four traffic tickets, two for speeding, one for driving an uninspected car, and one for illegal parking. He had reported as required to Traffic Court and bail was set at $150. Unable to raise the money, he had been put in jail as a scofflaw. He was to remain in jail until October 27, the date set for his trial.

Although Legal Aid rarely handles traffic cases, it was obvious that this family's survival depended on the father's release. Realizing also how frequently other defendants charged with far more serious crimes are paroled at the discretion of the Court, Legal Aid arranged for the defendant to be rearraigned and paroled until the date of the trial. By the date of the trial the defendant had accumulated enough funds to pay the fines imposed upon him by the magistrate presiding at his trial. After pleading guilty and paying his fines, he was released to go home with his wife and children.

# THE PROFESSION AND PRACTICE OF THE LAW IN ENGLAND AND AMERICA   By L. C. B. Gower and Leolin Price

## Organization of the Profession

*The English Divided.* It need hardly be said that the most important contrast of all is that the English distinction between barristers and solicitors is unknown in the States. There one qualifies as a lawyer and thereafter may be described quite indiscriminately as a member of the bar, as a counsellor-at-law, as an attorney-at-law, or just as a member of a law firm, and may engage in any or all of the types of work which in England are undertaken either by a barrister or a solicitor. In England "bar" is used only in relation to barristers. In America the word is used in connection with all legal activities; the entrant qualifies by passing bar examinations, the professional organizations are described as bar associations and the word "solicitor" is never used. This has often led to a tendency to compare the American legal profession with the English bar, thus giving rise to an impression that the contrasts between the two professions are far more startling than they really are. The fact is that the American profession is broadly similar to the solicitors' branch of the English profession and that anything comparable to the English bar is unknown in the States.

No attempt can here be made to describe the details of the English division into two branches. Basically it depends on two conventions: (1) that solicitors do not have a right of audience in the superior courts, and (2) that, in general, barristers do not have a right of direct access to the lay client. The result of these conventions is that solicitors are in the nature of general practitioners to whom the lay client goes in the first instance; barristers are specialists, primarily in advocacy and secondarily often in some particular branch of the law, whose services must be enlisted by solicitors if the matter involves litigation in the superior courts, and whose aid may be enlisted whenever specialist advice is needed. This, however, does not mean either that barristers have a monopoly of advocacy or that there is no specialization among solicitors. On the con-

---

Reprinted from *The Modern Law Review*, vol. 20, 1957, pp. 317–346, with the permission of the author and the publisher. Mr. Gower is a Solicitor and Professor of Commercial Law at the University of London and Mr. Price, of the Middle Temple, is a Barrister-at-Law.

trary, solicitors as well as barristers can, and do, appear as advocates in the courts in which the overwhelming bulk of civil and criminal work is undertaken, i.e., the county courts and the petty sessional courts, and in the many new administrative tribunals which have sprung up in recent years. And many solicitors, especially those who practice in partnership, specialize in particular branches of the law. A solicitor's office bears some resemblance to that of an American law firm, though it is likely to be more old-fashioned and dusty and less mechanized. A barrister's chambers are still more old-fashioned: of course they have telephones and typists, and today some barristers even use dictating machines; but office organization is minimal—most of the paper work being undertaken by the solicitor.

The English system has the advantage that a *corps d'élite* of specialist advocates is available to every litigant whatever lawyer in whatever town he may have consulted in the first instance. This is hardly true of the States. A lawyer in Oshkosh who doubts his ability to argue a case before the U.S. Supreme Court can enlist the services of a specialist in Washington and sometimes he does, but often he will feel it a matter of professional pride to handle the matter himself. Hence, it may well be, as many American observers have concluded, that the standard of advocacy is generally higher in England than in the States.

On the other hand, the English system means that a specialist has to be engaged, and paid, in every High Court case even though none is needed. There is little doubt that this is one reason for the high costs of litigation in this country. This is aggravated by the further division whereby there are two ranks of barristers: juniors and Queen's Counsel (otherwise "leaders" or "silks"). A barrister who has been outstandingly successful may apply to the Lord Chancellor to be elevated to the rank of q.c., and if his application is granted he will cease to undertake some of the bread-and-butter work undertaken by juniors (such as appearing in county courts and settling pleadings) and hope to earn a better living in a rather less exhausting fashion. When a q.c. is briefed, a junior must be briefed to appear with him and, by convention, the junior will be paid a fee equal to two-thirds of that paid to the leader. Accordingly, in the more important cases a minimum of three lawyers will be engaged (solicitor, junior and leader) and the fees payable to the junior, being proportionate to those of the leader, may be more generous than he could command if he handled the case without a leader.

*Professional Associations.* Each of the English branches has its separate professional organizations. The governing body of the solicitors is the Law Society, which has a number of statutory functions (for solicitors in contrast to the bar are subject to detailed statutory regulations) relating to admissions, professional discipline and the like. The Society also administers an indemnity fund, financed by levies on all practicing solicitors, to reimburse members of the public who suffer as a result of the misdeeds of the dishonest few. There are also regional Law Societies which are purely voluntary bodies without statutory powers or duties. Membership of neither the Law Society nor a local society is yet compulsory, but approximately 83 per cent of practicing solicitors are members of the Law Society.

The traditional organs of the barristers are the four Inns of Court which are still responsible for admission to practice and for discipline. They retain their independent existence with an agreeable club life, but have combined to form the Council of Legal Education which organizes the qualifying examinations and lectures and classes for students of the four Inns. More recently a democratically elected General Council of the Bar has been established to deal with matters of general interest to the bar as a whole, and, since the war, this has started to build up a secretariat. And there is now a Standing Joint Committee of the Bar Council and the Law Society which considers matters of interest to both branches of the profession....

The unified American profession permits of a somewhat simpler organization. The American Bar Association is a voluntary organization for the whole legal profession bearing some resemblance to the Law Society, but, it may be fair to say, distinctly more enterprising and active (especially in the field of law reform). In addition to its Annual Convention, attended by several thousands, it holds a number of Regional Meetings which are well attended also, and the various sections into which it is organized are in continuous operation making proposals for the improvement of the law and legal administration. In addition to the ABA itself there are numerous State and City Bar Associations, some of which are extremely active.

An organization, of which there is no English counterpart, is the American Law Institute, a product of the livelier interest in law reform to which reference has already been made. The Institute is responsible for the invaluable Restatements of the Law which are, perhaps, the English lawyer's favorite source of American law. It has also produced a number of model codes (e.g., of Criminal Procedure and Evidence) and has interested itself in the field of continuing legal education—a field little explored in England. Incidentally, the joint research—by judges, practitioners and law teachers—sponsored by the Institute is one of the reasons for the closer relationship prevailing in the States between the practicing and academic sides of the profession. Another reason for this is the nature of the legal training which American lawyers undergo.

*Legal Training.* . . . [I]n America law school training has almost completely superseded apprenticeship; in England the main emphasis is still on apprenticeship.

Though the regulations differ somewhat from state to state the overwhelming majority of American lawyers now qualify by graduating (after a first College degree) at the Law School of a University, thereafter immediately taking a bar examination and being admitted into practice. In England a university degree is in no sense a professional qualification. In the case of the Bar all that is needed to qualify to be "called to the Bar" is to "keep terms" at an Inn of Court (and "keeping terms" no longer has any educational significance) and to pass the examinations of the Council of Legal Education. To assist in passing these examinations, students can attend the lectures and classes of the Inns of Court Law School organized by the Council, but most (perhaps 59 per cent) of those who intend to practice in England instead combine keeping terms with reading law at a university. After call to the bar most would-be practitioners then read in chambers to obtain the practical "know-how" by becoming pupils of a practicing barrister. For this privilege they have to pay 100 guineas (£105) for a year's pupillage or 50 guineas for six months. During the whole of this time they are unlikely to earn anything at all, and the out-of-pocket expenses (excluding living expenses) are likely to be in the neighborhood of £200. Even thereafter, as we shall see, they probably will not earn enough to keep themselves for some years.

The requirements for admission as a solicitor are more stringent. The basic requirement is a period of apprenticeship (articles of clerkship), varying from three to five years, with a practicing solicitor. This can sometimes be combined with reading for a university law degree but the minimum period of articles (three years) is dependent on prior possession of a degree in laws, arts, or science and an increasing percentage of entrants (about 50 per cent) in fact read for a law degree first. Unless they do this they must, during their articles, attend for at least a year at an approved law school. For this purpose those articled in London attend for two six-month courses at the Law Society's own law school and those in the provinces go to classes organized by the law schools of the provincial universities—an arrangement which is proving increasingly unpopular with both the Law Society and the universities. Admission is dependent on passing examinations of considerable difficulty—more difficult than those for the bar.

During articles the clerk will not necessarily be paid anything; on the contrary, he may have to pay the principal a premium normally of 200 or 250 guineas. Happily this is increasingly coming to be recognized as anachronistic and, especially in London, it is now possible for a law graduate with a good degree to obtain free articles and often a small salary. Even in other cases the whole or part of the premium may be repaid by way of salary in the later years of articles, and probably about half the articled clerks are paid something, at least during a part of their articles. Out-of-pocket expenses (in addition to any premium, but excluding living expenses) will be in the neighborhood of £150.

In connection with the expense of qualifying either for the Bar or as a solicitor, it should perhaps be pointed out that in England most university students are now in receipt of State or municipal grants so that this part of the training presents less serious financial problems. In general, however, these grants are not available during the purely professional part of the training if this follows a university course and it is here that most students feel the financial rub, which is only slightly alleviated by the limited number of modest scholarships and bursaries provided by the Inns or the Law Society. In the States the problem is somewhat different. Once the student has graduated he can obtain a well-paid post immediately; he feels the pinch at the law-school stage—and the fees of some of the non-State universities are very high indeed. Fortunately, labor is so well paid in the States that he can generally finance himself through college and law school by part-time work supplemented, perhaps, by loans which most universities will make and which he has no fear of not being able to repay out of his later earnings.

*Number of Lawyers.* According to the Survey of the Legal Profession in 1951 the number of American lawyers engaging in some form of legal work was 202,037, of whom 176,995 were in private practice. Later figures for 1955 give a total of no less than 241,514, of whom approximately 190,000 were engaged in private practice. This means that there was one lawyer in private practice per 868 of population.

Comparable English figures can only be approximate. There are about 25,000 solicitors on the roll, but in the year 1955 only 17,966 took out practicing certificates. Many solicitors practicing as assistants ("associates" in American terminology) or in legal work in industry or the government service do not need to take out certificates and there may be as many as 4,000 more who are engaged in legal work of some sort. Of those who took out certificates some 15,500 were in private practice. Perhaps 3,000 should be added for assistants without practicing certificates, giving a total of solicitors in private practice of about 18,500. The number of barristers engaged in some form of legal work in England is probably under 3,000 and the number in full-time private practice has recently been estimated at 1,230.

Hence, the total English legal profession seems to number about 25,000, and those in private practice can hardly be more than 20,000, or one lawyer per 2,222 of the population—little more than one-third of the American ratio.

*Types of Legal Practice.* By convention, English barristers cannot practice in partnership. Each carries on an individual practice, though a group shares a set of chambers, a clerk, and a small secretarial staff. Solicitors, on the other hand, may practice in partnership or as assistants. . . . The English lawyer tends to regard as typical of his American colleagues the vast New York law firm with the number of partners approaching three figures. Certainly American firms may be much larger than any known in England, where the law imposes an arbitrary limit of twenty on the permissible number of partners—a limit which at present only one firm has attained. But these large New York firms are atypical; to a far greater extent than in England, the small-town lawyer practices on his own. On the other hand, the percentage of American lawyers in solo practice is declining rapidly and among partnerships there is a tendency towards larger firms; there does not seem to be any marked change in these respects in England.

As would be expected, in both countries the major concentrations of lawyers are in the large cities but the English lawyers are grouped in one city to a greater extent than in the States. Nearly 30 per cent practice in London as contrasted with only 12 per cent in New York City, and 20 per cent in New York City, Chicago and Washington D.C. combined.

*Lawyers not in Private Practice.* Of the lawyers not in private practice, the latest American figures give 21,300 in government service, 8,000 in the judicial service, 15,063 salaried in private industry, 1,350 in educational institutions, and 234 doing legal work in other private employment. We have no exactly comparable figures for the Englsh profession. Statistics in the possession of the Law Society show that of those solicitors who took out practicing certificates in 1955, 404 were in commerce, industry or a nationalized undertaking, thirty-seven in whole time central government service, 1,375 in municipal government and 309 in other whole-time employment. Each of these figures should probably be doubled to account for those who did not take out certificates, and for barristers (the number of whom in municipal government is negligible but appreciable in central government service and industry). Approximately 230 barristers and solicitors (mainly the former) are full-time teachers of law.

The main contrast here seems to be in the relatively small number of English lawyers in central government. This reflects the lesser extent to which a legal training is regarded as a preparation for public service. And this is brought out even more clearly if we contrast the role of lawyers in politics.

From the Seventy-first to Seventy-fifth Congresses lawyers provided between 61 per cent and 75 per cent of the total membership of the Senate and from 56 per cent to 65 per cent of that of the House of Representatives. And since the beginning of the century lawyers have comprised a quarter of the membership of state legislatures. In England the percentage of lawyers in the House of Commons since the war has been about 20 per cent only. Indeed, despite the training in public speaking which legal experience provides there is a widespread belief that to be a lawyer is a positive handicap towards the attainment of the highest political offices in England.

*Nature of Legal Work.* While in general the type of work undertaken by lawyers in the two countries is similar, a comparison between the *per capita* numbers of lawyers makes it clear that lawyers play a less persuasive role in England. In part this is accounted for by the less close relation between law and politics in a country which has no written constitution, for a rigid constitution, especially a federal one, tends to make all political problems legal ones. Hence, as we have seen, the greater role played by American lawyers in public life. But this alone cannot account for the whole of the difference. Of even greater importance, perhaps, is the more important part played by the American lawyer in industry and commerce. The "corporation lawyer," whether as a specialist in corporation law in private practice, or as a "tame lawyer" employed by a business corporation, has a dominant role in American commercial life to an extent unknown in England. Here, too, the specialist in company law enjoys considerable power and prestige but his status is far less elevated and he has far less prospect than his American colleague of attaining the presidency of one or more powerful corporations with the salary, retirement benefits and stock options which go with it. Here the chartered (public) accountant is more likely to attain these heights. A most significant difference between the position in the two countries is the greater extent to which the English legal profession has abdicated in favor of the newer accountancy profession largely, perhaps, because the lawyers are only just beginning to realize the importance of tax matters. We in England have at least avoided the unhappy disputes with the accountants which have recently come to a head in the States—but only at the cost of leaving the accountants in control of far more of the tax work.

Again, the English lawyer plays a far less important role in collective bargaining between employers and labor and in industrial relations generally. In the States this is an important and lucrative branch of legal practice; in England lawyers have been almost totally excluded from this field. Nor do we have anything exactly comparable to the "Washington lawyers"—lawyers formerly prominent in the government service who have left it for private practice. The nearest English approach is the ex-Income Tax Inspectors who become called to the bar and practice as tax experts.

*Earnings.* It would take us too far afield to attempt to describe the exact method of assessing permissible remuneration for legal work. It must suffice to say that in America for most legal work (other than probate, workmen's compensation, and court-appointed work) it depends largely on free bargaining and upon what the market will bear. So, generally, does barristers' remuneration in England. Solicitors' remuneration, on the other hand, depends to a large extent on fixed statutory scales dependent, in conveyancing matters, on the value of the property concerned, and in other matters on the amount of work involved. Only recently, and still only in non-litigation and nonconveyancing work, has some measure of flexibility been introduced so that remuneration can openly be graded according to the skill, specialized knowledge, and responsibility involved, the difficulty of the case, and the success and importance of the job.

The result is what matters for our purpose. And there seems little doubt that despite the fact that American lawyers are far thicker on the ground they yet contrive to be better paid. The average net income of all lawyers in the States in 1954 is said to have been $10,220, an increase from $9,375 in the year 1951. Even among associates in law firms the average income was $7,800; this is not surprising since a graduate with a good record at one of the better law schools can expect to obtain a starting salary of $4,000–6,000 and to double it in about five years. Salaried lawyers in private industry were the highest paid group, with an average net income of $13,770, but those in government employment did little better than associates, with an average of $7,920 and without, of course, the same prospects as associates. Full-time law teachers averaged $9,000; in universities they are generally paid rather more generously than their colleagues in most other departments, since they are appointed to full professorships at an early age without having to rise slowly to the top of the academic pyramid. There were significant regional differences, the Middle East being the best paying area and the North-West the lowest. But the highest average for any state was California ($12,180) and the highest average for a large city San Francisco ($13,157) and not, as might have been expected, New York or Washington. To an ever-increasing extent lawyers rely for their income on business clients rather than on individuals. Peak earnings are not reached until after twenty-five years' practice, between the ages of fifty-five and sixty, and provision for retirement presents problems. The ratio of net to gross incomes of private practitioners is about 61 per cent.

In contrast with these detailed figures we can offer for England little more than inspired guesses.

Out of some forty junior barristers in eight leading sets of "common law" chambers who in 1953 disclosed their earnings to a special correspondent of *The Times*, only one earned over £5,000 a year. Of the others six earned over £3,000, five between £2,000 and £3,000, and nine between £1,000 and £2,000. In these chambers the average earnings of juniors three years after call to the bar were under £250 a year. For juniors of five to nineteen years' standing the average was under £800 a year. For juniors of twenty years' standing and more the average was £2,700 a year. The over-all average for the chambers (excluding the newly called) was £1,400. These were the figures for the best sets of chambers in the Temple in 1953, when there was still something like a boom in litigation. In other chambers in the Temple and Lincoln's Inn earnings were probably substantially less; and since 1953 there has been a general falling off in work. Today the average barrister's earnings are probably lower than the figures quoted in this paragraph....

The largest legal incomes are made by a tiny number of q.c.s; and, once a junior is really well established, he will consider applying for "silk." Taking silk is an important and hazardous step; hazardous, because a busy and successful junior may have no success at all as a q.c.; and many who are eventually successful suffer a severe loss of income immediately after "appointment to the rank of Queen's Counsel." From time to time some brilliantly successful junior takes silk after only ten years of practice. More commonly the step is taken after fifteen to twenty-five years of practice or even later. With modern rates of taxation the newly-appointed q.c. is unlikely to have accumulated out of his earlier earnings as a junior any considerable savings to provide a "cushion" during his early days as a silk; and the modern tendency is to take silk later than in the past. At the same time many who are otherwise suitable now decide that they cannot afford to take the risk, and do not apply for silk.

It is believed that there are about 180 silks in practice; but not all of these can be regarded as full-time practitioners, and our guess is that the number of silks in effective full-time practice is about 130. Their earnings vary as widely as those of juniors. Some make little or nothing. Many probably earn between £3,000 and £5,000; and there are some exceptional and fashionable silks who make over £10,000 a year. One or two may make as much as £25,000 in a phenomenally good year. In recent years Sir Hartley Shawcross, q.c., was undoubtedly making more than any other practitioner at the bar. On his retirement from private practice, he was credited in the newspapers with having earned in some years as much as £50,000. When approached he would neither confirm nor deny this figure. It is interesting to note that in his fourth year at the bar, Sir Hartley Shawcross made only £130, and that his effective career in private practice as a q.c. lasted only five and a half years.

It would be wrong to conclude this general survey of earnings at the bar without emphasizing that except for the very few the financial reward is meagre, and that for everyone the rewards are uncertain and dependent on good health and constant application. But a career at the bar has many special attractions. One of them is the fact that the judges of the superior courts and the county courts are all appointed from the ranks of practicing barristers. Appointment to the bench is not only a great distinction; it is also financially worthwhile.

Nevertheless, in recent years, the bar has become less and less attractive. This is shown not only by the diminishing number of the new recruits but also by the increasing number of really distinguished barristers who leave the bar for well-paid appointments in the City and in business. . . .

We cannot speak with much greater precision about the earnings of solicitors. Having qualified, most entrants to the profession start as employed assistant solicitors. At present they can hope to receive a salary of about £600 in the provinces and rather more in London. Some time within five to ten years (when they are likely to be earning in the neighborhood of £1,000) most will be taken into partnership or will set up in practice on their own. If they remain as employed assistants in private practice they are not likely ever to rise above £1,500. On obtaining a partnership —which may initially be on a salaried basis—their earnings are likely to rise gradually, especially if they are taken into partnership in an established firm, but unless they have capital to bring into the partnership they will normally be expected to contribute to capital out of their share of profits so that, for some time, their actual drawings may be no greater than before. . . .

There is little doubt that English lawyers, like their American colleagues, rely increasingly on business clients rather than individuals, and it is probable that they, too, attain peak earnings after about twenty-five years' practice. The American percentage for overheads of only 40 per cent would be regarded with envy; in England it is probably over 60 per cent in most cases; but, of course, the two figures are not strictly comparable because an English firm is likely to have a much higher proportion of paid assistants. Retirement has not presented quite the same problems as it has in the case of the bar, for solicitors have a business or a share in it to sell when they retire but they, too, will welcome the recent tax concessions regarding retirement benefits for the self-employed. In fact most solicitors seem to die in harness at a ripe old age.

As with American lawyers, the increasing number of solicitors in industry and commerce (including the nationalized undertakings) probably have the highest average incomes coupled with generous pensions. And those in the government service seem to do rather better (relatively to the profession as a whole) than in the States. After a probationary period of one or two years they will start as legal assistants at a salary scale of £1,085 to £1,475 and may rise through Senior Legal Assistant (£1,500–£2,000), Assistant Solicitor (£2,100 to £2,600), perhaps attaining the post of Solicitor or Legal Adviser to a major government department at £4,250, once again with pension rights. The scales for solicitors in municipal government start rather lower, but there are more vacancies for the senior posts of Town or County Clerk, some of which are paid even more than the top salary in central government....

*Women Lawyers.*

When it comes to women who enter the law, the majority of large law offices still refuse (short of war) to interview them for jobs.... Women must work twice as hard as men for half the pay. And so far there have been relatively few women—although the number is steadily increasing—who have won positions of real distinction in practice, in legal service to the government or on the Bench.

Thus spoke Professor Barbara Armstrong, herself an exception to the rule which she enunciated, about the position in America in 1951. The position does not seem to have materially changed since; the nation's Portias are still the Cinderellas of the American legal profession, and constitute a very small proportion of it (said to be 2.48 per cent in 1951). Many of these are employed in government agencies where they seem to find it easiest to obtain employment.

In this respect England seems to be slightly more progressive. Here, too, there have been "relatively few women who have won positions of real distinction" but many have proved highly successful as solicitors in private practice and in the government service. They may find it more difficult to obtain employment but it is certainly not true that nothing short of war will secure them an interview for a vacant post. They seem to have made rather less impact at the bar, but three have attained the distinction of becoming q.c.s and one has become a Metropolitan Police Court magistrate. But, rather to our surprise, we find that the percentage of women in practice either as barristers or solicitors may be even smaller than in the States (about 2.1 per cent). As in the States there are a number of women in law teaching, but none has yet attained the rank of full professor as several have in the States.

*The Judiciary.* The most conspicuous contrast here is in the number of professional judges in the two countries. In the States there are about

8,600, or approximately 3.2 per cent of the whole profession. In England the vast majority of our judges are laymen acting as magistrates on a part-time unpaid basis. And many of our judges who are legally qualified act only on a part-time basis as recorders and chairmen of quarter sessions. The total full-time professional judges is under 300 or about 1.2 per cent of the whole profession.

Another great contrast is in the extent to which politics plays a part in the selection of judges. In the States it still plays a major role whether the judges are appointed or elected, and election by popular vote still prevails in more than two-thirds of the states. The bar associations have done their best to mitigate the worst features of a system under which a judge periodically fights an election, often on a party ticket, but in the opinion of many qualified observers it still constitutes the chief obstacle towards decent judicial administration.

In England all the judges are appointed. This, of course, does not necessarily mean that politics plays no part in their selection. It certainly does to some extent in the selection of those American judges who are appointed, and formerly it did so in England too. But experience over the last twenty-five years suggests that it has now been eradicated almost completely in the appointment of full-time judges in England.

Because of the smaller numbers of English judges and because of the method of selection, it would be expected that the over-all standard would be higher. We have little doubt that this is so. On the other hand, it must be emphasized that English judges are selected from a very small section of the profession, since nearly all the worthwhile appointments are open only to barristers in private practice and not to solicitors. Hence, the quality of county court judges and stipendiary magistrates has not always been high, and there have even been some disappointments on the High Court bench. Dismissal of an unsatisfactory Supreme Court judge is impossible; he can only be removed as a result of an address of both Houses of Parliament (which has only happened in one case when in the early nineteenth century a judge in Ireland was removed) and there is no retiring age. A county court judge retires at the age of seventy-two with possible extensions to seventy-five and is removable for misconduct or (theoretically) for inefficiency.

Having regard to the diversity of practice among the various jurisdictions in the States no meaningful comparisons can be drawn as regards judicial salaries. But American readers may like to know that as a result of recent increases Supreme Court judges are quite generously paid; they enjoy salaries of £8,000 per annum with excellent pension rights. But county court judges, with jobs which in some respects are more difficult and no less responsible, have, until now, been grievously underpaid at £2,800, (admittedly with pensions). The extent to which England relies on unpaid and underpaid judges is remarkable.

## Practice and Procedure

Having regard to the wide variations of practice as between the various states in America it is difficult to be specific on this aspect of our subject. Nevertheless, there are certain features which strike any English observer of the American scene and any American observer of the English. Among these the following may be mentioned.

*The Jury.* America has not only retained the Grand Jury in criminal cases but also the petty jury in civil as well as criminal cases. The fact that the normal civil proceedings, such as motor accident cases (which in both countries constitute so large a part of current litigation), are heard before a jury astounds an English lawyer who is accustomed to a system whereby the civil jury is a very rare occurrence, and where its disappearance is regarded as one of the great legal reforms of the century. Its retention in the States undoubtedly accounts for many of the subtler distinctions between the habits of the two professions; for example, to the very different type of forensic eloquence displayed by trial lawyers. In the States it is still common to hear real old-fashioned harangues, which have long since passed into disuse in England. On the whole, the English advocate gets his effects by understatement, the American by overstatement. In the States, too, there is a stricter observance of the technical rules of evidence, especially as regards what questions may be asked. An American trial lawyer will not consider that he has earned his fee unless he punctuates his opponent's examination of witnesses by objections to the questions he is asking. In England this is done seldom and circumspectly even in those cases where there is a jury.

Not only is a jury far more common in the States, but where there is a jury the role of the judge during the trial is far less important than in an English case heard with a jury. In England the judge's summing up is not limited to directions on the law but reviews the whole of the evidence. At the very least this minimizes the effect of emotional appeals in counsel's final speeches—which invariably precede the summing up and never follow it as occurs in some jurisdictions in the United States. Often it goes considerably further and means that the jury is subtly influenced towards returning a verdict favoured by the judge. Such a wide-ranging summation would be regarded as highly improper in the States; there the judge's role is limited to directions on the law and often he will do no more than read to the jury instructions agreed by the two parties. It certainly seems to English lawyers that the Americans, having saddled themselves with the incubus of the jury, have gone out of their way to ensure that the system operates with the maximum disadvantage.

There are also startling contrasts as regards selection of the jury. In the States, especially in criminal cases, days or even weeks may be occupied while each side catechizes the jurors and exercises its rights of challenging them until a jury acceptable to it has ultimately been selected. In a heterogeneous community selecting the "right" jurors is regarded as more than half the battle. In England each side accepts the jury provided, and challenges, except for obvious causes (such as acquaintance with the parties or their lawyers), are unheard of. Equally unheard of here is the American habit of finding out what has taken place during the deliberations in the jury room. Accounts of the jury's discussions are frequently reported in the American newspapers and it is not uncommon for the parties' lawyers themselves to question jurors in order to improve their trial technique by learning what arguments proved persuasive, or even in order to find a possible ground for an appeal. In England it would be regarded as the gravest professional misconduct for any lawyer to attempt to invade the secrecy of the jury room and it might be contempt of court for them or a newspaper to do so. This leads us conveniently to another contrast.

*Pre-Trial Publicity.* In any sensational American criminal trial anyone who reads the press, watches television or listens to the radio is likely to know before the trial what the prosecution hopes to prove and (more serious still) details on the accused's background and former convictions (whether admissible in evidence or not). And during the course of the trial the newspapers do not hesitate to express their views of the guilt or innocence of the accused. This scandal of "trial by newspaper" is not wholly unknown in England because of our habit of hearing in public the preliminary investigations before the magistrates and allowing full reports of these hearings to be published. But at least we restrict publication to what is actually put in evidence (without comments on its effect) and publication until after the trial of any other material is a serious contempt of court. No English newspaper would dare to publish anything approaching the sensational titbits which are commonplace in the States, and English editors have been sent to prison for publications which the most respectable of American editors would regard as models of restraint.

What is perhaps more disturbing is that in the States this abuse is sometimes connived at by the police and lawyers (who hand out press releases) and by the judges (who rarely attempt to restrain them). The organized profession is alive to these evils, but hitherto attempts to curb them have been successfully met with the arguments that the freedom of the press must not be curtailed and that the protection of the individual demands that law enforcement functions in the fierce light of publicity. Precisely the same arguments are raised in England when it is suggested (as at present) that we should conduct preliminary inquiries *in camera*. There is little doubt that in both countries the interests of the individual have been sacrificed to the public's thirst for sensation and that the freedom of the press has been confused with license. But these abuses have gone much further in the States than in England. On the other hand, the English restraint in criticizing decisions after they have been handed down may go too far.

*Professional Ethics.* Attention has already been drawn to a number of respects in which ethical practices differ in the two countries. In fact the main difference in this respect is not so much between the ethical rules themselves as between the ways in which they are formulated and the extent to which they are observed. The main difference in the content of the rules is that the American are not concerned with those which in England regulate the relations between the two branches. Some of the latter are surprising to American eyes; for example, the rule that the barrister himself must not interview the witnesses (other than experts and the client himself). There may be some force in the comment of an American critic that this rule destroys one of the main advantages of having a specialist corps of advocates.

The other main contrast is that handling an action "on spec" is utterly unprofessional in England, whereas payment by "contingent fee" is permissible and common in the States. The subtle difference which this makes to the whole mental outlook of the two professions can scarcely be exaggerated.

So far as formulation is concerned the American practice is in advance of the English. The rules are set out in two codes adopted by the ABA— the Canons of Professional Ethics and the Canons of Judicial Ethics. The former has been formally adopted by the bar associations of most states; the latter has received less widespread formal adoption but is generally recognized as providing an accepted standard. In contrast the English rules consist largely of unwritten conventions and of rulings and decisions by the professional bodies—another manifestation, perhaps, of our characteristic antipathy to written constitutions. But the English rules seem to be observed more strictly than the American. Thus, "ambulance chasing" is said to be a common practice in a substantial proportion of states but has now been almost, if not completely, eradicated in England. And, as already pointed out, press releases by district attorneys are common despite the fact that they are generally forbidden by Canon 20 of the Code of Professional Ethics. In this connection it must not be forgotten that not all states have integrated bars with compulsory membership of the Bar Association. In England every barrister has to be a member of an Inn and every solicitor is subject to the jurisdiction of the Disciplinary Committee whether or not he is a member of the Law Society. This, and the fact that the English profession is much smaller and closer knit, undoubtedly facilitate the maintenance of proper standards.

*Legal Aid for the Indigent.* Here England may now claim to be in advance of our American colleagues. Since the implementation in 1950 of the legal aid scheme set up under the Legal Aid and Advice Act, 1949, we have a nationwide scheme financed by the State whereby, in criminal cases, advocates are provided free for all those who need it and, in civil cases, legal representation is available to the poorer section of the community on payment only of what they can afford. This scheme is now in operation in all the regular law courts except in domestic disputes before magistrates and the principal step needed to bring it into full operation is the creation of the Legal Advice Centers where advice short of assistance in impending litigation can be obtained.

This scheme has not had too good a press in the States, where all too often it has been damned as "Socialized Law." One contribution towards Anglo-American understanding which the English lawyers at the Convention can make, is to point out to their American colleagues that the operation of the scheme is entirely in the hands of the organized profession who have lost none of their independence by participating therein. Indeed, a criticism which is often, if unfairly, made is that the lawyers have benefited more than the public. That the lawyers have indeed benefited is clear, for they now get paid, adequately if not always in full, for the work which they do and run no risk that the client will default. But it is clear that the public have also gained greatly and that the scheme is a highly successful and surprisingly inexpensive social service.

In contrast, the American provisions are primitive, though improving[a] . . . In civil cases it is only fair to emphasize that the practice of taking up cases on a contingent fee renders the need somewhat less acute than in England where, as already pointed out this is professionally improper. Similarly, the fact that generally in the States the loser does not have to pay the winner's advocates' fees (as he does in England) makes the burden of the costs of litigation seem less severe.

*Trial Procedure.* We conclude with a few general observations on the contrasting features of an American and an English trial. American lawyers must reconcile themselves to the fact that most Englishmen's impressions of an American trial are derived from the films and that we visualize an undisciplined slanging match between judge, counsel and

[a] The developing program for legal aid in the United States is discussed by Orison S. Marden, Esq., p. 427.

witnesses. In fact, of course, the average American trial is quite as dignified and orderly as, say, any English county court case. What is true is that it lacks the perhaps excessive awesomeness of an English High Court trial and that an American judge is not treated with the same, almost sycophantic, deference as is his English brother, and is less likely to forget that he is a fallible human being. Apart from this the main superficial contrasts are few: the fact that counsel are unrobed and prowl around when examining witnesses or addressing the jury instead of staying rooted to one spot, the presence of the Stars and Stripes instead of the Royal coat-of-arms, and the absence of the law books and reports which line the walls of an English courtroom.

This last contrast, however, reflects an important difference in procedure. Legal argument, in the States, is mainly written; whether in trials at first instance or in appeals the lawyers hand in written briefs to the judge and are only allowed a very short time (usually as little as half-an-hour) to supplement this by oral presentation to the salient points. Hence, there is rarely any reference to the actual authorities during the oral proceedings; the judge goes through the briefs in the seclusion of his room and may be aided in the needful research by a qualified law clerk.

In England, on the other hand, the argument is always entirely oral and during the course of it counsel will take the judge through the authorities on which he relies, reading out extracts from the judgments ("opinions" in American parlance) while the judge follows from a volume before him. Hence, an English trial involving any point of law necessitates the presence in the court of a sizeable collection of legal literature.

This, indeed, is but one illustration of the greater "orality" of the English trial. The judge is assumed (normally correctly) to be wholly ignorant of the case at its opening in court. Hence, counsel reads out the pleadings, the correspondence and everything else on which he wishes the judge to be informed. To an American it seems that although the English may have largely eradicated the jury they conduct the proceedings in a manner only explicable on the assumption that everything has to be explained to a bunch of laymen. Yet the same applies even to the type of proceedings in which there never was a jury; for example, in Chancery matters where, although the evidence will normally be contained in written affidavits, these will be read by counsel from beginning to end.

This orality extends even to the judge's decision. In England in the trial at first instance the judge will almost invariably give an oral judgment off the cuff. Even in the Court of Appeal this is the usual practice. Only in the rare cases which reach the House of Lords are written decisions normally given after mature consideration. In the States, on the other hand, it is almost invariable practice for the judges, whether at first instance or on appeal, to hand down considered opinions.

Another contrast is in the greater extent to which many American jurisdictions have succeeded in breaking down the veil of secrecy behind which each party is allowed to prepare its case. As a result of pretrial conferences before the judge, and pretrial examination of the opponent's witnesses, the element of surprise is eradicated from a civil case to a much greater extent than is necessarily so in England. On the other hand, jurisdictional disputes are far more common. American federalism has led to a most complicated arrangement of federal and State courts operating side by side with complicated rules as to their respective jurisdictions. In certain types of litigation, therefore, time- and money-consuming objections to jurisdiction and venue are recognized tactics. England is, at least, free from this.

## Conclusions

In this paper we have drawn attention only to the contrasting features of our two systems. But it cannot be too strongly stressed that the similarities derived from our common heritage are far more striking than the differences. Both systems are still based on judge-made law rather than upon codes, both draw their judges from the ranks of private practitioners rather than from a separate magisterial profession, both retain essential common-law safeguards of civil liberty such as habeas corpus and cross-examination. And the lawyers of both would recognize the following words as aptly applying to them:

From all outward appearances the . . . lawyer is much like everybody else. He is dressed no better than representatives of other occupations of businesses requiring contact with the public. . . . Certainly he possesses neither the house nor the car which corresponds to the income which others may think he earns based upon his many years of education and the hours he devotes to his profession.

And, alas, the following also:

Yet he is surprisingly unpopular. He has been unhappily described as one who gets two other men to strip for a fight and then takes their clothes.

# THE WALL STREET LAWYERS  *By Spencer Klaw*

For MEMBERS of the big law firms of downtown New York, a corps of practitioners generally known as Wall Street lawyers, these are agreeably busy times. In one thirty-day period last autumn, for example, Wall Street lawyers analyzed and approved an antitrust consent decree for Combustion Engineering, Inc.; represented American Express in the organization of an international car-rental system jointly owned with the Hertz Corp.; and helped set the stage for an $11-million swap involving two of New York's largest hotels, the Ambassador and the Sheraton-Astor. During this period they were called on to handle the legal aspects of one big projected merger—Climax Molybdenum and American Metal—and to defend in court an even bigger one—Bethlehem Steel and Youngstown Sheet & Tube—the legality of which had been challenged by the Justice Department. Working with bankers and company counsel, Wall Street lawyers also completed the laborious preparation of prospectuses and SEC registration statements for more than a dozen major corporate security issues, including a $288-million offering of common stock by Standard Oil (New Jersey).

As it has been over the years, the Wall Street legal corps was simultaneously active in nonbusiness affairs, too. In Washington, to give just one instance, a Wall Street lawyer, Edwin L. Weisl, was serving as counsel to a Senate subcommittee, one of whose principal witnesses was a former Wall Street lawyer, CIA Director Allen W. Dulles, who testified on Soviet progress in missile technology. The law firms of downtown New York have traditionally supplied the federal government with investigators, administrators, and policy makers. Wall Street lawyers, of whom John Foster Dulles and the late Henry L. Stimson are two outstanding examples, have been picked for major jobs by every President from McKinley to Eisenhower, and hundreds more have served two or three-year tours in Washington at slightly lower levels of government. Members of Wall Street law firms also sit on the boards of big foundations, among them the Carnegie Corporation and the Rockefeller Institute for Medical Research, and of universities, charities, civil organizations, and cultural institutions.

But it is in the world of business, which provides them with their principal livelihood, that Wall Street lawyers have their most pervasive influence. Indeed, many have moved from the position of corporate legal

---

Reprinted courtesy of *Fortune Magazine*, Vol. 57, No. 2, February 1958, pp. 140 *et seq.*

adviser to that of corporate executive. Today, Prudential Insurance, U.S. Steel, International Nickel, J. P. Morgan, Phelps Dodge, Chrysler, and Chase Manhattan are among the companies headed by former Wall Street lawyers. Even as a corporate adviser, the Wall Street lawyer often exerts considerable influence in the conduct of business enterprises (although these days, to be sure, he is no longer called on, as one New York attorney likes to put it, to teach the robber barons how to rob). The complexities of doing business within the framework of federal regulation and taxation have in fact created an unprecedented demand for his services, and the Wall Street lawyer, who will be examined here primarily in terms of how he earns his living, has never before had so many affairs of great moment to handle.

*Watching the Sun Rise over Wall Street.* What makes a lawyer a Wall Street lawyer? He doesn't have to have a Wall Street address, of course, but for purposes of this article he has to be a member of one of the big institutional law firms that are the distinguishing features of the downtown Manhattan legal community. In all, there are about 1,700 such lawyers—partners or salaried associates of . . . twenty large firms . . . and of four or five smaller firms that offer legal services of comparable scope and quality. The contemporary Wall Street lawyer characteristically practices as a member of a legal team consisting of fifteen to thirty partners, many of them specialists, and perhaps twenty-five to eighty or more associates. The individual practitioner and the small partnership have been giving way to the big institutional law firm in cities other than New York, but most lawyers all over the U.S. still regard the big law office of the New York financial district as being, as lawyers like to say, *sui generis.*

The big Wall Street firm generally handles bigger transactions, draws bigger clients, charges bigger fees (not infrequently $100 an hour or more for a senior partner's time), and takes in more money (up to $6 million a year) than law firms in other cities. Its legal craftsmanship is of the highest quality, and it is able and willing to assign whole squads of legal foot soldiers to a single antitrust case or bond issue. In some of the oldest firms, hard work and long hours are such an honorable tradition that young associates boast of watching the sun come up over Wall Street. Indeed, the prosperity of the partners in a big Wall Street firm depends in part on what Karl Marx would have classified as the systematic expropriation of surplus labor value. By hiring talented young lawyers, working them to a fare-thee-well, and in effect reselling their services to clients at a healthy markup, the partners—who often work just as hard as their associates—are able to earn an average of $80,000 or so each year, and in some cases as much as $200,00 or more.

This does not mean that the one hundred or more law school graduates who come to Wall Street each year are being cruelly exploited. On the contrary, the Wall Street firm offers bright young lawyers a postgraduate education of great value, at a salary starting at $6,500 and rising to around $18,000 after eight or ten years. For perhaps one out of every six or seven who qualify for starting jobs, the payoff is membership in the firm. For others, the reward is a partnership in a smaller New York firm or in a large firm in some other city. For still others, it is a job with a corporation—very often with one of the firm's clients, an arrangement that has the effect, of course, of strengthening the bonds between client and law firm.

There are some observers who feel that the big Wall Street firms have had their day. Their influence, the argument runs, has diminished with the decentralization of economic power that has deprived the Wall Street financial community of some of its old imperial splendor. Certainly Wall Street law firms have been facing stiff competition in recent years, both for business and for manpower. Law firms in other cities have begun to offer services to clients, and training to young lawyers, comparable to those once available only on Wall Street. For manpower the big New York firms are also getting competition from their own clients: many companies in the past twenty years have established or greatly expanded legal departments of their own, and in staffing them they have been able to offer benefits—notably tax-sheltered pension funds and in some cases stock options—not available to the employees or members of a partnership.

Nevertheless, the lights are burning late at night in the big law firms on Wall and Broad streets, a sure sign of prosperity. New firms have grown up to compete for business with the big old firms, while most of the big old firms have been getting even bigger. Simpson, Thacher & Bartlett, for instance, has doubled in size since 1936, and so has Cahill, Gordon, Reindel & Ohl. Indeed, the big Wall Street law firms have probably never had it so good.

*Hot Potatoes and Massive Situations.* The large institutional law firm is a fairly recent phenomenon. Its early history has been summarized in one mouth-filling sentence by Robert T. Swaine in his history of the firm of Cravath, Swaine & Moore. "The expansion of personnel and the tendency toward specialization, which began in the larger offices of New York and other cities in the early 1920s," Swaine notes, "accelerated during the boom, and, with little hesitation at the 1929 market collapse, continued as depression-induced bankruptcies and New Deal agencies engulfed business and created such demands on the profession that competent legal assistance was at a premium." Bankruptcies are no longer a major item of business. But the prosperity of the big Wall Street law firms, as Swaine suggests, has in effect been underwritten by New Deal and post-New Deal legislation, and for twenty years their main stock in trade has been advice on how to do business in a heavily taxed and closely regulated economy.

Corporations do not, of course, have to go to Wall Street for such advice. But in three important fields—antitrust work, corporate financing, and corporate reorganization (e.g., mergers)—and, to a lesser extent, in the field of tax law, the big New York firms are the recognized experts. "Take a merger problem," a Wall Street lawyer explained recently. "A company is planning a merger, and it wants to know if it will violate Section 7 of the Clayton Antitrust Act. This is a very hot potato, and the company's house lawyer, who may be an absolutely first-rate man, usually is still anxious to have someone else take the responsibility. Well, it makes sense to come to us. We're specialists. We've had a number of these Section 7 cases in the firm since the act was amended in 1950, and we've been doing antitrust work for years. We know what the law is, and we have a feeling for what it's likely to become. Another thing, we know all the people down at Justice who are involved. I'm not talking about influence—we don't deal in that—but it's our business to know what those people are thinking, and we've got a book on every one of them."

The big Wall Street firm has what amounts, indeed, to a national practice. Most of its corporate clients, naturally enough, are drawn from the New York area, where sixty-five of the two hundred largest industrial corporations have their headquarters. But they come from faraway points too. In a recent survey of forty-eight large companies located outside New York, twenty-six reported that they used Wall Street firms either regularly or on special occasions, usually in connection with financing, major litigation, mergers, or serious tax or antitrust problems. "Whenever a large, massive situation comes up," a senior partner of one big Wall Street firm observes complacently, "they come to New York. We have the shock troops to throw in—that's one of the services we sell."

One sort of massive situation that has come up with increasing frequency in the past ten years is the big antitrust case. To prepare and conduct a sound defense may require three to four years' work by as many as fifteen lawyers. In one recent case, in which RCA and General Electric were sued by Zenith for alleged patent monopoly, two New York law firms each rented an entire floor at the Palmer House in Chicago, where the suit was being tried, to accommodate lawyers, files, clerks, and stenographers. Litigation is not always profitable. "It's so damn expensive," one lawyer explains, "that often you just can't charge the client anything above your actual costs. But it's a service we have to provide, and at worst it can be looked on as a sort of loss leader." (The boom in antitrust litigations has, however, tended to improve the standing of the litigating partners of the big firms. At one time, mere barristers were rather overshadowed by office-lawyer partners, like the late Nelson Cromwell of Sullivan & Cromwell, and Paul D. Cravath of Cravath, Swaine & Moore, who seldom, if ever, went near a courtroom. Today, the reputation of some large firms—notably Cahill, Gordon, Reindel & Ohl, whose senior partner, John T. Cahill, was once a highly successful U.S. prosecutor—stems largely from their litigating skills.)

Another massive situation in which Wall Street firms specialize is the issuing of new securities. ("Anyone can read the SEC regulations," a Wall Street lawyers says. "Nine-tenths of the real work is reading between the lines, and that's what we're experienced at.") Registering a big stock or bond issue with the SEC is a complicated business, on which a team of lawyers, consisting of at least one partner and perhaps three associates, may work day and night for many weeks. Of course, this is not everybody's dish. "There's only a limited amount of creative splendor," says one New York lawyer, "that you can put into an SEC registration statement." But however unrewarding from a literary point of view, the composition of prospectuses and registration statements is a very profitable affair, and stock and bond issues are looked on with affection in the big Wall Street offices, where they are often referred to as lettuce, green vegetables, or the green-goods business.

*Recruiting the Troops.* The big Wall Street firms have traditionally chosen their associates (and future partners) mainly from the law schools of Harvard, Yale, and Columbia, and, to a lesser extent, from Michigan, Virginia, and Pennsylvania. Before World War II, the most promising seniors flocked to Wall Street each year at Christmas time and made the rounds of the big offices looking for jobs. "I didn't particularly want to work in New York," says a successful midwestern lawyer who graduated close to the top of his Harvard Law School class in 1937, "but I did want to practice law, and the Wall Street firms were the only ones who would take you on and pay you a decent salary even if you had no clients and no connections."

In the last few years this situation has changed. Hundreds of law students still make the annual Christmas trek to Wall Street, but many of them have already been tentatively sized up, or even offered jobs, by partners who have visited their law schools on recruiting trips. In 1956-57, 194 law firms and corporations sent recruiters to Harvard; at Yale, during one thirty-day period at the height of last fall's rushing season, recruiters included representatives of five corporations, seventeen big Wall Street firms, ten other New York firms, and twenty-four law firms located elsewhere in the country.

Since 1949 the big New York firms have raised their top starting salaries from $3,600 to $6,500 (they were about $2,100 prewar) and many large firms outside New York have been fairly closely matching these figures.

In the face of this competition, the big Wall Street firms are now hiring graduates of law schools at Minnesota, Chicago, Iowa, and other universities that used to be considered outside the pale. But the bulk of their associates still come from the traditional Ivy League recruiting grounds, where Wall Street continues to get a good share of the able and talented graduates. A recent Harvard Law School compilation, for instance, shows that of the five top men in the classes of 1950 through 1956, thirty-five in all, sixteen went to work for large New York firms. "The secret of Wall Street's power," says Dean Eugene V. Rostow of the Yale Law School, a former associate of Cravath, Swaine & Moore, "is its concentration of skill and experience. There is still a powerful pull toward Wall Street."

*The "White-shoe Outfits."* Who are the desirable recruits in Wall Street's eyes? One important criterion is academic standing, and a personable senior who has served on his school's law review—i.e., who is in the top 5 or 10 per cent of his class—can usually take his pick of the big Wall Street firms. (In contrast to pre-World War II days, this now applies even to Jewish students, though some Wall Street firms that in recent years have been hiring Jews have not yet made any of them partners. Many firms also take on women as associates, but partnerships are still for men only.)

But Wall Street firms also hire men with mediocre marks. In a sampling of recent Yale Law School graduates hired by big Wall Street firms, one-fourth—nine out of thirty-five—were in the botton two-thirds of their class, and three of these were in the bottom quarter. Actually, it takes a fair amount of brains just to get through a first-rate law school, and a Wall Street firm will often choose an attractive and socially mature student with a B-minus average in preference to a brilliant scholar with awkward manners and bearing. "Brilliant intellectual powers are not essential," the late Paul D. Cravath, generally considered the principal architect of the big institutional law firm, once told a group of Harvard law students in discussing the qualifications for becoming a lawyer of affairs. He added: "Too much imagination, too much wit, too great cleverness, too facile fluency, if not leavened by a sound sense of proportion, are quite as likely to impede success as to promote it. The best clients are apt to be afraid of those qualities. They want as their counsel a man who is primarily honest, safe, sound, and steady."

A few big firms—an outstanding example is Davis, Polk, Wardwell, Sunderland & Kiendl, sometimes known as the Tiffany of law firms—reputedly have a predilection for young men who are listed in the *Social Register*. These firms are called "white-shoe outfits," a term derived from the buckskin shoes that used to be part of the accepted uniform at certain eastern prep schools and colleges.

*Midnight at Mr. Cravath's.* The law-school graduate who signs up with a big Wall Street firm can count on working hours that would be regarded as pretty outrageous by management trainees at, say, General Electric or du Pont. At some Wall Street firms, indeed, night and weekend work was considered, as recently as the 1940s, to be not only normal but salutary. It is a tradition at Cravath, Swaine & Moore, for instance, that when Hoyt A. Moore (now, at eighty-seven, the firm's oldest active partner) was urged by his colleagues to take on extra help because the staff was under such pressure, Moore replied, "That's silly. No one is under pressure. There wasn't a light on when I left at two o'clock this morning."

Cravath himself often used to tell an associate to meet him at his house on East Thirty-eighth Street at eleven-thirty or so in the evening, when Cravath would have returned from the opera or the theatre. "Many nights," Robert Swaine writes in his history of the Cravath firm, "young lawyers from the office sat there awaiting his return, spent an hour or two past midnight going over papers or discussing a question of law with him, and then returned to the office with instructions to be back at eight o'clock in the morning with a new draft or the answer."

Since World War II the rigors of an associate's life have been greatly tempered—he now gets a full month's vacation, for example—and when a partner of one Wall Street firm remarked some time ago to a group of Harvard students that he kept a blanket in his bottom desk drawer so that he could catch catnaps when working through the night, most of his audience recognized that he was joking.

Nevertheless, in most big offices, unless an associate drops anchor in the relatively quiet waters of the estates-and-trusts department, he is likely to average one or two late evenings a week at the office, and a good deal of weekend work. At least one firm, Sullivan & Cromwell, keeps a suite in a Manhattan hotel to accommodate partners and associates who miss the last train home. And while few if any firms these days regard long hours in themselves as a desirable feature of a young man's legal training, it is usually made clear early in the game that slackers are not likely to be rewarded with partnerships.

"Sooner or later," the managing partner of one firm explains with chilling affability, "the young men come into my office and ask, 'Can I take Monday off next week?' I say, 'I don't know; *can* you?' They usually look surprised, and I say, 'If it won't interfere with your work, take Monday, Tuesday, Wednesday, Thursday, and Friday off. But if you have work to be done, you'd better be here all night if necessary.' They never ask the question again."

Cravath, Swaine & Moore is known as the hardest-working of the big firms. The firm's offices are at 15 Broad Street, in the same building as several other big law firms, among them Davis, Polk, and there is a standard joke about how to tell the Cravath lawyers from the Davis, Polk, lawyers. Going down in the elevator, the joke runs, the Cravath lawyers talk about what they were doing at the office so late the night before, while the Davis, Polk lawyers talk about what they're going to have for lunch.

A shrewd Wall Street observer points out, however, that any such differences may reflect nothing more than superficial contrasts in institutional styles. "The Davis, Polk lawyer," this observer comments, "may have worked just as late the night before as the Cravath fellow. He just doesn't boast about it. Davis, Polk people pride themselves on being gentlemen, and a gentleman doesn't brag about being a greasy grind."

*The Partner's Key.* The prize for which the young associate theoretically strives is, of course, a partnership. But only one out of every half-dozen or so who begin their apprenticeship in a big Wall Street firm is ever rewarded, figuratively speaking, with the key to the partner's lavatory.

Some associates are not really interested in becoming partners. They come to Wall Street for a two or three-year legal internship, and then move on to law firms in other cities. Other associates become fascinated by the business problems of a client, decide they would really like to make business decisions themselves, and leave to go to work for the client in an executive job. (At last count, former associates of just one Wall Street firm, Sullivan & Cromwell, included the presidents of eight large companies, among them International Nickel, American Radiator & Standard Sanitary, and Marine Midland; and vice presidents of a dozen more, including National Dairy Products, Crown Zellerbach, and Eastman Kodak.)

Some associates would like to become partners, but eventually conclude that the chances are slim. (Few Wall Street firms have an absolutely rigid up-or-out policy, but most of them discourage men from staying on indefinitely as associates.) Men with six or seven years of experience in a big Wall Street office are in great demand, however, to staff or even head corporate legal departments, and they usually have no trouble landing a good job—in most cases, as noted earlier, with a client.

*Dividing the Take.* For those who achieve a partnership in a big Wall-Street firm the financial rewards, compared with the earnings of the average U.S. lawyer, are quite dazzling. A very large Wall Street firm with, say, eighty or more partners and associates, may gross from $4 million to $6 million a year. Roughly half of this amount, however, is siphoned off in overhead expenses, which in the case of one large firm were divided as follows during its last fiscal year:

| | |
|---|---:|
| Employees' salaries: | |
| Legal | $1,030,000 |
| Non-legal | 825,000 |
| Total salaries | $1,855,000 |
| Pensions, social security, etc. | 195,000 |
| Rent depreciation, maintenance, etc. | 270,000 |
| Stationery, library, and telephone | 95,000 |
| Other expenses | 95,000 |
| Total expenses | $2,510,000 |

Assuming that such a firm grosses $5 million, nets $2,500,000, and has thirty partners, the average take per partner would come to about $83,000. By comparison, a U.S. Commerce Department survey in 1954 placed the average earnings of U.S. lawyers at $10,220, and of lawyers practicing in large firms (nine or more partners) at $36,100.[1]

Average figures, of course, are rather meaningless. Earnings vary from firm to firm, from year to year, and from partner to partner. Generally, though, a new partner in one of the very large Wall Street firms is given a percentage of the firm's profits calculated to yield from $25,000 to $30,000 a year. In many firms working capital is provided by the senior partners, who from time to time leave some of their earnings in the kitty, and new men are not required to contribute. In a few offices, however, a new partner is expected to put some money into the working-capital fund, usually a sum proportionate to his share in the firm's proceeds.

The distribution of earnings within a partnership is a very delicate matter. In many large firms it is handled by a committee of senior partners whose recommendations are usually accepted without question by their younger colleagues. Practices vary widely from firm to firm, but, generally speaking, a partner in a big firm can count on earning at least $60,000 a year by the time he is in his early fifties, and if he consistently attracts important new clients, a good deal more. In some Wall Street firms, indeed, there may be several senior partners whose shares in the firm's earnings range from $100,000 to $200,000 a year. But taxes being what they are, many senior partners prefer to spread the money around among the younger men. And in one large firm all partners, after their first seven or eight years in the firm, are put on an equal footing, each drawing around $80,000 a year.

[1] Probably the biggest money-makers among the approximately 250,000 U.S. lawyers are a few leading specialists in the art of representing plaintiffs in accident cases; some are reputed to net more than $300,000 a year.

The partners' share of the work in a big Wall Street firm is big, too. Partners often put in long hours on weekends when—as they point out with a certain masochistic relish—their businessmen clients are out playing golf.

Some Wall Street lawyers take a fierce pride in how hard they work. "I would rather work twelve hours a day as a lawyer and go to bed tired after a day full of interest," Paul Cravath once proclaimed, "than to work six dull hours as a stockbroker and have six hours left for bridge and society." But most partners seem to regard their heavy work load as a necessary price they pay for success in a very competitive field. "Wills-and-estates work is pretty leisurely," a tired-looking young partner observed recently. "But corporate practice is different. The lawyer can't just work from nine to five the way the client does. The client wants his problems solved quickly. He calls you Friday, and wants an answer by Monday. And in this league there's a terrific professional drive to do work as accurately and expertly as possible."

*The Art of Trapping.* Like other lawyers, those who practice on Wall Street are concerned with attracting and holding clients. Many Wall Street firms have members who specialize in what one senior partner calls "trapping," i.e., cultivating prospective clients through social contacts. But law firms cannot ethically operate new-business departments, and apart from buying theatre tickets on occasion for an out-of-town client, Wall Street lawyers do little business entertaining.

Actually, trapping seldom snares major clients. Most big companies are quite hardheaded when casting about for a Wall Street law firm, and their choice is likely to be made on the basis of the reputation of a particular senior partner. The best business-getters on Wall Street, in fact, are men whose reputations as trial lawyers, politicians, government officials, business advisers, or public citizens are such that they attract important clients to the firm without having to lift a finger to woo them. The late John W. Davis, one-time Ambassador to the Court of St. James's and Democratic candidate for the presidency in 1924, was an outstanding example of what one Wall Street lawyer calls "the public partner."[2]

Because of the institutional character of the big Wall Street firms, not every partner has to be a good business producer for a firm to prosper. The new generations of corporate managers are often content to pass along their legal business to the new partners of the same law firm that served the company before. The First National City Bank, for instance,

---

[2] Defeated presidential candidates seem to gravitate to New York law firms. Wendell Willkie became a member of the Wall Street firm now known as Willkie, Owen, Farr, Gallagher & Walton. Adlai Stevenson last year joined—primarily as its Chicago partner—the New York firm of Paul, Weiss, Rifkind, Wharton & Garrison, which differs from the big Wall Street firms mainly in that it is situated uptown (on Madison Avenue) and most of its partners are liberal Democrats.

has been a client of Shearman & Sterling & Wright since 1897, while Davis, Polk, Wardwell, Sunderland & Kiendl has represented J. P. Morgan & Co., for upwards of seventy years.

Many Wall Street lawyers sit on the boards of client companies. This is frowned on by some critics, who argue that a lawyer can't give a company really objective legal advice if he is also a director, but the client often expects it, the law firm likes this further hold on the client's legal business, and so the practice is quite widespread. John Cahill, for example, is on the boards of W. R. Grace & Co. and of RCA (RCA alone gives Cahill's firm around $425,000 of business each year.) Sullivan & Cromwell partners are on the boards of some dozen major companies.

*How to Lose a Client.* Even old clients can be lost, however, and remembering not to take them for granted is often the Wall Street lawyer's hardest job. "The greatest mistake," says Arthur Dean, senior partner of Sullivan & Cromwell, "is to think you're entitled to be consulted. Some lawyers get to be fortyish, fiftyish, living in the suburbs, playing golf on weekends—then suddenly the client is faced with some new and very tough problem, and he takes his business somewhere else. In many cases where a law firm loses a client, you'll find the lawyers had too comfortable an existence."

The fees charged by the big Wall Street firms, like most lawyers' fees, usually bear at least some relation to the time expended on the client's behalf, and partners and associates are required to keep close track of their time. A value is assigned to each lawyer's time, and these time charges may range from $5 to $35 an hour for an associate and from $50 to $100 or more for a partner. When a bill is being prepared, the hourly time charges of each lawyer who worked on the job in question are first added up. Then the total arrived at may be halved—or doubled—depending on factors such as the difficulty and novelty of the legal problems dealt with, and, in litigation, whether the client won or lost. "When we win a big case," a Wall Street lawyer points out, "we expect to share in our own success."

The size of the matter handled is also taken into account. In the green-goods business, for instance, legal charges are usually related to the size as well as to the complexity of a security issue. Thus total legal fees, paid by both issuer and underwriters, might range from $20,000 to $35,000 in the case of a small ($5 million to $10 million) stock or bond issue, up to several hundred thousand dollars in the case of a big and complicated financing. (Trans-Canada Pipe Lines, for example, recently paid legal fees of approximately $237,500 in connection with a $112,500,-000 issue of subordinated debentures and common stock; this sum excludes the amount, not a matter of public record, paid to counsel for the underwriters.)

*Never any Haggling.* Generally, Wall Street firms refuse to haggle with clients about bills; if a client complains about a fee, it is suggested that he pay whatever he thinks the job is worth. Bills are almost never itemized, and even within the office the time charges assigned to each partner and associate are sometimes treated as highly confidential—at least in so far as the associates are concerned. "But you usually find out sooner or later," one associate recalls. "I remember the day I hit on the formula. At the time, the firm was paying me about $3.75 an hour, and they were charging the client $21 for my services. I didn't know whether to feel flattered or sore."

Despite the fees they get, Wall Street lawyers, like most other Americans, feel that they don't make enough money—or, at any rate, that they aren't able to keep enough of what they do make. Lawyers are legally prohibited from practicing as corporations, of course, and so, unlike the executives of a corporation, members of a partnership get no stock options and no tax-sheltered pension funds. In the circumstances, a job offer from a corporation can look very attractive even to an $80,000-a-year partner in a Wall Street firm.

This is particularly true if the position offered is an executive one. Offers of jobs as company counsel, even in quite large corporations, are not usually so appealing. As a rule, they neither pay so well nor offer such exciting prospects for further advancement as, say, an administrative vice-presidency. To be sure, there has been a marked improvement over the past twenty years in the professional and social standing of corporate counsel. But Wall Street lawyers, like many others in private practice, are proud of the fact that they are not dependent on any single client, and tend therefore to be a little patronizing about what used to be called the "kept" lawyer who works for one company.

(Company lawyers, incidentally, don't take this lying down. One of their most effective spokesmen, Leon E. Hickman, vice president and general counsel of Alcoa, has observed tartly: "The files of Alcoa are replete with brilliantly reasoned opinions of general practitioners that have little or no value because of the incompleteness or the distorted emphasis of their factual assumptions.")

Their patronizing attitude toward company lawyers does not prevent private practitioners from envying some company lawyers the money they make. A notable example, one that brings a glazed expression into the eyes of some Wall Street lawyers, is that of William T. Gossett, a former member of the Wall Street firm of Hughes, Hubbard, Blair & Reed, who resigned in 1947 to become general counsel of the Ford Motor Co. (He is also a vice-president and director.) In 1956, the latest year for which figures have been made public, Gossett's salary amounted to $125,000. In addition, he had "supplemental compensation" due him amounting to

$145,000, and the company reported that under its stock-option plan, Gossett had bought 37,500 shares of Ford stock at $21 a share. Ford stock as of the beginning of the year was selling at about $37.

*Keepers of the Conscience?* The lure of corporate benefits has not resulted in any exodus from the big Wall Street firms or, as noted earlier, in any discernible falling off in the quality of their young apprentices and future partners. For all their complaints about high taxes, Wall Street lawyers seem quite content with their lot.

Most of them profess to find their satisfaction in the practice of law, and not in making business decisions for clients or in acting as their conscience-keepers—two roles that have sometimes been attributed to them. Many Wall Street lawyers naturally have a highly developed business sense, and in complicated transactions it is often impossible to sort out the legal from the business aspects. But even those Wall Street lawyers who are widely respected for their shrewd judgment in business affairs tend to minimize the lawyer's role as a maker of business policy. "If a lawyer wants to make business decisions," says one such partner, "let him resign from the practice of law and go into business."

Wall Street lawyers also deny performing any great prodigies in the public-relations or conscience-keeping line. In many cases, of course, a lawyer may be better read, better informed about social trends, and generally less parochial in his outlook than his client, and therefore in a position to advise him not only about the legal implications of his acts, but about other possible repercussions as well—e.g., unwelcome attentions from a congressional investigating committee. But a Wall Street lawyer, dealing largely with sophisticated executives of big banks, investment houses, and industrial corporations, may not often find himself in this position.

"In getting out a big securities issue," says a specialist in this field, "ethical problems hardly ever come up. It strikes me that the managers of big business are leaning over backward these days to do the right thing. It's the little fellows who are always trying to gouge each other's eyes out."

*What the Law Ought to Be.* Wall Street law firms are often asked for advice in situations not covered by existing law (a possible conflict of interest, say, between a corporation and one of its officers), and in such cases the client will be advised to do what is "right"—that is, to conform to what the lawyer believes the law ought to be. But in general, Wall Street lawyers spend very little time urging clients to behave themselves.

For the typical Wall Street lawyer there appears to be excitement enough in dealing in large (and gratifyingly complex) economic affairs, and in occupying a position from which the upper echelons of public service are readily accessible and which is at the same time close to the very center of U.S. business life. "When I came downtown in 1923," a highly successful Wall Street practitioner recalled recently, "everyone was talking about the golden Nineties. Now they're talking about the golden Twenties. Glamour is an elusive thing, and I don't know if they'll ever be talking about the golden Fifties. But for my money, this is still one hell of a business."

# REVIEW OF LEVY, CORPORATION LAWYER... SAINT OR SINNER?

By A. A. Berle

ALL LAWYERS are somewhat suspect. A Spanish conquistador-governor early implored the King of Spain to send no lawyers at all to his new territory: "They are all devils." A half-century later, Shakespeare (here is where Levy begins his book) in *Henry VI* makes Jack Cade agree to "kill all lawyers," while Plato had earlier asserted that the lawyer's soul is "small and unrighteous." But, Levy notes, Jack Cade was contemplating a dictatorship. Plato contemplated something like a Fascist republic. Once a government of laws becomes normal, lawyers are essential. This is no less true of corporation lawyers than of any other kind.

In the great decades of the growth of American corporations (1890–1930), their lawyers came to have a singularly sinister reputation. In that generation they were supposed to be, and often were, little more than highly paid, powerful mercenary agents of great technical competence, dedicatedly serving all-powerful financial tycoons. They were lieutenants of vast, insensitive and pitiless private interests on headlong march to personal plutocratic empires. In later appraisal, we know that the Vanderbilts, Goulds, Harrimans, Hills, Rockefellers and their lawyers in their ruthlessness also built a foundation of capital development later turned to useful account. Out of it our present unrivaled industrial productivity has emerged. The succeeding generation in milder mood has been content to let St. Peter pass judgment on their motives, has modified their methods and has ceased to ask whether the end justified the means. Even so the methods of the time cannot be called pretty; their ruthlessness was undeniable while their declared motive was desire to attain unlimited

---

Reprinted from *Harvard Law Review*, vol. 76, 1962, pp. 430–434 with the permission of the author and the publisher. (Copyright, 1962, by Harvard Law Review Association.) Biographical material on Professor Berle appears on p. 398.

private wealth. They were hated by the contemporary public. Lawyers were then "used" by these interests to see that they got what they wanted. They delivered against contract; often they were more economic royalists than the princes of property they served. Most of the older great corporation law offices functioning in New York today resulted from their deceased founders' success in providing the services required by one of the nineteenth century moguls. An unconsciously cynical book, *The Cravath Firm*, by Cravath's successor, the late Robert T. Swaine (privately printed in New York in 1948), sufficiently testifies to the methods used.

Corporation lawyers in the course of this development ceased to be the courtroom advocates of Lincoln's day. They hired trial specialists for that sort of thing. As a rule they made much more money than their barrister brothers. I do not think Levy is wholly accurate in dismissing as extinct the courtroom hero: the late John W. Davis was undeniably just that, especially in appellate work. But modern corporation lawyers do not have a high opinion of litigation—it is better than trial by battle, but not much—and their business is keeping their clients out of court, free to work at their economic job. Levy is undoubtedly right in observing that the "plush" law business is office counseling for well-paying business corporation clients (and he should have included the commercial and investment banks through whose influence much of this business is now received). He names as illustrative leaders of the corporation bar men like William Nelson Cromwell (survived by the firm of Sullivan & Cromwell), Paul D. Cravath (survived by Cravath, Swaine & Moore), John Foster Dulles, a later head of Sullivan & Cromwell, and a number of others. His list could easily be extended.

These law firms, once established, obviously responded to the growing demands and needs of their clients and in responding, changed. They are now, as Levy says, departmentalized: taxmen; "scriveners" (I owe the word to the late Roberts Walker of White & Case) of bond indentures; specialists in securities registration; cohorts devoted to administration of estates and personal trusts (the grist of a trust company client); litigation groups continuously engaged in courtwork; divisions whose members spend most of their time before administrative commissions in Washington (where branch offices provide local accommodation). Below these are galley slaves handling stock-transfer, proxy statement and periodic reporting problems in routine volume. A wry comment in *Fortune* magazine as far back as January 1931—quoted by Swaine himself— noted that "the lawyer is still sometimes a gentleman"—though overshadowed by a shopkeeper's business. At the top of these firms now there are apt to be one or two relatively unknown men always in demand when crises or great decisions of private or public corporate policy are in the making. Usually graduates from one or another of the specialized departments, these men have come to know not only formal corporation law but also to have developed wisdom—advising their most powerful clients in a higher range of problems. Such men not infrequently are asked to become heads of their corporation clients.

In this upper range, I think (and so does Levy) that the corporation lawyer has not departed from his profession. Rather he has extended it. He often operates in that no-man's land where law, economics and political science meet, and where new law is daily crystallizing. At Columbia we teach (sometimes over theoretical objection by our students of jurisprudence) that there is an inchoate law affecting corporations holding market power, or on which the community has come to depend for some essential function, and that this inchoate law has recognizable criteria and principles. The moment these principles are seriously infringed, the state predictably intervenes. In that case an explicit rule of law presently results. Great and powerful interests cannot afford to risk being caught in a major infringement even though the rule has not become explicit; the consequences are apt to be immediate and conceivably far-reaching. As an example: the existence of the "administered price" and the dangers involved in pushing it beyond a certain point are fairly well known to advanced students of corporations. The fact was dramatically illustrated in April 1962 when the steel corporations pushed price administration into a dangerous area—and suddenly found themselves the object not only of political action but of antitrust and various other investigations as well. Under the circumstances, this result was predictable. The top-range level of corporation lawyers, had they been consulted, perhaps could have prevented both the incident and the intervention; certainly a better approach could have been devised.

Yet, and no one has described it better than Mr. Levy, the institutional law offices (he names Sullivan & Cromwell; Davis, Polk, Wardwell, Gardiner & Reed; and the Cravath firm—or, as he calls it, the "Cravath system") now comprise hundreds of lawyers, few of whom will ever reach this upper status. In atrabiliar moments this reviewer sometimes wonders whether the "institutional" corporation law firms of New York and other cities do not accomplish a terrible waste of many of the ablest and best trained young minds American legal education produces. They attract the honor students of the best law schools; the young men vanish into these firms. Some have the courage to strike out on their own after three or four years, and these often give the best account of themselves. Others find well-paid but unrenowned jobs as corporation secretaries. Still others succeed, "making"—that is, becoming junior partners in—the firm. (In my younger days, the cliché was that to "win the race for the firm" cost two nervous breakdowns and a divorce. It was not just, but had an unpleasant amount of truth.) In later mid-career they might even emerge as senior partners, commonly without their names appearing in the firm title. After which they honorably die, leaving as their entire life-product modest fortunes, memberships in highly respectable clubs, and a certain amount of good, unspectacular work as trustees of suburban hospitals or community funds. This picture, though not wholly inaccurate, nevertheless is, as Beryl Levy observes, somewhat unjust. Through good fortune or external personal or political connection some of these men find opportunity in government. This one takes a tour of duty as member of an administrative commission in Washington; another is named delegate to some international conference; a third, more successful, perhaps, is appointed to a judgeship, a sub-Cabinet post, or occasionally to a top Cabinet job. My observation, however, is that a teacher in any respectable law school stands better chance of a brilliant legal career in government or on the bench (if that is what he wants) than do partners in most institutional law firms—though the financial rewards are obviously not as great.

I agree with Mr. Levy that a subtle change is going on in the makeup and functions of corporation practice. It may in time redeem the bulk of the corporation bar from the profitable but usually undistinguished bondage in which most of it lives. This is because the giant corporations it serves are, in fact, primary tools of American industrial supply and development. As their management is increasingly divorced from their ownership, they increasingly evolve into public rather than private institutions. Will-they, nill-they, they thus are becoming a vital part of the public structure of the economic republic comprised in the United States. Necessarily the men who manage them, and the lawyers who advise them, have an increasingly recognizable though nonstatutory position in the public life. Increasingly, too, the formerly despised but now respected staff lawyer or "legal" vice-president, or as he used to be called, "house counsel," of the large corporation gains stature, and jobs on his staff offer wider opportunity. He usually is in the councils of power when decisions are made. He more than any other understands explicit corporation law; but he also knows that beyond its limits there is an inchoate law waiting to become explicit when crisis comes. Understanding the corporation's business as well, he is increasingly likely to enter the business situation as legal and economic statesman as well as corporation employee. More consistently so, perhaps, than the businessman-executive.

An all-too-brief pair of chapters ("Leviathans in 'Partnership'" and "Corporation as Government") suggests in part at least this change in position, intimating (with less emphasis than I should give) that organized labor is now entering a like transitional period.

Finally, Levy poses the question of social responsibility. He gives an incomplete but suggestive roll of honor of lawyers who have met such responsibilities professionally and superbly, often by defending men and their civil liberties irrespective of personal consequences. He could have added that few lawyers, however successful, are long remembered merely for their commercial practice. The lawyer's luster and his title to esteem almost always comes from his extra-curricular, extra-commercial work. William G. Thompson in Boston defended Sacco and Vanzetti—to his loss. But he lives in history, while few recall the contemporary corporation lawyer-leaders of the Massachusetts Bar. Clarence Darrow, trying the Scopes case, made his reputation national, though few would recommend defense of an insignificant schoolteacher fighting a crackpot statute as a promising avenue to success. Going on the bench or into government almost invariably means financial sacrifice: Henry L. Stimson made his reputation, not his fortune, by becoming Secretary of State. As a rule men are not asked to defend civil liberties cases even as volunteers, or to enter high government service, or to take judgeships, merely because they have ground out a successful commercial corporation practice grist. In every case it would be found that these men—there are, happily, many of them —had early developed and long communicated a passionate interest in some aspect of the social, political and intellectual affairs of their time, and had demonstrated willingness as well as capacity to make a contribution thereto.

The late Harlan Stone—professor and Dean of Columbia Law School, later head of an "institutional" corporation law firm, thereafter Attorney General, Justice of the Supreme Court and finally Chief Justice of the United States, whose reputation will grow in history as more about him is known and understood—used to make this plain as teacher, as practitioner, and as judge, to his students and younger friends, including this reviewer. I am grateful that Levy refers to him in closing, and to Stone's invincible confidence that the "lawyer's age-old and resurgent capacity for leadership and idealism will reassert itself."

# THE EMERGING ROLE OF
# THE CORPORATE COUNSEL    By Leon E. Hickman

THE TOPIC for discussion is the role of the corporate counsel, the lawyer who functions for a corporation as a full-time, salaried employee. The practice of law within a corporation on a completely independent, fully professional basis is a relatively new development.

From a time antedating World War I and continuing through the 1920's, most high-ranking graduates of the good law schools practiced their profession as general practitioners, quite commonly with the large law firms. Beginning with the depression and carrying through World War II, a career in government was something of a fetish among the law school graduates who were good enough to have a choice. This is not surprising because it marked the beginning of the era of big government, the emergence of the welfare state. New concepts of government service had to be planned, enabling statutes of revolutionary scope drawn, lobbied through Congress and finally both administered and litigated. Government service is still a stimulating field for the lawyer because great responsibility comes relatively early in one's career.

The period since World War II has been the era of the salaried corporate counsel. His emergence was in response to the ever-increasing need for daily counsel on the legal intricacies of public regulation, both by statute and administrative agency. I am sure I need not labor the growing complexity of doing business lawfully in a period when regulation by the Securities and Exchange Commission, the Federal Power Commission, the Wage and Hour Administration and Robinson-Patman, not to mention the revitalization of such old-timers as the Sherman Act and the Clayton Act, followed each other in bewildering succession. The growth of corporations to a size where their impact on the social and economic well-being of the nation gave them public responsibilities of a vast but indeterminate nature also made the detached and trained viewpoint of full-time legal advisers quite indispensable. Today, most corporations which are more than local enterprises employ counsel on a full-time, salaried basis.

The gradual evolution of corporate counsel over this half-century can be roughly traced by the popular characterization of him. In the 1920's

---

Reprinted from *The Business Lawyer* (a publication of the American Bar Association), April 1957, pp. 216–228, with the permission of the author and the publisher. The author is General Counsel for Alcoa.

the occasional lawyer who drifted into corporate employment was rather derisively referred to by most of the general practitioners as a "kept" counsel. It was assumed that such a lawyer had sold his professional independence for a monthly pay check; that the hand which controlled the purse controlled his conscience and that he could not advise his corporation effectively because he was employed by it.

As we emerged from the depression, the corporate lawyer gradually assumed a greater variety of duties commensurate with the growing complexities of corporate life. In this period, he rose in professional stature to the dignity of "house counsel," a humbling but honorable title which implied employment on legal housekeeping tasks, the drafting of minutes or resolutions, the preparation or examination of routine papers, the drafting of contracts of a repetitive nature, but hardly responsibility for really complex legal problems.

Since World War II, house counsel has emerged as the "corporate counsel." The head lawyer has commonly become the general counsel, usually an officer of the company, not infrequently a member of the board, and, if circumstances are right, a party to the corporation's innermost councils and planning. . . .

### Some Popular Misconceptions

It has long been assumed by general practitioners that the corporate counsel forfeited his professional independence in accepting full-time employment, that he probably spent his time giving the advice that his nonlegal colleagues wished to hear and that at best he was no more than a slave to the dictum attributed to Elihu Root that

> The client never wants to be told he can't do what he wants to do; he wants to be told how to do it, and it is the lawyer's business to tell him how.

I doubt if that picture was ever true; certainly it is completely false today. I know well the general counsel of most of the larger firms and have discussed with many of them their professional position and freedom. "Kept" they may be in the sense that the corporation pays their salary regularly and generously; "kept" they are not if one means that someone is the keeper of their conscience or of their professional judgments. Freer men I have never known. Having staff rather than line functions, they are not subject to pressures to make a certain sales quota or to reach a production target. Often they alone are in a position within a corporation to stand out against wrongful business pressure. Their success does not depend on production or sales or a treasury balance; it depends upon being men of good judgment. The judgment must include a sound knowledge of law, the process by which both legislatures and courts make new law, and the ability to state one's convictions effectively but in good spirit. These corporate counsel can and do take the long view. They are not entitled to exercise a veto power over corporate action and they do not aspire to that role. But if they are competent, they are listened to as one voice in the corporate family which is detached, analytical and objective, and which is raised with the corporation's over-all and long-range interests always in mind.

I know of no corporate counsel who holds with Elihu Root's dictum. Mr. Root was probably right in his estimate that most corporate officials like to be told how to do what they have decided should be done, but the really responsible executives are equally appreciative of well-thought-out advice that a certain course of action is unsound, and that neither it nor anything like it should be undertaken. I suppose that many think he who controls the purse controls the mind, and that corporate counsel cannot have an independent judgment with respect to the plans of those who pay his salary. I have found it otherwise. A corporate counsel may not only reach an undesired conclusion, he can stay with it and reiterate it long after his brethren in the general practice might well find it the part of wisdom to rest on their record and the shield that the responsibility for error was not theirs.

The great danger to the professional independence of the corporate lawyer—and the only danger that I recognize—lies within the lawyer himself. It is that he may choose to subordinate his professional judgment to a commercial one; that he may forget that he is the lawyer but not the businessman. Yet if his interest in commercial considerations is kept in proper perspective, his value as a counselor increases. He becomes interested in keeping the company out of the red as well as out of the courtroom; in maintaining a trained, productive labor force as well as in Taft-Hartley; in employee safety as well as workmen's compensation; in effective salesmanship as well as Robinson-Patman; and in better production methods and new applications quite as much as in patents and infringements. This added comprehension improves his legal judgment. But he must never forget that his responsibility remains legal rather than commercial. Otherwise he is only the baseball pitcher who subordinates his concentration on his curve and his control to the twice-a-season double.

A second misconception is that the corporate lawyer has a captive clientele. I have not found it so. If his judgments are not respected, if he is not available for consultation when wanted, or if he runs with the ball and makes the nonlegal decisions as well as the legal ones, his nonlegal brethren simply do without the advice of counsel when the need next arises. Of course, those corporate officials who deal only in matters of ultimate responsibility and with questions of obviously grave legal consequences do not have this escape from lawyers; but nine-tenths of the matters that occupy the attention of a corporate legal department would simply be decided without the advice of lawyers if such counsel were not given cooperatively, promptly and competently.

Another piece of folklore is that corporate lawyers are employed on salary to save money. I doubt that such an assumption is valid. The usual corporation lawyer would be less than human if he did not notice that outside counsel occasionally charge as much for a month's work as he may receive in a year. But such thoughts overlook the fact that corporate counsel is not only assured of a salary—and usually a good one—but of an office, a staff, a pension, possibly a stock option and the variety of additional perquisites that go with his particular status as an official of his company. Corporate law departments have an increasing acceptance, not because of their relative cost, but because of the service they are in a position to perform.

If the corporate lawyer is to justify himself, the justification must be on the basis that he renders a superior service. This I believe he does; not because he is a better lawyer, but because he is in a more favorable position than the general practitioner. For example, I am satisfied that I am a much more effective counsel to my corporation in my present capacity than I was as an outside general practitioner devoting almost full time to its work. The corporate counsel holds all the advantage in position, whether viewed from the standpoint of access to facts, understanding of personalities, comprehension of issues or appreciation of long-range corporate policies and objectives.

### The Unique Advantages of the Corporate Counsel

In most ways the corporate counsel functions like any other lawyer. He negotiates, drafts and reviews contracts and written agreements of all sorts. He determines the legal meaning of statutes and written agreements. He participates in negotiations. He gives ad hoc judgments on an infinite variety of proposed corporate moves. He may or may not do courtroom work, depending largely on his own inclinations. He employs general law firms and works with them. But there are at least three aspects in which the corporate counsel is in a position to be uniquely effective. He may practice preventive law; he can be certain of his facts; and he can schedule his work on an acceptable timetable. How well he utilizes these advantages of his inside position is up to him, but the opportunity is there. If the possibilities in all three fields are fully developed, you have a lawyer at his maximum effectiveness.

*Preventive Law.* It has been said that "a corporation needs a legal department in order to avoid the need for lawyers." This is true for a variety of reasons. Corporate counsel can be and usually is called into consultation early. He commonly participates for weeks or months in the planning, the discussions, the development of the corporate projects before legal difficulties arise. He has maximum opportunity to anticipate trouble. He may meet such legal difficulties either by counseling action that he regards as legal or by suggesting a change in the program that avoids the issue altogether. He is consulted in advance of legal trouble on an infinite variety of spot decisions; and this comes easily, both because he is available and because the advice does not add to the cost of the project.

It is not so natural for outside counsel to occupy this forehanded position. Commonly he is only consulted after a legal obstacle has arisen. While he could have been consulted earlier, there are difficulties. The corporate official who foresees the possibility of a legal problem may deprecate the time it takes to give outside counsel a correct feel of the facts or may be reluctant to incur additional expense. And perhaps the problem will never arise anyway. None of these considerations militates against a telephone call, a memorandum or a conference with house counsel.

The long view is an important facet of preventive law. Much of a corporation's legal trouble arises from decisions to win today's battle and let tomorrow take care of itself. Consistent with this pragmatic philosophy, outside counsel, when retained, is frequently requested simply to construe a statute, draw a contract or advise on the legality of a proposed corporation decision without being made a party to the total course of action of which the decision is but one piece. It is not so easy to limit the frame of reference of the corporate counsel. No fellow employee is in a position to tell him that he is not being asked to consider the long-range implications of a course of action or the effect of one department's moves upon the legal position of another. The frame of reference within which he operates, and must operate, is as broad as the interests of the corporation itself.

*Certainty about Facts.* Most legal problems find their origin and their answer in the facts. One of the great values of corporate counsel is his ability to get the facts of a situation, not only promptly but accurately and fully. He has the advantage of devoting his full time to the affairs of a single company; and of knowing its over-all policies, programs and problems with the assurance born of day-to-day relationship with them. He has a rather accurate basis for appraisal of the ability of his nonlegal corporate colleagues to give him the facts on which he must act. He is in a position to know those who are objective and analytical, as well as those who are constitutionally optimistic or inclined to submit only those facts which will produce a predetermined answer. Additionally, house counsel is in a position to get data from any source within the corporation promptly and as a matter of routine.

Outside counsel does not commonly enjoy such advantages to an equal degree. His contact with the corporate organization usually cannot be as close or on as wide a scale. Normally, he cannot start with as thorough a knowledge of the company's over-all position. The very existence of factual investigations by outside counsel may arouse rumors, fears and occasionally an effort to cover up mistakes. With rare exceptions, the outside counsel considers only those problems which are brought to him and builds his factual background by a cross-examination of the corporate employee who consults him. His knowledge of the facts is not apt to be much better or broader than the knowledge of the man with whom he talks, one who commonly is not a lawyer. Such further investigation as he may direct is likely to be on the basis of leads developed in these conversations. The general practitioner's preoccupation with the affairs of many clients and his limited authority to probe behind the facts given to him tend to limit rather severely the factual background of the outside practitioner. The files of Alcoa are replete with brilliantly reasoned opinions of general practitioners which have little or no value because of the incompleteness or the distorted emphasis of their factual assumptions.

The fact-finding advantages of the corporate counsel should be fully utilized. They are an indispensable tool to the practice of preventive law.

*Acceptable Timetable.* I was somewhat shocked after twenty-six years in the general practice of corporate law to learn how little comprehension I really had of the importance of timing in corporate counseling. Litigation presents no problem, for the court determines the timing; nor does a Securities and Exchange Commission registration, for the underwriters and the Commission dictate the schedule. But in that great intermediate field of decisions on competitive problems such as the applicability of Robinson-Patman or the drafting of a contract or a deed, general practitioners, to a greater extent than house counsel, tend to view the assignment in isolation and as a timeless project. In a way this is not surprising, for the problem is usually submitted to them in isolation from the surrounding circumstances. And in the normal course of events, these legal assignments, artificially isolated from a current commercial struggle, take their place on the general practitioner's desk in competition with pending assignments, commonly for other clients.

Inside corporation counsel should have a better knowledge of timing. A Robinson-Patman Act question not uncommonly originates in a telephone call from a district sales office asking if a price may be cut or some other concession granted on a sale which, at that very moment, is being competitively sought by Alcoa and its competitors on the basis of comparative price or terms. Unless the general sales representative in Pittsburgh can get legal advice within a matter of minutes, or at most of hours, he does not need the advice for the sale has been lost to a competitor by Alcoa's inaction. It is here that house counsel has a great advantage. If a corporate legal department is well organized, there are at least two, and preferably three, lawyers in the department who are completely current on all decisions under Robinson-Patman and on the company's sales policies and problems. If certain commodities are under great competitive pressure, the corporate counsel should know it as a matter of daily liaison with the sales people with whom he regularly works, eats and plays. He is in a position to pass on the legality of a proposed sales gambit almost as soon as it is put to him. If more research is needed, he does it between legal assignments, knowing that the next problem in the same field will also come to him.

The ability to make the required legal decisions in timing with the nonlegal aspects of the same project is furthered by the common practice of assigning staff counsel to a corporate project at its inception, well in advance of any legal problem. Counsel sits in on the initial discussions between engineers, salesmen or accountants, as the case may be. When a point of legal doubt is reached, counsel is not only there but he is completely conversant with the factual background and the personalities involved. On most such occasions, he will have had days or weeks of forewarning that at a foreseeable point in the project certain types of legal problems are to be anticipated; and when they are reached, he should be able to pass upon them with a timeliness that would permit the project to continue without a break.

I cannot stress too much the importance to a dynamic, competitive enterprise of a prompt legal decision. Such speed is not often possible with outside counsel. Most corporations would be reluctant to retain a firm to absorb so much preliminary background before approaching the legal problem. The more normal method would be to proceed until the legal impediment were reached, then call in outside counsel, explain matters to him from the beginning, give him time to research the law, to get the matter on his own calendar in competition with assignments of other clients, and finally to give an answer. It is easy to see that the timetable is improved from the standpoint of the corporate official in that much less time must be spent with corporate counsel in explaining the problem than would be the case if a lawyer were called in from the outside. This makes the businessman much more ready to recognize a legal problem or the need for a lawyer's advice.

Another advantage to a corporation in the employment of corporate counsel is that these lawyers are available at all times for the company's work. More than that, their time can be marshaled so that they give priority to the problem that is more urgent. It is not always so with outside counsel who have a number of clients. It is no answer to one client to say that another's problem is more urgent or more important, for to the first client it is not. It is much easier within a single corporation to decide which problem is the most urgent, or, if there be a difference of opinion, to determine which corporate official takes precedence.

It is my experience at Alcoa that many more matters have been submitted to inside counsel than were ever given to outside counsel. I cannot avoid the suspicion that in the absence of lawyers prepared to give immediate and, at the same time, well-thought-out answers without added expense to the project, our nonlegal brothers in the corporate enterprise simply decide that they are not willing to submit to the delay, and that, consequently, it is not a legal problem that faces them. But, I would be less than candid with you if I did not reveal that Alcoa has its share of those who first discover their legal problems at the eleventh hour, and only then seek advice. Perhaps it would be more accurate to say that after a transaction has been fully planned and perhaps a program publicly announced, it is then submitted to counsel for the first time, not so much for help as for a benediction. And usually these are the very people who are most impatient of a lawyer's delay! However, I am led to believe that this is a vanishing breed that can be educated into better habits by an alert and cooperative legal department.

Thus far we have seen that the corporate counsel enjoys three unique advantages in working from within the corporate structure. If he lives up to his opportunities, he practices preventive law to the hilt; he understands the factual basis of his corporation's problems and their significance better than almost any man in the company; and he gives his counsel in a timely fashion that has an importance little understood outside the corporation. So much for the ability of the good corporate counsel to translate the advantage of his position into effective, day-by-day counseling.

## The Emerging Role of the Corporate Counsel as an Advisor on Corporate Citizenship

The position and status of the corporate counsel give him another role to play, perhaps more significant than the ones already discussed. This is his opportunity, his right, indeed his duty, to counsel and encourage good corporate citizenship. He is in a uniquely effective position to do so. The importance of this role can hardly be overstated. And the importance of an acceptable corporate citizenship in our delicately balanced capitalism cannot be overemphasized. Corporate freedom of action extends only so far as there is at least public acquiescence, and preferably public support; and the public is fickle. It is the corporate counsel's prime function to work toward maintaining the public's support and consent for the existing and evolving corporate form. I do not mean to imply that his is likely to be a voice in the wilderness. Every good management is well aware of the pressures on our evolving corporate capitalism and is extremely sensitive in its appraisal of the consequences of compliance with or resistance to these pressures. But a corporation can proceed into this difficult area with much more effectiveness if its corporate counsel is also alert to the problem. . . .

The corporate lawyer is in a strong position to counsel and encourage legal conduct that will merit public support. It is here that corporate counsel can perform his greatest role. He is a student of the gradual enlargement of our common and statute law. If he is worth his salt, he knows better than most those economic and social pressures that will find their way into law, as well as those that are false and predatory.

The post of corporate counsel is no role for an appeaser; he must know just as well when to advise a fight as when to yield a little in order not to lose a great deal more. More importantly, he must know how to deploy corporate forces so that on most occasions battle lines will never be formed. He must rise above the cautious role of the lawyer who simply advises that a proposed course of action is legal or illegal and leaves to others the wisdom of the corporate policy. The corporate counsel's voice should be insistent in favor of going beyond bare legal minima; when to do so will build for his company a reservoir of public good will, or minimize or eliminate what would otherwise be a widespread feeling of injury or injustice.

Corporate support of higher education, of hospitals and of community betterment—explained to and supported by the shareholders whose money is being spent—are illustrations that quickly come to mind. The equitable sharing of one's own production with customers in times of shortage is another. The insistence upon the letter of a contract when the consequence is widespread distress in certain areas of our economy is an obvious example of a course to be avoided. In the long run, a corporate policy or program is not justified, and will not benefit the company expounding it, unless it benefits consumer, supplier, employee and shareholder alike.

Corporate counsel is freer than anyone else in the corporate family from pressure, and his responsibility is correspondingly greater. He has no direct responsibility for production, sales or finance. He operates from a detached staff position. He is trained in analysis and is a student of the political processes out of which our laws and free capitalistic society have emerged. Like the abbot in the ancient monastery, the clerk to the feudal baron or the chancellor to the king, the corporation counsel is in a position to wield a unique influence. The fact that his number is rapidly increasing and the importance of his role recognized and utilized leads me to believe that, as a group, corporate counsel are exercising their prerogatives constructively. At least, that is my hope.

---

*COMMENT. Small-firm, Small-town Law.* It would be helpful to round out the picture of the bar in action by an introduction to law as it is practiced in small cities and small firms. However, at this level the practice of law is so individualized and variegated that we need refer the reader to other sources.

Highly recommended is a novel: Cozzens, *The Just and the Unjust* (New York: Harcourt, 1942). The late Professor Chafee, whose judgment on matters both literary and legal your editor deeply respects, in reviewing the book wrote: "This is one of the best legal novels the reviewer has ever read, and he is not given to superlatives. . . . When the reader reaches the last page, he has been given the best account I know of the daily life of ordinary lawyers." For a compact view, see Woodbury, "Shall I Practice in a Small Community" in *Listen to Leaders in Law*, Love and Childers, eds. (Atlanta: Tupper and Love, 1963). A more dismal view: Carlin, *Lawyers on their Own* (New Brunswick: Rutgers U. P., 1962).

Useful information will be found in Blaustein and Porter, *The American Lawyer* (Boston: Little, Brown, 1954); Chapter 2, pp. 41–63, helpfully describes legal work of varying types, such as private practice, corporate counsel, labor lawyer, and government attorney. A good suspense story with a realistic setting in small-town practice is Travers, *Anatomy of a Murder* (New York: St. Martin's, 1957) (the author is actually Justice Voelker of the Supreme Court of Michigan). See also Partridge, *Country Lawyer* (New York: McGraw-Hill, 1939). *Cf.* Hays, *City Lawyer* (New York: Simon & Schuster, 1942); Pepper, *Philadelphia Lawyer* (Philadelphia: Lippincott, 1944).

*Part Three*

# PERSPECTIVES

CHAPTER 9

# Beyond the Frontier

PERHAPS THE MOST DRAMATIC LEGAL development of this decade is the growing importance of transnational law. This is not so much innovation as renaissance; as we have seen, a cosmopolitan approach to law characterized early stages of English development and the early years of American independence.[1]

This early breadth of view rested in part on the thought that law was a science which employed moral or intellectual principles of general applicability. There are tentative indications of a current rebirth of this idea; more compelling are powerful forces of a pragmatic nature which are hammering at the legal isolation of the past century. One can now get to the opposite side of the world in less time than once was needed for the trip from New York to Washington; even greater speed is available for the transmission of information and the delivery of weapons for mass annihilation. American capital and goods are being exported in large quantities; even in inland manufacturing cities there is call for lawyers who know something of foreign legal systems. And, strangely enough, aspects of our own legal institutions, concealed from us by familiarity, can be more sharply seen in the light of other ways of approaching the same problem.[2]

We turn first to the civil law systems which provide the bases for law throughout the continent of Europe, in Quebec and Louisiana, throughout the American republics to the South, and in much of Asia and Africa.

[1] Chapter 1, pp. 10, 14, and 44–48, discussed continental influences in English Law; Chapter 2, pp. 70–71, discussed the use of civil law precedents in early American lawmaking. The struggle for codification, discussed in Chapter 3, was also influenced by continental experience, and a related theme reappears in the Restatement phenomenon considered in Chapter 4. *Cf.* Schlesinger, *Comparative Law* (Brooklyn: Foundation Press, 1952), p. 6.

[2] For a general introduction to the use of comparative law, see Gutteridge, *Comparative Law* (London: Cambridge U. P., 1946).

# THE CIVIL LAW SYSTEM:
# AN HISTORICAL INTRODUCTION   By Arthur T. von Mehren

THE LEGAL systems of the western world are, for purposes of comparison, frequently divided into two groups: the civil law system, seen in French and German law, and the common-law system developed in England. Two points of difference are usually emphasized in comparing the civil and the common laws. First, in the civil law, large areas of private law are codified. Codification is not typical of the common law. Second, the civil law was strongly and variously influenced by Roman law. The Roman influence on the common law was far less profound and in no way pervasive. These points of difference should not be allowed to obscure the extent to which the civil and the common laws share a common tradition. Both systems were developments within western European culture; they hold many values in common. Both are products of western civilization.

This section sketches in broad outline the development of the common and civil law systems with particular attention to the question of why the Continent had recourse to codification whereas England never codified its law.

Our sketch must begin with the Romans. Roman law, over its long history, was brought to a high level of juristic development. The Romans, with their genius for institution and their practical common sense, achieved excellent solutions for particular problems and combined these solutions into a remarkable body of law. This law, reflecting the relatively high development of Roman political, economic, and social life, met the requirements of a culturally and economically advanced society. After the fall of Rome, such a society was not to begin to re-emerge in Europe until the later Middle Ages.

Much of what is today Europe, including parts of England, had been romanized for some 400 years before the western Roman Empire was shattered by the German tribes and formally came to an end. . . . With the breakup of the Roman Empire in the West, the only political and cultural force capable of creating and maintaining legal and political unity disappeared. Highly effective organs of social control, the Roman

---

Reprinted from von Mehren, *The Civil Law System* (Boston: Little, Brown, 1957), pp. 3–12, with the permission of the author and the publisher. The author is Professor of Law at Harvard University, a member of the Conceil de la Faculté de Droit, Université Internationale des Sciences Comparés, Luxembourg, and a Director of the American Association for the Study of Law.

courts and administrators, were replaced by relatively weak and imperfect institutions. Large areas of human activity were no longer under law. Western Europe might, however, not have slipped back into a localized, agrarian society if to the fall of Rome had not been added the expansion of Islam.

The Mediterranean was the Roman world's great artery of commerce. The barbarian kingdoms, "founded in the fifth century on the soil of Western Europe, still preserved the most striking and essential characteristic of ancient civilization, to wit, its Mediterranean character." The great landlocked sea made communication and transportation relatively easy. It provided an essential basis for both the unity and the commercial life of the Roman Empire. Even after the breakup of the Empire, it fulfilled this function. Trade continued. . . .

The rise of Islam in the course of the seventh century changed this whole picture. By conquest, the Moslems obtained control of Africa and Spain and possession of the Balearic Isles, Corsica, Sardinia, and Sicily. Western Europe was cut off from the Byzantine Empire and lost its great avenue of communication and transportation. . . . The ending of commercial activity, the interruption of commerce, "brought about the disappearance of the merchants, and urban life, which had been maintained by them, collapsed at the same time." The Roman cities survived only as centers of diocesan administration, losing both their economic significance and their municipal administration. Some coasting trade remained along the shores of the North Sea until the end of the 9th century when the Norsemen destroyed it. The activities of first the Avars and then the Magyars prevented use of the Danube as an alternative artery of commerce.

These facts made profound economic, legal, and social changes inevitable in Western Europe. The legal and political order appropriate to the highly-developed commercial civilization that Rome had achieved could not survive the collapse of its political and later its economic basis. . . . Western Europe became essentially a rural civilization. An estate economy without markets developed. Sale and purchase were not the normal occupations of anyone; they were expedients resorted to only in times of bad crops or when it was necessary to obtain a few essential commodities, such as salt, which could not be produced locally.

Roman law was not entirely lost or forgotten during this period. Elements of Roman law persisted in memory or as custom and habit. The Church preserved in its law and culture much of Roman civilization. The system of personal law that prevailed in the German kingdoms subjected the Roman element of the population to Roman law, though this law became obscure and corrupted. . . .

The most important single event for the subsequent history of Roman law in western Europe occurred, paradoxically perhaps, after the fall in 476 of the western Empire. The Roman Empire continued in the East with its seat at Constantinople. It was there, in 528, that Emperor Justinian (527–565) ordered the great compilation, systematization, and consolidation of Roman law later known as the *Corpus juris civilis*. Justinian's "codification" comprises the Institutes, the Digest, the Code (or collection of imperial enactments) and the Novels (or collection of later imperial enactments). The Institutes, the Digest, and the Code were promulgated between 533 and 534. The Novels contain imperial legislation enacted after the Code was issued. This later imperial legislation was never officially collected. The Novels are based on private collections.

The Digest, also known as the Pandects, is for the history of western law by far the most important part of the *Corpus juris*. It is a compilation of the writings of the great Roman jurists, especially those of the classical period. As the Digest was to state the current law, changes had to be made in the original texts. A committee of sixteen, headed by Tribonian, accomplished the work of compilation, systematization, and abridgement in the short period between 530 and 533.

The Institutes is a systematic treatise intended for the use of law students. It is based in considerable measure upon an earlier work of the same type written by Gaius. A committee of three compiled the Institutes in the last year of the preparation of the Digest. It was published almost concurrently with the Digest.

Justinian's Codes were introduced into Western Europe in 544 when the eastern Empire reconquered Italy. They were not, however, of real significance for western European law until the twelfth-century "revival" of the study of Roman law at the Italian universities.

It was probably Irnerius who gave at Bologna, in the twelfth-century, the first lectures on the Digest. These lectures are a milestone in European legal history. They mark the discovery of the great compilation of Roman law and begin the development of a legal science around that body of law. Irnerius' lectures came at a time when profound political and economic changes were already under way in western Europe. . . . The 12th century saw a large-scale expansion of commerce along both the Mediterranean and northern coasts of western Europe. "The revival of maritime commerce was accompanied by its rapid penetration inland. Not only was agriculture stimulated by the demand for its produce and transformed by the exchange economy of which it now became a part, but a new export industry was born."

The twelfth century saw a rapid increase in the number of fairs. These fairs provided organized facilities for commercial exchange. Towns developed into commercial centers. . . . These and other developments led, from the twelfth century onward, to demands for a new law. Custom, "which had been gradually elaborated to regulate the relations of men living by the cultivation or the ownership of the land, was inadequate for a population whose existence was based on commerce and industry." The old law "had to disappear with the economic state that it reveals to us."

The creation of a new law and a legal science on the Continent and in England was a long, complex process. Its history is a part of the general history of the economic, political, and intellectual development of western Europe. The new law was woven from many strands: existing customs and practices, the customs of merchants, canon law, the revived Roman law and, at a later stage, natural-law philosophies. Various agencies contributed to its elaboration: practitioners, judges, administrators, scholars, men of affairs, churchmen, and philosophers. In the period from roughly the end of the eleventh to the beginning of the fourteenth century two differences, which were to be of crucial importance for the later history of the civil and the common laws, appear in the general legal situation on the Continent and in England. On the Continent the revived Roman law, based on study of the *Corpus juris civilis*, has a much greater impact than in England. During this same period, the English kings, in striking contrast to their French and German counterparts, create an effective, centralized administration of justice.

In the eleventh century, legal studies, especially in Italy and Southern France, begin to change in a remarkable manner. System and science gradually replace the primitive legal thought characteristic of earlier periods. Irnerius' lectures at Bologna on the newly discovered Digest were "an event arising out of the spontaneous growth of ideas and requirements in different localities of the more civilized regions of Europe." They came at a most propitious moment. Two areas of life, the political and the commercial, required new legal solutions. Politically, the great problem was to organize a sufficiently strong central power to prevent complete fragmentation of governmental power. Economically, it was necessary to develop legal techniques to permit the carrying on and further development of trade.

The local law had not proved adequate to these challenges. The administration of justice was very decentralized and lacked trained, specialized personnel. The feudal system, with its localizing tendencies, prevented the establishment of central judicial agencies that could develop a law common to the larger political and economic units that were emerging. Lacking trained, specialized personnel working in a tradition, the local, customary law had little growing power.

But the local law was not merely deficient. The newly discovered *Corpus juris civilis* had a claim to direct authority as the law of the *imperium romanum*. It also embodied the Roman cultural ideal. Rome, its glory and its unity, had lingered on in men's minds. Roman law was one of the expressions of that glory and that unity for which men still longed. Roman law favored centralized governmental authority. The *Corpus juris* contained a law capable of solving satisfactorily many of the problems of a more active economy and a more cultivated society. Roman law offered, if not the only, the best hope for a unified, common law. Roman law had also already formed and shaped, at least in part, many of the existing customs and social institutions of western Europe. The *Corpus juris civilis* came, therefore, not as completely strange and foreign but as part of a shared and not entirely forgotten past.

With the lectures of Irnerius at Bologna thus begins for western Europe the study of Justinian's lawbooks as a coherent, systematic body of law. The importance and influence of the revived Roman law spread rapidly. By the end of the twelfth century there were at Bologna alone 10,000 students in law. Students from the Italian schools carried the new learning throughout western Europe. Scholars of Roman law came to have such prestige that university doctors of law were appointed to the royal councils and made judges in many local courts. . . .

During the period between 1100 and 1500 the Roman law, the *Corpus juris civilis,* became the basis for legal science throughout western Europe. The *Corpus juris* also made important contributions to practice at the level of specific rules and solutions. The degree of Roman law influence, particularly in this latter respect, differed in the various parts of the Continent. In France, Roman influence was greater in the southern part of the country, the *pays de droit écrit,* than in the northern part, the *pays de coûtumes.* In Germany, a decree of Maximilian I in 1495 formally "received" the *Corpus juris,* as glossed by Italian scholars, as the law to be applied in the newly organized imperial court of justice, the Reichskammergericht. Roman law did not thereby become a general law. Particularism was recognized in the maxim that "Town's law breaks land's law, land's law breaks common law." The example of the Reichskammergericht was soon followed by the high courts of the various German principalities, states, and towns. Nevertheless, the law administered in the German courts was never fully romanized. However, German legal science, centered in the universities, was based almost entirely upon Roman materials.

By 1500 France and Germany, along with western Europe as a whole, had thus achieved the basis for a common legal science grounded on Roman law sources. In England, though English law was influenced by continental developments, this romanized legal science was never received. The revived Roman law had, of course, some influence on the developing common law. Vacarius was at Oxford teaching Roman law in 1151. The intellectual community of the period was small and international in character. It kept in relatively close contact, aided by the fact that learned conversation and learned writing were in Latin. It is clear that English lawmen borrowed from their continental brethren and found suggestive insights in continental learning. Roman law also influenced the common law through the canon law of the Catholic and later the Anglican church. At various periods in English legal history the ecclesiastical courts and judges, as well as lawyers trained in canon law, were active in the administration of the law relating to testamentary matters, domestic relations, and admiralty. In these branches of the law, Roman conceptions, as modified and molded by Christian ethics, were of particular importance in shaping the common law that we know today.[a]

The Roman law, though it influenced the rules and solutions of certain areas of the common law, never decisively shaped its techniques or habits of thought. There are no famous English glossators or commentators on the *Corpus juris*. The *Corpus juris* never became for English lawmen the starting point for systematic reasoning and investigation that it was for the lawmen of the Continent. How is this difference to be explained? The problem is related to the question of why France and Germany had recourse in modern times to legislative codification of the private law.

The basic fact of English legal history is the early creation of a national, efficient, and centralized administration of justice. This development was possible because in England political power was at an early date centralized, rationalized, and made effective. In 1066, the Norman invasion brought to England a class of capable administrators in the service of a lord who claimed central political power by right of conquest. In feudal theory England was one fief. Thus the feudal system, instead of tending to fractionalize political power as it did on the Continent, gave an acceptable basis for the development of effective organs of central power. The early English kings, many of whom were unusually capable and energetic, made the most of their opportunities. They early created institutions designed to secure and increase central governmental authority. The Domesday Book (1086) symbolizes both the administrative skill and diligence of Norman officialdom and William's determination to use the feudal system, with its confusion of government and property, to strengthen the royal, central power.

Among the most important institutions developed by William and his successors for the maintenance and strengthening of central authority was the king's court. At this period, a tripartite division of power between the executive, legislative, and judicial branches of government was unknown. The concept of conscious legislation had not developed and would

[a] For Professor Maitland's discussion of ecclesiastical influences see Chapter 1, pp. 15–16.

hardly have fitted the needs of a period during which change tended to be gradual. The royal courts held a large share of this undifferentiated governmental power.

In the twelfth century, Henry I (1100–1135) began the practice of sending his ministers around the country to hear cases in the local courts. Before the end of the century, the king's court, with its regular circuits, was the most powerful political institution in the country. These courts were staffed with trained officials, who regularly visited every part of England, but whose permanent headquarters were at the king's court and whose allegiance was to the central national political authority. "And because the royal court is very powerful in England, because it has very little seigneurial justice to fight against, because the old popular courts are already antiquated, the law of the royal court rapidly becomes the one law *common* to all the realm, the law which swallows up all, or nearly all, the petty local and tribal peculiarities of which English law, at the time of the Conquest, is full." "Between the accession of Henry I and the death of Henry III [1100–1272], this Court has declared the Common Law of England."

The institutional fact of a unified court system thus resulted in the growth of a law common to the entire realm. The common law, unhampered by a strict rule of *stare decisis,* was able to develop new rules and techniques adequate for a period in which the rate of change was relatively slow. The centralization of justice called forth an organized class of lawyers. The English bar soon established a tradition of law teaching. The universities never came to occupy the dominant role in legal education that they early achieved on the Continent. The existence of an independently organized bar with a vested interest in the law administered in the English courts may well be the basic reason why Roman law was never received in England.

England thus achieved a truly common law through a slow and organic growth. The English courts created, over many centuries, a unified law. The contrast with France and Germany is striking. Neither of these countries achieved until modern times a common law in the sense of a general body of law common to the whole country. The explanation for this difference between the legal situations of England and of France and Germany is fundamentally institutional. France and Germany achieved a centralized administration of justice at a much later period than did England.

Until the end of the fifteenth century, the history of the evolution of the organization and structure of the French legal system forms part of the struggle between the feudal system, with local, seignorial judges, and the emerging, ever-clearer fact of royal, central power. This picture is further complicated by a conflict between the Church and the developing State. Jurisdictions overlapped. The administration of justice was notoriously slow, complicated, and expensive. No institution existed with a sufficiently general and exclusive jurisdiction to permit the development of a body of common law. Between the end of the fifteenth century and the French Revolution, the royal, central power became increasingly dominant. An important step toward unification was one taken in the Ordinance of 1667, which gave France for the first time a truly uniform civil procedure. During the sixteenth century, the customs of northern France were "codified."

Unification was, however, not achieved during the *ancien régime*. Portalis well described the French scene on the eve of the promulgation in 1804 of the French Civil Code: "What a spectacle opened before our eyes! Facing us was only a confused and shapeless mass of foreign and French laws, of general and particular customs, of abrogated and non-abrogated ordinances, of contradictory regulations and conflicting decisions; one encountered nothing but a mysterious labyrinth, and, at every moment, the guiding thread escaped us. We were always on the point of getting lost in an immense chaos." The greatest achievement of the French Civil Code was to give France a national, unified, and coherent body of law. The newly found unity is symbolized by Article 7 of the Law of 30 Ventôse, An XII (March 21, 1804), which promulgated the various separately-enacted laws as a single Civil Code: "From the day on which these laws enter into force, the Roman laws, the ordinances, the general and the local collections of customs, the statutes (*statuts*), the regulations all cease to have the force of law in the matter covered by the laws which comprise this Code."

Legal unity was even longer delayed in Germany. Modern Germany did not achieve political unity until the final decades of the nineteenth century. Before the Civil Code became effective, at least six systems of law were in force within the territory of the new state. These systems were subject to change by local law and custom. The law as to succession, for example, often varied from one contiguous locality to another. Some of the laws in force were written in German, others in French, others in Greek, Latin, or Danish. The situation prior to 1900, the date the German Civil Code took effect, is well characterized by the observation "That such an anomalous state of things could have been tolerated for so long a time is a legal mystery which remains to be solved."

# THE CODE SYSTEMS  By Rudolf B. Schlesinger

*The Codes' Break with the Past.* In the legal history of almost every civil law country, we can identify a short period in which a more or less complete break with the past took place. In France, this was the period from 1789 to 1810; in Germany, from about 1870 to 1900. In both countries, the political temper of the time favored revision as well as national unification of diverse local laws. For reasons which will be explained below, this goal could be accomplished only by codification. At the beginning of the 19th century, the codification movement was forcefully supported by the bayonets of Napoleon's soldiers who subjugated a large part of the European continent; but even after Napoleon's downfall, the movement continued until virtually every civil law country had adopted a code system.

There are a few—very few—exceptions. Scotland preserved its civil law system in uncodified form. The Roman-Dutch law of South Africa, Ceylon, and British Guiana equally resisted the trend toward codification. As a result we find that a case coming up in a Scottish or South-African court today may turn on the interpretation of a passage from Justinian's Corpus Juris.

Under the codified systems of the great majority of civil law countries, the situation is very different. The draftsmen of the codes often followed one or the other of the pre-existing and perhaps conflicting local rules. It has been pointed out . . . and the point bears repeating, that very frequently they did not adopt the solution found in the Roman law. Sometimes they discarded all pre-existing rules on a given point as unreasonable or unsuited to modern conditions, and constructed a new rule which, perhaps after comparative research, they believed to be in accordance with their own concepts of reason and policy. Thus, when after comprehensive re-examination of the whole body of law the new systematic structure of interrelated substantive and procedural codes had been erected, much of the previous legal learning was relegated to limbo.

The new national codes, of course, presented problems of interpretation; but except for the construction of some terms of art which the codifiers had consciously used in their former sense, little help could be derived from precode authorities which were either too universal or too local in character, and often could not be fitted into the new national

---

Reprinted from *Comparative Law* (Brooklyn: Foundation Press, 1959), pp. 174–198, with the permission of the author and the publisher. The author is Professor of Law at Cornell University and a member of the Board of Editors of the *American Journal of Comparative Law*.

structure. This was true even in those instances in which the draftsmen limited themselves to rearrangement of pre-existing rules. Codification, in the civil law sense of the word, always implies a new start, regardless of whether the former rules are completely changed or merely remodeled.

In the area of substantive private law, the codifiers provided for flexibility and future growth by incorporating a certain number of broad, elastic formulations into the codes themselves. . . . The adjective codes, however, are meant to be essentially all-inclusive statements of judicial powers, remedies and procedural devices.

In common law jurisdictions, too, procedure is generally "codified"; but continuity is preserved by statutory safety valves such as § 64 of the New York Civil Practice Act which provides that "The general jurisdiction in law and equity which the supreme court of the state possesses under the provisions of the constitution includes all the jurisdiction which was possessed and exercised by the supreme court of the colony of New York at any time, and by the court of chancery in England on the 4th day of July, 1776; . . ." Such reference to the powers which in bygone days the courts possessed by virtue of their own pronouncements at law and in equity, makes us feel that at least some of such powers are *"inherent"* and quite independent of any statute.

For the continental lawyer it is hard to undertsand that judicial powers and remedies can exist without an express basis in the written law. This becomes apparent, for example, in cases in which civilian courts are asked to enforce American judgments. Many countries, including the majority of civil law jurisdictions, enforce foreign judgments only on condition of reciprocity. Therefore, if a New York judgment is sought to be enforced in Ruritania, the Ruritanian court will examine the question whether a New York court in the converse case would enforce a Ruritanian judgment. Actually, as we know, the answer to this latter question should be in the affirmative, because New York recognizes judgments rendered abroad as ordinarily conclusive. This liberal New York rule, however, is a creature of the common law, and is not embodied in the Civil Practice Act or any other statute. The Civil Practice Act is completely silent on the point. The court in Ruritania, a civil law jurisdiction, will carefully examine the pertinent New York "code" and will infer from its silence that in New York there exists no provision whatsoever for the enforcement of foreign judgments. The result is that under the Ruritanian reciprocity rule New York judgments fail of enforcement in Ruritania, although as a matter of fact Ruritanian judgments are enforced in New York. In practice, situations of this kind are not infrequent.

As the example shows, the very meaning of the word "code" depends on whether it is used by civilians or by lawyers brought up in the common law tradition. In the eyes of the latter, a code is supplemental to the unwritten law, and in construing its provisions and filling its gaps, resort must be had to the common law. To the civilian, a code is a comprehensive, and in the area of procedure often an all-inclusive, statement of the law. In its interpretation, the court is always conscious of the interrelation of all the provisions contained in the whole code, and indeed in the entire code system. The intention of the legislator, where it can be ascertained, will not be disregarded. Primarily, however, code construction is grammatical, logical and teleological; in any event, it is free from historical reminiscences reaching back into the period prior to the preparation of the code.

It follows that, for the bread-and-butter purposes of the legal practitioner in a modern civil law country, familiarity with the older history of his legal system is hardly necessary—certainly less necessary than for his common law colleague who in the middle of the twentieth century may win a case by citations from the Yearbooks. Modern civil law, as embodied in the great codes, was consciously created as something new, and its roots in logic and policy are many times stronger than those tying it to older historical developments.

History, however, although of limited "practical" value to the modern civilization, provides important clues to an understanding of the difference between common law and civil law. To present and to analyze some of these clues, is the purpose of the materials on the next-following pages.

## Common Law and Civil Law—A Historical View

*Case Law and Code Law.* In his "History of the English-speaking Peoples," Winston Churchill again and again drives home an important point: the focal role which the common law played in the process by which England was welded into a nation. It was the common law which brought about national unification of England's legal system. Neither reception of a professorial "Roman" law nor subsequent codification was needed in England to unify the law on a national scale.

The historical processes by which the leading continental countries attained nationally unified law, differ in at least two respects from those to be observed in English history:

(1) In England, unification was accomplished by the *bench* and *bar* of a *powerful central court* which succeeded in gaining the respect of the nation. Although they represented the central Government, and wielded the tremendous power of judicial lawmaking which became the mainspring of the common law, the royal judges by preserving the jury

system were able to dispense the people's own justice. Judicial arbitrariness was checked by the jury, and later by the rule of stare decisis.

During the critical revolutionary period in English history, bench and bar of the common-law courts successfully defended the law—their law, which they had created, and of which they were the institutional representatives—against the despotic encroachments of the Stuart Kings. "The law," which was the matrix of the writs of habeas corpus, certiorari and mandamus, was on the side of liberty during the great revolutionary struggle, and the common law courts were able to align themselves with the forces which transformed England from a feudal agricultural society into a commercial and industrial nation. England's legal institutions, still centered on a powerful and respected judiciary, thus entered the modern age without a violent break in their continuity.

Continental courts, by way of contrast, were unable to create nationally unified law. The reasons why no court on the continent attained the stature of the English Curia Regis, can be found in the divisive struggles between ecclesiastic and secular power, and between overlord sovereignty and local or regional independence which characterize the medieval period in continental history. In the absence of authoritative precedents set by a powerful central court, lawyers and judges had to turn to other sources of authority. Roman law was favored as such a source not only by the Church, which had absorbed the Roman system into its Canon Law, but also by the Emperor who under the theory of "Continuous Empire" claimed to be the legitimate heir of Justinian's imperial power and who could but benefit from the Byzantine doctrine: that only a written text approved by the Ruler was "the law." Nor were the other kings and princes of Europe, much as their claims to power competed with those of the Emperor, averse to the absolutist implications of this doctrine, believed to be enshrined in the Corpus Juris.

The seat of Roman law learning was in the Universities. While in England the bench and bar of the common law courts provided for the professional training of young lawyers, the continental rulers had to turn to the law faculties to supply them with men trained to become judges, lawyers and administrators. The Universities, in exchange for generous charters and privileges, willingly complied, and turned out large numbers of *doctores* well versed in Latin and in Roman law. Thus it came about . . . that a University-taught and University-developed version of Roman law became dominant (although perhaps in varying degrees) in almost every part of the continent. This domination (the exact period of which, again, varies from country to country) lasted for several centuries, from the late Middle Ages to the end of the eighteenth century.

During this whole period, continental courts not only failed to play a leading role in the development and the national unification of the law; by their Roman-canonistic, inquisitorial procedure, and by their failure to fashion legal remedies against official oppression, they lost popular support and respect. In France, in particular, they became identified with the hated *ancien régime,* and with it were swept away in the French Revolution. The Revolution, at the same time, released strong feelings of nationalism. New national law and new democratic (or at least nonfeudal) courts had to be created. They were created *by legislation.* Not a court, but a code became the instrument and symbol for the national unification of law in continental countries. Historically, therefore, it is true, though perhaps an oversimplified truth, that the common law postulates a law created by the courts, while to the civilian the court is merely a creature of legislated law.

(2) Another significant difference between the English and the continental way of attaining nationally unified legal systems becomes apparent if we consider the time element.

The growth of the common law has been a slow, gradual process which has continued from the time of William the Conqueror to this day. The institutions of the common law, therefore, bear the imprint of many different ages. Each of the continental legal systems, on the other hand, was shaped into a nationally unified structure at one stroke, by a more or less revolutionary act of codification. Each code, consequently, breaths the spirit of the particular age in which it was born.

The influential codes of France (1804) and of Austria (1811) were products of the age of enlightenment and of rationalism. That was an era which extolled reason over tradition. Reasonable rather than traditional solutions were sought by the draftsmen of the codes. True, the draftsmen often used the system and terminology of older authorities, and adopted many rules from laws or compilations of the precode period; but solutions which did not stand the test of reason, were eliminated without regret. The codes which thus emerged were no mere restatements but important vehicles of innovation.

The very idea of codification rests on the sanguine eighteenth century belief in the ability of the human mind by its reason to project the solution of future controversies, and to do so in a systematic and comprehensive manner. The great legal compilations of older periods, including Justinian's *Corpus Juris,* the *Siete Partidas* and the German *Sachsenspiegel,* had been restatements rather than codes. It remained for rulers and lawyers who understood the philosophy of rationalism, the teachings of the French Revolution and the practical needs of the nineteenth century to develop the technique of a true code, i.e., of a systematic, authoritative and direction-giving statute of broad coverage, marking a new start in the legal life of an entire nation. This *technique* is still part of the civilian mentality, even in those civil law countries in which the codes' *positive provisions,* adopted or revised at a later date, reflect philosophies of more recent vintage.

*Differences in Classification—The Great Dichotomies.* The common law had grown into a system at a time when men's ideas about law were still encased within rigid formulas. The eternal need for flexibility had to be met, at least in part, outside of "the law"; and this function was taken over by the Court of Chancery. The latter Court also served a political purpose by becoming a seat of countervailing power, used by the King as an antidote to the power of the common law courts. Thus originated the division between law and equity which is still one of the outstanding features of Anglo-American law.

On the continent, there was no central court possessing such independent power and prestige as to provoke the creation of another central court as an antidotal or countervailing instrument of judicial power. Furthermore, we must again remember that modern civil law, i.e., code law, is essentially a product of the last 160 years, i.e., of a period sufficiently free from ancient formalism so that the draftsmen of the codes have been able to combine both strict rules of law and broad equitable principles in a single unified structure. Thus, no need was felt for a separate system of equity courts and of equity jurisprudence. The result is that the law—equity division is unknown in modern civil law.

On the other hand, and again for reasons which only history can explain, civilian thinking is dominated by two great dichotomies which to us, if not unknown, are of minor significance.

In a civilian mind, all law is automatically divided into private law and public law. This dichotomy, recognized in Justinian's Digest and never questioned by Roman law scholars from Irnerius (about A.D. 1140) to Savigny, was left intact by the codifiers. The codes, if anything, deepened the chasm between the two spheres of the law, by reshaping private law in codified form, while leaving public law (except criminal law and procedure) in its generally uncodified condition. It must be noted, moreover, that many civilian countries live under a federal system of government. When such a country in accordance with constitutional provisions enacts a *national* civil code (such as the codes of Germany, Switzerland and Brazil), it thereby federalizes its private law, while a large part of its public law necessarily remains state law. This, again, adds emphasis to the dichotomy between public and private law.

The tremendous practical importance of the dichotomy lies in its jurisdictional aspect. The jurisdiction of the ordinary civil courts in continental countries is traditionally limited to disputes governed by private law. This tradition was well settled long before the nineteenth and twentieth century period during which public law controversies, that is controversies regarding the validity and propriety of administrative and other official acts, gradually became justiciable. As a result, it was felt necessary to entrust the adjudication of public law disputes to separate administrative courts.

The comparable development of the common law occurred much earlier in point of time and was little affected by the theoretical distinction between public and private law. By habeas corpus, certiorari, mandamus and prohibition, and by tort actions against public officials (sued in their individual capacity, to be sure), the common law courts asserted, and through centuries of political and indeed military struggles successfully preserved, their power to curb abusive official action. As a result of these struggles, which reached their points of climax in the days of Magna Carta and later of Lord Coke, the common law established the basic principle that the same court which decides a private dispute between two individuals also reviews the lawfulness of administrative acts. The different development in the civil law countries is not surprising if we remember that in those countries the law was not shaped by a powerful central court.

Another dichotomy which is of the greatest practical importance for civilian lawyers, is that between "civil" and commercial law. Historically, this division reaches back into the Middle Ages. Roman law, as developed and perhaps corrupted in medieval times, became unsuitable as a basis for business transactions. This was due to several features of medieval law, such as irksome interference with freedom of contract; restrictions on assignments and powers of attorney; usury laws which sharply limited and often prohibited the taking of interest; overindulgent protection of debtors; failure to recognize the mercantile concept of negotiability; and, above all, a cumbersome, expensive and irritatingly slow procedure. In order to avoid these fetters of an inadequate general law, the guilds and corporations of merchants developed a customary law of their own; in time they gained from secular as well as ecclesiastic authorities grudging recognition of the principle that this customary commercial law within its proper sphere should prevail over the general law. According to medieval views, the guild or corporation had the power to codify its corporate customs, and these codifications became known as *statuta mercatorum*. Confirmation of the *statuta* by the sovereign was frequently sought and granted; but it was the prevailing view that the *statuta* had the force of law even in the absence of such confirmation.

The *statutum* conferred on the individual member of the guild a status which he took with him wherever he traveled and which, at least in principle, had to be respected by any court before which he might appear. This liberal rule of conflict of laws made it incumbent upon the courts dealing with commercial matters to familiarize themselves with the *statuta* of many trades and countries, with the result that by the practical use of "comparative law" the commercial customs and laws of the Western world became more and more unified.

The guilds also had the power to elect their own judges. The jurisdiction of these special courts, originally limited to internal affairs of the guild, was later broadened to include all cases involving commercial disputes between merchants. The procedure of the merchants' courts was fair, rational and expeditious, in sharp contrast both to the primitive forms of trial (battle, ordeal, or wager of law) which until the Reception of Roman law prevailed in Germanic countries, and the delays and subtleties of canonistic procedure which in non-commercial matters dominated procedural thinking on the continent from the Reception until the nineteenth century.

The main characteristics of the substantive law which was created by the commercial courts, were emphasis on freedom of contract and on freedom of alienability of movable property, both tangible and intangible; abrogation of legal technicalities; and, most importantly, a tendency to decide cases *ex aequo et bono* rather than by abstract scholastic deductions from Roman texts. No wonder, then, that commercial law was a highly successful institution. Cosmopolitan in nature and inherently superior to the general law, the law merchant by the end of the medieval period had become the very foundation of an expanding commerce throughout the Western world.

Commercial law as a separate branch of private substantive law, coupled with the special jurisdiction and procedure of commercial courts, thus was well established before the time of the great codifications. In Napoleon's code system, and in most of the later codifications, the dichotomy between "civil" and commercial law was preserved by the enactment of separate commercial codes, and by provisions (either in the code of commerce or in the procedural codes) perpetuating the separate commercial courts....

In England, the law merchant was absorbed into the common law during the seventeenth and eighteenth centuries. The common law courts, always jealous of competing judicial bodies, proved powerful enough to displace the special commercial courts. In the process, many of the merchants' substantive rules and customs, especially those dealing with negotiable instruments, were transformed into common-law rules. This incorporation of commercial law into the fabric of the common law was facilitated by the fact that an inductive, pragmatic method was common to both systems. For the same reason, the merchants' resistance to the process of absorption was not too strenuous. On the continent, on the other hand, where at that time the general law was still dominated by scholastic thinking and by canonistic procedure, and where the courts of general jurisdiction were much weaker and less respected, the merchant class successfully resisted the merger of "civil" and commercial law.

*Surviving Traces of Pre-Codification Law in the Civil Law World.* Before the age of the great codifications, continental law had three principal characteristics:

(a) In most countries of the continent, it was strongly Roman-influenced.
(b) It was University-taught law.
(c) Based on a Romanistic University tradition which transcended regional and national frontiers, it was, to a considerable extent, a *ius commune* prevailing throughout most of the European countries and their overseas possessions.

We have seen . . . that codification deprived the Corpus Juris and the other Roman texts of their authoritative status, and in large measure even of their indirect influence on modern civil law. It remains to explore the question to what extent the two other characteristics of precode civil law, its professorial and its transnational nature, have survived the surgical process of codification.

(1) Codification certainly diminished the law faculties' position of leadership in the development of the law. In some countries, such as France, academic lawyers were not even asked to participate in the drafting of the codes. Elsewhere, e.g., in Germany and Switzerland, law professors did help to prepare the codes, either as single draftsmen or as members of a drafting team; but their proposals, of course, required the approval of legislative committees and of the legislature itself. The days when the professors literally were making law ex cathedra, were gone.

Academic influence on the law, to be sure, was by no means broken. The codes needed interpretation, and the authors of the majority of influential commentaries, treatises and monographs were members of law faculties. So long as a code is relatively new, the opinions of academic commentators (*la doctrine*, as the French expression goes) may constitute the only guide in the application of the code and in filling its gaps. Even later, when most of the important controversial questions arising under the code have been settled by court decisions (i.e., by *la jurisprudence*, as the French would call it), the commentator's role in collecting, explaining, systematizing and often criticizing the judicial decisions remains a significant one. There is no doubt that to this day the authority of leading textbooks and commentaries in civil law countries is considerably stronger than in the common law world. . . .

Another surviving trace of the formerly dominant position of the law faculties may be found in the fact that the young civilian, unlike his counterpart in most common law countries, simply cannot become a lawyer without having passed a course of University study. He cannot enter the profession by "reading law."

The precode tradition can be seen, also, in the law faculties' continuing interest in legal history as a subject both of research and of teaching.

(2) Of all the characteristics of precode civil law, its transnational nature was the one most radically changed by codification. The important codes enacted in the civil law world during the nineteenth and twentieth centuries were national codes. *Within* the enacting nation state, codification usually meant unification of diverse laws. But *as between* one nation state and another, the national codifications had the effect of impeding the interchange of legal thought and experience. Judges, practitioners and academicians in each country began to concentrate their efforts on the interpretation and development of their own code system, without paying much attention to the similarly isolated developments in other countries living under different codes. Linguistic and conceptual barriers between the lawyers of various civil law countries thus were bound to grow, with the result that the civil law orbit has lost its former coherence to a much greater degree than has been the case in the common law world. Only rarely can we speak today of "the civil law rule" on a given point, and the experience of international practitioners shows that the differences *inter sese* among civil law systems are even more pronounced than those among common law jurisdictions.

The intellectual isolation of each national legal system which resulted from the codifications, was somewhat mitigated by the fact that some outstanding codes were used as models by legislators in other countries. Thus, so-called "code families" . . . came into existence.

As between two civilian codes which do not belong to the same code family, differences in positive rules and principles, and even in the system of the codes, are apt to be marked. If, nevertheless, judges and legal writers continue to use the generic term "civil law," they must feel that in spite of the differences between the various codes there is a common approach or way of thinking, perhaps a common method and terminology, which binds all civilians together and sets them apart from their brethren practicing under different systems. . . .

Revival of the transnational features of the civil law is becoming a highly practical issue for our European brethren, in the face of the increasing economic integration of the continent and of the growing importance of supranational European organizations. European legislators may find it impossible, and perhaps not even desirable, to reunify the bulk of the written law of the continent, which would be tantamount to undoing the work of the national codifiers. The task of creating a new *ius commune* for Western Europe thus may have to be performed outside of the codes, by bench and bar, scholars and teachers.[a]

[a] Professor Donner, President of the Court of Justice of the European community, suggests that, within the treaty structure, his court may be beginning to perform this task. See Donner, "The Court of Justice of the European Communities," *The Record of the Association of the Bar of the City of New York*, vol. 17, 1962, pp. 232, 238–243.

Ultimately, the task reaches beyond the continent of Europe, and even beyond the civil law world. In our brief survey of the differences between common law and civil law systems we have found that most of these differences have their roots in the political and social conditions of bygone ages, and not in the realities of our day. No present-day schism separates the social, religious, moral and political presuppositions of the common law from those of the civil law. The terminological and institutional divergencies between the two systems, though they have become realities for the international practitioner and for the student of comparative law, are realities forced on us by the dead hand of the past. Behind the facade of these divergencies, comparative studies uncover more and more basic similarities in the actual handling of twentieth century problems. The conclusion to be drawn from our historical survey thus is an encouraging one: that with good will and intellectual effort, a solid bridge of understanding can be built between civil law and common law, and that, eventually, it may not be impossible to discover the outline of the general principles common to both systems.

### Geographic Expansion of Civil Law

Among the legal systems of the world, three large gorups may be discerned at first glance—civil law, common law and the Soviet orbit. The whole of continental Europe this side of the Iron Curtain (with the possible exception of Scandinavia) and the countries of South and Central America are looked upon as the core of the civil law jurisdictions. The common law system is generally thought of as coextensive with the English-speaking world. The Soviet orbit includes, in addition to the U.S.S.R., the satellite countries in Eastern, Southeastern and Central Europe, as well as the mainland of China, Mongolia, North Vietnam and North Korea in East Asia. Yet even these commonly accepted generalizations are subject to certain qualifications, some of which will be discussed below.

Outside the confines of these three blocs, even the most elemental generalizations are dangerous. The interpenetration of common, civil and indigenous law in many parts of the world has produced mixed systems which elude easy classification. . . .

The interpenetration of the common and the civil law may be observed even in the Latin American countries, whose fundamental civil law character, we have seen, has been the subject of judicial notice in the courts of this country. The impact of the common law has been felt chiefly in the area of constitutional law. The United States Constitution has been studied and many of its provisions incorporated into corresponding Latin American Constitutions. Even in the field of private law, it seems that common law influences on Latin American developments are not lacking, and in fact are growing of late, spearheaded by the relatively recent adoption of the express trust in a number of Central and South American countries.

The same mixed character of law in the Western Hemisphere is evident to an even greater extent in Puerto Rico ... as well as in Louisiana and Quebec, often referred to as civil-law enclaves in the common-law world. Of the two last-mentioned jurisdictions, perhaps Quebec has better resisted the encroachment of the common law, although the entire commercial law of the province, codified as well as uncodified, reflects English influence. Even Louisiana, laboring under the decadence of the French language and the impact of a federal system, still maintains a civil law flavor in juridical method as well as in legal substance.

Common law influences have been felt, also, in areas geographically remote from the United States and Great Britain. These influences, though originally perhaps imported during a period of conquest, colonization or occupation, usually persist even after the end of that period. Both India and Israel are now in the throes of creating a new legal order for their countries, but in doing so they are preserving the essential common law nature of their law of procedure and of their general legal method. Having won their independence, both countries are faced with new problems of constitutional law; in meeting these problems, their highest courts often choose between (somewhat conflicting) British and American solutions, thus strengthening the basic common law orientation of their public law, whether their preference in the particular case be for Dicey or for Holmes and Brandeis.

The American impact upon the law of the Philippines has been strong and apparently lasting; and Japan, essentially a civil law country, shows the strong American influence of the postwar period in its judicial organization and its constitutional and administrative law.

On the other side of the globe, we find in Liberia ... a legal system almost entirely patterned after its United States model. Some ancient features, such as strict common law pleading, which in the United States have been virtually abolished by statutes, are preserved in Liberia, where the pace of statutory change has been slower. The interior of the country is still partly governed by customary tribal law; but the people of Monrovia live under a legal system which to Blackstone, were he to revisit this planet today, would appear much more familiar than the present-day law of England or the United States.

The common law has worked, also, upon the uncodified civil law systems of Scotland, South Africa, Ceylon and British Guiana. Scots law retains much of its original character, particularly in the traditional fields of marriage, property and inheritance; but centralized legislative and judicial control, combined with the economic integration of the United Kingdom, have had the effect of anglicizing many facets both of substance and procedure. The law of South Africa, likewise, has been influenced by the common law; but it has preserved its basic Roman-Dutch character. Unlike Scots law, South African law is no longer subject to legislative and judicial controls exercised in Britain, and this fact, coupled with political sentiments, may assure the survival of the interesting Roman-Dutch system for the visible future. In Ceylon and British Guiana, on the other hand, the common law has widely replaced the former Roman-Dutch system.

The civil law, even though it has its core areas in continental Europe and Latin America, has spread into many parts of Asia and Africa. The main structure of the German Civil Code was adopted by Japan and Siam; the same Code strongly influenced the law of precommunist China. Turkey virtually copied the Swiss Civil Code and the Swiss Code of Obligations, and recently adopted a revised Commercial Code which, although largely German-inspired, was carefully integrated into the (Swiss) scheme of the two older codes; the Turkish Penal Code follows the Italian model, while the Code of Criminal Procedure shows German influence and the Code of Civil Procedure is patterned after the procedural code of the Swiss Canton of Neuchatel.

The Code Napoléon has enjoyed a wide sphere of influence, not only in the traditional civil law areas of Europe and Latin America, but also in North Africa and the Near East. Throughout this vast area, except in Turkey and Israel, French influence has been stronger than that of any other western legal system; but the depth of its penetration varies from period to period and from country to country. In contrast to Turkey, which under Atatürk's leadership consciously broke with the past and completely westernized its legal system, the Arab nations of that region show a strong (and in some instances recently revitalized) attachment to the Islamic traditions of their legal systems. In several countries, such as Saudi Arabia and Yemen, the law is still largely based on the Koran and other religious sources. The Civil Codes of Egypt (1949), Syria (1949) and Iraq (1951, eff. 1953), where western influences have been strong during the first half of this century, now seek to achieve a synthesis between Islamic teachings and the legal institutions of the West. These codes, modern in style and organization, reflect traditional religious views in dealing with family and inheritance law, and preserve the jurisdiction of religious courts in such matters. But in the law of obligations, and in the area of commercial law, which may be covered by a separate civilian-style commercial code, western influence is still strong. To the extent that they do adopt solutions taken from western (civilian) codes, Arab legislators tend increasingly to be selective; but while the *Code Napoléon* is no longer blindly followed, it is still the most potent source of western influence upon lawmakers in the Arab world.

The growing amalgamation of civil law and Islamic law in the Near East is well illustrated by Art. I of the Iraqi Civil Code, which reads as follows:

> Section 1. The code governs all questions of law which come within the letter or spirit of any of its provisions.
> Section 2. If the Code does not furnish an applicable provision, the court shall decide in accordance with customary law, and failing that, in accordance with those principles of Muslim law (Shari'a) which are most in keeping with the provisions of this Code, without being bound by any particular school of jurisprudence, and, failing that, in accordance with the principles of equity.
> Section 3. In all of this, the Court shall be guided by judicial decisions and by the principles of jurisprudence in Iraq and in foreign countries whose laws are similar to those of Iraq.

The "similar laws" of foreign countries to which Sect. 3 refers, are the codes and judicial decisions of Syria, Egypt and France.

The Islamic tradition is a factor, though a much less potent one, also in Indonesia, another oriental country touched by civil law influence. There, the Dutch introduced the so-called "dualist" system; the majority of the indigenous population lived under their own customary law ("Adat" law, varying from region to region), while Europeans, non-native orientals and others who voluntarily accepted European law were governed by Dutch codes. There was, also, a dual court system. Upon gaining independence, the Indonesian Republic created a substantially unitary court system, but the dualism of the substantive law has been preserved, and whatever the future may hold, it seems certain that the clock will not be turned back to the state of the law prior to the colonial period.

Similar dualistic systems prevail in many of the territories (mainly in Africa) which are still under colonial rule. The western component of such a system may be common law or civil law, depending on whether the colonial power is Great Britain or a continental nation. The non-Western component consists of indigenous tribal law, often classified under the heading of "primitive law," or of Islamic law which governs not only the many immigrant Moslem communities but in many parts of colonial Africa has become the equivalent of native law and custom, sometimes for whole areas and sometimes for certain tribes or other groups.

A survey of civil law and common law jurisdictions, even a most hurried one, would not be complete without some reference to the special position of the Scandinavian legal systems. While not classifiable as belonging to either group, Scandinavian law has some of the characteristics of both. It is progressive and largely embodied in fairly systematic statutes, some of them of broad coverage; these statutes, however, are not organized as a comprehensive whole such as the code systems of typical civil law jurisdictions. There are differences *inter sese* between the laws of the various Scandinavian nations; but many uniform statutes have been enacted by Denmark, Norway and Sweden, governing such matters as marriage, sales, checks, insurance, trademarks and air traffic. Social security has been a subject of inter-Scandinavian coordination, and uniform rules of conflict of laws for all five Scandinavian nations were adopted by treaty. Scandinavian lawyers and legislators thus created a model of cooperation among sovereign states which deserves close study by those facing similar problems in other parts of the world.

Finally, mention must be made of the large territories formerly governed, or at least influenced, by the civil law which were forcibly added to the Communist orbit since 1945. Our knowledge of recent legal developments in China, Mongolia, North Korea and North Viet Nam is incomplete; but there is no doubt that there have been radical changes in the direction indicated by the Soviet model. The same trend prevails in the Communist-controlled countries of Eastern and Southeastern Europe. The Baltic states, Bulgaria, Czechoslovakia, East Germany, Poland, Roumania and Yugoslavia belonged to the civil law world in precommunist days, while Hungary's somewhat unique legal system had at least many of the characteristics of civil law. With the exception of Albania, therefore, all of the Communist countries of Europe are ex-members of the civil law group. For varying periods of time, their precommunist codes, substantive and procedural, were preserved by the new rulers, in the sense that they were not formally repealed. In East Germany, some of the old codes are still on the books; but their meaning has changed. . . . Expropriations and planning measures have widened the area covered by public law, mainly in the form of administrative regulations backed by criminal sanctions, and have led to a partial atrophy of private law, at least in the economic sector.

There remain some significant differences between the legal systems of the People's Democracies and the Soviet model, and independent developments are discernible in those countries which are following their own "road to socialism." Nevertheless, it is evident that the "civil law" elements in the legal institutions of all communist countries have been reduced almost to the vanishing point.

In spite of this forcible contraction of its sphere, the civil law still reigns over more than half a billion people. The number of persons living under the common law may be even larger, if one includes India and

Pakistan among the common law jurisdictions. Accurate statistical comparisons are lacking, and perhaps impossible to compile. Certain it is, however, that legal relations among the people of the Free World are overwhelmingly governed by rules, principles and institutions stemming from common law or civil law.

---

We have just seen something of the extension through many areas of the world of legal systems based on French, German, and Soviet models. It will be useful now to observe a few of the salient features of these systems, for they present significant divergencies both from Anglo-American law and from each other. Our concern here is not the fact that a single legal problem may receive different solutions; our attention is directed to a more pervasive matter—significant differences in approach and technique for handling legal problems.

---

## FRENCH LEGAL TRADITION

### By René David and Henry D. deVries

IN OUR view, the French legal system, especially for the professional trained in the common law, serves as the nearest and most direct bridge to the civil-law world. French legal terminology is sufficiently akin to English to permit the acquisition of a reading knowledge with far less effort than is required by other languages of civil law countries. Historically, the contemporary French legal system has exerted an influence in almost every country which has sought substantial reform of or transition from internal multiplicity of legal norms. . . .

Reprinted from David and deVries, *The French Legal System* (New York: Oceana, 1958), pp. 6, 12–28, 45–46, and 77, with the permission of the publisher, the authors, and the Parker School of Foreign and Comparative Law, Columbia University. Henry D. deVries is Professor of Law at Columbia University and Associate Director of the Parker School of Foreign and Comparative Law. In 1949 he was Professor at the Academy of International Law, the Hague. René David is Professor of Law at University of Paris. Among his works is an important recent study of French Law, *Le Droit Français* (Paris, R. Pichon et R. Durand-Auzias, 1960).

## The Napoleonic Codes

A view commonly held abroad, and even to some extent in France, regards the codes of the early nineteenth century as representing a complete break in the continuity of French legal development. However, though marking a convenient dividing line between legal history and modern law for many purposes, the Napoleonic codification in France, especially in the deeper perspective of the past one hundred and fifty years, did not represent a violent departure from tradition.

The Napoleonic Codes were the fulfillment of a promise that had inspired jurists of prior centuries. In 1560, in 1576 and in 1614, the States General had voted to compile a single codification, but every attempt at innovation was rejected by the *parlements* of the provinces, the jealous guardians of local law. Their very lack of political independence made them cling to their *coutumes* as precious privileges. In Brittany, for example, any proposal of reform was treated as a violation of the original compact by which the duchy had become united to the Crown of France.

French law on the eve of the Revolution contained all the elements necessary to codification of private law. The primary objective was unification throughout French territory of those bodies of law which had remained in such fragmentary confusion that, to use Voltaire's phrase, the traveler changed law as often as he changed horses.[a] The Revolution, by abolishing the *parlements,* removed the greatest obstacle. Napoleon Bonaparte as First Consul furnished the final impetus. The French Civil Code was first contemplated by the Constitution of 1791, but the original drafts were rejected. It was not until 1800, when the fervid enthusiasm of 1789 to 1793 was waning in the first reaction against Revolutionary ideology, that a commission was named which was to achieve its purpose.

The Napoleonic Codes deal with those branches of the law which were already "written law," promulgated as legislation before the Revolution. The most famous of these Codes, the *Code Civil,* or *Code Napoléon,* contains: provisions from the Digest of Justinian, reworked over the years and embodied in the monumental work of Pothier in the eighteenth century (contracts and torts); *coutumes* (property, decedents' estates, matrimonial community property, capacity of persons); royal ordinances (gifts, wills); and the *corpus juris canonici* (marriage). The Code of Civil

[a] Professor Von Mehren (pp. 486–493), and Professor Schlesinger (pp. 494–509), compare the regional diversity which characterized the law within the continental nations prior to codification with the corresponding development of a unified common law in England. It may be worthwhile to consider whether there is any significant analogy to current divergencies among the laws of the American states. Does the march of history here suggest the possibility for the further extension of trends which we have already encountered at various points in Anglo-American law? See Chapter 1, p. 11; Chapter 2, p. 73; Chapter 4, pp. 145 *et seq.*

Procedure is a barely revised edition of the *Ordonnance* of 1667 prepared by Colbert. The Code of Commerce reproduces the *ordonnances* of Colbert on internal and maritime commerce.

The draftsmen of the Civil Code were not political theorists. They were judges and practitioners of pre-Revolutionary days, averaging sixty years of age. It was inevitable that they conceive of a code in terms of their own background, experiences and even prejudices. "Written reason" for them was the law they had always known. In contracts and torts, already essentially unified through the work of the French Romanists, practically no innovations can be found. In other fields, they confined themselves to choosing between differing bodies of customary law; in the case of matrimonial community property, for example, the draftsmen incorporated into the Code the traditional regime developed in the course of centuries at Paris. On the other hand, the landed aristocracy was disappearing, and innovations were inevitable in the area of feudal relationships. Thus, land law, family law, the law of persons and decedents' estates, were necessarily simplified by the elimination of feudal and canon law elements. Even here, however, the new provisions did not constitute as great a departure from basic legal principles of pre-Revolutionary days as is generally assumed.[b]

All public law matters except criminal law and procedure remained outside the scope of codification. Nevertheless, codification produced important effects on governmental organization and relations between the government and the individual, since public law jurists could hardly remain indifferent to the existence of a Code prepared in terms of universal justice and bearing the name of Napoleon. The ideological bases of codification provided ample reason for elaborating public law rules from analogous sources in the Codes.

Clearly inspired by notions of natural law, the draftsmen and sponsors of the Napoleonic Codes considered them the *"ratio scripta,"* the "written reason" capable of universal application. They believed, and it was the belief of their epoch, that they had succeeded in formulating a logical and rational exposition of principles and rules destined for the ages and independent of local conditions or social and economic changes. This belief, propagated by the Napoleonic conquests and France's prestige as a world power, coupled with the very real need codification served internally in unifying vital areas of private law, created a strong tendency in the nineteenth century to view the Codes, perhaps even more than their authors intended, as sacrosanct distillates of human wisdom. While differences between public and private law rules remained, the arbitrary nature of

---

[b] Compare Professor Schlesinger's emphasis on reform elements in codification, pp. 494, 498.

much of the public law development prior to the Revolution was replaced by a solid body of code provisions from which the nineteenth century jurists could extract underlying principles and apply them to a systematic and coherent organization of rules of public law.

Codification had not generally been favored by the legal profession. French law prior to the Revolution was a shoe that fitted many a judge's or practitioner's foot. The complexity of differing rules and procedures within a single national territory was not necessarily a source of concern to those whose occupational gain depended upon the increment of past experience. It required not only the political pressure of a Napoleon envisaging himself as another Justinian, but also the public awareness of the need for territorial unification of private law and the supporting ideology of natural law, to overcome the latent inertia—if not hostility—toward codification on the part of the legal profession.

With the Napoleonic codification, the pressure on the judiciary, which might otherwise have forced it to exert more influence on lawmaking, was removed. Though stemming from natural law theories which had rejected the omnipotence of legislature or sovereign, the Civil Code became in the nineteenth century the symbol of the desirability and effectiveness of creating law exclusively through representative assemblies rather than through courts. Private law, a systematic body of legislative rules reflecting natural law concepts of the epoch in familiar terminology, channeled legal scholarship into the task of literal interpretation, the exegetic method, without specific reference to other sources. The judiciary, under a statutory duty since the Revolution to express reasons for their decisions, found the most satisfactory starting point in the articles of the Codes. They thus avoided, at least formally, possible charges of arbitrary action or lack of legal basis for their decisions. Not until the end of the century, when code rules literally applied proved inadequate and even incompatible with social and economic changes in many cases, did the legislative positivist view begin to wane, opening the way to the increasingly dominant role of the courts.

In summary, the Napoleonic codification was an important and inevitable phase of French legal development. Its effects were to a large extent not anticipated by the draftsmen. Some of the consequences they desired —substitution of a "rational and logical" system of law for traditional customs, the creation of a law readily accessible and comprehensible to laymen—remained largely illusory. On the other hand, the terminology, style and classifications of the Codes, familiar to practitioners, judges and teachers, contributed to a relatively simple transition from pre-Revolutionary techniques of interpretation and elaboration of texts [the summaries and commentaries on Roman law] to the nineteenth century exegetic method. . . .

## The Law Professionals

One of the difficulties which may impede our understanding of a foreign legal system is the existence of a legal profession within that system whose functions are other than those to which we are accustomed. In England and in America, lawyers have had a profound influence on the development of political and economic institutions. Maitland has stressed the centralization of the teaching and practice of the law in the Inns of Court as a basic reason for the independent growth of the common law, without substantial reception of Roman law elements. Many peculiarities of our legal system—the expansion of remedial devices by legal fictions, the reliance on judicial precedents, formalism in pleading and modes of proof—testify to the development of Anglo-American law through the activities of the practicing lawyer....

In France, on the contrary, there are various law professions and, consequently, it is impossible to speak of the impact of the legal profession as such on the development of French law. The active practitioner has less influence on the growth of the law than certain other law professionals, such as the professors.

Generally speaking, in France the practice of law in the American sense is open to the public, except for those activities directly related to litigation. Anyone, whether trained in law or not, may give legal advice, prepare legal documents, and even appear on behalf of litigants before some courts. However, an agent for litigation (the *avoué*) must be formally appointed in courts of first instance and appeal, and the litigant has a right—though not an obligation—to retain a separate representative (the *avocat*) for consultation on matters of law and for the presentation of oral argument at the hearing. Reminiscent of the distinction between the solicitor and the barrister, the French dichotomy of function, which antedates the British, can be found as early as the thirteenth century.

In discussing the various legal professions in France, only those aspects essential to an understanding of French legal methods and traditions will be examined here.

*The Judiciary.* The close relationship between bench and bar, the one being chosen from the ranks of the other, is a basic characteristic of the Anglo-American legal tradition. In France, an electoral system for judges existed for a short time after the Revolution; this system was superseded by the development of a career judiciary whose training and aspirations are totally different from those of the members of the bar. Being a judge in France, with few exceptions, implies membership in a judicial civil service, whether as *juge de paix* or police judge, whether in a criminal court or a civil one, whether in a court of first instance or the *Cour de*

*Cassation.* A candidate for the judiciary can prepare by obtaining the *licence en droit* from a university law school, and then, after a short assignment of practical training, taking an examination to qualify either as *juge de paix* or as a judge of a court of general jurisdiction. As *juge de paix*, advancement is usually only within a limited hierarchy determined by the population of the district, but if he qualifies for the courts of general jurisdiction, he may win successive promotions, the apex being the position of Chief Justice of the *Cour de Cassation.*

In contrast, therefore, to England and the United States, where judgeship in any court is often the climax of a lawyer's or a barrister's career, in France[c] one can become a judge shortly after leaving law school, without prolonged practical experience. The result is that bench and bar are separated by a formidable barrier of differences in temperament, training and approach. The French judge feels a far closer kinship with the professor of law than with the *avocat,* whom he tends to regard as a mere rhetorician.

Another consequence of the French system has been the creation and maintenance of an *esprit de corps* of the judiciary. Isolated from the bar and steeped in a tradition engendering court solidarity rather than judicial individuality, the judges tend to consolidate as a group into guardians of general principles and concepts. In England and the United States, it is almost impossible to appraise the role of the judiciary without reference to the contributions of individual judges. In France, it is far simpler to discuss the nature of the *esprit de corps* of the judiciary as a whole.

The judiciary in France is bound to attract men and women who prefer the security of assured lifelong financial compensation to the risks of competition. The young French judge, often following a family tradition, can expect a tranquil professional existence—his first years, at least, being spent in a provincial town. His tenure of office in courts of general jurisdiction is for life, though he can be dismissed for cause by action of the *Conseil supérieur de la magistrature.* This body, set up pursuant to the 1946 Constitution and composed of representatives of the executive, legislative and judicial branches, supervises the appointment, promotion and discipline of the career judiciary.

Since the bench is normally composed of at least three judges (except in small civil or police cases where a single judge presides), the individual responsibility of each member is limited. The requirement of French law that all decisions be *per curiam,* dissenting or concurring written opinions being prohibited, acts as a formal deterrent to a French judge's assertion of his own views or convictions. Moreover, he is under a duty not to violate the principle of secrecy, or *secret des délibérations.*

French judges of the post-Revolutionary era, by virtue of their atti-

[c] And in many other European legal systems.

tudes and organization, are ill-equipped to fulfill the role of the Anglo-American judge in the development of the common law. Even less have they attempted to assume the responsibility of the American judiciary for review of legislation on constitutional grounds, although there is no express constitutional bar to such action. The French judiciary has willingly abandoned the tradition of the *parlements* of pre-Revolutionary France which, in the absence of a Parliament in the modern sense, intervened in governmental matters on the pretext of upholding the ancient customs of the realm.

The French judge's reliance on his university education as the main formative experience in his legal training accentuates his analysis of legal problems in terms of generalizations and abstractions which perplex the Anglo-American professional, accustomed to a judge's close scrutiny of the factual patterns of cases as the source of tightly drawn rules. Cases arising in the French courts often require decisions which, if handed down by Anglo-American judges, would formulate rules of law, and thus "create" law; but the French legal technique of formal resort to a text or of referring to general principles of law evidences judicial reluctance to assume the role which the members of the Anglo-American judiciary find rightfully theirs. There is ample recognition in modern France of the problem of *insuffisance ou silence de la loi*,[1] and legal theoreticians today do not view the judicial function as involving the mechanical application of pre-existing rules. But judicial habit, conditioned by training and career status, coupled with the Civil Code's prohibition against deciding cases by way of pronouncement for the future,[2] tends to maintain a formal pattern of reasoning which seeks to maintain at all times the appearance of making decisions within an established framework of general principles of written law. This judicial attitude is important in understanding the French techniques of interpreting statutes and codes.

The existence of a career judiciary in France eliminates the possibility of political pressure and maintains a tradition of impartiality in civil and criminal litigation. Though promotion may still depend upon personal relations with hierarchical superiors, the development of a civil service

[1] *Cf.* Civil Code, Art. 4: "A judge who refuses to decide a case, under pretext of the silence, obscurity or insufficiency of the law, may be prosecuted as being guilty of a denial of justice."

[2] Civil Code, Art. 5: "Judges are forbidden to decide cases submitted to them by way of a general and rule-making (*réglementaire*) decision."

See also the following Articles of the Law of August 16–24, 1790:

Art. 10. "Courts may not take part directly or indirectly in the exercise of legislative power . . . on pain of forfeiture."

Art. 12. "They may issue no rules (*règlements*), but must address themselves to the legislative body whenever they believe it necessary either to interpret a law (*une loi*) or to make a new one."

mentality reduces to a minimum the effect of favoritism on the part of any one person or department.

As a consequence, the French judiciary, despite a role clearly subordinate to that of its Anglo-American counterpart, enjoys the high standing due a profession whose aim is to insure respect for the law and independence from political and personal pressures.

*The Ministère Public.* Parallel to the hierarchy of the judges, there exists a hierarchy of public officials who are agents of the executive and yet, as part of the magistrature, are appointed and classified as judges. The office of *ministère public* originated in the fourteenth century. As in England, the king entrusted the presentation of his views on litigated matters of a public or general interest to a law-trained representative acting in his name. As the powers of the French monarchy expanded, the presence of such a representative before courts of first instance was provided for to assist in the dispatch of civil, political or criminal justice. The Revolutionary decrees formally recognized the officers of the *ministère public* as agents of the executive power before the courts.

One or more representatives of the *ministère public* (or *parquet,* as it is also known) is assigned to each civil or criminal court of France, with the exception of the *juge de paix* and the police court. In the court of first instance, he is known as the *procureur de la République;* elsewhere, as the *procureur général.* In criminal matters, the *ministère public* corresponds to the prosecutor or district attorney of Anglo-American law. In non-criminal court proceedings, the *ministère public* represents societal or community interests in general, rather than the specific interests of the State as a party in an adversary proceeding. In many matters of family law, personal status and capacity, it may assume responsibility for the presentation of independent arguments in pending cases.

Its representatives are considered magistrates because they must have the same qualifications as the career judiciary. Having passed the same examinations, the candidate has his choice of either career, a choice often determined by his temperament and ambition. (The difference between the judiciary proper and the *ministère public* is neatly delineated by the French terms for the two offices, the former being designated as the *"magistrature assise"* and the latter as the *"magistrature debout."* Unlike the other legal professions in France, however, the interchange of personnel between the judiciary and the *ministère public* is possible and not infrequent; although a judge rarely transfers to the *ministère public,* the representatives of the latter body are often appointed judges, especially to the higher courts. Undoubtedly the weaker role of the court as compared to its counterpart in Anglo-American countries is to some extent buttressed by the institution of the *ministère public,* whose arguments carry greater weight with the judges than do those of private litigants.

*The Avocat.* In France, the profession of *avocat* ranks with that of the *magistrat* and the law professor in terms of social prestige. In contrast to the *avoué*, who is an *officier ministériel* (a limited group having a monopoly in certain matters and appointed by the State), the *avocat* is primarily responsible to the *Ordre des Avocats,* the largely self-governing local bar association. There is also a difference in the functions of the two professions. The *avoué,* who, like the English solicitor, is the agent of the litigant, is concerned with procedural details; the *avocat* takes part only in the court hearing. Because of the differing concepts of the nature of evidence in the French and Anglo-American systems, the French *avocat* or *avoué* is not faced with many of the perplexing problems that lead Anglo-American lawyers to specialize in various aspects of trial practice. Since there is no direct examination or cross-examination of witnesses at the French trial or *audience,* the task of the *avocat* in litigation is much less comprehensive than that of the English barrister or the American trial lawyer.

The *avocat* . . . specializes in the oral development of argument. To the Anglo-American attorney, this oratorical specialization seems to place undue emphasis on rhetorical devices as the means of persuading the tribunal. Great freedom is permitted the *avocat* in his presentation, which is not unlike an American trial lawyer's summation to the jury, and many oral arguments or *plaidoyers* are hardly models of soberly marshaled reasoning. But often those aspects of a case which in Anglo-American trials are brought out by the examination and cross-examination of witnesses can be brought to the French court's attention only by the one who "speaks for" a litigant. In criminal cases, where the interrogation of witnesses is conducted directly by the court, it is often only the *avocat's* impassioned oratory which can point to the important discrepancies or contradictions in the testimony. The *plaidoyer* must, therefore, be viewed not merely as a formal means of summarizing the legal arguments in the case, but as an accepted channel for persuasion within a procedural framework which otherwise affords no such opportunity.

Nor should the *avocat* be regarded as having inherited the Roman orator's contempt for law as being work for dull minds and requiring knowledge of "just enough law to understand the legal advice obtained from a jurisconsult." Standards of knowledge of legal principles and skills are maintained by the requirements of a university legal education followed by a further examination, before the *avocat* can be licensed and admitted to the bar.

Except for cases before the *Cour de Cassation,* the *Conseil d'État,* and the criminal courts, the services of an *avocat* are not required by law; although the right is seldom exercised, a litigant is free to argue his own case with the permission of the court. Historically, and as part of the now extinct view that a profession suffers loss of prestige if its members depend on their professional activity for their livelihood, the services of the *avocat* were to be rendered without financial compensation, though he was free to accept a voluntary and spontaneous remuneration from the client. As a member of an "order," as a descendant of the *chevalier ès lois* of the Middle Ages, the professional ideals and bar regulations of the *avocat* bring back faint echoes of a class structure which has long since disappeared. In general, the profession of *avocat* is not calculated to attract young men of modest means. The restricted conditions for financial reward, the stress on niceties of professional behavior, the length of time required for acquiring a clientele might tend to discourage many without independent means. However, membership in the bar is now greater than ever—ample tribute to the prestige of the title of *avocat* and to the desire to compete for prominence in the only legal profession permitting the individual to receive public attention for his style, personality and achievements.

*Other Legal Professions.* Since the general practice of law is not restricted in France to persons with formal legal training, counseling on legal matters is often the work of individuals or firms who are not members of any regulated legal profession—self-styled *agents d'affaires, conseils juridiques, jurisconsultes, contentieux juridiques.* As legal advisers to business interests, they perform many of the functions of the American lawyer acting either independently or as house counsel. . . .

The *notaire* is a trained lawyer, completely removed from the area of litigation, who performs numerous and important functions in law administration that far transcend the duties of Anglo-American notaries. He is empowered by law to impart the quality of *"acte authentique"* to certain writings which must be executed before and by a public officer. He is, therefore, the official authorized to draw up and record antenuptial agreements, notarial wills, mortgages and gifts *inter vivos*. He is also usually retained to draw contracts of sale of real estate, for the administration of property in decedents' estates, and in the organization of companies. As family counselor, and thus often the informal arbiter of disputes, he is, especially in smaller towns, a solidly established, eminently respectable institution.

*Law Teachers and Law Schools.* Many attempts have been made to explain the difference between Anglo-American and French law by characterizing the former as "lawyers' law," which developed through practitioners' techniques, and the latter as "professors' law," growing out of university systematization. . . .

Legal education is regarded in France as a part of a nationally uniform system of free, secular, public education. . . . For admission to the school of law of a French university the student must successfully have passed the *baccalauréat* examination (popularly called the *bachot*), a series of comprehensive tests in such broad areas of knowledge as philosophy, literature, languages, natural sciences and mathematics, and finally an oral examination before a panel of professors. The *baccalauréat,* which is the culmination of years of instruction in subjects taught within a highly regulated framework of methods and materials, brings about a uniformity of approach and a strong feeling for form in analysis and presentation. Perhaps it leads also to excessive respect for the teacher's omniscience as well as his authority. In contrast to the American system, where the student accumulates credits toward his degree by passing examinations at the end of each semester, the French educational system not only prescribes periodic tests but also requires the sixteen- to eighteen-year-old student to effect a synthesis of his entire secondary school work in order to obtain the diploma of *bachelier.* Trained throughout in oral recitation, the young Frenchman's experience of exhaustive oral examinations is a test of the breadth of his knowledge and also of his ability formally to organize the oral presentation of ideas and information. The degree of success attained in the various stages of the baccalaureate examination often influences the candidate's choice of a career.

As there is no intermediate step between secondary education and professional training, the *bachelier* will enter the school of law at a period when his average American counterpart is still in college. The French school of law must, therefore, take into account the absence of an independent faculty of political and social sciences and the fact that its students number many who will never enter any legal profession. Where the American law school seeks to prepare its students for practice, the law school of a French university aims at far broader objectives. Although law studies proper predominate, a general informational approach to political and social sciences is also stressed. For those seeking a law degree, greater emphasis is placed upon legal method, with the traditional *droit civil* as the basic discipline.

The French technique of law teaching also reflects the emphasis on systematic oral presentation previously noted; lectures are almost always considered the superior pedagogic method. In the last twenty years, conscious efforts have been made to supplement formal lectures both by student research on concrete problems and group conferences between professors and students. But the discussion and exchange of views between the two groups, so typical of American education, is noticeably lacking in France. The law schools of French universities, other than that of the University of Paris, which has a huge student body, do afford an opportunity for contact between a professor and his students, but French students, generally speaking, are not inclined to raise questions, and they reveal the degree of authority exercised over them during their entire schooling by their restraint in taking any position which might be regarded as critical or disrespectful of the professor. He, in turn, finds it difficult to close the gap without yielding some of the authority which, in France, is deemed necessary to his effectiveness as a teacher.

*The Law Teachers.* The professional who teaches law is appointed by the State following a *concours d'agrégation,* a competitive written and oral examination. Having secured his *licence* after four years of study in law school, and his *doctorat* as the result of a more specialized program of courses and independent research culminating in a dissertation, the candidate competes for available teaching positions in one of four groups: Roman law and French legal history; private law and criminal law; public law; political economy. Once appointed a professor of law, the subjects he teaches will depend upon the openings at various universities, the summit of choice being that of Paris. Originally professor of criminal law at Aix-en-Provence, he may next become professor of commercial law at Caen, then professor of civil procedure at Lyon or Paris. As a system, the rotation in different branches of the law, in contrast to the higher degree of specialization in American law schools, tends toward a broader approach to law as a whole. A small number of professors may practice as *avocats* and thus be members of a bar, but in general the law teacher does not regard his total lack of practical experience as a handicap. On the contrary, because of the social prestige he attains as a professor and because of his notion of the professor's function, he views the litigious and routine aspects of the law as barriers to his major task of research in the law and the exposition of general legal ideas and principles. This traditional attitude underlies the role of *doctrine* in French legal development. The opinions of professors of law, though not binding on the courts, have great weight in influencing judicial decisions. Prepared with deliberate detachment from actual controversy and elaborated from general principles of law, these opinions are an important aid to the judiciary. In a legal system which does not formally recognize the doctrine of binding precedent and which assigns a prominent role to rhetorical argument, the opinions of legal scholars act as guiding threads in the overall pattern, leading to impartial decisions by the courts.

Clearly the requirement of a university education has influenced the outlines of French legal thought. From the Anglo-American point of view, French legal reasoning appears to start with a highly generalized proposition of law to which the facts are then fitted, rather than to begin with a detailed examination of the facts followed by application of a narrowly formulated rule. French legal method reflects the centralized and generally uniform teaching methods existing throughout the country. Inevitably, the approach of the French law professional is conditioned by his years at the *école de droit,* with its stress on law as part of a general university education and its awareness that it must relate its methods and courses to the needs of many who will never practice law. The factors which emerge in contrast to American university legal education are: a higher degree of abstraction, an almost complete absence of procedural analysis, and a strong consciousness of the interrelationship of the components of the legal system as a whole.

### Private Law and Public Law

For the French jurist, the fundamental division, the *summe divisio*, is between private law and public law. The dividing lines may be unclear, the logical bases may be disputed, but the traditional dualism recognized in Roman law remains the most significant division of French law. In legal theory this dualism, unknown to the ancient Germanic law, rests on the Roman law reference of Ulpian in the Digest (D.I.2.1.1.): *"Publicum jus est, quod ad statum rei Romanae spectat; privatum, quod ad singulorum utilitatem."* In theory, some rules of law concern the State—the rules of public law; others concern relations of private persons—the rules of private law. There is, of course, an appreciation of the fact that any body of law may be said to concern the State, since the State has an interest in the peaceful solution of controversies even though only private bodies are affected. Nevertheless, in France as in other continental countries, the separation of public and private law is an undeniable aspect of positive law. French jurists are *publicistes* or *privatistes* even though their fields of inquiry may occasionally overlap. There is a Supreme Court (the *Cour de Cassation*) for private law matters and another (the *Conseil d'État*) for public law matters, and different rules and procedures may be applicable to solution of the identical legal problem in public and private law.

The Law of August 16–24, 1790 expressed the Revolutionists' distrust of the judiciary by barring courts of the judicial power from criticism of administrative acts. This law created a vacuum which could only be filled by review of acts of the *Administration* within the broad confines of executive power. And the basic notion that the independence of the *Administration* from control by the ordinary courts could not be assured if the *Administration* were subject to the body of private law rules applied by those courts led to the gradual development of public law principles. The *Code civil* does not cover the question specifically, but from the beginning its provisions were considered inapplicable to situations in which the government or the *Administration* were involved. The *Tribunal des Conflits*, the court empowered to decide issues of jurisdiction and applicable law in cases of conflict between the administrative courts and courts of the judicial power, held in the leading case of *Blanco*, decided in 1873, that, in the absence of statutory authorization, the liability of the *Administration* "cannot be determined by the principles established in the *Code civil*."

A separate body of law today governs administrative activity; public law has developed side by side—at times merging with, and at times distinctly different from—private law. Since 1872, the *Conseil d'État* has been recognized as an independent tribunal; its decisions, which prior thereto had been merely advisory opinions requiring approval of the Chief of State to become binding, were given the force of judgments. The next important date was that of the *Cadot* decision in 1889; following the lead of the *Tribunal des Conflits* in the *Blanco* case mentioned above, the *Conseil d'État* held that it had general power to review administrative acts without need for a statutory grant of jurisdiction in specific cases. Since then, the *Conseil d'État* has continuously exercised the power to review administrative acts and decisions.

As a consequence public law, in the sense of a body of enforceable rules governing the validity of administrative acts and liability of the State for acts of its agents, has reached a firm stage of development. The evolution of judicial review of administrative acts, however, has not been extended to acts of parliament. Thus French constitutional law, in contrast to administrative law, is still essentially political science—a descriptive exposition of governmental institutions and their functions rather than a body of rules and principles supported by judicial control. It is the *droit administratif* developed by the *Counseil d'État* in the past seventy-five years which is the heart and core of French public law.

## Procedure and Evidence

In the early common law, as in classical Roman law, remedies preceded rights. In both legal systems, substantive rules were implied from the terms of the writs or forms of action. In Rome of the Lower Empire, the Rome of Justinian, the approach was in direct contrast. In contemporary legal systems which derive much of their technical organization as well as formal views of law from this later Roman source, court actions and the procedural aspects of law are incidental consequences of the system of rights, rules and principles elaborated by jurists without regard to specific procedures. In modern "civil law" countries, litigation has never been the heart of any definition of law as it has been in common law countries; the concept of a substantive right carries with it various consequences, of which the possibility of enforcement in the courts is only one.

To some degree, the same general reversal has occurred in the common law countries, especially since the fundamental procedural reforms in England and the United States in the nineteenth century. But even today these countries remain within a more definite procedural mold; this can be explained not only as a tenacious survival of a mode of lawmaking, but as a tendency on the part of leading Anglo-American jurists, stemming from training and professional habit, to emphasize practical experience in law rather than the theoretical organization of a legal system. In common law countries, consequently, there is more attention to procedure and evidence as branches of law study, reflecting a deep-rooted pragmatic approach which tests the very existence as well as the effectiveness of rights by their enforceability in practice.

The French *juriste* has a different approach. Reversing two of Mr. Justice Holmes' comments on the nature of law, he is more apt to consider *Droit* as a "brooding omnipresence in the sky" than as the "prophecies of what the courts will do in fact." The *juriste* maintains the distinction between *Droit*, the body of legal rules and principles by which rights and duties are defined, and the various procedural means by which practitioners seek to apply them on behalf of their clients. In the French notion of *Droit*, it is difficult to distinguish the IS from the OUGHT; in fact, the justification for the detached notion of *Droit* is that, in a legal system which formally denies a creative role to the courts, the lead in crystallizing rules and principles to guide solutions for new situations, in the absence of legislation, must come from the legal scholars and the *idée-force* of *Droit*. . . .

The study of civil procedure in the law schools consists of a semester's course at the end of the four-year course for the *licence*. Criminal procedure is dealt with as part of the year's course in criminal law. Administrative procedure is almost wholly ignored. Little effort is made to present or to explain legal problems against a procedural background. In the French view, procedural law is primarily a subject for practitioners, knowledge of which need be acquired only by those specializing in practice. The most important literary sources of procedural law are not the treatises of university professors, but the form books, digests and practice manuals prepared by practitioners. This gulf between the law faculties and practitioners often tends to obscure the proper analysis of court decisions by scholarly commentators; legal education without adequate procedural background to aid understanding of the precise issues involved tends toward the formulation of broad conclusions and generalizations which in actual practice are difficult to sustain.

Those rules paralleling the Anglo-American rules of evidence are even more neglected as a cohesive subject of study. If procedural law is to some extent dealt with as separate branches of civil, criminal or administrative law, the rules of evidence are a minor chapter in each of these branches; but, in reality, there is no French "law of evidence"; the last important study purporting to cover as a whole the *droit des preuves* is over one hundred years old. . . . There is no general analysis of rules of admissibility of proof. As a general proposition, the common-law rules of proof—i.e., the rules applicable in the absence of a specific statutory requirement—are found in the Civil Code articles relating to proof of obligations. The situation is more preplexing in *droit administratif,* and even in criminal law the rules of evidence appear extraordinarily fluid and imprecise. The question of proof of foreign law is treated only in sketchy fashion, if at all, in works on private international law.

One reason for the failure of French jurists to develop a body of rules of evidence has already been indicated—the separation between *Droit* and its application in practice. Other reasons of primary importance are the absence of a jury in court proceedings except in the *cours d'assises* [the court for the trial of major criminal offenses], and the prevailing notion in French law expressed in the principle of *"intime conviction"* of the judges. There is no need to elaborate upon the oft-mentioned point that the Anglo-American law of evidence is directly related to the institution of jury trial in civil as well as in criminal cases; and that consequently the rules so developed have no real counterpart in a legal system which need not concern itself with control of a jury of laymen in civil cases. As for the principle of *intime conviction* as applied in France, it is clearly inconsistent with a system of rules of evidence binding upon the tribunal itself. As a general principle, it operates to permit the tribunal to receive any offer of direct or indirect proof and to weigh the evidence submitted in its sole discretion. . . . For example, the court can without other justification base its judgment in nonreviewable form on a general formula of "serious, precise and consistent presumptions." And Anglo-American lawyers may be surprised to learn that issues of reasonable doubt in criminal cases may be resolved by evidence and argument bearing on prior convictions of the accused, his general behavior, even his family history. In fact, rules of evidence which are binding on the tribunal, and not merely guides to the exercise of discretion, appear only where the principle of *intime conviction* of the judges has not been fully admitted in French law, as in litigation involving personal status.

In criminal cases, the stress is on oral testimony presented to the full court during a public trial; witnesses are examined by the presiding judge, not by counsel or prosecutor. In non-criminal actions, the word "trial" is inappropriate; the securing of evidence, the development of the legal contentions, the definition of relevant issues, take place gradually over an extended period of time until the case is ready for final determination; the record so compiled is then submitted to the full court with oral argument. Thus, though formally accepting a subordinate role in formulation of rules of law, French judges are freer to exercise their discretion in resolution of issues of fact than their Anglo-American counterparts. The French believe that the protection of individual rights and the just and fair determination of issues of fact which the Anglo-American rules of procedure and evidence are designed to serve are equally well secured by a system which places responsibility for decision on professional judges whose personal evaluation is unencumbered by complex and detailed rules.

## THE APPROACH TO GERMAN LAW    By Max Rheinstein

THE RELATION between the law of [the Federal Republic of Germany] and the other Germanic laws is not entirely the same as that between the law of France and the other Romance laws, all of which consist of legislative enactments consciously based upon the model of the laws of France. Of the Germanic laws only a few constitute planned receptions. German laws and institutions were intentionally adopted in Japan and, through Japan, in Korea. The German Civil Code also served as the model for the modern codes of China and Greece. The Swiss Civil Code was taken over almost literally in Turkey. Austrian models have been influential in the Balkans. But the kinship between the legal systems of the German speaking countries, *i.e.*, Germany, both West and East, Austria and Switzerland, is due to the community of language, history, and tradition. This common tradition has had two roots, the customs of those Germanic peoples by whom Western and Central Europe was settled, and the Roman Law as it was rediscovered in the late Middle Ages.

Both these roots have also been those of the laws of France and the other countries of Western Europe. Varying in detail from place to place, the amalgam of Germanic medieval customary laws and techniques of Roman jurisprudence constituted that great body of the Civil Law which was split into its two modern components only by and since the codification of the private law of France in 1804. By this event the private law of France was transformed from a plurality of local variants of the basically uniform Civil Law into a new, great, self-sufficient unit, the cultivation of

---

Reprinted from *Indiana Law Journal*, vol. 34. 1959, p. 546, with the permission of the author and the publisher. The author is Professor of Law at the University of Chicago and Honorary Professor at the University of Freiburg, Germany. He practiced law in Germany prior to 1933 and more recently has been a member of the International Faculty of Comparative Law at Strasbourg and Helsinki.

which came to be centered around the Code. In Germany, national codification did not occur until 1896. During that period of almost a century, the old-style Civil Law continued in Germany. It was exposed to influences which caused the national codification of Germany to differ from that of France in some important respects.

Since the two systems have had such a long period of common development, since even after the French codification mutual influences did not cease to operate, and since politically both countries have come to be democratic republics, I can limit myself to those aspects of the law of Germany which significantly differ from French Law. Let it be pointed out, however, that one difference in the political structure of the two countries has had much less influence upon Germany's lawyers' law than an American lawyer might expect. France is organized as a strictly centralized country. There is only one government, that in Paris. When Germany was re-unified as a nation in 1871, the American pattern of federalism was followed and the constituent states were preserved, each with its own government. The federal pattern was continued in the reorganization of Western Germany after World War II, so that presently eleven state governments are operating in addition to the federal government in Bonn. The division between federal and state law in Germany is different, however, from that in the United States. In Germany, practically all private law, together with procedural law and criminal law, i.e., the bulk of the lawyers' law, is federal law. The uniform federal law is applied by state courts with one exception. The court at the top of the judicial pyramid, the *Bundesgerichtshof*, is federal, and as a general supreme court of, as we would say, law and equity, maintains uniformity throughout the fields of private law, criminal law, and procedure. It is a busy court with a large number of judges. At one time there were about 150; today [1959] there are about eighty. Ordinarily the judges sit in panels of seven, but when one panel wishes to overrule a decision rendered by another, the presiding judges of all panels have to convene. From this observation you can already conclude that precedent is important in the courts of Germany.

While the *Bundesgerichtshof* is the highest German court in which civil and criminal litigation is handled, it has, just like the French *Cour de Cassation*, no regular jurisdiction in matters of public law. However, the line between private law and public law is not drawn at the same point. Litigation arising out of government contracts is a matter of public law in France; in Germany, however, the government is not thus privileged and any litigation arising out of a government contract is handled by the civil courts just like litigation between private parties. The same principle applies to claims for torts committed by public officers in the course of their official activities. The state is liable but the litigation is handled by the civil courts. These courts cannot decide, however, matters of constitutional law. The mode of handling such problems in Germany is different from that of both France and the United States. In France ... the constitutionality of a statute cannot be questioned in any court. In the United States, I hardly need to remind you, the question of whether or not a piece of paper purporting to be a statute really is a statute is decided as an incident of each case in which it happens to be relevant. Review of the constitutionality of legislation rests with the regular courts and, in the last instance, with the Supreme Court of the United States. Since that Court has withdrawn almost completely from the exercise of jurisdiction in ordinary matters of law and equity, it has in reality become the constitutional court of the United States, and there no longer exists a judicial guardian of the uniformity of ordinary law.

In Germany the exercise of constitutional control has been taken from the regular supreme court of the nation and handed to a special Constitutional Court. Whenever there arises in a case a problem of constitutional law, especially of the constitutionality of a statute, the court must certify the case to the Constitutional Court, which thus constitutes the most august body of the judiciary. It is a small body composed not only of professional career judges, but also of law professors and other "jurists" of high standing who are elected to the Court by the federal parliament. These latter members, while being judges, are thus also men enjoying the confidence of the political party by the vote of which they have been elected. In this respect, as in that of constitutional structure, Germany differs from France. As far, however, as the lawyers' law goes, the differences are by no means so considerable as those between the Civil Law and the Common Law. They are not unimportant, however, and in the main they are due to the fact that German private law remained uncodified almost a century longer than French law.

*The Systematic Character of German Law.* The scholars of the Pandectist school ascribed primary importance to the building of a meaningful system of classification of the legal phenomena, i.e., a system which would not only, like an alphabetic arrangement, facilitate the search for the established law in point, but which would by itself help the lawyer find the right answer to new problems. That a "good" classificatory arrangement can be more than a framework for ready reference is strikingly illustrated in natural science. Information concerning the various kinds of matter in the world can be arranged in many ways, for instance under the heading of every single material to which it refers, and these headings then can be arranged alphabetically from aluminum to zinc. Such an arrangement is quite useful to one who wishes to obtain information on the characteristics of any particular mineral or chemical. But entirely new insights not only about particular species of matter but about matter in general emerged when all matter was divided into elements and compounds, and the elements were arranged according to their atomic weights. The mere fact that the elements were arranged in this periodic system of Mendeleyeff provided information which had not previously been available. It became known that an element's position in the system determines its physical and chemical characteristics. It became possible from an element's position to predicate characteristics which had escaped observation, to fill gaps in the system by the discovery of hitherto unknown elements, and to describe their characteristics accurately even before their discovery. Atomic weight turned out to be determined by the composition of an element's atomic nuclei, by which in turn, that element's physical and chemical characteristics are determined. Classification of the elements by atomic weight thus constitutes classification by their most essential aspect. It is far more useful to the scientist than an alphabetical arrangement or any other that is based upon criteria of an equally unessential character.

*The Contribution of the Scholars.* The material with which the man of the law has to work is constituted by controversial situations of social life and the rules which the legal order holds ready for their solution. Since both the controversies and the rules pertaining to them belong to the realm of ideas rather than that of physically observable objects, they are less easily ascertained and defined than are elements, plants or physical processes. The first task of a science of law is thus the observation and definition of the controversies and their rules of solution. That task is one of great difficulty. The quality of its solution is closely tied to the quality of performance in the lawman's second task, i.e., that of finding the "best" classification for the arrangement of the innumerable life controversies with which they have to deal. In a law which is dominated in its development by professors we shall find a greater approximation to the highest insight yielding system of classification than in a law dominated by judges, attorneys, conveyancers, priests, prophets, or administrators.

Ever since its rediscovery in the late Middle Ages, the law of the Roman *Corpus Juris Civilis* constituted the subject-matter of professorial concern, first in the school of Bologna, then, in the sixteenth, seventeenth and eighteenth centuries, of the legal scholars of Western Europe, especially of France and the Netherlands. The classificatory work of the scholars, particularly Pothier, constituted an essential basis for the arrangement of the materials in the French Civil Code of 1804. But that arrangement, while constituting an enormous improvement over that of the *Corpus Juris* or the collection of French customary laws, the *coutumes,* is crude when it is compared with that of the younger Civil Code of Germany.

The 2,281 articles of the *Code Napoléon* are divided into three books, of which 509 constitute the First Book on Persons, 195 the Second Book on Goods and the Various Modes of Property, and 1,571 the Third Book on Manners of Acquiring Property. The subject matters respectively dealt with in Books I and II are held together by intrinsic connection and are of fairly homogeneous character. The Third Book, however, contains a hodgepodge of such heterogeneous topics as torts, sales, matrimonial property rights, wills, mortgages, the statute of limitations, the general rules on contracts, etc.

Germany gave her legal scholars almost another century for work preparatory to codification, and during that period the German professors paid intensive attention to the problem of classification and arrangement. In consequence, the draftsmen of the Civil Code could resort to a "system" that is not only more elaborate than that of the French Civil Code but also more useful in the sense of yielding more information through the simple device of relative place.[a] The system is also more complicated in the sense that one has to have studied it thoroughly in order to be able to use it. From the mere reading of the Code, a foreign lawyer will seldom be able to deduce the solution of an actual case. For him, however, who has grasped that system, it constitutes an invaluable source of insight and information.

The essential feature of this "system" of the German Civil Code is the arrangement of the material from the specific to the more general and on to the highest possible generalization. A concrete example will help to illustrate this cryptic statement. Let us assume that in an action for the price of an automobile the buyer pleads the following defenses: that the car tendered by the seller was defective; that upon his demand for delivery of a properly functioning car the seller has done nothing; that the alleged contract had never been concluded at all because he, the buyer, had never accepted the seller's offer; and, if he should be held to have accepted it, his acceptance would not be binding because he had been induced to declare it by the seller's fraudulent misrepresentations.

Where in the Code do we have to look to find the provisions respectively concerned with the problems raised by each of these pleas? In the Code we find a title with the heading "Sales" and in that title we find a number of sections dealing with the problem known in American law as that of a seller's warranty of quality. If we thus wish to know whether or not under the facts of the case a buyer is entitled to reject the tender of goods because of an alleged defect of quality, we turn to these sections of the Code. The problem of determining in the case of a sale the re-

[a] It may be helpful to recall Professor Schlesinger's observation that, in contrast to the situation in Germany and elsewhere, in France law professors were not invited to participate in the drafting of the Civil Code. See p. 502.

spective rights of buyer and seller if the goods are defective, is peculiar to transactions of sale and is dealt with in the Code, together with other problems peculiar to sales, in the title on Sales.

But where do we find the provisions dealing with the next plea of the buyer, i.e., the plea that he does not have to perform his part of the bargain because the other party has not performed his? That problem is not peculiar to sales. It can arise just as well in a contract for services, in a construction contract, a contract of lease, or any other contract which involves mutual obligations of two or more parties. Consequently it is dealt with in that part of the Code which is concerned with problems common to all contracts of mutual obligations.

The plea that the seller's offer was not accepted raises a problem which can arise not only in contracts of mutual obligations but with respect to an alleged contract of any kind. Hence, it is dealt with in that part of the Code which deals with those problems which are common to all kinds of contracts, those containing mutual obligations as well as others.

Finally, the plea that the alleged buyer's acceptance of the seller's offer had been induced by fraudulent misrepresentations raises a problem that can arise not only in connection with contracts but also with a conveyance, a marriage, a will, a notice of termination, a rescission, or any other kind of declaration of intention. Hence, for its proper handling we have to look to that part of the Code which deals with those problems which can arise in connection with declarations of intention generally and of any kind.

This mode of arrangement results in a continuously increasing degree of abstraction.[1] It requires an intensive training and concentrated mental effort on the part of the user. It also results in a great economy of thought. The lawyer does not have to study and store up separately in his memory the rules on the effects of misrepresentation in sales, leases, insurance contracts, loans, conveyances, mortgages, etc. He only studies the rules on misrepresentation in connection with legal transactions of all and any kind, observing that they are the same except for some special transactions such as marriage, the execution of wills, or subscribing to corporate stock.

The method has an additional, and even more important, advantage. If the legal order has failed to enunciate a rule on the effect of misrepresentation on some peculiar transaction, for instance the confirmation of a letter of credit, such a rule is available in the general form in which it is stated as applicable to all legal transactions of any kind. The avail-

[1] The sequence of arrangement is such that the more general provisions precede the more special ones.

ability of the general rule does not, however, free the court of the duty to determine whether the general rule is really appropriate for the transaction in question or whether the transaction is so peculiar that an exception to the general rule ought to be made. Rules of broad generality are not to be applied mechanically but discerningly so that they serve the pursuance of those general lines of policy which have found expression in the Code and the legal order in general. The very statement of such basic policies is indeed the central task of the Code.

Let us return to the example of a sale and assume that, before or after the actual handing over of the car by the seller to the buyer, one or the other of them is declared to be a bankrupt, or that the car is attached by the sheriff for a creditor of the seller or of the buyer. The answer to the problem of whether the car may be so attached or whether it belongs to the bankrupt estate depends on the passage of title from the seller to the buyer. When and how does title pass? The rules concerning the passing of the title to chattels can, of course, hardly be expected to be much simpler in German law than in American law. At the moment we are not interested in knowing what these rules are, but only where they can be found in the Code. An American lawyer will expect to find them in the title on Sales. But he will not find them there in the German Code. A transfer of title may be made in connection with a contract of sale, but it may also occur upon the ground of a contract of donation, of partnership, of security for debt, of barter, of compromise, of factoring, or perhaps upon no particular ground at all. The problem is thus to be treated in a context broader than that of a sale. Indeed, it is regarded as being of a character quite different from that of determining what are the rights and duties of the parties to a contract. Promises, how they become legally binding, what duties they imply, how they may be discharged, etc. present problems of a kind essentially different from those which relate to ownership in things, what such ownership means, and how it is acquired, lost or encumbered. Problems of the former kind are treated in the Second Book of the Code, entitled *The Law of Obligations,* while problems of the latter are provided for in the Third Book, entitled *The Law of Things.* In the field of sales this treatment means that all questions concerning the mutual rights and duties of buyer and seller are dealt with in the *Law of Obligations,* while those which concern the passing of the title are dealt with in the *Law of Things.* To an American lawyer this separate treatment of the two sets of problems may appear artificial, but upon closer inspection he may find that it results in a deepened insight into the issues, interests and policies which are respectively at stake, and consequently a treatment of each of the two sets of problems more adequately serving the peculiar needs of each. After all, the problems concerning the mutual rights and duties of the parties are primarily of concern to these two parties, while the problems of title are of basic concern to third parties, such as creditors and subsequent purchasers.

*The Contribution of the Civil Service.* Acute analysis of problems, separation of issues, and elaboration of clearly defined and consistently used terminology have been the work of the professors. A second group which has placed its stamp upon the legal order of Germany is the high bureaucracy. With technical competence, occasional narrowness, but always with respect for the dignity of the individual and an earnest desire to do justice, the members of the high civil service influenced legal development in the pre-constitutional era, and continued to influence it, in close cooperation with the parliamentary bodies of the periods of constitutionalism and of post-World War I democracy. Even the Third Reich of National-Socialism could not function without their administrative skill and experience and could not entirely eliminate their moderating influence.

Like his counterpart in Sweden, France, or Italy, the high civil servant of Germany is a man of the law. The desire of the service for national uniformity of regulation constituted one of the most powerful incentives to legal unification, especially in Austria, Prussia, and France. The benevolent paternalism of the German civil service has found expression in the system of judicial organization in which the administration of justice has been made easily accessible, inexpensive, and in many cases completely free of cost.

In passing, it might be observed that German civil procedure is even more informal than French, especially because it relies less on documentary evidence. Juries were used in serious matters of crime between 1848 and 1924, when, with general approval, they were abolished during the course of an economy drive. Lay judges are used extensively, however, in criminal, commercial and labor cases, and in many proceedings of public law. They sit together with the professional judges, forming one unitary bench, and participating in all phases of the trial and decision. Criminal procedure, it may also be observed, presents elaborate safeguards for the accused, who is, of course, presumed to be innocent until his guilt has been proved by the prosecution.

Returning to the role of the high civil service, other expressions of its influence can be found in those numerous provisions of the codes and statutes which are designed to protect the economically weak and to secure justice for them in a social order of economic liberty and competition. It expressed itself also in the loving care expended upon the elaboration of such branches of the law as guardianship, illegitimacy, criminal law or installment buying, i.e., the law of the little man, which tends to be neglected in a legal system dominated by attorneys.[b] The tradition of the civil service has also been instrumental in securing in the German legal order a large place for considerations of good faith, fair dealing and good morals.[c] These considerations permeate the entire body of German law; they set limits to the exercise of every right; they prevent the abuse of the letter of the law for unconscionable purposes; they constitute the tools by which the laws, without textual changes, can constantly be adapted to changing conditions of even the most shattering kind. It may be appropriate to remember that in England the inventors of Equity, the Chancellors, had also been high civil servants.

In a very specific way the civil servants have influenced the law in their capacity of legislative draftsmen. Legislation is invariably drafted in the departments of the central government, all of which have staffs of skilled law-drafting specialists. The most proficient are likely to be those on the staff of the Federal Ministry of Justice, from which originates practically all legislation of lawyers' law.[d] These specialists are also the permanent watchdogs of the law, always scanning the total body of the law for defects and obsolescences for which remedial legislation is indicated. Such legislation will be carefully prepared in close consultation with the representatives of all interested groups concerned. The final political decisions rest, of course, with the cabinet and the parliamentary bodies, but the law is likely to be kept up to date and the technical properties of the pertinent legislation are usually of a high quality. In the face of pressing demands for speedy enactment during the years following World War II, the traditional standard could not always be preserved, but even in these times of legislative mass production it has by and large been remarkably high.

*The Contribution of the Judiciary.* A third group of men by whom the general character of German law has been markedly influenced is the judiciary. Ample room exists in the German legal order for judicial law making. In some fields, especially that of administrative law, the statute law is so sporadic that, just as in France, the major part had to be developed by the administrative tribunals.

[b] Compare the discussion of the technical competence and responsiveness of American legislatures in Chapter 6, the role of the bar reported in Chapter 7, and the American Law Institute's recent attention to statutory reform reported in Chapter 4, pp. 177–179.

[c] Our Uniform Commercial Code, § 1–203 provides: "Every contract or duty within this Act imposes an obligation of good faith in its performance or enforcement." *Cf.* UCC § 2–103(1)(b) ("reasonable commercial standards of fair dealing in the trade"). Although foreign parentage is not acknowledged, there is reason to suppose that European experience was of significance in the drafting of this provision. See also UCC 2–302 ("unconscionable" contracts).

[d] Compare Justice Cardozo's call for a "Ministry of Justice" and Judge Friendly's more recent appeal, reported in Chapter 6, pp. 283 and 337.

A wide room for judicial creativeness also exists in those fields which are covered by the Codes, especially the Civil Code, insofar as they contain broad statements of policy. Detailed provisions are, of course, used for the regulation of topics which require clear rules capable of immediate application, such as the statute of limitations, mortgages, marital property rights, intestate succession, or the formalities of conveyancing or the organization of business corporations. There are other topics, however, for which the drafters of the Codes found it more appropriate to limit themselves to the pronouncement of policies, more or less broadly stated, by which the courts should guide themselves. While the provisions on torts are not so completely vague as articles 1381 and 1382 of the French Civil Code, they are still sufficiently broad to require much judicial implementation. Even provisions going into narrow detail require judicial interpretation, and their application, as well as that of all law in general, must always be understood to be made so as to keep them in accord with the paramount principles of good faith and fair dealing and with public policy and good morals.

With the steadily increasing rate of political, economic and social change, the judges have also come to find themselves compelled to engage in judicial lawmaking in the sense of adapting the existing law to new conditions. Traditionally the task of changing law has been considered a function of the legislature. Lawmaking by judges appears to be repugnant to the principle of democracy by which the legislative power is entrusted exclusively to the properly elected representatives of the people. The parliamentary bodies have worked in close cooperation with the civil service of the governmental departments. But policy decisions were regarded as the exclusive domain of the legislatures.

This mode of division of functions between the legislatures assisted by the civil service on the one hand, and the courts on the other, has undergone a modification since World War I. The needs for adaptation of the law to rapid and constantly recurring changes of conditions have become so pressing that the legislatures have not been able to keep pace. At times there also emerged situations in which conflicting interests were so evenly balanced in a legislature that it found itself unable to act. Since action of one kind or another had to be taken, the task fell to the judiciary, which, after initial reluctance, has come to accept its expanded role as maker of the new law.[e]

The most spectacular occasion was presented by the catastrophic inflation of the German currency after World War I. . . . The currency law expressly stated that notes of the Reichsbank constituted legal tender. . . .

[e] Compare the role of the French judiciary discussed at pp. 513–516.

Every debtor, of course, availed himself of this opportunity. By the middle of 1923 long-term debts had disappeared. Of course, nobody had any investments either; savings had been wiped out. The result was wonderful for debtors and catastrophic for people who had to live on savings. As these results became apparent, savers and other investors began to press for remedial legislation that would require debtors to pay more than the mere nominal amount of their debts. However, debtor interests were strong enough to prevent the legislature from passing such a law. When the situation became intolerable, the judges acted. In a decision rendered on November 28, 1923, the Supreme Court held that the debtor had not discharged his debt until he would pay an additional amount so that his total payment would roughly approximate the original purchasing power. The Court could not, of course, change the wording of the currency law which still provided that the tender of notes in the nominal amount of a debt constituted a discharge. The Court did hold, however, that a debtor would violate the general postulate of good faith and fair dealing if he would invoke this law and refuse to pay his creditor as many notes of the now stabilized currency as good faith and fair dealing required him to pay under the circumstances of the individual case.

That decision was sensational, not only because of its impact upon the economy, but also because never in modern German law had a court so openly eliminated a rule of statutory law. It may well be said that the inflation cases initiated a new era of judicial method. The courts' attitude toward the texts of the codes and other statutes came to be one of much greater freedom than before, an attitude which turned out to be just the one required in times when the need for constant and quick adjustment of the law to rapid social changes was not fully satisfied by the legislature.

Case law has thus come to play a significant role. Although precedent is not formally binding, it is readily followed. The practicing attorney will look up cases as a matter of course, will cite to the court those which are favorable to his cause, and try to distinguish those which are against him; and the court itself will take notice of the cases and quite possibly devote much of its opinion to their discussion. So important is the role played by the case law that a lawyer is held liable for malpractice when in drafting a contract he fails to take into account a case having a decisive bearing on the judicial interpretation of a crucial clause.

Insofar as the significance of precedent is concerned, an American lawyer should not find it too difficult to understand the ways of his German colleague. He will not find it quite so easy, however, to follow him in his use of treatises and in the handling of statutes. The tone of argumentation is different. The starting point of legal reasoning is the statute, its particular provisions, their relative positions in the context of the legal system as a whole, and the principles to be derived from them. Legal discourse tends to be more attentive to the totality of the legal system and the policies underlying it, and concepts are apt to be used with greater sharpness of definition and greater consistency than in the United States.

# THE COMPARISON OF
# SOVIET AND AMERICAN LAW  By Harold J. Berman

IN ANALYZING the common foundations of Western legal systems, it is important, and perhaps even necessary, to view them from the perspective of a non-Western culture; and here the study of Russian law can be extremely valuable. For the law of Soviet Russia has many links with Western legal systems, and yet it has its roots elsewhere. It deals with problems very similar to those which confront our law—housing, automobile accidents, workmen's compensation, mass distribution of goods, family disorganization, inheritance, theft, homicide, and many others; and its legal solutions to those problems are in many respects similar to ours. Yet its roots are in a Communist political and social system, in a centrally planned economy, and in the historical tradition of Russia, with its Byzantine, Mongol, and Russian Orthodox heritage, on the one hand, and its window to the West, its adoption of Western institutions, on the other.

Let me speak first of some of the features of Soviet law which are more or less common to Western legal systems. Soviet law is found in constitutions, in legislation, in administrative regulations, and in judicial decisions—although the boundaries between these different forms of law are not as precise as in Western systems generally. The Soviet judicial system includes trial and appellate courts of general jurisdiction within each of the fifteen union republics, with a single all-union court, the Supreme Court of the U.S.S.R. Also there is a separate system of permanent military courts in the nine military districts into which the country is divided, culminating in the Military Division of the Supreme Court of the U.S.S.R. The basic instruments of Soviet criminal and civil law and of judicial procedure are in the form of codes (in addition to the criminal code, code of criminal procedure, civil code, and code of civil

---

Reprinted from *Indiana Law Journal*, vol. 34, 1959, p. 559, with the permission of the author and the publisher. The author is Professor of Law at Harvard University. Professor Berman has taught and studied law in the Soviet Union and written extensively about Soviet law.

procedure, there is also a family code, a labor code, and a land code); these codes are republican, rather than all-union, but the differences from republic to republic are slight, inasmuch as the codes of the Russian Republic served as a model for the other republics and inasmuch as all the codes are subject to all-union legislation. There are a substantial number of lawyers in the Soviet Union—some 60 to 70 thousand—as well as law-trained notaries who draw contracts, wills and other documents. A substantial amount of litigation is conducted in the courts over such matters as housing, divorce and alimony, workmen's compensation, discharge of workers, property rights in houses and other property which may be personally owned, inheritance, author's royalties, personal injury, and other similar matters. In addition, a special system of courts called Gosarbitrazh (literally, state arbitration) decides some 400,000 cases a year involving contract disputes between state business enterprises, which are juridical persons with substantial powers of disposition of goods and a limited power of disposition of capital.

Soviet criminal and civil procedure follow the pattern set by the Western European systems, a pattern which came into Russian history with the judiciary reforms of 1864. In contrast to Anglo-American law, the Soviet system of indictment of crimes—like the French, German, Italian and others—provides for investigation by an examining magistrate, who questions the suspects and witnesses at length over a period of time and presents the indictment. Trial both of criminal and civil cases is by a court consisting of a single professional judge and two lay judges, called people's assessors, who are chosen from the population to sit for ten days out of a year. In a criminal case the burden of proof of the allegations of the indictment is upon the prosecution, and the accused is entitled to a defense counsel. There is a right of appeal in civil and criminal cases; the appeal is heard by a court consisting of three professional judges. Review of the appellate court's decision by a still higher court is discretionary.

What I have been describing thus far are certain surface features of Soviet law. Of course we are concerned with what lies behind the surface. But the surface is also important, for it gives us a key to unlock the first door to what lies behind. An American law student does not have to feel entirely lost in starting out, at least, to understand Soviet law. He can read opinions of Soviet judges in decided cases—many of them have, in fact, been translated into English by American scholars. He can read legislative materials and codes which speak a language familiar to him— a language of property, contract, negligence, unjust enrichment, intent of the parties, fault, statute of limitations, right of appeal, burden of proof, damages, criminal intent, criminal negligence, right of self-defense, right to counsel, and, in general, the entire apparatus of concepts and institutions of Western legal systems. He can read treatises and textbooks by Soviet law professors—provided he knows Russian—written for the benefit of the Soviet legal profession (including judges and prosecutors) and of law students in the thirty-two Soviet universities, expounding and commenting on the various branches of Soviet law in a manner in many respects similar to that of treatises and textbooks with which he is familiar. The American student will confront serious problems in using these materials—including problems arising from their paucity as compared with ours, from the fact that some Soviet laws are unpublished, from the fact that much of Soviet legal literature is colored by Party jargon and from the fact that writers and courts are bound by Party policies which are not always explicitly stated. One must learn to read between the lines of Soviet writings. Yet it is of considerable value that the lines are there.

*Techniques of Adjudication and Legislation.* What lies behind this first door? Let us turn first to techniques of adjudication. Here the American lawyer does not feel nearly as much at home as would the French or German or Italian lawyer—though they, too, would encounter some surprises. Soviet adjudication is distinguished by its informality. A civil action is commenced by a written complaint which need state very little and may state as much as the plaintiff wishes. No written reply is required. There is no set procedure for formulating issues in advance of trial and no pretrial procedure for taking depositions or procuring documents. As in Continental European countries, the trial may continue at intervals over weeks or even months. The judge and, if they wish (which they seldom do), the two assessors take the leading role in questioning the parties and the witnesses, although the lawyers (and also the parties themselves) may interrupt with questions. There are no rules of exclusion of evidence; however, the judges are supposed to be guided by rules of evaluation of evidence. In criminal cases the complaining witness may also claim his damages for losses which he suffered as a result of the crime; again, the pattern is European. Upon appeal the case is, in effect, retried. The informality of the proceedings is emphasized by the fact that in a great many civil cases the parties prefer not to be represented by counsel.

The informality of civil trial procedure is bound up, of course, with the absence of the jury; both are connected with the conception of the trial primarily as an official investigation of the truth of the claims and defenses presented, rather than primarily as a forum for achieving justice through the clash of adversaries. This, too, is European—to a much lesser extent, English—and quite un-American. But the informality of Soviet civil and criminal trial procedure is also connected with a special feature of Soviet law, the paternal relationship of the judge to the parties; the Soviet judge is supposed to guide and discipline the parties and to help inculcate in them the attitudes and beliefs which the State seeks to encourage. (About this I shall have more to add later.)

Soviet judges are not bound by precedent and indeed it is prohibited by Soviet law for the lawyers to cite precedents. Statements of law by higher courts in decided cases, and especially by the Supreme Court of the U.S.S.R. are, however, binding upon lower courts; therefore Soviet lawyers can and do cite such statements. The difference is a subtle one. The distinction between the development of law by analogy of previous decisions and the development by analogy of code provisions, statutes, and doctrine may be of little practical importance to the outcome of a particular case. The absence of a doctrine of precedent in Soviet law is nevertheless significant in that it reflects the absence of a strong sense of the growth of law over time. There has been some organic development of legal doctrine in the Soviet Union, but on the whole Soviet legal development has been more fitful, and in many areas of law there have been wide swings back and forth. One wonders in any event whether the doctrine of precedent, in its strict form at least, could possibly be introduced into a system such as the Soviet, in view of the informality of pleadings. Without precision in the formulation of issues, it is impossible to achieve precision in the distinction between holding and dictum.

Finally, with regard to Soviet techniques of adjudication, it must be noted that Soviet judicial opinions reflect a rather mechanical mode of reasoning, a conceptual rather than a pragmatic logic. All flavor of "sociological jurisprudence" is missing from them. Law seems to be conceived in terms of fixed rules; its application is viewed as requiring accuracy, not policy. The opinions are short. Occasionally the facts of the case are developed at length, but rarely is there any elaborate discussion of the law. The opinion has more the form of a decree, and indeed is entitled a "decree" (postanovlenie). Typically it is in the following style: "This case is governed by Article Such-and-such. The contention that that provision is superseded by the statute of such-and-such date is unfounded, since the statute does not refer to that provision." And so on. On the other hand, where it is conceived that there is a gap in the law, the Soviet courts often do not hesitate to fill it. In fact Soviet codes and statutes are full of lacunae, and as a result much of Soviet law is avowedly judge-made. For Example, the Soviet courts, without any code or statutory provision on the subject, early decided that damages awarded in tort cases for loss of earning capacity should be paid in the form of annuities, and should cease to be paid if the plaintiff subsequently recovered his earning capacity. We know this practice in workmen's compensation, of course, but the Soviet judges introduced it in tort actions generally. Indeed, most of Soviet tort law has been spun judicially out of a few broad code provisions. To cite an even more striking example, workers found guilty under a law (repealed in 1956) imposing two-to-four months' imprisonment for quitting a job without permission of management, were held by the courts to be *not* obliged to return to the former job after serving their sentence, on the ground that by quitting, though unlawfully, they had dissolved the labor contract. This was surely "mechanical jurisprudence," though it made new law. Incidentally, the decision provided a strong incentive for otherwise reluctant managers to give insistent workers permission to quit.

Mechanical jurisprudence—in the sense of a logic which tends to read legal propositions literally, rather than in terms of their social purpose—is connected in Soviet law with the movement toward stability which began in the early 1930s and which has gathered considerable momentum since Stalin's death six years ago. Earlier Soviet jurisprudence had taught that law and policy are virtually indistinguishable, and that Soviet law in the period of construction of socialism should have maximum flexibility. Article 1 of the Civil Code of 1922, providing that rights are to be protected only to the extent that they are exercised in accordance with their social economic purpose, and Article 16 of the Criminal Code of 1926, providing that a socially dangerous act, though not specifically proscribed, may by analogy be punished under a provision proscribing similar acts, were reflections of the earlier conception of law as policy science. Since the mid-1930s these provisions have become obsolete. Article 1 has been severely restricted and the doctrine of analogy has been expressly repudiated. The reasons for this shift toward what Stalin in 1936 called "stability of laws" and "strict socialist legality" are complex. They are connected with a stabilization of social life generally, the strengthening of the family, the restoration of military traditions, the emphasis on the achievements of pre-revolutionary Russian history, and, in the economic sphere, a recognition that efficiency in an industrial society requires the kind of calculability and predictability which only a stable legal system can provide. Under Stalin legal stability did not extend to the political area and to a lesser extent the same is true under Stalin's successors. Where the top leadership has felt its own security threatened, it has resorted to terror—terror by abuse of law and naked terror without law. But in areas of social and economic life in which the supremacy of the Party leadership was not challenged, Stalin discovered that his dictatorial powers could be maintained more effectively with a system of law than without it. The dictator can easily enact statutes; his problem is to establish a system for their interpretation and application in a manner consistent with his will. For this purpose mechanical jurisprudence is safer than a more creative approach—safer for the leadership and safer also, and perhaps primarily, for the judges and lawyers.

Thus Soviet techniques of adjudication lead us to Soviet techniques of legislation. As in France after the French Revolution, so in the Soviet Union, restrictions on the doctrine of precedent as well as on liberal judicial interpretation of statutes are seen in terms of legislative supremacy. The difference is, however, that the Soviet legislature, the Supreme Soviet of the U.S.S.R., is hand-picked by the top leadership of the Communist Party, and its freedom of debate is extremely narrow. Only recently has there begun to function a committee system; there are now some thirteen standing committees for drafting legislation in various fields. But the initiative is with the Party leaders, and it is they who set the limits of possible action. It is the absence of due process of legislation, the absence of a genuine adversary system of enacting statutory law, which is the chief formal distinction between the Soviet legal system and the legal systems of the West. Here we find one of the principal links between Soviet law and Soviet autocracy.

The de facto legislative power of the top Soviet leader or group of leaders reflects a fundamental difference between the nature and function of law in the Soviet Union and in the West. It is a basic postulate of all Western systems that law is essentially a means whereby society exercises control over the political leadership; it is a basic postulate of the Soviet system, on the other hand, that law is essentially a means whereby the political leadership exercises control over society. We must remember, in this connection, that Russia has never had a deep-rooted tradition of a system of law which binds the ruler himself.

*Soviet Law and Social Order.* We must not confuse the rule of law, however, with the role of law. Despite their initial hostility to law both in theory and in practice, the leaders of the Russian Revolution learned, as leaders of the western revolutions in earlier centuries had learned, that the principles for which the Revolution was fought cannot be preserved unless they are institutionalized in law. In particular, the Soviet leaders learned that the system of planned economy cannot function without law; and they learned that a collectivized—one might better say, a mobilized—social order requires law.

Let me speak briefly first about the law of a planned economy. Soviet industry and commerce are largely in the hands of state agencies; and Soviet agriculture is under stringent state control. The plans under which the state officials who are thus in charge of Soviet economic activities operate come from higher administrative authorities and ultimately from the Council of Ministers of the U.S.S.R. and its State Planning Committee. Yet plans are not self-executing. It is all very well for Moscow to say, or for the new regional economic councils to say, that so much coal, so much steel, so many pairs of shoes, so many television sets, should be produced; but where are the managers to get the necessary resources to produce them? Labor must be paid; goods must be procured; the product must be distributed. The bottlenecks of planning are insuperable unless a rational system of incentives, of criteria which will guide individual decisions, is worked out. The Soviet leaders in the late 1930s worked out such a system—worked it out in orthodox terms of monetary rewards, contract law, corporate autonomy of individual enterprises, and in the case of the collective farms, cooperative sharing in the profits of the collective as well as personal ownership by the peasants of their household plots.

I have mentioned that there is a great deal of contract litigation between state business enterprises. Gosarbitrazh adjudicates disputes arising over failure to deliver, breach of warranty, and similar questions. The individual state enterprise has the same incentive to sue for breach of contract that a private firm in this country has: its losses will come out of its profits, a portion of which goes into bonuses. In addition there is an added incentive: if it can show that its failure to fulfill the plan is due to the fault of another enterprise, it can escape measures of administrative discipline. Finally, the State itself has a strong interest in an impartial determination of responsibility, as well as in the correction of the causes of breach of contract. Indeed, one of the most interesting aspects of the work of Gosarbitrazh is its educational role in so-called precontract disputes. If the parties cannot agree upon the terms of a contract which, under the general plan, they ought to conclude, they may resort to Gosarbitrazh which will determine how the contract should be written. It is apparent that here contract law and administrative law are intertwined, and that although Soviet contract law is often quite similar to our own in terms of the rules of formation, breach, damages, and the like, it fulfills a quite different function.[a]

Finally, I should like to say a few words about the functions of Soviet law in maintaining a collective social order. In comparison with the United States, Soviet society is more highly mobilized, more highly directed, not only for military purposes but also for social and economic purposes. It is the idea of Soviet society that each person in it must have a place, a job to do. The legal system is more immediately concerned than ours, therefore, with the allocation of duties, and although rights are of course correlative with duties, it is implicit in Soviet law that duties precede rights, that rights arise out of duties.

How is this manifested concretely? In the first place, it is manifested in the increased role of criminal law. The concept of "official crimes"—intentional or negligent abuse of authority by persons in responsible positions—plays a very important part in the control of the economic behavior not only of managers of state enterprises but even of persons quite

[a] Compare current proposals in the United States for compulsory arbitration of labor contract formation where strikes threaten basic industries.

far down in the official hierarchy, including, for example, waiters in state-owned restaurants. From 1940 until 1956 workers who quit their jobs without authorization of management were subject to two-to-four months' imprisonment. Recently in several of the smaller republics a law has been enacted whereby a person who is considered an "anti-social and parasitic element" may be exiled from two to five years to another part of the republic by an ad hoc body of neighbors with review by the executive authorities only.[b]

The role of law in maintaining a mobilized social order is seen also in the powers of the Procuracy not only to prosecute crime but also to supervise generally the legality of administrative acts. The general supervisory powers of the Procuracy make it the watchdog of the central government; it may protest any illegality of management, of local government, or of individual officials, to the next higher administrative authorities. Although the institution of the Procuracy is known also to other countries, only in Russia has it played so crucial a role in maintaining social order in general.

The Soviet courts, too, play an important part in maintaining the sense of collective unity and collective purpose in the society. Their task is conceived to a large extent in terms of educating people—the parties, the spectators, and the whole society—to be the kind of "new Soviet man" which the state is seeking to develop: hard-working, honest, resourceful, cooperative, and above all conscious of his membership in a socialist society and loyal to its leadership. Both substantive and procedural law manifest a jurisprudence in which the balancing of interests yields place to the shaping of interests. It is not merely that Soviet judicial decisions are thought to have an educational function, but rather that the educational purpose of judicial decisions becomes a central factor in the determination of rights and duties in particular cases. An American parallel may be found in the laws governing juvenile delinquency: here we are expressly concerned primarily with the effect of procedures and of decisions upon the person before the court. Something of the spirit of the law governing juvenile delinquency is carried over into all branches of law, civil and administrative as well as criminal, in the Soviet Union. This is not to say that Soviet law is benign. It is benign in some respects and ruthless in others. And it is not necessary to stress that the whole conception of a parental relation between the court, as an arm of the state, and the people as its wards, so to speak, lends itself to arbitrariness, to political interference in adjudication, and to a philosophy of historical relativism under which rights may be withdrawn altogether if circumstances so require.

[b] These developments are discussed more fully at pp. 555–557.

Yet it is a mistake to view Soviet law as merely an instrument of dictatorship. It is a genuine response to the crisis of the twentieth century, which has witnessed the breakdown of individualism—in law as well as in other areas of spiritual life. "Where today are the economically self-sufficient household and neighborhoods, where is the economically self-sufficient, versatile, restless, self-reliant man, freely making a place for himself by free self-assertion . . . ?" asked Roscoe Pound in 1930. "Where, indeed, but in our legal thinking in which it is so decisive an element." Since 1930 it has gone out of much of our legal thinking as well. The excesses of totalitarianism can teach us the dangers of rushing to the opposite extreme; nevertheless this is not a matter where we can afford to be smug. Our own law may be seen in the light of Soviet experience, as seeking a level which combines the virtues of individuality and collectivity, while avoiding the mythology of either "ism."

The preceding study is supplemented by the following report utilizing information and insight gained by Professor Berman while studying and lecturing in the Soviet Union during the academic year 1961–62.

# THE DILEMMA OF
# SOVIET LAW REFORM   By Harold J. Berman

SOME YEARS ago black-and-white thinking had so distorted America's vision of the Soviet Union that it was difficult to discuss Soviet law without an elaborate explanation that indeed there is such a thing as law in the Soviet Union; that in the mid-1930s, after a period of legal nihilism and naked terror, Stalin proclaimed the need for "stability of laws" and "socialist legality"; and that the legal system which Stalin established (with Vyshinsky's help) was designed not only to make people obey but also to encourage initiative and responsibility and, above all, to instill a belief in the rightness of the Soviet political, economic, and social order. It may be that today we have outgrown our fire-and-brimstone concept

---

Reprinted from Berman, "The Dilemma of Soviet Law Reform," *Harvard Law Review*, vol. 73, 1963, pp. 929–951, with the permission of the author and the publisher. (Copyright 1963 by the Harvard Law Review Association.)

of hell and our primitive notion that the devil rules by fear alone. If so, we are in a better position to assess both the strengths and the weaknesses of Soviet law.

Such an assessment is of critical importance for us as Americans. We have, strangely enough, a very great stake in the development of Soviet law. That stake is partly physical and partly spiritual. Physically, our very survival depends in part on the extent to which law can exercise a stabilizing influence both on Soviet internal developments and on Soviet foreign policy. The fact that the Soviet people, including the Soviet leaders, believe in law is therefore a cause for us to rejoice. The fact that the law in which they believe differs sharply in certain essential features from the law in which we believe is, by the same token, a cause for us to be greatly concerned. Indeed, never before in our history has the study of a foreign legal system been of such crucial significance to us, for no other people has ever lived so close to us as the Soviets. We are less than a half hour away from them by missile.

But even apart from the danger of atomic war, the destiny of the Soviet Union is intimately related to our own destiny. We are two revolutionary peoples in the world today—two peoples who have a worldwide mission. The struggle between us is only in part a power struggle. More basically, it is a spiritual struggle between two concepts—two developing concepts—of social order, each claiming universal validity. The spiritual struggle is more basic, for however the power struggle ends the spiritual struggle will remain. War would not settle the question of communism, no matter who is "victorious." The survivors of a war would still have to choose between something like the ideals reflected in Soviet law and something like the ideals reflected in American law.

## The Significance of Soviet Law Reform

The fact that the Soviet concept of social order is not a static but a developing one is dramatically illustrated in the striking changes which have taken place in the Soviet legal system in recent years. Indeed the reform movement in Soviet law is one of the most significant aspects of Soviet social development in the past ten years since Stalin's death.

In interpreting this reform movement, one must start with Stalin—however much the present Soviet leaders would like to expunge his name from the memory of their people. For despite the very substantial changes which they have introduced, the Soviet legal system remains Stalinist in its basic structure and its basic purposes. The organization and functions of the lawmaking, law-enforcing, and law-practicing agencies—the legislature, the Procuracy, the courts, the administrative organs, the bar—are not essentially different now from what they were when Stalin died. The main outlines of Soviet criminal law and procedure, civil law and procedure, labor law, agrarian law, family law, administrative law, constitutional law, and other branches of the Soviet legal tree, remain basically the same as before.

And if one looks behind the structure to the purposes of Soviet law, it remains a totalitarian law, in the sense that it seeks to regulate all aspects of economic and social life, including the circulation of thought, while leaving the critical questions of political power to be decided by informal, secret procedures beyond the scrutiny or control either of legislative or judicial bodies. It remains the law of a one-party state. It remains the law of a planned economy. It remains a law whose primary function is to discipline, guide, train, and educate Soviet citizens to be dedicated members of a collectivized and mobilized social order.

If this is so, it may be asked, what is the significance of the recent reforms? Indeed, many Western observers have treated each successive development in Soviet law during the past ten years as mere smoke without fire—or even as a smokescreen designed to conceal the absence of any fire. Others have viewed the reforms as half-hearted concessions designed to appease the appetite of the Soviet people without really satisfying their hunger. These grudging responses are reminiscent of Soviet interpretations of American law reforms: the New Deal, we are told by Soviet writers, did not really alter the fundamental nature of the American capitalist system; the Supreme Court decision in the *Segregation Cases* did not end discrimination against Negroes; American law remains "bourgeois."

Viewed from a sufficiently lofty height, the scene never changes. This may only mean, however, that the viewer does not see what is really going on. . . .

Of course, if the observer abandons all elevation and descends into the midst of the events, he loses all perspective and sees only flux. The foreign journalist in Moscow—and the reader of his articles at home—tend to see a whirling, eddying stream. The only solution is to seek a composite picture, from various perspectives.

Such a composite picture would reveal, I believe, six major tendencies in Soviet law reform since 1953:

First, there has been a tendency toward the elimination of political terror.

Second, there has been a tendency toward the liberalization both of procedures and of substantive norms.

Third, there has been a tendency toward the systematization and rationalization of the legal system.

Fourth, there has been a tendency toward decentralization and democratization of decisionmaking.

Fifth, there has been a tendency to introduce popular participation in the administration of justice.

Sixth, there has been a tendency in the past two years to threaten those who will not cooperate in building communism with harsh criminal and administrative penalties.

*The Tendency Toward Elimination of Terror.* Stalin's system since the mid-1930s was based on a coexistence of law and terror. Law was for those areas of Soviet life where the political factor was stabilized. Terror, either naked or in the guise of law (as in the purge trials of the late 1930s), was applied when the regime felt itself threatened. But these two spheres were not easy to keep separate either in theory or in practice. It was not a peaceful coexistence. In the first place, the borderline shifted: the crime of theft of state property, for example, which was supposed to be dealt with by due process of law, could easily merge with counterrevolutionary crime and thereby become subject to repression by the secret police. In the second place, even though terror diminished after 1938, it continued to have a deleterious effect on the legal system itself. Urgently needed law reforms were delayed and sidetracked because of people's fear of being labeled "deviationist."

A month after Stalin's death in March 1953, his successors began to proclaim the "inviolability" of Soviet law and to denounce "arbitrary procedures" and "violations of socialist legality," particularly in connection with the so-called "Doctors' Plot," which many have supposed Stalin trumped up in the last months of his life as a pretext for a new wave of purges. After the arrest of Beria in July 1953, many of the excesses of Stalinist terror were attributed not to the dictator himself but to his chief of secret police. This deception wore thin, however, and in February 1956 Khrushchev attacked Stalin by name at the 20th Congress of the Communist Party of the Soviet Union, denouncing him for the "cult of personality" and for persecution of loyal party members in violation of their legal rights. In October-November 1961, at the 22d Party Congress, the attacks on Stalin were renewed with even greater vigor. The inviolability of socialist law was again proclaimed. Vyshinsky's name was added to Stalin's as coauthor of a legal system which permitted falsification and distortion of legality for the persecution of people innocent of any crime.

In implementation of these attacks upon the "cult of personality" important steps have been taken since September 1953 to eliminate those features of the preexisting Soviet law which permitted the disguise of terror in legal form.

First, the Special Board of the Ministry of Internal Affairs has been abolished. It was this Special Board which had been the chief instrument of terror. It was a three-man administrative committee—the Russians called it a *troika*—which was empowered by a 1934 statute to send people to labor camps without a hearing, in a secret administrative procedure, without right of counsel and without right of appeal.

Second, the security police have been deprived of the power to conduct investigations of crimes under their own special rules without supervision by the Procuracy.

Third, the special procedures for court cases involving the most serious antistate crimes have been abolished. The laws of 1934 and 1937 permitting persons charged with certain such crimes to be tried secretly, in absentia, and without counsel, were repealed.

Fourth, the military courts, which had previously had a wide jurisdiction over civilians, particularly in the case of political crimes, have been deprived of all jurisdiction over civilians except for espionage.

Fifth, the law permitting punishment of relatives of one who deserts to a foreign country from the armed forces—though they knew nothing of the desertion—has been abolished.

Sixth, Vyshinsky's doctrine that confessions have special evidentiary force in cases of counterrevolutionary crimes—based on the transparently false notion that people will not confess to such crimes unless they are actually guilty—has been repudiated; confessions are now treated as having no evidentiary force in themselves, and the matters contained in a confession must be corroborated by other evidence.

Seventh, Vyshinsky's doctrine that the burden of proof shifts to the accused in cases of counterrevolutionary crimes has also been repudiated. The new Soviet codes place the burden of proving the guilt of the accused squarely on the prosecutor. Although the phrase "presumption of innocence" is avoided in the codes, all that we mean by that phrase is spelled out in Soviet law.

Eighth, Vyshinsky's broad definition of complicity, borrowed from the Anglo-American doctrine of conspiracy, has been repudiated. Innocent association with others who are planning an illegal act can no longer constitute a crime under the new Soviet legislation.

Ninth, the law on so-called "counterrevolutionary crimes" has been slightly narrowed and made a little less vague. The term "counterrevolutionary" has been eliminated and the term "antistate" substituted. The crime of "terrorist acts," which hitherto had been interpreted to include any violent act against a state or party official or, indeed, his close relatives, whatever the motive, has been restricted to murder or serious bodily injury of the official himself committed for the purpose of overthrowing or weakening the Soviet authority. The law on state secrets has been substantially relaxed—though it is still far wider in its scope than we would consider tolerable. And a new list of information constituting state secrets has been enacted which is less broad and more precise than the earlier list.

Finally, there took place from 1953 (or 1955) to 1957 a systematic reexamination of all cases of persons previously convicted of counterrevolutionary crimes and the release from labor camps of the overwhelming majority of such persons as fully rehabilitated.

The restoration of procedural due process of law in political cases is a signal achievement of the post-Stalin regime. The Soviet citizen is now protected against police terror, false charges, and faked trials to a far greater extent than ever before in Soviet history. No longer need he fear the midnight knock on the door as a prelude to transportation to a Siberian labor camp without a fair hearing.

Yet one cannot speak of the total elimination of political terror so long as open opposition to Communist Party policy—the "Party line"—can lead to criminal sanctions, however "objectively" and "correctly" imposed. The 1958 Statute on State Crimes carries over from the earlier law on counterrevolutionary crimes the provision against "agitation or propaganda" directed against the Soviet system. To defame the Soviet political and social system, or even to possess written materials of such defamatory nature, if for the purpose of weakening Soviet authority, is punishable by deprivation of freedom of up to seven years. In 1961, for example, certain leaders of the Jewish community in Leningrad were convicted for the crime of circulating anti-Soviet literature obtained from a foreign embassy, presumably the Israeli. We would call this a denial of "substantive" due process of law.

The law of antistate agitation and propaganda is only one of many features of the Soviet system which keep alive the fear of Soviet citizens that the terror may return. Later I shall speak more fully of this fear, and of some of the conditions which give rise to it. But it is important to stress at this point that the fear of a return to terror is itself a form of terror. Therefore, one must view the developments of the past ten years as reflecting only a tendency—though an extremely important tendency —toward the elimination of terror.

*The Liberalization of Procedural and Substantive Law.* Even apart from political crimes, Soviet law has undergone substantial liberalization in the past ten years. It would be impossible to list the hundreds, indeed thousands, of needed reforms which have been introduced. Let me speak very briefly of some of the most important, first in criminal law and procedure, then in criminal punishment and the system of detention, and finally in some other fields of law.

In criminal law and procedure, the "tightening up" of the rules with respect to burden of proof, evaluation of confessions, and the doctrine of complicity, which have already been mentioned in the discussion of political crimes, have given increased protection to persons accused of other crimes as well. In addition, the right to counsel prior to trial, though still limited, has been significantly extended; the time for supervisory review of acquittals in criminal cases, formerly unlimited, has been reduced to one year; powers of search and seizure have been somewhat restricted; the doctrine of analogy, whereby a person who committed a socially dangerous act not specifically made punishable by law could be sentenced under a law proscribing an analogous act, has been eliminated; penalties have been substantially lightened for many crimes—for example, new laws imposing lighter sentences for petty rowdyism ("hooliganism") and petty theft of state or public property have removed the necessity of many long years in labor camps for conviction of trivial offences; and some crimes have been eliminated altogether—for example, abortion, absenteeism from work, and quitting one's job without permission. The large-scale amnesties of 1953 and 1957 released all except those sentenced for, or charged with, the most serious offenses. . . .

Liberalization has not been confined to criminal policy. Since 1953, and especially since 1955, there has been a reexamination of every branch of law and a weeding out of many of the harshest features. For example, a new civil right has been created to obtain a court order for public retraction of a newspaper libel. Equal rights of foreigners under Soviet law have been declared—subject, of course, to statutory restrictions. (It would be interesting to put those two provisions together and to have a suit by a foreigner in a Soviet court demanding a retraction of a newspaper libel against him.) In labor law the rights of trade unions have been enhanced and the procedures for settlement of workers' grievances have been improved. In family law, a new code is expected to be enacted shortly which will, among other things, ameliorate the position of the child born out of wedlock. Similar examples could be multiplied from many other fields of law.

In 1961 and 1962 there has been a contrary trend, away from liberalization, in certain areas. These recent backward steps, however, cannot, yet at least, be considered to have stopped the liberal momentum of the post-Stalin reforms.

*Systematization and Rationalization.* The general tendency toward liberalization of law is, of course, an important supporting buttress of the tendency toward elimination of political terror. For such tendencies to have permanence, however, deeper foundations are required in the legal system as a whole. From that standpoint, the efforts of recent years to systematize and rationalize the Soviet legal system are of great significance.

The Stalin Constitution of December 1936, and the Vyshinsky jurisprudence which surrounded it, rehabilitated the various republican criminal, civil, labor, and family codes of the "New Economic Policy" period of the twenties which had largely fallen into disrepute in the period from 1930 to 1936. Of course the NEP codes, designed for a transition period of mixed capitalism-socialism, were inadequate for the new period of full socialism with its planned economy. The Stalin Constitution therefore called for the creation of all-union codes to replace the earlier republican codes. But until such new all-union codes were adopted, the earlier ones were to prevail, together with the thousands of statutory and administrative changes introduced into them.

During the remaining sixteen years of Stalin's reign, however, new all-union codes were not adopted, although many drafts were produced. Only with the removal of the political and ideological pressure of Stalinist autocracy did it become possible to introduce new codes, and, together with them, a reorganization of the entire system of legal administration....

In 1957 the constitution was amended to provide for separate republican codes to be based upon new all-union Fundamental Principles. In December 1958 the Supreme Soviet of the U.S.S.R. adopted a series of Fundamental Principles of various branches of law—Fundamental Principles of Criminal Law, Fundamental Principles of Criminal Procedure, and Fundamental Principles of Court Organization—together with new comprehensive statutes on state crimes, military crimes, and military tribunals. Subsequently, in December 1961, the Supreme Soviet adopted Fundamental Principles of Civil Law and of Civil Procedure. Fundamental Principles of Family Law and of Labor Law are now in preparation; indeed, a statute on the procedure for the hearing of labor disputes adopted in 1957 is itself a systematization of many aspects of labor law.

On the basis of the Fundamental Principles, the various republics have adopted their own new codes of criminal law and criminal procedure and are now in the last stages of work on new codes of civil law and civil procedure....[a]

Two other items cannot be omitted from this very brief account. The Juridical Commission of the Council of Ministers of the U.S.S.R. has been given the function of determining which laws have lost their force in the light of the new legislation. In the twenty years between 1937 and 1958, the U.S.S.R. Supreme Soviet enacted over 7,000 statutes, edicts, and decrees, and the U.S.S.R. Council of Ministers issued about 390,000 de-

[a] Compare the work toward uniform law among the states of the United States discussed in Chapter 6. It must be remembered that in the Soviet Union, uniformity of action by the republics, on matters thought to be important, can be obtained through control by the Communist Party. See p. 555.

crees and regulations. Few of these were formally declared to have lost their force. Yet in 1960 only about 15,000 of these approximately 400,000 normative acts actually remained in force. The Juridical Commission has been attempting to cleanse the Augean stables of Soviet legislation by systematically listing, little by little, those laws and other normative acts which are no longer valid.

In connection with this, it is important to note two new laws on the publication of laws. Of the more than 7,000 laws of the Supreme Soviet enacted between 1937 and 1958, only some hundreds were published. Of the 390,000 decrees and regulations of the Council of Ministers, only a few thousand were published. The rest were merely distributed to the appropriate officials concerned with their enforcement and to other authorized persons. A 1958 law requires publication of all acts of the Supreme Soviet. Edicts, decrees, and acts of the Presidium of the Supreme Soviet are required to be published only if they are of "general significance" or have a "normative character." Also a 1959 decree of the Council of Ministers requires publication of all its decrees and orders which are general or normative. The determination of which acts are general or normative and which are not is left to the Presidium and the Council respectively.

The systematization and rationalization of Soviet law is not something which can be accomplished in a few years. Indeed, it is something which must go on continually. The recognition of its importance, and the very great efforts being devoted to it, are an encouraging sign of the determination of the post-Stalin regime to establish a far higher degree of legal security than that which existed in the past.

*The Tendency Toward Decentralization and Democratization.* Khrushchev has committed himself to the view that the harshness of the Stalinist system cannot achieve the purposes of socialism as he envisages it, and that cooperation with the policies of his regime cannot be secured without a systematic and rational legality. Implicit in this conviction, and necessary to its implementation, is the belief in the possibility of a wide decentralization of decisionmaking and a still wider participation of the public in the formulation of issues for decision.

Two qualifications must be made at the outset, however, in discussing the tendency of the post-Stalin period of Soviet history toward greater decentralization and democratization. The first is that there is no sign that the present Soviet leadership has any intention of allowing this tendency to go beyond its power to control it. The limits of decentralized decisionmaking and democratization are set by the central authorities. The second qualification is that this theory of "democratic centralism"— centralization of authority combined with decentralization of operations —was also Stalin's theory. The difference today is a difference in degree.

The tendency toward decentralization and democratization has been greatly accelerated since Stalin's death, however, by the very nature of the tendencies toward elimination of political terror, toward liberalization, and toward systematization and rationalization of the law. Apart from all other considerations, these tendencies have imposed an absolute requirement of help from hundreds of thousands of people at various levels of the official hierarchy and in various parts of the Soviet Union. In addition, the main purpose of these tendencies—to overcome the rigidities of the system inherited from Stalin, to stimulate local and individual initiative and enthusiasm—has necessitated the enlistment of maximum cooperation from the maximum number of people.

When we think of America we think of 180 million people of diverse outlooks, traditions, and interests, scattered across a great continent which includes not only New York City and Washington, D.C., but also Texas and California and Mississippi and Vermont and a host of other very different kinds of communities. But too many of us, when we think of the Soviet Union, stop with the Kremlin. It should not need demonstration that even if we imagined the entire Soviet population to be a disciplined army, the commander-in-chief would be greatly in need of subordinate units of command with considerable autonomy of action. He could not run the lives of 220 million people, including thirty or forty major nationalities, spread across one-sixth of the earth's surface, by push-button from Moscow....

This is not to say that centralization is not the major fact of the Soviet political and economic system. "Bolsheviks are centralists by conviction...."

The decision in 1957 to abandon the rule of the 1936 Constitution calling for all-union codes and to substitute a rule calling for separate codes in each of the fifteen Soviet republics, based, however, on all-union Fundamental Principles; the earlier decision to dissolve the all-union Ministry of Justice into separate republican ministries of justice and the later decision to do the same with the Ministry of Internal Affairs; and, most important of all, the decision in 1957 to split the economy of the country into about one hundred economic regions, each with its own Council of National Economy, and to divide among these regional councils some of the functions of the former economic ministries with their central offices in Moscow—these decisions in the direction of decentralization were called for by the enormous bureaucratization of Soviet social and economic life, which had become almost too stifling to endure.

Yet decentralization in itself is not democratization; it may be, and to a certain extent it has been, simply a moving of the center to the localities, a stretching of the chain of command. It has also been more than that, however. The lower links in the chain have unquestionably been given more initiative. And even where ultimate decisions have been reserved for Moscow, a far greater hearing has been given to the voices of the localities.

This is illustrated by the process of law reform itself. Khrushchev and his immediate associates could give the word that the time had come for substantial law reforms and could indicate the lines along which the reforms should run. But the word could not become a reality without an enormous effort by the people who would be directly affected by these reforms. These include not only the professional lawyers who would have to draft them and the officials who would have to administer them, but also the various people who would have to live under them.

The comprehensive legislation enacted in recent years has been worked on by representatives of hundreds, indeed thousands, of organizations. All the major governmental agencies have expressed detailed views on their various provisions. There has been endless discussion of them in the universities, in research institutes, in economic organizations of various kinds, in scholarly journals, and in the daily press. . . .

In addition, popular participation in lawmaking has been stimulated by the expansion of the committee system of the Supreme Soviet of the U.S.S.R. and of the Supreme Soviets of the fifteen republics. Tens of thousands of expert consultants have reported to these committees. And apart from major all-union and republican legislation, there has been a substantial increase in the powers of the local municipal councils and a vast amount of activity of local governmental organizations, involving the participation of literally hundreds of thousands of Soviet citizens.

Of course it would be a mistake to suppose that Soviet federalism and Soviet democracy involve—as ours do—a struggle between opposing political units and groups, a competition for political leadership. In the Soviet Union all power resides in the Communist Party, which remains, as stated in the constitution, the "central core" of all organizations, whether they be state organizations or social organizations. Despite the development of greater intra-Party democracy in recent years, the Party remains a disciplined elite, subservient to its leadership. Decentralization and democratization of decision-making in the spheres of government, law, and economic administration is not a threat to Party supremacy; indeed, it is required by the Party as a means of maintaining its supremacy.

Yet Party control is, in a much deeper sense, challenged by the development of autonomous centers of discussion and initiative, even though it remains the "central core" of such centers. One of my strongest impressions in a year of intimate association with Soviet jurists of all kinds is that of their cohesion. Whether they are judges, procurators, Ministry of Justice officials, law professors, research workers, legal advisers of state institutions and enterprises, or advocates, the seventy to eighty thousand jurists of the Soviet Union are bound together by the closest professional ties. They meet together in many different kinds of activity; they discuss and debate common problems; they work together; and they are bound not only by their common legal education but also by their common vested interest in the preservation of legality. As a class, they have grown greatly in importance during the past ten years.

*Popular Participation in the Administration of Justice.* In describing the movement away from political terror, harshness of punishment, chaos and irrationality of legislation, and overcentralization of decision-making, one runs the risk of leaving the false impression that the Soviet legal system is becoming just like ours. It is true that Stalin's successors have sought to eliminate the dualism of law and terror which formerly characterized the Soviet system, and in so doing they have taken important steps in the direction of a more humane, more rational, and more democratic legal system. Yet they have sought to do this without abandoning the dynamic revolutionary development of the Soviet state and of Soviet society; indeed, their purpose has been to instill new vitality into that revolutionary development by softening the motive force of fear and strengthening the motive force of common effort, struggle, and enthusiasm. The Soviet people are now being asked voluntarily to make sacrifices which formerly were evoked from them in part by threat of force. No doubt both the leaders and the people are greatly relieved at the decrease in emphasis upon terror and coercion and the increase in emphasis upon the liberal, rational, and democratic elements in their legal system. But these elements are not—for the leaders, at least—ends in themselves but rather a means toward lifting their society to new heights of economic progress, political power and social solidarity.

Law is conceived of as a major instrument for achieving these goals. Law is conceived of, above all, as a means of educating Soviet people to be the type of socially conscious, dedicated members of society which are required if socialism is to be maintained and if communism is to be achieved. This concept of the dynamic function of law in molding not merely the conduct of men but also their morality and their very characters is, in my view, the greatest challenge which Soviet law presents to the world. I wish to consider now, however, only one aspect of this concept, namely, its reflection in recent years in a greatly increased participation of ordinary Soviet citizens—of society, the public, *obshchestvennost'*, as Soviet terminology has it—in the administration of justice.

It is Soviet theory that under communism the functions of state organizations (which operate in part by coercion) will be turned over entirely to social organizations (which operate only by persuasion). In anticipation of this glorious day, the role of social organizations has been greatly increased. Neighborhood and factory meetings have been convened for a variety of purposes and have been given certain semijudicial functions. Also a voluntary auxiliary police force has been organized—the so-called *druzhiny*, or bands—to help keep order; they direct traffic, take drunks into custody, and in general make themselves unpopular among the people on the streets. In addition many special volunteer commissions have been formed and given semi-official status—to observe conditions in the labor colonies and to make recommendations, to report to municipal councils on housing questions, to report on local observance of "socialist legality," and for a host of similar purposes. Trade unions and the Young Communist League (*Komsomol*) are also considered to be social organizations, and their functions have been extended.

Many of the functions of Soviet social organizations are also performed in the United States by volunteer workers and social organizations. Indeed, no country in the world can match the United States, I would venture to say, in the amount of public-spirited activity of volunteer social organizations. Yet there is a difference in kind between Soviet social organizations and their American counterparts—a difference which is striking. In part it is a difference in the scope of the activities of Soviet social organizations and especially their powers over the lives of their members; in part it is a difference in the amount of official pressure that can be brought upon them, due especially to their links with the State through the Communist Party.

For example, the *Komsomol* organizations in the universities call for student volunteers to work during the summer holidays in the so-called "virgin lands" of the East. The volunteers are recruited, however, by lists posted on bulletin boards, and refusal to go courts expulsion from the *Komsomol* and probably—at least it is so assumed by the students—from the university. A second example may be found in the activities of "comrades' courts," now operating under a recent statute, which meet in apartment houses or in factories to consider minor offenses committed by neighbors or fellow workers. Their punitive powers are limited to a ten-ruble fine. Mostly they issue reprimands and warnings. However, they may also recommend eviction from the apartment or disciplinary action (including demotion) by the factory management. Such eviction or disciplinary action may be resisted through regular court proceedings, but nevertheless the recommendation of the comrades' court is a serious matter. One other example: Soviet courts sometimes go "on circuit," so to speak, to apartments or factories, to hear criminal cases involving persons in those places. The purpose is to demonstrate to the entire "collective" and to the public the social danger of the offenses charged and to educate people in the requirements of the law. But the tendency to convict and to mete out harsh punishment is very strong when such an educational purpose is in the forefront of the procedure itself.

Some Western students of the Soviet scene have, in my opinion, exaggerated the evils of this kind of new "social justice." One must put oneself in the Soviet situation, where true social cooperation in informal voluntary groups, entirely independent of the State, hardly exists. The comrades' courts that I have seen in action have impressed me by the good spirit with which they act and with which they are received. Especially important is the fact that their powers are very limited and that these limits are enforced by the courts and by the legal system.

The great danger, of course, is the potentiality of abuse of these social organizations by the Communist Party and the State. The still greater danger is the dream of a far-off time when there will be no legal system and no State but only one vast social organization, one vast Communist Party. It is, I am sure, a dream which can never be realized; but so long as it is held it inhibits the achievement of true legal security.

*The Return to Harsh Criminal and Administrative Penalties.* A sixth major tendency in Soviet law in the post-Stalin period is the return in 1961 and 1962 to harsh criminal and administrative penalities against those who refuse to cooperate in building communism.

In May and June 1961, the three largest republics, comprising three-fourths of the Soviet population, finally enacted the notorious antiparasite law which had been first proposed for public discussion in 1957 and later adopted in the smaller republics from 1957 through 1960. This law, in its final form, provides for "resettlement" in specially designated localities, for two to five years, of persons who constitute "antisocial, parastic elements" and who are not performing socially useful work but are living on unearned income. Persons may be sentenced under this law by the judges of the regular courts in a summary procedure and without the usual guarantees of the criminal law, or else by general meetings in the factories or apartments, with review by the local municipal council.

In 1959 I was told in Moscow by the principal draftsman of the 1958 Fundamental Principles of Criminal Procedure that in his opinion the antiparasite laws contradicted the provision of the Fundamental Principles that no person may be punished for a crime except by sentence of a court; and that there was a good chance they would not be adopted in the three largest republics and that they would be repealed in those republics where they had already been adopted. His optimism proved unjustified. The laws have now been reconciled with the Fundamental Principles on the more-than-tenuous theory that the offender is not being punished for a crime, nor is he being confined; he is simply sent to another place where he must take a socially useful job!

In the first year of the operation of this law in the R.S.F.S.R., as I learned last May at a lecture by the Minister of Justice, 10,000 people in Moscow were charged under the antiparasite law. Eight thousand, he said, received only warnings; 2,000 were sent out of Moscow; of these, only fifteen were subjected to confiscation of property. It may be inferred from the relatively few instances of confiscation that the law is principally a device for getting rid of vagrants and putting them to work.

Also the extension of the death penalty in 1961 and 1962 to a wide variety of crimes, many of them economic crimes not involving violence, reflects the regime's determination to take extreme measures against those who most flagrantly violate the tenets of Communist morality. In a case tried in July 1961, one of the statutes imposing the death penalty was applied retroactively by a special edict of the Presidium of the Supreme Soviet authorizing the retroactive application "as an exception" in the specific case. (The edict was never published as it was not considered to be "of general significance." ... There is reason to believe that there were other such cases of retroactive application of the death sentence, specially authorized by similar edicts.) Judging from Soviet press accounts of individual trials probably over 250 Soviet citizens were executed for economic and other crimes in the year from May 1961 to May 1962, and probably an equal or greater number were executed from June to December 1962. One can only say "probably" because Soviet crime statistics are a state secret! (In 1961, forty-three persons were executed in the United States.)

This harsh policy was also reflected in increased penalities for lesser crimes. Soviet jurists have publicly criticized the tendency of some procurators and courts to treat the imposition of the death penalty for serious crimes as a signal for reversing the entire trend toward liberalization.

What significance should we attach to these developments? As is so often the case with violations of basic principles of judicial precedure, the particular individual victims do not command our affection. They were, presumably, scoundrels. It is rather the abuse of the integrity of the legal process that concerns us, for one abuse suggests another.

When I asked how he could explain the decision of July 1961 applying the death penalty retroactively, one leading Soviet jurist replied, "We lawyers didn't like it!"—an answer as interesting for the "we lawyers" as the "didn't like it." Another prominent lawyer told me that he did not believe in the use of the death penalty in peacetime in any case. Not only lawyers, however, were concerned about these measures. An engineer said to me when I raised the question of what was so bad about getting rid of the scoundrels: "If they start with scoundrels, what is to stop them from going on to political opponents?" Whether the majority of Soviet citizens make this connection, however, is something that cannot be known. Many, at least, seem to support the regime's new policy of ruthless repression of large-scale economic crimes.

## Conclusion

We have heard much of "the thaw"—to use Ehrenberg's phrase—the unfreezing of Soviet life in the years since Stalin died, the reduction of terror, the increased freedom to criticize, the greater encouragement of individual initiative, the relaxation of tensions. But the *long-range* problem of government in the Soviet Union is whether the Soviet leaders are willing and able to establish not merely a season, or a climate, or a policy, of freedom and initiative, but also a legal and institutional foundation which will make freedom and initiative secure from their own intervention. Until that problem is solved, the fear of a return to Stalinist terror will haunt the Soviet people, and especially the intellectuals. In research institutes and universities, as well as among educated people generally, debates rage over the "liquidation of the consequences of the cult of personality" which is Party jargon for preventing a recurrence not only of violence but also of all the rigidities that went with it. Nobody—presumably from Khrushchev on down—wants such a recurrence. But nobody can guarantee that it won't happen—if it becomes "necessary."

A Soviet professor said to me: "I am not proud of the book I wrote in 1952. But in those days, if you said anything objective on that subject you would be told, 'Enough!'—and if you persisted you might disappear." Then he paused, and added, "And you know, nine years is a very short time in the light of history!"

Khrushchev has replaced the Stalinist dualism of law and terror by a new dualism of law and social pressure; one is free from arbitrary arrest by the secret police, but one is not free from the social pressure of the "collective"—whether it be the more innocuous pressure of the collective of the neighbors in the crowded apartment houses or the less innocuous pressure of the factory, one's co-workers, or the local Party organization. The new dualism still stands in the shadow of the old.

In 1960 I wrote that "Krushchev's great contribution to Soviet politics is his belief that terror is inefficient and unnecessary and that, by a common effort of will and enthusiasm, the Soviet people can lift their society to new heights. So far he has been enormously successful. But the doubt remains as to how he will respond to setbacks and crises, whether at home or abroad"; 1961 and 1962 have been years of such setbacks. Domestically, the setback in agriculture deeply upset not only the economy but also the confidence of the people; the failure to grant the usual spring price decreases in 1962, followed by drastic increases in prices of meat and butter (30 and 25 per cent respectively), produced a great shock among the city-dwellers. In addition, the renewed attack on Stalin caused great consternation, not only because many people loved Stalin, but also, and more important, because many could not understand what Khrushchev's purposes were: they asked, was he moving Stalin from the mausoleum only to make room for himself? Internationally, there was the split with China, the Berlin crisis, the resumption of atomic tests, the talk of war.

It is not surprising, therefore, that the Soviet leadership responded to discontent at home with a stepping up of social pressure and with such harsh legal measures as the death penalty for economic crimes.

Yet it would be a great mistake to assume that the "thaw" has ended. Such an assumption underestimates the importance of the legal and institutional changes which have in fact taken place. The law reforms have already counted. They have acquired a momentum which is hard to stop. A vast structure of procedures and rights has been built, and though its foundations need to be greatly strengthened it is not something which can easily be toppled.

The question remains, does the Soviet leadership wish to carry the process of law reform to its conclusion? Is it willing to establish guarantees against the reversal of this process? If it does not do so, it will have great difficulty in maintaining—especially in the face of domestic and international failures—the sustained drive, the sustained will and enthusiasm, which alone can make the Soviet system work. If it does establish such guarantees against a return to arbitrary measures, it will lay a basis for the gradual overthrow of that system.

---

*COMMENT. Civil Law Trials.* A keen disappointment for your editor has been the failure to find a vivid but realistic account of a criminal-law trial in a civil-law jurisdiction. Of particular interest to an American lawyer is the preliminary investigation before a judge at which the evidence is compiled from the point of view of both prosecution and accused; this proceeding has particular relevance to the still rudimentary, but developing, devices for pretrial discovery in American criminal procedure.

A good insight into European trial procedure may be gained from Bedford, *The Faces of Justice* (N.Y.: Simon & Schuster, 1961), a warmly human account of specific criminal trials in England, Germany, France, and Switzerland; "The Case of Dr. Brach" (pp. 101–151) is especially recommended. The trials are presented in a literary style which makes delightful reading, but one who seeks to appreciate continental criminal trials should be aware of the fact that they are greatly affected by crucial pretrial procedures. For a Kafkaesque account of a French trial, see Besnard, *The Trial of Marie Besnard* (N.Y.: Farrar, Strauss & Cudahy, 1963), and for a literary masterpiece which sidelights French criminal procedure, your editor warmly recommends Camus, *L'Étranger* (New York: Pantheon, 1946), translated as *The Stranger* (New York: Knopf, 1951) and as *The Outsider* (London: H. Hamilton, 1946).[1]

*Readings on Foreign Legal Systems.* In addition to the books by Von Mehren, Schlesinger, and David & deVries, from which extracts were quoted, helpful introduction to civil law systems may be found in Lawson, Anton, and Brown, *Introduction to French Law* (Oxford: Clarendon Press, 1963). The origins of continental law are explored in Munroe Smith's *The Development of European Law* (New York: Columbia U.P., 1928). An American lawyer planning to work with legal materials of France, Germany, or Switzerland will find indispensable help in Szladits, *Guide to Foreign Legal Materials: French, German, Swiss* (New York: Oceana Publications, 1959).

Developments in Soviet law are thoroughly examined in Gsovski & Grzybowski, *Government, Law and Courts in the Soviet Union and Eastern Europe* (New York: Praeger, 1959). See also Hazard, *Settling Disputes in Soviet Society: The Formative Years of Legal Institutions* (New York: Columbia U. P., 1960), covering the years before 1925; Hazard and Shapiro, *The Soviet Legal System: Post-Stalin Documentation and Historical Commentary* (New York: Oceana, 1962) contains a wealth of materials on law reform during the post-Stalin period. See also Hazard, "Soviet Codifiers Release The First Drafts," *American Journal of Comparative Law*, vol. 8, 1959, p. 72; Grzybowski, "The Powers Trial and the 1958 Reform of Soviet Criminal Law," *American Journal of Comparative Law*, vol. 9, 1960, p. 425.

*"Mixed" Systems.* Particularly instructive are jurisdictions, like Scotland, Quebec, and Louisiana, which have civil law traditions but which have been linked with and influenced by related common-law systems.

---

[1] General discussions of criminal law procedures under various continental systems will be found in the following: Vouin, "The Protection of the Accused in French Criminal Procedure," *International and Comparative Law Quarterly*, vol. 5, 1956, p. 1 (prior to the 1958 revision of the French Code of Criminal Procedure); Anton, "L'Instruction Criminelle," *American Journal of Comparative Law*, vol. 9, 1960, p. 441 (emphasizing the impact of the 1958 revision on pretrial procedures); Hamson, "The Prosecution of the Accused—English and French Legal Methods," *Criminal Law Review*, 1955, p. 272; Keedy, "The Preliminary Investigation of Crime in France," *University of Pennsylvania Law Review*, vol. 88, 1940, pp. 385, 692, 915; Meyer, "German Criminal Procedure: The Position of the Defendant in Court," *American Bar Association Journal*, vol. 41, 1955, p. 592 (a refutation of common misconceptions: that guilt is presumed; that the accused is compelled to testify; that there is no right against self-incrimination; and that an accused can be convicted on hearsay).

See Walker, *The Scottish Legal System* (Edinburgh: W. Green, 1959); Smith, *British Justice: The Scottish Contribution* (London: Stevens, 1961) (the civilian heritage of the Scottish legal system and its contributions to English and British Law); Groner, "Louisiana Law," *Louisiana Law Review*, vol. 8, 1948, p. 350; Laverty, "Some Differences between the Common Law and that of Quebec," *Canadian Bar Review*, vol. 9, 1931, p. 13. *Cf.* Lee, *Introduction to Roman-Dutch Law* 5th ed. (Oxford: Clarendon, 1953), discussing the legal systems of the Union of South Africa and of Ceylon, which were derived from Roman law as applied in Holland prior to codification. Further references on "mixed" systems appear in Schlesinger, *Comparative Law* (1959) Scotland: 525; Quebec: 190–191, 524; Louisiana: 9, 288, 522.

*International Legal Practice*. At an accelerating pace modern law practice is encountering not only the legal systems of other nations but also international legal structures built upon a multitude of treaties and upon organizations like the United Nations and the European Common Market. A realistic, first-hand report on the significance of these developments to the practice of law is Arthur H. Dean's "The Role of International Law in a Metropolitan Practice," *University of Pennsylvania Law Review*, vol. 103, 1955, p. 886. See also Cowles, "To What Extent Will American Lawyers Need an Understanding of International Law to Serve Clients Adequately during the Last Half of the Twentieth Century," *Journal of Legal Education*, vol. 7, 1954, p. 179; Jessup, *The Use of International Law* (Ann Arbor: U. of Michigan Law School, 1959).

Among the growing body of literature on the growth of transnational law and legal institutions within the Common Market are Stein & Hay, "Legal Remedies of Enterprises in the European Economic Community," *American Journal of Comparative Law*, vol. 9, 1960, p. 375; Donner, "The Court of Justice of the European Communities," *The Record of the Association of the Bar of the City of New York*, vol. 17, 1960, p. 232; Lagrange, "The Role of the Court of Justice of the European Communities as Seen Through Its Case Law," *Law and Contemporary Problems*, vol. 26, 1961 p. 400; and Behr, *Judicial Control of the European Community*, (New York: Frederick A. Praeger, 1962).

There is good writing, interesting and not too technical, which introduces the wider international structures. A good starting point is R. Y. Jennings' lecture, "The Progress of International Law," *British Year Book of International Law—1958* (1939), pp. 334–355; republished (1960) in pamphlet form by the Cambridge University Press. Books which can serve as an introduction include Jessup, *Transnational Law* (New Haven: Yale U. P., 1956), based on a series of lectures; Brierly, *The Law of Nations*, 6th ed. (Oxford: Clarendon Press, 1962), a short, classic text; McNair, *The Development of International Justice* (New York: Oceana,

1954), containing lectures by the President of the International Court of Justice on the work of the Court. See also Stone, "International Law and Contemporary Social Trends," *Rocky Mountain Law Review,* vol. 29, 1956, p. 149 (an evocative analysis of current problems of international law in terms of scientific, psychological, moral, and cultural trends); Covey T. Oliver, "The American Law Institute's Restatement of the Foreign Relations Law of the United States," *American Journal of International Law,* vol. 55, 1961, p. 428.

CHAPTER 10

# The Goals of Law Study

THOSE CONSIDERING A CAREER IN LAW often wonder what law school is like. Is it nothing more than memorizing a complex set of rules? Students in the midst of law school sometimes lose sight of the objectives of their study. And practitioners of law may be interested in the reasons for the changes which are occurring at their Schools: Does legal education reflect the rapid developments in law and society?

This brief chapter is designed to sharpen these questions and to suggest a few tentative answers.

**TAUGHT LAW IS TOUGH LAW**     *By Robert A. Leflar*

BACK IN 1927 when I first heard Dean Roscoe Pound use the expression "taught law is tough law," the words caught my imagination and, as apt aphorisms do, conjured up broad vistas of thought and some insight into ultimate truth. I was then about to embark upon a career of teaching law, and the words in that context gave me a personal sense of prospective participation in the great glacial process by which law and legal system are handed down through the centuries from generation to succeeding generation in our common law society. I was about to take part in the transmission of our legal heritage. The law I was about to teach would be "tough law;" it would be hard, persistent, enduring law. (That made me feel important.) If I had any doubts about the "toughness" of the law which I would teach, they were resolved by my reflection on what I

---

This paper was presented as the Hepburn Memorial Lecture at Wayne University Law School on May 14, 1962, and is reprinted from *Wayne Law Review*, vol. 8, no. 4, 1962, pp. 465–480, with the permission of the author and the publisher. The author is Distinguished Professor of Law at the University of Arkansas and a former Associate Justice of the Arkansas Supreme Court.

could teach, which was certainly not much more than my own teachers had just attempted to teach to me. There was one generation of persistence established already.

As I thought more about it, however, I realized that Dean Pound was speaking of something much larger than the effects of law school classroom teaching on successive generations of law students, and of something even larger than the congenital laziness and conservatism of lawyers which makes many of them natural opponents of almost any kind of change in the law. He was speaking of the self-perpetuating nature of our law, the doctrine of precedents and stare decisis, the fact that law, particularly the common law, patterns itself upon itself almost perpetually, even to the extent of disregarding changes in the society and in the civilization upon which the law operates. He was speaking, for one thing, of the attitude which induces many citizens, both lawyers and laymen, to criticize appellate courts—the Supreme Court of the United States, the Supreme Court of Michigan, the Supreme Court of Arkansas—when these courts break away from old lines of decision, overrule old precedents, look beyond stare decisis to liberalize the law. We have heard much of that sort of criticism in recent years. "Tenacity of a taught legal tradition is much more significant in our legal history," says Pound, "than the economic conditions of time and place." Rules of law sometimes persist simply because they have once been announced as rules of law, regardless of changes in society that have made the rules practically unexplainable except as bits of history. Referring to the continuity of the common law, Pound points out that "it has a real unity at least from the age of Coke to the present. As a mode of thinking, as a mode of reasoning upon legal subjects, it is the same in England, the United States, Canada, and Australia. It is the same in its technique of decision, in its judicial and juristic craftsmanship, and in its characteristic institutions. It is the same in its reasoning by analogy from decisions rather than from statutes. It is the same in its distinction of law and equity. . . . [It] is the same in substance in one century and in the next. And yet between Coke and the present, equity has developed; the law merchant, which Coke had not much more than heard of, has been absorbed into the common law. . . ." Uncounted other rules have been brought into and taken out of the body of the common law. Yet a common law decision from Arkansas or Saskatchewan can be understood and respected in Michigan or in New Zealand, because the system is the same. A contracts case written in Queensland might read almost the same as one written in Michigan. And a criminal law case decided in England or in Massachusetts 150 years ago might be cited as authority by a court sitting in Illinois today.

We all know about the common law's background in history and tradition, and how the decision in one case is drawn from the decision in another, or others. This is the common law method, the method of preserving and continuing established custom and tradition. It is the historical method. That is pretty fully discussed in the textbook and in first year law classes, and it is not what I want to talk about principally today, though I needed to refer to it. What I want to dwell on now is growth and development in the law, change as distinguished from constancy, the way in which the tough old trunk of our body of taught law puts out new shoots and branches and leaves and even new stalks that grow up from its roots, the way in which these new growths themselves become tough taught law, and something about the relationship of legal education to tough law and tender law.

In the early days of our Republic, young men studied law by reading Blackstone and Kent and Story. When there were no law schools, or few law students in few law schools, the study of the law was by the mastery of textbooks, which was for the most part the acceptance of what was in the textbooks. Originality and imagination in the student were no virtue in that kind of study; they could only get a young man into trouble when he was examined on the texts. In the later 1800s and well into the present century, for most young men who attended a law school, the lecture method of law teaching was used, and it, too, put a premium on memory rather than on original thought. Those days were the great days for the toughness of taught law; those were the days when the textbook and the lecture were *the law*, the Gospel according to Saint Blackstone and Saint Greenleaf, or sub-saint local lecturer.

Then came Langdell and his case system for law teaching. At first it made small difference, for more than one reason. The most obvious reason was that for thirty or forty years there were few students in case system law classes. A more important reason was that the case system itself, in the hands of Langdell and his immediate successors, did not encourage students in the classroom to question the social policy of a case, but only to question its logic, its historical verity, its correlation with other cases. The early case system under a good Socratic teacher compelled the law student to think for himself, which mastering textbooks and listening to lectures never did compel him to do, but to think for himself *about what?* Mostly about the analytical structure of the law and how a case fitted into that analytical structure, the legitimacy of its historical antecedents, the factual and probative accuracy of its syllogisms. There was little in that mode of teaching that would encourage young lawyers to seek improvement in the law, to strive for changes that would make law fit better the needs of the society. That casebook teaching left the law that was taught as tough as ever, and only taught it better. Emphasis in case teaching was on cases which were supposed to follow the precedent of prior cases, leaving improvement in the law to legislatures whose ephemeral product was no proper subject for serious law study until it had lain in the books for 100 years.

On the face of it this does not describe what takes place, or is supposed to take place, in the classrooms of today's law schools, though we still say that we use the case system of law study. What has happened?

We have all heard it said that there are as many case methods for teaching law as there are law teachers using casebooks, that each teacher devises his own system. That of course is not quite true; there can't be 2,000 genuinely different systems. But with 2,000 law teachers in the United States, each on his own and with no obligation to do homage to Langdell, we do get teaching methods that are pretty far away from what the men of Harvard envisioned three-quarters of a century ago. It is a rare law teacher who today would ask a second or third year class to state a case, discuss it, state another and discuss it, and so on to the end of the class period. That routine procedure has real value for beginning students, but we know that the value quickly wears out, and even the second semester man begins to demand something that goes deeper beneath the surface. The law teacher today can assume, or should be able to assume, that the student has read the assigned cases, and has them in his mind as background and foundation, so that we can take off *from* there. Take off *for where?*

I suspect that the big break in American law teaching came with the development of what Roscoe Pound called Sociological Jurisprudence. This new school of thinking about law placed emphasis on the idea that law's function is to serve the best interests of the society which it governs —to serve that society's interests in terms of its culture, its economics, its social institutions, its life, and its aspirations. This was in contrast to Analytical Jurisprudence which treated law almost as an end within itself and was content to study the systemic character of law and the interrelationships of its parts with each other. It was in contrast too with Historical Jurisprudence which studied law primarily in terms of its past, its origins and lines of prior growth more than its future. Perhaps Sociological Jurisprudence should not be classed as a separate school, and is only one of the forms of Philosophical Jurisprudence. There have been many philosophers, and few of them have avoided the temptation to philosophize about law. Most of them have centered upon some ultimate ideal, some end of ends that human life should serve, such as individual freedom, or the greatest happiness of the greatest number, or virtue in mankind, or the survival of the fittest, or a finer civilization, or equality in the distribution of economic goods, or the like. Many, though not all, of these were abstractions, as broad or as narrow as the beautiful large words in which they were phrased, or as the content which the particular philosopher read into the beautiful large words.

Sociological Jurisprudence, though it could be called a philosophy, or part of a philosophy, was different from most of these. It was concrete. It dealt not just with ideas and ideals, but with the facts of life, the facts of our society. Sociology is the study of our society and all its institutions—economic, cultural, familial, religious, political, its ways of life and living. Sociological Jurisprudence sees law as the servant of the society of the time and place, the body of norms which that society creates for itself to further and effectuate the perceived interests that accrue from its activities and its aspirations. This is a conception of law that unites the study of law with the study of society. It is one that forces the student of law to look outside the law itself for his justifications. It directs the student to look not merely at Coke's "the reason of the law," which was a rather specialized kind of logic; not merely at the history of the law, which in some areas has more to do with the folkways of the past than with the living present; but to look at the job that the law has to do today. The law student now is allowed to believe, under the Sociological Jurisprudence that has come to be generally accepted in America, that he is entitled to ask whether the law, or any particular rule of law, is doing its job in *this* society well or poorly. He feels that he is entitled to ask first what the job really is, then to check on how the job is being performed, then to compare, to see whether that is the best and most effective way in which the job can be performed.

That is what general acceptance of the theories of Sociological Jurisprudence has done for us. I say "general acceptance" deliberately, though I realize that far fewer than all the lawyers, judges, and law professors in America would go along with what Roscoe Pound and his disciples have written under the head of Sociological Jurisprudence. The Natural Law philosophers would never agree that they had accepted the materialistic implications of a functionally-tested jurisprudence, yet the fact remains that most of the Naturalists have come in practice to advocate essentially the same approach to actual legal problems though they still idealize other ultimate values and condemn sociological jurists for not idealizing those values. At another extreme the so-called Realists also proclaim their differences and disagreements, yet their point in fact is that they accept the function-tested sense of Sociological Jurisprudence but would temper it with something of the opportunist's crassness and the cynic's defeatism. Nor does the Sociological jurist deny the reality of this Realism; he merely refuses to make it the central feature of his legal philosophy. What we have in America today, despite debate about ultimate ideals at one end and courthouse practicalities at the other, is a general agreement among legislators, judges, and ordinary citizens, plus law professor jurisprudes and a few others chiming in with their own minor discords, that the function of law is to serve the functions of society, and that every society is free, or at least should be free, to remake its law in the society's own functional image.

A corollary to this societal emphasis in legal theory is well expressed in another of Dean Pound's favorite phrases, "the efficacy of effort." If a body of law ought to serve well the needs of a society, then the effort to make it serve those needs well is a worthwhile effort. If that is the nature of law and its function, then we as members of the profession of the law are under a professional obligation to do what we can to make sure that not only in the law's administration but in its substance these ends are served. This is an effort in which every one of us may properly engage. More than that, it is an effort in which success, at least some measure of success, is possible. That is what we mean by "the efficacy of effort;" we *believe* that the law's administration and its substance can be improved, will be improved if we work at it with enough intelligence and energy. This belief in the efficacy of effort is a basic part of the Sociological jurist's creed.

Is it not inevitable that the tough taught law of generations past becomes a little less tough when the law's devotees maintain toward it the questioning attitude and the belief that conscious effort can improve it?

I am still talking, of course, about the growth and development of law, about changing law in a changing society, about how we in America were once less hospitable to changes in our substantive law, especially judicial changes in it, than we are now, and why we are more hospitable to changes now than our fathers were a few decades ago. And I am trying to show that our methods of legal education, influenced in turn by new jurisprudential theory, have had a great deal to do with our changing attitudes toward law itself. I'd like to pursue this influence of methods of legal education a little further, as it bears not only upon the attitudes of American law students but upon those of mature lawyers and judges, and even law professors. (I will assume, incidentally, that lay attitudes toward law will in general follow those of the legal profession, perhaps a generation late.) What I want to do is to look at the attitude-producing effects of some specific features of modern legal education.

One never-ending feature of modern legal education is casebooks. That is what we law teachers still call the books we use as teaching tools in our courses, though Langdell and Ames wouldn't recognize many of them as casebooks in the classic sense. Today they are mostly labeled "Cases and Materials on" whatever the subject may be. The "Materials" parts of these books normally deal with the business situations, the social, political, economic, psychological, cultural problems which the law works with in the particular field, the factual difficulties inherent in these problems, differing points of view as to how the best interests of society can most effectively be served in connection with these problems, and the like. The choice of cases to be printed in most casebooks today is based on the adequacy of discussion in the reported case of such "facts of life" as are relevant to the case. If an opinion relies merely on authority, without analysis of the social or economic problems inherent in it, it is likely to be regarded as "not a good casebook case," whereas the current cases that are selected for inclusion in the new casebooks are likely to deal both with the legal authorities and with the sociological considerations ("sociology" is a word that properly covers the whole waterfront of social studies) that bear on the legal question in the case.

Furthermore, the parts of the good new casebooks that deal with cases do not today just print the cases plus related citations, nor do they just raise questions about the logic of the case and what answers that logic would call for in slightly different sets of facts. They raise questions of policy. Their textnotes and footnotes call upon the law student not only to differentiate deductive from inductive reasoning, to formulate or complete the formulation of syllogisms, to reason from analogy after a fashion, or after various fashions, and to enjoy a good reductio ad absurdam. These materials actually require students to make value judgments, to make choices as to what the law ought to be, to make up their own minds as to whether particular cases were rightly or wrongly decided not just in the light of earlier decisions but in the light of all the considerations that a free-wheeling jurist might bring to bear on the case. These considerations are at least partly the same ones that a statesmanlike legislator would take into account in dealing with the same broad substantive problem. It is pretty obvious that this student experience does not make for an attitude of reverence toward old law. . . .

The increased awareness of law faculties that other academic disciplines have much to contribute to law study is another major development that has significance here. Increasingly we are recognizing that law is not an academic occupation complete within itself, to be studied altogether in isolation from other academic fields. Interdisciplinary study and research is becoming the rule rather than the exception in our good law schools. We have much of it in upperclass and graduate seminars on medico-legal problems, family law, law and psychology (including insanity), criminology generally, the treatment of juvenile offenders, urban housing and land use problems, the economics of taxation, labor relations and labor law, civil rights, trade regulation and antitrust laws, corporate promotions, and a dozen other fields. Information concerning installment buying and financing practices relates the law of Sales to the facts of daily life. A fairly thorough understanding of liability insurance policies and statistics is essential to any realistic appreciation of the law of Torts. A course in Crimes and Criminal Procedure has infinitely greater meaning when it includes something more than the third-hand materials of appellate cases. Law teachers and casebook editors today realize this, and are acting accordingly. Seminars conducted by law teachers jointly with economists, or with criminologists, or psychologists, or physical scientists, or with experts in some special area of government or private industry, are increasingly common. Whenever this interdisciplinary study occurs, either in separate seminars or as a part of regular law school courses, it tends to break down the law's stolid insularity, it makes law students understand that law justifies itself only by its sensible relation to the problems that arise in our daily lives, that the function of our law is to serve the needs of our society.

Furthermore, legal education today is by no means limited to work with undergraduate or even graduate law students. Postadmission study, so-called continuing legal education, has come to be a major activity in many law schools, and a fair fraction of all the lawyers in America occasionally go back to law school in one way or another nowadays, to bring themselves up-to-date on new developments in the profession. Much of what is dealt with in these postadmission short courses is, of course, of the "how to do it" type, almost mechanical in character, involving forms, techniques, and procedures for dealing with one kind of special situation or another in the trial of personal injury cases, the development of an oil and gas lease program, the operation of a prosecuting attorney's office, the evaluation of lands to be taken by condemnation proceedings for public uses, or the like. These do not much change popular attitudes, nor lawyer attitudes, about the nature of law and its function in society, but only help lawyers to do specific jobs a little better. Also, a lot of lawyers come to legal institutes and short courses primarily to get a tax deductible vacation, preferably on a football weekend. That is not typical, though. The fact remains that, along with the "how to do it" courses and the "fun and games" aspect of continuing legal education, there is mixed into these lawyers' seminars a great deal of discussion that calls for new analysis of the law's function in a changing society. . . .

There is one other area of legal education that I must mention. This is what may loosely be called "outside reading," sometimes grandly spoken of as "legal research." It is what law students do when they want to get perspective on their courses; it is what practicing lawyers do when they prepare trial or appellate briefs or seek a better understanding of some part of the law to which a case in the office directs their attention. . . .

In the old days, this kind of research took the reader to the cases. The cases were the original sources, and save for a few texts such as Blackstone and Story there was nowhere else to go Then the cases, in America especially, began to multiply. The time came when no one could keep up with all of them. There were just too many. There was talk of limiting publication to the more important cases, but nothing has come of that—not yet, at least. Some acceptable method of digesting, summarizing, distilling the essence from them had to be discovered.

For a time it looked as though the *Corpus Juris*—Ruling Case Law—American Jurisprudence—A.L.R. type of encyclopaedic digest and annotation might take over the field. And we must recognize that their day, and their special sort of usefulness, have certainly not passed from us.

But the Restatements and the high quality textbooks which embrace a sociological approach to the problems of the law have, along with the law reviews, come to constitute the major secondary materials for serious extracurricular law study today. Wigmore's Evidence, Corbin's or Williston's Contracts, Davis' Administrative Law, Harper and James' or Prosser's Torts, Scott's Trusts, and a score of other good books in smaller fields are our great texts today, and they are no manuals of slavery to the past. We may even be moving away from the case law stage of the common law, toward a commentator's stage, comparable to that of the Glossators and text writers of the old Roman Law, when the writings of the Jurists superseded the texts about which they wrote.

At any rate, this is another aspect of our current concern with re-examining the law, almost with taking it apart and putting it together again, in the light of the kind of job that today's society expects today's law to do for it.

That brings me close to my conclusion. I referred near the beginning of my remarks to the spate of current criticism of our appellate courts for their asserted disregard of stare decisis, for their willingness today to overturn old precedents and to liberalize the law. We know that some judges are called "activists," because they are willing deliberately to question old legal rules, not follow them blindly merely because they are old rules, and in some quarters "activist" is a nasty word. In another camp today are judges who are loosely identified as favoring judicial restraint. The late Judge Learned Hand shortly before his death publicly aligned himself with this group. Their position stated broadly is that judges should abide by precedent and established doctrine as far as possible, should restrain themselves for the temptation to remake the law as it ought to be, should in general leave to the legislatures the task of improving the law. But this group itself readily enough engages also in judicial renovation of the law, a bit more slowly and subtly than the avowed activists, but just as surely. They are more likely to do it by distinguishing older decisions, or by finding a thread of growth already present in them, or by dropping warnings of prospective overrulings before the fatal step is taken and then citing the warning as authority for the final departure later. However they do it, I am not much inclined to distinguish between great judges like Schaefer and Traynor today and great judges such as Cardozo, Hand, and Holmes in a slightly earlier generation. All of them are or were engaged in bringing our law up to date. Only in their judicial techniques do they differ.

None of them have sought to abandon the past. The past is a part of the present. The past is a part of all of us today, and a part of all our law today. No great judge urges that we should abandon stare decisis, the rule of precedent, today or ever. There may be some theorists who would be willing for justice to be administered on a completely ad hoc basis, without law as we know it save in statutory form. But I do not know any major jurists who advocate such a thing, despite occasional loose talk, and I am certain that there are no appellate judges in America who operate that way.

By the same token, on the other side of the scale of theoretic talk, there are lawyers and judges who say that they oppose all judicial change in the law. If you considered their talk, by itself, you would conclude that they opposed all judicial promulgation of rules that were not already firmly embedded in the concrete of prior adjudication. Yet a reading of the judicial opinions of judges who talk like that almost invariably reveals that what they really oppose are changes in directions that they don't like, which often enough are the directions of current societal change. The same judges are often quite willing to promulgate "strong opinions," going beyond what is required by earlier ones, in directions they do like, which quite often are toward societal views that have prevailed in times gone by.

There is no appellate judge in America who is not an "activist," in one realistic definition of the term. This is in the sense that the judge believes in improving the law, according to his lights, and affirmatively tries to do so. There are very real differences among judges, both as to what are the true directions toward where improvement lies, and as to the proper rate of judicial movement toward them. But there are more today who are willing to move with fair speed, and to admit that they do so, than there were a judicial generation ago.

The old "taught law" has ceased to be such "tough law" as it once was, as far as specific doctrine is concerned, and a new toughness of the taught question-asking technique is taking its place. It is the taught question "Why?" that, we may hope, toughly persists today.

# THE TAPESTRY UNFOLDS  *By Oliver Wendell Holmes, Jr.*

WHAT A subject is this in which we are united—this abstraction called the Law, wherein, as in a magic mirror, we see reflected, not only our own lives, but the lives of all men that have been! When I think on this majestic theme, my eyes dazzle. If we are to speak of the law as our mistress, we who are here know that she is a mistress only to be wooed with sustained and lonely passion—only to be won by straining all the faculties by which man is likest to a god. Those who, having begun the pursuit, turn away uncharmed, do so either because they have not been vouchsafed the sight of her divine figure, or because they have not the heart for so great a struggle. To the lover of the law, how small a thing seem the novelist's tales of the loves and fates of Daphnis and Chloe! How pale a phantom even the Circe of poetry, transforming mankind with intoxicating dreams of fiery ether, and the foam of summer seas, and glowing greensward, and the white arms of women! For him no less a history will suffice than that of the moral life of his race. For him every text that he deciphers, every doubt that he resolves, adds a new feature to the unfolding panorama of man's destiny upon this earth. Nor will his task be done until, by the farthest stretch of human imagination, he has seen as with his eyes the birth and growth of society, and by the farthest stretch of reason he has understood the philosophy of its being. When I think thus of the law, I see a princess mightier than she who once wrought at Bayeux, eternally weaving into her web dim figures of the ever-lengthening past—figures too dim to be noticed by the idle, too symbolic to be interpreted except by her pupils, but to the discerning eye disclosing every painful step and every world-shaking contest by which mankind has worked and fought its way from savage isolation to organic social life.

---

This excerpt is taken from a speech, "The Law," presented before the Suffolk Bar Association on February 5, 1885, and reprinted in Holmes, *Collected Legal Papers* (New York: Harcourt, 1921), pp. 25–28.

A biographical note on Mr. Justice Holmes is given on p. 3.

# INDEX

# INDEX

ADMINISTRATIVE AGENCIES
Administrative Procedure Act, 361–362, 385, 387, 413
Changing attitudes toward, 381–394
Consistency with American legal system, 376–380
Development, 351–380
Effect of A.B.A. on, 358–360, 362–363, 374–376, 413
FTC, 357, 364, 366, 369
Growth, reasons for, 370–374
ICC, 354–356, 362, 364–367, 373, 375
Judicial review of, 380
NLRB, 353, 359, 360, 364, 372–373, 375
NRA, 359
Opposition to, 370–376
Political groups, effect on, 354–363
Role, 351–380
SEC, 360, 373, 375
Social Security Administration, 353
States, 354
Veterans Administration, 353–354, 369

AMERICAN BAR ASSOCIATION
Administrative Agencies, influence on, 358–360, 362–363, 374–376, 413
Selection of judges, see JUDGES, Selection

AMERICAN LAW
Blackstone's influence, 51
Case reports, 74–75
Comparison with Soviet law, 536–544
Criminal law in 19th century, 59
Early history of, 48–51
Equity
  Administered through common law forms in Pennsylvania, 79–85
  Preserved by treatises, 73–74
Formative period
  Adoption of English law, 49–51, 53–54
  Common law influence, 64
  Distrust of judges, 75, 76

European Codes' influence, 58
Lay judges, 65–66
Legislation, 56–61
Natural law influence, 55–56
Roman influence, 57–58
Rousseau, 58
Treatises and reports, 54–55, 68–76

AMERICAN LAW INSTITUTE, see RESTATEMENTS

BENTHAM
Offers to codify American law, 100–102
Opposition to Blackstone, 29, 30

BLACKSTONE
American law influence, 28, 29, 51, 63
Commentaries, 28, 29, 51

BRACTON, 17

CALIFORNIA
Civil Code, see FIELD, Codification

CANUTE, 8, 9

CARDOZO, 347

CHANCELLOR, see EQUITY

CHANCERY, see EQUITY

CIVIL LAW
Code Systems, 494
Codification
  Austrian Code, 498
  French Civil Code, 493, 498, 528
  German Civil Code, 529–532
  Napoleonic Code, 507, 510–512
Compared to common law, 486, 496–509
Early development
  Austrian Code, 498
  French Civil Code, 493, 498, 528
  Germany, 493
  Pre-codification, 502–504
  Roman influence, 486–491, 497–501

577

Expansion into other countries, 504–509
France
  Legal Profession, 513–521
  Napoleonic Code, 510–512, 528–529
  Private *vs.* public law, 521–522
  Procedure and Evidence, 522–525
Germany
  Civil Service, 532
    Judiciary, 533–536
  Codification, 529–532
  Development, 525–527
  Scholars' contributions, 528
  Systematic character, 527–528
Ministry of Justice, 284, 533
Soviet Union, 508–509

CODIFICATION
Advisability in America, 140–143
Bentham's offer to the United States, 100–102
Common law, 115–133
Field, 113–115
  California, 122–133
  New York, 109–113
  Opposition, 115–121
  Pomeroy, 123–125
  Reasons, 106–115
  Western states, 104–106
Massachusetts, 102–103
Problems, 133–139
Restatements, *see* RESTATEMENTS
Roman law, influenced by, 109–110

COKE, 27, 500

COMMON LAW
Adoption by American courts, 49
Check on official action in America, 64
Codification, 115–133
Compared to civil law, 486, 496–509
Conflict with equity, 36, 37
Conflict with legislation, 60–61
Continuity, 6
Development
  Chancery, 21, 22
  Christian influence, 7, 8
  Coke, 27
  King's Bench, 21, 22
  Language, 12, 13
  Norman influence, 11, 12, 491
  Procedure, 9
  Roman influence, 10, 11, 15, 16
  Unified court system, 491–492
"Folk-right," 9
Henry II, 13, 14
Jury trial, 17–19
Restatement of, 145–183

CONSTITUTION
Social and economic consequences, 87–88

ECONOMIC LEGISLATION, *see* LEGISLATION, Social and economic

EDWARD I, 20

EQUITY
Administration through common law forms in Pennsylvania, 79–85
Chancellor, early role of, 28, 31, 32–34
Common law, relation to, 36–43
Defined, 30, 31, 37
Precedent, role of, 35, 39, 40
Procedure, 33
Reformations of wills and agreements, 41
Remedies, 41, 42
Roman influence, 35
Saved in America by treatises, 73–74
Trusts and uses, 34–36, 42, 43
Writs, 22–23, 31–32

FIELD
Codes related to Restatement, 172–173
Codification
  California, 122–133
  New York, 109–113
  Opposition, 115–122
  Reasons, 106–115
  Western states, 104–106

FRANCE, *see* CIVIL LAW

GERMANY, *see* CIVIL LAW

GLANVILL, 16, 17

HALE, 27, 28

HAND (Learned), 338, 344

HENRY I, 492

HENRY II
Legal reforms, 13, 14
Legislation, 24, 25

HISTORY
Effect on law, 66–68
Place in study of law, 3–4, 572–573

JUDGES
Early American distrust of, 75, 76

Germany, 533–536
Lay judges in early American law, 65–66
Magistrate system
  New York City, 219
  Philadelphia, 220–235
Need to work with legislators, 283–290
Political activity
  New York City
    Contributions to party, 207–209
    Distribution of prizes, 195–198
    Source of patronage, 203–206, 215
  Pennsylvania, patronage, 235–240
  Philadelphia, magistrate system, 233–235
Popular dissatisfaction with
  Causes, 186–189
  Judges resist controls, 193
  Results
    Brief tenure, 189–194
    Impeachment, 190–191
    Popular election, 184–194
    Reduction of salaries, 191
Remuneration and other benefits, 198–203
Role contrasted with legislature, 337–350
Selection
  American Bar Association plan, 249, 250, 255–268
  Bar Association influence, 215–216, 240–246
  Bipartisanship, 248
  England
    Inns of Court, 273–275
    Lord Chancellor, 269–273
  Federal courts
    Eisenhower administration, 255–262
    Kennedy administration, 262–268
    Standards, 257–258
  General evaluation, 276–279
  Governor's interim appointment, 235
  Judicial Nominating Convention, 246
  Missouri Plan, 250, 254
  New York City, 209–217
  Newspapers, 216
  Nonpartisan primary, 246–248
  Pennsylvania, 235–240, 247
  Pennsylvania Plan, 250–252, 255
  Politicians, 203–206, 235–240
  Sitting judge principle, 240–242, 245–246

JURY TRIAL
Delay and cost, 426
Role at common law, 17–19

JUSTINIAN CODE, 488

LAW SCHOOLS
Association of American Law Schools, 406
Case method, 421, 566–567, 569–570
Emergence of, 65
Goals, 564–574
History, 572–573
Post-graduate education, 571–572
Public-policy considerations, 567–569
Treatises in teaching, 69, 76–78, 572

LEGAL AID, see LEGAL PROFESSION

LEGAL PROFESSION
Bar examination, 407
Effect on legislation, 288–289, 403–426
France, 513–521
Inns of Court, 25, 26
Law schools, see LAW SCHOOLS
Legal Aid and Defender Association, 427–436
Organization, 404–415
Practice
  Corporation lawyer, 468–482
  English and American, compared, 437–454
  General, 398–403
  Wall Street, 455–468

LEGISLATION
America
  Conflict with common law, 60–61
  Criminal law, 59
  Formative period, 56–61
  Separation of powers, 62–63
  Treatises used as basis for, 71–72
British Royal Commission
  Organization, 331–333
  Personnel, 333–336
Codification, see CODIFICATION
Conflict with royal prerogative, 25
Consumer protection, 95
Early common law, 20–24
Executive product, 291–292
Judge as lawmaker
  Contrast with legislature, 337–350
  Ministry of Justice, 293–315, 342–343, 347–348
  Restricted by statutes in United States, 338–343
Lobbyists, 292, 319
Ministry of Justice, 293–315, 342–343, 347–348
Modern legislator and his problems, 315–318
Natural resources, 89–90, 95
New York, 347, 412

580 INDEX

Product of cooperation between courts and legislators, 293–315
Research, 292–293, 307–315
Social and economic, 93–95, 351–394, 418
Structure of legislature
  Comparison of state legislatures with United States Senate, 322–324
  Problems, 318–324
  Proposed changes, 320–324
Uniform State Laws, see UNIFORMITY OF LAW
Unsolved problems, 96–99

LEWIS (William Draper)
Restatements, 145–153

MAGISTRATES, see JUDGES, Magistrate system

MAGNA CARTA, 20, 21, 500

MASSACHUSETTS
Codification, 102–103
Early law in, 48–51

MINISTRY OF JUSTICE, see LEGISLATION

MISSOURI PLAN, see JUDGES, Selection

NATURAL LAW
American law influence, 55, 56, 66
Rule of law, 379

NEW YORK
Civil Practice Act, 494–495
Codification, 104–106
Commission on Administration of Justice, 294–295
Commission to Investigate Defects in the Law, 293–294
Law Revision Commission
  Bills in legislature, 301–303
  Drafting and approval, 300–301
  Emergence of, 347, 412
  Organization, 296
  Problems
    Conflicts of interest, 304–305
    Fear of "Super-Legislature," 303–304
    Political, 303
  Research, 298–300, 307–315
  Salary for members, 310–311
  Source of projects, 296–298
  Uniform Commercial Code, 306–307

PARLIAMENT
Emergence of, 24, 25

PENNSYLVANIA
Equity administered through common law forms, 79–85
See also JUDGES, Selection

PENNSYLVANIA PLAN, see JUDGES, Selection

PHILADELPHIA, see JUDGES, Magistrate system

POMEROY
California Civil Code, 123–125

POUND, 564–565, 567, 569

PRECEDENT
Binding effect, 44–45
Bracton, 17
Case reports, need of, 46
Continental countries, 45
Equity, 35, 39, 40
Role of judge, 46, 47

RESTATEMENTS
Acceptance, 171–172
Authority, 154, 160–161, 165–168, 170–171, 173–174
Collateral benefits
  Code of Criminal Procedure, 177–178
  Code of Evidence, 177–178
  Uniform Commercial Code, 178
Common law, clarification of, 174, 175
Conflicts, 152–153
Contracts, 153, 157–159
Defects in American law prior to codification, 145–147
Planning
  Finances, 151
  Organization of work, 151–152
  Personnel, 171
Plans altered, 152–153
Property, 159–168
Relation to Field Code, 172–173
Result compared to the plan, 154–156, 162–168
Retrospective view, 175–177
Second, 169
State annotations, 164, 174
Torts, 153
What was needed, 148–150

ROMAN LAW
American law, formative period, 57–58
Codification, influence on, 109–110
Effect of Roman rule, 11

English law, 15–16
Mediaeval Europe, 14

RUSSIA, *see* SOVIET LAW

SEPARATION OF POWERS
Constitutional law development, 491–492
Formative period, 56–59, 62–63

SOCIAL LEGISLATION, *see* LEGISLATION

SOVIET LAW
Appraisal, 559–560
Civil Law, 508–509
Comparison with American law, 536–544
Reforms, 545–559

STARE DECISIS, *see* PRECEDENT, Binding effect

STATUTES, *see* LEGISLATION

TREATISES
America in formative period, 54–55, 68–76
Incorporation in state codes, 71–72
Law schools, 69, 76–78, 572
Preserved equity in America, 73–74
Preserved unity in American law, 72–73
Use in America in 19th century, 71–72
Use in American law schools, 76–78

UNIFORMITY OF LAW
New York
  Law Revision Commission, 295–315, 347, 412
  Uniform Commercial Code, 306–307
Uniform State Laws
  Desirability, 324–325
  National Conference of Commissioners
    Achievements, 329–331
    Organization and procedure, 326–329

VOLUNTARY DEFENDER ASSOCIATION, *see* LEGAL PROFESSION, Legal Aid